APOSTLES OF REVOLUTION

· · ·

JEFFERSON, PAINE, MONROE, AND THE STRUGGLE AGAINST THE OLD ORDER IN AMERICA AND EUROPE

JOHN FERLING

BLOOMSBURY PUBLISHING
NEW YORK · LONDON · OXFORD · NEW DELHI · SYDNEY

BLOOMSBURY PUBLISHING
Bloomsbury Publishing Inc.
1385 Broadway, New York, NY 10018, USA

BLOOMSBURY, BLOOMSBURY PUBLISHING, and the Diana logo are trademarks of
Bloomsbury Publishing Plc

First published in the United States 2018

Copyright © John Ferling, 2018

ISBN: HB: 978-1-63286-209-9
       eBook: 978-1-63286-211-2

Library of Congress Cataloging-in-Publication Data is available

2 4 6 8 10 9 7 5 3 1

Typeset by Westchester Publishing Services
Printed and bound in the U.S.A. by Berryville Graphics Inc., Berryville, Virginia

To find out more about our authors and books visit www.bloomsbury.com and
sign up for our newsletters.

Bloomsbury books may be purchased for business or promotional use. For information on
bulk purchases please contact Macmillan Corporate and Premium Sales Department at
specialmarkets@macmillan.com.

To Bill Morton
Physician, lawyer, author, and friend

CONTENTS

PREFACE

Some who were part of the protest against Great Britain before 1776 never wanted the American colonies to leave the British Empire. Some who wished for independence in 1776 were soon horrified by the extent of the domestic changes that accompanied the break with the mother country. Some among America's revolutionaries saw American independence as only an essential first step in the realization of a social and political transformation that could never be achieved so long as the American colonies remained part of the British Empire.

Thomas Jefferson, Thomas Paine, and James Monroe were among the latter, and their involvement in the American Revolution, and subsequently in the French Revolution as well, is the focus of this book. Of course, many other colonists also thought that England was irredeemably corrupt and that the American colonies were displaying symptoms of the corruption that had plunged the mother country into decline. There were others, too, who longed for the ideals of the American Revolution to spread to England and Europe, sparking far-reaching reform movements or revolutions that would sweep away the evils inherent in the old order of monarchical and aristocratic rule. Later, after the American Revolution had succeeded, there were others besides Jefferson, Paine, and Monroe who resisted what they saw as a counterrevolution that threatened the democracy and egalitarianism unleashed in 1776.

So, if there other apostles of revolution, why are Jefferson, Paine, and Monroe the cornerstones of this book? No individual of their era strove harder than these three to bring an end to a world where wealth and power were restricted to the few. Different as they were, the three shared radical visions of a democratic future, a new age purged of entrenched privilege. To a degree seldom seen among their contemporaries, they understood the harmful ramifications of a grossly unequal distribution of wealth. They sought a world in which individuals were judged according to their merits, not on the social strata into which they were born. While Jefferson, Paine, and Monroe championed less intrusive governments, each nevertheless believed that governments could enhance the opportunities available to ordinary citizens, and Jefferson and Paine articulated plans through which the government could increase individual independence, freedom, or security. Each struggled to create a world in which people would be liberated from age-old superstitions through the pursuit of reason and the untrammeled freedom of thought and expression. Each embraced the idea of progress—though perhaps not the notion of humankind's perfectibility—and presumed that the conditions in which humans lived could be improved. Each literally risked his life in pursuit of these ideals. Becoming a revolutionary is not always a safe undertaking. Paine experienced combat in the Revolutionary War and came very close to dying during the Reign of Terror in 1794 in France. Monroe fought in several engagements during the War of Independence and suffered a near-fatal wound at Trenton in 1776. Jefferson was almost captured by the king's soldiers in 1781, and would have faced a life-threatening imprisonment if he had been taken captive.

Jefferson and Paine made major contributions to the lives and outlooks of their contemporaries, and their writings remain influential today. Jefferson's Declaration of Independence captured the spirit of his countrymen in 1776, and for generation after generation of Americans—and for many non-Americans as well—it has encapsulated the principles of human rights and freedom. Thereafter, Jefferson collaborated with French reformers in the preparation of the enduring Declaration of the Rights of Man and of the Citizen, and in the 1790s he led a political party that battled antidemocratic forces in the United States. No writer in the twenty years after 1776 came close to reaching the vast numbers that read Paine's books and essays, and none rivaled the cutting-edge ideas for which he was renowned. Monroe was something of an everyman among those shaped by the American Revolution. Only eighteen in 1776, Monroe was radicalized by the rhetoric of the American Revolution—including ideas expressed by Jefferson and Paine—and by his exemplary and often dangerous military service in the Revolutionary War. His attachment to the revolutionary ideals, and his propulsive ambition, motivated and steeled him to fight the foes of the spirit of 1776 and to see the revolutionaries in France as comrades.

Jefferson, Paine, and Monroe were real revolutionaries who longed for a genuine revolution that would lead to profound alterations in America's fabric. For them, and the most radical of America's insurgents, the American Revolution was the means through which to escape royal and aristocratic rule, replace Britain's oppressive dominion with governments in which the people were sovereign, free the colonists from the incessant warfare of the British Empire, and set Americans on a path toward equal rights and opportunities.

Jefferson, Paine, and Monroe traveled different routes on the road to the revolution. Jefferson's years in college and his subsequent studying and reading, as well as his experiences while a provincial assemblyman, pulled together his thinking. By his thirtieth birthday, Jefferson was convinced that Virginia was victimized in myriad ways through its connection with London. Paine's radicalism grew from untold hours of listening to the lectures and debates among activists in the English reform movement. Monroe was influenced by the force of the stirring insurgent rhetoric in the air as he came of age in the mid-1770s, and like the other two, he was driven by a gnawing ambition for recognition and acclaim.

When independence was declared, Paine was the most radical of the three. Paine not only rejoiced in an American Revolution that he expected to usher in great changes, but also he hoped it would cleanse England and the Old World of monarchy, titled nobilities, and the fallacies and superstitions that sustained the old order. He dreamed that the American Revolution was the first step in the creation of a new world free of autocratic governments, oligarchical elites, widespread inequality and deprivation, and the seemingly perpetual menace of war. He envisioned the birth of a world in which the poorest would be elevated to a more comfortable station and that at long last they, too, would enjoy the natural rights that were their due. In time, Jefferson and Monroe caught up with Paine's thinking, and so, too, did many other Americans who were radicalized by the Revolutionary War and the revolutionary credo made widely known at least in part through the writings of Jefferson and Paine.

Jefferson, Paine, and Monroe played important roles in the American Revolution: two as writers, two as soldiers, one as the occupant of high offices before peace came in 1783. Significantly, all three were active in the French Revolution as well. Jefferson, who spent five years in France in the 1780s, collaborated with French aristocrats galvanized by the American Revolution. Paine was in and out of France on several occasions during the initial years of the French Revolution. He wrote favorably about the early radical events of the Revolution and was among the first in Paris to publicly urge the establishment of republicanism. He eventually served for nearly two years in the National Convention, France's revolutionary legislature, where in 1793 he took public stands in the debates on the fate of the monarch, Louis XVI. Monroe, appointed by George Washington to be the United States minister to France, arrived in Paris in the summer of 1794. He openly acclaimed the French Revolution and throughout his stay worked to bring about closer relations between revolutionary France and the United States.

Each of the three rejoiced at having the good fortune to be part of what Paine effusively labeled the "age of revolutions" and Jefferson branded "an age of revolution and reformation."[1] Each believed that the French Revolution had been inspired by the American Revolution. Each hoped the example of a republican France, together with that of the American Republic, would prompt radical changes across the European landscape. Above all, each prayed that the nation they regarded as the great scourge, England, would be swept with the liberating spirit of a republican revolution. And each felt that drastic changes in France and beyond would inspire additional changes within the United States.

While none of the three urged violence in Europe, none shrank from it. Jefferson and Paine justified some of the French Revolution's early carnage. None of the three foresaw the turn toward terror that eventually tainted France's revolution. Some conservative Americans—including John Adams, George Washington, and Alexander Hamilton—early on looked with misgivings on the events in France. A part of this book is an examination of the shortcomings of Jefferson, Paine, and Monroe in failing to foresee the collapse of the moderate republican revolution that they had expected and cherished.

As the French Revolution advanced from heartening reforms to ghastly, blood-soaked horrors, Jefferson, Paine, and Monroe grew disillusioned and abandoned all hope that Britain and Europe would become republicanized in their lifetimes. By the mid-1790s the American Revolution—and the America that the Revolution was still creating—had for them become even more momentous, since by then it was clear that America alone stood as a beacon of hope to the oppressed. But as that crucial decade progressed, Jefferson, Paine, and Monroe grew convinced that those they saw as reactionary American Anglophiles, led chiefly by Hamilton and his patron Washington, were bent on wiping out many of the changes ushered in by the American Revolution. The goal of these "Tories," the trio was certain, was to fabricate the United States on the model of monarchical and oligarchical England. Seemingly, all that had been achieved since 1776 was imperiled, a widely shared belief that led the politics of the 1790s to be waged with a supercharged passion evident in only two or three other decades in American history. For Jefferson, Paine, and Monroe—and for their adversaries—what was at stake was nothing less than the shape of America for generations to come.

Jefferson, Paine, and Monroe knew one another, though all three were never together at the same moment. They corresponded with one another; Paine lived for a time with Monroe; Monroe once shared a house with Jefferson. Each had a genuine affection for the other two, but their feelings transcended mere warmth. Monroe revered his elders Paine and Jefferson. Jefferson admired Paine's unequaled gifts as a writer and endorsed the radical ideas he espoused. Both Jefferson and Paine looked on Monroe as a zealous, dedicated, trustworthy, and diligent stalwart of enlightened change. By 1800, Paine and Monroe had come to think of Jefferson as America's best, and perhaps only, hope for preserving the revolutionary American world that had sprung to life in 1776.

These three were not always successful. While in their late thirties, each appeared to be an utter failure. Paine at thirty-seven was unemployed and nearly destitute. When he was thirty-eight, Jefferson's political career was in tatters, leaving him to think that his public life was over and that he would live the remainder of his years in isolation at Monticello, his hilltop estate. At age thirty-eight, Monroe was rebuked by President Washington, a veritable kiss of death for anyone with political ambitions.

Each despaired when his dreams for France did not play out as hoped, but none ever lost faith in the American Revolution. Each went to his grave confident that the changes brought about by the Revolution would endure, thanks in no small measure to Jefferson's election as president in 1800, but also because none of the three ever lost confidence in the American people's commitment to republicanism.

For all their shared hopes, the three were different in many ways. Paine hailed from a working-class background, and of the three his climb to renown was the most spectacular. Monroe's father was a minor planter with little money, but it was James's good fortune to have well-connected and influential relatives who laid the groundwork for his ascent. Only Jefferson came from a truly privileged background. But whether from humble or elite origins, no one's rise to the pinnacle is guaranteed, and this book explores the assorted factors and personal qualities that accounted for the ascendancy of each of the three.

In the early 1790s, Paine may have been the best-known American revolutionary in Europe, and in America only Washington was better known. Later in the decade, once Americans at last became aware of Jefferson's role in writing the Declaration of Independence, his popularity within the United States soared and exceeded that of Paine. By 1796, when the first contested presidential election took place, only Washington was held in higher regard than Jefferson. Outside Virginia, Monroe's name was familiar only to political junkies until a few years into the nineteenth century, and even then, unlike Paine and Jefferson, he was never a celebrated figure who drew the curious and hero-worshippers to his door.

Jefferson, Paine, and Monroe shared some common links. All were published authors. All wrote things that they came to regret, or in Paine's case that he should have lamented having written. Two of the three fell heavily into debt and the third faced money struggles throughout his life. Each also grew jaded toward George Washington. It is not too much to say that Paine and Monroe came to despise him. Jefferson struggled to maintain a more balanced understanding of Washington, but he, too, came to see the first president as deceitful, even disingenuous.

It is a daunting challenge to come to grips with earlier historical figures and their times. John Adams doubted that future historians would ever be capable of adequately understanding the American Revolution. Jefferson agreed, and he told Adams that the "life and soul of [the] history" of the Revolution "must be for ever unknown."[2] His comment was seemingly underscored by John Jay, revolutionary congressman, diplomat, and first chief justice of the United States, who late in life reflected that many of the Founders "were not at all what they seemed, nor what they were generally believed to have been."[3] But more can be known than Adams and Jefferson believed. Among other things, the Founders left behind voluminous collections of letters and writings, and some wrote useful memoirs. This treasure trove of material opens a window onto the American Revolution and the lives of Jefferson, Paine, and Monroe.

It is difficult to imagine more exciting times than those in which Jefferson, Paine, and Monroe lived and acted. They were a part of the struggle for American independence, the long and desperate Revolutionary War, the momentous French Revolution, the creation of the new American nation, the intense partisanship of the 1790s, including the battles waged by America's first political parties, and the pivotal election of 1800. Larger-than-life figures marched across the stages on which these three played, from Washington to Hamilton, from Louis XVI to Napoleon Bonaparte, from Benjamin Franklin to John Adams to James Madison. Our trio knew early on that they lived in the most stirring of times. Each was anxious not merely to be part of the times, but to play vital—and memorable—roles in the great events of the day. Each understood that making huge personal sacrifices was the price to be paid for his activism, and each willingly did so. Tragedy struck the private lives of each of the three. Two suffered the early deaths of spouses, and all three coped with the demise of at least one child. Activism brought heady successes. It also produced ruthless, menacing adversaries. Each lost friends because of his public role, and at times the payoff for public engagement was to suffer the grievous hand of loneliness and despair.

Each of the three had ample virtues and blemishes. Jefferson was manipulative, although through good and bad times he remained steadfastly affectionate and loyal toward Paine and Monroe. Paine and Monroe understood the ins and outs of politics, but neither possessed Jefferson's uncanny ability to divine political trends and the motivations of others. Paine could be prickly, and his gargantuan ego alienated many. Hands down, he was the most dissolute among the three. But he was also the most forward-thinking and the one whose mind always seemed to be actively searching for new and untried ways to lighten the burdens of the downtrodden. Paine may also have been the most generous of the three and the one most likely to provide enjoyable company during a night of convivial conversation. But that came with a catch: It was for the most part a companionable evening only for a male. Paine was not a misogynist, but whereas Jefferson and Monroe thoroughly enjoyed the company of women, he sometimes froze in their presence, finding it nearly impossible to converse. Monroe exhibited many traits that won the respect of others. He was brave and daring, not the type to be intimidated or brow-beaten, exceedingly industrious, loyal, and adept at winning and maintaining friendships. But where Paine and Jefferson were capable of shrugging off savage criticism, Monroe was hypersensitive. To the point of irksomeness, he was unable to cope with the least slight, not the best attribute for one engaged in the rough-and-tumble game of politics. To a degree unseen in Jefferson and Paine, Monroe at times was consumed with suspicion toward his friends and a bubbling anger, even loathing, for political enemies.

This book is first and foremost about three American revolutionaries who in time became apostles of ever wider revolutions. It is not intended as intel-lectual history, but as an examination of the lives of three politically engaged Founders who shared a sense of hopeful possibilities about liberating and empowering ordinary people. It looks into what shaped and drove these three, examines their actions and ideas, and seeks to explain their successes and failures, their good judgments and bad choices. While a student many years ago, I read Bertram Wolfe's *Three Who Made A Revolution*, a book that told the story of the Russian Revolution by making Lenin, Trotsky, and Stalin the focal point of the account. Wolfe's book inspired me to sometimes take a comparative approach when teaching, and on occasion it has influenced my approach to thinking and writing about the American Revolution. Compara-tive history prompts the historian to ask questions that might not otherwise be asked, to travel pathways of inquiry that might not otherwise be taken, and to draw conclusions that might otherwise never be drawn. I hope this book, and this approach, will shed light on the Age of Revolution while at the same moment open a window onto the thinking, challenges, and complex activi-ties of Jefferson, Paine, and Monroe.

Debts accumulate in the course of writing any book. I am grateful to Barbara Oberg and Andrew Burstein, whom I pestered with questions about Jefferson, and who always responded cheerfully. Edith Gelles, James Sefcik, Charles Lipp,

Keith Pacholl, Arthur Lefkowitz, Michael de Nie, and Robert Schaefer also provided help with my queries. Matt deLesdernier has helped me with many books and on this one, too, he provided assistance on military matters. Physicians Laura Lamb Larson and William Morton offered guidance concerning Paine's illnesses. Lorene Flanders and Chris Huff graciously supported my research and writing by providing an office that I have used daily. Angela Mehaffey and Margot David in the interlibrary loan office of the Irvine Sullivan Ingram Library at the University of West Georgia provided crucial help in meeting my frequent requests for books and articles, and Gail Smith and Billy Willey saw to the acquisition of items that were important to my work. Once again, I am grateful for the help, guidance, and kindness of Peter Ginna, who edited this manuscript, as he has done with all but one of my books over the past twenty years. This was my first book with Anton Mueller, and I found him a delight to work with. Grace McNamee and Laura Phillips were wonderful to work with during the production stage of the book. Maureen Klier is a splendid copy editor and it was my good fortune to work with her yet again. Julie Dobbs and Chris Harris helped me out of more than one scrape with my computer. I owe so many debts of gratitude to Catherine Hendricks that to list them would double the length of this book.

Geri Thoma, my literary agent, was crucial in the fulfillment of my dream to write the book.

I don't think Sammy Grace, Simon, Katie, and Clementine care much one way or another about Jefferson, Paine, and Monroe, but they enrich my life, which makes the often trying work of writing a book a bit easier.

As always, Carol, my wife, was supportive, understanding, and patient throughout the forty-two months that I spent on this book.

PROLOGUE

JAMES MONROE'S CARRIAGE BOUNCED NOISILY over the cobblestone streets of Paris on the sunny afternoon of August 15, 1794. He was the new United States minister to France, and his destination was the Salle des Machines, a vast theater in the northern wing of the splendid and sprawling Tuileries Palace. Once used for concerts and by the Paris Opera, and more recently the Comédie-Française, the palace for more than a year had been home to the Convention, France's national legislature. Older than any building in the United States, and flanked by lavish gardens and an immense park that was more or less a public venue, the Tuileries sat a short walk from the gently flowing Seine.[1]

Monroe was likely overwhelmed by the size of Paris, which was more than ten times larger than the largest American city and bore no resemblance in manner or design to New York or Philadelphia, both of which he had visited. Parts of Paris retained a medieval look, with narrow, winding streets and huge ancient churches, but thanks to a building boom during recent decades, numerous grand and ornate structures dotted the landscape, many situated on new and expansive boulevards. Here and there stood a building influenced by the Italian and German rococo style, though most of the recent construction proudly bore evidence of tasteful and smart French classicism. Jean-Jacques Rousseau complained that Paris was a "dirty and stinking" metropolis bulging with "ugly black houses," a city awash with "filth, poverty, beggars, carters, sewing women, women hawking tisanes and old hats."[2] Monroe likely took in some of the squalor in the course of his carriage ride. He may also have seen the guillotine on the Place de la Révolution, a large square adjacent to the Tuileries—an instrument that lately had been put to considerable use.

Monroe, now thirty-six years old, was a striking individual. Sturdy, perhaps a bit rough-hewn, he stood slightly over six feet, nearly five inches taller than most fully grown American men and even more imposing than European men, who on average were shorter than their counterparts across the ocean.[3] Monroe had always been svelte, and he was considerably slender now, having just completed an arduous sea voyage from Baltimore. Monroe was part of the Virginia gentry, educated and somewhat refined, although he brought to mind more the rugged man of action than the elegant and urbane diplomats more commonly seen in European courts.

Monroe's objective on this day was to present his credentials and be officially received as the representative of the United States, a country with which France sixteen years earlier had signed treaties of alliance and commerce. Ordinarily, the reception of an important foreign emissary was conducted by the nation's executive, but five days before Monroe's arrival in Paris, Maximilien de Robespierre—leader of the Committee of Public Safety, France's executive branch for the past several months—had fallen from power and gone to the guillotine. Thereafter, in what Monroe characterized as "a derangement of their affairs," the Committee of Public Safety had for all practical purposes ceased to exist, leaving France without an executive.[4] The turmoil was but the latest upheaval in a French Revolution that had begun with moderation in 1789. However, following the 1792 outbreak of war with Austria—and a growing list of enemies in the ensuing months—France had careened into bloody violence. In the atmosphere of fear and hysteria that beset Paris in the first year of the war, people thought to be priests and aristocrats had been dragged from jails and murdered, and in time the king and queen had also been executed. During what the French called "the Terror," which peaked while Monroe was crossing the Atlantic, more than 2,500 had been executed in Paris. Sometimes scores had climbed the scaffold daily in the course of the six weeks that his ship, the *Cincinnatus*, had been at sea. It had been even more ghastly in the provinces, where many times the number that died in Paris perished by order of revolutionary tribunals, so many that the guillotines could not keep pace and firing squads had been pressed into action.[5]

Five years earlier, Monroe, a fervent republican, had greeted word of the French Revolution with joy. He felt that the American Revolution had inspired the French, and that the driving force behind both upheavals had been a desire to thwart oppressive monarchs and cruel aristocracies that were indifferent to humankind's natural rights. Now, in mid-afternoon on this warm day in Thermidor (as August had been renamed in France's revolutionary calendar), Monroe was to address France's government.

"Citizen Monroe," as he was referred to in the Convention's journal, alighted from his carriage in the midst of a large and friendly throng. Once he was escorted into the legislative chamber, Monroe beheld an assembly hall unlike any he had ever seen. The Salle des Machines was long and narrow, with sixty-foot ceilings. Hundreds of deputies occupied seats in sharply rising, semicircular tiers. Thousands of noisy spectators filled galleries overlooking the rostrum and legislators. As soon as Monroe entered, he was welcomed with applause and cries of "Long live the Convention, long live the United States of America, our brave brothers." A member of Monroe's party felt that the Americans had been greeted "like beings of a superior nature."[6]

As the hall grew quiet, Monroe prepared to read his address. He was in an awkward position. France had been at war for thirty months, about half of that time in a life-and-death struggle with a coalition that included virtually every major power in Europe save for Russia. Alliance with France did not require that the United States aid its ally, and in fact from the war's outset America had been officially neutral in the European conflict. Neutrality required delicacy on the part of the American minister, but Monroe was a novice diplomat and had hurriedly written his speech only the night before. Its contents reflected his sentiments and those of his political party back home, the Republican Party, more than a strict adherence to neutrality, the steadfast position of the administration of President George Washington.

In a tone that he subsequently described as "suitable solemnity," Monroe began by saying that "Republics should approach near to each other." Nothing could be more true, he went on, than that the French Republic and the American Republic "cherish the same principles and rest on the same basis, the equal and unalienable rights of men." The bond between the two nations, he continued, had been cemented through French assistance in America's War of Independence, as well as by the prevailing hope in the United States that France would triumph in its own "noble" war on behalf of the "cause of liberty." Indeed, "America is not an unfeeling spectator of your affairs in the present crisis." It was eager to "perpetuate the harmony" that had long existed between "the two Republics."[7]

When Monroe completed his remarks, the president of the Convention embraced him and declared that France and America—which he said had been "freed by each other"—were the closest of "friends." They were not merely allies. Theirs was a union of what he called the "sweetest fraternity," a bond that "will be forever the dread of tyrants, the safeguard of the liberty of the world, and the preserver of all the social and philanthropic virtues." Next, the Convention voted to hang the American flag next to the French flag within the chamber. Monroe was overcome with emotion, calling the ninety-minute ceremony a time of "distressing sensibility." Never had he been part of anything so impassioned or moving, he said.[8]

What touched Monroe most deeply was that the stirring formalities seemed to him to be the fulfillment of the dream that had guided him through the War of Independence and his political activism following hostilities. In his mind, the American Revolution was about more than breaking with Great

Britain and creating an independent American nation. It had been a struggle waged to bring on seminal political and social change, and not just in America. Like some other rebels, Monroe had hoped the American Revolution would shine as a radiant beacon, spurring reforms in Europe's bastions of monarchy and aristocracy.

Monroe's dream had been realized with the eruption of the French Revolution. With unbridled fervor, he wished for the French Revolution to succeed and for its example to lead others to embrace republicanism, a radical ideology that would transform subjects into citizens and unleash substantive social changes. But Monroe was not dreaming only of change in Europe. Just as the American Revolution had inspired dissidents in France, Monroe believed that if the French Revolution succeeded, it would spawn still more change within America.

At the moment when Monroe arrived in Paris, the French Revolution was threatened by an array of conservative European powers that sought nothing less than the restoration of the French monarchy and aristocracy. Monroe realized that if they were successful, it would cease the spread of the "spirit of liberty . . . in other regions."[9]

Monroe knew full well that his views were anathema to American conservatives. He understood, too, that his most conservative countrymen prayed that the conservative European powers would defeat France and demolish all that the French Revolution had wrought. Monroe had to know that, as he spoke to the Convention, he was on thin ice in making excessively friendly remarks about the French Republic and in encouraging closer Franco-American ties. His address, he told his friend and fellow Virginian James Madison, was certain to "be scanned with unfriendly eyes by many in America." Nonetheless, Monroe, filled with ardor, had not hesitated to speak his mind, hopeful that the "citizens of both Republicks" would benefit from "cementing more closely their union."[10]

Thomas Paine, though a native Englishman, had played important roles in both the American Revolution and the French Revolution. He had moved from England to America in 1774. Two years later, in *Common Sense*, the most important work published during America's revolution, Paine had condemned monarchies and called on the colonists to break with Great Britain and establish a republic, the form of government best suited for "Securing freedom and property to all men." At stake, Paine had written, were "*the RIGHTS of MANKIND,*" not merely in America, but in Europe as well. If the American Revolution succeeded, nothing less than the "birthday of a new world" would dawn.[11]

Paine was back in England when the French Revolution erupted. The news from France had reawakened "the ardour of Seventy six" in his soul, he said, for it held the promise of the triumph of the ideals of the American Revolution in England and throughout Europe.[12] He had hurried to France and soon became a player in the dangerous events unfurling about him. He had been one of the first in France to appeal publicly for the creation of a French republic and one of the first to openly call the French king by his given name rather than as Louis XVI. He had even been elected to the Convention, the very assembly that Monroe addressed. He rejoiced at the opportunity to take part in a second great revolution that, like its predecessor, was being waged on behalf of "the cause of all mankind."[13]

Paine had never heard of Monroe. But Monroe, and all Americans, knew of Paine, and the new American minister had read *Common Sense* and other works that Paine had produced during America's Revolutionary War. Monroe knew, too, that Paine had come to France and had read with admiration what Paine had written in the 1790s about human rights. That was all he knew, save that Paine was not in his seat in the Convention. Monroe probably guessed— though he did not know for sure—that Paine's involvement in the French Revolution had drawn him into the vortex of peril. For certain, Monroe was unaware that as he was cheered in the Salle des Machines, Paine languished with hundreds of other inmates in the Luxembourg prison. He had been incarcerated eight months earlier in the heat of the Terror, and as Monroe delivered his rapturous speech to the French assemblymen, Paine's life hung by a thread.

Paine and Monroe may not have known each other, but Paine knew Thomas Jefferson, having met him in Philadelphia and in Paris, and Jefferson was especially close to Monroe. In fact, Jefferson was a patron of Monroe's. The two had met nearly fifteen years earlier, and Monroe, ambitious to make his mark, had understood that Jefferson could be crucial in facilitating his rise to importance in political circles within Virginia. Jefferson in turn had seen promise in Monroe, a bright, industrious, and above all loyal young man. By 1786, Jefferson had discerned in Monroe "a man whose soul might be turned wrong side outwards without discovering a blemish to the world."[14]

Eight years later, on this day in 1794, Monroe was literally following in Jefferson's footsteps. Jefferson had served as the second United States minister to France, and while living in pre-revolutionary Paris he had attended concerts a dozen times or more in the Salle des Machines.[15] Like Paine, Jefferson had played a role in the early events of the French Revolution, though his activities had been covert. But no less than Paine, or Monroe, Jefferson hoped that the French Revolution would bring republicanism to France, and that it in turn would both annihilate the "enormous inequality producing so much misery to the bulk of mankind" and restore the "rights of man" throughout Europe and in England.[16]

Jefferson was back in America in 1794, but he watched the French Revolution closely, and he had read Paine's public and private defense of the radical, and sometimes bloody, upheavals in France with great pleasure.[17] Jefferson was convinced, as was Monroe when he alighted in France, that the American Revolution had been the spark that ignited the French. But as the twentieth anniversary of American independence approached, both Jefferson and Monroe feared that ultraconservatives menaced many of the gains won in the American Revolution, much as French royalists and aristocrats wished to annihilate the reforms that France's revolutionaries had implemented over the past five years. Jefferson and his acolyte Monroe were also filled with foreboding that those who plotted against the promise of the American Revolution likewise wished to use their power and influence to frustrate America's friendship with France and destroy the French Revolution. The threats they beheld only increased their fervor for the success of the French Revolution, as they were convinced that a flourishing French republic would nurture, and perhaps reawaken, the idealism that had swept over America in 1776.

For Jefferson, Monroe, and Paine, the battles they fought after 1776, and especially during the tumultuous 1790s, were waged for nothing less than the dignity, equality, and rights of man in America and throughout Europe and England.

CHAPTER I

"The Destinies of Life"

On the Road to Bigger Things

No blueprint exists for the making of a revolutionary. If there were such a pattern, one or more among Thomas Jefferson, Thomas Paine, and James Monroe would not have matched it, for the three had quite different early-life experiences. Indeed, perhaps the greatest common link among the three was that little or nothing in their earliest years appeared to mark them as future apostles of revolution.

Thomas Jefferson was fortune's child. Born in 1743 on Virginia's mountainous western frontier, he was the son of a prosperous tobacco planter, Peter Jefferson, and his wife, Jane, from the prestigious and powerful Randolph family. Together with their eight children, the couple lived at Shadwell, a six-room, one-and-a-half-story farmhouse that sat on a sprawling estate of fourteen hundred acres worked by a large number of slaves. Already six years old at the time of Jefferson's birth, Thomas Paine was born and raised in Thetford, England, a country market town of some two thousand inhabitants situated about seventy-five miles northeast of London. His father, Joseph Pain—as the family name was originally spelled—was a Quaker; his mother, Frances, who was Anglican, was the daughter of the village attorney. Thomas was their only child to survive infancy. Joseph earned his living as a skilled artisan, making stays for women's corsets and waistcoats, a pursuit that enabled the little family to live comfortably in a small, thatch-roofed house that included the shop. James Monroe was born fifteen years after Jefferson in a region of Virginia that hugged the lower Potomac River. Monroe's paternal ancestors had emigrated from Scotland a century earlier, and his father, Spence Monroe, had inherited five hundred acres that had been nearly exhausted by three or four generations of tobacco planting. Elizabeth Monroe, James's mother, was the daughter of a Welsh immigrant. A farmer who owned the amount of property that Spence possessed was considered by Virginians to be of the gentry class, but a few hundred acres was a trifle compared with the holdings of the great planters in the colony. Even so, Spence Monroe was thought to be affluent by his neighbors, yet his family of seven—there were four boys and a daughter—lived in a rustic two-story frame house whose square footage was not appreciably larger than today's two-car garages. Any frills the Monroes enjoyed came because Spence worked on the side as a carpenter, cabinetmaker, and home builder.[1]

Jefferson, Paine, and Monroe, unlike many of their contemporaries, each received a formal education, and each spent more years in school than his father. After studying at home with a tutor for several years, Jefferson was sent off for his college preparatory schooling at age nine. For the next eight years, while a student in two Latin schools that offered a classical education, he lived much of the time away from home. He emerged ready for the rigors of college, but of no less importance, Jefferson's ambition had been quickened along the way. By age seventeen, when he enrolled in the College of William and Mary in Williamsburg, Virginia, Jefferson already craved to stand apart from others intellectually, cherished the hope of becoming distinguished by his grace and refinement, and was keen to be seen as a natural leader by virtue of his enlightenment, taste, and urbanity. Jefferson's first-rate education was crucial to his evolving aspirations, but his temperament, longings, and self-esteem were first shaped by his father. Young Thomas loved and revered his father, who through the accumulation of a large library and disciplined self-study had smoothed the rough edges of his intellect and persona. Jefferson remembered him as a bright, ambitious, physically impressive, passably culti-vated man of "strong mind, sound judgment, and eager after information." Peter Jefferson had by steps risen to be a justice of the peace, sheriff, and county surveyor. A favorable marriage catapulted him to greater prominence, including election to the Virginia colonial assembly, the House of Burgesses. But Peter had not attended college and that may have inhibited his rise to a leadership role in an assembly dominated by great planters and lawyers.[2]

Through his father's influence, and that of James Maury, one of his prepa-ratory school teachers, young Jefferson found joy through study and learning. Maury possessed the largest private library that Jefferson had ever seen, and the schoolmaster gave his young student free run of it. Maury doubtless saw young Jefferson as an exceptional student, and several faculty members at William and Mary concurred. One, William Small, a Scotsman and the only member of the faculty who was not a clergyman, introduced young Jefferson to rational and scientific ways of thinking. So influential was Small that Jefferson later remarked that it was his "great good fortune" to have been taught by him, for he had "fixed the destinies of my life."[3] Small was not solely responsible for molding the young student, but the Jefferson that emerged from college was intellectually curious, committed to inquiry, and open to new ideas, including the reconsideration of conventional practices.

Early on, Jefferson knew that someday he would inherit considerable wealth, and following his father's early death in 1757, Thomas inherited some five thousand acres and slightly more than twenty slaves. His inheritance set Jefferson apart from the great majority of free whites in the South, for in many counties no more than 30 percent were landowners, and among them not many possessed much more than two hundred or three hundred acres; in Virginia and Maryland, considerably less than half the free population owned a single slave. Though Jefferson understood early on that he could live comfortably, even as an adolescent he knew that he wanted more than the obscurity that attended a life of simply managing a plantation. At age sixteen he had beseeched his guardian for permission to attend college, as the doors it opened would, he said, "hereafter be serviceable to me." He made the most of college. Describing himself as "a hard student" who studied for several hours each day, Jefferson was nevertheless popular and fashioned lifelong relationships with several fellow students. In some respects, his collegiate habits resembled those that he exhibited throughout the rest of his life, as he daily set aside time from studying for violin practice and exercise, which included walking, running, and swimming. By the time he graduated in 1762, Jefferson yearned not merely to "be admired" but also to achieve a "*very* high standing." He thought that would be within reach if he became a planter-lawyer. Planting would generate wealth, while practicing law was a possible avenue to power and prestige.[4] Following graduation, Jefferson read law with George Wythe, an esteemed Williamsburg lawyer and a member of the House of Burgesses.

Jefferson passed the bar exam at age twenty-two, but he did not immediately launch his legal practice. He spent most of the next two years at Shadwell, living with his mother and siblings and engaged in still more study. Some in the eighteenth century, such as Patrick Henry and Alexander Hamilton, opened legal practices after only a few weeks of preparation, and few attorneys displayed a particularly studious side once they were licensed to practice. But Jefferson, who had already spent more than two years studying under Wythe, delayed starting his practice for another twenty-four months while he immersed himself in further studying law, history, science, and classical philosophy, and reading eminent Enlightenment thinkers. The love of learning and ideas, which would be an enduring characteristic, had already taken hold, but more than that accounted for what one scholar called Jefferson's "monastic" period. Jefferson hoped that through a deeper understanding of the law he could rapidly gain distinction once he opened his legal practice. In addition, he recognized that his limitations as a public speaker would be a formidable handicap when arguing cases before juries in county courts. That led him to set his sights on practicing before the General Court of Judicature, where cases were tried before a panel of judges and greater intellectual rigor was required.

What is more, Jefferson not only wanted his father's old seat in the Burgesses; he aspired to greater prominence than his father had attained. Jefferson coveted a leadership role in the Virginia assembly. A close friend thought something else also drove Jefferson. Edmund Randolph, his cousin, believed that Jefferson dreamed of becoming a gifted writer as well as of winning admiration as a sophisticate. Indeed, Randolph thought Jefferson undertook his painstaking studies so that he could comfortably converse with learned individuals everywhere, but also from the hope that by becoming a brilliant conversationalist, he would enjoy a well-rounded social life.[5]

Jefferson may have loved his books, but he was living the life of a recluse and he yearned for love and companionship. His first stab at courtship, while in college, had ended unsuccessfully because of his social awkwardness. Eight long years passed before Jefferson sought the hand of another woman. At one point, the miserably lonely Jefferson proposed to his closest college chum, John Page, that Page, his wife, and Jefferson become a threesome to "pull down the moon." Page apparently understood that Jefferson was proposing a ménage a trois and did not answer the letter for a very long time; when Page finally responded, he ignored the shocking proposition. Jefferson once referred to youth as a time of "colonial subserviency," and he never looked back fondly on this period of his life. Whereas Benjamin Franklin and John Adams each devoted about forty pages in their memoirs to the first thirty or so years of their lives, Jefferson glossed over his in two brief paragraphs.[6]

In 1767, at age twenty-four, Jefferson began to practice law, mostly handling cases involving land claims and titles in the lower courts and, from the beginning, arguing cases in Virginia's highest court. He succeeded almost at once, and his caseload more or less doubled each year during the next five or six years. By the early 1770s, Jefferson was earning about £175 annually, roughly seven times the yearly income of most craftsmen in, say, Philadelphia. His legal practice required considerable travel, though Jefferson was at home most of the year, and in his spare time he drew up plans for Monticello, the mansion he had long dreamed of building. He selected the top of a tall hill on the other side of the Rivanna River from Shadwell—an unconventional site, as hilltops were susceptible to damage in severe storms, roads had to be cut upgrade through the dense and tangled forest, and digging a successful well atop a mountain was always problematic. But Jefferson saw his mountain as strong and inaccessible, an asylum "above the storms," a shelter from "those who have not talents to occupy themselves." (Long after the house was constructed and the gardens and landscaping tended to, a visitor not improbably thought Monticello's site was "something grand & awful," a place that most would "rather look at . . . than live at.") His legal practice and, in time, politics might occasionally take him away, but for most of each year the independence-seeking Jefferson planned to sequester himself in his mountain lair and pursue whatever he wished. During his second year as a lawyer, Jefferson set a team of his slaves to work clearing and leveling the top of the mountain, and soon, work began on the house.[7]

About eighteen months after taking up the law, Jefferson turned his attention to what Virginians called "burgessing," seeking election to the House of Burgesses. He ran for election to his father's old seat. It was the earliest opportunity to do so, as there had not been an election in the three years since he had completed his studies with Wythe. It is unlikely that Jefferson made any stump speeches during the campaign, as that was not a common practice in eighteenth-century Virginia. But like other candidates in other elections, he probably enlisted friends to round up support for him, and to assure success, he held rallies at which voters were treated to food and strong drink. One contemporary described the practice as "swilling the planters with bumbo." Hustling for votes must have been an ordeal for Jefferson, who disliked fraternizing with strangers.[8] But he did it, and he won.

A couple of weeks after turning twenty-six, Jefferson took his seat in the assembly. The House was run by its Speaker and clerk. Every member served on at least one committee, but the assembly's crucial business was performed by five key committees. Some assemblymen never got a place on one of them, and for those that did, years were usually required to win such a coveted post.[9] Jefferson landed on two of the major committees on his first day as a burgess, thanks to Peyton Randolph, the Speaker of the House and a relative from his mother's side of the family. Few who sat on a leading committee ever became its chair. George Washington served in the assembly for sixteen years and never obtained such a plum assignment. But Jefferson rose rapidly to become the head of one of the powerful panels. However, before the Revolutionary War he never ascended to the leadership team. Not the expansive type, Jefferson shrank from the arm-twisting, coaxing, and wheeling and dealing incumbent on legislative leaders. Something else also got in Jefferson's way. Roughly a year after entering the assembly, he met and began to court Martha Wayles Skelton.

Martha was a twenty-two-year-old widow with a three-year-old son. She lived with her father at the Forest, a plantation near Williamsburg, where

Jefferson was spending about a quarter of each year grappling with his legal and legislative responsibilities. Descriptions of Martha vary, ranging from short to tall, though most observers agreed that she was attractive and good-natured, loved books and music, and played the spinet and harpsichord. One thing is beyond dispute. Martha was the daughter of a man who had amassed a fortune from his legal practice, as well as from tobacco, slave trading, and land speculation.[10]

Jefferson was smitten immediately, telling a friend that he planned to "take to himself a wife." But there were delays, and the courtship lasted some fifteen months. Not only did he face obligations in Williamsburg and Albermarle County, but the couple may have wished to know each other better before committing to matrimony. As Shadwell had burned a few months prior to their first meeting, Jefferson additionally had to await the completion of at least a small portion of Monticello so that he and his bride would have a residence. He also faced a reelection campaign in 1771, which kept him at home more than usual. Once all obstacles were removed, the couple wed on New Year's Day 1772 in an Anglican ceremony at the Forest. Nearly twenty-nine on his wedding day, Jefferson married at a later age than most males in colonial America. It was not unusual for an ambitious young man to postpone marriage until he had established himself. John Adams and George Washington were only a year younger than Jefferson when each of them married.

Jefferson was convinced that marriage would bring him "every scheme of happiness," and apparently it did.[11] It offered an escape from years of solitude and isolation, and from the beginning he found "comfort and happiness" with Martha. The manner in which he constructed his memoirs—he skimmed over his first twenty-nine years in four paragraphs—suggests that Jefferson may have thought his life began when he and Martha married. There is no reason to question his later remark that Martha had been the "cherished companion of my life, in whose affections, unabated on both sides, I . . . lived . . . in unchequered happiness." The couple seemed well suited for each other. They shared an interest in music and books, and she brought to the marriage her previous experience in managing a plantation household.[12] While her son from the first marriage died not long after she and Jefferson married, the couple ultimately had six children, though only two lived to adulthood.

The wealth that Martha brought to the marriage enabled Jefferson to immediately abandon the law. Not only had he come to see his legal practice as boringly repetitive, but he also grew to think that an appallingly large number of his fellow lawyers were lazy, ignorant, and corrupt men who preyed on the malice and avarice of others. Martha's wealth additionally permitted Jefferson to build the magnificent mansion he had dreamed of for himself and his family.[13]

Before he wed, Jefferson was producing tobacco as a cash crop in Albemarle County, where he owned some 2,650 acres, and on an additional 2,500 acres scattered throughout other counties. The death of his father-in-law in 1773 brought several thousand additional acres. By age thirty, Jefferson had become a land baron and—given the scores of chattel that Martha brought to the marriage—the owner of some 175 slaves. He may not have been the wealthiest resident of Albermarle County, but Jefferson was on the way to becoming extraordinarily rich.[14]

Jefferson's wealth was crucial for attaining the status and lifestyle that he had long craved. So, too, was political office, though there was nothing beyond sitting in the Virginia assembly to which Jefferson could aspire. Virginia's royal governors were appointed in London, and residents of the colony were never considered for the position. No seats for colonists existed in Parliament, no American had ever risen to a ministerial post—the secretary of state for American affairs, say, or chancellor of the exchequer—and gaining an important imperial office such as a seat on the Privy Council or Board of Trade was out of the question. The colonial assembly was the ceiling for a politically active colonist. Young Jefferson's aspirations are unknown. He may have dreamed of making a name for himself, as Benjamin Franklin had done, with his pen. All that can be known with assurance is that as Jefferson turned thirty in the spring of 1773, the vista before him was one of overseeing his planter pursuits, indulging his intellectual interests, luxuriating in his family life, managing the ongoing construction of Monticello, and basking in what he saw as the delicious respect that went with sitting in the assembly.

By the time Jefferson entered the House of Burgesses in 1769, the assembly faced a matter of unprecedented urgency. Anglo-American problems had festered for several years and had grown to the crisis stage. The first signs of trouble had come early in the 1760s, when London abandoned its traditionally slack enforcement of imperial trade laws and lackluster collection of customs charges in colonial ports. Tensions flared when London tightened its control, and a crisis came in 1765 when Parliament enacted the Stamp Act, its first attempt to levy a direct tax on the American colonists. Protestors surged into the streets in the major colonial cities, nearly every assembly denounced the legislation, and the Stamp Act Congress—attended by delegates from seven colonies—remonstrated against what Parliament had attempted.

Virginia had been the first to inveigh against parliamentary taxation. Following a resounding speech by Patrick Henry in which he assailed the Stamp Act as unconstitutional and a violation of the rights of the colonists, the burgesses adopted a series of resolutions censoring the law. Jefferson, a twenty-two-year-old student at the time, had stood in the lobby outside the assembly chamber listening to Henry's address and was swept with passion. The speech made an enormous "impression . . . on me," Jefferson later said, and he never wavered in his somewhat misplaced belief that Henry's fiery oratory had sparked the American Revolution. The speech may have been electrifying to Jefferson, but he was busy with his studies and within days returned to Shadwell and began his cloistered years of preparing to practice law.

Parliament repealed the Stamp Act in the face of the colonies' defiance, but in 1767 it imposed another set of taxes on the colonists, the Townshend Duties. The following year London posted more than two thousand British soldiers in Boston, the city that imperial leaders identified as the epicenter of colonial unrest. The troops were sent to assure that taxes and trade revenues were collected. A new wave of protests flared, and not solely in Boston. Trade embargoes sprang up in several major American ports, as had been the case earlier in protests against the Stamp Act. But this time the boycotts were more widespread and better enforced. In Virginia, George Washington took the lead, urging that the province embargo British trade until the taxes were repealed. (Jefferson, a fledgling assemblyman, voted for the ban on trade.) The colonists' strategy largely succeeded. In 1770, Parliament backed down a second time, repealing all colonial taxes except a duty on tea.

Seeking to avoid provocation, the British ministry, headed by Frederick, Lord North, refrained from further taxation. Quiet prevailed for three years—such tranquility in fact that the royal governor of Massachusetts reported to London that the "late incendiaries are much fallen" and the days of colonial protest were at an end.[15] The lull in American disturbances began just when Jefferson first called on Martha and continued until the couple had been married for eighteen months and had started a family. The one exception occurred in 1772, when Rhode Island protestors boarded and burned the *Gaspee*, a customs vessel, wounding the ship's captain during a brief melee. The North ministry's wrong-footed response to that incident included an attempt to arrest and try the perpetrators in London. Alarm spread throughout the colonies. To this point, Jefferson had been so absorbed by personal matters that he appears to have barely noticed the earlier disturbances. Now, however, he saw Lord North's step as an unmistakable usurpation of the colonists' authority.

In January 1773, Jefferson, working hand in hand with his assembly colleagues Patrick Henry and Richard Henry Lee, succeeded in having the House of Burgesses transmit its concerns to Massachusetts. Of greater importance, Jefferson helped induce the assembly to establish a committee of correspondence to facilitate communication between the colonies and foster the beginnings of a united front against imperial abuse. Boston's Committee of Correspondence responded promptly, and within a year every colony but Pennsylvania had created a similar body. Thereafter, the provincial insurgents shared ideas and information, adding to the suspicions of the British government, and as Samuel Adams of Massachusetts remarked, reinforcing the belief that the "Colonies are all embarked in the same bottom. The Liberties of all are alike invaded by the same haughty Power."[16]

The year 1773 was crucial in another respect. To save the nearly bankrupt East India Company, North's government enacted the Tea Act, legislation that reduced the six-year-old tax on tea and gave the beleaguered company a monopoly on tea sold throughout the colonies. Radical leaders in the colonies, such as Samuel Adams, understood immediately that if the colonists became accustomed to paying the duty on tea, it would break the back of the protest movement. The colonial insurgency, quiescent for years, was ramped up again to prevent the sale of the duderetied tea. Protest mobs turned out in several cities, but the most memorable response was in Boston. On the night of December 16, a carefully organized and managed crowd boarded the three tea ships docked in Boston Harbor and destroyed 340 large chests of tea worth several million dollars in today's money. The Boston Tea Party set in motion a spiral of events that ultimately led to war between Great Britain and its colonists.[17]

Jefferson had not been a major player in the colonial protest, but he lived in a troubled colony and its tribulations shaped his thinking regarding the British Empire and Virginia's—and America's—place in it. Boom times for tobacco, Virginia's staple, had come to an end around midcentury, plunging many planters into debt and threatening others with ruin. By the time Jefferson finished college, many planters were speaking of tobacco as a "worthless weed" and a "precarious commodity" that appeared to be reducing Virginia to "a declining State." Part of the problem stemmed from the vagaries of the marketplace, but some of it was due to imperial policies. Britain's trade laws mandated that American planters could sell their tobacco only within the British Empire. This policy had generated little stir so long as tobacco fetched a healthy sum, but once prices declined, indignation grew swiftly in Virginia. Provincial planters watched helplessly as English and Scottish merchants resold American tobacco at higher prices in European markets. Long before Jefferson entered the assembly, the House of Burgesses had petitioned the Crown to permit Virginians to export their tobacco to foreign markets. The appeal was turned down. Resentment built within the Old Dominion, expressed by Arthur Lee—a member of one of the colony's most powerful families—in a 1764 pamphlet that argued the best hope for Virginia's planters was to be independent of "the arbitrary impositions" of British trade restrictions that "fix, like cankers, on their estates, and utterly consume them." Around the same time, an exasperated George Washington exclaimed, "Our whole substance does already in a manner flow to Great Britain." Jefferson agreed, and later reflected that "debts had become hereditary from father to son . . . so that planters were a species of property, annexed to certain mercantile houses in London."[18]

Unable to persuade London to reform its trade laws, the burgesses moved in a different direction in 1772, Jefferson's fourth year as a member. They petitioned the Crown to end the African slave trade within the British Empire. Shrinking the labor supply would drive up the price of slaves. Given the inevitable shortage of bonded labor in rice-producing—and economically healthy—South Carolina and Georgia, Virginia's planters could realize windfall profits (and liquidate their debts) by selling their surplus chattel to the Low Country. But the Crown spurned Virginia's entreaty. Jefferson supported the step taken by the assembly, though it is not clear whether he joined the call to end the slave trade as a matter of economic expediency or that he saw it as the first step toward ending slavery in Virginia, or both. What is apparent is that London's intransigence on matters of trade, and the king's disallowance of Virginia's call to stanch the African slave trade, were crucial in the formation of Jefferson's thinking about America's place in the empire. He shared with other Virginians the growing belief that the colonists were burdened by an intolerable lack of autonomy.

Jefferson's views were not formed solely by Britain's contributions to Virginia's tobacco woes. The Currency Act, passed by Parliament in 1764, prohibited Virginia from issuing legal tender paper money, a step that confronted land-speculating planters with difficulties in borrowing and accumulating capital.[19] After 1763 the imperial government also prohibited the colonists from settling west of the Appalachians, crippling colonial land companies that had sprung up to gain title to the lush, virgin prairies west of the mountains. Jefferson was a stockholder in one such company.[20]

Economics alone did not shape Jefferson's thinking about the British Empire. Scores of pamphlets and newspaper essays had appeared in the decade since London had taken its first steps to raise revenue and tighten its enforcement of imperial laws, and many had focused on the limits of Parliament's authority. In addition, most of the colonial assemblies had adopted declarations assailing parliamentary taxation and asserting the colonists' right to be taxed only by their elected representatives. George Wythe, Jefferson's legal mentor, drafted a 1764 declaration for the burgesses along those lines, and the following year Richard Bland, a Virginia assemblyman steeped in constitutional theory, produced a pamphlet that expanded on the case against Parliament's claim to possess unlimited authority over its colonies.

Jefferson was familiar with the line taken by the American protestors, and he was no less acquainted with the sources that many of the pamphleteers and petitioners drew on. He, too, had read Algernon Sidney and his seventeenth-century contemporary John Locke, the former a republican theorist, the latter an exponent of the notion that all men were "equal and independent" and that all possessed the natural rights to life, liberty, and property. Like many educated provincials, Jefferson as a student had also read tracts produced in eighteenth-century England by writers that he called "true Whigs." These English writers, some of whom were leading literary figures, depicted England—and Parliament—as having grown hopelessly corrupt as a result of the rapid commercialization of English life. They contended that England was being led toward destruction by a national bank, rampant and hazardous speculation, and swiftly mounting national indebtedness. These writers not only blamed recent kings for having facilitated England's out-of-control venality, but also warned that monarchs were bent on restoring the influence they had lost in England's Glorious Revolution.

By Jefferson's time, writers in this tradition were alleging that the current monarch, George III, had through patronage and the systematic manipulation of Parliament made great strides in his sinister plan to regain nearly unlimited monarchial authority. That Parliament had attempted to levy taxes on the colonists and encroached on their autonomy, together with the king's complicity in dispatching a standing army to Massachusetts to enforce parliamentary policies, led Jefferson to the conclusion that England had fallen sway to an unholy alliance of monarchical despots and an oligarchic nobility. By 1774, he and a great many of his fellow Americans were convinced that the liberty long enjoyed by the colonists was in grave danger.

While Jefferson's precise outlook prior to 1774 is unknowable, it is clear that by the time of the Boston Tea Party he was convinced that the imperial authorities had no regard for the colonists' wishes. He yearned for a republican state, which he defined as "a government by its citizens in mass, acting directly and personally, according to rules established by majority."[21] In hindsight, it appears that Jefferson's thinking had taken an exceptional turn even before the colonists learned in May 1774 of London's response to the Boston Tea Party. Jefferson had come to believe that many of the elements that corrupted England were embedded in Virginia's politics, economy, and society, and in time they would have the same toxic impact on Virginia as they were having within the mother country. He had come to see the colonial insurgency as crucial not just to thwart British tyranny, but as the sole means of instituting change within the provinces.

Among the English and Europeans, America was reputed to be the land of equality, and indeed property ownership and the opportunity for upward mobility were more widespread in the colonies. Nevertheless, those living in the America of Jefferson's early years were accustomed to social inequality. In the words of one historian, it was a time of "a place for every man and every man in his place." Some historians have labeled pre-revolutionary America as a "premodern" time that still "bore traces of the medieval world." To be sure, it was a strikingly class-conscious time when those at the top were seen as "Gentlemen in the first rank of Dignity & Quality" and those in the lower reaches of society were often categorized as "inferior," the "meaner sort," or the "ignorant vulgar." John Adams thought of farmers and laborers as the "common herd," and George Washington in the 1750s spoke of them as the "grazing multitude." It was a time, too, when class distinctions were readily apparent. While those in the lower rungs of society wore clothing made from coarse and cheap fabrics, their social superiors wore silk stockings, wigs, lace ruffles, and shoes with silver buckles. The more affluent owned horses and chariots, and those beneath them did not. Those at the top were thought of as "gentlemen" and addressed as "Mr." or "Sir," and those down the line had no title. Corporal punishment was restricted to those in the lower orders. Only property owners could become militia and army officers, and for the most part only the largest property owners could hope to be a field officer, such as a major or colonel. People were expected to show deference when encountering their superiors by bowing, doffing their hat, or stepping aside. A Maryland physician may have exaggerated when he said that the inferior were to "fawn and cringe" in the presence of a social better, but he captured the essence of cultural expectations. So rife were the visible privileges of status that even church pews were assigned according to rank.[22]

Although Jefferson did not expound on the inequities in American life before 1776, his soon-to-be commitment to egalitarianism suggests that he already yearned for changes. To be sure, whereas a more conservative insurgent such as John Adams denigrated as "gross" and "absurd" the premise of "the natural Equality of Mankind," Jefferson embraced the validity of the proposition. Furthermore, while Adams early in the American Revolution took umbrage when a "Wretch" and "common Horse Jockey" dared approach him as an equal and applauded the changes unleashed by the insurgency, there is nothing in Jefferson's voluminous writings to suggest that he would have responded similarly.[23]

Like many other colonists, young Jefferson saw himself as an American, though that hardly meant he was Anglophobic. Inspired during adolescence by the stirring events of the Seven Years' War—when Virginia fought on behalf of the British Empire and annually raised an army of some two thousand men, under the command of Colonel George Washington—Jefferson had grown up holding Great Britain in the highest esteem. Nonetheless, he was a native Virginian. His family had resided in the province for three-quarters of a century, his father had served the colony, and Jefferson was convinced—not entirely incorrectly—that Virginia had survived and flourished since its founding in 1607 with little assistance from England. Throughout his life, even after the establishment of the United States, Jefferson spoke of "my country, Virginia." He naturally saw Britain's new colonial policies, which had commenced as he was coming of age, through the prism of a Virginian with a passionate concern for the well-being of his province. By 1774, Jefferson had come to see with crystal clarity that when the wishes of powerful forces in England—whether merchants, businessmen, financiers, or land speculators—collided with the desires of colonists, the Crown would always side with those in the metropolis against what Jefferson called "the lasting interests of the American states." By then, too, Jefferson understood that the Anglo-American crisis was likely to be a great historical event, perhaps the epochal happening of his lifetime, and he wished to play a greater role in it.[24]

The year 1774 was the tipping point of the imperial crisis. Learning of the Boston Tea Party, North's ministry considered, but rejected, the use of force. Instead, it levied fines on Massachusetts and shut Boston Harbor until restitution was made for the tea that had been destroyed. Massachusetts immediately appealed to the other colonies for assistance, and during that taut summer twelve colonies agreed to send delegates to a Continental Congress that was to meet in Philadelphia in September to determine a unified American response. The hour of the showdown had arrived. At stake was defiance or surrender, war or peace. Jefferson prayed that he would be chosen to be part of Virginia's delegation and that he would go to Philadelphia that fall—the very autumn, as it turned out, in which Thomas Paine arrived in the city.[25]

Unlike Jefferson, who was virtually assured of a life of affluence and some measure of prominence, Paine's English childhood was a time—or so he once remarked—when "all the inconveniences of early life" were "against me."[26] The writer and journalist Daniel Defoe, who died about the time of Paine's birth, said that English society could be divided into seven divisions, ranging from the "great, who live profusely" down to the bottom rung, the habitation of the "miserable, that really pinch and suffer want." Paine's family were part of what Defoe called the "working trades, who labour hard, but feel no want," an element that made up about 4 percent of England's population.[27] Defoe was correct that those in the working trades were not penurious, but they enjoyed few luxuries. It was also true, as historian J. H. Plumb noted, that "trade was fickle and the chance of hunger and poverty threaded the lives [of craftsmen] with anxiety." Plumb was on target as well when he wrote that among those who slipped into poverty, or had the misfortune to be born into indigence, there were "few winners and a multitude of losers."[28]

Great gaps in wealth separated the various divisions of English society. The average annual income of those in the nobility has been estimated at £2,800. The gentry rubbed along on between roughly £300 to £1,000 yearly. Craftsmen and farmers earned only about £40 for a year of hard work, while laborers did not make half that amount. Those at the top—royalty, nobility, gentlemen, and the educated minority—constituted an oligarchy that controlled English politics, which, in the words of historian John Harrison, was "essentially a practical business whose object was to produce tangible advantages" for those within the oligarchy. The business of politics did not include widening the suffrage, making Parliament more representative of society, reforming the tax system so that it was more fair and diverse, or using the power of government to improve the lives of workers and society's "losers," to use Plumb's pithy terminology.[29]

The English took pride in what they saw as their liberties, though in fact England was replete with inequities. Those not in the upper levels of English society "experienced daily social frictions," as one historian tactfully put it.[30] The chafing included the realization that many at the top not only looked on those beneath them as inferior, but also that some noblemen openly manifested a hauteur-laced air of scorn toward those in the lower orders. Some may have accepted this as the way of the world, but nothing was more galling to Paine than being seen as second-class, and much of his first forty years— and all those that followed—were consumed with his quest for recognition as a man of merit who was deserving of acceptance.

Like Jefferson, Paine said little about his youth, though he believed that the Quaker ethic imparted by his father had given him a good "moral" grounding and he was thankful for having received a few years of formal education. Thomas's parents scrimped and saved to send him to Thetford's Grammar School, doubtless hoping to save their son from a lifetime of hunching over a workbench for about fourteen hours every workday like his craftsman father.

Paine attended the school for six or seven years, and as he later said, he acquired "a tolerable stock of learning." He displayed a keen interest in science and mathematics, but otherwise Paine was a lackluster student, which he never denied. Late in life he characterized himself as self-taught, once remarking that "every person of learning is finally his own teacher" and also claiming that he had "seldom passed five minutes . . . in which I did not acquire some knowledge." Given his humdrum performance in grammar school, Paine's formal education abruptly ended at age thirteen. He was apprenticed to his father and earmarked for a lifetime as a staymaker.[31]

Unlike Jefferson, Paine had not been a methodical, disciplined student. Later, in adulthood, he displayed streaks of industry, but the traits that most observers discerned throughout his life were a passionate need for the company of others, a throbbing curiosity, restless ambition, and impatience for recognition. Those attributes were more a hindrance than a help to a craftsman, and early on he found the stultifying repetitiveness of his trade painfully disagreeable. He ran away twice, both times hoping to enlist on a privateer. His first flight, at age sixteen, was foiled by his father, who caught up with him in Harwich and brought him home. Three years later, in 1756, when England and France commenced hostilities in the Seven Years' War, Paine fled again. This time he succeeded in enlisting as a crewman on the privateer *King of Prussia*. It captured eight prizes, earning a handsome commission of thirty pounds for a lowly hand such as Paine.[32] When the vessel docked in Dartmouth late in the summer of 1757, Paine did not reenlist. He lazed about for six months, living off what he had made at sea, a habit that was to be a lifelong characteristic. When his money ran out, Paine drifted. Between 1757 and 1759, when he passed from age twenty to twenty-two, he lived in London for a spell, then in Dover, Lincolnshire, and Sandwich, earning his keep at the workbench.

Young Paine was a striking individual. He stood five feet ten inches, about four inches taller than the average English male. He was always slender, or "spare," as one observer noted. Yet, perhaps because of his work as an artisan, he was so broad shouldered that he impressed some as "rather athletic," though others thought he was "stooped a little." He sported long, wavy brown hair and bright blue eyes that were so lustrous one observer thought no painter could ever come close to capturing them. He did not smoke, though he used snuff and was fond of strong drink, and some thought it remarkable that he was never heard to curse, tell ribald jokes, or off-color stories. People thought him amiable and unpretentious. That, and his easy-going geniality, led nearly everyone to address him as "Tom," not "Thomas." (However, after he became famous only his enemies called him "Tom.")[33]

Paine met his first wife during his residence in Sandwich. At age twenty-two, he wed Mary Lambert, a maid in the household of a prominent businessman. She died a few months into the marriage, almost certainly as a result of complications from a childbirth that was also fatal to the child. Thereafter, Paine attempted to make a clean break with his past, seeking to put behind him his days as a craftsman. He sought employment as an exciseman, or tax collector, with the customs service, the calling that Mary's father plied. More than a year passed before Paine was hired, a long stretch that he spent at home in Thetford, marking time back at the workbench. In the fall of 1761, with his twenty-fifth birthday rapidly approaching, Paine began his new calling. He patrolled the Lincolnshire coast by boat and horseback, on the lookout for smugglers. But in 1765 Paine was fired for slipshod work. He returned to Thetford and his old craft yet again. After an unhappy year of making stays, Paine moved to London in search of an alternative. He spent two years teaching poor children and, having for a time been caught up in the Methodist movement that was gaining traction in England, preaching for a spell. But in 1768, at age thirty-one, he was reinstated as an excise collector in Lewes, a hilly market town of five thousand in Sussex near the English Channel.

Paine kept the job for six of what may have been his happiest—though not trouble-free—years in England. Surpassingly pleasant and gregarious, he blended into the life of the town and was readily accepted, in time even securing appointment to the unelected town council. He joined social clubs that met in local pubs and rapidly stood out as a dominant force in the lively disputations on politics and assorted other topics that were the customary fare of such gatherings. A friend later recalled that Paine was "tenacious of his opinions, which were bold, acute and independent." Associates found him to be both jocular and unflappable, and one said he never displayed a niggle of doubt when taking a stand during a political debate. He also had a flair for composing droll poems and songs that landed him at the center of attention. Paine later said that he enjoyed a wide range of acquaintances and made many warm friends among both the "rich and poor" in Lewes.[34] His chums nicknamed him the "Commodore" for the skills he displayed as a sailor when tracking down tax evaders on the River Ouse and the nearby craggy coast. One friend recollected him as being "very respectable, sensible, and convivial," adding that he always "entertained with his witty sallies," but also that he educated others with his "more serious conversations." Paine was such a fierce debater in the clubs that his compatriots crowned him the "most obstinate haranguer."[35]

Three years after arriving in Lewes, Paine married Elizabeth Ollive, the daughter of a recently deceased shopkeeper. It appears to have been a marriage of convenience, for the couple often lived separately and the union was never consummated, a fact that Paine acknowledged but refused to discuss. As he had already been managing her late father's store for a couple of years, matrimony enabled Paine to acquire the shop and possibly to augment his income. Elizabeth, who was just short of turning twenty-two—nearly thirteen years younger than Paine—may have thought wedlock offered the best available means of support for her and her widowed mother. If so, she misjudged her husband. Paine not only lacked the discipline necessary for success in business, but he was also overburdened by the multiple demands of running the shop and attending his duties as a customs agent. His once thriving little tobacco and grocery emporium failed.[36]

The death knell for the shop arrived after Paine, in 1772, got caught up in a campaign among south coast excise officers to increase their meager salaries. He had not had a hand in starting the movement for greater pay, but was drawn to it and likely spent considerable time listening to the ideas of those who had organized the initiative. For reasons that are obscure, veteran excise officials in and around Lewes approached Paine about writing an appeal to Parliament that called attention to the tax collectors' plight.[37] Paine had never written anything for the public, but it may have been that in coffeehouse conversations he articulately expressed the grievances of the tax collectors. Or perhaps Paine volunteered himself to draft the appeal.

His petition displayed signs of the writing skills for which he later became famous. His essay was lucid, assertive, and succinct, and he marshaled a persuasive case: the wages of excisemen had not been increased in a century, causing "pinching circumstances" that raised the danger of "negligence and indifference," not to mention a "corruption of manners and principles" that could result in fraudulent practices.[38] Paine completed the appeal late in 1772. It was circulated among excise collectors throughout England, who greeted it with enthusiasm prior to its submission to Parliament early the following year.

Shortly before the appeal was to be presented, Paine hurried to London to promote his tract and the tax collectors' crusade. Despite not having received a leave of absence, Paine lingered in the city. He was caught up in the urban swirl, especially by the astounding variety of public talks and the give-and-take between knowledgeable speakers and their audiences. Much that Paine heard were bits of the "Radical Enlightenment," notions that had evolved during previous decades and were only now gaining currency in public discourse. These included ideas of egalitarianism and democracy, the belief that government's purpose was to advance the worldly interests of people, that all men possessed natural rights, and that all had the right to pursue happiness. The essential precept that reached Paine was that government was to seek to advance the general good, disregarding theological touchstones and breaking with centuries-old habits of serving only monarchy, aristocracy, and ecclesiastical authority.[39] Intermingled with these notions were critiques of Britain's system of governance and its deplorable indifference— even its antipathy—to the plight of the bulk of the citizenry.

At age thirty-five, Paine appears to have been captivated by the many things a big city offered, and in fact he would spend most of the rest of his life in urban environments. A New Yorker visiting London about the same time wrote that it was awash with debating societies, clubs, and coffeehouses which every moment provided "a contemplative mind . . . some new matter" to consider. Still brimming with the interest in science and mathematics that he had displayed as a student, Paine attended numerous lectures on natural philosophy, as science was called at the time. But he was also drawn to talks by political activists, and he frequented pubs and coffeehouses where every shade of political opinion was bandied about. One that he surely patronized was St. Paul's Coffee House. On Thursdays, the Club of Honest Whigs—a group that included Benjamin Franklin and several English natives who during the American protests were thought by the colonists to be "friends of America"—gathered at St. Paul's to explore and debate topics that ran the gamut from science to religion to politics.

Not everything that Paine heard in London would have been new to him. Lewes, a hub of republicanism during the English Civil War in the mid-seventeenth century, remained a site of political dissent and radical ideas. In Paine's time, this took the form of circumspectly questioning the extent of monarchical authority, more boldly urging the reformation of Parliament, and emphatically deprecating regressive taxation.[40] Exactly when and why Paine's radicalism crystallized remains a mystery, although clues abound. Since his youth in Thetford, he had witnessed much that was despicable in the England of the time: an uncaring and domineering oligarchy, ruinous poverty, cruel exploitation, and a pitiless judicial system stacked against the lower classes. To Paine's eyes, the malign effects of privilege for a tiny nobility were all about, deeply etched in the fabric of the English nation and conspicuous in its government, church, universities, and military.[41]

Paine had struggled and foundered throughout his life, and if he attributed his failings to a political and social system beyond his control, he would not have been the first to do so. His untiring ambition and hunger for acknowledgment were already present by his midthirties, forming the spectrum through which Paine saw—and judged—the world around him. It would have been nearly intolerable for one like Paine to settle for the dead end that lay in wait for a journeyman staymaker or a customs official, or to live with the reality that a scornful public mostly looked with contempt on tax collectors.

Paine's temperament and condition may have made him receptive to the ideology of change and reform. However, not every person who experiences failures, disappointments, despair, and distress becomes a political and social reformer. The power of ideas themselves can be transformative, and Paine was listening to speakers and reading authors who put forward ideals of human freedom and dignity. Moreover, throughout his stay in London the city was engulfed in political turbulence, and it is likely that in that environment the assorted shards of his experiences and thinking came together and took on a radical contour.

Resentment at the concentration of power in the hands of England's ruling oligarchy stretched back at least a century before Paine's birth, but the radical movement in England grew substantially in the eighteenth century. Its growth was spurred by the country's expanding middle class, dislocation of trade brought on by England's seemingly perpetual warfare, and parliamentary restrictions on mercantile and manufacturing activities. At the time, an explosion in the number of newspapers and mushrooming urban centers, where people could meet and share ideas, added fuel to the fire.

Radicals in the 1760s and 1770s focused mostly on broadening the rights of Englishmen. Influenced by the same writers who had found an audience among those in the colonial protest movement, the starting point for most English radicals in Paine's time was that God had created all men equal, that no man had a right to govern another without his consent, and that even within a civil society the people retained their sovereign authority. Most radicals continued to embrace the notion that the best government was a mixed government—a blend of monarchy, aristocracy, and democracy. For the most part, they centered their attention on the deplorably unrepresentative House of Commons. They assailed Parliament's malapportionment, which left urban centers and manufacturing towns severely underrepresented, and they urged the secret ballot and more expansive suffrage rights. (In Paine's Thetford, for instance, less than 1 percent of the two thousand adult residents could vote.) But the radical movement in England was hardly monolithic. Some critics probed deeper, pointing to a political system characterized by the "arbitrary power of . . . grandees" in league with the monarch, and others rejected monarchy altogether, contending that it inevitably injected unnecessary forms of corruption into the body politic. Some argued that the king and powerful aristocrats had built "an artful and corrupt" system distinguished by the creation of hordes of unnecessary offices, most filled by members of the peerage and all paid for by heavy taxes. For years, these assorted criticisms sputtered along attracting little attention.[42] But the John Wilkes affair changed things.

Wilkes, a member of Parliament and the publisher of a newspaper, the *North Briton*, had been arrested in 1763 on charges of seditious libel growing from his strongly worded attacks on ministerial policy and the king. Tried and convicted, he fled to France to avoid incarceration. Five years later, Wilkes returned to England and appealed to the king for a pardon. Before any action was taken, Wilkes successfully stood for election to the House of Commons in a district in Middlesex County, a portion of which included London. Almost immediately following his election, Wilkes's appeal was rejected and he was sentenced to two years in prison. Although no law prevented a convicted criminal from serving in Parliament, the Commons refused to seat Wilkes. Protestors took to the streets. The members of one crowd, estimated by some to have swelled to forty thousand, chanted: "Wilkes and Liberty! No Liberty, No King!" While incarcerated, Wilkes was reelected on three subsequent occasions in 1768 and 1769, but in each instance the House of Commons—with the king and his ministers pulling the strings—expelled him. Once, it seated the opponent that Wilkes had defeated.[43]

Parliament's action created a firestorm of indignation, provoking charges that a toxic oligarchy—"a profligate junto of courtiers supported by the mere authority of the Crown"—posed a deadly threat to England's constitution. The Wilkes affair not only sparked mob activity; it was the trigger for the creation of the Society of Supporters of the Bill of Rights. The Society demanded full and equal representation of the people, annual sessions of Parliament, and the exclusion of all peers from the House of Commons. It churned out an avalanche of literature that assailed the entire system of English government, including the "obsolete and vexatious claims of the crown," and warned of the danger of "court influence" over Parliament. It was a staple of reform-minded screeds to suggest that in no age since the fall of the Roman republic had "venality and corruption [been] so prevalent as at this time in Britain."[44] Paine read some of this radical literature—as did Jefferson in Virginia—and heard even more extreme ideas tossed about in the public houses he frequented.

Paine spent most of the winter of 1772–1773 in London, and he returned frequently thereafter, attracted by the vibrancy of the city, including its swirling political ferment. The failure of the excisemen's campaign—predictable though it might have been in a nation of Bible readers attuned to the Scriptures' conflation of "sinners and tax collectors"—further radicalized Paine, who most likely held the king responsible for the defeat. That was only the first blow Paine suffered. Having ignored his work for days, even weeks, at a time, Paine was fired from the excise service in the spring of 1774. As this was his second dismissal, Paine knew that he was finished as a tax collector. He had also carelessly neglected his shop in Lewes, which came to grief around this same time. In June, Paine and his wife broke up. They did not divorce, but entered into a legal agreement under which they would live separately, the shop and assorted household possessions were to be auctioned to meet debt obligations, and Elizabeth was to pay him thirty-five pounds, in return for which Thomas agreed to make no claims on whatever goods she acquired in the future.

At age thirty-seven, eighteen years after first leaving Thetford and going into the world on his own, Paine was jobless, with little prospect of finding work unless he returned to the artisan's bench that he detested. Deep into middle-age by eighteenth-century standards, Paine had little to show for his life. Should he stay in England, he had no reason to hope for anything better in the remaining time allotted him. Probably for the first time, he thought of moving to America, where many a down-on-his-luck individual had gone in search of a second chance. With the funds he had secured in the legal settlement with his wife, Paine had the wherewithal to make the move. On one of his sojourns in London, Paine likely discussed the notion with Benjamin Franklin. Paine knew of Franklin's remarkable ascent. Franklin had also once been an artisan, but in the American colonies his natural talents had been recognized and he gained fortune and renown. Inspired by Franklin's example, Paine hurried to London late in the summer of 1774 to request a letter of introduction from him, something akin to a stamp of approval that would be of considerable help when he disembarked in Philadelphia, a city where everyone would be a total stranger.

Franklin, who wrote letters for six Philadelphia-bound immigrants in 1773–1774, readily consented. Having been a penniless stranger in an unknown city on two occasions himself, Franklin was willing to provide a helping hand. He relied largely on the endorsement of George Lewis, a mathematician and member of the Royal Society who was better acquainted with Paine and evidently thought him bright and purposeful. Just prior to Paine's departure, Franklin wrote to his son-in-law in Philadelphia, Richard Bache, himself an immigrant from Yorkshire. Franklin described Paine as an "ingenious, worthy young man," though one with little money, who would require assistance in finding temporary employment "as a clerk, or assistant tutor in a school, or assistant surveyor, (all of which I think him very capable)."[45]

Franklin may have persuaded him to select Philadelphia, though given the Quakerism in Paine's background, he was probably drawn toward the city all along. The town and the surrounding colony had been founded by Quakers a century earlier, and Pennsylvania was noted for its liberality. In addition, Philadelphia was the fastest-growing city in the colonies and its economy was booming, making it a magnet for immigrants. Philadelphia also boasted several newspapers and printing presses, which may have tempted Paine to try his hand at additional writing, given the enthusiasm with which his appeal had been greeted by his fellow excisemen.

Paine never said that the American revolt against British governance was a factor in his decision to abandon England for the colonies, but it must have been on his mind, and he probably questioned Franklin about Anglo-American relations. As 1774 unfolded, Franklin grew to expect the worst, and he counseled the colonists to *"Behold . . . where matters are driving,"* warned that the English government had turned its back on "retreating or changing . . . Measures," and advised colonial leaders to never "tamely submit to the Yoke prepar'd for you" by the authorities in London.[46] Franklin, as was his wont, may have been guarded in responding to Paine. Even so, there was no hiding the fact that imperial tensions had reached the crisis stage, and the mooring lines between Great Britain and America seemed ready to break. The Boston Tea Party had sparked unbridled fury in England. Talk of using force to suppress the colonial rebellion was widespread, and many inside and outside the government thought war with the colonies was inevitable.

Paine made the decision to come to Philadelphia knowing full well that hostilities might be in the offing, and might in fact have already begun by the time he landed. But he came nonetheless, a man at a dead end in his life who was probably driven as much or more by his storehouse of radical ideas as he was by the desire to find employment. With Franklin's letter of introduction in his bags, Paine boarded the *London Packet* in October 1774, bound for Philadelphia.[47]

James Monroe was probably taught to read and write by his parents, though for a time he studied under a private tutor. At age eleven he enrolled in Campbelltown Academy, a nearby school. He lived at home, though he daily faced a long walk to his classes, some of it through a thick forest. During his first year at the academy, Monroe was a classmate with John Marshall, later the chief justice of the United States, who had been sent from his home one hundred miles away to study with Archibald Campbell, an Anglican priest and headmaster of the academy—and purportedly a strict disciplinarian. Monroe studied under Campbell for nearly five years, one of twenty-five pupils admitted to his school. Near his sixteenth birthday, Monroe was deemed sufficiently advanced in Latin to gain admittance to the College of William and Mary. The small, leafy campus had not changed since Jefferson's days as a student nearly fifteen years earlier. Three buildings dotted the grounds, structures that Jefferson—with his eye for exquisite architecture—disparaged as "rude, mis-shapen piles, which, but that they have roofs, would be taken for brick-kilns."[48] The main building, three quarters of a century old, served as a classroom and dormitory; the president's house stood opposite; and an adjacent building was utilized by a dozen or so Indian students, who studied a different curriculum. Monroe chose to live on campus rather than in town, and he lodged in or near the room that Jefferson had occupied.[49]

Monroe arrived on campus in June 1774, the month when Boston Harbor was closed and Massachusetts was fined by Britain as punishment for the Boston Tea Party, and a few weeks before Franklin wrote his letter of introduction for Paine. Word of Britain's draconian actions reached Williamsburg just days before Monroe set foot on campus. The news led Jefferson, in concert with Patrick Henry and Richard Henry Lee, to introduce a resolution in the House of Burgesses denouncing London's uncompromising stand. When it passed, Virginia's governor—the last royal governor the Old Dominion— would have dissolved the assembly. The defiant assemblymen met at Raleigh Tavern late in May and agreed to embargo dutied tea. They also agreed to meet again in August to select delegates to the Continental Congress that would consider America's response to British coercion.[50]

In September, as Monroe was settling in as a student, the Continental Congress gathered in Philadelphia. During the pivotal summer and fall of 1774, Jefferson, Paine, and Monroe faced life-changing choices. Jefferson, eager to play an important role in the epic events of the day, strove to be chosen for the Continental Congress. Paine sailed to the crisis-laden American colonies and to a city where he knew not a soul. Monroe, still in his teenage years, continued his studies while keeping abreast of the exciting drama swirling all about him. Nor was it just these three who faced critical choices. The American colonies stood on the abyss in 1774. It was to be America's last year of peace for a very long time.

CHAPTER 2

"THE BIRTHDAY OF A NEW WORLD IS AT HAND"

REVOLUTIONARIES

JEFFERSON SPENT THE SPRING and summer of 1774 doing what he could to secure his appointment to Virginia's delegation to the Continental Congress. It would have gone against his grain to campaign openly, so he played to his strength. He committed to paper his ideas on the Anglo-American crisis, doubtless hoping that an insightful analysis of the threat faced by the colonists would lead to his selection. He probably intended to read the tract at the August meeting of the body that was to select the delegates to Congress, the Virginia Convention—as the former House of Burgesses now called itself.

Jefferson set off for Williamsburg at the height of the summer, but he never reached the capital. He fell ill during the journey and turned back to Monticello. Later, he sent copies of his essay to close friends in the Convention, including Patrick Henry. Jefferson knew that his absence meant he would not be a congressman, but he wished to make the Convention aware of his position and to influence those who would be delegates. He must have also hoped that someone would arrange for the publication of his composition, and he was not disappointed. Toward the year's end, his tract was published in Williamsburg as *A Summary View of the Rights of British America*—a less-than-fetching title that someone other than Jefferson concocted—and soon thereafter it appeared in print in Philadelphia and London.

Jefferson's argument was one of the most radical that had yet appeared. It was so militant that Jefferson later conceded that he was "unable to get anyone to agree" with some of his arguments, and in fact most members of the Virginia Convention and some in the Congress that met in September thought him "too bold."[1] But timing is everything in politics. When Jefferson's pamphlet finally appeared, companies of militia were drilling here and there throughout the colonies on cold, muddy fields and committees of safety were springing up, many bent on harassing those who remained loyal to the king, and sometimes even driving the Tories into exile. Jefferson's *Summary View*, which not a few had thought far too bold in the summer of 1774, touched the pulse of many colonists by early the following year.

Some portions of *A Summary View* were old hat. As with many earlier pamphleteers, Jefferson asserted that whereas a lone menacing act by the imperial government might have been seen as accidental, one ministry after another had adhered to the same course, laying bare a pronounced pattern of oppression. He additionally argued that Parliament lacked any jurisdiction over the colonies, a position taken by numerous previous writers. No justification existed, Jefferson wrote, for 160,000 eligible voters in England to "give law" to four million Americans. The Continental Congress, which met that autumn, was unwilling to take such a radical position. It recognized Parliament's authority to regulate imperial trade, whereas Jefferson, in *A Summary View*, insisted that the colonists had a natural right to "a free trade with all parts of the world." Jefferson, in fact, argued that Parliament and "a few worthless ministerial dependents" had carried out the designs of avaricious English interests bent on "extort[ing]"America's wealth. Theirs was "a deliberate, systematical plan of reducing us to slavery."

Jefferson's argument veered into more or less unchartered waters when he turned to the monarch. While he, like others, maintained that the king was America's sole link to the British Empire, Jefferson took the position that the monarch could only exercise authority consented to by the colonists. He argued that the colonists recognized the monarchy as the "mediatory power" between their interests and the interests of those within the mother country and other parts of the British Empire. Not only was Jefferson's argument cutting-edge, but his tone was unfamiliar. Virtually no one in the colonial insurgency had openly assailed the king, but Jefferson censured George III for his "deviations from the line of duty." By refusing to disallow legislation in which Parliament had overreached its authority, the king was part of the unlawful attempt to exploit the colonists. Jefferson additionally reproached the king for having rejected "salutary" laws enacted by colonial assemblies. Surely thinking of the Crown's veto of Virginia's legislation regarding slavery and the slave trade, Jefferson characterized such royal subscriptions as a "shameful . . . abuse of . . . power." He also blamed the king for sending a large British army to occupy Boston in 1768, an act of despotism pure and simple. However, by making the civil authority in Massachusetts subordinate to the army, the king had additionally taken a step that was "criminal against our laws." Conscious that most of his countrymen still spoke in polite and respectful terms when referring to the monarch, Jefferson said that he had used the "language and sentiment which becomes a free people," adding that to flatter from "fear . . . is not an American art."[2]

Jefferson was also one of the first to challenge the conventional view in England, and in America, that the colonies had survived and prospered as a result of British power and sacrifices. Indeed, several ministries since 1765 had insisted that the price Britain had paid to create and maintain the colonies justified the imposition of taxes on the colonists. Jefferson painted a completely different picture, one that was not entirely an exaggeration. He contended that "America was conquered, and her settlements made and firmly established" by the colonists with little help from the mother country. The colonists "own blood was spilt" and their "fortunes expended" in the process. Said Jefferson: "No shilling was ever issued from the public treasures of his majesty or his ancestors for their assistance, till of very late times, after the colonies had become established on a firm and permanent footing." Nor had the colonists' sacrifices ended with the ordeal of establishing colonies in the forbidding American wilderness. The colonists had unilaterally undertaken the often bloody work of opening successive new frontiers during the past century and a half. Furthermore, in war after war that began in Europe and spread to America, the colonies had fielded armies to assist the mother country.[3]

Jefferson's essay seethed with a rage seldom matched in the many earlier pamphlets written by colonists. At bottom, his anger grew from a realization that the colonists would never be more than second-class citizens within the British Empire. They were without a voice in the imperial government. No important ministerial post was occupied by an American and, for that matter, no such official had ever been "taken from among us." The colonists' perpetual inferior status led imperial leaders to sacrifice "the rights of one part of the empire to the inordinate desires of another," shorthand for saying that if the interests of the colonists conflicted with those of powerful entities within England, those in the homeland would always be favored.[4] The bedrock of Jefferson's thinking was that the empire must be radically reconstructed if America was to remain within it. It is inconceivable that he could have thought that London would peacefully consent to anything of the sort.

Recovering from his illness and with no immediate role to play in Virginia's troubles with London, Jefferson remained on his hilltop until early spring, when he set off for the next meeting of Virginia's legislature, this time scheduled for Richmond. By then, the imperial crisis had reached the abyss. The Continental Congress had denounced the Coercive Acts—Parliament's retaliation for the Boston Tea Party—adopted an immediate embargo on imports from the mother country, prohibited exports to England after the summer of

1775, and urged each colony to prepare its militia for possible hostilities. By March, when the Virginia Convention was gaveled to order, every member knew that Congress's defiance had probably made war inevitable. Given the absence of several leading figures who were delegates to the soon-to-meet Second Continental Congress, Jefferson played a greater role than he had in any previous legislative session. He helped write a plan for Virginia's militia and drafted his colony's rejection of a peace plan proffered by Parliament that in fact conceded nothing demanded by the first Congress.[5]

In May, news arrived that Britain had responded with force to Congress's defiance. On April 19, blood had been shed in Massachusetts when the British army attempted to destroy a provincial arsenal in Concord. Militiamen from several hamlets in the Bay Colony had turned out to resist the king's soldiers, and a long day of fighting had occurred during the army's retreat to Boston. Britain's redcoats might never have reached their destination had not a thousand reinforcements been sent to their rescue. By day's end nearly three hundred British soldiers had been killed or wounded, and its army was pinioned in Boston by armed forces from all four New England colonies. War had broken out.[6]

The war produced an immediate change in Virginia's delegation to Congress. Four members left, including George Washington, who had been named commander of the just-created Continental army. The Convention named only one replacement to its delegation—Jefferson. He hurriedly put his affairs in order, among other things selling four thousand pounds of his tobacco so that it would get it to market before the embargo on exports took effect in the fall. Before departing, Jefferson wrote to William Small, the Scottish professor at the College of William and Mary whom he so admired. If Jefferson had written to him previously in the thirteen years since his graduation, the correspondence has not survived. Obviously hoping that Small would not think ill of him for supporting the colonial insurgency, Jefferson maintained that an accommodation between the colonies and the parent state had been within reach. Had not a majority in Parliament "made sale of their virtue," he wrote, and had the king acted as an arbiter rather than "blowing up the flames" of hatred toward America, war could have been avoided. Jefferson closed with the wish that Small's feelings for him "may be preserved inviolate," though to make amends he sent along three dozen bottles of Madeira.[7] Not long thereafter, Jefferson set off for Philadelphia, home to Congress and, for the past six months, the residence of Thomas Paine.

The *London Packet*, the vessel that carried Paine to America, docked in Philadelphia on the last day of November 1774, a month after the First Congress adjourned, shortly before the appearance of *A Summary View*, and about five months before war erupted. Not everyone on board had survived the Atlantic crossing. What Paine called a "putrid fever"—probably typhus—had swept the ship, killing 5 of the 120 passengers and leaving Paine at death's door. He was carried ashore on a stretcher and, because of Franklin's letter of introduction (or so Paine thought), cared for by a Philadelphia physician. He was bedfast for days and too weak to get about for a while thereafter.[8]

Despite what he had told Franklin about his aspirations for work in America, Paine may all along have hoped to support himself through writing. If he had not seriously considered that pursuit before he sailed, Paine's enfeebled condition following his arrival virtually drove him to it. Weak and wan, and still tethered to his room, Paine began to write. He did not call on Richard Bache, to whom Franklin had written on his behalf, until about six weeks after disembarking. By then, Paine had made a more important acquaintance: Robert Aitken, an engraver, printer, and bookseller who planned to publish the *Pennsylvania Magazine*, destined to be one of the first magazines to appear in the colonies. After seeing an example of Paine's writing, Aitken selected him as the publication's editor. This was perfect for Paine. He edited the magazine for several months, making decisions on what submissions to use and simultaneously writing essays of his own. He could devote as much, or as little, time to his work as his energy permitted and his mercurial temperament willed.

Paine was prolific. He churned out two essays during his first month in Philadelphia and nine in half a year, as well as five poems. His productivity slowed as his recovery progressed, possibly an indication of how easily he could be distracted once he was well enough to get out and about, though his duties as an editor also ate into his time. His essays covered numerous topics. His first, written early in his convalescence, confronted the day's burning question: Would the British government respond with force to the colonial insurgency? Imagining a conversation between General James Wolfe, who became a legendary figure following his death while leading the British army in the Battle of Quebec in 1759, and General Thomas Gage, commander of the British army in America in 1775, Paine had Wolfe denounce Parliament's "corruption and error" in seeking to reduce the colonists to the status of an "inslaved people." The glory of England required that Britain abandon its destructive course in favor of "the sweets of peace and liberty." There was nothing new in his piece, and Paine likely wrote it mostly as a means of bringing himself to the attention of those in Philadelphia's protest movement. It at least caught Aitken's eye and led to the business relationship between the two men.[9]

Paine next turned to a topic that had sparked little outrage in America: slavery. Throughout his life as a writer, Paine was often the first to take a stand on a controversial issue. Slavery had endured in the colonies for well over a century, spreading like a dark stain into every province. While an occasional writer had questioned its existence, nothing like an organized anti-slavery movement had come into being. Benjamin Rush, a Philadelphia physician, had assailed slavery in a pamphlet two years before, a step that led to what he called "the most virulent attack that was ever made on me," not to mention a staggering loss in the number of his patients. Paine had to know that he would win few friends by denouncing slavery, but he did so nonetheless, displaying the courage that would always be his hallmark. Paine not only cataloged slavery's wickedness; he challenged Christians to square slavery with the teachings of Jesus. He urged the emancipation of those held in bondage and called for public subsidies for those who were freed. Six weeks after the appearance of his essay, the first abolitionist society in North America was established in Philadelphia, though Paine's piece was probably not a factor in its creation.[10]

Paine took his duties as editor seriously, and the early issues of the *Pennsylvania Magazine* included essays by John Witherspoon, president of the College of New Jersey (now Princeton), and Francis Hopkinson, a lawyer who would become a signer of the Declaration of Independence. The magazine flourished, tripling its subscription list within a few weeks, and the multifarious pieces that Paine wrote contributed to its success. He censured the practice of dueling and urged lawmakers to make it a felony to issue a challenge. He attacked the royal practice of awarding "pompous titles" to noblemen, arguing that some reprobates who had been honored were more deserving of designations such as "plunderer of his country" or "murderer of mankind." In another piece, he waxed on about the causes of unhappy marriages, seemingly concluding that wedlock was virtually assured to result in misery. Early on, he took up Britain's exploitation of India, though discerning readers would have understood that "India" was a metaphor for an America threatened with "plunder" by the unmatched "avarice" of those British "nabobs" responsible for driving the empire's rulers.[11]

In the poem "Liberty Tree," drafted for the *Pennsylvania Magazine*, Paine wrote of how the colonists in war after war had fought England's battles in the belief that the mother country stood for freedom. But now tyrannical England threatened the previously "Unvexed" colonists, forcing them to defend themselves: "From the East to the West blow the trumpet to arms / Thro' the land let the sound of it flee / Let the far and the near all unite with a cheer / In defense of our Liberty Tree."[12]

Learning of the recent bloody events in Massachusetts, Paine rushed an essay into print. Although he meant to endorse the colonists' military resistance at Lexington and Concord, Paine was cautious. A stranger in a strange land, he was still trying to fathom the colonists' mind-set, intentions, resolve, and capability of waging war against a superpower. Besides, the Second Continental Congress would not meet for another two weeks, and no one knew how it would respond to the bloodshed in New England. Paine crafted the piece as a dream in which a traveler passes through an idyllic land that first faced a blight and next a "tempest," before eventually surmounting its adversities. As if Paine feared that his readers would not understand where he was going, he explained all at the end: the beautiful country was early America, the blight it endured had been brought on by imperial policy, and the tempest was Britain's resort to force. At the end of his dream, America prevailed to "rise with new glories and her fame . . . established in every corner of the globe."[13]

Once Congress reassembled on May 10, it took step after step to ready the colonies for war, including the creation of the Continental army and its corps of general officers. If there had been any doubt about whether the events in Massachusetts meant war, all uncertainty was removed. Paine wasted no time composing his own response to London's decision to crush the colonial rebellion, and this time he was bold and resolute. He argued that powerful elements in the homeland were bent on the economic exploitation of the colonies. England, "red with the blood of her children," was an "unprincipled enemy." It had taken up arms neither to repel an invasion nor to defend the natural rights of its citizenry, but for the "vilest" of reasons. Avarice, he declared, had driven it to plunder the wealth of the colonists. Paine pounced on a statement by the Earl of Sandwich, the first lord of the Admiralty, widely reprinted in the colonial press. Declaring that the "American heroes" were "cowardly men," Sandwich had predicted that they would take flight at the "very sound of a cannon." So craven were the colonists, said Sandwich, they would never resist Britain's show of force. Paine's answer was that the Americans would fight. They would go to war to defend their "spiritual freedom and political liberty."[14]

As Paine had written nothing about the imperial crisis before leaving England, his views on the colonial insurgency down to 1775 are unknown. But given his introduction to English radicalism during his last few years in the homeland, there can be little doubt that Paine had long since come to see the British government as corrupt and evil, and bent on victimizing the American colonists as it had long victimized Ireland and commoners within England. Whatever his own ideas, Paine had not been in Philadelphia long before he discerned that the pro-independence elements within the colonial insurgency hoped to follow the break with the mother country with the establishment of their own republican nation. An American republic, Paine was certain, would be a bright ray of hope for those in the homeland who sought to reform England. To Paine, republicanism at the very least meant supplanting monarchical and aristocratic governance with elected officials who were representative of the interests of the people. For many, including Paine, it meant even more. The classical republican ideal foresaw a simple and virtuous society, one composed of small governments and citizen-farmers and workers, a golden alternative to the traditional English and European-wide culture in which the few exercised power over the many, and those few selfishly put their interests ahead of the interests of society as a whole.[15]

The advent of war may have increased Paine's restiveness. What is clear is that as Philadelphia's customary sweltering summer settled in during 1775, he was eager for a change. Little time had passed before he wearied of the burden of getting out a magazine while writing his own pieces, and his relationship with Aitken had been strained from the outset, as both were headstrong individuals with conflicting views about the magazine's content. Paine also wanted a greater salary and, given the publication's success, he believed that he deserved a raise in pay. There may have been more. Rumors were making the rounds that Paine was drinking heavily and could no longer cope with the challenge of editing the magazine. Tattle about his affinity for strong drink followed him throughout his life, and it is not inconceivable that a fondness for alcohol may have contributed both to his checkered background in England and to his ability to function as an editor.

However, persuasive evidence of alcoholism at this juncture of Paine's life does not exist. Paine was in contact with Franklin, John and Samuel Adams, and Dr. Rush—who later authored one of the first books in America on the dangers of abusing alcohol—and none mentioned Paine's alleged addiction to drink. If Paine was a hopeless alcoholic, it seems likely that John Adams, who filled his diary and letters home with gossip about his colleagues in Congress and assorted Philadelphians, would have mentioned Paine's dipso-mania. Nor did the perceptive Franklin appear to think Paine was a drunkard. He wrote a letter of introduction on Paine's behalf, saddling his son-in-law with the task of helping the newcomer get started in Philadelphia, and in 1775 and 1776 Franklin himself encouraged and aided the writer. What can be said with assurance is that Paine was single and lonely, that he looked forward to relaxing with acquaintances in the evenings in coffeehouses and taverns, and that on some occasions he was drawn to tippling.

Something else may have pulled Paine away from the magazine and in other directions. He had not known a soul in Philadelphia when he arrived.

By summertime, seven months after his arrival, Paine's writing and engaging manner had brought him into contact with a considerable number of influential men. No one was of greater importance to him than Dr. Rush, whom he met at Aitken's bookstore and with whom he formed a close relationship. They were an odd couple, separated in age by nine years—Rush was the younger of the two—and economically and educationally by a wide crevasse, for Rush was a college educated physician and comfortably affluent. However, the two shared an interest in writing, and their views on slavery and the American rebellion were nearly indistinguishable. Rush also found Paine to be a wonderful conversationalist. Through Rush, Paine met other Philadelphia gentlemen. On his own, Paine developed friendships with successful craftsmen who had emerged as important political activists. Rush and the others were drawn to Paine through what he had written, and their acceptance of him increased his self-confidence. He had ventured into unchartered waters in leaving England for Philadelphia. Wishing for more freedom, he cut his ties with Aitkin, eager to see where that would lead.[16]

Accompanied by two slaves and four horses, and riding in an elegant phaeton, Jefferson arrived in Philadelphia in June following an exhausting nine-day journey from Richmond. He rented rooms in the home of a cabinetmaker on Chestnut Street between Third and Fourth, which put him in close proximity to Paine, who lived at the corner of Front and Market Streets, two blocks east and one north of Jefferson's residence. There is no indication that the two met during Jefferson's fifteen off-and-on months in the city. But as Jefferson shopped at Aitken's store and became friends with at least two other acquaintances of Paine's—Franklin, who returned to America in 1775 and joined the Pennsylvania delegation shortly before Jefferson took his seat in Congress, and Dr. Rush—the possibility exists that the two were introduced.[17] Jefferson ran in different circles from Paine, and he was busy. Congress met for six or more hours daily, except on Sunday, and committees did their work before or after the day's congressional session. While Jefferson was hardly a recluse, he was reserved in the company of strangers, and if he and Paine met that summer or fall, it likely would have been a brief and forgettable encounter, at least from the congressman's perspective.

Most congressmen were unknown outside their colony. Jefferson was an exception. The "famous Mr. Jefferson" had entered Congress, said a Rhode Island delegate two days after the Virginian's carriage clattered into town. Most members of Congress had likely read *A Summary View*, a pamphlet that John Adams—not given to effusive praise—lauded as a "very handsome public Paper" penned by "a fine Writer." Adams later recollected that Jefferson entered Congress with a "reputation for literature" and "a happy talent of composition."[18]

Jefferson's new colleagues, and most others who met him throughout his long life, discovered a strikingly impressive individual. At six feet two inches tall, Jefferson towered above most other men. He had reddish hair and a somewhat ruddy complexion. His eyes were "light grey." He was slender, but struck many as strong and sinewy. One who met Jefferson described him as "bony" with "broad shoulders, a true Virginian." Another was struck by his "uncommonly long" arms, "wrists of . . . extraordinary size," and "very large" hands and feet. He tended to stand ramrod straight, though he slouched while seating, leading some to comment on his poor posture. His gait was "not precise and military, but easy and swinging." Strangers remarked on his "mild and pleasing countenance," though he was so unforthcoming in the presence of strangers that some initially thought him "reserved even to coldness." But acquaintances that got to know Jefferson usually described him as gentle, polite, kind, humble, thoughtful, gracious, cheerful, and good-humored. One summed up his impression of Jefferson as a man who "arouse[d] esteem and affection." Indeed, throughout his adult life, onlookers commented on the "dignity in his appearance, and ease and graciousness in his manners." Nearly every observer was struck by his profound intellect, and many who spent any length of time in his presence came away thinking him perhaps the most engaging conversationalist they had ever met. One with knowledge of Jefferson characterized him as "a very sensible spirited fine Fellow," and he struck others as diligent, industrious, and well-organized. John Adams, who as a congressman from Massachusetts came to know Jefferson better than most, portrayed him as "prompt, frank, explicit, and decisive." What most surprised his colleagues in Congress was Jefferson's hesitancy to join in debates, a trait he shared with Washington and Franklin. While serving on small committees, however, Jefferson was less reluctant to discuss and dispute matters.[19]

Jefferson had entered a deeply divided Congress. All agreed on the need to wage war, but there was disagreement over the ends for which the colonists were fighting. At an early session, prior to Jefferson's arrival, South Carolina's John Rutledge asked the question that would harry Congress for the next fifteen months: "do We aim at independency or do We only ask for a Restoration of Rights & putting Us on Our old footing" that had existed before London initiated its new colonial policies a decade or so earlier?[20] When Jefferson came to Philadelphia, those who favored reconciliation were in the majority. John Dickinson of Pennsylvania was their leader and his message, asserted time and again, was that American security and prosperity hinged on maintaining the imperial ties. He was confident that military resistance would bring Britain to the negotiating table, and he believed that if Congress petitioned the king to intervene, George III would do so, perhaps by asking a friend of America's, such as William Pitt, the Earl of Chatham, to form a new government. But according to Dickinson, should the "evil day" ever come when independence was declared, America would "taste . . . deeply of that bitter Cup" of adversity. A war for independence would be longer and more difficult than a war waged to force concessions from London, and in all likelihood such a conflict would be unwinnable. With striking foresight, Dickinson laid out the woes that would accompany a lengthy war: battles would be lost; casualties would be steep; camp diseases would stalk soldiers and civilians alike; the northern colonies would be invaded from Canada; the Royal Navy would suppress American trade; slaves in the South would rebel or run away behind enemy lines; and American morale would be unsustainable. If by some miracle America won a war for independence, the new, weak nation would be prey for Europe's predatory powers. It would be far better, said Dickinson, for Congress to fight this war to achieve the demands spelled out in the Declaration of Colonial Rights that the First Congress had adopted—reconciliation, but on terms that restricted Parliament's authority over the colonies to the regulation of imperial commerce.[21]

There were those in Congress who doubted that reconciliation on favorable terms was possible, and the more radical among them no longer wished to remain part of Great Britain. British actions had fostered a desire for independence among some congressmen, and so, too, had a longing for a degree of autonomy that could never be realized within the empire. Some who favored independence understood that America's economic interests could never be fully secured so long as Great Britain called the shots, and still others believed that an independent American republic would offer Americans the best hope of achieving freedom, happiness, and greater personal opportunities.

John Adams much later reflected, "The Revolution was effected before the war commenced. The Revolution was in the minds and hearts of the people," noting that the transformation occurred prior to bloodshed, though he never said precisely when the metamorphosis took place.[22] Adams's comment, one of the most famous made by a Founder, may have been true for him and Boston's radicals, but it was not an accurate analysis of the state of mind throughout the colonies. Those who favored reconciliation remained a majority in Congress until the spring of 1776—twelve months or more after the war commenced—and even at that juncture the foes of independence maintained control of Pennsylvania's assembly in the colonywide elections. Indeed, no congressman who favored independence dared say so openly prior to January 1776, for to do so was to risk shattering the brittle unity essential for waging war.

While Dickinson led the anti-independence faction within Congress, Adams in the summer of 1775 emerged as the leader of the covertly pro-independence congressmen. He disagreed vehemently with Dickinson's notion of petitioning the king. Adams thought it certain to be unavailing. He agreed with his cousin, Samuel Adams, who long before had remarked that the imperial leaders would offer "cakes and sugar plums" to "sooth America into a state of quietness," but they would never concede the colonists' rights.[23] John Adams additionally feared that an appeal to the monarch would send the wrong message to any nation in Europe—and especially France—that might consider providing the colonists with much-needed military assistance. "I dread like Death" petitioning the king, Adams remarked, but "We cant avoid it. Discord and total Disunion would be the certain Effect of a resolute Refusal to petition."

Congress passed and sent off to London what would be called the "Olive Branch Petition." In the face of the setback, Adams clung to the hope that the king would turn a deaf ear to Congress's entreaty. The war and the king's refusal to negotiate, Adams reasoned, would further radicalize the colonists. In the meantime, Congress's "Progress must be slow. It is like a large Fleet sailing under Convoy. The fleetest Sailors must wait for the dullest and slowest." Adams's adroit leadership impressed Jefferson, who in time reflected that his colleague, and soon-to-be friend, had been the "ablest advocate and defender" of American independence.[24]

Jefferson almost certainly favored independence before the war began, but he, too, silently adhered to the course that Adams charted. In the meantime, Congress put Jefferson to work. Given his reputation as a writer, Congress appointed him to craft its response to Britain's unacceptable peace plan, something he had already done in the Virginia Convention. The draft he wrote for Congress was even more strongly worded than the one he had prepared in Richmond ninety days earlier, and it was accepted with few substantive alterations. Congress also immediately assigned him to a committee that was to prepare what today would be called a declaration of war. The committee members asked Jefferson to write the draft, and he composed a muscular statement that was too strong for Dickinson, who also sat on the committee. Dickinson hurried out a draft of his own, and Jefferson accepted it without a fight. A combative sort—such as John Adams—would have found Dickinson's action intolerable, but Jefferson typically shied away from personal confrontations. He also admired Dickinson. On his fifth day in Congress, Jefferson had ridden two miles north of Philadelphia to call on his new colleague at his estate. Dickinson toned down some of Jefferson's rhetoric, but the Declaration of the Causes and Necessity of Taking Up Arms remained a strongly worded statement. Its immediate purpose, after all, was to induce the citizenry to serve and sacrifice, and even Adams acknowledged that the final document had "some spunk in it."[25]

While Jefferson served on many committees, he played only a minor role in Congress during his first year as a delegate. In fact, he was not even in Philadelphia much of the time. Thirty-five days following his arrival, the weary and heat-stressed Congress adjourned until autumn. Like nearly every other delegate, Jefferson set off for home, in his case after a visit to his barber and the purchase of chocolate for his family at Monticello. He returned on September 30, but three months later departed for home once again, a luxury afforded those from colonies that sent multi-member delegations to Congress. Jefferson was accompanied on his second trip home by an indentured servant, a stonecutter whose labor he had just purchased in Philadelphia; he planned to put him to work making the columns at Monticello. Jefferson had anticipated remaining at home for about two months, but concern for the health of Martha and the sudden death of his mother in late March delayed his return.[26]

Jefferson came back to Philadelphia in mid-May 1776, confessing to a friend that he had "been so long out of the political world that I am almost a new man in it." The political world had in fact changed enormously during his long absence. Once hostilities had commenced, Jefferson had said that "after colonies have drawn the sword there is but one step more they can take"—a declaration of independence.[27] But when he left Philadelphia at Christmas, those seeking reconciliation were still firmly in control and independence remained an unlikely prospect. That was no longer true in May.

As Adams had foreseen, war radicalized the colonists as had nothing else during the Anglo-American crisis. Many colonists felt betrayed in the wake of Britain's recourse to force, a sentiment best expressed by George Washington. Almost his first words on hearing of hostilities were "a Brother's Sword has been sheathed in a Brother's breast." The sacrifices made necessary by war also hit home more directly than had parliamentary taxes or the Coercive Acts. Men were wrenched from their civilian pursuits to bear arms. Wives and children were left at home to fend for themselves and maintain farms and shops, and in rare instances to take up the trade the husband had pursued. Sometimes the men who soldiered never came home. Sometimes they did not come home in one piece. Diseases spread from armies into nearby hamlets, at times taking a terrible toll among the civilian inhabitants. War led nearly every colonial assembly to suddenly and dramatically increase taxes, disrupted provincial economies, sliced the incomes of many farmers and workers, and precipitated shortages of many coveted commodities.

Events of the war eroded the desire to reconcile with England. Fear and outrage gripped towns all along the Atlantic coast after the British navy in October 1775 bombarded and utterly destroyed Falmouth, Massachusetts (now Portland, Maine), in reprisal for the town having fired on a royal vessel; the wanton act left residents homeless in the face of the approach of New England's fearsome winter. Southerners were still digesting that news when a bombshell dropped in their laps. In late autumn, Virginia's royal governor, the Earl of Dunmore, who had raised a small force of Tories augmented by a couple of vessels and upwards of 150 British regulars, issued a proclamation promising freedom to all rebel-owned slaves who escaped their patriot masters and joined him. Within a week, five hundred slaves fled behind Dunmore's lines, and another five hundred reached him during the next thirty days. Ripples of terror eddied throughout the South. General Washington called Dunmore "the most formidable Enemy America has," and Edward Rutledge, a South Carolina congressman, said that Virginia's governor had done more "to work an eternal separation between Great Britain and the Colonies, than any other expedient, which could possibly have been thought of."[28]

On January 7, 1776, an express arrived in Philadelphia with the text of an October address by George III. It was a war speech. The monarch declared that the American insurgents embraced "opinions repugnant to the true constitution of the colonies, and to their subordinate relation to Great Britain." Vowing "to put a speedy end to these disorders," George III pledged "decisive exertions" of force, and he rebuffed Congress's Olive Branch Petition.[29]

Thirty-six hours later, in the creeping light of a cold winter morning, Thomas Paine's *Common Sense* was put on sale in a Philadelphia shop. It was not only the most important pamphlet published in the American Revolution; it was the most influential political pamphlet issued in America during the seventeenth and eighteenth centuries. Not until the appearance of *Uncle Tom's Cabin* nearly three-quarters of a century later would any American publication have such a profound impact. Jefferson had benefited from the timing of *A Summary View* a year earlier. Now the moment had come for Paine. He was aided by the news from the military front and the happy coincidence of having his tract hit the streets in the same heartbeat that the text of George III's pugnacious speech appeared in colonial newspapers.

Paine had been almost entirely inactive as a writer since the summer. This was the time of his break with Aitken and the swirling speculation that he had cozied up to the rum pot. But Paine had hardly forsaken writing. He expected to take up his pen again soon, planning a history of Anglo-American troubles down to the outbreak of war. Franklin was providing guidance and furnishing needed source materials. While he prepared for that grand undertaking, Paine wrote a brief essay, a 250-word newspaper piece that appeared in mid-October. In it, he revisited the horrors of slavery and also considered the barbarity visited on generations of American Indians. Unconvincingly, Paine attributed those horrors to Great Britain, not to the colonists. His effort was forgettable save for two incisive lines in which he professed to see better days ahead when "the Almighty will finally separate America from Britain. Call it independence or what you will."[30] He had crossed into territory where others shrank from going, and it caught the attention of influential individuals, including some in the pro-independence faction within Congress. All that can be known for certain is that more than one individual called on Paine and encouraged him to write a full-blown essay urging American independence.

Only Dr. Rush subsequently acknowledged having broached the idea to Paine, and he recalled having been brutally candid in his entreaty. So what if writing a tract urging independence exposed Paine to "popular odium," Rush remembered asking. What could a man without a job, a family, an income, or property lose? Rush hardly had to resort to arm-twisting. Given the stock of radical ideas that Paine had acquired before leaving England, American independence was alluring to him for many reasons.

During his year in Philadelphia, Paine had come to understand that many colonists who favored breaking with the mother country also hoped to accompany independence with the establishment of an American republic. If the prospective American republic succeeded, it might inspire remarkable reforms in England. He also believed that the difficulties Britain would face in waging a long, difficult, and ultimately futile war to prevent American independence might provoke a political tsunami within England, precipitating major reforms, perhaps even a revolution. Paine heard out those who beseeched him to take up his pen, and he readily consented, intent on not merely sounding the trumpet for independence, but of proclaiming all that was corrupt in England's political system and all that was marvelous about republicanism. Those who courted Paine had to convince him of only one thing. He initially planned to write three newspaper essays on the topic, but his suitors persuaded him to think in terms of a pamphlet. A pamphlet would not only reach a national audience; it might possibly reach readers in England as well.[31]

Paine could write quickly, and in this instance he appears to have written his pamphlet within about six weeks. Rush, who may have had a vivid imagination, later maintained that he perused the chapters as they were written and that he alone lent Paine a helping hand in composing the first draft. Rush also acknowledged that Samuel Adams and Franklin read the manuscript prior to its publication. Rush made one additional claim. Paine, he said, intended to call the pamphlet "Plain Truth," but he persuaded him to title it "Common Sense."[32]

Those who had encouraged Paine to write likely envisaged an essay only on reconciliation versus independence, and some doubtless had not wanted anything more than that. But Paine was a true revolutionary. He believed that the very structure of England's political system was rancid, spawning villainy against both the English people and the colonists. Like other English radicals, Paine felt that republican government alone could excise the festering misery and hopeless despair faced by most residents of England. Paine's *Common Sense* would largely introduce America to these radical notions. Before Paine, as historian Eric Foner noted, republicanism had been "an unarticulated strain of political radicalism" in the colonial press. No American writer had so comprehensively lashed together the reasons underlying the commonplace assertion that "corruption was destroying English liberty."[33]

Paine opened with a tutorial on government that synthesized much of English radical thought. The people were to create their government, and its purpose was to provide for their freedom, happiness, and security. The citizenry had been without a voice in the creation of the English government, and the result was "a rotten constitution" in which power was divided between three branches: monarchy, nobility, and commoners. The contrivance may have saved England from monarchical absolutism, but the complexity of the system—he called it "a house divided against itself"—inevitably led to a "clog" that frustrated the interests of all but the most powerful factions in society. The worst feature was monarchy, as it was inevitable that kings would be the "overbearing part" of the system. It was always within the grasp of the king as the "the giver of places and pensions" to bring a sufficient number of lords and commoners under his sway. Kings, in fact, "hath little more to do than to make war and give away places," and the favors they bestowed bought sycophantic support needed for waging the interminable wars beloved by monarchs. Monarchy had "empoveris[ed] the nation," as one king after another had "laid . . . the world in blood and ashes."

Republicanism was Paine's antidote to monarchy and aristocracy. He limned a constitution in which the government consisted of a limited executive and a unicameral legislature, chosen in annual elections by a broad citizenry. His formula would result in the creation of a democratic republic, though he avoided the word "democracy" and emphasized "republican." The republic that he outlined would be unimpeded by hereditary nobles and, to be sure, by the "corrupt influence of the crown," which throughout history had always and inescapably "poisoned" republics. Government, said Paine, was "a necessary evil" given the "inability of moral virtue to govern the world." But if government was essential, republican government—and a limited one at that— offered the best hope for putting in place rulers who would pursue "good and wise purposes," preserve peace, and secure "freedom and property to all men." The alternative was stark. When a republic did not exist, authoritarianism and tyranny ensued.

Paine moved next to his examination of whether America's interests would best be served through reconciliation with the mother country or through independence. He called reconciliation "a fallacious dream." Item by item, he challenged the argument that the colonists would be better off by remaining within the British Empire: To continue under Britain's jurisdiction was to guarantee that the colonists' trade would be circumscribed for England's benefit; to remain in the empire would assure that Americans would be dragged into whatever wars London thought it desirable to make or to enter; so long as Americans were colonists, their interests would be only "a secondary object" to Britain's rulers; meanwhile, London would "suppress" anything in the colonies that rivaled, or someday might contend with, powerful interests within the homeland; and remaining tied to Britain would assure that the colonies would continue to be contaminated "by European corruption." The colonies, wrote Paine, were now capable of supporting themselves without British assistance.

To those who said that a war for independence would be unwinnable, Paine responded: "'Tis not in the power of Britain or Europe to conquer America." The colonists could field large armies, build a considerable fleet, and obtain assistance from Britain's European rivals. Above all, America was three thousand miles away from London, which would have a crippling effect on Britain's military efforts.

"I challenge the warmest advocate of reconciliation," concluded Paine, "to show a single advantage that this continent can reap by being connected with Great Britain." Paine's answer to those who sought reconciliation: "'TIS TIME TO PART."

Paine charged that the foes of independence in Congress were not merely timid. They were "interested." That is, the reconciliationists in Congress represented potent interests that would benefit from remaining tied to Britain, and they ignored the well-being of vast numbers of their countrymen. In addition, for Congress to make reconciliation the aim of the war was misguided. Paine trod gingerly in this portion of *Common Sense*, for having contended that Britain could not win the war, he had to say—without quite saying so—that the colonists might be incapable of winning the war alone. As "we may quarrel on for ever," the day may come when the colonists "in our present state" might need help from France or Spain. Yet, so long as reconciliation was the aim of the war, "those powers would be sufferers" should the contest end in "strengthening the connection between Britain and America." Only if America declared independence would those nations "give us any kind of assistance."

Paine's argument for American independence was breathtaking. He transformed the meaning of America's struggle with the mother country from what many had seen as a quarrel over taxes and Parliament's authority to an epic event in which Americans were summoned to fight for the survival of liberty—their liberties and the liberties of others, and the liberties of generations yet unborn. "O! ye that love mankind! Ye that dare oppose not only the tyranny but the tyrant, stand forth." Freedom had been destroyed in Europe, Asia, and Africa, "and England hath given her warning to depart."

Few generations in history had ever had the opportunity to do something so epochal, so meaningful, as that which was presented to those living in 1776. The salvation of freedom was in their hands, and Paine captured the meaning and majesty of what they might achieve in a spellbinding manner:

> The sun never shone on a cause of greater worth. 'Tis not the affair of a city, a county, a province, or a kingdom; but of a continent—of at least one eighth part of the habitable globe. 'Tis not the concern of a day, a year, or an age; posterity are virtually involved in the contest, and will be more or less affected even to the end of time, by the proceedings now.
>
> Now is the seed-time of continental union, faith and honor. The least fracture now will be like a name engraved with the point of a pen on the tender rind of a young oak; the wound will enlarge with the tree, and posterity read it in full grown characters. . . . [A] new era for politics is struck—a new method of thinkings has arisen. . . . We have it in our power to begin the world over again. . . . The birthday of a new world is at hand.[34]

During the decade-long crisis with Great Britain, hundreds of pamphlets had been published on both sides of the quarrel, but Americans had never seen one like this. Paine wrote in an accessible, engaging manner, free of legalistic jargon and devoid of the unfathomable Latin passages that had punctuated so much of the lawyerly pamphleteering. Historian Sophia Rosenfeld noted that Paine's "language . . . was by turns unadorned, satirical, prophetic, metaphoric, and violently indignant, but never dry." No one summed up the secret of the success of *Common Sense* better than Jefferson, who wrote that Paine was unsurpassed in his "ease and familiarity of style, in perspicuity of expression, happiness of elucidation, and in simple and unassuming language."[35] One historian surmised that Paine wrote with the intention that his composition was to be "read aloud." It was more likely that *Common Sense*'s suitability for being read to public gatherings by leather-lunged patriots was simply a happy by-product of Paine's graceful facility as a writer. Paine was consciously seeking a wider audience than the small number of educated elite who customarily purchased and read the pamphlet literature, and he found it. Benjamin Rush noted that Paine had "a wonderful talent of writing to the tempers and feelings of the public" as well as the skill to fill his composition with "splendid and original imagery." Paine never denied the importance of timing to *Common Sense*'s success, and in fact he once claimed to have deliberately planned his tract's publication to coincide with the arrival of word of the hostile intransigence of king and Parliament. That was a fib. It was simply his good fortune that *Common Sense* appeared at a moment when the colonists' rage toward the mother country had reached the boiling point. Paine said as much within his pamphlet: "the time has found us."[36]

Dickinson's *Letters from a Farmer* had been the bestselling pamphlet published in America during the ten-year-long imperial crisis, but within only a few months *Common Sense* had sold upwards of seventy-five times more copies. (Congress's management aided sales, as individual legislators prevailed on newspaper editors to mention or advertise the tract, and at least one congressman shipped home large numbers of the pamphlet for distribution.) However, *Common Sense* created such a sensation that it needed little assistance. In addition to its brisk sales, many read excerpts in newspapers and others heard at least portions that were read on village greens, in the ranks of the army, and by pastors in their pulpits. One congressman, who was delighted that someone had finally dared to publicly use the "frightful word *Independence*," happily noted that *Common Sense* was being "greedily . . . read by all ranks of people." General Washington acknowledged that the pamphlet was "working a powerful change . . . in the Minds of many men." Franklin said that its impact had been "prodigious" and Dr. Rush thought it had "burst from the press with an effect that has rarely been produced by types and papers in any age or country." During the ensuing weeks, Paine's arguments were repeated time and again in addresses, resolutions, and instructions adopted by local bodies.

Paine had excited a clamor. Twenty-five editions of the tract appeared in the colonies in 1776, perhaps prompting Paine—who at times was known to exaggerate—to claim that hundreds of thousands of copies were sold during the first year, a boast once accepted by some historians. Recent scholarship, however, has demonstrated that the print technology of the day would have limited sales in America in 1776 to roughly seventy-five thousand copies. Nevertheless, as *Common Sense* was soon published in England and France, and later during the Revolutionary War in Warsaw, Rotterdam, Copenhagen, Moscow, and Berlin, the pamphlet in time probably enjoyed enormous sales somewhat along the lines suggested years later by Paine. Yet, despite his work's remarkable sales, America's lack of copyright laws—and Paine's shortcomings in negotiating a deal with an experienced and tough-nosed printer—cost him a princely sum. Paine once said that had he received his fair share in royalties, he might have realized £1,000 a day in Pennsylvania alone during much of 1776. He likely wildly overestimated what he had lost, though there can be no doubt that his tract might have made him wealthy. But he was not bitter, and over the long haul he took great pride in not having benefited financially from his public service. Indeed, Paine not only donated his modest earnings to the Continental army for the purchase of gloves for the soldiery, but thereafter he declined substantial portions of the royalties earned from his subsequent writings, a sacrifice so out of the norm in his time—and so equally unconventional among today's public servants who author a book or find someone to write it for them—that it set Paine apart from his fellow Founders, save for General Washington, who had agreed to serve without pay.[37]

General Washington immediately expressed his joy on reading what he called Paine's "unanswerable reasoning" and predicted it would hasten the approach of a declaration of independence. Charles Lee, the number two general in the Continental army, called it "a masterly irresistible performance" that would "give the coup de grace to G. Britain," a conclusion echoed by many others. (Lee, who met Paine that winter, said he thought the writer "has genius in his eyes.") *Common Sense*, it was said, had made American independence a "delightful theme" that now was endorsed with "rapturous praise." "Nothing else is now talked of," said those in the know.[38] John Adams, a political conservative, loathed Paine's advocacy of unicameralism and his thinly shrouded advocacy of democracy, which since Aristotle had been thought by nearly all political philosophers to be a form of government that would inevitably deteriorate into civil disorder and dictatorial rule. Nevertheless, Adams rejoiced that the pamphlet was certain to make independence "the common Faith." He, too, praised "the Strength and Brevity of his [Paine's] style," especially his "elegant Symplicity." Years later, laced with envy and resentment, Adams railed that "History is to ascribe the American Revolution to Thomas Pain."[39]

Paine was never so vain as to claim responsibility for the American Revolution, although then and later he insisted that his tract "gave a turn to the politics of America" that hastened Congress's decision to declare independence. Paine was dead on target in taking considerable credit for reshaping attitudes within Congress and outside of it. Later, in 1779, he additionally declared that had it not been for *Common Sense*, American independence would not yet have been declared. Whether or not independence would ever have been declared had not *Common Sense* been written can never be known, but its appearance was crucial to the break with Great Britain happening when it did, in July 1776. Given the repeated military setbacks that America experienced in the second half of 1776, it is entirely possible that had independence not been declared during that summer, Congress might not have taken the step for a very long while thereafter.[40]

A month after the appearance of *Common Sense*, John Adams gleefully exclaimed that there was "no Prospect, no Probability, no Possibility" of reconciliation.[41] A confluence of occurrences between the autumn of 1775 and the spring of 1776—*Common Sense* among them—had indeed propelled the colonies toward severing ties with Great Britain. Military adversity was paramount in the timing of the break. Two American armies suffered cataclysmic defeats in the course of an invasion of Canada, one on the final day of 1775, the other in a series of disasters in May 1776. But America's military woes went deeper. Prior to the second calamity, Congress learned that its army in Canada was shamefully defective. A congressional committee sent to investigate found that many officers were "unfit" and the soldiery untrained, undisciplined, unpaid, and woefully provisioned. News of the second thrashing in Canada reached Philadelphia early in June, at the very moment that a huge British armada was known to be bearing down on New York. Congress recognized that "Our Affairs are hastening fast to a Crisis." It also realized that Paine had been correct in warning that foreign assistance was necessary if the war was to be won, and that aid could be had only if America declared independence. On June 11, six months and two days after *Common Sense* appeared, Congress appointed a committee to draft a declaration of independence.[42]

That Jefferson was added to the committee was something of a fluke. Typically, Congress created multi-member committees composed of representatives from each of the three sections of the colonies. In this instance, it put two New Englanders on the committee, John Adams and Connecticut's Roger Sherman, and two from the mid-Atlantic region, Pennsylvania's Benjamin Franklin and New York's Robert R. Livingston. The fifth member would be a southerner and Virginia's Richard Henry Lee seemed a shoe-in, as he not only led Virginia's delegation but on June 7 had introduced the motion calling for Congress to declare independence. But Lee wanted to return home to participate in writing his state's first constitution. Recognizing Jefferson's talent as a writer, Congress appointed him to what the congressmen soon called the Committee of Five. Probably at its initial meeting, the other members of the committee asked Jefferson to compose the draft.[43]

Jefferson was a fast writer, and in this instance he appears to have completed his assignment within four days. His drew on numerous sources, including the literature of the Enlightenment and English Whig polemicists, the text of Lee's resolution calling for independence, what one scholar labeled the "war crimes" charges that Dickinson had included in the Declaration of the Causes and Necessity of Taking Up Arms (Britain's instigation of hostile acts by Indians and African Americans), and what Jefferson himself had written and sent to the Virginia Convention a few weeks earlier as a draft for the state's first constitution. The latter included both a lengthy compilation of charges against George III and a commitment "to re-establish such antient principles as are friendly to the rights of the people." However, nothing influenced him more than Virginia's Declaration of Rights, which as luck would have it appeared in a Philadelphia newspaper on the very day that Jefferson likely began to write. George Mason's draft of Virginia's Declaration had been adopted in committee in May and printed in the *Virginia Gazette*, even though it had not yet been accepted by the Virginia Convention. Among other things, Mason had written that "all men are born equally free" and possess "certain inherent natural rights, and that governments ought to produce "the greatest degree of happiness and safety" for the people.[44]

Before the week was out, Adams and Franklin had read Jefferson's draft and recommended only a handful of minor stylistic changes. In all, twenty-six alterations were made to Jefferson's draft, some possibly by Sherman and Livingston, and some probably by Jefferson, who, like most authors, here and there reconsidered his original wording. The modifications notwithstanding, the document that was presented to Congress late in June was to be sure the handiwork of Jefferson.[45]

After a brief preface asserting that the time had arrived to "dissolve the political bands" with the mother country, the best-remembered section followed, Jefferson's lyrical passage on egalitarianism and natural rights, including the right to revolution:

> We hold these truths to be self-evident; that all men are created equal; that they are endowed by their Creator with inherent and inalienable rights; that among these are life, liberty, and the pursuit of happiness; that to secure these rights, governments are instituted among men, deriving their

just powers from the consent of the governed; that whenever any form of government becomes destructive of these ends, it is the right of the people to alter or to abolish it, and to institute new government, laying its foundation on such principles, and organising its powers in such form as to them shall seem most likely to effect their safety and happiness. Prudence indeed will dictate that governments long established should not be changed for light & transient causes, and accordingly all experience hath shewn that mankind are more disposed to suffer, while evils are sufferable, than to right themselves by abolishing the forms to which they are accustomed. But when a long train of abuses and usurpations, begun at a distinguished period, & pursuing invariably the same object, evinces a design to reduce them under absolute despotism, it is their right, it is their duty, to throw off such government, & to provide new guards for their future security.

That melodic paragraph was followed by a lengthy, reproachful bill of indictment that cataloged the despotic acts of Britain's rulers and denounced the Crown's refusal to receive the colonists' petitions for redress. Jefferson marshaled more than twenty charges of illegal and tyrannical actions by the king and nine by Parliament. The final paragraph announced that the colonies had become "FREE AND INDEPENDENT STATES" that could do all that independent entities "may of right do."

There was nothing new in Jefferson's document. He never claimed there was. In fact, he later said that his intent had been to follow's Congress's wish to capture the "tone and spirit" of "the American mind," the outlook that had crystallized over the past decade of ferment and built to a crescendo since the eruption of hostilities. Parts of what Jefferson wrote had appeared in *Common Sense*. Paine had written of "Mankind being originally equals in the order of creation," whereas Jefferson said simply that "All men are created equal." Paine had said that humankind deserved a government that provided "the greatest sum of individual happiness," while Jefferson identified "the pursuit of happiness" as among the natural rights of man. Both Paine and Jefferson indicted the king, though the arraignment in the Declaration of Independence was both more comprehensive and more specific.

John Adams subsequently complained that it was "a juvenile declamation" in that there was not "an idea in it, but what had been hackneyed in Congress for two years," and some historians have suggested that given Jefferson's lack of originality, his achievement has been "overrated."[46] But both Adams and the scholars misunderstood what Jefferson had achieved. Abraham Lincoln understood. "All honor to Jefferson," he said," for having had "in the concrete pressure of a struggle for national independence . . . the coolness, forecast, and capacity to introduce into a merely revolutionary document, an abstract truth, applicable to all men and all times." Historian David Armitage also appreciated what Jefferson had achieved, observing that he had used "his forensic and rhetorical skill to forge an instrument for declaring independence without any earlier models to guide him."

It is not likely that any other congressman could have matched the literary artistry of Jefferson's Declaration. In a clear and simple manner, Jefferson's document flowed like a gentle stream, yet delivered its message with forceful eloquence. He was a penman with a genius for the cadence of the written word, a writer conversant with music who had a feel for what one scholar has called the "rhythmical pauses . . . comparable to musical bars."[47]

People read the Declaration in newspapers and broadsides, and many heard it read by army officers or local officials in town squares and on village greens. No other congressional pronouncement during the Revolutionary era was as widely read by contemporaries, and aside from constitutional amendments nothing else ever issued by Congress has reached such a large contemporary audience, nor has continued to inspire subsequent generations of Americans and non-Americans.

The year 1776, in contrast to any other year in American history, witnessed the appearance of two written works that profoundly altered the immediate course of events and went on to influence future generations. *Common Sense* and the Declaration of Independence were written for radically different reasons, but despite the dissimilarities in the two documents, their authors shared an ideal. Paine hoped that the American Revolution would create an American nation unlike any in existence and that it would inspire a sea change in England's society and governance. Jefferson was not fully apace with Paine, but his hope for the American Revolution was more radical than that of most colonial insurgents. A great many colonists prayed that despite the severance of ties with Great Britain, and the termination of all vestiges of royal authority, the social and political fabric of the colonial world would remain intact. But for Jefferson, the American Revolution involved more than breaking with the mother country. It was the essential step that had to be taken before major changes could be made within Virginia's domestic landscape.

When it created the Committee of Five in early June, Congress agreed to take up the question of independence on July 1. On Friday, June 28, the committee submitted the document that Jefferson had written. It was ignored until the following Tuesday. On Monday, as planned, Congress debated independence, spending that long sweltering day going back and forth on the momentous issue, not stopping until the pink light of sunset bathed the Pennsylvania State House where Congress was meeting. Although many delegates spoke, there is no evidence that Jefferson joined in. The following morning, Congress returned to the question of breaking with Great Britain, but little was left to be said. Around noon, Congress declared independence by a unanimous vote. At that point, the congressmen at last turned to Jefferson's draft. Altogether, they spent about ten hours in the course of three separate sessions poring over his handiwork, finally completing their work on July 4. The congressmen were unsparing editors, excising roughly a third that Jefferson had written. Few authors can watch with equanimity as their compositions are chopped apart, and Jefferson was no exception. But a good editor can improve what an author has written, and Congress proved to be quite good at its task. It made the Declaration of Independence leaner and more readable. Yet despite the pruning, Jefferson's literary masterpiece survived. Jefferson anguished as he watched his colleagues wielding their axes, and he subsequently complained about it to friends. However, as Richard Henry Lee sagely replied, what Jefferson had composed was "in its nature so good, that no Cookery can spoil the Dish."[48]

News of the Declaration triggered celebrations from New England to Georgia, and in several locations crowds destroyed royalist trappings, including the king's arms and pictures. On July 9, the day that word of independence reached Manhattan, a crowd gathered in the evening and pulled down an equestrian statue of George III. The "IMAGE of the BEAST was thrown down . . . and his HEAD severed from his Body," it was reported. Later, the lead from the monument was shipped to Litchfield, Connecticut, where it was melted and converted into forty-two thousand musket balls by local women.[49]

Once the Declaration of Independence was written and approved, Jefferson was ready to leave Congress. As quickly as he could get away from Philadelphia, Jefferson returned to Virginia and rejoined the legislature, anxious to change his state for the better.

Paine and James Monroe took another course. Both men—one soon to turn forty, the other barely eighteen—went to war.

CHAPTER 3

"THESE ARE THE TIMES THAT TRY MEN'S SOULS"

PAINE AND MONROE GO TO WAR

BETWEEN THE APPEARANCE of *Common Sense* in January and the Declaration of Independence in July, Thomas Paine took up his pen for several additional sorties on behalf of separating from Great Britain, though he had little new to say on the topic. One biographer thought Paine approached the issue "as if bored," but his essays nevertheless attracted considerable attention. That was due in part to his newfound fame, though he benefited again from fortunate timing. His newspaper essays in April and May were read as word spread of the second military debacle in Canada and at a time when the final political battles over declaring independence were waged in several provinces. It was a tempestuous time that John Adams equated to riding in a "Whirlwind."[1]

Once Congress declared independence, Paine left Philadelphia to soldier. News had traveled that a huge British armada had been sighted off Long Island. The fourteen-month-old war was about to heat up, with the action centered in New York. General Washington had been preparing for it since January. He had correctly surmised that the enemy would abandon Boston and turn its attention to New York, seeking first to take Manhattan Island and then to gain control of the Hudson River, the spine of the new United States. Britain's control of the river would sever ties between the four New England provinces and the nine states to the south, virtually assuring a British victory. By July, a large Continental army, augmented by militia from several states, was in place to defend Manhattan and Long Island. Paine did not hesitate to do his part. There was a risk-taking streak in his makeup: He had served on a privateer, his job as an exciseman had not been without hazards, and he had braved an Atlantic crossing, not an undertaking for the fainthearted. In this instance, Paine was willing to face danger because of his commitment to America's cause, but as an immigrant who had lived in Philadelphia for only eighteen months, he may also have viewed answering the call to bear arms as a means of solidifying his status in this new land.

Paine enlisted in the Philadelphia Associators, a volunteer unit separate from the Continental army, though it, too, was subject to General Washington. The body that Paine joined was designated a "flying camp," a mobile force primed for rapid deployment. But the Philadelphia Associators never moved after making a one-hundred-mile march to Perth Amboy, New Jersey. Washington left the men in New Jersey across from Staten Island, strategically placed in the event that at some point he wished to include them in an attack on the British rear. Paine was with the Associators for three months while the campaign for New York played out, apparently serving the entire time as the secretary to its commander, General Daniel Roberdeau, a successful Philadelphia merchant.[2]

The New York campaign did not go well for the Americans. After a series of errors and misjudgments by Washington, including a rout on Long Island from which the army barely escaped, the callow army in mid-October withdrew from Manhattan, save for its maintenance of one post, Fort Washington, in the island's northern region. By then, the Associators' short-term enlistments had ended and the men had marched home. Paine did not accompany them. Indeed, he went north toward the front. His destination was Fort Lee, on the New Jersey side of the Hudson River, an installation positioned almost directly across the river from Fort Washington. The two posts had been created to prevent British naval vessels from sailing north of Manhattan; in addition, Fort Lee served as a huge supply depot. Paine came to Fort Lee hoping to sign on as a civilian aide to General Nathanael Greene, one of the original thirteen general officers appointed by Congress when it created the army. Greene had been given command of this sector in mid-September, shortly before Paine arrived and offered his services.[3] Greene accepted, and for the next sixty days or so Paine was with the Continental army, and some of that time in harm's way.

Paine ran errands, took dictation, and drafted some of Greene's letters and orders. When the bulk of Washington's army retreated north of Manhattan in October, Paine had enough time on his hands to also serve as a correspondent for a Philadelphia newspaper. Paine and Greene got on well together, forming an enduring relationship. Only five years separated them—Paine was the older of the two—and both had been reared as Quakers, but Greene was also drawn to Paine because he found him to be competent and useful. Others around headquarters thought Paine strikingly unconventional. He was considerably older than most of the men, and in bearing and temperament nothing like a spit-and-polish soldier. Paine was teased by some of his comrades and at times he was the butt of their practical jokes, but they appear to have liked him, and he bore their good-natured baiting without rancor.[4]

In November, the war caught up with Paine. The British army, under General William Howe, had pursued Washington's Continentals following their withdrawal from Manhattan, and the two forces collided in a sharp one-day engagement at White Plains on October 28. In the aftermath of the inconclusive encounter, Howe marched his men back to Manhattan and Washington divided his army into four parts: One division of Continentals was to guard the Hudson north of Manhattan; a second was to remain near White Plains and stand ready to march in whatever direction it was needed; Washington crossed into New Jersey with two thousand men; and Greene was given three thousand men for the defense of Forts Washington and Lee.

The decision to defend Fort Washington was misguided, and some of the generals in the council of war that Washington convened told him as much. Washington wavered indecisively until the British attacked on November 16. The skeptics had been right. The installation fell within five hours. More than 3,100 American soldiers were lost. Paine, in the company of Washington and Greene at Fort Lee, watched the disaster unfold. In the aftermath of the debacle, Washington—neither for the first nor the last time—looked for a scapegoat. He found it in Greene, maintaining that his subordinate had persuaded him that the fort was defensible. Greene had indeed advised that a British attack could be repulsed or, in a worst-case scenario, all of the fort's defenders could escape across the Hudson to New Jersey. But the final decision was Washington's, and from the outset he had been far more eager to defend the installation than he subsequently acknowledged.

Fort Washington was not the last catastrophe of the autumn. Four days later a British force led by Lord Cornwallis scaled the rugged Jersey escarpment, moved speedily in the face of little resistance, and seized Fort Lee. For a force as ill-provisioned as the Continental army, the loss was staggering. Cornwallis captured 12 cannon, 6 mortars, 4,000 cannonballs, 2,800 muskets, 400,000 cartridges, 500 entrenching tools, upwards of 300 tents, 1,000 barrels of flour, and untold amounts of baggage. In one week, America's army had lost 20 percent of its soldiery, 146 pieces of artillery, and tons of weaponry, munitions, and other stores.[5]

Greene immediately claimed that most of Fort Lee's contents had been removed before Cornwallis arrived. Paine knew the truth, but he went along with the fable in his account for the Philadelphia newspaper. The war effort required that the truth be hidden. Paine knew, too, who had made the decision to defend Fort Washington and who was responsible for failing to order the removal of the precious supplies from Fort Lee, but public morale required— as he would write a quarter century later—that he remain silent regarding Washington's "series of blunders that had nearly ruined the country."[6]

General Cornwallis, who had spent half his thirty-six years in the British army, was not one to waste time. He came after Washington's army the day after Fort Lee fell. Knowing that Cornwallis would stalk him, Washington had already begun to retreat, but not before he summoned help from militiamen, the division in White Plains, and some among the remnants of the army that had been driven out of Canada. In the aftermath of his two most recent calamities, Washington had 5,410 men under his command, much of his manpower due to the rapid mustering of militia; Cornwallis had nearly twice that number. Washington's plan was to fall back, awaiting the arrival of the units that he had ordered to join him. If sufficient numbers arrived, he hoped to make a stand behind one of the rivers that sluiced through New Jersey. Some in Congress and elsewhere carped at yet another retreat by Washington, but Paine publicly defended the commander's tactics, correctly pointing out that to have stood and fought would have resulted in the "entire destruction" of the army and probably of the American Revolution. Once again, too, he lauded the American commander, presciently telling his readers that not only would future generations call Washington's strategic retreat "glorious," but also that it would earn him "eternal" fame.[7]

Paine was with the soldiers as they began the retreat under a sullen November sky. So, too, was James Monroe, a young Virginia lieutenant whose unit was part of the small force that withdrew southward with Washington immediately after the contest at White Plains.

Monroe had abandoned his college studies sometime in the spring or summer of 1776. Ardent and idealistic, he enlisted in the Third Virginia Regiment. It was hardly surprising that Monroe signed on to soldier. Virginia pulsated with important events. The American rebellion, and now the war, were the most exciting—and clearly the most consequential—things that had occurred in Monroe's, or any living person's, lifetime. As was true of Paine, there was an adventurous side to Monroe, a yearning to be where the action was, a willingness, even an eagerness, to run risks, to face peril, to test himself. Also, like a great many others who aspired to rise to something better, Monroe saw soldiering as a crucial necessity if his keenly ambitious cravings were to have any chance of fulfillment.

Monroe had already been active in the cause, at least as much as was possible while he continued his studies. Since April of the previous year, when Governor Dunmore had confiscated the gunpowder stored in Williamsburg's magazine, the little college town had been swept with rumors that a British invasion was imminent and that Virginians would use force to regain possession of their powder. Monroe, caught up in the mood of the times, attended open meetings where resistance to British provocations was discussed. He also purchased a musket. During the summer of 1775, Monroe was part of a band of twenty-three men that broke into the governor's palace and seized two hundred firearms and three hundred swords, which were promptly turned over to the local militia. Thereafter, Virginia remained relatively calm until September, when skirmishes occurred between Tories and rebels near Hampton Roads. By then, Virginia had created a regular military establishment consisting of two regiments, and some in the army trained on a field behind the college. Monroe must have watched and listened as the men marched and drilled, and a martial band sometimes played. By December, open warfare raged in Norfolk between Virginia's soldiers—including the men that Monroe had watched go through their exercises—and an army composed of British regulars, Tories, and the runaway slaves that Governor Dunmore had raised that autumn. When it became clear a few weeks later that the British high command was sending a large fleet and army to the Carolinas to reestablish royal control, Congress created a southern department of the Continental army and put General Charles Lee in command. Lee arrived in Williamsburg to take command in March 1776 and was greeted with fanfare. Williamsburg and the bucolic little campus were alive with military fervor.[8]

Before Lee's arrival, the Virginia Convention created seven additional regiments, though some seventy-five days would be required for them to become operational. Once they were up and running, some of the new regiments trained daily that spring and summer in Williamsburg on a field in the shadow of Monroe's dormitory. After six weeks in Williamsburg, General Lee departed for the Carolinas, but he left the Third Regiment behind. Together with the militia, it was to guard against the possible return of Dunmore's armed force. Lee put Brigadier General Andrew Lewis, a fifty-six-year-old immigrant from Ireland and veteran of two earlier Virginia wars, in charge of the Third Regiment, which throughout the spring continued its daily training. This was the moment when Monroe signed on to soldier. He turned eighteen in April and probably went into the army around the time of his birthday or at the end of the school year. He was commissioned a lieutenant.[9]

Monroe experienced only a few weeks of training, marching on the sunbaked drill field and barking out orders. He wore a hunting shirt made of durable osnaburg and carried a tomahawk in his belt, attire ordered by General Lewis. In July, learning of a renewed threat posed by Dunmore's army, the Third Regiment marched toward the Chesapeake. Some on the trek were posted in Jamestown and Yorktown, but most of the seven hundred men in the regiment slogged on under the merciless summer sun, wearied not only by the heat but also by insufficient water. Many men avoided drinking from wells they passed along the way, having been told that Dunmore had ordered that the smallpox-laced bodies of dead runaway slaves be dumped down the shafts. Word also spread that Dunmore had inoculated some of the former slaves in his little army with smallpox and sent them amid the civilian population in a rudimentary stab at germ warfare. What was known for sure was that when Dunmore's troops were not conducting raids up three small rivers that emptied into the Chesapeake, they were digging fortifications on Gwynns' Island, near the mouth of the Piankatank River. Lewis wasted no time confronting his adversary with an artillery bombardment; Dunmore answered in kind. When Virginia's soldiers invaded the island the next morning, Dunmore fled with his force. It had been a small engagement. Only one Virginian died, in an accident when his homemade mortar burst. But if Monroe was in the action, it was his baptism of fire.[10]

Dunmore sailed away from Virginia for good on August 7. Within a few days, the Third Virginia was back in Williamsburg, but not for long. Anticipating that the first blow in General Howe's campaign to take New York was imminent, Washington summoned the First and Third Virginia Regiments. (Three others were ordered to New York in September and a fourth in December.) In mid-August—not long after Paine and the Philadelphia Associators arrived in Perth Amboy—Monroe and his comrades began the long, dusty march northward, past verdant farms and ragged, overgrown fields, a trek of some four hundred miles made under the searing summer sun. The men were tired and hungry when they arose each morning, hungrier and ready to drop when the day's march ended, though before catching a few hours of sleep they first had to prepare the evening mess over a low fire and clean their pots and utensils. Each night, a few of the unlucky drew a shift of guard duty.[11]

In August, Jefferson in Philadelphia noted that the Third Virginia was "on the road hither," though in the end the regiment skipped its planned parade through the city when it was learned that smallpox had broken out among the town's residents. Averaging roughly fifteen miles each day, the Virginians completed their march in twenty-six days, a pace that took its toll. The brigade commander reported that a third of the men were unfit for duty when at last the regiment crossed onto Manhattan on September 12, although one low-ranking officer claimed that the men in his company "reached this place in good spirits and generally speaking healthy."[12]

Around this time, the Third Virginia became part of the brigade commanded by Brigadier General George Weedon, a forty-one-year-old native of the same county in which Monroe had been raised. A child of the minor gentry, Weedon had not attended college. Instead, like Monroe, he had gone to war while in his late teens, soldiering for nine years during the French and Indian War. Afterward, he ran a tavern in Fredericksburg until he answered the call to arms again in the Revolutionary War.

The Virginians arrived in Manhattan too late to take part in the disastrous opening battle on Long Island, and they were posted too far north on Manhattan Island to see action when a superior British force landed at Kip's Bay in mid-September, promptly routing the American defenders. The Virginians were a cocksure bunch, proud of being southerners, convinced of their superiority as soldiers to the New Englanders, even persuaded that the Yankees thought them special and greeted their arrival with "great joy." Not long passed before they had an opportunity to show their mettle. On their fifth day on Manhattan Island, three companies from the Third Virginia saw combat when advance units of the British army penetrated Harlem Heights. The Virginians were plugged in to strike at the enemy's rear during its retreat through a green and white field of buckwheat. It was the first good outcome for the Americans in any engagement of consequence in the Battle of New York. The redcoats had been "cursedly thrashed," boasted Weedon, and Washington lauded those who had fought, telling them that not only had their valor "greatly inspirited the whole of our Troops," but they had demonstrated what American soldiers could achieve when "Officers & soldiers will exert themselves . . . to support the Honor and Liberties of their Country." One of the Virginia company commanders could not have agreed more. His men had "behaved like soldiers," he boasted, adding that the Marylanders had performed just as valiantly, but that some Yankees had acted "shamelessly" under fire. Some twenty Americans died in the Battle of Harlem Heights, including men in the Third Virginia, and more than one hundred rebels were wounded or captured. If Monroe had not come under fire on the Chesapeake, he most likely did in this battle.[13]

A month later, the Continental army—save for the ill-fated men at Fort Washington—withdrew from Manhattan, and a few days after that, portions of the rival armies clashed in an inconclusive confrontation at White Plains. Washington committed only a small portion of his army to the battle, and the Virginians were not included. But they had been in skirmishes prior to the bigger encounter, battling armed Tories and Hessians, the German mercenaries hired by Britain. The Virginians performed ably, driving away the enemy force, inflicting heavy losses, capturing much-needed weapons and blankets, and helping to secure the area at White Plains so that Washington could make a stand. These southern boys had even come to conclude that the Yankees had now "plucked up a heart" and were fighting "lustily."[14]

It was following the battle at White Plains, and the division of the army, that Washington set off with two thousand men for New Jersey. The Virginians were part of Washington's depleted army. Already weary from hard campaigning, and deprived of an adequate diet and other essential supplies, the men faced yet another wearying tramp. Before they set off, Weedon spoke of the "Sufferings of my poor men." They had faced danger for weeks, and many were without shoes and stockings, while "almost all [were] without Shirts." Despite New York's bone-chilling autumn nights, scores lacked a blanket. The regiment had shrunk by about 15 percent since departing Virginia—it now stood at six hundred men—and barely half of those still in the field were fit for duty. Early in November, the Third Virginia and their comrades from other units were on the move. After crossing to the west side of the Hudson, another week of hard marching brought them directly across from Staten Island. They arrived on the day of the disaster at Fort Washington and could hear the faraway artillery blasts.[15]

Through what remained of November, the Virginians were on the march almost every day as Cornwallis pursued the Continentals across New Jersey's bleak late-autumn landscape. Early in the chase, every Virginia regiment was dispatched to Brunswick to stand guard against a possible British landing in Perth Amboy. After only a couple of days, they were ordered northward to Newark to join the main army. When the Virginians entered Newark, Monroe and Paine were in the same location for the first time, but it was unlikely the two encountered each other then or at any stage of the retreat. Paine remained in the presence of the highest-ranking officers, while Monroe, a lowly lieutenant, tended to his duties in a small company.

The Virginians were in Newark for only a few hours before Washington's force moved southward yet again. Monroe later recalled standing on the side of the road and counting heads as his regiment departed Newark. To his surprise and consternation, only three thousand men marched past him. The army had shrunk. Some of the shrinkage came about because many soldiers had left for home the moment their enlistment expired. In addition, large numbers of men were unfit for duty and had been sent to Morristown to recuperate. A substantial number of those yet on duty must have barely met the test for fitness. The rigors faced by the soldiers can hardly be exaggerated. Atop the harsh and demanding conditions they had already faced between August and October in the campaign for New York, the soldiery spent much of November on the move and frequently under fire. Each day was "melancholy," said one of the Virginians, as the men slogged mile after mile along "deep miry road[s]." All the while, the men endured an inadequate diet, threadbare clothing, and lack of shelter, as the army had abandoned its tents during its hurried retreat from Manhattan. Weedon said the men's lives were "uncommonly hard." Washington embroidered only slightly when he said that "many of 'em" were "entirely naked," and another observer was sadly accurate in describing the men as "animated scarecrows." Washington did not mention that the morale of the men had ebbed. The Virginia captain who had crowed about southern superiority ten weeks earlier now wrote friends at home: "You will wonder what has become of the good army of Americans you were told we had. . . . They were in some degree imaginary." No one at the time could have imagined that among these gaunt, unkempt, unshaven raga-muffins—many with "disfigured" faces "full of sores"—were two men who would be presidents of the United States, three who one day would be cabinet officials, and three who would be state governors.[16]

The American army reached Brunswick on November 29 and remained there for forty-eight cold hours, the men's breath visible, the aroma of wet, decaying leaves filling every campsite. At some risk, Washington tarried in the hope that reinforcements from the division he had left in White Plains would arrive, possibly enabling him to make a stand, but as it turned out, they were still days away from joining him. He was frustrated, too, by the poor turnout of New Jersey's militia, and on his second day in Brunswick, Washington dejectedly told Congress that he no longer expected that "any considerable aid will be derived from them." The next day he ordered his men to fall back once more. They escaped Brunswick unscathed, but only barely. "Our Rear . . . got out" as the enemy's "advanced Guard were entering the town," Washington reported to Congress. The army eluded Cornwallis yet again in part because the enemy's pursuit was slowed by a barrage laid down by Continental artillerists, including those in Captain Alexander Hamilton's company. The British answered that cannonade—as they had often before—and it is a good bet that from time to time both Monroe and Paine came under fire. Paine, in fact, claimed that he faced "the whistling of a cannon ball" on enough occasions that he came to "stand it with . . . little discomposure."[17]

The following day the little rebel army entered the tiny college town of Princeton, about ten miles above the Delaware River. Although Washington was not immediately aware of it, Cornwallis's pursuit had ended and his army was resting at Brunswick. The redcoats were nearly as bedraggled as the Continentals. The men were tired, the horses exhausted after four months of arduous campaigning capped by the grueling attempt to catch the fleeing rebels, and the army's supply line was worryingly extended. But Cornwallis, a fighter if ever there was one, had not ended the chase of his own volition. With late autumn's first snowfall expected any day, General Howe had called a halt, opting to put his men into winter quarters. The reprieve was a godsend for the Americans. Washington's army had now dwindled to merely 2,500. Had the British not stopped, Washington in all likelihood could not have risked the slow and tedious business of getting his diminishing army across the Delaware. He probably would have marched his tattered force to Morristown and entered winter quarters, ending the campaign of 1776 and changing both the course of the war and how Americans would look at George Washington. Instead, in the predawn darkness of December 2, Washington started for the Delaware with a bit less than half of his army. He left the remaining 1,500 men, which included the wet and cold soldiers of the Third Virginia, in Princeton. They were to wage a holding action against any enemy pursuers that arrived.[18]

Around noon on December 2, the first rebel soldiers reached the slate-gray Delaware River at Trenton and immediately started across to Pennsylvania. Five days and nights were required to make the crossing, a time-consuming operation under any circumstances, but especially for soldiers who had to wrestle heavy cannon, wagons, and cumbersome supply chests onto vessels about to make the slow passage. Those who went over at night crossed in the eerie orange-yellow illumination provided by giant fires set along each shore. The last American trooper set foot on Pennsylvania soil on December 7, and it might have been a man from the Third Virginia. Monroe was among the 134 men in the Third Virginia that crossed, a mere 14 percent of those who had marched north from Williamsburg some 125 days earlier. They got across unimpeded by the enemy. Cornwallis had remained in Brunswick, some twenty-five miles away, for a week. After a leisurely march, the British regulars arrived in Trenton just hours after the last rebel soldier had safely crossed the Delaware.[19]

If Monroe may have been one of the last to pass into Pennsylvania, Paine was likely among the very first. He was on a mission. With the army and the country confronted by what he subsequently, and variously, called the "black times" and the "blackest stage of affairs"—Paine would always think this period had been the very nadir of the Revolutionary War—he again took up his pen to rally the citizenry. Paine once said that the idea to write was his alone, but he also said on one occasion that he did so "on the advice of several principal officers." Paine said that he worked on his composition in the evenings at "every place we stopt" during the army's nine-day trek from Newark to the Delaware River. Though he was cold and weary, using a campfire for illumination—and according to legend a drum for a desk—his essay little by little took shape. What is beyond dispute is that once he reached Trenton, if not earlier, Paine was ordered to hurry to Philadelphia, where he could finish the job more quickly.[20] It was the end of his days of soldiering.

Paine reached the city—about thirty miles from Trenton—sometime in December, and on the nineteenth his tract appeared in a newspaper. A week later it was issued in pamphlet form as *The American Crisis*. Not much of his essay is any longer remembered, save for the first two sentences, an opening flourish that few writers have ever equaled:

> These are the times that try men's souls. The summer soldier and the sunshine patriot will, in this crisis, shrink from the service of their country; but he that stands it *now*, deserves the love and thanks of men and women.

Paine's essay covered the recent campaign, but he did not dare reveal the most damaging things he had seen. He papered over the enormity of the disaster at Fort Lee, portraying what had been captured by the enemy as inconsequential. He depicted Washington—who appeared to some surrounding him as habitually and perilously indecisive—as a commander whose deepest talents were "unlocked" by the greatest trials. For the most part, Paine looked forward, not backward, and he addressed the manifold crises facing America in 1777. The army, already undermanned, was melting away as the twelve-month enlistments expired. It would have to be replenished by fresh enlistees, though recruiting would be more difficult than ever. Not only would it be a formidable challenge to induce men to serve in an ill-equipped army that had suffered a long string of defeats, but Congress had recently voted to transform the Continental army to a standing force in which the soldiers would have to serve for three years or longer. Paine appealed to the citizenry to display "perseverance and fortitude," as his stirring opening lines indicate.

In the wake of the poor turnout and dispirited performance by the New Jersey militia, Paine pitched some that he wrote at militiamen, claiming that these citizen-soldiers should be "the best troops in the world for a sudden exertion." He warned that disaster waited should Americans fail to serve and sacrifice. They would face defeat and "slavery without hope" under the rod of the "sottish, stupid, stubborn, worthless, brutish" British monarch. But if they stood behind the cause, a "glorious issue" would follow in the wake of an American triumph in this war, which he fancifully told his readers could be realized through just one major American victory in 1777.

Paine centered less on the threat of military defeat at the hands of the British army than on an internal problem. The mid-Atlantic states—New York, New Jersey, Pennsylvania, and Delaware—were "infested with Tories" who preached a "servile, slavish, self-interested fear," he wrote. There was a palpable danger that the citizens of those states would succumb to the insidious message of this internal enemy and drop out of the war. Paine exhorted the authorities in those states, and in Congress, to respond with "determined hardness," including the "confiscation of the property of disaffected persons."[21]

Some historians believe that Paine's *American Crisis* rekindled hope during the season of despondency, a view expressed that winter by an unfriendly Philadelphia publisher who nevertheless conceded that the pamphlet had "rallied and reanimated" sagging morale.[22] It alone was not responsible for rekindling the war effort. A week after the pamphlet hit the streets, Washington scored a great victory, a triumph that aided recruiting and revived spirits dashed by the defeats of 1776.

During the retreat across New Jersey, Washington had wanted to make a defensive stand. Once he crossed the Delaware, he began instead to contemplate an action that would take the fight to the British. In fact, for the time being there was nothing to defend, for General Howe had put his redcoats in winter quarters early in December. Howe divided the army that Cornwallis had commanded, posting it in seventeen cantonments throughout New Jersey. The three most forward posts, one at Trenton and two others nearby at Bordentown and Burlington, were assigned to Hessians. As the British and German mercenaries marched into their respective bases, reinforcements trickled into the American camp. Toward the middle of December, Washington's force had swelled to 6,104 men fit for duty, roughly equaling the combined total of Hessians garrisoned in the three cantonments just north of the Delaware. Washington steadily warmed to the notion of a strike.[23] With the "fate of America . . . trembling on the point of suspense," as Paine subsequently put it, Washington ultimately decided to hazard a surprise attack on Christmas night against the Hessian garrison at Trenton.[24]

Washington planned a three-pronged strike. One division was to cross the Delaware and attack Trenton from the south. A second was to cross the river and seal off the roads leading from the hamlet. Washington, meanwhile, was to take 2,400 of his most seasoned veterans on a long roundabout march of some twenty miles. They were to cross the Delaware above Trenton and advance on the little village from the west. Lieutenant Monroe's unit was with Washington. Christmas Day had been clear and cold, but near sunset, as the march began, the temperature rose and conditions deteriorated. It began to rain, then to sleet, and finally to snow. A keening wind that one soldier imagined to be nearly hurricane strength cut through the men. Near midnight, the units with Washington reached Johnson's Ferry and McConkey's Ferry on the Delaware River, where they crossed the ice-swollen, rushing river. Horses and eighteen pieces of artillery, and some men, went across on ferries, though many soldiers made the passage in Durham boats, sturdy vessels ordinarily used to transport heavy cargoes of freight. In the most famous painting of the event, Emanuel Leutze's *Washington Crossing the Delaware*, rendered three-quarters of a century later, Washington is shown standing and holding a spyglass, a heavy sword strapped round his waist. Next to him, struggling to hold an American flag that is blowing wildly on this blustery night, is Lieutenant Monroe. Leutze's speculative depiction of Washington might have been more or less accurate, but he erred in placing Monroe in the same boat with the commander. No Virginians were in the vessel with Washington. The commander likely crossed with Colonel John Glover and his troopers from Marblehead, Massachusetts, men who had been mariners prior to the war and a contingent that the commander often called on when daring action was required.

Monroe, in fact, did not even cross with the main body of troops. He went over earlier, part of a fifty-man unit of Virginians commanded by Captain William Washington—a divinity student before the war who had been dangerously wounded in the fighting on Long Island ninety days earlier—that was tasked with sealing the Pennington Road above Trenton. If they succeeded, word of the rebel attack would not reach the enemy forces in Princeton and Brunswick until after the battle of Trenton had been fought. Monroe's unit remained alongside the road throughout the bitter night, taking several prisoners going to or coming from Trenton. In the course of their undertaking, Dr. John Riker, a neighbor whose dogs had been awakened and sent up a howl at the intruders, emerged to complain, which he did by unleashing a stream of expletives. However, on learning that the troublemakers were American soldiers, Dr. Riker brought them food and volunteered to accompany them as a surgeon-physician. Following orders, the Virginians and Dr. Riker did not start toward Trenton until the earliest sign of gray morning light appeared in the eastern sky. Despite the poor visibility in the relentless snow, they found and rejoined the main body of Washington's force sometime before seven thirty. There were two wings to Washington's attack force. General John Sullivan commanded the right wing, Greene the left, which included the Third Virginia and was assembled near where the Pennington Road entered Trenton.

Now the men waited, nervously going through time-honored pre-combat rituals while thinking the things that soldiers about to go into battle think about. Time crawled. The day grew lighter. It was quiet, eerily but thankfully so. The Hessians were unaware that the adversary was at their door. Then, in a flash, the battle began. Just after eight A.M., American artillery opened fire. Both wings of Continentals surged forward. Captain Washington's little company was in the van of the men under Greene, charging as hard and fast as they could run in the snow. Monroe recalled seeing the Hessian officer of the day "shot down" in the street in the initial gunfire. The Hessians had been taken by surprise. Nevertheless, they recovered with startling speed, rushing outdoors in an attempt to save their cannon and open fire on the oncoming attackers. It was a desperate fight, and early on Captain Washington was hit with musket fire, balls slicing through both hands. Monroe was now the commander of the company, though not for long. While running full tilt, he was hit and knocked down by a gunshot. As horses and men stormed past, Monroe, in pain, his comprehension blurred, was likely aware of the red stain in the snow where he lay. He had been cut down by a ball through his breast and shoulder. It was a dangerous wound. An artery in his shoulder had been severed. Not long passed before Monroe, bleeding profusely, his coat stained crimson, was carried from the field to safety. He was attended by Dr. Riker, who in the nick of time clamped the artery, after which Dr. John Cochran, a physician from New Brunswick, New Jersey, who had recently volunteered to accompany the army, dressed the wound. Monroe's life was saved, thanks to a train of events that had started with Dr. Riker's howling dogs.[25]

The battle was over in an hour. Of the 1,500 Hessians in Trenton, 106 were killed or wounded and 896 captured. The entire garrison would have been taken had the two other Continental forces succeeded in crossing the Delaware. Still, it was a magnificent American victory, the first since the initial weeks of the war in the spring of 1775, a triumph made even grander in that the Americans suffered so few casualties. The Americans, in the words of one of Washington's staff officers, had "pounced upon the Hessians like an eagle upon a hen." Washington immediately apprised Congress of his stunning victory and happily reported: "Our loss is very trifling." One of his aides reported that two privates had been killed and two wounded, an ensign from the Fourth Virginia had been slightly wounded, and "Capt Washington and his Lieutenant" suffered more serious wounds. Upwards of five others appear to have perished from exposure.[26]

There was no surrender ceremony. It was imperative that the men, with their prisoners, get back across the icy river. If time was lost, there was a danger that enemy troops from nearby camps might swoop down on the victorious rebels. The lack of formalities did not deter the artist John Trumbull, who painted several famous events in the American Revolution, from imagining some twenty years later how a ceremony might have looked. Monroe is in the background in the painting, to the rear of Washington, who sits astride his chestnut charger. Lieutenant Monroe is seated, leaning on Dr. Riker and clutching his bloody shoulder. Captain Washington is shown bandaged and standing before several mounted officers, including General Weedon.

Monroe had been among the first to cross the Delaware and he was one of the first to be taken back across to Pennsylvania. That night, he was carried to the home of John Coryell in what now is New Hope. He remained there for two weeks or more and was bedfast during the initial ten days. Monroe was eventually taken to the residence of forty-year-old Henry Wynkoop—a former assemblyman who later served in both the Continental Congress and the first U.S. Congress—in Northampton Township, Bucks County, where he continued his lengthy convalescence, attended daily by Dr. Riker. When Monroe returned to soldiering, in May, he was promoted to the rank of captain.[27]

During the first weeks that Monroe's hosts were nursing him back to health, Paine, a few miles away in Philadelphia, set to work on follow-up pieces to his *American Crisis* essay. However, even as the wordsmith worked, the black mood of December lifted. On December 31, Washington, in his most audacious act of the entire war, crossed into New Jersey yet again and in the span of seventy-two hours fought two additional battles. The first—often called the Second Battle of Trenton—was a perilous clash with Cornwallis, for the Continental army was backed against the Delaware River and retreat seemed impossible. Five years later, in a tract on aspects of the American Revolution, Paine captured the moment: "If ever the fate of America depended on the event of a day, it was now." It was a savage fight, as the Continentals repulsed one bloody charge after another by the British. It was also, in the words of one American soldier, "a great Slaughter." As night descended, some five hundred redcoats lay dead or wounded on the cold, wet soil along the banks of the Assunpink Creek. Under cover of darkness that evening, Washington's men escaped to the north, where the next day they fought an engagement against a smaller British force. The Battle of Princeton was even more lopsided. British losses exceeded four hundred, while the Continentals lost about thirty-five men. Altogether in the week that began with the Christmas-night crossing, nearly two thousand British soldiers were lost. At most, the Americans had lost about one hundred and fifty men.[28]

After word of the American successes reached Philadelphia, Paine shifted gears in two new essays that appeared in January 1777. While he showered Washington with praise for his "master stroke of generalship" from Christmas onward, Paine's paramount objective was to do what he could to help with the recruiting of a new army in 1777. Among other things, Paine sought to demonstrate that Britain could not win the war. Its prowess was exaggerated. Yes, Britain had a magnificent naval history, but its armies had always been mediocre. Furthermore, Britain's best chance of defeating the Americans was gone. If it could not defeat us "in the summer when our army was less than yours, nor in the winter when we had none, how are you to do it now." It was a mocking jab at General Howe, who had to know that he now would have to face America's new standing army, a force that was larger than it was previously and composed of veteran soldiers commanded by more experienced officers. Granted, the redcoats might win more battles, wrote Paine, but they could never subdue and control a country as vast as that of the United States. Nor could the British defeat a Continental army that employed a Fabian strategy of committing only a portion of the army to any engagement rather than hazarding the entire force. The redcoats could not inflict "a total defeat" on their adversary, and all the while the British would suffer attrition and the escalating costs of waging war. Paine acknowledged that trouble and sacrifice loomed for America's soldiers, but he asked, "What are the inconveniences of a few months to the tributary bondage of ages?"[29]

Neither Paine's exhortations nor enticing cash and land bounties offered by the states led to a groundswell of enlistments. Congress hoped to raise seventy-five thousand men for the campaign of 1777, but the army peaked that year at thirty-nine thousand. No one was more aware than Captain Monroe of the difficulty in recruiting men to serve in the new standing army. In the spring, fully recovered from his wound, Monroe returned to Virginia to procure men for his company. He beat the bushes for several weeks but failed to raise a single soldier. In mid-August, Monroe returned to the army, which was in Pennsylvania, and called on General Washington at headquarters. Though he had returned empty-handed from his recruiting foray, Monroe came back with a letter to Washington, written by his uncle, Joseph Jones, a member of Congress and an old acquaintance of the commander's. Jones told Washington that his young nephew possessed the "Character [of] a Gent[leman]" and that his failure to raise a company was due to the "present disposition of the people" and not to a lack of diligence on Monroe's part. Washington had met Monroe previously. In May, he had used him as a courier for delivering a letter to a physician in Philadelphia. Impressed with the young man, Washington sometime in August appointed him to be an aide-de-camp to Major General Lord Stirling. Monroe was about to go back into harm's way. For the first time since Trenton and Princeton, Washington's Continental army was on the verge of a major battle.[30]

In the weeks after word reached London of the devastating culmination of the campaign of 1776, Lord George Germain, the American secretary, devised a careful plan for 1777. General John Burgoyne was given a large army with which to invade northern New York from Canada. While he moved south, General Howe was to move north, bringing the main British army up the Hudson from Manhattan. The Americans could not permit the two British armies to unite, for the enemy would then control the Hudson. Washington would have to fight, and when he did, he would be caught in a pincer movement between the two British armies. But given the lag in communications between America and London, Britain always gave its commanders in the field considerable freedom to act as events dictated. Howe chose to ignore the plan that Germain had formulated. Convinced that Burgoyne could reach Albany unaided, Howe opted to campaign for Philadelphia, a move that he believed would compel Washington to stand and fight in defense of the city that was home to the Congress.[31]

Toward the end of July, about three weeks before Captain Monroe knocked on his door, Washington discovered that Howe planned to try to take Philadelphia. Washington knew immediately that a great battle loomed. Earlier, he had sent Stirling's brigade to Peekskill to stand guard against Howe's likely advance toward Albany, but on learning to his surprise that Howe planned a Philadelphia campaign, Washington ordered Stirling to rejoin the main army for the defense of the city. Monroe took up his duties as one of Stirling's aides late in August, around the time that Howe's army came ashore at Head of Elk, Maryland, some fifty miles west of Philadelphia.

Lord Stirling—actually William Alexander of Basking Ridge, New Jersey, who brandished the title sixth Earl of Stirling despite the disallowance of his claim by the House of Lords—had entered the Continental army in 1775 as a colonel and had risen to the rank of major general. At age fifty-one, Stirling had already led men in several major engagements. Vain and noted for his affinity for strong drink—at least one congressman thought him an alcoholic and told Washington as much—Stirling was never regarded as brilliant, but no one doubted his bravery under fire, and Washington thought him steady and reliable. Stirling, who had served as an officer's aide in the Seven Years' War, was outgoing and good-natured, and he treated his aides decently. He rapidly won Monroe's loyalty and respect.[32]

Like Alexander Hamilton, who had become an aide to Washington a few months earlier, Monroe had longed for a field command. Nothing was available, due in some measure to the large number of French volunteers vested with field officer ranks by Silas Deane, a former congressman sent to France in 1776 by the Continental Congress. Deane's job had been to persuade France to provide arms, munitions, clothing, and military engineers to the American rebels, but unable to resist the entreaties of ambitious and adventurous French soldiers who were willing to fight the British in America, he went far beyond his instructions. The nineteen-year-old Marquis de Lafayette, who had never experienced combat—and, in fact, had been forced from active duty when France's army was reorganized to emphasize merit, not social influence—was among the officers that Deane appointed. Many thought it ludicrous that Lafayette should have been made a major general, but some congressmen, and General Washington, realized that he could be useful. Thinking the young marquis would serve only briefly in America before returning to France, where he could use his influence to "Secure to us" invaluable assistance, Washington cultivated Lafayette.[33]

Monroe may have been disappointed in having to settle for being an aide to a general officer. It was not a way to win fame, which Monroe craved, but serving someone of Stirling's stature had its rewards. It was a means of meeting important officers and dignitaries who came to camp, and for numerous aides the post was a stepping stone to becoming a brigade commander. The day-to-day routine of an aide was to take dictation, draft the general's letters, accompany him as he made the rounds, maintain brigade records, disseminate the general's orders, and not infrequently serve as his courier. The routine changed during an engagement. The aide rode at his general's side during a battle, often coming under fire and facing a multitude of dangers.

Monroe could not have served under Stirling for more than three weeks before Howe's army faced off against the Americans on September 11 near Kennett Square on Brandywine Creek, some thirty miles west of Philadelphia. Since the disaster on Long Island a year earlier, Washington had vowed to never hazard his entire army in an engagement. Perhaps because the two armies were roughly the same size, but more likely because he felt pressure from some congressmen to make a stand that might prevent the enemy from taking Philadelphia, Washington elected to put his entire army on the line. Because of the seeming wisdom of Washington's previous strategy, Paine had told his readers not long before that a total defeat was not possible. In fact, at Brandywine, General Washington ran the risk of a colossal drubbing and it almost occurred.

Thinking that Chadds Ford, which lay across the road from Head of Elk to Philadelphia, was the most likely place where Howe would try to cross Brandywine Creek, Washington posted his army on the east side of the stream and waited for the showdown. The commander deployed militia on his left wing, the least likely site of an attack, and a force under General John Sullivan on his right wing to guard against a flanking maneuver. The bulk of the American force was in the center, where Washington expected Howe's blow to fall. Stirling's brigade, and one or two others, were held in reserve, prepared to move in any direction. The Americans were ready—or so it seemed. Howe did precisely what he had done in the engagement on Long Island in the summer of 1776. He launched the fighting by attacking the center of the American lines, just where Washington had expected the blow to fall. But it was a diversion.

Howe, together with Cornwallis, took half the British force, about 7,500 men, on a long march to his left, Washington's right, and crossed the Brandywine unopposed at Jefferis Ford two miles above Sullivan's overextended force. Just as on Long Island, Washington had failed to properly reconnoiter the area, and both he and Sullivan were unaware of the ford. Eight hours into the fighting, Howe's redcoats suddenly appeared as if an apparition. They marched out of the woods and launched a flank attack on Sullivan's surprised and vulnerable force.

Washington had received credible warnings that Howe was on the move long before the redcoats struck Sullivan. For hours, Washington discounted the reports that flowed into headquarters. Even after the flank attack commenced, the American commander—swamped with contradictory intelligence— remained indecisive for what was nearly a fatally long time. Finally, as Sullivan's force buckled and was fast approaching a total disintegration, Washington ordered the reserve divisions under Stirling and General Adam Stephen to hurry to the assistance of the Continentals' beleaguered right wing. The fight that followed was furious, and desperate. If Howe overwhelmed Sullivan, the British would be poised to envelope the American center, quite possibly leading to the annihilation of Washington's army. A British trooper, thinking it one of the hottest battles he ever experienced, spoke of the "infernal fire of cannon and musketry . . . The balls plowing up the ground. The trees crackling over one's heads. The branches riven by artillery. The leaves falling as in autumn by the grapeshot." Less articulately, but with no less feeling, an American private captured the fury of the battle: "The Battel was . . . Cannons Roaring muskets Cracking Drums Beating Bumbs Flying all Round, men a dying wounded Horred Grones which would Greave the Heardist of Hearts to See our [comrades] . . . Slain in such a manner." It was a "Dolfful Sight," he said.[34]

Outnumbered two to one, the men on the American right fought, fell back, and fought again. The redcoats were held off for a time, in part by a staggering artillery barrage levied by Stirling's brigade. Stirling's men stood "firm as a rock in the middle of a wild ocean of carnage," according to a contemporary report. But the enemy had the numbers, and the Americans fell back a third time. At this juncture, Stirling's force was, as one historian put it, "in the hottest corner of the entire battle front," not to mention the most perilous. Lafayette was part of this desperate fray, and at its height, while standing beside Stirling and Monroe, he took a ball in the leg. Many of Monroe's old chums from the Third Virginia were killed or wounded.[35] Stirling's force buckled once more and, yet again, was nearly overrun. It was saved from disaster when Washington rushed in further reinforcements that stanched the British advance. Finally, and fortunately, darkness fell, bringing an end to the fighting. During the night, Washington's army retreated to safety.[36] Brandywine had been one of the hottest battles of the war, and Monroe had been in the thick of it during the three hours or so that Stirling's division saw action.

After yet another close brush with disaster, Washington was no longer keen on risking the army to prevent the enemy from taking Philadelphia. However, he hardly wished to communicate his intentions to Congress. In the days following Brandywine, Washington repeatedly told Congress that he had a "firm intent of giving the Enemy Battle," and he advised the legislators that he planned to make Howe pay a heavy price for attempting to take the city.

Monroe, through Stirling, knew the truth. Washington was posturing, creating the impression that he was eager for another face-off. Washington was not cowardly. His strategy was prudent, and Monroe understood that as well. The American army could not prevent Howe from getting hold of the city and the hazards of another engagement were too great. As a result, no more major battles were fought before the British marched into Philadelphia. Washington protected himself by fibbing to Congress that the British had won their prize without further bloodshed because of the shortcomings of those who provided him with intelligence. Congress had fled the city before the redcoats, on September 26, paraded triumphantly through Philadelphia's cobblestone streets. Congress set up shop in York, Pennsylvania. They were not alone in fleeing. Paine had gotten out of town too.[37]

Howe immediately divided his army, posting about half his men—some eight thousand—in Germantown a few miles north of Philadelphia while the remainder went about the grim, and bloody, business of clearing the American forts along the Delaware River that linked the city to the outer world. Washington wasted no time in preparing a surprise attack on the British force in Germantown, hoping to close 1777 with a spectacular victory reminiscent of his successes at Trenton and Princeton at the end of the previous year's campaigning. The attack was set for October 4. The New Jersey brigade under Stirling was once again held in reserve.

Stirling's force had played a key role at Brandywine, but it never got into action at Germantown. A dense fog scudded in, blanketing the Pennsylvania landscape as the Americans readied for the fight, and once the battle got under way, the combination of fog and thick smoke from thousands of guns so reduced visibility that Stirling's force could not be found and brought into the fray. Despite the problems that arose, including the failure to take the enemy by surprise as at Trenton, the Americans came close to scoring a major victory. But victory eluded the rebels and, in the estimation of many officers on both sides, Washington failed because of his flawed leadership. Early in the engagement, when momentum was on his side, Washington squandered a precious hour trying to take a large mansion occupied by slightly over one hundred redcoats, a target of trifling significance. Had the Continental army and its artillery been employed more wisely, the outcome of the engagement might have been different. As it was, after three hours the American army withdrew, having lost three times the number of its adversary.[38]

While Washington was fighting the two battles in Pennsylvania—and suffering a 20 percent attrition rate—another American army, led by General Horatio Gates, destroyed General Burgoyne's army in northern New York. Two weeks after Germantown, Burgoyne at Saratoga surrendered what remained of his defeated army that had launched the campaign five months earlier with some 7,500 men. Some in Congress were frustrated by Washington's repeated blunders, and not a few were angry that he had not fought a second battle to prevent Howe from taking Philadelphia. Inevitably, some thought the American cause would be better off with Gates at the helm of the Continental army. Whether an organized conspiracy to dump Washington actually existed has never been proved, but many in Congress carped that fall and winter about the commander. For a time, his stature sank so low that the president of Congress noted that Washington's opinions were greeted in Congress with "much indecent freedom & Levity."

But if there was a cabal to replace Washington, it came to nothing. Most congressmen recognized that Washington had faced the more formidable of the two enemy armies in 1777, and most still thought him a talented and virtuous leader.[39] Monroe was one whose faith was unshaken, and over the years he never wavered in his belief that Washington was the best man to lead the Continental army. From his first glimpse of Washington, Monroe had been impressed by his "countenance and manner." He praised Washington's "integrity, fortitude, and firmness under the severest trials." To that, he added: "A deportment so firm, so dignified, so exalted, but yet so modest and composed, I have never seen in any other person." Monroe likely was influenced by Stirling, who was certain that even despite the failure to win the clash at Germantown, Washington's courage in launching the strike would sow the impression in Europe that "we Can out General our Enemy, that we dare Attack them." Stirling was proven correct when John Adams subsequently reported from Paris that Washington's audacity was a key factor in France's decision to enter the war as an American ally.[40]

Monroe was not in a position to publicly comment on Washington or political issues, but Paine was. Although some of Paine's most important

Philadelphia benefactors, including Dr. Rush, were among the commander's harshest critics, he rushed into print two new *American Crisis* essays that vindicated Washington. Many years later Paine would write that the "black times of '76 were the natural consequence of [Washington's] want of military judgment," and his inadequacies in 1777 and later had "nearly ruined the country." But he said none of this at the time. "Nothing but mischief" would have come from revealing what he believed to be true, he later remarked. Making command of the army into a political football would have led to bitter and possibly lethal divisions within both the army and Congress. While not effusively praising Washington in his two *Crisis* pieces, Paine claimed considerable American success at Brandywine, took issue with those who had criticized the commander's generalship at Germantown, and defended him for not being baited into what might have been disastrous battles in the weeks following Germantown. Paine added that under Washington's leadership, the Americans had not been conquered, even though Great Britain had wielded a professional army that was nearly always numerically superior to the Continental army.[41]

Late in December, Washington's army, disheveled and hungry, took up winter quarters at Valley Forge, beginning a stretch of four months that many have regarded as the period when American fortunes bottomed out. There may have been worse times, though it would be difficult to imagine greater misery than the common soldiers endured that Pennsylvania winter. The men were poorly furnished and ill-housed, faced two lengthy food shortages, and suffered waves of camp diseases. Ultimately, one man in seven among those who marched with Washington into Valley Forge perished before spring arrived. Monroe survived. He also stuck it out while upwards of three hundred of his fellow officers quit the army and went home. Monroe was promoted to the rank of major that winter.[42]

Monroe did not mention Valley Forge in his memoirs. Perhaps that horrid winter was not etched into his consciousness as it was for others. After all, as an aide to a general, he escaped the privation and woes visited on the enlisted men. The general officers secured lodgings in substantial dwellings in the area and, together with their aides, took the day's main mess at the well-provided table set at Washington's headquarters. The aides, who lived in the same house with the general they served, usually occupied cramped quarters, and some slept on the floor for lack of a bed. Yet, compared with the men in their rude huts, the aides were warm and well fed. Nevertheless, Monroe during that winter and spring was wearily disenchanted. For the first time he acknowledged that soldiering had become "infinitely more disagreeable." But his despair arose less from the deplorable conditions than from a realization that what many called the "Spirit of 1776"—a sacrificial and patriotic frame of mind—had been superseded among a large number of high-ranking officers, businessmen, and congressmen by an obsession with personal advancement. "The principles on which the war is carried on now is intirely different from what it was at first," said Monroe. "Patriotism, publick spirit and disinterestedness have almost vanish'd; and honor and virtue are empty names."[43]

Paine came to Valley Forge shortly after the army entered the site and before the first deadly crisis unfolded. He was impressed by what he saw. The soldiers, "like a family of beavers," were busy felling trees, splitting logs, and building their huts, which he mistakenly assumed would provide adequate shelter.[44] But Paine could not linger. He had a job, his first real employment since Robert Aitken hired him as an editor three years earlier. A few months before Brandywine, Congress created the Committee for Foreign Affairs, and John Adams had nominated Paine to be its secretary, a position that paid seventy dollars a month, adequate for a comfortable lifestyle for a single person. Although the two had clashed over political philosophy, Adams felt compassion for the penniless writer and thought he deserved recompense for all that he had done for the cause.

Paine had a checkered work history, but he took this job seriously. He needed the money. In addition, the position enabled him to network with important political figures and it held the promise of access to materials that he would need for the history of the American Revolution that he planned to write someday. The job was also ideal for someone of his temperament. Since the United States as yet had no ties with any foreign nation, the committee met infrequently, leaving Paine with considerable free time. He occasionally visited Colonel Joseph Kirkbride, with whom he established a close relationship that would continue for the remainder of his life. The two had met late in 1776 when Kirkbride commanded a Pennsylvania militia regiment; after Tories burned his home, Pennsburg Manor in Bucks County, Kirkbride moved across the Delaware River to Bordentown, near Trenton, and purchased a five-acre estate that he called "Hill Top." Kirkbride shared Paine's political outlook, liked and admired him, and looked forward to his visits. On one occasion during 1777, when Paine was crossing over into New Jersey to call on the Kirkbrides, he came under fire from a small party of enemy soldiers. A companion said that Paine had been "very gallant" despite the danger. Now and then, Paine also visited old army acquaintances, including Washington, with whom he breakfasted at headquarters on the morning after Germantown. Paine and Washington could not have been more unalike, but when time permitted, the commander welcomed a visit. He thought Paine was useful. Paine probably knew he was being used. Much later, he spoke of

Washington's inability to form companionate relationships and his habit of appraising others only in terms of how they might best serve him. Following Germantown, Washington provided Paine with an embroidered rendering of the recent battle, and that was the version that Paine disseminated.[45]

Paine's job was in York, to which Congress had decamped, but he chose to live in Lancaster, roughly twenty-five miles from Congress's temporary home. It was a larger village and the residence of numerous Philadelphia expatriates, as both the state assembly and Committee of Safety set up shop there. Besides, the committee that Paine worked for rarely met. Paine and two other refugees moved into a house owned by local gunsmith. The landlord's son subsequently deprecated Paine for "indolence" and, of all things, his "vacuity of thought." Paine, he said, followed breakfast with a walk lasting several hours; he returned in the early afternoon for the day's largest and longest meal, after which he napped for a couple of hours before taking yet another long walk. (His list of Paine's supposed flaws did not include alcohol addiction or abuse.) What the observer witnessed, but failed to understand, was Paine's regimen for productivity. Paine thought through his compositions while alone and unimpeded on his strolls. Benjamin Rush, a writer himself, understood Paine's habits, and he, too, later recollected Paine's solitary walks, noting that his friend "retired frequently from company to analyze his thoughts and to enjoy the repast of his own original ideas." Instead of having idled away his time in Lancaster, Paine in fact wrote perhaps the longest of his *American Crisis* essays, a piece that ran some four thousand words.[46]

The war changed forever during Paine's six-month stay in Lancaster. France signed treaties of alliance and commerce with the United States in February 1778, assuring its entrance into the three-year-old conflict. Since 1776, France had secretly furnished the American rebels with weapons, munitions, and other essentials, but it had not wished to enter hostilities until it was confident that Britain could not win the war. Burgoyne's catastrophic defeat at Saratoga, as well as Washington's pluck in attacking at Germantown, convinced the French that they would be betting on a winner. Word of the treaties trickled into the United States as the spring vegetation burst into bloom at Valley Forge. Delighted to have the horrid winter behind him and swept with euphoria by news of the French alliance, Washington ordered "a day of . . . General Joy." Washington may have thought the day was a joyous affair, but Monroe, probably like many another soldier, carped about the hours of "extreme fatigue" and "stubborn labour" that the celebration entailed. The soldiers gathered on Valley Forge's parade ground under a bright, warm sun and marched past the Continental army's general officers and the French volunteers, such as Lafayette, who had come to fight for America during the past two years. When the last company passed the reviewing stand, the assembled troops, accompanied by successive cannonades from the artillerists, cheered: "Long live the King of France; God Save the Friendly Powers of Europe; and To the American States." Thereafter, the enlisted men returned to duty or to their bleak huts, while the officers, including Major Monroe, gathered under canopies for a feast that featured cold meats and an assortment of liquor and wine.[47]

No one knew precisely what the French alliance meant. Paine thought Great Britain might be so anxious to avoid a ruinous war with France that it would recognize American independence and make peace. In fact, Lord North's ministry never considered conceding independence, but after Saratoga it offered peace terms. The ministers additionally resolved that in the event the Americans rejected its offer, Britain would press on with the war, gambling that it could avoid another cataclysmic defeat and slowly wear down its enemies. North's government also understood that if hostilities continued, France's entry into the war would result in considerable ripple effects requiring major changes in Britain's grand strategy. Troops would be needed in the homeland as a safeguard in the event of a French invasion and in the Caribbean to defend the precious sugar islands against almost certain French attacks. The latter eventuality would compel London to redeploy nearly half its army from mainland America to the Caribbean. With fewer regular troops available to fight in North America, Britain would have to create new regiments fleshed out with newly recruited American Tories—possibly including liberated slaves—and it would have to turn to a southern strategy. In effect jettisoning its northern provinces, Britain would henceforth focus on reclaiming Virginia, Georgia, and the Carolinas. If successful, Britain would emerge from the conflict with a large American empire that stretched from Canada to the West Indies, and included trans-Appalachia, the reconquered southern colonies, and East and West Florida, which Britain had won in the Seven Years' War. The first priority, however, was to seek an immediate end to the conflict and forestall French belligerence. As spring approached, North's government dispatched the Carlisle Commission to America to offer peace based on the demands made by the First Continental Congress six months prior to the outbreak of hostilities. Congress in 1774 had been twenty-two months away from declaring independence. Rather than independence, it had sought greater autonomy for the American colonies within the British Empire. Seemingly, that was the best that Lord North could hope for at the approach of 1778.[48]

A month after the festivities at Valley Forge, Washington learned that the British army was relinquishing Philadelphia, the first step in the implementation of Britain's new strategy. Sir Henry Clinton, the newly appointed successor to General Howe, marched his army across New Jersey toward Manhattan. Washington's army of some twelve thousand men shadowed the slightly larger enemy army. As the two armies moved slowly across New Jersey, Monroe led parties that were charged with keeping an eye on the enemy's movements; at one point, he and his "70 men who are now fatigued much" succeeded in capturing three British regulars, and he intimated in his report to headquarters that had he been assisted by half a dozen horsemen, he could have taken several additional captives.[49]

Meanwhile, Washington wrestled with his choices. Several councils of war urged a cautious approach that involved little more than harassing the enemy. But in the end, Washington opted for something between extreme caution and a clash in which he risked his entire army. At Monmouth Courthouse on June 28, 1778, he ordered an attack by more than half his army on the two-thousand-man rear guard of Clinton's force. The Battle of Monmouth that resulted was the last major engagement fought in the North during the war and the final time that Monroe experienced combat.

At first, things went well for the Americans, who began the contest with a three-to-one manpower advantage. However, once Clinton rushed in reinforcements, the British enjoyed superior numbers. Late in the morning, under a merciless sun that drove the temperature above one hundred degrees, the Americans began to fall back. Stirling's brigade had not been in the early fighting, but around noon, when the Continentals took up defensive positions behind a ravine that sliced through the battlefield, Stirling's men anchored the American left, and Greene's the right. Clinton probed for weaknesses in each wing, hoping to break through and turn the rebels' flank, scoring a major and unexpected victory. Stirling's force was first to feel the brunt of Clinton's assault, and it faced a severe test, but it withstood several attacks. Once it even temporarily drove the British back by counterattacking with a bayonet charge. At another point in the desperate fight, Monroe led a party of seventy men on a reconnaissance mission. He discovered that Clinton was massing for an assault on the American right. Washington responded quickly, rushing reinforcements to Greene. The American lines held until night fell over the blood-soaked landscape, and Clinton, taking a leaf from Washington's well-worn book, stole away. The Americans had suffered some 360 casualties, the British about 500. While Monroe came through unscathed, both Alexander Hamilton and Aaron Burr, who was part of a new regiment composed of New Yorkers, had horses shot from beneath them, and Burr was felled by heatstroke. In the wake of the fighting, Hamilton praised the "coolness and intrepidity" of Stirling's men, and James McHenry, another

of Washington's aides, lauded the "evident and unequivocal . . . and effica-
cious" bravery of the men under Stirling. In his report to Congress, Washington made clear that the men under Stirling had "put a stop to [the British]
advance."[50]

Monroe's war was nearly over. For ages, he had wanted something more
than serving as an aide-de-camp, though he wished to continue soldiering.
Monroe said that he "would still prefer that mode of life attached with its
usual fatigue and danger" to a role as a civilian, at least while his country was
at war. He pleaded for a field command, but there were no openings. He said
he would consider other options that involved serving his country, and a few
weeks after Monmouth, Monroe—who had just turned twenty—traveled to
Philadelphia, once again home to Congress. He came in hopes of gaining
some sort of appointment in Europe. He may have sought to become the
secretary to an American envoy in France, though he said that he preferred to
go "in the character of an officer."[51] Nothing was available. Monroe remained
at Stirling's side throughout the fall and, as both armies were idle, he was
posted all the while in New Jersey. However, at year's end he resigned and
returned to Virginia in hopes of attaining a field command in the state line or
militia. Both Stirling and Washington wrote letters on his behalf, a rare step for
the commander. Washington said that Monroe was eager to serve in the South,
a theater "where a new scene has opened" given that Britain had initiated its
southern strategy by invading Georgia six months after Monmouth. Washington spoke of his "high opinion" of Monroe, remarking on his "zeal" for the
cause and lauding him as "a brave active and sensible officer."[52]

Monroe was awarded the rank of lieutenant colonel in the state's militia,
but the regiment that he was to command was eventually disbanded, as it
never came close to filling its enlistment quota. Monroe kept searching. When
Colonel John Laurens, one of Washington's aides and a South Carolinian,
conceived the idea of raising an army of liberated slaves to defend his state
against a British invasion, Monroe eagerly sought a command post in the
proposed army. Hamilton, who was close to Laurens and acquainted with
Monroe, wrote a letter of recommendation on his behalf. Hamilton told
Laurens that Monroe was a "night errant," an "honest fellow," a "man of honor,"
and "a sensible man and a soldier." Alas, the South Carolina assembly balked at
what Hamilton had labeled as Laurens's "black scheme," and the army of
former slaves never came into being.[53]

Monroe was at loose ends throughout 1779. The war still raged, but it was
far away. He also said that a "variety of disappointments" in his "private
fortune" had occurred, thwarting his "plan of life." Monroe never divulged
what had dashed his hopes. It is a good bet, however, that all along he had

anticipated financial assistance and, eventually, a handsome inheritance from his uncle Joseph Jones, an affluent, London-educated lawyer and judge. Monroe likely dreamed of someday becoming a Virginia planter. He may have hoped to follow the trajectory of George Washington: soldiering as a young man, and becoming a gentleman farmer, businessman, and political figure following his military service. But at about this very moment Jones, at age fifty-two, suddenly and quite unexpectedly fathered a son. As 1780 approached, Monroe was jolted by the realization that the future he had envisaged had vanished.[54]

Though adrift, Monroe had been shaped by his Revolutionary War service. He had been with an army, and frequently in harm's way, for thirty months, and for much of what remained of his life he would often be addressed as "Colonel Monroe." He had come of age in the army, passing from a teenager when he first bore arms to a twenty-two-year-old in 1780. Tall, muscular, and trim, with penetrating gray-blue eyes, he was a striking figure who impressed others as earnest and grave, at least until he smiled and his features brightened, and then acquaintances saw a happy and friendly visage.[55] During his service, Monroe had met an array of powerful figures, including many up-and-coming young men destined to play substantive roles in the postwar period. Though separated by a yawning chasm with regard to rank, Monroe and Lafayette—who were only six months apart in age—had a convivial relationship. In many ways, however, Monroe's most important wartime relationship was with Pierre S. Du Ponceau, another Frenchman who served with the Continental army.

Two years younger than Monroe, Du Ponceau—like his Virginia counterpart—had abandoned his college studies to serve in this war. He came to America in 1777 with Friedrich Steuben, a Prussian and veteran soldier. When Congress sent Steuben to Valley Forge to train the Continental soldiery, the teenaged Du Ponceau accompanied him as an aide-de-camp. Du Ponceau spoke fluent English and was surpassingly amiable, and he almost immediately became Monroe's closest companion. The two young men were so close that they exchanged letters on the days they did not see each other in camp. Du Ponceau also became something of a mentor to Monroe. Inspired by the Enlightenment, Du Ponceau had wanted to serve in America's revolutionary conflict, as he hoped the American Revolution could be the spark that would free humankind from its despotic shackles. There is no evidence that Monroe had previously looked on the colonial insurgency as anything other than an escape from British tyranny and a stab at American independence. His relationship with Du Ponceau changed his thinking about the war and the American Revolution, and in time it would influence his political outlook as well.[56]

Paine, like Du Ponceau, had long hoped the American Revolution would inspire change in England and Europe. Paine, in fact, was one of the first to think of the American rebellion as something greater than merely a quest for American independence. He knew, too, that if the war was lost, all hope for progressive change in America and Europe would be lost as well. When Paine returned to Philadelphia with Congress in July 1778, a month after Clinton abandoned it and a week after the action at Monmouth, he and a great many others no longer believed that Britain could win the war. French belligerency had made that impossible, or so many thought. What worried Paine was that North's peace offer, and civilian weariness with the three-year-old war, might entice Congress to end hostilities short of independence. Washington harbored the same concerns, and in a mood of gloomy apprehension he publicly characterized Lord North's peace offering as "more dangerous than [Britain's] efforts by arms." Paine wasted no time in sounding the alarm. He wrote that for Britain to propose peace short of independence was grasping at straws, akin to "madmen biting in the hour of death." Anticipating that Britain's diplomats in the Carlisle Commission would play on the Americans' inveterate fear and hatred of France, Paine tried to explain geopolitics to his readers: "Even wolves may quarrel, still they herd together" for security. Without much conviction, he portrayed France as peace-loving while England "cannot . . . live long at peace with any power." Above all, he sought to persuade his fellow countrymen that if the war continued, it must inevitably end for England in "loss and disgrace" and "impenetrable gloom." Washington and Paine need not have worried about Lord North's proffer of peace. Congress refused to meet with the Carlisle Commission.[57]

If Americans were resolutely committed to "rub and drive on," as Paine claimed late in 1778, support for the war in England had been badly shaken by Burgoyne's surrender at Saratoga. Numerous writers, including American Tories—some of whom had fled to London—sought to bolster Britain's commitment to continue fighting. That was sufficient inducement for Paine to become involved. He produced two long essays addressed to the "People of England." His object was to convince them of the folly of continuing the war. Four years of fighting had come and gone, and each had conclusively demonstrated "the impracticability of conquering America." Paine had said this before, but in this essay he moved to fresh ground. Given his understanding that English politics involved differences between competing economic interests, Paine directed his argument toward "the mercantile and manufacturing part" of England. He sought to convince those whose lifeblood included commerce with America that they would be better off trading with an independent partner. From America's "flourishing must your profits arise," he wrote. In addition, he advised those in the commercial sector that they had suffered long enough from the "misconduct and misfortune" spawned by the king's and Parliament's deluded American policies, and that their situation would only worsen through going to war with France. At this point, Paine added what had been on his mind for years: "Your present king and ministry will be the ruin of you; and you had better risk a revolution."[58] Paine would never waver from his belief that bringing an end to monarchical and oligarchical rule, and that alone, could overcome the widespread misery that oppressed so many in his homeland.

While some had expressed concerns about his ruminations on government in *Common Sense*, and one or two had even questioned his commitment to the American Revolution, probably owing to his background in England, Paine to this point had enjoyed the approbation, even patronage, of important figures in Congress, the army, and in Philadelphia. But beginning late in 1778 he waded into partisan domestic matters, and he paid heavily for it.

First, he stepped into the imbroglio over Pennsylvania's constitution. Three months after independence was declared, a constitutional convention dominated by artisans had drafted the most radical constitution adopted in Revolutionary America. As historian Eric Foner has written, Pennsylvania's constitution "symbolized the utopian aspects of the Revolution—a radical break with the British past." It also threatened the hegemony long exercised by Philadelphia's merchant elite. Property qualifications for holding office were eliminated, and something close to universal manhood suffrage was instituted, as voting rights were extended to all adult male taxpayers. Opposition came swiftly from conservatives, who attributed the constitution to the handiwork of "coffee-house demagogues" and "political upstarts."[59] Paine had written about the constitution as early as March 1777, simply urging that a "squabbling spirit"—an attempt to replace it with a new constitution—be deferred until after the war was won, lest partisanship impair the war effort.[60]

But war or no war, opponents of Pennsylvania's constitution in 1778 mounted a full-scale assault in which they proposed a referendum on whether to hold another constitutional convention. Paine took a stand in four essays in December. Much of the conservative cant against the constitution had played on class antagonism, but Paine refused to go there. He was drawn to this battle because at bottom what he saw at stake was nothing less than the meaning of the American Revolution. Paine had always seen the American rebellion as a struggle for the liberation of humankind, and he defended Pennsylvania's constitution as a recognition of human equality. The freedom to govern should not belong exclusively to the rich or the poor. "I consider freedom as personal property," he wrote. The "floor of Freedom is as level as water. . . . It is this broad base . . . that gives security to all and every part of society. . . . I consider freedom to be inseparable from the man as a man." Paine had in essence amplified Jefferson's Declaration of Independence by asserting that independence meant freedom and that dependence was the antithesis of freedom. In ringing terms, Paine endorsed Jefferson's natural-rights passage. As Jefferson had in the Declaration of Independence, Paine had also maintained that the American Revolution—and the new nation of entities that once had been imperial colonies—was fundamentally about establishing "equality of rights."[61]

Paine made powerful enemies among conservatives everywhere. Soon enough, he antagonized still others, including some in Congress, through his involvement in another matter that he saw as crucial to both the Revolution and the eventual shape of the new American nation. Four months before independence was declared, Congress—in the immediate aftermath of America's first defeat, the December 1775 debacle at Quebec—sent Silas Deane, a former congressman from Connecticut, to Paris to purchase materials for the war effort. Deane entered a snake pit. The French agent with whom he was dealing acted unscrupulously, marking up the price of the arms and munitions that he sold to Deane in order to increase his profit. During 1777, Arthur Lee, an American diplomat in Paris, charged that Deane, too, was engaged in war profiteering. Deane, according to Lee, had acted with the intent of defrauding the government of the United States. Lee's allegations raised suspicions in some quarters that Deane might have been acting in concert with Robert Morris, Philadelphia's leading merchant and until recently a Pennsylvania congressman who chaired the committee charged with purchasing war materials from abroad. Congress recalled Deane and in August 1778 launched an investigation that produced deep divisions among the congressmen. When Deane, toward year's end, publicly defended himself in the press, Paine jumped into the white-hot tempest.

At first glance, the matter was of no concern to Paine. But as secretary to the Committee for Foreign Affairs, Paine had seen documents that convinced him of improprieties by Deane and others. For a man who thought it dishonorable to make money off the Revolutionary cause—and who had in fact forsworn the stupendous royalties earned by *Common Sense*—Paine was outraged by what Deane had supposedly done. Paine could see what General Washington saw when he was summoned from headquarters to Philadelphia at this very moment to confer with Congress. For Washington, who had not been away from his army for fifteen months, his five-week stay in Philadelphia was revealing. While Continental army soldiers suffered every conceivable deprivation, Washington discovered that the richest Philadel-phians lived in luxury as if there were no war. Indeed, according to Wash-ington, many affluent Philadelphians, propelled by an "insatiable thirst for riches," viewed the war as something "for their own private emolument." Washington suspected that "various tribes of money makers" in other cities were acting similarly. What Washington saw convinced him that the Amer-ican Revolution was in "eminent danger" unless "things [were brought] back to first principles"—that is, back to the spirit of 1776.[62]

Washington's chief concern was about winning the war, and Paine, too, feared that hedonism might cripple the war effort. But Paine additionally worried that when public officials used their power for private ends rather than for serving the public good, the result would be fatal for republicanism. Paine thought that a public official who behaved in this manner was corrupt, and that such corruption would ultimately destroy civic virtue, the bedrock of republicanism. Paine was hardly alone in believing that bribery and corrup-tion had destroyed what once had been the promise of republicanism in England. The literature of the American insurgency during the previous fifteen years had been filled with the message that a deeply rooted iniquity had "corrupted" England, dooming it to groan under oligarchy. Hand in glove with this notion was the belief that republicanism's downfall throughout history had been brought on by the intractable quest for ever greater riches and luxuries by the wealthiest members in society. Whatever others saw in the Silas Deane affair, Paine saw the behavior of Deane and Morris as that of "avaricious and ambitious men" who "laugh at virtue." Their conduct was incompatible with selfless, disinterested patriotism, and in his judgment it could only prove fatal to the dream that the American Revolution was the birthday of a new world. Paine was in step with half the members of Congress, those who thought it necessary to expose Deane and his "Tory friends and Mercantile Abettors."[63]

With these thoughts swirling in his mind, Paine rushed into print more than a dozen newspaper essays. He charged Deane with "embezzlement," blasted his "unfitness for a public character," and obliquely accused his defenders of being driven by "a selfish attachment to their own interest." In addition to Deane, Paine took on Robert Morris. He accused the merchant of "corruption" for having used his post as a congressman for private gain, and Paine insisted—much as had Washington in private—that such malfeasance would "be fatal both to public interest and public honor."[64]

In one of his initial essays, Paine said that he "expected . . . to be abused" for what he had written.[65] He was prescient. One dark night, he was waylaid in the street, thoroughly beaten, and left in an "offensive and filthy" gutter.

Paine recovered from the drubbing, but he soon suffered longer-lasting damage. Unwarily, Paine had divulged in one of his essays that France had promised aid to the Americans prior to Deane's arrival in Paris. Paine had been made aware of this through documents he had seen in his role as secretary to the congressional committee; but by revealing France's hidden intentions, Paine violated his oath of secrecy. The French minister to the United States—who was eager to preserve the fiction that his country had provided no assistance to the United States prior to the Treaty of Alliance—protested, providing Paine's foes in Congress with the wedge they needed to push for his dismissal from his secretarial post. Gouverneur Morris, a peg-legged New York congressman who always sided with the elite, took the lead in excoriating Paine. Morris, an American facsimile of an English peer—he was the grandson and son of royal officials in New Jersey and New York and the owner of a sprawling manor near Manhattan—assailed Paine on the floor of Congress in sulfurous class terms. He characterized Paine as "a mere adventurer from England, without fortune, without family connections, ignorant even of grammar." Congress ultimately deadlocked on what to do with Paine, as it did on the question of Deane's conduct. But as Paine was unable to secure a hearing before Congress—indeed, he said that he not only had been "censured unheard," but was also in the dark as to what he had written that had provoked such an "unfavorable disposition"—he simply resigned as secretary to the committee.[66]

As with that of James Monroe at about the same time, Paine's future appeared to unravel during 1779. For the first time in two years, he no longer had a steady income. He was also deeply hurt that so many had turned on him. The bitterest sting was his discovery that some in America, where the Revolution had supposedly given birth to a new world, looked on him as a lower-class upstart, much as supercilious English noblemen disdained commoners. On his way out the door, Paine told Congress: "I have obtained fame, honor, and credit in this country. I am proud of these honors."[67] But the scorn he felt was so corrosive, the gnawing emptiness that gripped him so overwhelming, that Paine sank into a dark, melancholy state. He did not leave his lodging for two months. "I fell, all at once, from high credit to disgrace, and the worst word was thought too good for me," he moaned. In private, he anguished over how Gouverneur Morris had "hopped round upon one leg" arrogantly besmirching his integrity.[68] Thereafter, a bitterness toward his adopted country seeped into Paine's correspondence, for he felt betrayed by those who had displayed "disagreeable ingratitudes" toward him despite his service to "the Cause itself." For the first time since his arrival in Philadelphia five years earlier, Paine spoke of leaving America. Of one thing he was certain. After having drifted for most of his adult life, Paine had found his calling while in America. "I know but one kind I am fit for," he said, "and that is a thinking one, and, of course, a writing one."[69]

It was at this very moment that Jefferson, too, was turned upside down. He had returned home soon after Congress declared independence, but in March 1779, General Washington—fresh from his eye-opening stay in Philadelphia— wrote to George Mason, his neighbor in Virginia, to tell him that the United States and the war it was waging had sunk into a "critical period." State and federal printing presses had for years churned out boundless amounts of paper money in a frantic effort to pay the soldiery and buy arms and supplies. Inevitably, the currency depreciated, until by 1779 something on the order of $125 in paper money was needed to purchase what had cost $1.00 three years before. The economic collapse menaced America's army in more far-reaching ways than any threat posed recently by Britain's armed forces. Washington spelled out the peril that had arisen. But the commander went further. In this hour of great crisis for the American Revolution, Washington pointed out that many who had served at the national level in 1775 and 1776 had returned home, abandoning the struggle. He asked: "where are our Men of abilities? why do they not come forth to save their Country?" And to that, Washington additionally asked: Could "Jefferson & others" continue to remain at home and "let our noble struggle end in ignominy[?]"[70]

Mason, as Washington knew would be the case, passed along word of the commander's displeasure to Jefferson. Jefferson never commented in writing on what Washington had said, but it struck him with the shock of an electric jolt. Jefferson's life immediately changed.

CHAPTER 4

"DEFENDING OUR FANES AND FIRE-SIDES"

WINNING THE REVOLUTIONARY WAR

JEFFERSON LEFT PHILADELPHIA NOT LONG after independence was declared, and before the summer of 1776 ended he was back in Virginia, having exchanged his seat in Congress for one in the state assembly. Most political activists throughout American history have preferred to serve at the national level. But Jefferson understood that for the foreseeable future Congress would focus almost exclusively on supervising the war, managing the economy, and conducting foreign relations. Domestic matters, including any reforms, were to be the province of the states, and once independence had been declared, the focal point of Jefferson's thinking was on bringing change to Virginia.

Most American revolutionaries in 1776, including the most conservative, called themselves republicans. Republicans were foes of monarchies and titled nobilities, and committed to the notion of the sovereignty of the people. In the glow of independence, republicans in every state set about refashioning the colonial governments under which they had lived. They longed for a society in which free people would have greater opportunities than had been the case in British colonial America, and they wished to limit government's infringement of liberties. By and large, the first state constitutions broadened suffrage rights, provided better and more equitable representation for those living in the backcountry, limited executive authority, and structured the new governments in such a manner that legislatures were unlikely to be manipulated by governors. By the first anniversary of independence, the state legislatures hardly resembled the colonial assemblies they had replaced. Nearly everywhere, the percentage of extremely wealthy delegates had been reduced by half or more.[1]

Jefferson fully approved of these reforms, but he wanted even more from the American Revolution. That was not true of every revolutionary. Only hours after Congress declared independence, for instance, an exultant John Adams in a letter home praised the "Greatness of this Revolution," as it meant the "People will have unbounded Power." But in the very next sentence, Adams wrote: "the People are extreamly addicted to Corruption and Venality. . . . I am not without Apprehensions from this Quarter."[2] In the coming years, Adams worked tirelessly to build bulwarks against the exercise of untrammeled power by the people. Jefferson shared some of Adams's misgivings, but he had more confidence in the people's judgment, and like Thomas Paine, he thought of the American Revolution as a watershed event waged for independence and securing people's inherent rights, political and otherwise. What is more, Jefferson in the summer of 1776 believed the time was right for securing substantive change. The public was suffused with the "Spirit of 1776," the gratifying sense that the most malign remnants of British rule were being swept away; so pervasive was the mood that in the summer of 1776 even conservative John Adams rejoiced, if only briefly, that never before had so much been "so totally eradicated from so many Minds in so short a Time." Jefferson felt that if Virginia was to be truly transformed, it must be now or never.[3]

Jefferson's ideas about changing Virginia were in place by the spring of 1776 when he drafted a constitution for his state and submitted it to the Virginia Convention. His draft constitution arrived too late to be considered, but what Jefferson put to paper demonstrated his hope of substantially reshaping political authority within the state. By apportioning representation according to population, he sought to shift power from the Tidewater counties in the east to the historically underrepresented Piedmont and frontier counties farther to the west. By proposing grants of land to all free, adult landless males, Jefferson would have instantly established universal manhood suffrage. His draft constitution additionally called for the abolition of the African slave trade, freedom of religion, and freedom of the press. The comprehensive domestic reforms that Jefferson envisaged were more radical than anything proposed in *Common Sense*. For all Paine's ringing rhetoric, for pragmatic reasons he had focused primarily on independence and the evils of monarchy and aristocracy. Jefferson was less constrained, and the social, economic, and political reforms that he put forward for Virginia were more advanced than the reforms made by any constitution adopted during the American Revolution. Indeed, if realized, Jefferson's propositions would have threatened the previously assured hegemony of the gentry class in Virginia.[4]

Jefferson never explained the reasons behind his radical views, and as one of his better biographers concluded, it was likely that he "did not understand them himself."[5] Jefferson said only that his convictions grew out of a "life of inquiry and reflection," beginning in his college years when he "heard more good sense, more rational" thought than in all the remainder of his life.[6] Throughout his life, Jefferson was both intellectually curious and a disciple of the Enlightenment. He took it for granted that nothing should be taken for granted. Everything was ripe for questioning, including the colonists' position within the British Empire and the nature of Virginia's society and political practices. His outlook, like that of Paine, was tinctured with rage. Jefferson, too, was troubled by British corruption, but he was also vexed by the imperial government's intrusiveness in domestic American matters and especially by the colonists' inescapably second-class status. In addition, Jefferson believed that Britain's detrimental influence was instrumental in the growth of what he called a "Pseudo-aristoi"—a burgeoning nobility—within Virginia.[7]

In the tempestuous years leading to independence, Jefferson, much like Paine, came to think that Great Britain groaned under a "vicious . . . Patrician order," an "aristocracy of wealth" that was "of more harm and danger, than benefit, to society." Having become "privileged by law," this artificial nobility had perpetuated its elite status through wealth in land, but also through the patronage of monarchs who "habitually selected [the] counselors of State" from the ranks of the aristocracy. The nobility reciprocated by facilitating monarchy's insatiable quest to advance the "interests and will of the crown." Royalty and aristocracy had colluded first in abusing the people of England, then those in Ireland, and with the Stamp Act in 1765 they turned to the victimization of the American colonists.

Like Paine, Jefferson burned with hatred of inherited privilege, the bedrock of monarchical and aristocratic power in England. Both were convinced that these entitlements sustained abuse by royalty and nobility, a grand ruse that made possible—inevitable, in fact—their systematic "treasonable crimes against their people." Jefferson and Paine harbored an implacable belief in egalitarianism, a conviction that Americans were the equal of the English, and indeed that free men everywhere were equals. Unlike any of the other major Founders, Jefferson and Paine believed, as historian Gordon Wood has noted, that "all men were *created* equal" and that "all men *remained* equal throughout their adult lives."[8] Paine's and Jefferson's antipathy to inherited privilege was a major component in leading both to see independence as the colonists' only recourse for escaping exploitation at the hands of Britain's predatory elite. Jefferson was also convinced that Virginia had come to bear an uncomfortable resemblance to Great Britain itself. A handful of "great families" dominated the colony, just as an entrenched oligarchy monopolized power in the mother country. As was true in England, Jefferson knew that Virginians of "virtue and talent" who were not wellborn were unlikely to ever reach their full potential. Nor would the "interests of society" be served so long as an aristocracy "founded on wealth and birth, without either virtue or talents," predominated and perpetuated itself through the "transmission of [its] property from generation to generation." Jefferson believed that after a century and a half as an English colony, Virginia was on the road to mirroring the political and social rot that blighted England.

England's political and social culture, Jefferson wrote, was one in which "dependence begets subservience and venality, suffocates the germ of virtue," and rendered commoners "fit tools for the designs" of the elite who wielded ultimate power. Jefferson saw the American Revolution as the colonists' only hope of escaping the same fate and their best hope for reordering Virginia socially and politically. To achieve this required attacking a system that enabled one element in society to utterly predominate. Vesting all free men with the right to vote, he thought, would lay "the axe to the root" of a potentially all-powerful American oligarchy.[9]

Jefferson was so set on his revolutionary mission that he spurned a congressional appointment to join Benjamin Franklin and Silas Deane on their diplomatic assignment in Paris. He told Congress that he could not leave Martha, whose health was precarious. Not everyone believed him. Richard Henry Lee, writing in the midst of the Continental army's disastrous New York campaign, told Jefferson with pitiless candor that he should abandon his "private enjoyments" and serve the national interest.[10] Already in his seat in the state assembly in Williamsburg when Lee's scorching letter reached him, Jefferson was unmoved. He remained in Virginia, and before 1779 his correspondence suggests that hostilities hardly intruded on his thoughts. More than one observer mistakenly thought Jefferson had abandoned the cause altogether. Lee was among those who reached such a conclusion, and in the summer of 1777 he struck again. Lee wrote to Jefferson while Burgoyne's army was advancing on Albany and Howe's was on the move to take Philadelphia. His missive dripped with sarcasm: "It will not perhaps be disagreeable to you in your retirement, sometimes to hear the events of war, and how in other respects we proceed in the arduous business we are engaged in."[11]

While others faced danger and deprivation, Jefferson spent most of his first three years after leaving Congress at home. He supervised the ongoing construction of Monticello, planted orchards and gardens, and oversaw the production and marketing of his crops. In addition, when the British and Hessian soldiers who surrendered at Saratoga were moved to Albemarle County early in 1779, Jefferson frequently hosted the captive officers at dinners, opened his library to them, and invited them to Monticello for philosophical discussions or to play music and sing with him and Martha. Jefferson made no attempt to hide what he was doing or his inclination to treat the prisoners of war "with politeness and generosity."[12] Jefferson was motivated by compassion, but his behavior was politically wrong-footed. Jefferson foolishly compounded his error by talking incessantly of retiring altogether from public life. For one who was thirty-six years old, and whose country was in the midst of a life-or-death struggle, talk of this sort was the height of imprudence, and it prompted Edmund Pendleton, one of the most powerful Virginians, to lecture him on the inappropriateness of wishing for a "happy quietus from the Public" when his services were so badly needed by his country.[13]

Jefferson eventually paid the piper. His conduct and rhetoric aroused an undying enmity among many, though in some respects the hostility was undeserved. Martha did experience two difficult pregnancies between 1776 and 1778, and she recovered very slowly, if at all, from the second.[14] The time and energy that he devoted to securing better conditions for the Hessian prisoners of war may have saved the lives of countless young men. In truth, despite the public's perception, Jefferson neither retired nor abandoned all public responsibilities. He annually attended the spring and fall sessions of the assembly, spending upwards of a quarter of each year in Williamsburg, and he tended to his legislative duties while at home, work that resulted in some of the American Revolution's most important reforms. But he contributed nothing toward winning the war that, with his own pen, he had helped to launch.

Disappointed at failing to gain approval for the constitution that he had drafted for Virginia, Jefferson did the next best thing. Five days after reentering the state legislature, early in the fall of 1776 (at about the same moment as the Forts Washington and Lee debacles), he proposed a review of the state's legal code, aiming toward new laws that would mesh with "our republican form of government." The assembly immediately appointed him to a five-member Committee of Revisors that was to scrutinize Virginia's laws and recommend changes. Two members who were not lawyers quickly dropped off the panel, leaving Jefferson to work with George Wythe, his legal mentor, and Pendleton, formerly a congressman and president of the Virginia Convention and now the assembly's speaker. After the members of the committee agreed to divide the workload equally, each returned to his home and set about what was to be a three-year undertaking.[15]

Among other things, Jefferson took up the criminal code. His labors resulted in a staggering reduction in the number of capital crimes, leaving only treason and murder to be punishable by death. Unfortunately, the bill that he brought forward also proposed an array of macabre punishments, including castration, branding, flogging, and maiming. Years later, Jefferson acknowledged the "revolting" nature of what had been proposed, though he shifted blame to his colleagues. The legislature, in a rare display of enlightenment, spurned the harsh penalties. Work on Virginia's slave code also fell to Jefferson. While he did not propose slavery's immediate end, Jefferson leaned toward the gradual emancipation of all slaves and the removal of all that were liberated from the state. In the end, however, he never introduced the measure. His excuse, which was no doubt accurate, was that the "public mind would not yet bear the proposition." Jefferson and his committee were responsible for three important changes in Virginia's slave code that the assembly adopted. Henceforth, it was illegal to bring slaves into Virginia, easier for slave owners to manumit their slaves, and mandatory that those who were freed must leave the state.[16]

Jefferson sought profound changes in three additional areas. He thought the committee's educational recommendations were "the most important . . . in our whole code." In addition to urging that the state provide three years of free schooling for all white children, he and his colleagues advocated the establishment of publicly funded college preparatory schools, a free college education for those who excelled, and the creation of state-endowed libraries. None of the proposals were enacted. The "wealthy class [was] unwilling to incur" the expense of educating the poor, said Jefferson.[17]

Jefferson attained more through his push for land reforms. In his draft constitution, Jefferson had proposed land grants to the landless, a proposition that stood hardly a chance of passage in an assembly composed largely of land speculators. However, Jefferson and others successfully pushed the opening of the West, closed by the imperial government since 1763. The new county of Kentucky—with fertile and cheap, if not free, land—was created.[18] In addition, Jefferson secured the repeal of the existing law of entail, an ancient English practice that prohibited those who inherited entailed property from selling their patrimony. England's nobility had designed entail as a means of assuring that property (and power) remained concentrated in the hands of a few families. Jefferson additionally managed to bring an end to primogeniture, another English law that mandated that a father's property be bequeathed to his eldest son. In going after these long-entrenched practices, Jefferson was chopping at the roots of the power of the Tidewater planters. The great planters knew precisely what he was doing, and some hated him ever after.[19]

Jefferson's assorted proposals for land reform were his initial expressions of what was to become perhaps the most famous aspect of his outlook—his belief that an agrarian way of life was best for both people and republics. Although much that he wrote on the subject came later—after he had experienced life in urban environments—the best-remembered articulation of his philosophy was in all likelihood written in the early 1780s:

> Those who labour in the earth are the chosen people of God, if ever he had a chosen people, whose breasts he has made his peculiar deposit for substantial and genuine virtue. It is the focus in which he keeps alive that sacred fire, which otherwise might escape in the face of the earth. Corruption of morals in the mass of cultivators is a phenomenon of which no age nor nation has furnished an example. It is the mark set on those, who not looking up to heaven, to their own soil and industry, as does the husbandman, for their subsistence, depend for it on the casualties and caprice of customers. Dependence begets subservience and venality, suffocates the germ of virtue, and prepares fit tools for the designs of ambition. . . . While we have land to labour then, let us never wish to see our citizens occupied at a work-bench, or twirling a distaff. . . . Let our work-shops remain in Europe. . . . The mobs of the great cities add just so much to the support of pure government, as sores do to the strength of the human body. It is the manners and spirit of a people which preserve a republic in vigour. A degeneracy in these is a canker which soon eats to the heart of its laws.[20]

Later, Jefferson spoke of how farming promoted "permanent improvement, quiet life, and orderly conduct," and still later he expounded on how it not just led to "a comfortable existence," but that almost alone among ways to earn a living it provided for ease and security in old age. Unlike those in virtually every other manner of work, farmers enjoyed an astounding "degree of freedom" from dependence. A farmer was his own boss, free to decide what to plant, when to work, and how long and hard to toil. Not only was farming the "wisest pursuit" for an individual, but a republic was more likely to flourish when the great majority of its citizens were farmers. With a stake in society, farmers were innately "interested in the support of law and order." In contrast to exploited and downtrodden urban laborers, who because of their "ignorance, poverty and vice" were easily manipulated by others with their own agendas, self-reliant citizen-farmers lived ordered lives governed by nature's rhythms. Independent and virtuous, farmers made up the sturdy—and stabilizing—foundation in which republics thrived.[21]

Jefferson's most far-reaching success came in the realm of religion. Many colonies had an established church, meaning that one denomination was officially linked to the state. In Virginia, the Church of England had been the state church throughout the colonial period. Virginia's pre-Revolutionary legal code required attendance at Anglican services and payment of tithes for the support of the church, and recognized only those marriages performed by Anglican priests. Dissenters faced persecution, including imprisonment. Though an adherent of the teachings of Jesus, Jefferson was not a Christian. Not surprisingly, given his outlook, he thought religion a personal matter and regarded government's intrusion into the realm of religious belief as certain to be "injurious" to some. He famously declared: "it does me no injury for my neighbor to say there are twenty gods, or no god. It picks neither my pocket nor breaks my leg."

Dissenters in Virginia were pushing for reform before Jefferson came home from Philadelphia. He soon joined the fight, which he subsequently called the "severest contest in which I have ever been engaged." As part of recodification, Jefferson in 1777 drafted a statute for religious freedom, though he waited two years before submitting his proposed law. The legislature tabled his proposal until the end of the Revolutionary War. When it finally took up the bill in 1785, Jefferson was abroad and James Madison shepherded it into law. It guaranteed religious freedom for all and terminated compulsory tithes. Once it became law in Virginia, it served as a model for statutes in other states and for the guarantee of religious freedom in the Bill of Rights under the United States Constitution. From the outset, Jefferson prayed that what Virginia had achieved might have some influence in Europe in ameliorating what he privately called the "ignorance, superstition, poverty and oppression of body and mind" inflicted by churches.[22]

Jefferson had not achieved all that he had hoped for in reshaping Virginia, but what he had wrought in a brief span that began in 1776 was breathtaking. Only Thomas Paine had come close to equaling Jefferson's influence in the ways Americans thought. Through the Declaration of Independence, Jefferson would exert sway over how generations yet unborn—in America and around the globe—would think of themselves and the world they inhabited, including an intractable belief in God-given rights and the natural equality of humankind. In addition, the reforms he had pushed in Virginia expanded the opportunities available to free men. No single public official during the American Revolution could reasonably claim to have been responsible for more domestic change than Jefferson. He had been a colossal figure in giving shape and meaning to the American Revolution. Late in his long life, Jefferson wondered "whether my country is the better for my having lived at all."[23] The answer was readily apparent.

Nevertheless, if Jefferson's country and his free countrymen were better for his having lived, he had done next to nothing to improve the lot of those in bondage, including the two hundred or so that he owned. Privately, Jefferson characterized slavery as a "moral evil" and a "blot in our country," but his reputation as a dreamy-eyed visionary notwithstanding, Jefferson was very much the pragmatic politician. He understood that Virginia at this juncture was not about to start down the road to ending slavery, and to push for slavery's abolition would sow divisions that might prove fatal to both reformism and waging the arduous war. Even so, he might have emerged from the shadows and denounced slavery, as had others, including Paine. He might also have freed some or all of his slaves as an example to others of what the American Revolution meant to him. Such a sacrifice—and it would have been an immense sacrifice, akin in a sense to Paine's having relinquished his royalties—was not in Jefferson.[24]

It was probably in April 1779 that Jefferson learned from George Mason of General Washington's lacerating letter about those who were not serving their country during the national crisis. Jefferson had heard the accusation before, but it was different coming from Washington. Jefferson admired Washington—and feared him as well, for no ambitious individual could wish to incur the commander's enmity. In his heart of hearts, Jefferson must have recognized the truth in what Washington had written, but the timing of the general's denunciation was crucial too. The war was changing and in such a way that Virginia was likely to face greater dangers than at any time since the outbreak of hostilities. Britain's new southern strategy virtually assured that. The war in the South, confined at this juncture to the region around Savannah, Georgia, was a long way from Virginia. But it was clear that every southern province was now in London's bullseye.

Virginians came face-to-face with Britain's southern strategy that spring. In May, three dozen Royal Navy vessels, carrying eighteen hundred redcoats under Sir George Collier, struck near Portsmouth on the Virginia coast. Collier's force sowed a wide path of destruction and panic as it torched shipyards and tobacco warehouses, plundered numerous plantations, and liberated and took away some fifteen hundred slaves. The war had reached Virginia in earnest, and it prompted numerous influential Virginians to appeal to Jefferson to stand for election as governor. Richard Henry Lee set aside his earlier mordant tone and simply urged Jefferson "to suffer every thing rather than injure the public cause." Jefferson knew that his political future was on the line. Though he admitted that the temptation to remain at Monticello was "almost irresistible," he consented. Jefferson was chosen governor by the legislature early in June.[25]

Jefferson had exchanged his placid retreat for an office that was to bring him much hardship and anxiety. No Revolutionary War governor encountered greater challenges, none had to make more momentous decisions, and none came face-to-face with more harrowing danger. Jefferson had hardly taken the oath of office before despondency set in, leading him to tell others that the day he left office would be the happiest of his life. But he was a diligent chief executive during his two years in the past.[26] Aside from two brief visits home, he remained in the capital: Williamsburg initially and later Richmond. Day in, day out, he met with the eight-member Council of State, drawing close to one of its youngest members, twenty-eight-year-old James Madison, with whom he had previously had only a passing acquaintance. Jefferson worked with legislators during the assembly's two annual sessions, and he dealt with a seemingly endless stream of paperwork. Nearly his every action was war-related.

Jefferson took office in a state wracked with fear that Collier's raid would be followed by similarly costly incursions. As it turned out, eighteen months passed before another British armed force appeared, affording Jefferson time to plan for another enemy foray. His administration erected armories, stockpiled weapons and powder, constructed batteries on the coasts and redoubts at strategic inland sites along the state's most important rivers, and devised a network of sentinels and express riders as a safeguard against another surprise. Jefferson also worked tirelessly to meet the state's quota of troops to be furnished to the Continental army. Congress had set Virginia's annual manpower allocation at six thousand men, and early in the war the state did a credible job of raising soldiers. But Jefferson took office four years into the conflict. The grueling war had exhausted the state, compelling it to offer land and cash bounties to attract recruits. When those ploys were not terribly successful, Virginia resorted to conscription, and in utter desperation it began offering a healthy male slave to those who volunteered. Even so, Virginia never met its assigned allotment during Jefferson's governorship. Finding money with which to fight the war was another great headache. Not only was the state's economy suffering from the war's disruption of trade, but the citizenry had long since been burdened with heavy wartime taxes. Jefferson had some success on this front, thanks to his commitment to increasing taxes on the wealthiest Virginians.[27]

As Jefferson approached the end of his first term in June 1780, the achievement of American independence, once thought assured following France's entrance into the conflict, seemed far less certain. For two years or more the new nation's economy had been in tatters, due largely to the depreciation of the currency brought on by the record amount of money dumped into circulation to meet the war's endless needs. Washington hardly exaggerated when in 1779 he lamented that a "wagon load of money will scarcely purchase a waggon load of provision."[28] The military situation had unraveled as well.

Early that year the British invaded South Carolina, and with disastrous results for the Americans. A huge British army, led personally by General Henry Clinton, disembarked in the coastal barrens below Charleston in mid-February. By April, Charleston was besieged. Washington exhorted Jefferson to send all the help he could spare to those defending the city, and Virginia's legislature authorized a commitment of up to two thousand men for its struggling neighbor to the south.

As governor, Jefferson was the state's commander in chief. Whether or not to send men to Charleston was his call, and it was a difficult one. Should another British raiding force attack Virginia, every soldier would be needed at home. Jefferson ultimately dispatched 400 Virginia soldiers, though before they reached Charleston, Britain's siege was ironclad. The Virginians never entered the city, which surrendered in May. The defeat was a catastrophe for the United States. Not only was a key city lost, but some 225 Americans died during the siege, 6,700 were taken prisoner, and the British captured 5,000 muskets and 400 pieces of artillery.

More disasters were on the horizon. Within days of taking Charleston, British forces occupied posts from Georgetown, sixty miles north, to Augusta on the Georgia–South Carolina border, an arc that extended nearly 175 miles.[29] By June 1780, when Jefferson was elected to a second yearlong term, it appeared certain that the British would reclaim all of South Carolina before the summer ended. As there was no longer a Continental army worthy of the name in the South, Jefferson feared that it could not be long before Lord Cornwallis, whom Clinton had left in command in the southern theater, would invade North Carolina. If that state fell, the British army would be on Virginia's doorstep.

Jefferson swung into action. He wished to establish an express system to link his state and North Carolina, hoping to gain intelligence and see what could be done to keep the fighting from reaching Virginia. He turned to James Monroe, a former soldier whom Jefferson had met early in his first term, as a courier and agent. Impressed with the young man, Jefferson had taken him on as a legal apprentice. Now, in the gathering emergency in the South, Jefferson wanted "a gentleman in a confidential business" that required "great discretion, and some acquaintance with military things." Monroe immediately accepted the challenge. Jefferson sent him to communicate with civilian authorities and the handful of Continental officers in North Carolina. Monroe was also to secure intelligence about the enemy. Jefferson instructed him to "hang as near" as possible to the "enemy's principal post" and to observe their movements. He also gave Monroe responsibility for bringing the express system into being. As Jefferson calculated that three hard-driving express riders could cover 120 miles in twenty-four hours, Monroe established "stations" at forty-mile intervals below Richmond. Monroe also conferred with Governor Abner Nash of North Carolina, spent several days in Hillsborough at the headquarters of General Johann de Kalb, the highest-ranking Continental in the South, and inaugurated the express by using it to funnel word of what he was learning to Jefferson.[30]

Only days after Monroe completed his mission, General Horatio Gates, the hero of Saratoga, arrived in Hillsborough to take command of what was to be yet another new Continental army in the South. Though shocked by the degree of war weariness that he found—in his view, southerners displayed a "Deficit in Public Spirit"—Gates badgered Jefferson and Nash for men and supplies. Jefferson did what he could. He ordered two thousand men to march to North Carolina, five times the number he had dispatched to Charleston's defense, and worked feverishly to locate the supplies Gates wanted. Jefferson sent him horses, livestock, wagons, leather, canvass, axes, tomahawks, powder, flints, cannonballs, and three thousand muskets, all of which he somehow obtained "without a Shilling of Money." He also did something that few would have had the nerve to do. Jefferson told Washington, whose army had remained largely inactive since Monmouth two years before, that Britain's paramount threat was to the South, not the North, and he beseeched the commander to provide greater help to Virginia and North Carolina.[31]

Gates had performed cautiously, and successfully, in the Saratoga campaign, but in the South he was reckless. His principal mistake was in moving too quickly and risking his entire force. Twenty-two-year-old James Monroe had told Jefferson six weeks earlier that the prudent course against such a powerful adversary was to "keep on their left Flank and harass and retard their Movements," but not to hazard all in a great clash.[32] If Gates's advisors proffered the same sound advice, he did not listen. Though his army was small and poorly furnished, Gates set off almost immediately after what he thought was a small enemy force at Camden, not far across the border in South Carolina.

Gates arrived to find Cornwallis with a force five times the size he had expected, containing both numerous regulars and a large cavalry arm. A considerable percentage of those under Gates were militiamen who had never experienced combat. In the Battle of Camden that followed, on August 16, Gates was routed. More than six hundred Americans were lost, as was all the rebel artillery, hundreds of muskets, and the southern army's entire baggage train. For the second time in ninety days a Continental army in the South had suffered a devastating defeat. In this instance, it was what one Virginia officer described as the "Cowardly Behaviour" of the militia that opened the door to catastrophe. Moments into the battle, the twenty-eight hundred North

Carolina and Virginia militiamen broke and "ran like a torrent and bore all before them," as Jefferson described it. The engagement was followed by "Great Desertions" among the surviving Virginia militiamen who had been with Gates, half of whom did not stop running until they reached home, or so reported one disgusted official.[33]

Unless Congress rapidly assembled yet another army, nothing could stop Cornwallis from marching into North Carolina. Reluctantly, Jefferson dispatched another two thousand militiamen, though he told Congress that most of the men would reach their destination "unarmed, unless it is in your power to furnish arms."[34] Six weeks later, after most of the Old Dominion's militiamen had tramped off to defend another state, Virginia was struck by British raiders not unlike those who had sowed widespread destruction on the eve of Jefferson's governorship. This force was commanded General Alexander Leslie. Collier's raid in the spring of 1779 had been conceived by the British high command in New York, but the genesis for Leslie's assault came from Cornwallis, who was indeed about to invade North Carolina. Cornwallis envisaged the sortie as a feint to prevent further Virginia reinforcements from being sent southward. A diversion it might have been, but it was a considerable one. Leslie's ships bristled with more than one hundred guns and carried 2,200 regulars, including horse soldiers. They came ashore at Portsmouth, Newport News, and Hampton during the third week in October 1780.

Washington had alerted Jefferson that Leslie's fleet had sailed from New York, but he thought it was en route to the Carolinas to buttress Cornwallis. The commander believed that another attack on Virginia, if it occurred at all, would not come before December or January, when the armies in the northern theater were immobilized by the winter weather. Jefferson took Washington at his word and was caught by surprise, but he reacted quickly. He summoned six thousand militia to arms and put them under the command of officers who had served in the Continental army. Monroe was among those who rushed to take up arms, securing the rank of lieutenant colonel and command of a regiment. Jefferson also appealed to Washington and Congress for help, telling them that the state's response would inevitably be "lamentably inadequate" due to its "want of the means of defense." In fact, even a well-armed militia would have faced an unfair fight, for foot soldiers were no match for cavalry and a fast-moving adversary, transported by Royal Navy vessels that some American generals labeled Britain's "canvass wings." Facing little opposition, Leslie's force swept through the state's eastern end and across the peninsula between the York and James Rivers. British troopers stormed across the dark green fields of one plantation after another as far inland as Yorktown, burning crops, liberating slaves, and looting rebel-owned dwellings. Along the coast, meanwhile, others torched vessels and windswept ship-construction sites.[35]

Leslie might have caused more harm, but after three weeks he was summoned to North Carolina by Cornwallis. Even so, Leslie's foray had been damaging, as much to morale as to property. The unrelenting calamities of 1780 turned America's hopes for victory to bleak despair. The catastrophe at Charleston had been the first, followed by Camden. Then, in September, on the eve of Leslie's raid, General Benedict Arnold sold out to the enemy, and nearly succeeded in giving America's indispensable post at West Point to the British. Even worse was word from abroad. Credible sources in Europe cautioned that France would likely make peace with Great Britain if the allies did not score a decisive victory before the end of the campaign in 1781. Should France seek a negotiated end to hostilities, America would face a stark choice: continue the war alone or accept the peace terms offered by a conference composed of Europe's monarchical states. Neither choice would offer much hope of securing American independence. Indeed, if the allies failed to win a conclusive victory within the next twelve months, the Americans were no longer assured of peace terms as generous as those offered by Lord North early in 1778.

Jefferson had long known that America's cause was in trouble, leading him to conclude that changes had to be made to how the war was prosecuted. He remained convinced that the "attachment of the people to the cause . . . and their hatred to Great Britain remain unshaken," but America's resources were nearly depleted and its "money has almost lost its circulation." He believed the series of defeats in the South had resulted less from poor leadership than from a dearth of manpower and supplies, and that the cataclysms at Charleston and Camden were a foretaste of what was coming if Virginia and North Carolina did not obtain more help from Congress and the Continental army. Jefferson appeared to understand better than Congress or General Washington that the greatest threat to America, and America's greatest opportunity for scoring a decisive victory, lay in the southern theater. Midway through 1780 Jefferson appealed to Washington for "considerable aids . . . from your army." Without them, he added, more military disasters could be expected, for a toxic "spirit of disaffection" was growing in Virginia. Not only were some refusing to serve in the militia, but hundreds of men from five counties had enlisted in Britain's Loyalist regiments and taken "oaths of allegiance" to "serve his Britannic majesty." In September, Jefferson advised Congress that if America suffered yet another major defeat in the South, "the consequences will be really tremendous."[36]

* * *

Thomas Paine, a private citizen, was not as well informed as Jefferson, but he, too, fathomed the deepening crisis. Since losing his job as secretary to the Committee on Foreign Affairs early in 1779—a few months before Jefferson's election as governor—Paine's life had been a severe struggle. He had battled depression, lived reclusively, and for a long stretch had written nothing. When Paine's money ran out, he hooked on as a secretary to Owen Biddle, a Philadelphia merchant, Quaker, and political radical who sympathized with the destitute writer, though he paid him only the barebones salary of a clerk. Paine could have obtained a better income. The French minister had offered him an annual salary of one thousand dollars to turn out essays promoting France's interests, some of which clashed with the interests of the United States. Paine refused. He would do nothing that was detrimental to his adopted homeland, and he would not advocate ideas with which he disagreed. Any "wretch who will write on any subject for bread" was no better than a "prostitute who lets out her person," he declared.[37]

Though Paine wrote nothing in 1779—it was his first year without a publication since coming to America—he was active in the battle against runaway inflation. Early that year, when Washington had first been awakened to what he privately denounced as the lack of "virtue and patriotism" among Philadelphia's elite, the commander had raged at those who ignored the nation's plight in their insatiable quest to "acquire a little pelf." Paine was unaware of Washington's anger, but he had already drawn the same conclusions. Paine in fact went further than Washington. He was convinced that many powerful businessmen were war profiteers who inflated prices to maximize their profits. With the price of wheat, flour, and corn zooming into the stratosphere—corn prices increased by 1,255 percent that year—some Philadelphians demanded that the government control prices on essential commodities. Businessmen denounced the notion. They insisted on a free market economy—Robert Morris maintained that trade must be "free as air"—and argued that any regulation would worsen inflation and lead to scarcities.

Paine, the very embodiment of self-sacrificing virtue, could not have disagreed more. He thought government—and especially, republican governments that represented the people and their interests—must intervene in economic matters, and above all it must do so in a time of crisis. It must act to sustain morale on the home front, which would be demolished if the free market economy that Morris and others sought broadened poverty and relentlessly widened the gap between the rich and all those beneath them. At an open meeting in May on the State House grounds, after several speakers had denounced blood-sucking "monopolizers and forestallers"—the very epithets that Washington had used in confidence to castigate greedy

merchants—those in attendance elected Paine, together with several distinguished Philadelphians, to an extralegal panel to regulate prices. It was the first
of three such committees that Paine served on that summer. In the end,
however, the businessmen prevailed, and the city, in September, rescinded price
controls. Though Paine's views did not change, he took the defeat silently.
Around this time John Armstrong, a fellow Pennsylvanian who, like Paine, had
soldiered in a volunteer company and later served as an aide to a Continental
army general, depicted "Poor Payne" as "not the most prudent man in the
world." Armstrong may have been generally accurate, though in this instance
Paine's silence was the model of circumspection. He realized that not only was
this a fight he could not win, but that the resulting divisiveness could only harm
the war effort.[38]

Paine's short-lived activism on behalf of price controls had aroused the
friends and followers of Robert Morris, some of whom had already laid into
Paine during the Silas Deane affair. Paine was not mauled again on a dark
street, but enemies assailed him in the press with scurrilous allegations,
including that he was a closet Tory who had used his connections to prevent
arms and equipment sent by France from reaching the Continental army.
One scribe advised Paine, "Go home, thou scoundrel, to thy native soil."
Another said, "Go, wretch, hide thy pitiful head in oblivion."[39]

If Paine was distressed by these attacks, he found the emerging partisan
differences within Congress to be even more alarming. Intense battles were
nothing new in Congress, but since independence the ongoing military emergencies had somewhat tempered wrangling. That changed in February 1779,
when France's minister to the United States asked Congress to determine the
terms it would seek whenever a peace conference took place. Incredibly, the
United States had waged war for four years without ever setting out what it
hoped to gain from hostilities, save for independence. The French request
ignited a firestorm within Congress unlike anything since the last-ditch fights
over declaring independence.

New and ardent divisions sprouted along economic and sometimes
sectional lines. The disputes intensified when the French minister intruded in
an effort to protect his country's North American interests as well as those of
its ally Spain, which was about to enter the war. Soon, it was clear that not all
Americans would get everything they hoped for from the eventual peace.
Though Congress met in secret, Paine appears to have learned a bit about
what was happening—enough to understand that the divisions posed a threat
to American unity and victory, and ultimately to the hope of a new world that
he had cherished from the beginning.[40]

The year 1779 was a miserable one for Paine. By September, his personal affairs were in such desperate straits that he wrote to Henry Laurens, the president of Congress, begging for his help. Reminding Laurens of what he had done for the cause, Paine told him of his impoverished state. "I think I have a right to ride a horse of my own," he said, "but I cannot now even afford to hire one." He had never been in such a precarious situation, he maintained, adding that he feared further deprivation would utterly destroy his health. Already that year he had been struck down by a fever and a relapse, illnesses that had left him bedridden for weeks. Now that he was better, he told Laurens, he hoped to publish his collected works and a history of the American Revolution. But he needed money for both endeavors, and he beseeched Laurens to use his influence to obtain assistance from Congress. He also appealed to the Executive Council of Pennsylvania to grant him a pension based on his disinterested service as a soldier and writer. Congress gave him nothing, but the Pennsylvania assembly offered Paine a position as a clerk, and at a better salary than Biddle was paying. He immediately accepted and started the job late in the year, about five months after Jefferson became Virginia's governor. Ebullient and reenergized, Paine rejoiced that the "idleness, uneasiness, and hopeless thinking" that had weighed so heavily on him for so long had come to an end.[41]

It is likely that while serving as the assembly's clerk, Paine helped draft some pieces of legislation, including Pennsylvania's gradual emancipation act of 1780, the first such law enacted by any state. The position also gave Paine greater access to news about the war, leading him to conclude, as had Jefferson, that an American victory seemed less likely than at any time since the darkest days of 1776. He rushed out an *American Crisis* essay, his eighth in the series and first in eighteen months. Paine once again addressed his essay to the English people, seeking to play on the war weariness that he believed was growing in his former homeland. He sought to persuade the English that their cause was hopeless. New generals and new strategies would prove unavailing, for years of warfare had already "lessened [Britain's] ability to conquer." In fact, if the history of the war demonstrated anything, it was that "America is beyond the reach of conquest." To continue hostilities would guarantee Britain only "a legacy of debts and misfortunes."[42]

Within ninety days of the essay's publication, Paine was made aware that America's situation was immeasurably worse than he had dared imagine. At almost precisely the moment in May 1780 that Philadelphia learned of the American surrender in Charleston, an alarming letter from Washington reached Joseph Reed, Pennsylvania's chief executive. It fell to Paine, as the assembly's clerk, to read the letter to the legislature. Whatever you may imagine about the army's distress, Washington began, "will fall short of the reality." The patience of the unpaid and ill-provisioned soldiery "begins . . . to be worn out." Mutinies were not unlikely. Given the nation's "insensibility and indifference" toward the war, the army as a viable force had reached the "decisive moment." In modern wars, Washington went on, the winner would invariably be the country with the "longest purse," and Great Britain had a sturdy economy. If a decisive victory was not won in the coming months, he cautioned, the United States would have no choice but to "confess to our allies that we look wholly to them for our safety. This will be a state of humiliation and bitterness against which the feelings of every good American ought to revolt." Pennsylvania "is our chief dependence," Washington told Reed, and he called on Pennsylvanians to "take a tone of energy and decision."[43]

Reed answered that he would do all he could, but added that the "Shock Paper Money has received" would retard the state's efforts. In a pointed reference to the war profiteers, Reed told Washington that the state's resources were at the "Caprice of interested or perverse Individuals."[44]

The gravity of the situation, as well as the recognition from on high that America's despair arose in part from what Paine saw as internal corruption, galvanized him. He immediately wrote to Reed and a leading Philadelphia merchant outlining steps that each might take to meet the emergency. Asserting that upwards of ten thousand men must be raised to supplant those killed and captured in Charleston, and that money must be found if the Continental army was to remain intact, Paine proposed that the "richer of the Whigs" voluntarily contribute to an army support fund; their sacrificial example, he said, would make it more "palatable" for ordinary Pennsylvanians to offer themselves up for military service. He additionally recommended that draconian taxes be levied on those Pennsylvanians who had refused to sign an oath pledging loyalty to the cause. Paine knew that an appreciable portion of the citizenry—including Tories and some Quaker neutralists—would never sign the loyalty oath. It was a distasteful step, but unavoidable. "We want rousing," Paine declared, and he did his part to revive the spirit of earlier, better days.[45] He immediately subscribed five hundred dollars to the army relief fund, virtually exhausting his meager savings. In June, Paine also published another *Crisis* essay. Not since the emergency occasioned by the calamitous New York campaign had Paine written two *Crisis* essays in such a short span.

The American Crisis IX pulsated with a feeling and urgency lacking for ages in Paine's compositions, although it was flimflam through and through. His goal was not veracity, but rousing the country and resuscitating morale. The "decline of the enemy is visible," he claimed. Britain's capture of American cities was "piece-meal work" that would not win the war. News of the "fate of Charleston, like [word of] the misfortunes of 1776," was "kindl[ing] into action the scattered sparks throughout America" of what once had been the "blaze of 1776." A "spirit of exertion" was gathering within all sectors of society in Philadelphia, including among the "enterprising part." America had stood alone in 1776, but now France was on its side, and the energized allies, backed by an "enterprising spirit" on the part of Americans on the home front, would guarantee "ravages" inflicted on the enemy." Paine did not, could not, assail Washington for not having taken the field during the past two years, though he mentioned that the "dangerous calm" in the northern theater had "lulled" the citizenry into "the lap of soft tranquility." Between the lines, Paine seemed to say that the cause cried out for what he called the "ardor . . . of a campaign" akin to Trenton-Princeton, when America had "snatched" victories that left "undone" all that the enemy had achieved in the previous months.⁴⁶

Paine's literary flourish, coupled with Reed's leadership and the troubling war news from South Carolina, stirred nearly one hundred well-to-do Philadelphia merchants to contribute to the army support fund. (Given Paine's well-known penurious state, the merchants also saw to it that his five-hundred-dollar contribution was returned to him.) Altogether, about three hundred thousand dollars was raised that summer, though in the end little went directly to the soldiery. The fund became the seed money for the nation's first bank, the Bank of Pennsylvania, which was underwritten by Congress. In addition, during that summer Reed's wife, Esther, published a broadside urging women to be "really useful." Acting in that spirit, she organized the "Association," female volunteers who made clothing and candles for soldiers, arranged drives to gather essential items, and appealed for funds that were to be used to acquire shirts for the soldiers. In a few weeks her efforts netted contributions from sixteen hundred Pennsylvania donors, which resulted in the purchase of two thousand shirts. The Association eventually established chapters in six states and spurred churches here and there to join the effort to help the soldiers.⁴⁷ The funds raised that summer were useful, but woefully inadequate. The news only worsened. Before the summer ended, the country was jolted by word of Gates's defeat at Camden and Arnold's treason a month later.

Paine issued another *Crisis* essay, this one unnumbered. Instead, borrowing from a line in Washington's letter to Reed, Paine titled it *The Crisis Extraordinary*. It was one of his lengthiest and driest efforts. (Paine himself said the essay was "tedious.") He urged a national impost—a revenue tariff on imported items—but the core of his piece was a call to the states to levy new taxes. He recognized the pain that would be caused, but contended that higher taxes now would be the cheapest alternative for the long run, as a well-funded army could bring the war to a speedy end. He warned, too, that if the war was lost because of lack of funds, the victorious British would pick the pockets of the defeated Americans. Although his proposal for an impost fell on deaf ears, the Pennsylvania legislature almost immediately responded by meeting the tax quota recently set by Congress.[48]

Just after Arnold's treachery, and about the time of Leslie's raid in Virginia, Paine conceived the harebrained idea of traveling to England. His plan was to sneak into the country and, while hiding with friends, write an essay "capable of fixing in the minds of the people of England" that their disastrous war must be brought to an end. Once a publisher had been found, he would "escape." Hubris had gotten the best of him. Attaching magical qualities to his pen, Paine appears to have harbored the fantastic notion that writing his piece in England would topple Lord North's government and bring an end to hostilities.[49]

Paine was so serious about his misguided scheme that he abandoned his position as clerk of the assembly and set about searching for some means of getting to England. Only a visit from General Nathanael Greene, who was in Philadelphia for a few days late in October to meet with Congress, changed his mind. Greene convinced Paine that the undertaking was far too risky. Should he be taken into custody in England, said Greene, he might become "an object of retaliation," inasmuch as the American military had just captured and executed Major John Andre, a British officer complicit in Arnold's treasonous scheme.[50]

Paine scrapped the trip, though soon enough he did cross the Atlantic. Given the grave state of affairs, Congress in January 1781 voted to send an emissary to France to beg for another loan. America's condition had grown steadily more desperate in the seven months since Washington had appealed to Joseph Reed. Not only had the campaign of 1780 ended without a decisive allied victory, but Washington's army had yet again remained inactive. Rumors buzzed that a faction committed to peace was growing in Versailles, and that the French might drop out of the war if the allies failed to score a decisive victory during the campaign of 1781. Many in Congress were swept with fear, especially as America's chances of winning a great military victory had seldom seemed so unlikely. France's navy was in the Caribbean, where for the most part it had remained during the past three years. In the summer, a French army of sixty-five hundred men had disembarked in America, though it, too, had remained inactive. America's plight only worsened when the Continental army was rocked by two mutinies in the first days of the new year. A Massachusetts congressman pithily summed up the dire situation: "We are bankrupt with a mutinous army."[51]

Congress selected Colonel John Laurens to sail for France. Laurens in turn asked Paine to accompany him as his secretary. Paine attributed the invitation to "Col. Laurens' passionate attachment to me." Possibly, though it was more likely that Laurens recognized that Paine was an experienced secretary and that *Common Sense* was widely celebrated in France. Besides, the two had known each other for a couple of years and had gotten on well together. But if Laurens wanted Paine, many in Congress had other ideas. Some congressmen likely shared the sentiments of Sarah Bache, Benjamin Franklin's daughter. In January 1781 she told her father that "there never was a man less beloved in a place than Payne is in" Philadelphia. Paine had made enemies, she said, because he had "disputed with everybody." To that, she added: "the most rational thing he could have done would have been to have died the instant he had finished his Common Sense, for he never again will have it in his power to leave the World with so much credit."[52] Aware of the opposition to his being a part of the crucial mission, and unwilling to risk delaying Laurens's departure while the congressmen wrangled over him, Paine asked his friend to withdraw the invitation.

But Paine so badly wanted to make the trip that he agreed to pay his own way. He collected the back pay owed him by the assembly, sold nearly all his possessions, and settled his debts. Just prior to their departure, Laurens brought the Marquis de Lafayette and Chevalier de Chastellux, a French soldier and acclaimed author, to Paine's cramped quarters to meet his soon-to-be traveling companion. Chastellux noted that Paine's untidy apartment bore "all the attributes of a man of letters; a room pretty much in disorder, dusty furniture, and a large table covered with books lying open and half-finished manuscripts. His dress was in keeping with the room," he added. Chastellux applauded the "vivacity" of Paine's "imagination and the independence of his character," noting that he found him an "animated" conversationalist and all in all an "agreeable" individual. Soon thereafter Paine and Laurens were on their way. They stopped at army headquarters in New Jersey for a briefing by Washington, who told Laurens the "patience of the army" was "nearly exhausted" and the "people are discontented." A French loan, he added, was the only hope of breaking the military stalemate. After leaving Washington, the two travelers hurried to Boston, from which they sailed on the *Alliance* in mid-February. Paine's last letter before beginning the crossing was to Greene. "I leave America with the perfect satisfaction of having been to her an honest, faithful, and affectionate friend," he said, adding, "I go away with the hope of returning to spend better and more agreeable days with her than those which are past."[53]

General Greene was in South Carolina in February 1781 when Paine wrote that letter. The previous October, when he had met with Paine and urged him not to sail for England, Greene had been named Gates's successor as commander of the Continental army in the South. Soon thereafter he called on Jefferson in Richmond and gave him a list of things his army would need: ten thousand barrels of flour and five thousand of beef or pork; two hundred hogsheads of rum or brandy; one hundred wagons, each furnished with four horses and an experienced teamster; skilled workers from assorted trades; five thousand pounds in specie; and an entire corps of militia adequately supplied for a winter campaign. He additionally told Jefferson that Virginia must furnish three thousand men to the Continental army. Greene added that he had appointed General Friedrich Steuben to command the Continentals in Virginia and drill the state's troops. Jefferson was staggered by Greene's shopping list, but he set to work to find what he could. After securing the assembly's authorization to confiscate civilian property, Jefferson—perhaps America's most prominent exponent of weak government—announced that if need be, he would "provide cloathing and blankets for the troops by seizing" them.[54]

Since 1778, each of Greene's three predecessors in the southern theater had failed, but a sliver of hope could be found when he arrived in North Carolina to take command. During the scorching summer of 1780, in the aftermath of Charleston's fall, bands of rebel guerrilla fighters had formed in the South Carolina upcountry. These mounted troopers moved rapidly, emerging from nowhere to strike small detached British parties and waylay enemy supply trains. Their work completed, they just as suddenly disappeared into the fastness of dark swamps, thick forests, and tall green hills. Before summer ended, Cornwallis reported that the "whole country" was "in an absolute state of rebellion." Within ninety days, he had lost 1,000 men, 15 percent of the army that Clinton had left with him. Some were lost at Camden, but much of the attrition was due to the partisan war. Cornwallis's situation soon worsened. Though ordered by Clinton not to leave South Carolina until the state was fully pacified, Cornwallis at the brink of autumn took 2,200 men into North Carolina in hopes of finding Tory volunteers and of checking the flow of supplies southward to the partisans. He marched into disaster. In October, about the time that Paine was contemplating a voyage to England, one-half of Cornwallis' army was isolated and defeated in the Battle of King's Mountain. Cornwallis had lost another 1,200 men. It was that debacle that had led Cornwallis to summon General Leslie from Virginia, cutting short his destructive raids.[55]

Jefferson's focus at that juncture was on doing what he could "to keep the war from our own country." That hope ended on the last day of 1780. A courier in Virginia's express system brought the governor word that a flotilla of twenty-seven vessels had been spotted in the Chesapeake. Twice that fall Washington had written to alert Jefferson that an armada was sailing "Southward" from New York, though its destination was unknown. Jefferson was reluctant to summon the militia to service yet again. Militiamen been called to duty four times since the spring. Not only was it expensive to call up the militia, but as recent mutinies indicated, it could be dangerously unpopular to wrench men away from home and hearth—all the more so if the emergency proved to be yet another false alarm. Leaders in wartime often have to make decisions based on hunches. In this instance, Jefferson guessed that the British would not dispatch another force of raiders so soon after Leslie's departure, and he did not muster the militia. He guessed wrong, and Virginia was utterly unprepared for what was coming. That was bad enough, but Jefferson compounded his mistake by inexplicably failing to act for fifty hours after the courier brought word of the fleet in the Chesapeake. Jefferson claimed to have bided his time as he sought to learn whether the ships carried friend or foe, but a better explanation might be that he was frozen with indecision at a moment when a rapid response was imperative.[56]

The squadron carried foes, a newly created force of Tories commanded by Benedict Arnold, who had been rewarded for his treason with the rank of brigadier general and compensation that today would be the equivalent of around one million dollars. More than 1,600 green-clad soldiers in Arnold's American Legion were scattered among the fast-approaching armada of frigates, sloops, brigs, and transports. By the time Jefferson finally acted, Arnold's force had entered the James River and was within five miles of Williamsburg. Jefferson called 4,600 militiamen to arms and ordered most to gather in Richmond, now Virginia's capital. Arnold got there first. Six days after Jefferson had been notified of the armada's approach, some 900 of Arnold's infantry and cavalry disembarked under a gloomy winter sky in Richmond and nearby Westham, the site of a foundry. As Jefferson watched through a spyglass from atop a knoll across the river, Arnold's Tory marauders sowed destruction and captured six field artillery pieces, nearly forty vessels, large and small, and extensive stockpiles of grain. Nor was this the only damage spread by Arnold. While one of his divisions plundered Richmond, another pillaged James River plantations and liberated slaves. Arnold's devastating sweeps ended quickly. Within a week after arriving in Virginia, Arnold, as ordered, had put his army into winter quarters in Portsmouth. Presumably, he would strike again when the weather permitted.[57]

In the wake of the calamity, Jefferson's enemies in Virginia—new and old—assailed him, branding him lethargic and neglectful. Old friends, including Patrick Henry, turned on him. Edmund Pendleton told Washington that Jefferson had not been "sufficiently attentive" to his duties. Steuben advised the commander that a good governor would have had the state better prepared for the raid. Jefferson claimed to have been the victim of poor intelligence. Washington had on occasion made such a claim. He always got away with it. No one believed Jefferson.[58]

Jefferson's future in politics was suddenly uncertain, though he had five months remaining as governor, and Virginia, as never before, faced imminent danger. Not only was the American Legion still in the state, but the British high command soon dispatched a force of regulars under General William Phillips, one of the British officers that Jefferson had entertained at Monticello. (Jefferson, in fact, had sent a friendly missive to Phillips three weeks after becoming governor in which he reflected on his fond memories of their once "agreeable circle.") Now Phillips, long since released from captivity, was to supplant Arnold as commander of a force of more than three thousand enemy soldiers on Virginia soil. In February, near the time that Laurens and Paine sailed for France, Washington tried to help Virginia by ordering the Marquis de Lafayette, with twelve hundred Continentals, to the state. At very nearly the same moment, General Greene advised Jefferson that before long Cornwallis would probably invade Virginia.[59]

All the while, Jefferson was confronted with baffling choices and the most difficult decisions. Throughout the winter, Greene and Steuben bombarded him with calls for men and supplies. Washington joined in as well, appealing to Jefferson to be mindful of the "common cause" by sending still more men to North Carolina. "You will consider the necessity and act accordingly," Greene told Jefferson in the same vein, and as if to stir him into trying harder, he added that there were laurels to be won if the outcome of the war turned on Cornwallis's defeat in the South. When Steuben requested tents, kettles, clothing, tools, munitions, workers, boats, and wagons, Jefferson in a torrent of activity did his best to comply. But when Steuben leaned on him to seize horses from civilians, Jefferson refused, and he also shrank from requesting authority from the legislature to seize farmers' livestock.[60] Despite his earlier vow to confiscate civilian property, Jefferson now feared that such a heavy-handed approach would destroy what little spirit remained for waging war. What Jefferson did do was tell Congress, in language as diplomatic as possible, that it was "inconsistent" for Virginia to have dispatched abundant aid to the northern states during their crisis years before 1778 only to have those states now ignore the plight of their brethren below the Potomac. Complaining did little good.[61]

While Jefferson's spirits tumbled, Greene waged a brilliant campaign in the Carolinas during the first seventy-five days of 1781. Greene acted with a combination of prudence and daring not seen among Continental army generals in the long years since Washington's attacks on Trenton and Germantown. Greene's bold initiatives inflicted an unsustainable toll of casualties on the enemy. In mid-January, in a pitched battle at Cowpens, not far from King's Mountain, the rebels killed and captured some eight hundred enemy soldiers and a cornucopia of weaponry, ammunition, horses, and specie; American losses were merely 5 percent of those of its adversary. Thereafter, Cornwallis went after Greene, pursuing him in a futile race across North Carolina that depleted his own force. Cornwallis could not catch him, and Greene slipped into Virginia late in February. All the British commander had to show for his dogged chase was a further loss of manpower, as one-tenth of the soldiery present when the pursuit began were dead or unfit for duty when it ended. To this point, Greene had adhered to a Fabian strategy. But in March, he brought his army back into North Carolina for a showdown with Cornwallis, and in mid-month Greene's army fought the British at Guilford Courthouse. Greene had the numbers on his side, though the majority of his soldiers were militiamen and most of those under Cornwallis were regulars. The bloody fray, one of the more ghastly of the war, continued throughout a spring-soft afternoon, and when it ended, Greene had retreated and Cornwallis had won the field. But that was all that Cornwallis won. At day's end, the British had lost 532 men, a staggering 28 percent of those he had led onto the battlefield, and twice the number lost by Greene, who was more capable of replenishing his troops. Cornwallis had lost some 1,700 men in a bit over two months. In nine months of pitched battles and assorted actions against Carolina partisans since the capture of Charleston, roughly half the soldiers left to Cornwallis by Clinton had been lost.[62]

Right after the brawl at Guilford Courthouse, Greene told Jefferson that the enemy was hurting and American militiamen were turning out in record numbers. He also confided that he sensed the opportunity to score a major victory, but much depended on Virginia. "I have committed my life and reputation to your service," Greene said, and in effect he pleaded with Jefferson to be a leader and do what must be done in this emergency. With Jefferson's help, Greene went on, he could pin down Cornwallis in North Carolina, possibly even drive him back into South Carolina. In either case, it would keep "the war at a distance from you."[63]

Greene had a plan. Jefferson was to commit every man he could spare to act in concert with Lafayette in a campaign to tie down in Virginia the enemy forces under Generals Phillips and Benedict Arnold. But that was only a portion of the strategy Greene envisaged. He also wanted Jefferson to send two thousand additional militiamen to North Carolina. This would give Greene the needed manpower to attack Cornwallis. Many found Greene's strategy appealing. Lafayette endorsed it, Richard Henry Lee thought it would be "one of those master strokes," and George Weedon, now commander of Virginia's militia, believed it might "terminate the war."

However, Jefferson and his Council of State were filled with foreboding. Without a naval arm, they thought it improbable that Lafayette, together with Virginia militiamen, could prevent Phillips from taking his army to North Carolina to rendezvous with Cornwallis. It was even more likely, Jefferson reasoned, that with so many of the Old Dominion's militiamen deployed in North Carolina, Phillips would go on the offensive in Virginia. The result could be catastrophic. Lafayette's army might be annihilated; Virginia's militia might suffer a crushing defeat. To Jefferson's way of thinking, Greene's plan was less likely to score the long-sought decisive victory than to result in yet another American debacle in the South. Jefferson rebuffed Greene, and his decision sparked outrage. Steuben charged that Jefferson failed to understand the depth of America's crisis. Weedon privately carped that Jefferson had "not an idea beyond local security." An angry Greene raged that "Nothing can be more ruinous to the public welfare, and dangerous to the public safety" than a governor who lacked the boldness to risk acting to help a "continental plan." However, Lafayette who was on the scene and understood the Virginians' perspective, told Washington that "Jefferson has been too severely charged."[64]

The fracas increased Jefferson's bitterness. He felt abandoned by Washington and Congress. He had been left to make unsavory choices for his enervated and war-weary state. Yet again, Jefferson complained about the northern states turning a blind eye to Virginia's plight. The North's discordant behavior was all the more egregious considering that Great Britain's southern strategy—now nearly thirty months in operation—was a tacit admission that it no longer planned to campaign above the Potomac. "The Northern States are safe," said Jefferson. He privately questioned Washington's acumen as a strategist. For three long years Washington's army had sat idle outside Manhattan while the British plundered southern states. Washington, he thought, had a fetish about retaking New York, an obsession that he compared to Spain's fixation on regaining Gibraltar, and Jefferson predicted that America's commander would enjoy no more success than had several Spanish kings. Nor was Jefferson alone in telling Washington of the "distressed State" of affairs in Virginia or in apprising him that "the great scene of action" is the southern theater. James Monroe's uncle, Joseph Jones, wrote to the commander begging "your interposition" lest Virginia and all the southern provinces fall to Great Britain, and Richard Henry Lee implored Virginia's congressional delegation to inveigh Congress to order Washington to come south. In Washington and his army, said Lee, Virginia "can alone find the remedy" for preventing British victory.[65]

Jefferson's rancor increased when General Phillips swung into action in mid-April. Britain's commander in Virginia dispatched three heavily armed schooners and several smaller craft up the Potomac. They sailed unopposed and destroyed property, seized livestock, and liberated slaves, including seventeen of Washington's chattel at Mount Vernon. Three weeks later, Phillips struck up the James River in fourteen vessels. Accompanied by Arnold and 2,500 men, including cavalry, Phillips's force sowed what Jefferson called a "Circle of Depredation" from Williamsburg to Richmond. Jefferson wasted no time summoning the militia, but it was ineffective. In some places it responded slowly, and nearly everywhere the militiamen were poorly equipped, outnumbered, and outmatched by an enemy with cavalry and naval arms. The British wrought destruction in the vicinity of Williamsburg, burned shipyards on the Chickahominy River, torched vessels and tobacco warehouses in Petersburg and along the James River, and incinerated some two million pounds of tobacco up the James. Phillips planned the total devastation of Richmond, but on learning that Lafayette and his Continentals were marching on the capital to link up with militiamen already posted there, the British commander reconsidered and withdrew to Portsmouth to await orders.[66]

Jefferson had only a bit more than a month left to serve as governor when Phillips launched his strike. The governor was as exhausted as his sapped state. He was frustrated by the "Spirit of disaffection" that had taken hold of so many Virginians and pained by his powerlessness under the state constitution. But nothing gnawed at him more than the lack of help given Virginia, especially as the war "falls at present on Virginia only." He pleaded with Washington to bring his army to Virginia. The commander's presence, wrote Jefferson, would restore confidence to the point that the governor's only "difficulty would then be how to keep men out of the field." The war had taken its toll on Jefferson, and not only politically. Twice he had been compelled to flee the capital and on both occasions to send his wife and three daughters scurrying to safety into the backcountry. When his youngest daughter, four-month-old Lucy Elizabeth, died in mid-April, Jefferson would have been less than human had he not wondered if those arduous flights had proven fatal to the child's already precarious health.[67]

During Jefferson's final weeks in office, Virginia's plight worsened. Following the bloody encounter at Guilford Courthouse, Cornwallis had withdrawn to Wilmington, North Carolina, to rest his soldiers and refit his battered army. While there, Cornwallis wrestled with his choices. He could remain in North Carolina, return to South Carolina, or march his fourteen hundred men to Virginia. He chose the latter, acting on the assumption that in the southern theater an "offensive war . . . can be carried on" in Virginia alone, and that on entering the Old Dominion his army would swell to around five thousand men, as he would take command of Phillips's force. That might be sufficient to destroy Lafayette's little army and shut down the supply routes through which the partisan bands in the Carolinas were sustained, but Cornwallis advised General Clinton that to take "and keep possession of the country" would require "a considerable army." Without ample reinforcements, he continued, the "beginning might be successfull," but "the business would probably terminate unfavorably."[68]

Cornwallis set off with his rested army at the outset of May, crossed into Virginia during the second week of the month, and linked up with the redcoats already in the state on May 20. Cornwallis immediately sought to bring Lafayette to battle. But given the unfavorable odds, the young Frenchman wanted no part of it, and Cornwallis had no appetite for another grueling chase after another Continental army on the run. The British commander responded by dividing his force. He sent one division to Point of Fork, where the Rivanna and Fluvanna Rivers met to form the James, and where Virginia maintained supply depots. Having also discovered that the Virginia legislature had fled Richmond to meet in safer Charlottesville, just a stone's throw from Monticello, Cornwallis late in May dispatched 250 British legionnaires under Colonel Banastre Tarleton to ride hard for Albemarle County.

Virginia's legislature convened in Charlottesville on May 28, and among the tasks it faced was the selection of Jefferson's successor, as he had informed them that he planned to step down when his second term ended in seven days, on June 4. Jefferson spent the week at Monticello, where he tended to his correspondence, conferred with a visiting Kaskaskia sachem from the Illinois country, and met daily with assemblymen. On Sunday, his last full day in office, Jefferson closed the books on two years of nearly unremitting anguish.

Neither Jefferson nor the assemblymen knew that Colonel Tarleton and his green-clad horsemen were coming, and coming fast, toward Charlottesville.

Tarleton's troopers galloped seventy miles in twenty-four hours, and they would have captured the prizes they were after had it not been for John Jouett, a twenty-six-year-old native of Charlottesville who was tippling at the Cuckoo Tavern in Louisa when Tarleton's Tory cavalrymen thundered past. Realizing instantly that Virginia's officials were in dire peril, Jouett—something of a Paul Revere for the Old Dominion—leaped on his horse and outraced the enemy to Charlottesville.[69]

Jouett pounded loudly on Monticello's front door at about four thirty A.M. Jefferson dressed, posted trusted slaves as lookouts on the steep, winding road up to his hilltop home, ordered a carriage readied for his wife and daughters—who were to be taken to a friend's house fourteen miles away—stuffed some state papers in his saddlebags while burning others, and hid several household valuables. Though taken by surprise, Jefferson had known that such an emergency could happen and he likely had previously fashioned an escape plan. Sometime that morning, after the departure of his family, Jefferson climbed aboard Caractacus, a horse that some thought the fastest in the state, and fled into woods too thick for the sun to penetrate. Later—no one knows how much later—a party of some twenty enemy soldiers under Captain Kenneth McLeod arrived and burst into the residence. They found a slave or two, but not the governor. Jefferson had escaped, and so, too, had all but seven laggard assemblymen in town, who had been slow to run for their lives after Jouett sounded the alarm following his stop at Monticello.[70]

It later became a staple of partisan politics to portray Jefferson's flight as an act of cowardice, but he had plenty of company when it came to running to avoid capture. Samuel Adams and John Hancock bolted from Lexington as the British army approached on the first day of the war, every congressman twice fled enemy armies bearing down on Philadelphia, more than once legislators and members of Revolutionary councils in several states scurried for safety, and General Washington and his army retreated on numerous occasions. All acted prudently. Capture meant a lengthy confinement in a British prison, and possibly worse.

Sometime during that unnerving June day, Jefferson rendezvoused with his family and began an arduous, and anxious, ride to a friend's residence some fifty miles away, never knowing whether he might encounter a party of British soldiers. He, Martha, and the children arrived tired and discomfited, but without incident. After five days, Jefferson gingerly returned home and, to his great relief, discovered that Monticello had been left intact. Only his wine cellar had been plundered by the British troops. Soon enough, however, he got the bad news that for ten days Cornwallis's army had encamped on his property on the James River, reducing it to "an absolute waste" before departing with about thirty of his slaves. Jefferson may also have learned that as a result of the British army's joint raids into the backcountry during his final hours as governor, Virginia had lost forty-three hundred stand of arms, twenty-three artillery pieces, and hundreds of barrels of power and food.[71]

Additional weeks passed before Jefferson brought Martha and the children home. By then, and probably long before, he had decided to take a "final leave" from public life.[72] At age thirty-eight, Jefferson's political career appeared to have come to an end. He had no interest in any government post. It is not clear what Jefferson intended, save for a comfortable life at Monticello surrounded by his family, though he may have contemplated doing as Benjamin Franklin and Thomas Paine, at about the same age, had done. It is conceivable that Jefferson envisaged a life at least partially devoted to writing, authoring an occasional essay or book on some scientific or philosophical matter, or on some political issue of the moment.

But one political matter required his immediate attention. A few days after Tarleton's raid, the legislature reconvened in Staunton. In the wake of yet again having had to take flight, and perturbed by their close brush with being taken prisoner, the assemblymen were in a fever for retribution. The assembly voted to investigate what it called Jefferson's "Catalogue of omissions, and other Misconduct," especially his performance over the past nine months commencing with Leslie's incursion. The inquiry was scheduled to take place during the assembly's fall session. Hurt and angry, Jefferson was grimly suspicious that a witch hunt was being concocted by those who sought to settle old scores or wished to ruin a future rival. Patrick Henry was a major player in the assembly's action, and ever after Jefferson looked on him as a disloyal former friend.

Vowing to be present during the probe in order to defend himself, Jefferson stood for reelection to the assembly and won. He was in his seat when the assembly convened in Richmond deep into the fall of 1781, and ready for the fight of his life. Jefferson seethed with cold resentment. But the inquiry never materialized. Those who had been his vocal accusers in June remained silent in December, possibly because of Jefferson's presence or maybe as they thought it not worth their trouble to go after a man who appeared to have no future in politics. In addition, the acrid passions of the spring had waned with the passage of time, especially as the war had taken a favorable turn between late spring and autumn. Even though there was no inquiry, Jefferson took the floor and spoke in his own defense. He read the charges and answered each allegation. When he was done, the legislature by a unanimous vote fulsomely thanked him for his service as governor and removed from the record "all *former* unmerited Censure." Vindicated, Jefferson immediately resigned and left for home, cherishing the ambrosial belief that throughout what remained of his life he would enjoy the "independence of private life."[73]

The war turned in the allies' favor during the weeks after Jefferson left office, in part because of Colonel Laurens's successful mission to France, an undertaking that culminated on very nearly the same day that Tarleton's horse soldiers rumbled into Charlottesville. The trip had not gotten off to a good start. Paine, who had barely survived his previous ocean crossing in 1774, had another close brush with death on this voyage. On the fifth night out of Boston, the *Alliance* was suddenly rocked by what Paine described as a "tremulous motion" that was "attended with a rushing noise." The captain and crew thought the vessel had somehow run aground, but in fact it was "surrounded with large floating bodies of ice against which the ship was beating." To make matters worse, the wind had begun to blow at gale force. The captain's only choice was to "lay the ship and let her take her chance." Two hours into the terrifying tempest, the "larboard quarter gallery was torn away" only a minute after Laurens had exited it. For seven hours on that stygian night, Paine and his fellow passengers were "plunging in an unguided ship to we knew not where." Suddenly, at four A.M., Paine later recollected, all on board heard the "agreeable noise of the water round the sides of the ship and felt her roll easily, which to us were tokens of escape and safety."[74]

After twenty-three days at sea, the voyagers alighted in L'Orient. Laurens hurried to Paris, but Paine traveled to Nantes for a bit of sightseeing. He arrived unkempt and unclean, and suffering from a dermatitis likely caused by vermin that infested the *Alliance*. Elkanah Watson, a somewhat priggish New Englander who was in France as an employee of a Rhode Island mercantile firm, met Paine on his arrival and served as a translator during a little ceremony arranged by Nantes's mayor, a devotee of *Common Sense* who was euphoric at the visit of such a famous individual. (Three years earlier, John Adams on his arrival in France had discovered that *Common Sense* was "received in France and in all of Europe with rapture.") The haughty Watson took an instant dislike to Paine, calling him "coarse and uncouth in his manners . . . and a disgusting egotist." Nevertheless, he saw to it that the grimy traveler got a hot bath—"he was nearly par-boiled," according to Watson—and clean clothes. Paine soon made the trek from Nantes to Paris, accompanied by Jonathan Williams, a merchant and relative of Benjamin Franklin's. Williams's impression of Paine could not have been more different from that of Watson. "I confess I like him as a Companion because he is pleasant as well as a sensible man," said Williams.[75]

While Laurens carried on negotiations in Paris and Versailles, Paine lived in Passy, the Paris suburb where Franklin resided. Paine played no role in Laurens's negotiations. He occasionally traveled into the city, possibly to make contact with like-minded Frenchmen whom Franklin had tipped him off to. He appears to have also spent considerable time with Franklin, the American minister to France, who was somewhat incapacitated from a recent episode of gout. It was a difficult time for Franklin, and not just with regard to his health. He was profoundly hurt when Congress ignored him, turning instead to Laurens to seek the loan. Paine, who was all too experienced in having suffered what he once called the "faults, follies, prejudices and mistakes" of Congress, commiserated. Paine's six weeks in the French metropolis, as well as his reasons for going in the first place, remain a mystery. Paine said only that he had tagged along as a "companion" to Laurens and because a stay in France would somehow present "a convenient opportunity to get out" his long-intended essay on inducing England to end the war. Neither was a convincing explanation for hazarding an Atlantic crossing in wartime. It may be that he hoped Franklin would retain him as his secretary or that he hoped to collect royalties in Paris from the sale of *Common Sense*. But with rumors swirling that France would drop out of the war after one more campaign, it is more likely that Paine envisaged writing a pamphlet to reanimate the French. He could gather information while living in France, much as his initial year in Philadelphia had been crucial in his preparation for writing *Common Sense*, and he might even make contact with French officials who would provide assistance, as France's minister to the United States had once offered to subsidize essays helpful to France.[76]

Prior to Laurens's arrival in France, Franklin had already secured a loan, but the young officer succeeded in obtaining even more. France was generous. The United States received the equivalent of £500,000 sterling, as well as clothing, ammunition, and sixteen thousand muskets. Before departing, Laurens went shopping with some of the money and purchased supplies for the Continental army. In late May, with the mission concluded and Laurens packing for the return home, Paine broke the news to his companion that he would not be accompanying him. He told Laurens that he could better serve the wartime United States by remaining in France, but Paine additionally confided that he simply had "no heart to return back" to America. The contempt with which he believed he had so often been treated, and the "hardships and difficulties" under which he had so long lived, had left him with jaded feelings for his adopted homeland.

In the end, Paine changed his mind and returned with Laurens. Paine later claimed that Colonel Laurens pleaded passionately for his company on the return voyage. So "pressing and excessive" were Laurens's entreaties, said Paine, that he relented. Almost everything that Paine subsequently said about this curious episode, from why he undertook the hazards of an ocean crossing to why he changed his mind about returning to Philadelphia, stretches credulity. In all likelihood, whatever he had hoped to find in France had proven illusory. Early in June—just as Jefferson's term as governor was ending—he and Laurens boarded *La Résolute* and set off for America.[77]

Eager to get the money to General Washington as quickly as possible, Laurens and Paine had hoped for a rapid crossing. Though their trip was free of death-defying excitement, they were at sea for a dreadful eighty-six days. Some eight months passed between Paine's departure from Philadelphia and his return, but when he reached the city in mid-September 1781 he discovered an altered military situation. "I think we are now in the fairest way we have ever yet been," he exclaimed, and he foresaw that "full success" was possible.[78]

No major fighting had occurred that summer, but transformative events had nonetheless taken place. In May, Washington had met in Connecticut with the commander of the French army in North America, Comte de Rochambeau. The purpose of the meeting had been to plan the campaign of 1781. Much to Rochambeau's disgust, the intransigent American commander had insisted on trying to retake New York. The French general thought Washington's idea untenable. The city was too well fortified to be taken in an attack, and so well stocked with provisions after Britain's five-year occupation that a siege operation was doomed to fail. Rochambeau was blunt, at times speaking to his counterpart in a tone that no one had dared in years to use with him, but Washington would not budge. As he had been ordered by Versailles to consent to whatever Washington wanted, Rochambeau relented, agreeing that the allies would target New York City that summer.[79] However, the moment that Washington departed, Rochambeau covertly urged Admiral François de Grasse, commander of France's navy in North American waters, to bring his fleet not to New York but to Virginia. Rochambeau had his eye on scoring a decisive victory over Phillips's army of 3,500. It was later that Rochambeau learned of Cornwallis's arrival in Virginia, and still later that he became aware that Clinton had sent reinforcements to Virginia. Cornwallis was ensconced at Yorktown, near Williamsburg, on the peninsula between the York and Rappahannock Rivers. His army, having now swelled to 7,000 men, had taken up residence there soon after leaving Jefferson's James River property, and he was busily seeking to make it a "safe defensive post."[80] By early summer, it was Cornwallis's large army that was in Rochambeau's crosshairs, for he glimpsed the possibility of a truly decisive allied victory if de Grasse did in fact reach the Chesapeake.

In mid-August, about ten days before Laurens and Paine finally came ashore in Boston, the allied commanders learned that de Grasse's fleet was in the Chesapeake. The armies under Washington and Rochambeau marched immediately for Virginia, lumbering through New Jersey in a choking dust and making the now-familiar laborious crossing of the Delaware. Less than a week before Paine arrived back in the city, the allied armies paraded through Philadelphia. Thereafter, in the course of their heat-laden march through the rural countryside south of Philadelphia, Washington and Rochambeau learned that de Grasse, with a decisive superiority of warships, had defeated a British fleet in what came to be known as the Battle of the Virginia Capes. The victory gave de Grasse control of the Chesapeake. Cornwallis could no longer escape by sea. Before setting off for Virginia, Washington had ordered Lafayette to do everything he could to keep Cornwallis bottled up in Yorktown, preventing his escape to North Carolina.[81] It was getting on to late September when the allied armies, with some nineteen thousand men, reached Yorktown. They found that Lafayette had done his job. Cornwallis's escape routes by land and sea were closed. His army was doomed. The full success that Paine had thought possible was, in fact, certain.

Early in October, the allies launched a siege operation. Its outcome was "reducible to calculation," Rochambeau told Washington, a novice at sieges. Soon it was clear that Rochambeau was spot-on. "We have got [Cornwallis] in a pudding bag," exclaimed one American soldier, while another boasted that the Allies had "holed [Cornwallis] and nothing remained but to dig him out." Hour after hour through day and night, Cornwallis and his men, now living a mole-like existence, were subjected to a shuddering, deafening bombardment. Closely following the news in Philadelphia, Paine said that Cornwallis had been "nabbed nicely," and indeed he had. On October 19, six and one-half years to the day since the war began on the village green at Lexington, Massachusetts, Cornwallis's army paraded in their gaudy red uniforms to the field of surrender and laid down their arms. A few weeks later, Lord North's government fell from power. The end that Paine had envisaged bringing about through his pen had been accomplished by arms at Yorktown.[82]

Jefferson had spent a lonely summer and fall, isolated and largely ignored. Few old friends had written, and none had offered to help during the assembly's scheduled investigation of his conduct as governor. Feeling deserted and forsaken, Jefferson told a relative that "nothing will ever more separate me" from "my farm, my family and books." His sorrow and resentment evident, Jefferson wrote to Lafayette of his hope that the "independence of private life" would "yield [him] that happiness" that he had not found in public service. So embittered was Jefferson, and so lasting were the deep and painful memories of his two years as governor, that when he wrote his memoirs forty years later, he devoted fourteen pages to his year in Congress that culminated with the Declaration of Independence, but only a single sentence to his two years as Virginia's wartime governor.[83]

Nevertheless, Jefferson was justly proud of his Revolutionary War service. In time, he boasted that his Declaration of Independence had captured the "tone and spirit" necessary for establishing the new nation and waging a desperate war. As an assemblyman, moreover, he had not only eliminated the "many very vicious points" encoded in Virginia law "under the regal government," but he had secured reforms that eradicated "every fibre . . . of ancient or future aristocracy" within the state's political system. Jefferson was keenly aware of the dangers he had faced and of his grinding toil in "defend[ing] our fanes and fire-sides from the desolations of an invading enemy." Invidious tongues had savaged him for his refusal to consent to Greene's stratagem for destroying Cornwallis, but the victory at Yorktown six months later was greater than anything that could have been won back in the spring, and it came about when Washington at last brought his army southward, as Jefferson had so often requested. Jefferson wished only for a proper recognition of the sacrifices he had made, the grief he had endured, the difficult decisions he had made, and the wisdom of his judgment in calling on Washington and Congress to focus on the war in the South. However, he kept his anguish under wraps, though it eddied out ever so briefly in one sentence to his young protégé James Monroe. On learning of Cornwallis's surrender, which surely meant a victorious end to the war, Jefferson said, "As an American, as a Virginian, I . . . covet as large a share of the honor in accomplishing so great an event." But he knew that his was a forlorn wish.[84]

Jefferson's agony ran deep, though he did have family and fortune to fall back on. Paine had nothing. Unemployed and penniless, his future appeared more bleak than ever. With the war apparently won, he did not even have a cause to write about. He approached the president of Congress about a paid position. He was met with deafening silence. Paine had not wanted to return to an America that had shown him such "thankless treatment." But he was back, shunned yet again and with insufficient resources to live on or to book passage for a return to France. Late in 1781 Paine wrote to Washington begging for help. He had "generously and honorably" served America's cause, he reminded the commander, and he had hoped "she would deal the same by me." He knew not where to turn, he said, save to "disclose myself to one who can sympathize with me."[85]

CHAPTER 5

"THE TIMES THAT TRIED MEN'S SOULS, ARE OVER"

PEACE AND NEW DEPARTURES

As 1781, that bleakest of years for Paine and Jefferson, ebbed away, neither could imagine the profound changes that soon would occur in their lives. Paine would shortly be hobnobbing with old foes, and it would not be long before both he and Jefferson would leave the United States. At the close of 1781, James Monroe was also at loose ends. Throughout that epic year, Monroe had chased after a field command, eager for action, avid to fight in defense of Virginia, lusting for military glory. On two occasions, in June and in September, he had unsuccessfully approached the Marquis de Lafayette about a post in the Continental force the latter commanded in Virginia. As the allied armies gathered for the siege of Yorktown, Monroe sought a command position in Virginia's militia, but that bid failed as well. Instead of being a part of the force that would compel Cornwallis to surrender, Monroe was at home anguishing that he "liv'd a very sedentary life" far from the fight and the laurels that others would reap. He continued his legal studies, but dreamed of traveling to France, thinking it might provide him with helpful "acquirments" for getting ahead as a lawyer or in politics. With the war seemingly near an end, Monroe was unsure which way to turn. But as was true of Paine and Jefferson, Monroe's life would soon be reshaped.[1]

Paine had written to General Washington for help almost as soon as the siege guns fell silent at Yorktown, and the commander was more than willing to assist. He was grateful for all that Paine had done for him and the cause, and he thought so gifted a writer might be helpful in overcoming what he saw as the thorny problems that plagued the new nation and its army. While the Continental army went into winter quarters in New York following Cornwallis's surrender, Washington came to Philadelphia late in November and remained there for five months. Early in his stay, Washington on two separate occasions brought up Paine's plight with Robert Morris, hardly a friend of the writer. But Morris, now the United States superintendent of finance, also thought Paine might be useful. Besides, he had met Paine and seemed to like him. They were the about same age and both were English immigrants who had come a long way from their once-obscure statuses. In February, at a wine-soaked meeting attended by Morris, Washington, Robert R. Livingston, who was the secretary of foreign affairs, and Gouverneur Morris, who was the assistant superintendent of finance, Paine was offered an annual salary of eight hundred dollars (more than sixty-five thousand dollars in today's money) for writing newspaper essays championing revenue-raising measures supported by Morris's friends in Congress. Paine had once vowed never to prostitute himself as "a hireling writer," but he accepted the terms.[2]

All parties to the agreement wanted the same thing: money and a stronger national government. As far as money was concerned, Paine was desperate for a livable income. Washington feared that his unpaid and destitute soldiers would mutiny again and abandon the cause before peace was negotiated. Morris wanted money so that the restless holders of federal securities could be paid their interest, solidifying their commitment to the national government. All three recognized that a stronger government was needed to safeguard the postwar United States and its interests. Adequate funds were wanting because Congress had no power to tax under the Articles of Confederation. It could only requisition money from states exhausted by the war and consumed with provincial matters. Morris and his allies in Congress thought the immediate solution was an impost, a revenue tariff on imported goods. Their plan was for the impost to raise money for paying the bondholders while the states, through the taxes they levied on their citizenry, tended to the army and their own accumulated war debts. Congress, in 1781, had sent to the states for ratification an amendment to the Articles vesting Congress with the authority to levy a 5 percent impost. Under the bargain that Morris and Paine reached, Morris pledged to never seek private or "selfish" gains from what Paine would be asked to write. Having publicly championed an impost nearly eighteen months earlier—and like Washington and Morris apprehensive about the fragility of the inchoate American union—Paine was comfortable with that part of the bargain. Paine also agreed to try to persuade the states "to grant sufficient taxes," advocate strengthening Congress's power of taxation, "prepare the minds of the people for . . . taxes and imposts," and trumpet the "bravery" and "good conduct" of soldiers, officers, and civil officials.[3]

It may seem puzzling that Paine, who had vilified the colossal power and reach of Great Britain's central government, would be an advocate for strengthening America's national government. Yet as far back as *Common*

Sense he had stressed the need for a "continental form of government" that could protect against foreign threats and civil wars, and he had urged those in authority in the thirteen revolutionary governments to remember "that our strength is continental, not provincial." In 1780, when Paine first turned his attention to the need for revenue, he had urged federal control over all the "vacant western territory," arguing that the sale of western lands would provide the national government with the funds it needed for waging the war. As the nation's economic woes mounted, Paine observed that "a link [is] wanting in the chain of union." The missing link was a strong national government. Above all, Paine wanted the American Revolution to succeed. His considerable vanity burning brightly, Paine told Morris that he ranked himself "among the founders of a new Independent World." He spared Morris his most fervent hope—that the newly independent, republican United States would survive and flourish, and that its success would spawn republican revolutions in England and Europe.[4]

The ink was hardly dry on the accord that Paine had signed before he rushed into print both a series of newspaper essays and *The American Crisis* XI. For some of his work, Paine was paid by the French minister to the United States, a step he may have taken without the knowledge of Washington and Morris, though not much escaped their attention. What Paine wrote served the interests of both France and the United States, for his ultimate goal was to assure that Americans did not let down their guard. Cornwallis's surrender, Paine cautioned, must not result in the "delusive hope" that "the business is done." The war would continue until a peace treaty was negotiated and ratified. In May 1782, when *The American Crisis* essay appeared, great uncertainty existed within the American government as to Britain's intentions. Paine took the tack that London's game—its worst "act of baseness" thus far, he charged—was to "seduce America" into believing that Britain was desperate for peace and the war was all but over. He warned that Britain's leaders were "Beaten, but not humble; condemned, but not penitent; they act like men trembling at fate and catching at a straw." Britain's king, whom Paine charged with having committed a "crime" in making war on Americans, now in his "ignorance and obstinacy" wished to continue the fight.

Paine exhorted his readers to remember that "we [must continue to] feed, clothe, arm, provide for, and pay an army sufficient for our defence." That could be done only if each state met its taxation quota set by Congress. At its heart, Paine's message affirmed what Washington had long said: Salvation could come only through a collective effort. The Revolutionary War, Paine reiterated, was the "war of the people . . . not the war of Congress," and to this he added: "The union of America is the foundation of her independence, the rock on which it is built."⁵

These were Paine's first publications in nearly two years, and they lacked the verve of much that he had written previously. But during the summer he recaptured his spark, producing what he regarded with considerable justification as his most important work since *Common Sense*. He wrote in response to a history of the American Revolution written by Abbé Raynal, a veteran French author, journalist, and historian, who had depicted the uprising as a rebellion by colonists who had come of age and sought nothing more than to be independent of their mother country. Many historians since then have seen the American Revolution in a similar light, but Paine—like Jefferson and Monroe—did not share that outlook. Morris put Raynal's history in Paine's hands and may have encouraged him to respond, though Paine required no arm-twisting. He had long planned to write his own history of the Revolution, and though he still said the time was not right for such an undertaking, Paine believed the moment was right for setting the record straight about the meaning of the American Revolution. Morris, praying that Paine's pen still had magic in it, must have hoped that the writer could reawaken the sacrificial passion that *Common Sense* had helped ignite.

Paine's *Letter to the Abbé Raynal* opened with a lengthy explanation of the colonial insurgency. It had begun as a "political revolution." Born in the face of British "despotism" and "insolent severity," the rebellion—which the colonists had neither sought nor wanted—had been carried forward in defense of "the Americans' most precious and sacred rights." Those rights were subsequently embodied in the republican governments that came into being with independence. Paine moved on to the gutsy decision to resist by arms a superpower "against which more formidable nations had failed." Wars in Europe were the wars of kings, and were waged for the benefit of royalty and aristocracy. Not in America. "This war is the public's war—the country's war. It is *their* independence that is to be supported; *their* property that is to be secured; *their* country that is to be saved. Here, Government, the army, and the people, are mutually and reciprocally one." His account of hostilities was little more than a succinct recounting of General Washington's heroic Trenton-Princeton campaign and the briefest of nods toward Nathanael Greene's brilliant generalship in the South.

The most memorable portion of the *Letter* was Paine's appraisal of the effects of the American Revolution. The American people, he wrote, had been transformed by the long, cruel struggle against Britain. "Our style and manner of thinking have undergone a revolution more extraordinary than the political revolution of the country. We see with other eyes; we hear with other ears; and think with other thoughts." Americans were once another people. But in escaping the "shackles" that restrained their thinking as English colonists, they "enjoy a freedom of mind" that enables them to "combat and expel" the "prejudice[s]" of their royalist past. The Revolution had truly been the birthday of a new American world. England, in contrast, remained unchanged, and it faced "decay" and "decline." Only a "total reformation" could change its fate. Like the United States, England could acquire "an expanded mind" and "a heart which embraces the universe," leading it to "renounce forever those prejudiced inveteracies" that for so long had sowed misery among her own people and countless numbers abroad. If England was to be reformed, it must be done by Englishmen, and likely by Englishmen who had been inspired by the American Revolution, which held the promise of "opening a new system of extended civilization." Should that occur, it would be one more reason why the American Revolution would "receive from heaven the highest evidence of approbation."[6]

In the early going, Paine consulted with Washington and Morris about the line he planned to take in each essay, once even inviting them to his tiny and unkempt apartment "to spend part of an Evening . . . and eat a few oysters or a crust of bread and cheese," and to listen to what he had "been turning over in" his mind.[7] Both accepted his invitation. Early on, too, one or both read the drafts of some of Paine's manuscripts, and on at least one occasion the author revised what he had written so that it would be amenable to his paymaster.

That routine was short-lived, and at least in one instance Paine might have saved himself some heartburn had he consulted others. Weeks after his cautionary springtime essays about a false peace being dangled before Americans, news arrived that Lord North's ministry had collapsed and been replaced by a government that was prepared to negotiate. As the year progressed, Paine became aware that talks between the belligerents were under way in Paris, but he also heard the rumors buzzing in Philadelphia that Britain would make peace only on terms of a more autonomous America remaining within the British Empire. In an effort to persuade war-weary America to spurn any accord that did not recognize American independence, Paine hurried *The American Crisis* XII into print. Warning that London's promises could not be trusted, Paine in his incandescent prose pleaded with his readers to never forget what Britain's leaders had done. They had sowed "wanton destruction" and committed acts of "insolent barbarity" throughout America. "We can look round and see the remains of burnt and destroyed houses. . . . We walk over the dead whom we loved . . . and remember by whom they fell. There is scarcely a village but brings to life some melancholy thought, and reminds us of what we have suffered, and of those we have lost by the inhumanity of Britain." America "is already independent," Paine told his readers, and the peace treaty must preserve America's independence. The essay was well received in the states, though Benjamin Franklin, one of America's four peace commissioners, feared that what Paine had written might make his job more difficult. Thinking the essay could not have appeared at a worse time, Franklin apologized to his British counterparts for Paine's "rude" remarks about British officials. But if Franklin was displeased, General Nathanael Greene, who had spent years fighting the British, was delighted. Greene exclaimed to Paine: "Your name, from your writings, will live immortal."[8]

Throughout 1782, the proposed impost amendment—which under the Articles required ratification by all thirteen states—seemingly made its way toward becoming law. Toward year's end only Rhode Island's consent was needed. Alas, it spurned the amendment, mostly from unwillingness to surrender to Congress any authority to enact—and collect—taxes. Congress quickly implored Rhode Island to reconsider, and Paine joined in with six essays. In an argument that was indistinguishable from Parliament's prewar insistence on supervising imperial trade, Paine stressed that the common good was morally of greater consequence than the provincial good. The United States could survive only if the states recognized that America's commerce must be subject to the "regulation and protection" of "the confederated patronage of all the States." If the American union failed, he warned, all the benefits won by the American Revolution would be lost. In this crisis, as in the war crises, Paine did more than write essays. In December, with Morris's financial backing, he made a long, cold horseback ride across the barren winter landscape from Philadelphia to Providence. His hope was to appeal directly to old acquaintances who once had been part of the state's delegation in Congress, but it was quickly apparent that his mission was futile. Paine was hammered in the local press as a "mercenary writer" employed by those who hoped to enrich themselves, a not entirely untrue claim. Paine's mission did not just fail; it proved to be unnecessary. While in Providence, he learned that Virginia had repealed its earlier ratification of the amendment. The impost was dead.[9]

As bleak as matters seemed when Paine saddled up for the ride home, he and good news reached Philadelphia at about the same moment at the dawn of spring. A preliminary peace treaty had been negotiated in Paris. Not only had Britain recognized American independence, but nearly every term in the accord was generous. The treaty had to be approved by the respective governments, but Paine and most other Americans believed that "the war is now happily and prosperously closed" and that Britain's army would withdraw from the United States.[10]

Paine greeted the news of impending peace with *The American Crisis* XIII, the final installment in the series. Timing its publication to coincide with the eighth anniversary of the day the war began, Paine struck a more reflective and personal tone than he had in any other piece, though this essay also contained an unmistakable message for the times. He began by borrowing from—and modifying—the memorable line that had launched his initial *American Crisis* essay in 1776: " 'The times that tried men's souls,' are over—and the greatest and completest revolution the world ever knew, gloriously and happily accomplished." He pondered neither the events of the Revolution nor its war, perhaps because after answering Abbé Raynal it would have been redundant to do so. Or he may have held back from fear of stealing the thunder from his planned history of the American Revolution. Or maybe he meant what he said at the outset of the tract: sudden word of the peace settlement had been so "stunning" that it required "a gradual composure of the senses to receive it."

Breathing a sigh of relief that the "complicated dangers" that had dogged Americans for nearly twenty years were behind them, Paine argued that the preservation of the United States hinged on safeguarding what had been won. Having written in *Common Sense* that "We have it in our power to begin the world over again," Paine now wrote that it was "in our power to make a world happy" by exhibiting "a character hitherto unknown." To do so, however, America must have "importance abroad and security at home," ends that could be attained only through a "well and wisely regulated and cemented" Union. For the safekeeping of the Union—the "great palladium of our liberty and safety"—Paine wrote that "something must be yielded up," and that something was that each state must surrender ultimate sovereignty to a national government.

Both the war and *The American Crisis* series were closing, and with their conclusion the most important chapter in Paine's life to this point was coming to an end. Perhaps suspecting that he never again would have such a large audience, Paine meditated on what had drawn him to support the Revolution. He had been unable to remain silent in the face of British tyranny and the threat in 1776 of "an impossible and unnatural reconciliation" with Great Britain. But there was more: "It was the cause of America that made me an author." From the first he had believed that America's cause was "the great cause of mankind." Now, faced with a future more uncertain than ever, Paine closed the book on his role in the American Revolution: "whatever country I may hereafter be in, I shall always feel an honest pride at the part I have taken and acted, and a gratitude to nature and providence for putting it in my power to be of some use to mankind."[11]

* * *

The trying times brought on by the war may have been over, but when Paine wrote his final *Crisis* essay, Jefferson was coping with his greatest trial. In June 1781, at the end of his second term as governor, Jefferson had once again become a private citizen. Two months after laying down his burden—and about two months prior to the beginning of the siege at Yorktown—Jefferson learned that Congress wanted him to join the team of American commissioners abroad who might someday negotiate the peace treaty. He declined, pleading the necessity of getting his economic affairs in order after a two-year absence from Monticello. There were additional reasons that he did not go into. Not only did he want to confront his detractors in the Virginia legislature when it met in December, but also his unambiguous private remarks about never again wishing to hold public office may have been sincere. Declaring in confidence that he had been "cured of every principle of political ambition," Jefferson expressed his seasoned conviction that "public service and private misery [were] inseparably linked." His plan, and his wish, was to spend the remainder of his life "in mental quiet."[12]

During his first year at home, Jefferson spent some of his time writing *Notes on the State of Virginia*, his only book. He began the undertaking while governor, responding to an inquiry by a member of the French legation in Philadelphia. What Jefferson had originally envisaged as a lengthy private letter grew into a manuscript that would eventually be published in 1785. He seldom strayed from Monticello during its composition, and in April 1782—about the same time that Paine entered into the accord with Morris—Jefferson was visited by Chevalier de Chastellux, the French soldier who, with Colonel Laurens, had paid Paine a visit shortly before his voyage to France. Chastellux had liked Paine, but he was captivated by Jefferson. Describing his host as "tall and with a mild and pleasing countenance," Chastellux added that Jefferson was "never spoken of" in Virginia "without respect." Within two hours, Chastellux felt that he and Jefferson had been lifelong friends. Not only was Jefferson's conversation "always varied, always interesting," but Chastellux was astounded by the breadth of Jefferson's interests and knowledge. They conversed deep into the night on myriad topics. When Chastellux departed, Jefferson accompanied him for sixteen miles and apologized for not riding farther, explaining that Martha was eight months pregnant and he did not want to be away from home for even one night.[13]

This was Martha's seventh pregnancy, her sixth in ten years with Jefferson, and she had experienced difficulties during earlier instances of childbearing. That she should never again have gone through the ordeal of bearing another child was immediately apparent. Soon after the birth of Lucy Elizabeth— the child was given the same name as the daughter born in 1780 who had lived barely one hundred days—Jefferson said his wife was "dangerously ill." Martha's health never improved, and four months later, on September 6, 1782, she died.

Jefferson had been deeply in love and happily married, and when he relinquished the governor's office he was looking forward to a long life at home with Martha and the children. Now, as Paine had twenty-two years earlier, Jefferson had lost his wife to the terrors of birthing a child. What Paine experienced when Mary Lambert lost her life has been lost in time, but Jefferson was consumed with grief at what he called "the catastrophe." His eldest daughter, Martha, also known as Patsy, later recalled "the violence of his emotion." Cast into a black depression, Jefferson did not leave his bedchamber for three weeks, and for a long, agonizing spell thereafter he would suddenly burst into tears and on occasion faint. Day after day, he spent hours in what Martha called "melancholy rambles, long and solitary horseback rides" about his estate. A month after his wife had been "torn from him"—as he inscribed on her tombstone—Jefferson said that life was "too burdensome to bear," and indeed some who were close to him feared that his bottomless despair might result in suicide. If he ever contemplated ending his life, his hand was stayed by what he said would be the "infidelity of deserting" his three daughters.[14]

Fearing the worst, Jefferson's friends thought he must abandon Monticello, with its gloomy memories. No one worked harder to persuade him to leave his grief-shrouded home than James Madison, Jefferson's young friend who had held a seat in Congress for the past three years. Two months after Martha's death, Madison prevailed on Congress to yet again ask Jefferson to join the peace negotiators in Paris. This time, Jefferson jumped at the opportunity. Just before Christmas, about one hundred days after his wife's death, Jefferson trekked to Philadelphia for the first time since 1776. He was in the city for about thirty days and probably met Alexander Hamilton, who was a member of Congress and close to Madison. He did not see Paine, as it was at this point that he was on his errand to Providence. At the end of January, commission in hand, Jefferson rode to Baltimore, from which he planned to sail for France. He booked passage on the *Romulus*, but adverse weather prevented its departure. During his weeklong wait for better weather, word of the preliminary peace arrived. Jefferson returned to Philadelphia to learn Congress's decision regarding his mission. This time, Jefferson spent some forty days in Philadelphia and in all likelihood encountered Paine, who returned from Rhode Island on March 20. Ultimately, with peace apparently assured, Congress released Jefferson from his commission. Soon thereafter, he left Philadelphia, though he was in no hurry to return home. He traveled to Richmond, where he probably sought to be added to the state's congressional delegation. He reached Monticello on May 15, five months after his departure.[15]

Jefferson's growing desire to return to public life was fueled in part by his wish to escape Monticello, though he was also eager to visit Europe, something he had first contemplated while in college. In addition, he remained ambitious and longed to rehabilitate the standing he had lost while Virginia's governor. The post in Europe would have been ideal, but if serving abroad was not in the cards, Jefferson welcomed a return to Congress, a step he would never have considered a few years earlier. But in 1783 a seat in Congress was more palatable. He had friends in Philadelphia, including many who, like him, were well versed in science and philosophy. What is more, with peace and true independence at hand, many contours of the new American nation were to be determined, and Jefferson, with his visionary yet orderly mind, was filled with ideas.

Following the arrival of word that he had been added to Virginia's congressional delegation, Jefferson returned to Philadelphia. But Congress was not in town. It was meeting instead in Princeton. Jefferson stayed just long enough to enroll Patsy, his eldest daughter, in school before he traveled to the tiny New Jersey college town. On arriving, however, he discovered that the peripatetic Congress intended to adjourn the next day and move to Annapolis. He was immediately on the road again. Finally, on November 25, 1783, he took his seat in Congress.[16]

It had been a year of anguish, misery, and frustration for Jefferson and Paine, and with the war coming to an end, both faced a future clouded with uncertainty. For the United States, much of 1783 had been similarly vexed and unsettled. Without revenue, it could not pay its soldiers and struggled to feed and clothe them. Mutinies, and the disintegration of the army, were distinct possibilities. With some twenty thousand British redcoats still in New York, the collapse of the Continental army would have been catastrophic. But tensions eased somewhat after April when an armistice mandated by the peace treaty went into effect. In June, with unrest becoming more widespread within the army, all but about eighteen hundred soldiers were furloughed and sent home. The pockets of the discharged were stuffed with a final paycheck signed by Robert Morris. In reality, the payment was a worthless IOU that the soldiers contemptuously called "Morris notes." Nevertheless, the sense of crisis receded. It ended entirely in September when it was learned that all sides had ratified the peace treaties.[17]

Paine had hardly been an active writer since turning out his final *American Crisis* piece in April. No longer under Morris's patronage, he had seldom been in Philadelphia, residing instead with his friends the Kirkbrides in Bordentown, New Jersey. He arose late, scoured the available newspapers, napped in the afternoon, and took a long daily walk that often ended at a tavern down the road. Paine's lack of productivity was not due entirely to indolence. He was felled in the autumn by scarlet fever. Quite ill for a week, Paine was feeble throughout a month's convalescence. However, as soon as he felt better, Paine—possibly inspired by Washington, who in the spring had authored two lengthy addresses urging that the national government be vested with greater powers—wrote an essay echoing the general. To "act as a nation," Paine wrote, the states (which he called a "medley of [thirteen] individual nothings") must surrender at least a portion of their sovereignty so that the United States government could become a "well-centered power" capable of advancing the national interest.[18]

When he was not sleeping or on a ramble, much of Paine's time was consumed by his quest for remuneration for his service in the American Revolution. He pleaded with several state legislatures or asked well-connected acquaintances to do so for him. Jefferson consented and appealed to the Virginia assembly to award Paine an annual pension, while Washington and Madison also requested some sort of benevolent gesture from that legislature. (Washington said that "poor Paine['s] . . . views are moderate" and he merely wished sufficient money to enable him to live in a "decent independency.") Their entreaties were in vain. Paine had better luck in Pennsylvania, which allotted him £500. New York was even more generous. It granted him a three-hundred-acre farm and farmhouse confiscated from a Tory in New Rochelle. Late in 1783, France's minister to the United States bestowed approximately $800 on Paine, with which he immediately purchased a modest house with seven acres of meadowland near the Kirkbrides in Bordentown.

Yet Paine remained grindingly poor and still at loose ends. Deep into middle age—he turned forty-eight at the outset of 1784—Paine was without an income or a cause. He told a friend that he felt like a prisoner with no future. As always, too, he seethed over the lack of recognition for which he hungered. Despite his belief that he had been one of the "founders of a New Empire," he felt ignored. He had sacrificed so much for the Americans, he fumed, and they had repaid him by taking little notice of his plight.[19]

Paine additionally poured his energy into a campaign for a pension from Congress and a position as the historian of the United States. He rehashed arguments that he had made in earlier appeals, though he also reminded the congressmen that whereas virtually every field-grade officer, high-ranking state official, and delegate to Congress "had estates and fortunes to defend . . . and now have them to enjoy," he had nothing. He had come penniless to this "troubled country" and, after years of toil and peril on behalf of America's cause, he remained impoverished. He might have become rich from the sales of *Common Sense*, but he had turned his back on its extraordinary earnings, thinking it the best way to show his commitment to "a just and good cause." He had written, soldiered, and at his own expense made a hazardous Atlantic crossing on behalf of that cause. Now the war had been won and he had nowhere to turn. He was neither a businessman nor a farmer. Appealing to Congress to redress the "cold conduct of America towards me," he asked for a pension of $6,000. Why he lit on that sum is a mystery, but the answer may be that as the French minister had paid him $800, he thought he was justified in asking for $800 for each of the eight years since 1776 that he had been active in America's cause. With that money, Paine told Congress, he would write three histories of the American Revolution, one that was a true account for adult readers, one tailored for children, and one that was to be earmarked for "Europe or the world." Congress did not act for two years. When it did, it gave Paine half the pension he had requested, but it did not hire him to write history.²⁰

Although Paine would have preferred a grander settlement, he had done remarkably well, especially given the indebtedness that choked the states and the national government. Remuneration for his services exceeded $4,000, about forty times what he might have earned annually had he continued to ply his trade as a skilled artisan. In addition, he received rent from a tenant on his New Rochelle farm. Thanks to a gift from Robert Morris, he also now owned a horse, Button, that he appears to have loved as much or more than any person.²¹

While Washington waited for the belligerents to assent to the peace accord, he continued to command what remained of the Continental army throughout 1783, imprisoned with duties that he longed to escape. He could not go home until the British army finally left the United States, and that was not going to happen until London ordered its departure. The British soldiers, now posted entirely in New York City, did not stir throughout the spring or summer. While they awaited orders, Congress—concerned about the nation's postwar defense needs—invited Washington to Princeton in August for consultation. Three weeks into his stay, the general wrote to Paine, who lived not far away, and invited him to come for a visit, adding: "I shall be exceedingly happy to see you." Though not given to flattery, Washington also forthrightly told Paine that he had "a lively sense of the importance of your Works." The general's invitation arrived during Paine's illness, but as soon as he was well, he rode to Princeton. Paine moved in with Washington at Rocky Hill, a large country farmhouse on a 320-acre estate dotted with orchards. He stayed for about two weeks, until Washington—having learned in mid-autumn that the British army would soon abandon New York—departed for West Point to rejoin his army.[22]

On November 25, Washington, with some eight hundred American soldiers—very nearly all that remained in the army—entered what the departing British commander persisted in calling "York Island." Paine may have been in New York that day. He may even have been among the civilian dignitaries who joined the soldiers for the grand victory parade down Broadway. All that is known for certain is that Paine was in the city during at least a portion of the nine days that Washington spent in Manhattan. During that stretch, Washington hosted, or was the guest, at one dinner and celebration after another. Whether Paine was invited to any of the festivities is unknown.[23]

Thereafter, all that remained for Washington was formally to resign as the army's commander. Deep into December, he rode to Annapolis, Congress's latest stop. Only one congressman had been a member of the Continental Congress in 1775 when Washington left that body to take command of the army. That was Jefferson, who had reentered Congress on the day of the army's victory parade through New York City. Congress hosted a dinner for Washington one night and a ball the next. It asked Jefferson to write the text of its acceptance of the general's resignation. Jefferson's statement declared that America's victory was due to Washington's leadership and perseverance, and to French aid. Washington, in his formal remarks, said that victory had come through the assistance he had received from Providence, his countrymen, and his officers. (He mentioned neither his soldiers nor his French ally.) With that, Washington left for home two days before Christmas in 1783. The long war had ended.[24]

More than ten weeks passed following Washington's resignation before Congress, which rarely had a quorum, took up any business. Nevertheless, Jefferson, thinking his days in Congress might be numbered should he be chosen for an overseas diplomatic assignment, spent the idle time tending to his committee duties. He drafted thirty-four reports in a bit over one hundred days, including a paper on the new nation's coinage, which Congress adopted in 1785. His most important work dealt with the West, which had suddenly become a matter of urgency. Settlers had been flooding across the mountains since the publication of the preliminary peace treaty, eager to acquire fertile land in the huge trans-Appalachian domain that the United States would gain in the accord. To maintain order, some form of governance was essential, and Jefferson was ready with a plan. He recommended the creation of several largely self-governing territories in which all adult white male residents were to have suffrage rights. In Jefferson's scheme, the national government was to have virtually no role in the governance of the territories. He additionally proposed that after 1800 slavery and indentured servitude were to be illegal in every territory. Congress eventually adopted most of his recommendations, although by a single vote it rejected a ban on slavery. "Heaven was silent in that awful moment!" he subsequently exclaimed.[25]

On May 7, Congress learned that John Jay, who together with Franklin and John Adams had been appointed to seek commercial treaties throughout Europe, was coming home. That same day Congress chose Jefferson as his successor. He did not tarry. Jefferson gathered Patsy in Philadelphia and the two hurried to Boston, hoping to join Abigail Adams, who was known to be planning to sail that summer to join her husband in Paris. Jefferson's hoped-for rendezvous with Abigail Adams did not pan out, but early in July he and his daughter sailed for France on the *Ceres*. It was the sort of voyage that travelers wished for, an uneventful three-week Atlantic crossing.[26] The *Ceres* set sail three years almost to the day since that dreadful morning when Jefferson had fled from the British soldiers galloping up the hill to Monticello. Now forty-one years old, Jefferson hoped the mission abroad would rehabilitate his reputation, but he also wished to experience Europe and—Jefferson being Jefferson—to broaden his horizons in every conceivable manner.

Jefferson left behind James Monroe, his sometime student and also his lodging mate, as the two had shared a house in Annapolis for six months while both served in Congress.[27] Monroe had almost simultaneously completed his legal studies and been elected to the Virginia legislature back in the spring of 1782, several weeks prior to Martha Jefferson's death. Monroe had struck his legislative colleagues as a man of merit, much as he had favorably impressed his superiors in the army. But in an assembly dominated by veterans who had risen to leadership positions before the war—including the likes of Patrick Henry, Edmund Pendleton, Edmund Randolph, and George Mason—Monroe, like every newcomer, was destined to be a backbencher. Besides, Monroe was distracted by the launch of his legal practice. In fact, Monroe regarded his service in the assembly as of such secondary importance that he would have resigned his seat and accompanied Jefferson to France had his patron been added to the team of America's peace commissioners early in 1783. But when Jefferson's first stab at becoming an envoy fizzled, Monroe stayed on, and soon enough his legislative colleagues elected him to the Governor's Council. He joined, among others, William Short, whom Jefferson would take with him to France as his secretary, and John Marshall, who, like Monroe, had soldiered and endured the winter at Valley Forge. Serving on the council enabled Monroe to play an influential role in the state's western policies.

Nothing could have been more agreeable to him, as through purchase and the award of bounty lands he had accumulated thousands of acres, chiefly in Kentucky.

After he had served just one year in the legislature, the assemblymen added the twenty-five-year-old Monroe to Virginia's congressional delegation on June 6, 1783, the same day it elected Jefferson. Monroe was delighted. He was "young & reputation is only to be acquir'd" through exemplary service in the highest offices, he told a friend. He added that James Madison "hath acquir'd more reputat[ion]n by a constant & laborious attendance upon Congress than he wod have done" had he remained in the state legislature. Confined to Virginia for the formalities of qualifying for the bar, Monroe did not take his seat in Congress until it was meeting in Annapolis in December, and he, too, was present when Washington surrendered his commission.[28] Once in Congress, Monroe became part of a distinguished team of Virginians. In addition to Jefferson, the delegation included the Lee brothers, Richard Henry and Arthur, and John Francis Mercer, whose career paralleled that of Monroe. They were the same age and had been college classmates. In addition, they had served together in the Third Virginia and both had suffered dangerous wounds in combat; both had also served as an aide to a general officer in the Continental army. Others in Congress included New Englanders Elbridge Gerry and Roger Sherman, who had signed the Declaration of Independence, and Maryland's James McHenry, a former soldier who would later serve in two presidential cabinets.

Young and politically inexperienced, Monroe was acutely aware that he had entered "a theatre to wh[ich] I am a perfect stranger." From the outset, he made clear that Jefferson was to be his pilot. Monroe felt that he was "under obligations to him." In addition, the "affection of my heart" disposed him to back everything his friend and mentor favored. When his patron set off for France, Monroe felt a keen sense of loss. "I very sensibly feel your absence . . . in the solitary situation in wh[ich] you have left me," he wrote to Jefferson. Monroe so missed Jefferson's guidance that he wrote to him half a dozen times seeking direction before finally learning that the *Ceres* had sailed. Monroe even wished to settle close to Monticello, and within weeks of Jefferson's departure he journeyed to Albemarle County to look for a suitable tract of land.[29]

Jefferson arrived in Paris in August 1784, beginning a five-year residence that in many ways appears to have been the happiest period of his life, save for his years with Martha and the children before he became Virginia's governor. His work as a diplomat was challenging, though stimulating, and for the most part it was not terribly arduous. Left with an abundance of leisure time, he learned all that he could about Paris. He studied its architecture, attended concerts and the theater, dined out frequently, traveled beyond the city and even outside France, and—given that he was a world-class consumer— shopped unrelentingly for books, furniture, gadgets, tools, and art that he would one day take back to Monticello. Salons—centers for debate and the exchange of ideas—were all the rage among Paris's educated upper class, but Jefferson seldom visited them, probably because his skills with the native language were so poor. He called on Franklin now and then, but drew espe- cially close to his other fellow envoy, John Adams, as well as to Abigail and their children, Nabby and John Quincy. Until Adams departed a few months later for London to take on his assignment as the first American minister to Great Britain, Jefferson spent many evenings with the Adamses at their resi- dence in Paris. Jefferson and Adams had become friends during their year together in Congress, but now they drew so close that Abigail found that Jefferson was "the only person with whom" her husband "could associate with perfect freedom, and unreserve." For his part, Jefferson discovered that Adams's stubborn irascibility was offset by his overall companionability and profundity. "He is so amiable," Jefferson gushed to Madison, "that I pronounce you will love him." Jefferson liked Abigail just as much, and she clearly enjoyed being with him, pronouncing him "an Excellent Man" who was "one of the choice ones of the Earth." She shopped for Jefferson at times and accompanied him on some of his outings, and she was delighted that he was eager to spend considerable time with her children.[30]

Jefferson's first winter in Paris was difficult, and his close ties to John and Abigail helped him through it. Like many travelers, he endured a period of "seasoning," a time of illness and indisposition while acclimating to a strange environment. Jefferson continued to grieve for Martha, and there were times on murky days when he felt the heavy hand of melancholy. During that winter he learned that little Lucy Elizabeth, the two-year-old child Martha had carried during her fatal pregnancy, had died of whooping cough shortly after his arrival in Paris. (Jefferson immediately decided to bring his six-year- old daughter Mary to Paris, eventually ordering that she be sent in the company of an older female slave.) Abigail Adams, who had also once lost a young child, felt Jefferson's sorrow and provided solace in her gentle way.

About the time that the Adamses left for London, in May 1785, Jefferson learned that Congress had appointed him to succeed Franklin, now nearing his eightieth birthday, as minister to France. Jefferson had gone to Europe to seek commercial treaties, but all that had come of his and his two colleagues' efforts was a pact with Prussia. The European nations adhered intransigently to mercantilism, the opposite of free trade, and America's decentralized system—which left each state to formulate its own commercial policy—posed a formidable barrier to the conclusion of trade agreements. In his role as minister, Jefferson found that the lion's share of his diplomacy consisted of trying to persuade France to broaden its trade with the United States. Increasing commerce with France was crucial, for Great Britain had ushered in the postwar period by severely restricting what Americans could sell within the British Empire. London's harshest step had been the closing of its ports in the West Indies to the United States, shutting off what had been the principal pre-Revolutionary market for much that the northern colonies had exported. Jefferson quickly learned that by 1785 three-fourths of America's exports went to France, but the volume of that trade was tiny in comparison with the colonists' prewar trade with Britain. So critical was the need to significantly expand trade with France that America's minister at Versailles in the 1780s was not only the young nation's most important diplomat, he was the new nation's single most important official.

Jefferson established a positive relationship with the Comte de Vergennes, Louis XVI's foreign minister. Where Franklin had been passive and deferential, and Adams was assertive and confrontational, Jefferson was diligent, industrious, well informed, and engaging. He won Vergennes's respect. From the outset, Jefferson was optimistic. He believed that Vergennes's inordinate fear of Great Britain would provide leverage toward working out favorable commercial deals that, in turn, would break Great Britain's near-total monopoly of the American market. If he could achieve that, Jefferson foresaw a more satisfactory balance of trade for the United States and the likelihood that American exporters—and especially southern planters—could at last disentangle themselves from their long-standing bondage to British creditors. Jefferson additionally understood that if the United States achieved economic independence, sectional tensions in American politics might be reduced, which could only be a positive development for the fragile American union. Alas, while Vergennes was amenable, he was stymied by France's implacable ancient monopolies, Byzantine restrictions, cumbersome fees and duties, and, atop all else, an economic system thought to be too fragile to endure much change. Jefferson's dreams proved to be beyond his reach and that of his successors for years to come. Nevertheless, to the very end of his stint in Paris, and far beyond, Jefferson saw France as the rock of American safety. "Nothing should be spared on our part to attach this country to us," he said, and he added that France was "the only [nation] on which we can rely for support under every event. It's inhabitants love us more I think than they do any other nation of earth."[31]

When time permitted, Jefferson tried to see as much as possible of France and western Europe. Altogether, he spent about 10 percent of his time in travel outside France. His longest journey was to northern Italy, a three-month overland excursion that took him through western and southern France, a trip that he made alone, save for a servant that he picked up in Dijon. On another occasion, he spent seven weeks touring the Netherlands and Rhine River towns, and while in Frankfurt he called on one of the former Hessian prisoners whom he and Martha had entertained at Monticello.[32] In many ways, the highlight of his traveling came when he crossed the English Channel in 1786, his first and only visit to Virginia's former parent state. It was an unplanned odyssey that happened suddenly when Adams, thinking that negotiations for commercial treaties with Portugal and Tripoli had reached the crucial stage, implored him to come. Although the commercial pacts failed to materialize, Jefferson stayed on for six weeks. He frequently visited with John and Abigail, and at one point he and John took a weeklong, three-hundred-mile tour of the English countryside, inspecting the architecture and visiting gardens and historic sites, including Shakespeare's house. Little about England favorably impressed Jefferson. He came away with a sour opinion of the English people, mostly because of their contempt for Americans. The English, he remarked, "require to be kicked into common good manners." English officials were even worse. Jefferson concluded that the prime minister and his cabinet "hate us," and that the king disliked Americans as much or more than his ministers. The story later circulated that when Adams introduced him to the monarch, George III turned his back on Jefferson, who had excoriated him in *A Summary View* and, of course, in the Declaration of Independence. The yarn was probably apocryphal, or at least embellished. Jefferson never mentioned it, but the monarch evidently displayed a noticeable lack of civility, prompting Jefferson to say that the king and queen had been "ungracious." England, he said subsequently, "fell short of my expectations," though he acknowledged that Englishmen were unrivaled as farmers and gardeners, its artisans were better off by "about a third" than their counterparts in France, and London was "handsomer" than Paris, though not so appealing as Philadelphia.[33]

Some four months after he returned to Paris, Jefferson met Maria Cosway, the twenty-six-year-old wife of a renowned English artist. She and her husband, Richard, were visiting the city. Blonde and attractive, she was like no woman Jefferson had ever known. Maria was well educated, fluent in six languages, an accomplished musician, and a notable painter who exhibited her work. Her marriage had been arranged by her parents, and she was clearly unhappy. She was drawn to Jefferson and he was bewitched by her. In the course of six weeks, the couple spent numerous days together exploring Paris, visiting galleries and museums, attending concerts and the theater, and ranging out into the countryside. Four years had passed since Martha's death and for the first time Jefferson confessed that he was a "mass of happiness." Every second that he was with her "filled [him] with something agreeable." He told her that since his wife's death he had lived the life of a "gloomy Monk, sequestered from the world," left to face "unsocial pleasures in the bottom of his cell!" But the instant he met her he "felt the solid pleasure of one generous spasm of the heart." He never wished to return to his "frigid" existence.[34]

Her husband, knowing or suspecting what was going on, cut short their stay in Paris and took Maria back to London. But the couple corresponded furtively, as Jefferson routed his letters through John Trumbull, an American artist living in London. Jefferson urged her to return to Paris. He also probed to learn her feelings. "Write to me often. Write affectionately, and freely. . . . Say many kind things and say them without reserve." The love he felt for her was evident. "I am always thinking of you" and "I am determined not to suppose I am never to see you again." He implored her to "Think of me much, and warmly. Place me in your breast with those who you love most." He also spoke of "our dear Monticello," where together they could "ride above the storms," living happily not "in the shade but in the sunshine of life." Maria was more guarded in her responses, and her fractured English made the meaning of some things she wrote difficult to unravel, though it was readily apparent that she believed the two shared "trait[s] of character" and that both were "suffering" from loneliness in their respective situations. She also said that Jefferson must decide whether he wished to spend the remainder of his days alone "on the beautiful Monticello tormented by the shadow of a woman" or whether he was prepared to live elsewhere, enjoying a happy and productive life with the woman he loved.[35]

Ten months after returning to London, Maria came back to Paris. This time, she came alone and stayed for more than three months, living with a friend, a Polish princess. Jefferson had asked her to dare to show her feelings. In returning, Maria had boldly revealed what she felt. She and Jefferson saw each other frequently. Then something happened. They were together on her last night in Paris. They were to meet for breakfast the following morning prior to her departure for London. Jefferson showed up. Maria did not. The previous evening had not gone as Maria had hoped. It ended, she said, as she had "suspected" it might.[36]

That is all that can be known about what transpired. Possibly, Jefferson never wished for more than an occasional tryst. Or his feelings for her may have changed during the months they were separated. Conceivably, Jefferson asked her to divorce her husband, but as a devout Roman Catholic she refused to consider such a step. Maria may have been willing to leave her husband, but urbane and thoroughly urban in orientation, she was unwilling to spend her life atop a lonely mountain in a strange land. It is no less likely that the break came because Jefferson would not consent to abandon Monticello and join her in a metropolitan environment. What is most likely is that Maria was prepared to leave—but not to divorce—her husband and to live with Jefferson in an adulterous relationship, but that he shrank from such an arrangement for myriad reasons, not the least being its toxic effect on his political ambitions. They never saw each other again, but they never forgot each other. Seven years later she told Jefferson that she still kept his picture beside her bed, and he responded that he continued to think of her "often and warmly." When he returned to Virginia, about thirty months after that last fateful night together, Jefferson told her, "I will always love you."[37]

Jefferson's responsibilities included assisting his countrymen who came to Paris. Students, such Thomas Lee Shippen of Philadelphia, who was making a grand tour of Europe, were among those who went to him for help. Young Shippen met numerous important figures on his trip, but he thought Jefferson was "without exception the wisest and most amiable man I have seen in Europe." Through Trumbull, Jefferson met and drew close to Angelica Church, the daughter of General Philip Schuyler and sister-in-law of Alexander Hamilton, who had come to Paris from her home in England in search of a more healthful climate. As one who doted on children, Jefferson seemed not to mind lavishing time and attention on the sons of Nathanael Greene and his former congressional colleague John Rutledge and the children of many other acquaintances who came to Paris. Near the end of his mission, several Americans living in Paris paid tribute to Jefferson's "particular kindness and attention to every American" that needed assistance, adding that Jefferson's "noble and generous" behavior had won their "love and admiration." One who repeatedly asked Jefferson for help was Gouverneur Morris, Paine's old nemesis, who had gone abroad on business. Morris met with Jefferson thirteen times in a span of six weeks, and on several occasions the two dined together. Though they had "only a slight Acquaintance" beforehand, Jefferson showed Morris around the city, making observations on Parisian architecture all the while, and even providing tips on shopping. Morris noted, "Mr. Jefferson lives well, keeps a good Table and excellent Wines which he distributes freely and by his Hospitality to his Countrymen here he possesses very much their good Will." He added, too, that Jefferson was "very much Respected" by the French, who held him in high esteem because of his habitual "good Sense and good Intentions." Morris's only criticism—which appears to have been unique with him—was that Jefferson was a poor judge of character, a flaw that led him to "assign too many to the humble rank of fool."[38]

Jefferson was living a life that many would have thought idyllic, but after thirty months in Paris he confessed: "I am burning the candle of life without present pleasure, or future object."[39] Jefferson not infrequently overstated things, and he may have exaggerated his unhappiness in late 1786, though he wrote that sentence shortly after Maria Cosway returned to London the first time. Without a doubt, however, Jefferson's anguish at having no future plans was heartfelt, for he remained as politically ambitious as ever, but he knew that in the United States of that day no public office existed that was superior to the one he held.

Soon after he returned to Paris in June 1787 from his lengthy journey through southern France and Italy, Jefferson, to his surprise, found Thomas Paine on his doorstep. Paine had crossed the ocean yet again, though this journey was unrelated to political matters. Paine, who had been living off the beaten path in Bordentown since getting his financial house in order, had not been active in public affairs for some time. He had written little during the past four years, and to the dismay of many old comrades, Paine had not been involved in the wide-ranging reform movements that swept Pennsylvania soon after the war.

Between 1783 and 1787 Paine addressed only two issues, and in both cases he had raised eyebrows—and hackles—among many old friends. During the Continental army's last days, the officers had formed the Society of the Cincinnati, portraying it to the public as a fraternal organization. Many republicans were immediately suspicious. As future membership was to be hereditary, some feared the Society would morph into a formal American aristocracy. Others saw the organization as a lobbying tool to advance the interests of America's most affluent and politically conservative citizens. No one was more hostile than Jefferson. He even complained to Washington, who was known to be sympathetic toward the Society. Given the "mass of evil which flows" from aristocracies, Jefferson cautioned Washington that tolerating the Society was too great a risk to run. But Paine—possibly because he had soldiered, or perhaps because of his ties to Washington—openly supported the Cincinnati, composed a song for it, and embraced it as the most probable means of providing support for the widows and orphans of fallen officers and enlisted men.[40]

Paine published nothing with regard to the Society of the Cincinnati, but in the winter of 1786 he wrote newspaper essays and one pamphlet in defense of the Bank of North America, a private institution chartered by Congress in

1781 and indirectly—but effectively—controlled by Robert Morris. The bank had helped stabilize the nation's finances during the last few years of the war, but the end of wartime defense spending was followed by an economic recession. Pennsylvania was especially hard hit. Money dried up, land values collapsed, and many debtors feared the loss of their property. The state assembly urged the bank to put more money in circulation. When it refused to do so, the Pennsylvania assembly issued £150,000 of paper money and repealed the bank's charter. Paine jumped into the fray, arguing—as a defender of the Federal Reserve System might do today—that the bank was essential for determining the proper amount of money in circulation and that it alone could forestall a recurrence of the runaway inflation that had nearly destroyed the war effort after 1778. Paine lost the fight. He was savaged in the press as Morris's lackey, though in fact he was no one's hireling in this contest. Other detractors labeled him a two-faced scoundrel, a turncoat who had abandoned the cause of freedom. One critic wrote: "*Janus* is our own, Who props a bank, altho' he scorned a throne." So harsh was the criticism that some of Paine's friends feared for his safety, and on one occasion when he could not be located for a time, an acquaintance, wringing his hands, was certain that Paine's "enemies . . . have shown him foul play."⁴¹

If Paine wrote little during the four years following the war, it was not due to indolence. He had begun to channel his energy into a feat of engineering. In his schooldays, Paine had displayed a flair for mathematics, and while residing in London he had been drawn to scientific lectures. The spirit of his time, the Age of Enlightenment, was to question dogma. Many of the great eighteenth-century philosophers celebrated the scientific revolution that would make humankind, in Descartes's phrase, the "masters and possessors of nature." In his answer to Abbé Raynal, Paine had toasted science as the "partisan of no country . . . patroness of all," and he had extolled those who had both labored "to extend and complete the civilization of nations" and had taken a "seat in the temple of science." The greatest of men were not those who made wars and empires, he had added, but those who pursued the "arts, sciences, agriculture and commerce, the refinements of the gentleman, the principles of society, and the knowledge of the philosopher."⁴²

Paine doubtless hoped to make money from the venture that he had embarked on, but striving for wealth had never been a fetish with him. In turning his focus to engineering, Paine was driven by his lifelong scientific curiosity. But that was not his only motivation. He still brooded over the condescension he had suffered at the hands of wealthier and better-educated gentlemen during the Silas Deane affair back in 1779. Paine hungered to be seen as both the famous author of *Common Sense* and, like the venerated

Franklin—a former artisan who had risen to the heights on two continents as a man of letters and of science—the inventor and builder of things that would improve humankind's quality of life. Paine had set his sights on bridge building, a venture that he hoped would lead to his recognition as a man of true distinction.

It was serendipitous that at the time several leading Philadelphians were seeking a solution to the long-standing problem of bridging the four-hundred-foot-wide Schuylkill River, a step that would result in increasingly lucrative ties between the city and the backcountry. Happily for Paine, late in 1785 he met John Hall, a recent immigrant from Leicester, England, who had made the ocean crossing bearing a letter of introduction to Paine. Hall, Paine discovered, had formal experience as a builder, among other things having worked for companies in England that built steam engines.

Going back to Roman times, bridges had been constructed in one of two ways: the post-and-lintel method in which flat beams were positioned on columns that in turn rested on piers, and the semicircular masonry method in which arches made of stone or brick bore the load. Paine envisaged an alternative method—a single-span iron bridge that would require no piers. It could be prefabricated in a foundry and put together at the site chosen for the bridge.[43]

Paine's initial plan was to build a bridge across the Harlem River, a surefire revenue maker. Farmers would pay tolls en route to New York's lucrative markets, while urban merchants and artisans would be no less eager to traffic their wares in the backcountry. Unfortunately, the only suitable location for straddling the river was on Gouverneur Morris's property in what today is the southern boundary of the Bornx; fearing what he regarded as the ne'er-do-wells who would tramp over his estate, Morris refused Paine's entreaties. Paine next turned to the Schuylkill River site. He had better contacts in Pennsylvania anyway, and in time gained sufficient funding to rent a loft in Philadelphia that served as his workshop. By the spring of 1786, he and Hall, with the assistance of a few hired laborers, were working on a thirteen-foot-long cast-iron model of the prospective bridge. Aside from managing the workers—which he acknowledged was easier than he had imagined—Paine thought through the step-by-step details of the model's design, always working in conjunction with Hall, who appears to have performed most of the manual labor. Hall's diary contains passages such as "With much pain . . . pinned 6 more arches. . . . I sweat at it; Mr. Pain gives me some wine and water as I was very dry." Just after Christmas, the completed model was put on display on the grounds of the Pennsylvania State House, where the Declaration of Independence had been signed and where, in just five months, the Constitutional

Convention would meet. It remained on exhibit for weeks and was studied by both the curious and potential investors.[44]

Paine had said that he had "no doubt" about the efficacy of his bridge, but others were wary. Many were skeptical of his design, and given the dearth of iron forges in the region, some had reservations about the cost of building an iron bridge. Few private investors stepped forward and, in light of Pennsylvania's postwar financial straits, public funding had been problematic from the outset. Seeing Paine's plight, Benjamin Franklin—who had returned home from France in 1785—encouraged him to seek the endorsement of the prestigious Royal Academy of Sciences in Paris, a sanction that almost certainly would calm the fears of American investors. It is quite likely, too, that Franklin and Paine believed that the Academy's approval might lead to the adoption of the bridge in France. Now fifty and with the war a thing of the past, Paine had for some time also mulled the notion of returning to Thetford to see his parents one final time. Franklin's advice convinced him that the time was right for making another ocean crossing. His plan was to sail for France and to visit England once his business in Paris was completed. In April, Paine—with his model bridge in the cargo hold—began his journey. He had crossed to America in 1774 bearing a helpful letter from Franklin. He sailed in 1787 with a dozen letters of introduction from Franklin in his pocket, missives written to notable philosophers, scientists, and government officials. Franklin described Paine as "an ingenious, honest man" and "a Friend of mine." He also carried a letter from Franklin to Jefferson asking that he assist Paine. Shortly before departing, Paine told Franklin that he would be back in Philadelphia within a few months. Fifteen years passed before he returned.[45]

Paine's voyage was fast and safe, and he spent four months in France, three of them in Paris, where he received a "cordial and friendly" welcome, quite unlike what he had viewed as the uncivil treatment he had long experienced in Philadelphia. It was during his stay in Paris that Paine surprised Jefferson with a visit. Thereafter, he dined with Jefferson at least once at the minister's residence and elsewhere on one or more occasions.[46] Most of Paine's time, of course, was consumed with his attempts to win approval for his bridge. Franklin's letters opened doors for him, but so did the reputation Paine had earned from his writings. He soon met with a host of luminaries, and he quickly became a regular at the salon of the Marquis de Condorcet, a mathematician, philosopher, and renowned figure in the French Enlightenment, not to mention a member of the Royal Academy of Sciences. In July, Paine submitted his plan to the Academy, explaining that on Franklin's recommendation he was seeking the members' approval as a necessary step toward obtaining funding for building the bridge across the Schuylkill River in Pennsylvania.

Following a month of study and deliberation, the Academy reached a positive conclusion—it judged Paine's bridge to be "sound," "strong," and "ingeniously conceived"—though only time could tell whether iron could withstand wind and extreme temperatures.[47] But if there was any chance of the bridge being built in France, a favorable ruling by the Corps of Bridges and Roads, a body venerated in Europe for its expertise concerning the design and construction of bridges, was necessary. Later in the summer, Paine failed to win their approval, as its members were disposed toward masonry construction. Earlier, one of the Academy's judges had informed Paine of an iron arch that had been constructed in Coalbrookdale, England, and that gave him a second reason to cross the Channel. He set off in September. He would briefly return to Paris in 1788, hopeful that his proposed bridge might be one of several chosen to span the Seine, and make several crossings for a very short stay during the early period of the French Revolution, but for the most part Paine remained in England for the next five years.

On alighting in England, Paine hurried to Thetford, where he discovered that his father had died nearly a year earlier. He spent several weeks with his ninety-year-old mother. After years of receiving assistance from others, Paine dipped into his resources to see that she would receive a weekly stipend for as long as she lived. Two individuals who spent time with Paine during his stay in England left descriptions of him, but as is so often the case with such things, their accounts were steeped in contradictions. One thought him slender and of average height, possibly even a tad below average, while the other remembered him as standing about three inches taller than most Englishmen, and that he was "rather athletic" and "broad shouldered," though slightly stooped. One recalled that he "wore his hair cued, with side curls, and powdered," but the other, who thought Paine's outward appearance was "contemptible," said he wore an aged and ragged wig. Only one mentioned his social graces, and he allowed that Paine's "manners were easy and gracious." Both agreed that he was a sprightly conversationalist, stocked with a rich supply of anecdotes and stories, and an ability to hold forth on a wide range of subjects, so many in fact that one was convinced that Paine's "knowledge was universal and boundless." The other concluded that Paine delighted in shocking his listeners. One said that Paine avoided "common chit chat" (a trait he shared with Jefferson; one visitor to Monticello discovered that his host was "revolted by idle chatter"). Paine was normally garrulous, but he fell silent in "mixt company and among strangers," and any interruption—even a loud party at a nearby table or a waiter dropping a tray—might cause him to "retire into himself and no persuasion could induce him to proceed." While both noted that Paine was given to pronounced mood swings, only one spoke of his lifestyle. He recollected that Paine read little, loved to walk, took a late-afternoon nap nearly every day, enjoyed music and singing, and played chess and dominoes, but disdained card games of any sort. As not a word was said about Paine's drinking habits, neither acquaintance apparently glimpsed a problem.[48]

By the end of 1787 Paine was once again vigorously engaged in his bridge campaign, a passion that consumed him during his first three years back in his homeland. As had been true in Philadelphia and Paris, he faced a series of ups and downs. Paine found an investor willing to fund the construction of another, larger model, something the Royal Academy in Paris had recommended. He also secured a patent, a necessary step in procuring a builder. Paine spent much of 1788 in Yorkshire working with a notable iron manufacturer, only to be stopped in his tracks when his principal backer went bankrupt. Paine hurried to London in search of help. Again, he had some success, though he was also compelled to risk his own capital, a chunk of which he garnered from the sale of his stock in a Philadelphia bank and £200 loaned him by Jefferson. (Jefferson additionally commissioned a painting of Paine by Trumbull, an honor that Paine relished all the more when he learned that Jefferson was collecting paintings and sculptures of those who had played notable roles in the American Revolution.)[49] Paine's initial notion had been to construct a giant 250-foot model, but he scaled back, and toward the end of 1788 work began in Rotherham on a 90-foot prototype.

In September 1790, the model was at last ready for public display. Exuberant and optimistic, Paine described his inspiration as a thing of "elegance and beauty" and said that the investors had "full as much confidence in the work as myself." The mammoth model, which weighed several tons, was exhibited in a grassy field on Lisson Green, a bucolic but heavily traveled area not far from downtown London. Finding residence nearby in a tavern called Yorkshire Stingo, Paine could meet with the curious visitors who came to see the structure and paid a shilling to walk across it.[50]

Paine's high expectations were not realized. Some critics, like those in Paris, were skeptical of iron bridges, and others pointed to what they saw as design flaws. In the spring of 1791—forty-eight months after arriving in England and five years after he and John Hall had begun work on the initial model in the Philadelphia loft—Paine all but conceded that his quest for notoriety as an engineer was hopeless, at least in the near run. He gave the order for his workers to disassemble the model and take it back to Rotherham. Six months later, Paine wrote to Hall confessing that the prototype was imperfect but insisting that with time and funding the defects could be overcome. While he never said that he was abandoning bridge building forever, the tenor of his letter suggested that was his mind-set. "I am engaged on my political Bridge," he wrote, and nine-tenths of his missive was devoted to his efforts to change the political "tide," which "yet [ran] the wrong way."[51]

Paine's long battle for his bridge had come to naught. Yet, for one without formal training as an engineer, his creativity and structural understanding were remarkable. In some respects, he was ahead of his time. Fifty years down the road, iron bridges designed for the most part by professional engineers would be commonplace. Indeed, in 1905 the president of the American Society of Civil Engineers said that "Paine's experimental bridge became the prototype of the modern steel arch."[52]

In the spring of 1787, the time when Paine arrived in Paris to display his bridge, Jefferson had been anxious for news from America. In one of Jefferson's last letters before sailing from Boston three years earlier, he had acknowledged that "nothing can save our Confederacy," and possibly the American union, unless the Articles of Confederation was changed to strengthen the authority of the national government.[53] Jefferson did not want an all-powerful central government, but he understood that a national government without the power to tax or regulate commerce was untenable. Fortunes were being lost, ambitions thwarted, national security was jeopardized, and the economic woes that had carried over from the war years were not being adequately addressed. Powerful interests had sought changes in the Articles before the war ended, and by the time Jefferson crossed the sea, bands of what historians would later call "nationalists" or "consolidationists" had begun to organize and campaign for constitutional reform.

Jefferson relied on Madison and Monroe to keep him informed. He did not realize how disappointing Madison would be on this score. Not long elapsed after Jefferson's departure before Madison, a committed nationalist, was absorbed in a thoughtful search for the means of balancing "stability and energy" in the national government in such a manner that the seminal interests of the more urban, commercial North and those of the agrarian, slave-holding South could be realized within a republican framework. Madison's starting point was that the states must be inhibited from any longer "invad[ing] the national jurisdiction." He was just as adamant about restraining the "tyranny" of "popular" opinion, a condition that he labeled a "disease." By 1786, Madison sought a constitutional convention that would discard the Articles of Confederation and replace it with a new constitution establishing a national government "arm[ed] . . . with a negative in all cases whatsoever on the local Legislatures." He hoped, too, that the new government would include a chief executive with such extraordinary powers that the official would—as Madison said privately—possess a "Kingly prerogative." Above all, he sought to make it difficult to bring about change, slowing (if not altogether ending) the creeping democratization set in motion in 1776.

Madison did not breathe a word of this to Jefferson before the Constitutional Convention met in May 1787. Knowing that Jefferson would be aghast at nearly everything he was working toward—and not wishing to have to choose between loyalty to Jefferson and the pursuit of ends he thought necessary to save the Union—Madison merely wrote to him about "dangerous defects" in the Articles that sowed commercial chaos and left the national government with insufficient revenue. He knew that Jefferson recognized the need for reform in both quarters. On the eve of the Convention, assured that he would not hear back from Jefferson before the delegates had completed their work, Madison at last divulged his commitment to a national government with nearly absolute sovereignty over the states.[54]

Monroe was little better at reporting to Jefferson. He hardly wrote to Jefferson about national politics after mid-1785, though his lack of communication was due to very different reasons. Monroe remained in Congress for two years after Jefferson's departure and was distracted by his numerous responsibilities, one of which was the time-consuming effort of shepherding into law much of Jefferson's earlier plan for the West. Monroe also still believed that Congress would adopt and send to the states for ratification amendments that would strengthen the hand of the national government and make a constitutional convention unnecessary. His naïveté blinded him to the power of the consolidationists and the shortcomings of those in Congress who opposed a powerful central government. But the chief reason that Monroe provided Jefferson with little useful information was that he was busily getting his personal affairs in order. Now in his late twenties, Monroe was still laboring to put his law practice on an even keel. He was also deeply involved in land speculation and made two extended journeys to the frontier. One excursion ranged through the Mohawk Valley and beyond to Niagara Falls. Accompanied "by a guard of six Mohawk chiefs," the travelers made much of their trek in bateaux. Securing Native American bodyguards proved to be a prudent measure, for some who started out on the expedition ventured across the Niagara River to "the Canada shore," where they were killed by a party of Indians. Monroe's second expedition carried him down the Ohio River and into Kentucky.

Monroe was also ready to settle down, and his thoughts were focused more on the numerous young women he was squiring than on Jefferson.

Monroe was quite the eligible bachelor. A young Philadelphia woman described him as the embodiment of "every perfection that a female can wish or a man envy," and she ticked off Monroe's notable features as including that he was "rich, young, sensible, well read, lively, and handsome," and even that the "dimple on his chin" added to his "beauty." She was off the mark with regard to Monroe's wealth. He was far from rich, although his legal practice and landholdings gave him the potential for someday becoming quite well-to-do. During 1785, while Congress was meeting in New York, he found the woman he had been looking for. He began to woo Elizabeth Courtright, the twenty-year-old daughter of a once-wealthy merchant who had lost most of his fortune during the war. She swept Monroe off his feet, and the two were married in February 1786. Monroe was on the cusp of his twenty-eighth birthday, essentially the same age as Jefferson had been when he married. When Monroe's congressional term came to a mandatory end in November, the couple hurried to Fredericksburg, Virginia, where Monroe, for the first time, practiced law unhindered by public office. But Fredericksburg was only a stopover. More than ever, Monroe wanted to live near Jefferson. After making several trips to Albemarle County in search of land, he purchased eight hundred acres and a house in Charlottesville in 1788.[55]

Truthfully confessing to Jefferson in 1787 that for more than a year he "had little to do" with "the political world," Monroe wrote his confidant a troubled letter shortly after the Constitutional Convention began. As its sessions were closed, Monroe had no idea what was transpiring. Nonetheless, he was anxious. He feared the delegates would be unable to come to agreement, but he was far more worried that the Convention would produce a constitution that vested the national government with so much authority that the document would never successfully run the gauntlet of ratification. He knew only that the "*affairs of the federal government*" were "*in the utmost confusion*" and that the convention was a last-ditch effort to save the Union. Either it would produce a constitution that would save "*us from our present embarrassments or complete our ruin*." Monroe's great hope was that General Washington, who had agreed to attend, would force compromises or "overawe" the extremists.[56]

Jefferson was a long way from home with only a sketchy knowledge of the political machinations that had occurred in America during his three-year absence. He confessed to having only the scantest awareness of the thinking of many of the delegates to the Convention. In fact, Jefferson must have wondered how well he knew Madison once he learned that his friend favored giving Congress virtually complete jurisdiction over the states. "I do not like it," Jefferson shot back. But all he could do was wait and, like Monroe, hope that what he called the "demigods" in attendance (Jefferson was thinking largely of Washington and Franklin) would stay the hand of those who would go too far.[57]

Jefferson's beliefs about governance had taken shape by the early 1770s. He had turned to revolution against Great Britain as the only means of protecting the American provinces from a central government that demanded control over the colonies "in all cases whatsoever," as the Declaratory Act had put it in 1766. With independence secured, he persisted in the belief that freedom could endure only where governmental power was limited. Like most other republicans, Jefferson saw an inevitable clash between power and liberty, for power was thought to be inherently expansive: If not contained, it would ineluctably infringe on liberty. The preservation of life, liberty, property, and what he had termed "the pursuit of happiness" in the Declaration of Independence, hinged on the restraint of government. Convinced that local government could more easily be constrained than a central government, the core of Jefferson's outlook was that America's national government must remain small and noninvasive. His bedrock belief was strikingly similar to what Paine had written in *Common Sense*:

> government, even in its best state, is but a necessary evil; in its worst state an intolerable one; for when we suffer, or are exposed to the same miseries by a government, which we might expect in a country without government, our calamity is heightened by reflecting that we furnish the means by which we suffer. Government, like dress, is the badge of lost innocence; the palaces of kings are built upon the ruins of the bowers of paradise. For were the impulses of conscience clear, uniform and irresistibly obeyed, man would need no other law-giver; but that not being the case, he finds it necessary to surrender up a part of his property to furnish means for the protection of the rest; and this he is induced to do by the same prudence which in every other case advises him, out of the two evils to choose the least.[58]

Jefferson additionally shared with Paine a belief that the American Revolution was about both American independence and the realization of wholesale change, nothing less than beginning "the world over again." For Jefferson, as for Paine, the American Revolution was a turning point for humankind, the repudiation of a dark, sordid past in which people for centuries had been the political and social victims of tyranny. But above all else, Jefferson believed that to sustain the new world brought into being by the American Revolution, governmental powers must be kept to a minimum and, in particular, the authority of the central government must be limited.

Not for nothing did Jefferson anxiously remark that he hoped the proposed American constitution would preserve the autonomy of the states in 99 percent of their acts. He was also hopeful, he said, that the states would be autonomous in domestic matters and that the national government's sovereignty would be restricted almost solely to matters of foreign policy and commerce. Nor would it have come as a surprise to anyone who knew Jefferson well to learn that in private he had described the Articles of Confederation as "a wonderfully perfect instrument" for enabling "the opinion of the people"— what at times he called the usual "good sense of the people"—to be heard and acted on.[59]

Toward the end of 1787, Jefferson at last saw a copy of the proposed constitution and was "stagger[ed]" by what he read. This constitution, he believed, looked to the past. It was more akin to the prerevolutionary colonial governments than to the state constitutions adopted after 1776. It would grant what he thought was a menacing degree of sovereignty to a remote central government, not unlike what the distant imperial government in London had sought to establish over the colonies after 1763. The new national government would also be incredibly "energetic," and Jefferson believed such entities were "always oppressive." The framers, he feared, had overreacted to congressional weakness under the Articles of Confederation, much like an errant tailor who "mend[ed] a small hole by covering the whole garment." Jefferson was aghast at the extraordinary powers given to the executive and at the presidency's lack of term limits. In time, he feared, the presidency would morph into a monarchy.

Nothing disturbed him more than the absence of a bill of rights. He knew that Lafayette and his coterie of aristocratic reformers in France were eager to secure a declaration of rights for their country, and that they thought it a setback to their struggle to learn that the proposed American constitution lacked such a document. Jefferson was also aware that Paine had criticized the lack of a bill of rights in the proposed constitution. Paine and Jefferson learned the results of the Constitutional Convention at roughly the same moment, and from England Paine wrote to him that those who defended the omission of a bill of rights were taking their defense from the Tory playbook. It was a staple of the archconservative mentality, said Paine, to claim that the more natural rights "we resign . . . the more security we possess," but their argument was fallacious. It was essential, he added, for the constitution to safeguard all natural rights, including "the rights of thinking, speaking, forming and giving opinions."

A "bill of rights," Jefferson immediately wrote to Madison, "is what the people are entitled to against every government on earth . . . and what no just government should refuse." Indeed, the lack of a bill of rights in the proposed constitution reflected an alarming "degeneracy in the principles of liberty" within America since 1776.

Jefferson never wavered on the inclusion of a bill of rights, but his intensely unsettled initial reaction to the Constitution gave way within a month to a more accommodating perspective. By then, he had declared himself a "neutral" with regard to the document's ratification, saying there was much good in it, though it contained "a bitter pill, or two." Months later, after Washington told him that the Constitution had been a necessary and "tolerable compromise . . . to save us from impending ruin," Jefferson moderated his stance even more. Later still, on learning that Washington, who had never abused his power while commanding the army, would be the first president, Jefferson felt even better. Ultimately, he claimed to have always been closer in outlook to the document's proponents than to its foes.[60]

Although Jefferson's fundamental views about government did not change during his five years in France, he came to look at some things in new ways. More than he was willing to admit, Jefferson found that he loved much about urban life, including the ready availability of recitals and the theater, not to mention the endless array of enchanting shops filled with beguiling treasures. He was surely swept up by the rich intellectual ferment that was commonplace in a major metropolis. As his command of the language improved, Jefferson, through Franklin, gained admittance to the circle around the duc de la Rochefoucauld, like himself an urbane gentleman-farmer with liberal predilections; those who gathered at the Hôtel de La Rochefoucauld— among them Chastellux, Lafayette, and Condorcet—discussed scientific, political, social, and philosophical issues, with much attention focused on the hope of securing reforms within France. He also frequented the salon of Madame de Tessé, whom he met through Lafayette. Jefferson found her to be an enlightened sophisticate, an outspoken republican who loved gardening and public affairs, and the two drew so close that they would continue a lengthy correspondence beyond his Paris years.

His affection for France stretched beyond consumerism and highbrow discussions. "I do love this *people* with all my heart," he exclaimed a year after his arrival. Jefferson was charmed by their culture and tastes, and he believed they were committed to pursuing happiness to a degree not to be seen among those of English stock. He loved the French, too, because he believed that they—or at least the most enlightened among them—were enchanted with America. Although he once remarked that he was "savage enough to prefer the woods, the wilds, and the independence of Monticello, to all the brilliant pleasures of this gay capital," Jefferson subsequently expressed his adoration for France by incorporating much that he had discovered while abroad into his life and home in Virginia.[61]

But Jefferson also found much that was abhorrent about the autocratic France of the ancien régime. Its nobility—which made up far less than 1 percent of the population, yet owned roughly a third of all the land and held seigneurial rights over the rest—was a separate order and its members were empowered with privileges unknown to England's aristocracy. They were entitled to separate courts and either escaped the lion's share of some taxes, such as the *gabelle*, the detested salt tax, or were exempt altogether from other levies, including the *taille*, the basic direct tax. They were not liable to conscription in the militia, quartering troops, or the *corvée*, the hated forced labor on roads. They were entitled to a portion of the harvest (as much as one-quarter in some provinces) within the *seigneurie* and in many instances were additionally permitted a share of the grapes, olives, and bread produced within the village. Like everyone else, the nobility faced mandatory tithes for the maintenance of the parish, but for the wealthy the tithe was not the staggering burden it was for the poorest citizens, the 80 percent or so of the population that made up the French peasantry. To many, the tithe was particularly despised because the church owned about 10 percent of the land. Nor was there much opportunity for those in the bottom rung of society to overcome their plight. Upward mobility in French society was possible, but unlikely, as the crafts were exclusive and gaining entrance to a skilled trade was difficult, and the great majority of landless peasants lacked the resources and education that might have elevated them. The results of these ancient practices were stunning inequities and crushing poverty, a degree of victimization on a magnitude that Jefferson had never witnessed among the white inhabitants of America.[62]

Strangely, Jefferson said little about the dire conditions faced by the urban workers all about him in Paris, but he was deeply moved by the "suffering under physical and moral oppression" that he beheld among the peasants and rural poor throughout the countryside. These were more his kind of people, and he was appalled at how they lived. They were "ground to powder" by a repressive autocracy, he said. More than anything else that he observed in "the vaunted scene of Europe," it was the plight of rustic French families that had the greatest influence on the shape of his political philosophy, forming the prism through which he judged the ancien régime, and for the remainder of his life the state of affairs in America. It was not that Jefferson's fundamental convictions were transformed. It was more that what he saw corroborated beliefs that before 1776 had made him a revolutionary. In some areas of southern France—which he toured in the spring of 1787—Jefferson found "a general poverty." He observed landless peasants working some of the best land he had ever seen, but despite their unremitting toil many were "ill clothed and looked ill," lived in "hovels," and dressed "in rags." Their diet of bread and the same unvarying vegetables seldom included meat. "What a cruel reflection," he remarked, "that a rich country cannot long be a free one." He was struck by the profound disparities in the distribution of wealth, or what he called an "unequal division of property" that resulted in "numberless instances of wretchedness"—indeed, "misery to the bulk of mankind." Here was a country in which one aristocrat, the duc d'Orleans, received 7.5 million livres in annual rent while many laborers earned but 1 or 2 livres from a day's work. Never, said Jefferson, had he encountered such corrosive, brutish distress among the free peoples of America.[63]

Jefferson never doubted for a moment that monarchy was the root cause of the deplorable conditions he observed. "I was much an enemy to monarchy before I came to Europe. I am ten thousand times more so since I have seen what they are," he said. Aghast at the "wretched . . . accursed . . . existence" that he witnessed among "the class of labouring husbandmen," Jefferson came away convinced of the "truth of Voltaire's observation that every man here must be either the hammer or the anvil." Like Paine, who had expounded on the iniquities that flowed from the pernicious alliance between monarchy and aristocracy, Jefferson, too, came to believe that the "deplorable" state of humanity throughout Europe could be traced only to monarchs that were propped up by "great standing arm[ies]" and allied with an ultraconservative church and nobility driven to maintain "the property of this country . . . concentrated in a very few hands." Through the maintenance of a rigid class system and a vexatious maldistribution of wealth, monarchies and the parasitic privileged elements preserved their power, entitlements, and unimaginable luxuries while suppressing the bulk of the population.

Jefferson advised his friends at home that if any American "thinks that kings, nobles, or priests are good conservators of the public happiness, send them here. . . . They will see here with their own eyes" that those who rule are a "confederacy against the happiness of the mass of people." Throughout Europe, the "dignity of man is lost" amid a "horror of evils." When he learned that some of his affluent countrymen now doubted republicanism, Jefferson wrote home again with the admonition to "Send those gentry here to count the blessings of monarchy." They will return home "good republicans." He added: "My god! How little do my countrymen know what precious blessings they are in possession of, and which no other people on earth enjoy. I confess,

I had no idea of it myself." Concluding that in monarchical Europe there were but two social classes, "wolves and sheep," Jefferson was so revolted by what he found that it led him to the conclusion Paine had long ago reached: The "evils of monarchical government are beyond remedy."[64] The only antidote for the miseries sown by royal rule was the eradication of kingship.

Jefferson's resentment of British authoritarianism had led him down the road of revolution, but so, too, had his abhorrence of the growing inequities in wealth, power, and opportunities among the free people in Virginia. His residence in Europe had provided a firsthand look at the result of an "enormous inequality producing such misery to the bulk of mankind" within Europe. It aroused Jefferson's fear that in time the same evil would take hold in his country and eradicate the sparkling promise of revolutionary America. He had not been in Europe long before he wrote to Madison that despite the earth having been "given as a common stock for man to labour and live on," one generation of the elite after another had wielded their authority "to invent" legal "devices" for hoarding their wealth and denying others the opportunity to improve their status. Safeguards must be taken in America, he said, to see that the few who possessed great wealth could not engender the same "numberless instances of wretchedness" that their counterparts had caused on the Continent. Living in Europe only strengthened his belief in the worthiness of the American Revolution, and more than ever he came to believe not only that rulers must listen to the people, but also that the people had a "duty"—as he had written in the Declaration of Independence—to act against the "abuses and usurpations" perpetrated by their rulers.[65]

When Shays' Rebellion, an uprising by debt-ridden farmers in western Massachusetts flared in 1786, many conservative Americans were horrified. Jefferson's response could not have been more different. A rebellion, "like a storm in the Atmosphere," clears and refreshes the air, he said. "[A] little rebellion now and then is a good thing" if it added to the "happiness of the mass of the people." It was healthy for the people to rise up against their rulers at least once each generation. "The tree of liberty must be refreshed from time to time with the blood of patriots and tyrants. It is its natural manure." Given what he had seen in Europe, as well as what he learned of the hysterical reaction of his own country's most conservative citizens to the Shaysites, Jefferson's thinking increasingly turned to the question of "Whether one generation of men has a right to bind another." He knew that in Virginia and elsewhere those who resisted change often defended laws as inviolable, insisting that the preservation of order and maintenance of a flourishing society required that the present generation must abide by—must be constrained by—the wisdom, decisions, and achievements of past generations. Jefferson's answer was akin to an exclamation point to his divergent, and more radical, point of view. The "earth belongs to the living, and not to the dead," he said. And to this, he added: "the dead have neither powers nor rights."[66]

Jefferson and Paine had the unique experience of being part of the two great revolutions of the eighteenth century, the American and the French. Each was delighted at his good fortune, as each instinctively understood the epoch importance of the upheavals. Paine, in fact, rushed across the Channel from England in the fall of 1789 to see with his own eyes what was happening in France, and soon thereafter he wrote to Washington, "A Share in two revolutions is living to some purpose."[67]

Jefferson in 1784 had arrived in a France that historians, with the benefit of hindsight, have generally portrayed as ripe for revolution. Jefferson turned out to be a fair historian himself. The account he left in his memoirs—long before many histories had been written—saw deep roots to the French Revolution. He painted a picture of popular exploitation. The people were victims of "the monstrous abuses" of monarchs, the aristocracy, and an indolent and immoral clergy. The citizenry, he wrote, groaned under "the weight of their taxes, and the inequality of their distribution," and by the "oppressions of the tithes" they were compelled to pay to the church. In addition, commerce was shackled by monopolies and industry by guilds, and "freedom of conscience, of thought . . . of speech . . . of the press" was severely restricted.

In his judgment, French officers who had served in America during the War of Independence brought home word of the breathtaking changes effected by the American Revolution, tidings that "awakened the thinking part of the French nation . . . from the sleep of despotism in which they were sunk." Jefferson never wavered in his belief that the American uprising was the spark that lit the French Revolution. The idea was not unique to him. During America's Revolutionary War, some European observers thought that the "flame [of liberty] that burns in America will spread quickly engulfing all of Europe." A Boston Club was formed in Paris during the war, and its members praised America's rebels, while Condorcet and other enlightened philosophers lauded the Declaration of Independence as a "sublime exposition of sacred rights that have too long been forgotten." Other reformers were more impressed by the first state constitutions in America. As early as 1777, Benjamin Franklin—like Jefferson later—noted that some in France believed that America's "Cause is *the cause of all* Mankind," and not a few looked on the defense of liberty by America's revolutionaries as laying the ground-work for the struggle for liberty within France. But whatever the influence of the American Revolution, Jefferson never lost sight of the fact that it was a deep fiscal crisis that set in motion the events that would topple the ancien régime.[68]

By Jefferson's third year in Paris, France was overwhelmed with debt stem-ming in large measure from a series of costly wars that stretched back a century and included the Seven Years' War. France's expenditures in support of the American revolt added to the nation's mounting indebtedness. War after war exacerbated the economic damage done by France's disjointed and ineffectual method of collecting taxes, a system that had been privatized with what turned out to be disastrous results. By the late 1780s, France's debt had climbed to four billion livres, and fully one-half of the annual budget was consumed by debt service. Revenue had to be obtained somewhere. With further borrowing no longer an option, taxation seemed to be the only viable solution. In hopes of finding a source of revenue, the comptroller persuaded the king to call into session the Assembly of Notables, 144 of the most powerful men in France. The comptroller also made public what had previously been the secret details of France's debt crisis and the state's taxation policies. King and comptroller expected the delegates to surrender some of their privileges before creating a national bank and adopting a land tax, a levy that would fall almost exclusively on the nobility, France's primary landowners. But the Assembly of Notables adjourned the day before Paine disembarked in 1787 having taken no remedial steps.

The comptroller's revelations about the economy caused an awakening—what one historian called the politicization—of the surprised and outraged populace. Jefferson rapidly divined "a revolution of public opinion." He noted that the "highest pitch of discontent" blanketed France and that "the royal authority has lost" much of its previous standing. He was delighted. He neither sensed nor craved violence, but in the wake of the Assembly's inertia, Jefferson foresaw that France was "advancing to a change of constitution." Sentiment for a constitutional monarchy was "ripening fast," he declared. Bubbling with optimism, and naïveté, he told Monroe in the summer of 1788 that revolu-tionary change would come "without its having cost them a drop of blood."[69]

Left with few good choices, Louis XVI summoned the Estates General—the French parliament that no monarch had convened for generations—to meet in Versailles in the late spring of 1789. An ebullient Jefferson again predicted a constitutional "revolution" that would result in "great modifications" in the king's authority. Broaching an idea that he would repeat again and again,

Jefferson in high spirits wrote to Washington that France "has been awaked by our revolution."[70]

Jefferson had watched closely as events unfolded. In fact, Jefferson had not merely been an observer; he was meeting frequently with Lafayette, whom he characterized as "a most valuable auxiliary to me." Theirs was a fascinating relationship, as each sought to use the other to his own advantage. Both were world-class players when it came to manipulation. Lafayette had demonstrated his talent in his handling of General Washington. To the consternation of many Continental army officers and the amazement of Comte de Rochambeau and his staff, Washington frequently entrusted Lafayette, who had not yet come of age and had never experienced combat before his arrival in America, with important assignments. Jefferson's artful twisting of American politicians would in time become legendary, and he worked his magic on Lafayette. Jefferson saw much that he admired in Lafayette, especially his "zeal," republicanism, and native intelligence. He also discerned flaws that many others failed to perceive, defects that would not be without consequence in Lafayette's ultimate crash. He thought Lafayette's overall education had been inadequate—the bright spot was his capability "to comprehend perfectly whatever [Jefferson] explained to him"—but his most egregious "foible" was his "canine appetite for popularity and fame." Lafayette, meanwhile, often entertained Jefferson in his Left Bank home, a mansion whose furnishings were in part inspired by what he had seen at George Washington's Mount Vernon. In the end, Jefferson appears to have been the superior manipulator. "I am More and More pleased with Mr Jefferson," Lafayette wrote to Washington on New Year's Day 1788. "His abilities, His Virtues, His temper; Every thing of Him Commands Respect and Attracts Affection. He . . . does the Affairs of America to perfection."[71]

As the date for the meeting of the Estates General neared, Jefferson met regularly with Lafayette and other reform-minded aristocrats, sometimes offering advice and on occasion even hosting meetings at his residence in which he participated in the discussions. Jefferson appears to have aired his thoughts on the contents of a French bill of rights and advised these acquaintances on what powers the Estates General should seek for itself. On at least one occasion, he hosted a dinner for the purpose of bringing together warring elements among the reformist aristocrats. Some who sat in the Estates General subsequently described their experience that summer, perhaps including their discussions with Jefferson, as a "school of Revolution." In the end, Jefferson was disappointed with the draft of a Declaration of Rights produced by Lafayette, as it included neither freedom of religion nor a Jeffersonian proclamation of the right of the people to alter or abolish a government. Jefferson counseled that the "Noblesse . . . will always prefer men who will do their dirty work for them," and he urged Lafayette not to be their tool.[72]

The Estates General convened on May 5, 1789, and in the span of a few weeks it carried out a revolution. Reconstituting itself as the National Assembly, it adopted the Declaration of the Rights of Man and of the Citizen that went beyond Lafayette's final draft and included recommendations that Jefferson had made in his many meeting with reformers. Several leaders in France's legislature acknowledged the influence of the Declaration of Independence and a radical Parisian journalist spoke for many in declaring that the American Revolution had "opened our eyes about the true destiny of peoples," especially their "natural rights, and the equality of everyone's rights." The National Assembly went further than Jefferson had gone in the Declaration. The French Declaration proclaimed that humankind was "born and remain free and equal," enumerated individual rights as including "liberty, property, security, and resistance to oppression," declared that "Liberty consists in the freedom to do everything which injures no one else," and included what was tantamount to a bill of rights. In what one legislator called the "electric whirlwind" of progressive activity during that summer, the Assembly abolished serfdom, mandatory tithing to the church, and the tax exemptions enjoyed by the elite, and embraced the principle of meritocracy through its declaration that "careers [are] open to talent."[73]

Jefferson wasted little time in informing Paine, who was still in England, that France's reformers had "prostrated the old government" and laid a "superb edifice" for "a new one." Confident that the reformers had succeeded in "cutting the Gordian knot," Jefferson advised Paine that the resolute National Assembly was prepared "to set fire to the four corners of the kingdom and to perish . . . rather than to relinquish an iota" of what it had achieved. Indeed, early that summer he thought the French Revolution, as both he and Paine rapidly labeled the events that were transpiring, was largely over, and deep into the summer of 1789 Jefferson continued to believe that carnage could be avoided. But he could no longer say it had been a "bloodless" revolution. Early in May he acknowledged the first instances of bloodshed, and one day in July, while out on business, Jefferson himself witnessed a bloody clash between the king's soldiers and a mob. He wrote to Paine immediately to say that the ultimate success or failure of the reformers "will depend on the army." The very next day, July 14, another mob stormed the Bastille, where for generations the monarch's prisoners had been confined and sometimes tortured. After a battle that raged for hours, leading to the death of ninety-eight attackers and one soldier among those defending the jail, the crowd penetrated the facility. Once the Bastille's seven prisoners were released, several guards were butchered. The Bastille's governor was slain, too, after which his head was sawed off, affixed to a pike, and paraded triumphantly through the streets of Paris.

Louis XVI had largely remained quiet, not to mention ineffectual, throughout the previous six weeks, seemingly unaware of the momentous events taking place. Even the importance of the fall of the Bastille escaped him. After the king had characterized the mob's activity as a riot, the duc de la Rochefoucauld-Liancourt corrected him: "Sire, this is not a riot, it is a revolution." In the days that followed, other inflamed mobs took control of Paris, demonstrating, plundering, and killing. Hoping to stop the unrest, the king formally accepted the existence of the National Assembly, though not the Declaration of Rights, and on July 17 he rode into Paris accompanied by the members of the National Assembly, who walked in two ranks on each side of the royal carriage. The king came not to conquer Paris, but to bow symbolically to it and to the legislature, hoping against hope that his gesture would end the violence and the Revolution. Jefferson was part of the throng that lined the streets to see the king. Many in the crowd that he estimated at sixty thousand carried "pistols, swords, pikes, pruning hooks, scythes, &c" that they had pilfered from the Bastille three days earlier, but they were peaceful. Jefferson reported home that many along the streets and looking down from upstairs windows saluted Louis with "cries of 'vive la nation.' But not a single 'vive la roy' was heard."

Lafayette immediately grasped the meaning of the day. The monarch had "turned himself over" to Paris and the National Assembly as its "prisoner." For neither the first nor the last time, Jefferson similarly displayed his striking ability to rapidly—and independently—divine the meaning of what had happened. In a jubilant mood, he wrote to Paine that same day, exclaiming that the king had "surrendered as it were" and that the National Assembly was "absolutely out of reach of attack." It now had "carte blanche" to make further changes, he exuberantly added. To another correspondent, Jefferson exclaimed that the "National assembly have now a clean canvas to work on here as we had in America." What Jefferson had immediately discerned became apparent to the ill-fated monarch only much later. In 1792 Louis reflected: "I know I missed my opportunity" to crush the Revolution, which he believed he could have done had he used military force in July 1789.[74]

Despite what Jefferson called an occasional "summary execution," Paris grew quieter as the summer wore on. Jefferson fretted about a monarchical and aristocratic counterrevolution, though he considered such a turn of events feasible only if the royalists were "supported . . . by the money of England."

He thought London's intervention was unlikely, but if Britain did come to the aid of the old order, Jefferson appeared to hope that the United States would provide help to France's revolutionaries. After all, France had "engaged herself in a ruinous war for us, has spent blood and money to save us, has opened her bosom to us in peace," whereas England had "moved heaven, earth and hell to exterminate us" and "has insulted us in all her councils in peace." France's revolutionaries had also looked on the American Revolution "as a model . . . on every occasion."[75]

As summer faded toward autumn, Jefferson grew more confident that British intrusion was unlikely. He advised Paine that "no possibility" existed that the assembly would be prevented from establishing a "good constitution" that would be "a middle term between that of England and the United States." He predicted that the French government would "resemble that of England in its outlines, but not in its defects." Jefferson was euphoric, not just pleased with the changes that had swept over France, but confident that if the French could make their new revolutionary government work, republican revolutions would "spread sooner or later all over Europe." He told a correspondent that the French Revolution had amounted to nothing less than the *"first chapter* of the History of European liberty." To that he added: "I will agree to be stoned as a false prophet if all does not end well in this country."[76]

September 1789 found Jefferson packing to come home. A year earlier he had requested a temporary leave of absence to return to Monticello, which he had last seen in 1783. Though he planned to return to Paris in the summer of 1790, he had urgent reasons for going home. He hoped that his daughter Patsy, now seventeen, might marry a Virginian. In addition, he had recently learned that he was alarmingly mired in debt, a turn of events brought on in some measure by the economic dislocations sown by the American Revolution as well as by his extravagant lifestyle. He believed that in a few months at home he could implement the necessary changes in operations to make his estate more productive. It is not inconceivable that Jefferson also wished to look into obtaining an important office in the new national government under the new Constitution. In fact, before he sailed—though long after he requested the leave to come home—Jefferson had learned from Madison that President Washington wondered if "any appointment at home" would be agreeable to him.[77]

Jefferson's reputation, which had nearly been fatally shattered during his last disastrous months as governor, had been rehabilitated within Virginia. Outside his state, however, few were aware of him or his grandest achievement, his authorship of the Declaration of Independence. Neither of the first two histories of the American Revolution—William Gordon's in 1788 and

David Ramsay's the next year—even addressed the authorship of the Declaration. Washington and other revolutionaries were praised at Independence Day banquets in the 1780s, but no record exists that toasts were raised to Jefferson. Startlingly, Jefferson had done nothing to make the public aware of his accomplishment. Whereas Franklin had devoted a lifetime to self-promotion and Washington, after the war, had retained a biographer and guided him in smoothing over the military disasters that had occurred on his command in two wars, Jefferson had shied away from advancing his standing. Responding to questions about the Declaration of Independence raised by a French historian in 1786, he said only that a committee had drawn up the document. A year later, when the *Journal de Paris* credited John Dickinson with having written the Declaration, Jefferson had drafted a corrective to the editor, but he said only that the Paris newspaper was incorrect in crediting Dickinson. After thinking it over, Jefferson opted to not mail the letter.[78]

A few weeks before he sailed home, Jefferson invited a group of Americans living in Paris to his annual Independence Day gala. On this occasion, the guests paid tribute to Jefferson as the author of the Declaration of Independence. Their ringing written statement acknowledged that Jefferson's "elegance of thought and expression" had "added a peculiar lustre to that declaratory act which announced to the world the existence of an empire."[79] This was the first real step toward making the public aware of his achievement, and thereafter word of Jefferson's feat spread far and wide.

Late in September 1789 Jefferson left Paris and a few days later crossed the Channel. Almost a month after beginning his journey, Jefferson's party—which included his two daughters, two slaves, and a dog he had acquired in France—sailed from Yarmouth. Twenty-six days later, on November 23, Jefferson set foot on Virginia soil.[80] He would never again leave the United States.

Paine was hardly uninterested in the frenetic events in France, but he had not been active in anything that occurred. Between the time of his arrival from America in May 1787 and Jefferson's departure for home twenty-eight months later, Paine had spent nine months in France in the course of two separate stays, but he had published nothing about the dramatic revolutionary events. He was consumed with his bridge, which he candidly confessed was his "principal object." He surely realized, too, that blundering into politics in a strange land could be ruinous for his engineering aspirations.[81]

But the bridge alone may not have entirely accounted for Paine's inactivity. Unlike the American Revolution, which from the time of Paine's arrival in Philadelphia in 1774 held at least the possibility of triggering worldwide transformative changes, the French Revolution in its earliest period seemed likely at best to result in a constitutional monarchy along the lines of what existed in England. The epic events of 1789 aroused him. Suddenly, he "rejoiced" that France was "getting into the right way," and he held out hope that in the end the French king would be less powerful than the English king. Above all, as the National Assembly became a republican body—a unicameral legislature without a separate house for the aristocracy—Paine was enlivened, clutching at the possibility that the English, like the French, would turn "their eyes toward the aristocrats." For the first time, the events in France appeared to him to hold the prospect that the French Revolution might be a beacon that would produce revolutions elsewhere, including in England. In the autumn of 1789, after an absence of fifteen months, Paine hurried back to France. He arrived in Paris just days after Jefferson's departure.[82]

CHAPTER 6

"MY COUNTRY IS THE WORLD"

PAINE AND THE EARLY YEARS OF THE FRENCH REVOLUTION

PAINE'S MOST RELIABLE SOURCE ON events in France had been Jefferson, who in turn was provided with invaluable information by the Marquis de Lafayette. By the time Paine returned to Paris in the fall of 1789, Lafayette was not merely an important player; he was one of the Revolution's leading figures, the vice president of the National Assembly and commander of the National Guard, the Parisian civic militia created by the Assembly to restore and maintain order within the city in the wake of the bloody assault on the Bastille. Lafayette's power increased after Louis XVI failed to use his army to smash the revolutionaries in July, and he became even more powerful when the king capitulated yet again in October, at nearly the very moment that Paine arrived back in Paris.

At the outset of the month, large numbers of Parisians—at first mostly women, though in short order they were joined by throngs of men—marched on Versailles in the wind and lashing rain. Initially, they were prompted more by a severe shortage of bread in the city's markets than by political issues. The crowd got onto the palace grounds and eventually into the palace itself. Although there were seven hundred rooms in the royal residence, some intruders found the bedchamber of Marie Antoinette, causing the queen to flee in her bare feet for safer quarters. But the king and queen were not hurt and a bloodbath was prevented, in large part because Lafayette and his National Guard established a measure of control.

Lafayette convinced the king that the time had come to accept the Declaration of the Rights of Man and of the Citizen. Assisted by the milling and unpredictable crowd, Lafayette also persuaded the monarch to move from Versailles to the Tuileries Palace in Paris. Escorted by some ten thousand National Guardsmen and the sixty thousand or so joyous Parisians who had descended on Versailles, the king and queen made a seven-hour trek to Paris, bumping along in their luxurious carriage on a journey that began under a bright autumn sun and ended after night had enveloped the city. Throughout the trip, the crowd treated Louis XVI and Marie Antoinette with respect, as did the crowds lining the streets of Paris. But the dwindling authority that Louis had clung to since the summer shrank even more in the course of the fateful twenty-four hours between the crowd's appearance in Versailles and the royal couple's arrival in Paris. Real power now belonged to the National Assembly, and no one in the legislature was more powerful than Lafayette, who was exalted as the "Hero of Two Worlds."[1]

Like Jefferson before him, Paine appeared to think that the French Revolution was now over, and he was ecstatic at the sweeping changes that had occurred. The demolition of the Bastille, which Paine labeled "the high altar and castle of despotism," symbolized the eradication of the "spoils of despotism." As Lafayette, whom he described as his "very good friend," had the reins of power in his hands, Paine was confident that affairs would continue on the right track. He knew that Lafayette had been profoundly influenced by the American Revolution and he believed that the general and his circle were virtuous and enlightened reformers. Nothing cheered Paine more than his belief that the changes wrought in 1789 were the "first ripe fruits of American principles transplanted into Europe." Not only had the monarch's authority been substantially diminished, but before 1789 ended, the National Assembly had placed the church's property at the disposition of the nation and abolished monastic establishments.[2] Paine shared his joy with numerous correspondents, including his newfound friend Edmund Burke.

Now nearly sixty, the paunchy, jowly, inveterately rumpled Burke had come to London from his native Ireland nearly three decades earlier to study law and pursue a literary career. His early success as a writer brought him to the attention of Lord Rockingham, a power among the Whigs in Parliament. Burke served as his secretary for a time, after which he won a seat in the House of Commons with Rockingham's backing. In time, Burke came to be seen as a major player on behalf of parliamentary and financial reform. By 1776, because of three major speeches denouncing the American policies of Lord North's ministry as misguided, Burke had become extremely popular among the colonists. Paine was anxious to meet this defender of the colonists' rights, whom he called "a friend to mankind." Burke was no less eager to make the acquaintance of the famed author of *Common Sense*, whom he called "the great American Paine." Sometime after Paine's return to England in 1787 the two met for dinner, brought together through a letter of introduction by Paine's friend Henry Laurens, the former president of the Continental

Congress. Paine subsequently spent several days at Burke's large country house outside London, prompting him to tell Jefferson that he was "in some intimacy with Mr. Burke." It was a close and affable relationship, based on mutual admiration and what both thought was a similar political outlook—a dislike for England's ruling party. But as is often the case with those who are politically active, each wanted something from the other. Paine in 1789 was not only angling for support for his bridge, but at Jefferson's request he was also seeking information about Britain's policies and intentions. Burke and his friends in the commercial sector hoped that Paine's connections across the sea might help in the normalization of Britain's relations with America.[3]

Paine badly misjudged Burke, believing that he, too, would rejoice in the changes afoot in France. Indeed, Paine could not understand how Burke, who had not condemned the American Revolution, could oppose the changes that had taken place in France. Paine was additionally confounded as most of Burke's Whig comrades had reacted positively to the events in Paris of 1789, including Charles James Fox, the faction's leader, who had called the storming of the Bastille "the greatest event . . . that ever happened in the world!" In January 1790, while still in Paris, Paine wrote to Burke about the events in France, elation in his tone. Paine praised the National Assembly for its "coolness" and "Wisdom," and confided that the assemblymen harbored a "Plan of a total Change of Government." He noted the antipathy toward the aristocracy that had surfaced, writing that "the term Aristocrat is used here" as was the "Word Tory in America." More ominously, from Burke's point of view, was word from Paine that the "Revolution in France is certainly a Forerunner to other Revolutions."[4]

Burke, who was far more conservative than Paine realized, was startled by what he read, and even more alarmed by events in France that occurred soon after he received Paine's missive. The National Assembly had abolished feudalism, put an end to the privileges enjoyed by the nobility, and renounced all differentiations in status, abolishing titles such as count, marquis, and baron. Henceforth, each person was simply a "citizen." Having already confiscated church properties, the assembly adopted the Civil Constitution of the Clergy, which dramatically reorganized the church and mandated that the clergy must swear loyalty to that Constitution. The political changes brought on by the Revolution caused Burke no less consternation. France had in name become a constitutional monarchy, though the discerning could see that it was close to having become a full-fledged republic. Indeed, one historian of the Revolution has noted that by early 1790 the "bedrock of democratic modernity was in place." Sensing the danger that lurked down the road, some seventy-five thousand aristocrats and clergy had fled into exile that year, and they were joined by a roughly equal number of other émigrés from the lower social orders.[5]

About the time that Paine wrote to Burke, he also wrote to Washington. The packet he sent included a key to the Bastille, a gift from Lafayette. In an accompanying missive, Lafayette said that he was presenting the key to "that fortress of despotism . . . [as] a tribute Which I owe as A Son to My Adoptive father, as an aid de Camp to My General, as a Missionary of liberty to its patriarch."[6] The president, enraptured like most Americans by the dramatic events in France, would proudly hang the key in the entrance hall at Mount Vernon. Paine's letter to Washington displayed a lack of concern about the course of the French Revolution, save for his worry that Parisian mobs might cause "Tumults" that would provoke foreign intervention. Above all, he worried that Great Britain might take up arms against France, as the Crown was driven by "an aristocratical hatred against the principles of the French Revolution." Perhaps leaning too heavily on Lafayette's understanding of things, Paine advised the president that Louis XVI saw himself as the "head of the revolution," continued to exercise a measure of executive authority, and was "on good terms with the Nation and the National Assembly." With Burke, Paine had taken a slightly different tack. The king, he had said, was not uncomfortable with what had transpired. Indeed, he was happier than he had been in years, for the uncertainty that had dogged him during the approach of the Revolution had at last been resolved and he no longer was "accountable" for all the woes that plagued France.[7]

If Paine actually believed this, Burke saw things quite differently, and with greater clarity. He understood that the king had lost his authority and was the captive of Paris and the National Assembly. The class-conscious Burke was riled by what he regarded as the monarch's humiliation at having been forced by a mob of lowly Parisians to leave Versailles. Moreover, unlike Paine, Burke did not believe the Revolution was over. Once a "mentality of insurrection" was planted, he prophesied, it could be expected to take on a life of its own. With the monarchy in shambles, Burke was convinced that there was no longer an authority in France with sufficient power or wisdom to control the unbridled fury of mobs. Even more, Burke felt the day was coming when more fanatical revolutionaries would gain control and take the Revolution to more extreme lengths.[8]

But what mostly gnawed at Burke was the fear that the French Revolution would spread far and wide, and would inspire "wicked persons" to provoke unrest within England. There can be little doubt that Burke thought of Paine, with his persuasive pen, as among the villainous who might stir up trouble. However, Dr. Richard Price worried him even more. Price was a dissenting clergyman with a wide following in London. (He was so popular that Abigail Adams liked to listen to his sermons when she resided in the city.) Jefferson had long corresponded with Price and dined with him at least twice during his 1786 visit to England. Paine was familiar with him, for Price had been a major player in the English reform movement that two decades earlier had given shape to Paine's thinking. He regarded Price as "one of the best-hearted men that lives." Around the time that Burke read Paine's troubling letter, he also read a sermon that Price had recently delivered in which he predicted that the French Revolution would ignite a "reformation of the governments of Europe." Price had gone on to urge parliamentary reform in England and to proclaim that England's monarch should be the "*Servant*" of the people, not their sovereign—the very sentiment Jefferson had propounded in his *Summary View* essay.⁹

Certain that Price and Paine, and other firebrands, were bent on sowing revolution within England, Burke responded early in February with a lengthy speech in the House of Commons. He called the French revolutionaries "architects of ruin" who had "pulled down to the ground" the monarchy, church, nobility, and more. France was in the grip of "a relentless despotism" piloted by mobs and "irrational, unprincipled" radicals committed to the menace of a "confiscating, plundering, ferocious, bloody, and tyrannical democracy." France had adopted "a bad constitution," whereas before 1789 it was "absolutely in possession of a good one." With "the most atrocious perfidy and breach of faith," France's revolutionaries had "laid the axe to the root of all property." Burke asked his colleagues in Parliament to consider how they "would like to have their mansions pulled down and pillaged, their persons abused, insulted, and destroyed; their title deeds brought out and burned before their faces, and themselves . . . driven to seek refuge" in foreign countries. Three days after the speech, a London publisher announced that he soon would publish Burke's book-length analysis of the French Revolution.¹⁰

No one was more surprised than Paine by Burke's unsparing assault on the French Revolution. During his stay as Burke's guest a couple of years earlier, Paine had predicted that there was going to be a revolution in France, basing his forecast largely on insights provided by Jefferson.¹¹ Paine had not thought Burke was anguished by the likelihood of drastic change in France. Now, however, little guesswork was required to anticipate that Burke's forthcoming book would be a defense of monarchy, a sortie against reforms of any sort, and a full-blown attack on all that had been achieved by the French Revolution. Paine had already begun writing what he must have intended to be a history of the stirring events of 1789—"Common Sense is writing a Book," Lafayette had informed Washington in January 1790, adding that "there you will See a part of My Adventures"—but Burke's speech caused him to shift his emphasis to a defense of the French Revolution and a call for reforms in England. Having composed *Common Sense* within a few weeks, Paine expected that a gifted writer like Burke would complete his tract rapidly and that it would appear during the spring of 1790. Wishing to have his vindication of the French Revolution available immediately after the publication of Burke's work, Paine hurried to London, ending a three-month stay in Paris. Late in March, three months after Jefferson's arrival in Virginia, Paine took up residence in Soho Square, near the center of London, and set about writing his newly conceived book.[12]

Burke's book was much slower in coming out than Paine had anticipated. It was not that Burke was a laggard. He was writing at a moving target, trying frantically to keep apace of events in France. He found it necessary to discard and rewrite entire sections in light of new developments, and also to take a wait-and-see approach before tackling some topics. Like many good writers, he was also given to meticulous revision. Spring passed and summer as well. Burke's book still had not appeared. Paine waited with growing impatience, as he wished to read Burke's book before completing his own. Nevertheless, Paine continued to write as the year progressed from season to season. He probably completed the bulk of his manuscript within a few weeks, though he put down his pen until he could read Burke and fashion a worthy rebuttal.

Nine months came and went. Sometime during that period, Paine moved to the Angel Inn in Islington, a bustling, mostly working-class neighborhood that was reputed to be a quieter location with fewer distractions. He devoted some time to writing and some to his bridge, and from time to time he checked with Burke's publisher to learn if his book's release was imminent. The book was progressing ever so slowly, the publisher confided, and he revealed that Burke was given to vacillation and rewriting, having reworked some sections of his draft as many as nine times. Paine passed some of the time in taverns and coffeehouses conversing and swapping stories with friends and acquaintances. One evening he dined with Mary Wollstonecraft, the feminist pamphleteer, and her eventual husband, novelist William Godwin. Wollstonecraft had recently returned from Paris, having traveled there to observe the Revolution. She, too, would produce a critique of Burke's book; in fact, hers was in print before Paine's. It is likely that much was said that evening over dinner about Burke and the French Revolution, though Paine characteristically said little while in the presence of women, and Wollstonecraft typically dominated every conversation in which she took part. Godwin subsequently recollected that Paine was "no great talker . . . though he threw in occasionally some shrewd and striking remarks." At meal's end, a "displeased" Godwin—he had accepted the dinner invitation because of his "very great curiosity to see Thomas Paine," whom he had not previously met—lamented that Wollstonecraft had so "ventilated" that Paine could hardly get in a word.[13]

With time on his hands, Paine frequently called on Gouverneur Morris, who arrived in London from Paris at very nearly the same time in the spring of 1790 that Paine returned from France. Following the Constitutional Convention, to which he had been sent as a delegate by Pennsylvania, Morris had spent a year in France alternately working for Robert Morris and a private company. Early in 1790, President Washington asked him to serve as an informal emissary to the British government. During the time the two were in Paris, Paine had often called on Morris. Given the exasperated tone of Morris's diary, Paine likely had dropped by entirely too often, boring him with incessant talk of his bridge. Paine also had a proclivity for overstaying his welcome, and more than once an irritated Morris scribbled in his journal that the visits left him with little time for more important things. Atop the inconveniences brought on by Paine's visits, Morris looked with disdain on Paine, a man whom he had openly deprecated in Congress in 1779 for his plebian origins.

Now that both were in London, and not living far apart, Paine resumed his visitations, on occasion twice a day. He had an additional reason for appearing at Morris's door: Paine was avid for word about British intentions that he might pass on to Jefferson. There were times when an exasperated Morris showed him the door and once he even told Paine that he was "a troublesome Fellow." On one occasion, Paine, perhaps under the misapprehension that Morris was now his friend, reminded him of the time when he had been "among those who were his Enemies." Morris acknowledged the truth of Paine's observation. Morris's diary reveals his incredibly busy social habits, visiting and dining often with a wide range of friends—including Maria Cosway, whom he found "vastly pleasant" and intriguing, and at whose home "dangerous Connections may be formed" between the sexes—but he never once called on Paine, never asked him to stop by, and never invited him to dinner. Nothing deterred Paine. He continued to show up, once dropping in when Morris was preoccupied with "a Leg Maker" who was fashioning a new "Stump" to replace his old wooden leg with a copper one. Many times, at least from Morris's perspective, Paine spoke of nothing of importance. Of course, he waxed on about his bridge and frequently asked Morris to come see it. Finally, in September 1790, Morris did make the trip to Lisson Green to look over the bridge and concluded that it was neither "so handsome as he [Paine] thinks it is" nor strong enough to accommodate heavy traffic.[14]

While awaiting Burke's book, Paine crossed twice for brief stays in Paris. In July, Paine and John Paul Jones, among others, composed an American delegation that marched in the Festival of the Federation, commemorating the first anniversary of the fall of the Bastille. He returned in October to carry the American flag in a ceremony celebrating France's new constitution. Paine cut short his second stay in Paris when he learned that Burke's long-awaited book was set for publication on November 1. He dashed back to London and was one of the first to purchase *Reflections on the Revolution in France*. During the first week in November, Paine brushed the dust from what he had thought was his nearly completed manuscript and began work on his defense of the French Revolution.[15]

Paine had thought he could get his book out hard on the heels of Burke's, but his also took longer to complete than he had imagined. He had to puzzle out his response to unanticipated portions of Burke's argument. In addition, *Reflections* roused numerous published rejoinders—about a dozen immediately and nearly seventy-five within a couple of years—and Paine wished to read some before completing his own work.[16] Time was also required to digest Burke's two-hundred-page treatise.

Burke's *Reflections* has remained a treasure trove in the hearts of conservatives through the ages. It passionately defended patriarchy, class domination, and inequalities of every kind that had safeguarded the old order in France and buffered England's political system. It included swipes—sometimes overt, sometimes less transparent—against English reformers such as Reverend Price, whom he mentioned repeatedly as the "political Preacher." (Burke did not refer to Paine in his text.) But the bulk of *Reflections* was an unrelenting onslaught against the French revolutionaries and a passionate argument against abrupt and radical change.

Burke reasoned that societies and governments took shape through long stretches of history, laying the groundwork for order, building an edifice based more on obligations than on individual rights, and instilling in the citizenry respect for the social and political world into which they were born. Burke argued that the end result was a government and culture that served the needs and well-being of the citizenry. "Society" and its government, he wrote, is "a partnership not only between those who are living, but between those who are living, those who are dead, and those who are to be born." He likened it to a "primeval contract of eternal society . . . connecting the visible and invisible world," a contract that is not subject to the will of the living. Indeed, the living "are bound to submit their will" to that immutable contract. Burke did not deny that change should at times occur, but he maintained that mutations should take place gradually so that the fabric of the state and society remained intact. Change in the fashion that Burke envisaged would leave those best prepared for governance—a ruling class drawn from the propertied elite and including a monarch and aristocracy—in place and continuing to wield power.

Burke did not offer merely a philosophical treatise on the necessity of maintaining the status quo. For the most part, *Reflections* was a philippic directed at the French Revolution, which had severed France's ties with its past and ushered in radical political, social, religious, and economic transformations. Paine labeled Burke's appraisal a "tribute of fear," and in fact it was just that. Fear is often the bedrock of the conservative mind-set, an unsettling anxiety that change leads to the unknown, that any departure might not be manageable, and that any adaptation might touch off a whirlwind of volatility that in the end could obliterate all that the privileged had come to enjoy. Burke's mission was to awaken England's ruling class to the peril it, too, would face should reformers such as Price and Paine succeed—as had the revolutionaries in France—in cutting "loose the reins of regal authority" and opening the floodgates to "a ferocious dissoluteness in manners, and . . . an insolent irreligion" that would endanger the possessions and entitlements of the privileged. Page after page of Burke's *Reflections* was a compilation of cruel revolutionary acts that had resulted in "bathing in tears, and plunging in poverty and distress, thousands of worthy men and worthy families." France was in the grip of "levellers" who had "change[d] and pervert[ed] the natural order of things," extinguishing "all orders, ranks, and distinctions," handing down edicts little better than "polluted nonsense."

Monarchical France, Burke contended, had made "power gentle, and obedience liberal," furnishing a "decent drapery" that "harmonized the different shades of life and . . . incorporated into politics the sentiments which beautify and soften private society." The ancien régime, and the attributes it had brought to France, was gone, "dissolved by this new conquering empire of light and reason." Men such as Lafayette, imprudent aristocrats whose "mischiefs" had arisen "from conspiracies, irregular consultations, seditious committees, and monstrous democratic assemblies," had opened Pandora's box. Once their "imbecility" had set things in motion, the "swinish multitude"—Burke's contemptuous term for working-class protestors—had taken to the streets. Mobs driven by "Rage and phrenzy," and reveling in wickedness, had run amok, seeking to clear "away as mere rubbish whatever they found." Through "violences, rapines, burnings, murders . . . and every description of tyranny and cruelty," they had succeeded in "pull[ing] down more in half an hour, than prudence, deliberation, and foresight can build up in an hundred years."[17]

The section in Burke's work that attracted the most attention among some critics was his lachrymose response to the plight of the queen, Marie Antoinette, who he thought had been treated with insolence during the royal family's forced removal to Paris. He was beside himself that commoners and armed National Guardsmen had burst into her bedchamber at Versailles, obliging her to flee "almost naked" through a secret passage. Later that day she had been compelled to "taste, drop by drop, more than the bitterness of death, in the slow torture" of the mob's derision throughout the lengthy trek to Paris. Now the queen, "distinguished for her piety" and "lofty sentiments," was a captive of the revolutionaries. Burke, who had seen the queen once, recalled that he had never caught sight of "a more delightful vision." She was "glittering like the morning-star, full of life, and splendor, and joy." He could never have imagined

> such disasters fallen upon her in a nation of gallant men, in a nation of men of honour and of cavaliers. I thought ten thousand swords must have leaped from their scabbards to avenge even a look that threatened her with insult.—But the age of chivalry is gone.—That of sophisters, economists, and calculators, has succeeded; and the glory of Europe is extinguished for ever. Never, never more, shall we behold that generous loyalty to rank and sex, that proud submission, that dignified obedience, that subordination of the heart, which kept alive, even in servitude itself, the spirit of an exalted freedom. The unbought grace of life, the cheap defence of nations, the nurse of manly sentiment and heroic enterprize is gone! It is gone, that sensibility of principle, that chastity of honour, which felt a stain like a wound, which inspired courage whilst it mitigated ferocity, which ennobled whatever it touched, and under which vice itself lost half its evil, by losing all its grossness.[18]

Not everyone shared Burke's enchantment with Marie Antoinette. Paine did not seethe with hatred for her—a year earlier he had written to Washington to ask that he "congratulate the King and Queen of France (for they have been our friends)" on having provided a "happy example . . . to Europe"—but he was roiled by Burke's lament for the queen. It was not so much Burke's fulsome praise that incensed Paine, but that he had ignored the plight of millions who suffered from the iniquities of powerlessness. Of the passage on the queen in *Reflections*, Paine's telling response to Burke was, "He pities the plumage, but forgets the dying bird." Jefferson took even greater exception to the "rhapsodies of Burke." Convinced that Marie Antoinette was the power behind the throne, Jefferson felt that her misrule had produced "crimes and calamities which will forever stain the pages of modern history." Two years before the Estates General met, Jefferson remarked that "the queen cries but sins on." Later, he said that "had there been no Queen, there would have been no revolution." Not even Gouverneur Morris, who was so conservative that he wept at hearing Louis XVI address the Estates General, was particularly troubled by the queen's humbling experiences at the hands of the Parisian crowd. Unlike Burke, who had been swept off his feet on first seeing the queen, Morris's initial impression was that Marie Antoinette was cold, hard, contemptuous, and vengeful. He believed that most French citizens hated her, and when she and the king were forced to move to Paris, the most that the prescient Morris could muster for the ill-fated queen was: "Poor Lady. This is a sad Presage of what is too likely."[19]

Aside from his overwrought solicitude for France's queen, two things leaped from the pages of *Reflections* that especially angered numerous readers. Many in England who had applauded the changes in France, thinking them a step in the right direction both for the French citizenry and for the improvement of Franco-British relations, found Burke's tone intemperate. Others, including Jefferson, were put off by Burke's utter indifference to the widespread suffering and despair within France, and were shocked by his lack of pity and outrage at the plight of the poor. Burke was incensed only at the losses suffered by the privileged. Whereas Jefferson had reacted with horror at the wretchedness he saw throughout France and Europe, Burke was unmoved. Paine put it best. "It is power, not principles, that Mr. Burke venerates." So biased was Burke toward the ruling elite, and so indifferent was he toward their victims, that Paine concluded "he is unfitted for the subject he writes upon."[20]

Following the appearance of *Reflections*, three months passed before Paine completed his book. He wrote the final sentence of what he titled *Rights of Man*—taking his title from the Declaration of the Rights of Man and of the Citizen—on his fifty-fourth birthday near the end of January 1791. After a festive night celebrating the completion of his labors, Paine delivered the manuscript to his friend Joseph Johnson, a London publisher who had previously issued numerous radical tracts and a progressive magazine. Their plan was to bring out *Rights of Man* three weeks down the road on Washington's birthday, and in fact Paine dedicated the book to the president and sent him fifty copies in gratitude for his "exemplary virtue" and in the hope that he would "enjoy the happiness of seeing the New World regenerate the Old." After turning out a small run—probably no more than a few hundred copies—Johnson got cold feet. He was apprehensive that Paine's radicalism might lead the police to shut down his shop. Paine then shifted to J. S. Jordan, whose backbone was not only stronger, but who also likely sensed that *Rights of Man* would result in excellent sales. Jordan issued an edition in mid-March.[21]

Paine's publisher might have foreseen that *Rights of Man* would be a money-maker, but no one could have imagined the sales it would generate. Before summer, six editions had been printed and fifty thousand copies had been sold in Great Britain, fifty times more than the most popular novels or general works customarily sold. And that was only the beginning. By summer's end, the book was available in America (where, according to one estimate, more than fifty thousand copies soon were in circulation), and translated editions were selling in France and throughout Europe, including Transylvania. It outsold the sensational tracts of the English Reformation era nearly 250 years earlier, and it may have been the bestselling book of all time in England, with the exception of the Bible. Interest in the French Revolution was widespread, which helped sales, though among the scores of others who wrote about it only Burke realized truly noteworthy sales. How much Paine actually earned from the book can only be conjectured, although it is known that Burke realized today's equivalent of nearly one million dollars from the sale of nineteen thousand copies of *Reflections* within Britain and abroad, including in France. Paine said only that following the sale of all sixteen thousand copies of the first edition of *Rights of Man*, he intended to "make a cheap edition, just sufficient to bring in the price of the printing and paper." His comment suggests that, as usual, Paine was more interested in the dissemination of his ideas than in making money.[22]

The phenomenal sales of *Rights of Man* were due to Paine's unrivaled talent as a writer. As he had with *Common Sense*, Paine consciously sought a wide readership, and this former artisan without much schooling had an intuitive feel for what those who were similarly circumstanced could and would read. They were his target and he scored a bull's-eye.

Paine moved into new territory in *Rights of Man*, including areas that most English radicals had not visited. Before the 1790s, the ideal of English radicalism had remained a mixed government of monarchy, aristocracy, and democracy. Paine's stance fifteen years earlier in *Common Sense*—an exhortation for full-blown republicanism in which there was no place for monarchy—had been more radical than the public stance taken by England's radical reformers. By the 1790s, inspired by the American and French Revolutions, more English radicals wished to advance the general liberties of humankind, but even then few were true democrats who favored suffrage rights for what many thought were the unseemly masses. Most English radicals continued to champion a mixed government that included a House of Commons chosen by a broader electorate.[23] Paine had gone far beyond that in his thinking. He was concerned with the universal rights of man and of permitting the living to shape their world "*in all cases*" as they saw fit.

The nuts and bolts of *Rights of Man* included the bold assertions that the age of kings and titled nobilities had ended: All people possessed natural rights and all were citizens, and those citizens not only created governments, but determined government's power in written constitutions that could be altered only by the people. There was more. Paine wrote *Rights of Man* in a rage. His anger at France's ancien régime was palpable and so, too, was his vexation at what he called Burke's "outrageous abuse" and "flagrant misrepresentations" of the French Revolution. But, like Burke, Paine wrote with fear in his heart. His dread was the inverse of Burke's: It was that Great Britain would join other conservative nations in making war on France to destroy the Revolution and prevent its spread. Convinced that Burke was "afraid that England and France would cease to be enemies," and that *Reflections* had been written in part to create a sentiment within England for hostilities with France, Paine in turn wrote to cultivate friendship toward France and bolster the spirit of reform among ordinary Englishmen.

Where Burke had made change seem threatening and insisted that it must come at a glacial pace, Paine demonstrated that "no mode of redress had existed" in autocratic France for the elites' abuses of the common people. But the heart of Paine's argument was that each "age and generation must be free to act for itself." No generation possessed the "right or the power of binding and controlling posterity to the 'end of time,'" as Burke, "the trumpeter of . . . order," had asserted. Said Paine: "The vanity and presumption of governing beyond the grave, is the most ridiculous and insolent of all tyrannies." For Paine, it was "the living, and not the dead, that are to be accommodated. When man ceases to be, his power and his wants cease with him. . . . I am contending for the rights of the living. . . . Mr. Burke is contending for the authority of the dead over the rights and freedom of the living. . . . Although laws made in one generation often continue in force through succeeding generations, yet they continue to derive their force from the consent of the living."

Paine knew that Burke had exaggerated the degree of violence that had occurred in France, and he felt that the depiction of a hostile and threatening mob dragging the royal couple from Versailles to Paris was absolutely untrue. Paine accurately pointed out that the palace in Versailles had been left intact and he truthfully observed that "not an act of molestation was committed" against Louis XVI or Marie Antoinette during their journey to the city. (Paine, however, failed to mention that the royal couple had endured the disconcerting sight of the heads of two of their bodyguards atop pikes carried by members of the throng.) He countered Burke's delineation of the blood-soaked French countryside with a graphic account of the barbarous punishments meted out by the British government, especially the "terror" visited on "the lowest class of mankind" as the means of maintaining order.

In defending France's Declaration of Rights, Paine assailed monarchy, mostly revisiting familiar arguments from *Common Sense*, though he now called kingship "a fraud," a "useless thing" that provides nothing worthwhile to a nation. That "monster, aristocracy," must be eliminated everywhere as well. All titles of nobility, which he called "gewgaws," must be "brought . . . to the altar" and made "a burnt offering to Reason." Titles, which were "like circles drawn by the magician's wand," should be replaced by one term for all people—"citizen." The demolition of kingship and aristocracy would not lead to ruin and disorder. Americans had neither a king nor a titled nobility and they were "living in a style of plenty unknown in monarchical countries."

Like Jefferson, Paine saw a direct link between the revolutions in America and France. French soldiers who had served in the War of Independence returned to France aflame with the "cause of liberty" and longing to light its torch in France. Their time had come. Indeed, the "revolutions of America and France have thrown a beam of light over the world, which reached into man." Aware that nothing filled Burke and his fellow conservatives with greater dread than the spread of revolution, Paine added that once man began to reason and to understand his natural rights—once "the veil begins to rend," as he put it—"it admits not of repair." Change became inevitable. The French had rethought their lot. Now "every court in Europe, dreading the same fate" among its people, "is in mourning." No one grieved more than Burke, a "fawning character of that creature known in all countries, and a friend to none, a Courtier. . . . Nothing can be more terrible to a court or a courtier, than the Revolution of France. That which is a blessing to nations, is bitterness to them; and as their existence depends on the duplicity of a country, they tremble at the approach of principles, and dread the precedent that threatens their overthrow."

As his readers must have anticipated, Paine built to a stirring climax:

When we survey the wretched condition of man under the monarchical and hereditary systems of government, dragged from his home by one power, or driven by another, and impoverished by taxes more than by enemies, it becomes evident that those systems are bad, and that a general revolution in the principle and construction of government is necessary. . . .

As it is not difficult to perceive, from the enlightened state to mankind, that hereditary governments are verging to their decline, and that revolutions on the broad basis of national sovereignty, and government by representation, are making their way in Europe, it would be an act of wisdom to anticipate their approach, and produce revolutions by reason and accommodation, rather than commit them to the issue of convulsions.

From what we now see, nothing of reform on the political world ought to be held improbable. It is an age of revolutions, in which every thing may be looked for.[24]

Paine crossed the Channel once again in the spring of 1791, his first trip to France in six months, one that appears to have come about by his wish to see to the French translation of his sensational new book and, in all likelihood, to collect his royalties. He lodged initially with an eagerly hospitable American he had met on a previous visit, sharing an apartment that Gouverneur Morris, who for once called on Paine, thought "wretched." Paine did not stay with his friend for long, possibly because his roommate—who thought him "a little mad" (which, said Morris, "is not improbable")—asked him to move on. In any case, Paine had his own reasons for moving elsewhere. He had decided to write a sequel to *Rights of Man*, a book he originally intended to title *Kingship*. Paine was certain that another book would also reach a huge audience, though that was not all that prodded him. Just after he arrived in Paris, a tract by Burke was published in France under the title *A Letter to a Member of the National Assembly*, a brief essay in which he answered critics of *Reflections*. What would have caught Paine's eye was that Burke openly urged Britain to declare war on France. Unleash the "hell-hounds of war," Burke wrote, for not only was resistance "from without" the sole means of destroying the French Revolution, but Britain's rulers must act to provide "safety to themselves." Early in May, Paine moved with Lafayette's assistance to a private apartment in quiet Versailles and began to write.[25]

Six weeks later, on June 21, Lafayette burst into Paine's bedroom. "The birds are flown," he announced, unable to contain his excitement.[26] The king and queen, concealed in disguises, had sneaked out of the Tuileries and were making a run for the border, but not before leaving behind a manifesto that repudiated the Revolution. They had long since realized that they were captives in Paris. The king had gradually been deprived of virtually all authority and freedom, including free rein to hunt, his favorite pastime. In April, when he and the queen had attempted to vacation at a retreat outside Paris, their exit from the Tuileries had been blocked by a large, mistrustful crowd that had showered them with insults. Now they wanted out, and many who had the king's ear, and longed for a restoration of full monarchical authority, helped lay plans for the royal couple's flight.

In an instant, both Lafayette and Paine knew that the king and queen's decision to flee had changed everything. The notion of constitutional monarchy had been dealt a fatal blow. What was more, if the king succeeded in escaping France, foreign intervention to restore the old regime was a virtual certainty. That meant war, and hostilities would almost inevitably trigger a civil war. Paine hurried to Paris to get a better feel for things. He found that crowds, boiling with rage, had poured into the streets around the Tuileries and were tearing down all symbols emblematic of royalty. One wag had affixed a "For Rent" sign on the gate to what had been the royal residence. Paine met up with an old Scottish friend, Thomas Christie, a progressive London banker who had also written a rebuttal to Burke's *Reflections*, and the two walked to the Tuileries, where a proclamation by the National Assembly was to be read. According to a dubious account left by an unfriendly English source, when the reading ended each man in the throng waved his hat with the tricolor cockade, a sign of support for the Revolution. But in his haste to get to Paris, Paine supposedly had forgotten his hat. The crowd turned on him. People pointed toward him and shouted, "Aristocrat! Aristocrat! Hang him to the lamppost." The story goes that men grabbed Paine and dragged him toward the makeshift gallows, but Christie, who spoke French, shouted above the din that Paine was an American. The lynch mob in a flash backed off. Paine allegedly was bruised and badly shaken, but released.[27]

Meanwhile, the royal couple's flight continued. After leaving behind a statement that, among other things, implored the people to "come back to your king; he will always be your father, your best friend," the king and queen had carefully adhered to a plan that had been months in preparation. They managed to get out of the palace, but not until after midnight, an hour or more behind schedule. A speedy carriage conveyed them to the residence of a wealthy Englishman on the Rue de Clichy, where they transferred to a larger carriage. That, perhaps, was their fatal blunder. The berline they chose had been built especially for their escape attempt, but it was huge and slow, constructed more for luxury than speed. Built to carry an enormous amount of luggage, it also included picnic equipment, racks for bottles, padded seats, even a leather-covered chamber pot. Nor were the king and queen, and their son, the only ones on board. They had brought along servants and three bodyguards attired in conspicuous yellow garb and, of necessity, perched in the open near the driver. Though the black and yellow coach was drawn by a team of six horses, this conveyance was not going to move fast, and the escapees had to traverse 150 miles to reach their hoped-for destination, the fortress border town of Montmédy. Starting its journey in the dark of night, the coach exited Paris—a feat the planners had thought would be the greatest obstacle of all—and lumbered down the highway at a top speed of ten miles per hour. A nonstop trip would have taken about fifteen hours, but stops had to be made for fresh horses at nineteen relay stations. Each stopover took at least twenty minutes. After hours on the road, the carriage suffered a damaged wheel, which necessitated a thirty-minute delay for repairs.

Around eleven P.M. on June 21, nearly twenty-four hours after stealing out of the palace, the carriage stopped for the final change of horses at Varennes, an Argonne Forest village of fifteen hundred inhabitants some thirty miles from Montmédy and the border of the Austrian Netherlands (today's Belgium). It was there that Louis and Marie Antoinette ran out of luck. They were recognized and detained. Once the preparations for their return to Paris were completed, the king and queen were escorted back to the city by thousands of armed citizens and guardsmen. The return trip consumed four agonizing days in what turned out to be the hottest spell of the summer. When the plodding carriage at last reached Paris, tens of thousands of mostly silent citizens lined the streets, or watched from rooftops and trees, as the mammoth vehicle crept through the city streets.[28]

Thereafter, Paine lingered in Paris for only a fortnight. These were to be his last days in France for some fifteen months, and it was a busy time. To form a republican club and publish a magazine, Paine joined with the Marquis de Condorcet, whose salon he had frequented; Jacques-Pierre Brissot de Warville, a journalist and rising figure in the legislature; Étienne Clavièrre, later to be France's minister of finance; and Achille du Chastelet, a devil-may-care aristocrat who was fervidly anti-monarchical. In the wake of the king's flight, Paine thought the time was right for a publication urging the termination of France's monarchy. Republican France, he said, would "contribute to the advancement of the entire world."[29]

Paine quickly fired off essays for the club's short-lived magazine and a Parisian newspaper. In one, Paine proclaimed his "attachment to humanity" and reaffirmed his "avowed, open, and intrepid" enmity toward monarchy and aristocracy, the sowers of "the calamities, the exactions, the wars, and the massacres" that have "crushed mankind." Those efforts were temperate in contrast to "A Republican Manifesto." Dashing it off a week after the captured king and queen were returned to Paris, Paine and Chastelet raced about the city posting the fiery broadside on walls and doors. (It was reprinted the following day in a Paris newspaper.) Paine asserted that the monarch's flight was "equivalent to abdication." Previously, Paine had argued in print for the constitutional monarchy that Lafayette and his fellow aristocrats had always sought—and that Jefferson had hoped for—but in the "Manifesto" he wrote as if the monarchy had ceased to exist. In fact, Paine was the first into print to drop the royal title "Louis XVI" and refer to the presumptive monarch by his birth name, Louis Capet. Paine wrote another tract that summer, though inexplicably Condorcet withheld its publication for a year. It was a lengthy essay in defense of the constitution that the National Assembly had drafted and that the king had denounced in the statement he left behind before taking flight.[30]

From time to time during the ten weeks or more that he was in France, Paine saw Gouverneur Morris. Washington had appointed him to be Jefferson's successor as the United States minister, and he arrived in France at very nearly the same time as Paine. Not a few who sympathized with the French Revolution thought Morris a poor choice—a monarchist whom many, including Madame de Lafayette, sized up as an "Aristocrat." Morris was unpopular with the government for sheltering aristocrats, though Paine, never an advocate of wreaking injury on foes of the Revolution, did not criticize the minister on that score. But Paine was among those who thought Morris's appointment "*most unfortunate,*" and he told Jefferson, "I shall mention the same thing to him [Morris] when I see him." All too aware of Morris's extreme conservatism, including his concurrence with much in Burke's *Reflections*, Paine had hoped for an American envoy who would be enthused about republican France's steps to sever its ties to the royalist past.

Morris had always disliked visits by Paine, though he now thought his annoying caller a useful source of information, given his contacts among the revolutionaries. The last time the two were together during the summer of 1791 was at an Independence Day party attended by several Americans and Lafayette. Morris, who was easily nettled by Paine, was vexed again, finding him not only "big with a Litter of Revolutions" but "inflated to the Eyes" with his own importance. Morris was not alone in taking offense at Paine's conceit. Earlier, a Parisian acquaintance had mentioned that Paine was "drunk with vanity. If you believed him, it was he who had done everything in America."[31] Over the years, many would think Paine was insufferably egotistical. It was a decided flaw in his character, though it is not difficult to understand his need for worthiness or why he saw himself as consequential. He had become an important person on two continents, and his dizzying ascent was nearly unrivaled. Paine had started only a step or two above the bottom rung in England's stratified society, and into middle age he was penniless with a track record of repeated failure. *Common Sense*, *The American Crisis*, and *Rights of Man* made him famous, so renowned that by mid-1791 virtually no one in England was better known. The articulate in France were also aware of Paine's writings, and of all living Americans only Washington was as widely known.

Paine returned to England within a week of the Independence Day bash, beginning what was to be his last residence in his native land. The manuscript that he had begun while in Versailles was in his bags, though it was far from complete and would not be finished for another seven months. Paine happily discovered that *Rights of Man* continued to sell at a brisk clip in England and that it was also doing well in Ireland. A few weeks after he returned to London, Paine received a warm note from Jefferson informing him that *Rights of Man* "has been much read" in America and that it was being devoured with "avidity and pleasure." For the most part, Paine lived quietly and out of sight during his first months back in England, spending much of his time on his new book, which his old bridge-building compatriot John Hall, back for a visit in his homeland, called "Burke's Funeral Sermon." Paine told Washington that this would be his last book. The president was probably skeptical, as Paine added that he had been rejuvenated by the renewal of the "ardor of Seventy-six" within France. Paine also implied that the objective of the book he was writing was to ignite a similar fervor for reform within England. In typical Paine fashion, he said that he longed to lay down his burden and return to America, but that he would do so only if "there was some person in this country [France] that could usefully and successfully attract the public attention."[32]

One of Paine's hallmarks was audacity, and he showed his pluck by occasionally giving public speeches in London. A month after returning to England, he addressed a meeting of the Friends of Universal Peace and Liberty in the Thatched-House Tavern. Paine hurled a few barbs at Burke and his fellow "partisans of arbitrary power," defended republicanism and the French Revolution, and denounced the British government's indifference toward the "very numerous poor." Moving into territory that neither he nor many other English radicals had previously visited, Paine asserted that rulers had a "moral obligation" to provide for children, the elderly, and those in the iron grip of poverty. Later, in remarks before the Revolution Society, Paine toasted "THE REVOLUTION OF ALL THE WORLD."[33]

The British government was not happy to see Paine again, but it took no public notice of him, restrained by the sobering likelihood that any overt move on its part might only provoke trouble for itself. The government's lone major initiative was to subsidize a hostile biography by George Chalmers, a Scotsman who had emigrated to Maryland in 1763. In America, Chalmers had practiced law until, like thousands of other Tories, he fled for the safety of England during the American Revolution. In England, Chalmers obtained an influential government post on the Committee on Trade and published extensively, including biographies of Shakespeare and Daniel Defoe. His *Life of Thomas Paine* was written under the pseudonym "Francis Oldys," a fictitious character whom Chalmers endowed with a faculty position at the

University of Pennsylvania. He exhaustively researched his subject and was the first writer to shine a light on Paine's past. Among other things, readers learned of Paine's English origins. Perhaps most of his readers, like Burke, had supposed that America was his homeland. But Britain's vengeful government was paying Chalmers to be a literary assassin, not an objective biographer, and he did his best to render Paine an object of loathing. Chalmers cataloged Paine's earlier failures, including his loss of jobs and the breakup of his second marriage. About a quarter of his 128 pages was cut and pasted from previously published diatribes against *The Rights of Man*. Chalmers interspersed this with innuendo and unsubstantiated allegations, claiming among other things that Paine had refused to assist his elderly parents and mistreated both his wives.[34]

Paine, well steeled by now against invective, let it pass. He remained at work on his manuscript, which he had now decided to title *Rights of Man. Part the Second*. He wrapped up his writing after Christmas, but once again had problems with his publisher and the book did not appear until mid-February 1792. Paine dedicated this volume to Lafayette: "in gratitude for your services to my beloved America, and as a testimony of my esteem for the virtues . . . which I know you possess." To that, Paine added that should the despotic powers of Europe make war on France, and should Lafayette take the field to defend his country, "I will come and join you."[35]

Paine's preface included another attack on Burke, who during the previous summer had authored *Appeal from the New to the Old Whigs*, a pamphlet provoked by riots in Birmingham that, to Burke, bore the scent of revolution. But Paine did not linger over Burke's latest effort, and he said relatively little about recent events in France. Instead, he moved into an uncharted region, yet again staking out positions far in advance of most English radicals. Paine interpreted the unrest in Birmingham and elsewhere as a sign that the pillars were cracking and England was approaching the brink of widespread disorder. As always, Paine wished to do what he could to stir tumult within England. The rainbow that he chased was an English revolution, but even if that did not occur, domestic turmoil might at least prevent England's government from attacking revolutionary France. In fact, during the previous spring, when many thought Britain was about to enter the war against France, Gouverneur Morris had been informed that William Pitt—"Pitt the Younger," the son of the Earl of Chatham and now the prime minister—"does not hazard a War" because "Payne's Book works mightily in England." Paine doubtless heard the same rumor, though probably not from Morris, and it was further incentive in getting out a second volume.[36]

Paine opened *Rights of Man. Part the Second* by telling readers that earlier so-called European revolutions were not revolutions at all, but unimportant events carried out by courtiers in the royal court. The result was that the supposed insurrections "had nothing in them that interested the bulk of mankind." The American Revolution and the French Revolution were different. Based on principles, these two modern revolutions had brought about profound change. Government "ought to have no other object than the general happiness," Paine went on, and a true revolution would have as its "object a change in the moral condition of government." That set the stage for what Paine really sought. He wished to expand the focus of English radicalism, which for a half century or more had emphasized the need for parliamentary reform and not much else. Not that Paine ignored Parliament. He limned the legislature as useless to the mass of the population, a body composed of one house that represented only a tiny electorate and another chamber that consisted of noblemen who inherited their seats. As such, Parliament was little more than a contrivance for piling taxes on the backs of the least fortunate.

Paine then focused on England's system of taxation and the harsh burden it imposed on the poorest in society. England, he wrote, was a country dominated by a powerful elite of great land owners who exercised total sway over the poor and downtrodden. The elite lived "apart from distress, and the expense of relieving it." They were separate from the manufacturing towns and laboring villages—doubtless including his own Thetford—where the burdens spawned by England's class system "press the heaviest." So bad was the situation in many hamlets that "one class of poor" was compelled to support another. None fared worse under this system than children and the elderly, for the landed elite, through its control of Parliament and its unholy alliance with the Crown, had succeeded in "throw[ing] so great a part of [taxation] from their shoulders" and onto the backs of others. This privileged class did not bear its fair share of the burden of taxation.

The elite controlled the political system, which it had rigged in its favor and to the detriment of the great body of the citizenry. Ministries changed, but putting new faces in power "amounts to nothing. One goes out, another comes in, and still the same vices, and extravagance are pursued. It signifies not who is minister. The defect lies in the system. The foundation and superstructure of the government is bad." Paine added that the time had come when the people of England must no longer "be governed like animals for the pleasure of their riders." Instead, urging a compassion that even today is decried by some, he argued that the time had come to steeply increase the taxes levied on the wealthiest and, in particular, to hike their property taxes. The latter step would induce the land barons to rid themselves of a portion of their sprawling estates, and that in turn would make land available to the landless. The enhanced revenue derived from restructuring the system of taxation would provide the English government with the funds to provide for the most vulnerable. The uses that Paine proposed were unorthodox in his time and for generations to come: subsidies for the aged and poorest citizens, free education for children of the impoverished, and economic assistance at the time of marriage for the neediest.

Paine was relatively restrained toward England's monarchy, having amply assailed it in previous works. But he did not ignore it entirely. He impugned the "arbitrary power" implicit in royalty and the "profligate and prodigal" habits of kings. England had spent seventy million pounds "to maintain a family imported from abroad," with much of the money raised through taxes levied on "thousands who are . . . pining with want, and struggling with misery." In contrast, President Washington eschewed a lavish lifestyle. "His sense of honor is of another kind," wrote Paine.

In *Part the Second*, Paine focused more on the aristocracy, which he got to in a roundabout fashion. Unlike France and the United States, he wrote, England lacked a written constitution. As a result, "the whole has no bounds." There was no charter "that either gives or restrains power," or "regulate[s] the wild impulse of power." One key to instituting "a change in the moral condition" of England was a written constitution that checked the capriciousness of rulers. Though chary, what Paine wrote could be interpreted only as a call for a constitutional monarchy that limited royal authority, as the United States Constitution established limitations on the power of the presidency and France's new constitution circumscribed monarchical authority. But in calling for a unicameral assembly—one with staggered terms as a safeguard against rash actions—Paine was unmistakably advocating the elimination of the House of Lords, an entity reserved for one class for the purpose of "protecting that class's distinct interest." Yet another step that he championed was for England to institute inheritance taxes and a system of "progressive tax[ation]." Both were designed to ensure that the wealthy paid their fair share. In addition, these taxes would whittle away the "overgrown influence" of the aristocracy. Paine thought all this might be possible, especially when other European nations, inspired by the examples of America and France, went through real revolutions that terminated "despotism and bad government." When that occurred, the "present age will . . . merit to be called the Age of Reason, and the present generation will appear to the future as the Adam of a new world."[37] His message rang with forthright idealism:

> I speak an open and disinterested language, dictated by no passion but that of humanity. . . .

Independence is my happiness, and I view things as they are, without regard to place or person; my country is the world, and my religion is to do good.[38]

Judging from its sales figures, *Part the Second* electrified readers just like its predecessor, perhaps even more so. Paine estimated that sales in England and Ireland exceeded fifty thousand copies. The book also sold well in America and France. No one will ever know exactly how many copies of the two volumes of *Rights of Man* were purchased, but hundreds of thousands had been sold by the mid-1790s. Gouverneur Morris was one of the first to buy *Part the Second*, and he quickly advised Paine that this time he had gone too far and "will be punished." Paine laughed at his warning, leading Morris to conclude that Paine thought himself too big for the government to take on. "He seems Cock Sure of bringing about a Revolution in Great Britain," Morris noted in his diary, and he again cautioned Paine, telling him that "the disordered State of Things in France" would thwart "all Schemes of Reformation" in England.[39]

Paine had been vilified before and he was unlikely to have been surprised, or especially disturbed, by the plentiful attacks on him that immediately dotted newspapers throughout England. "Brother Fustian," who claimed to be a skilled artisan, cautioned workers not to be "humbugged by Mr. Paine." Other writers branded Paine an "American spy," "foreign emissary," "renegade Englishman," "unnatural son of Britain," and—a charge with which he would have agreed—a "burning republican" who sought "complete and universal revolution." Still other writers, including some that were government hirelings, portrayed Paine as a foul-smelling, hideously ugly, uncivil—even downright brutal—individual. If these assaults did not particularly trouble Paine, he must have found the response of Charles James Fox to be disconcerting. Fox, the leader of the Whigs, a longtime foe of the king, and an advocate of reform, had from the first warmly embraced the French Revolution, even lauding France's constitutional monarchy as "stupendous and glorious." But Fox repudiated Paine after *Part the Second* appeared, charging that the author's radicalism "was a libel" on British reformism.[40] Soon enough, too, Paine discovered that Morris had been correct in having foreseen the harsh response of the British government.

Almost from the moment that *Part the Second* appeared, Paine was shadowed by government agents. The ministry not only sponsored meetings at which his book was denounced; it harassed publishers of radical literature and subsidized both writers and publishers that attacked Paine. One printer was so lavishly endowed by the government that he printed twenty-two thousand copies of a pamphlet lambasting both volumes of *Rights of Man*.

Effigies of Paine were hung and macabre posters went up, among other things showing "TOM THE STAYMAKER" on the gallows. On May 21 Pitt's government took its most serious step. It issued a proclamation against "wicked and seditious writings," which the prime minister acknowledged before the Commons was directed at *Rights of Man* for its having advocated the "total subversion" of the British system of government. Soon thereafter Paine was summoned to court to answer charges of sedition, though his court appearance was eventually postponed until December, probably because Pitt feared sweeping riots in the event that Paine was actually tried. What Pitt really sought was to make Paine so uncomfortable that he would quit the country.[41]

Paine responded to the pressure during the summer of 1792 by going into hiding. He left London and stayed with friends in small neighboring towns, where he was careful not to call attention to himself. But he was not silenced. He wrote letters to several officials defending his action in having authored a "virtuous" and "meritorious" book, even elaborating on his attack on Britain's "hereditary system." He also wrote one long pamphlet, though it was not published while he remained in England. Containing nothing new about revolutions or reforms, it was through and through an assault on England's "phalanx of placemen and pensioners"—he referred to them as a "whole train of court expectants"—who from fear of losing their sinecures had joined in the onslaught against him.[42]

If Paine was wise enough not to publish anything else while still in England—assuming he could have found a publisher—he also saw the wisdom of getting out of the country. According to one story, Paine's decision to flee came after the poet William Blake cornered him following a now-rare public appearance and said, "You must not go home, or you are a dead man." Paine took the advice to heart. Accompanied by two friends, he set off immediately for France, departing under cover of darkness. The party took a circuitous route in the hope of throwing off any government agents that might be on their tail, but at every turn they looked over their shoulders. On reaching coastal Dover, Paine breathed a sigh of relief, certain that he had eluded danger. But during his last night in England—the last he would ever spend in his homeland—agents entered his hotel room, searched his bags, and rifled through his papers, which included a missive from President Washington and several letters that the United States minister in London had asked him to deliver to various parties in Paris, including Gouverneur Morris. The agents kept him on pins and needles interminably, but in the end Paine was not detained. The next morning, while a large crowd heckled and jeered him, he boarded the ferry for the short crossing to Calais.[43]

* * *

Paine fled England to escape danger, but in returning to France he entered the lion's den. The France to which Paine crossed in mid-September 1792 was far different from the one he had left fourteen months earlier. Following the king's return to Paris after his failed escape attempt, the legislature had deliberated the monarch's fate. In the end, it agreed that if Louis consented to the constitution just then being completed—after two years in the making—he could remain on the throne. If he rebuffed the constitution, a regency would be established until the king's son came of age. Not everyone was happy with the Assembly's decision. The legislators were flooded with addresses from throughout France that denounced the monarch and bristled with outrage that he was being allowed to retain even a scintilla of his previous authority. But the more conservative revolutionaries had prevailed, and they prayed that their victory would bring to an end the French Revolution. Their prayers went unanswered.

Much that occurred thereafter during Paine's absence was driven by the war that erupted in the spring of 1792, just weeks after the appearance of *Part the Second*. War clouds had gathered in the aftermath of the king's flight. During the summer of 1791, Austria and Prussia threatened hostilities should the royal couple be harmed, and Austria eventually, and provocatively, moved troops near the French border. By late 1791 war fever was growing within France, driven by nationalism, the foreign threat to the Revolution, and—among those who thought like Paine and Jefferson—zeal to spread the Revolution throughout Europe.

That autumn, the members of the French assembly had collectively stood, raised their hands, and taken an oath to "live free or die." Jacques Brissot, Paine's earlier collaborator in the founding of a republican club and magazine, was among the most vocal in clamoring for war. Now the leader of the Girondins, a republican faction within the assembly, Brissot had long claimed that his faction embodied the "new republicanism," influenced by what he saw as the American example: a national legislature composed of prominent and meritorious individuals and a weak, nonhereditary executive. By the dawn of 1792, Brissot, fearing for the future of the republican gains of recent years, had cried on the assembly floor: "To war, to war! Such is the cry of all patriots." Brissot and his fellow Girondins thought war was necessary to save the Revolution, but not solely from foreign enemies. They imagined that going to war would silence those in France who conspired against the Revolution. In addition, they expected that hostilities would prove fatal for France's monarchy, the end game for the most radical republicans. Not a few Girondins were nationalists who from the outset supported war as the means of French expansion, including the annexation of Prussia's Rhineland territories. They kept this motive under their hats. They told the public that this war would be different. It was not a war of conquest. It was a war of liberation, a struggle to free those subjugated by autocrats and aristocrats. In January, the Girondin-dominated assembly sent an ultimatum to Austria. Ninety days later—five months before Paine fled England—France declared war.

Two of France's heroes in America's Revolutionary War, Lafayette and comte de Rochambeau, were given command of two of the three wings of the French army sent to the frontier for what was supposed to be a short and glorious venture. But, in the words of one historian, the war did not go badly so much as "it went nowhere at all." France's generals faint-heartedly moved their forces into the Austrian Netherlands, after which—despite a considerable numerical superiority—they crumpled at the first display of enemy resistance and retreated back across the border. Thereafter, the French army did nothing. Anger and fear gripped Paris, which buzzed with rumors that the war effort had been sabotaged from within France by counterrevolutionaries composed of aristocrats, clergy, and the king. By early summer, the streets were filled with Parisians made anxious by the war and inflamed by the talk of reactionary plots to destroy the Revolution. On June 20 a crowd somehow burst into the king's residence in the Tuileries Palace. Pistols were thrust in his face and swords were brandished. Someone hoisted a pike adorned with a calf's heart dripping with blood and stuck it under the king's nose. During the course of four excruciating hours, Louis was called a villain, made to don the *bonnet rouge*—a red hat, the symbol of loyalty to the Revolution—and compelled to drink a toast to the Revolution. After suffering countless indignities, the king was finally rescued unharmed, but the monarchy was in tatters.

Soon the reputation of General Lafayette was also fatally damaged. Once perhaps the most popular figure in France, Lafayette's standing suffered a blow when the king attempted to escape. Some unfairly suspected him of complicity in the planned escape. Others, just as undeservedly, blamed him for having failed to prevent the royal couple's run for the border. In addition, many distrusted Lafayette, discerning in him the same incorrigible obsession with popularity and fame that Jefferson had instantly spotted. But Lafayette's fundamental problem was that as the Revolution spun onward, he came to be caught in the middle. Royalists, including the queen, thought him a schemer bent on gaining for himself the king's authority, while radicals hated him for his unswerving commitment to a constitutional monarchy. One radical published an attack comparing him to Washington and contending that "the American hero, the great general, the immortal restorer of liberty," had successfully dealt with the crises of the American Revolution whereas Lafayette had failed in the critical moments of the French Revolution.

But it was Lafayette's actions during the crisis-laden summer of 1792 that ruined him. On a prickly hot July day, Lafayette's National Guard fired into a large crowd that had gathered at the Champ de Mars (now the site of the Eiffel Tower) to urge an end to the monarchy. Fifty died in the unfortunate incident which bore some of the trappings of the Boston Massacre in America's Revolution. A month later, after learning of repeated affronts visited on the king, Lafayette left his army and hurried to Paris to address the assembly. Telling the legislators that the war could not be waged so long as chaos prevailed in Paris, he demanded the punishment of those who had assaulted the king, the suppression of radical Parisian clubs such as the Jacobins, and the restoration of the authority that the king had wielded during the first year of the Revolution. Some would never forgive Lafayette for having abandoned his army, but for others Lafayette's fatal blunder was that they interpreted his presence in Paris as a threat to use his army to roll back many of the gains of the Revolution. In the midst of the white-hot hysteria over a counter-revolution, not a few now believed that Lafayette posed a greater threat to the Revolution than France's foreign enemies, and some fancied a conspiracy involving the king, Lafayette, and Austria to destroy the French Revolution.

Lafayette survived a bit longer, but his days in power were numbered. So, too, was the existence of France's monarchy. Early in the summer, as bad news from the military front eddied into the capital almost daily, the assembly summoned to Paris volunteer national guardsmen from throughout the country. By July, thousands of Fédérés, as these citizen-soldiers were called, were in the capital. Aflame with revolutionary fervor, they were, in the words of one historian, "high pressure patriots." Another scholar characterized them as "the yeast in the revolutionary dough in the summer of 1792."[44] Vast numbers from Marseille marched through the city streets singing "Song of the Army of the Rhine," soon to be renamed "La Marseillaise." Before long, the Marseille Fédérés joined with other guardsmen to petition the legislature for an end to the monarchy, proclaiming that "the very name of 'Louis XVI' now means 'treason to us.'" Section after section in Paris followed with petitions of their own urging the dethroning of the king. One charged that since 1789 the king's actions amounted to "perjury, treason, and conspiracy against the people." Ridding themselves of the monarch, said another, would be akin to severing "the first link in the chain of Counter-Revolution."

Amid this frenzy of alarm and rage, word arrived that Prussia not only had joined Austria in the war against France, but that this new enemy—renowned throughout Europe for its splendid army—had issued the Brunswick Manifesto, a pledge to inflict "exemplary and ever memorable vengeance" on France's revolutionaries following the Prussian victory. Now there were daily demonstrations and new calls for the king's removal. Paris was a powder keg. The lid blew off when France's assembly both failed to act on the question of the monarchy and gave Lafayette a vote of confidence. On August 10, two days after its vote on Lafayette, a heavily armed crowd of thousands stormed the royal palace in the Tuileries. The mob was driven by loathing for the monarchy—many screamed "Down with the fat-head!"—and scorn for the Old Regime, and perhaps most of all, as Alexis de Tocqueville put it in one of the earliest histories of the French Revolution, by an "indomitable hatred of inequality" that "forced itself on their attention," as "they saw signs of it at every turn."[45] Although the king's bodyguard of Swiss mercenaries had recently been quadrupled, it was heavily outnumbered and some six hundred of these soldiers were hunted down and slaughtered. The king and queen escaped by hiding in the legislative hall with the cowering assemblymen.

Some historians have called the events of that bloody August 10 "the second French Revolution," though not solely because of the carnage at the Tuileries. That same day the Assembly—pronouncing that France's internal woes during the past several years were due to the monarch's repeated betrayal of the Revolution—issued an emergency decree that stripped the king of his constitutional authority. Three days later the king and queen were removed to a medieval fortress in the northern reaches of Paris. In essence, they were under house arrest. With some speaking of the king as "Louis the Last," all seemed to understand that France's monarchy was at an end. In the days that followed, streets, gardens, and palaces with royal tags were renamed throughout country, and authorities removed statues, portraits, and emblems of all kinds that venerated royalty or any member of the aristocracy. However, the legislature did not proclaim France a republic. It called for the election of a new national assembly, and for the first time in a national election in any nation—including the United States—extended suffrage rights to all adult male citizens. The new assembly was to be called the National Convention, and it was to convene six weeks later, on September 20. It was directed to write a new constitution for France and it was to decide the fate of the monarchy.

Perhaps Louis XVI and Marie Antoinette understood that they were doomed. For certain, Lafayette realized that the constitutional monarchy was dead, and likely the monarch with it. He sought to march his army to Paris and save the monarchy. But Lafayette had lost his army. The soldiery would no longer follow him or the king. Nine days after the storming of the Tuileries Palace—and thirty-five days before Paine spent his last night in England—Lafayette, accompanied by several officers and their servants, crossed the border into the Austrian Netherlands, hoping to reach the coast and sail for America. He did not make it. He was captured by the Austrians. For the next five years, Lafayette was a prisoner of the foreign enemies of the French Revolution.

Meanwhile, Paris remained in the grip of palpable fear bred by a steady diet of bad news from the military front and a blizzard of rumors. The coalition armies—accompanied by numerous armed émigrés, ultraroyalists who had fled France during the past three years—easily captured two major French fortresses: Longwy, on the border of the Austrian Lowlands, and Verdun, some thirty miles deeper into France. Around the same time, several nations, including England, broke off relations with France in protest of the suspension of the monarchy. Some suspected that all were on the cusp of taking up arms against revolutionary France. In this milieu of foreboding, the Paris Commune, created in July by radical Parisians, posted inflammatory placards about the city: "To arms! The enemy is at our gates." Police searched the city for those suspected of counterrevolutionary activities. More than five hundred were arrested, including numerous journalists and refractory priests.

The police dragnet did not quash the rumors. Reports spread of plots to restore the monarchy. Some gave credence to stories of a conspiracy to liberate the king and queen and somehow spirit them to the safety of the invading armies. Many believed what came to be called the "prison conspiracy." Supposedly, incarcerated counterrevolutionary aristocrats and priests were involved in a deep conspiracy with like-minded persons who had been driven underground. In this already combustible atmosphere, radicals such as Georges Danton, an influential assemblyman, broadcast the warning that France's enemies—aided by the "traitors in your bosom"—were poised "to carry out the last blows of their fury." The predictable explosion came early in September 1792, hard on the heels of news of the Brunswick Manifesto and word that Verdun had fallen. Barely a week before Paine's stealthy flight across the Channel, the "September Massacres"—sometimes called the "First Terror"—erupted. Over five days, prisoners were slaughtered. Noblemen, clergy, common criminals, some forty prostitutes, and just as many adolescents (one as young as thirteen) were put to death, most hacked to pieces with swords and axes that appear for the most part to have been wielded by fanatical Fédérés. More than fourteen hundred in all perished in an orgy of savagery driven by fear, hatred, retribution, and zealotry. The carnival lust for killing spread across France that month. Seventy-five bloody incidents occurred in thirty-two departments, including the butchery and decapitation of forty-four royalist prisoners at Versailles.

The killing spree likely would not have occurred had it not been for the war and that summer's anxious belief that the French Revolution hung by a slender thread. The Revolutionaries' panic was not entirely misplaced. Had Austria and Prussia committed larger armies, France might have been defeated and the French Revolution destroyed. Although France had nearly four hundred thousand men under arms, the allies sent only about seventy thousand to the front. By September, France had twice that many men under arms in the war zone. Even so, as late as September 12, a week after the First Terror concluded, the road to Paris lay open. During the next week, on September 20, a combination of egregious errors by the allied commanders and the arrival of French reinforcements resulted in a major French victory at Valmy in the Argonne Forest region. Even more spectacular French triumphs followed. Decimated by disease and facing a growing French army—one that briefly included an "American Legion" composed of free blacks who originally hailed from the French Caribbean—the Prussians retreated, relinquishing all that they had taken. As summer faded into autumn, the French defeated the Austrians at Jemappes and in no time took control of the Austrian Netherlands. In the weeks that followed, one French army crossed the Rhine and took Mainz and Frankfurt, while another seized Nice and Savoy in the Kingdom of Sardinia to the south. Revolutionary sentiment appeared to blossom from Corsica to Geneva, from Brussels to Westphalia. Some assemblymen in Paris spoke of taking Berlin, Poland, and Spain during the campaign of 1793. What in the minds of most had begun as a war to save the Revolution in France was now being described by many as a "revolutionary war" that clasped the "wonderful possibility of destroying tyranny throughout the whole of Europe."[46]

Paine arrived in Calais one week after the September Massacres and a week before the French victory at Valmy. A year earlier he had hinted to Washington that he planned to return to America in the near future, but instead he chose to move to France after fleeing England. Less than a month earlier, just after the decisive August 10 events at the Tuileries, the Legislative Assembly had bestowed French citizenship on twenty foreign "allies" of France who had distinguished themselves in fighting tyranny. Three Americans and six Englishmen were among those honored. In addition to Washington, the Americans were Alexander Hamilton and James Madison, chosen for their work in securing the new United States Constitution. Paine was included in the slate from England. Only Paine and Anacharsis Cloots—a Prussian nobleman who had also shuttled between his homeland and Paris to support the French Revolution, which he, too, believed was the opening salvo in the transformation of Europe—exercised the privilege bestowed on them. Before leaving England,

Paine appears to have also known that Calais had elected him to be part of its delegation to the forthcoming National Convention. He was thrilled by the prospect of serving in a national legislature that was to determine the fate of France's monarchy and craft a new constitution. When Paine fled to France, he believed that the war confronted the French Revolution with a crisis no less alarming than that faced by the American Revolution during the bleak autumn of 1776. The first installment of Paine's *American Crisis* had been issued during that dark moment of America's war, and he envisioned deploying his literary talent to help the cause of the French revolutionaries.

Following his hurried flight and the unnerving night in Dover, Paine had alighted at the foot of the gangplank in Calais in such a disheveled state that one observer thought he looked like a laborer coming off a three-day drunk. But Calais greeted its guest with worshipful esteem. Despite a cold, driving rain, the authorities rolled out the red carpet. They embraced and cheered him, put a national cockade in his hat, and honored him with ceremonial gunfire. As he walked to his inn, a large crowd shouted, "Vive Thomas Paine! Vive la Nation." In the afternoon, he was hailed again and escorted to the city hall for another ceremony, where he made a speech pledging to devote his life to the Revolution. In the evening, still another adoring audience gathered to salute him at the town meeting hall. His arrival in France was breathtakingly unlike his departure from England.[47]

Paine was also acclaimed in joyous festivities in each of the three towns in which he stayed while traveling from Calais to Paris. Not even Benjamin Franklin had been so warmly received on his arrival in France, nor would any other American be so rapturously welcomed by the French before Woodrow Wilson's arrival following the armistice in World War I. Paine finally reached Paris on his sixth day in France. It was to be the last day of the existence of the outgoing legislature, and he hurried to its chamber, where the deputies received him with one more rousing welcome. The next afternoon, after visiting Gouverneur Morris, Paine met in the Tuileries Palace with the other delegates to the National Convention—all 748 of them—and marched through the gardens in a drenching rain to the Manège, once the royal riding school and now the hall in which this new legislature would meet. It was not the most suitable site for a legislative body. A long rectangular structure, it was scorchingly hot in summer and brutally cold in winter, when the vast building's only heat was provided by a single porcelain stove (made to resemble the Bastille). The lighting was poor, the seating was cramped, the acoustics were miserable, and the lack of ventilation made for a noxious environment.[48]

Once the procedural chores were out of the way, the Convention, with little of the speechifying customary in legislatures, voted to abolish the monarchy and establish the French Republic. The vote was unanimous. Paine, who had played a key role in creating an American republic, could now truthfully say that he had a hand in making France a republican nation.

It is likely that Paine would not have endorsed going to war had he been in France several months earlier when the decision was made. In *Rights of Man*, Paine had depicted the Revolution's termination of monarchical autocracy as having eliminated the cause of wars. But now that France was at war, and the Revolution was imperiled, Paine pitched in to help with the war effort. By the end of his first week back in Paris he published in French— thanks to the translation by a friend—an essay on the war crisis, *Address to the People of France*. As he had often done during America's war, Paine exhorted the revolutionaries to put aside their differences and focus on gaining victory. Telling them that this was a winnable war, Paine wrote, "it is impossible to conquer a nation determined to be free!" In *Common Sense*, Paine had given a new meaning to the American resistance, and in this piece he advised the French that they were engaged in a new kind of war, a struggle unlike the "paltry cause of kings." This was a war waged in "the great cause of ALL" and for the "establishment of a new era" devoid of monarchs. The object of this war was to secure "the great Republic of Man."[49]

During the first year of America's war, Paine had believed the colonists' cause suffered because many could not imagine an alternative to monarchy. He found that France's war effort was impaired by royalists who pined for Louis's restoration. A month after the appearance of his first essay, Paine penned a second tract that bore more than a passing resemblance to the antimonarchical section in *Common Sense*. The Revolution had dethroned not merely Louis, but the very "absurdity of Royalty," he wrote. A "swamp breeds serpents" and monarchy "breeds oppressors." Kings were "monsters in the natural order." The history of monarchy was replete with "hideous wickedness" and "horrible cruelties." French kings had displayed an inescapable proclivity for waging wars. Little was accomplished by the bloodshed they caused, save that the citizenry was made to "pay dearly" for their grandiose ambitions. Nations can endure and prosper without monarchs, he argued. To believe they cannot is to "treat our posterity as a herd of cattle" unable to think for themselves.[50]

Paine was busier than he had been in years, scribbling essays, attending the lengthy daily sessions of the National Convention, and coping with his legislative committee assignments. But he found time for socializing with English-speaking French friends—one was Edmond Genêt, who soon would sail for Philadelphia to become France's minister to the United States—and assorted foreigners, including Mary Wollstonecraft, who had moved to Paris three months after Paine arrived and stayed on until 1795. When word came of fresh French victories in the war, Paine and friends celebrated, sometimes at the Hôtel de Philadelphie, where he resided, drinking, rejoicing, and singing "La Marseillaise" and other popular revolutionary songs. Paine drew especially close to Lord Edward Fitzgerald, an Irish aristocrat, the cousin of Charles James Fox, and a former British army officer who had been severely wounded in the Revolutionary War fighting in South Carolina against the army of Nathanael Greene. Fitzgerald, who came to know Paine better than most, found him to be kind and generous, given to a "simplicity of manner," a "goodness of heart and a strength of mind . . . that I never knew a man before to possess."[51]

The war and his writing were not all that was on Paine's mind. He was absorbed by two trials, one his own. Paine was tried in absentia in London, a one-day affair a week before Christmas. It has been noted that no ruling class ever deliberately committed suicide, and those who ruled England were not about to watch idly as their wealth and privileges were endangered by Paine's *Rights of Man*. Pitt's government charged him with "seditious libel," a capital crime. Though Paine was gone and in all likelihood never coming back, the government wished to make sure that he stayed away. It also sought to make an example of him, and by securing a conviction the government would possess the legal right to suppress *Rights of Man*. Paine was represented by a noted criminal defense attorney, but to no avail. In a matter of minutes, the jury returned with a guilty verdict. England's conservatives and their toadies had to be content with hanging Paine in effigy and selling medallions bearing a depiction of him swaying in the gallows. In Leeds, where he had spent several happy years, a ceramic pitcher was issued adorned with a depiction of Paine's head on the body of a serpent. An inscription beneath the image proclaimed: "Observe the wicked and malicious man / Projecting all the mischief that he can." Immediately following the trial, the proprietor of a bookstore was sent to jail for selling *Rights of Man*.[52]

Paine had been the defendant in the trial in London, but he was to be an active participant—and a juror—in the trial of Louis XVI in Paris. The National Convention purposefully delayed bringing forward the delicate question of trying the deposed king until early November. A series of questions were taken up, each sparking a lengthy debate. It was quickly apparent that many assemblymen opposed a trial, though not because they thought the monarch was innocent. In fact, nearly everyone thought that if Louis XVI was tried, a guilty verdict was inevitable. That in itself led some to oppose a trial. Those delegates feared that a formal determination of the king's guilt would create troubles that might otherwise be avoided. Many who thought this way advocated foregoing a trial and simply punishing Louis by incarceration or exile. Roughly one in ten legislators thought the monarch, and presumably any monarch, was inviolable. Others believed that the king was guilty of crimes against humanity and did not merit a trial; those delegates thought he should immediately be put to death. Still others who saw dethronement as tantamount to a guilty verdict argued for summary execution. Days into the debate, Paine weighed in. He drafted a lengthy statement and, as he still did not speak French, had it translated and distributed to the delegates.

Paine argued in favor of a trial, but he took a position unlike most of his colleagues who voted to try Louis. Paine's touchstone was that a court proceeding would produce dark revelations about the "disastrous system of monarchy," provoking uprisings against repressive governments elsewhere in Europe. He also thought it crucial that the world learn of the royal "horde of conspirators" responsible both for the villainy of the ancien régime and sinister intriguing against the French Revolution. It was imperative, he continued, that the English people learn that their king had provided "clandestine assistance" to the enemies of the French Republic. Paine thought that what would come out in a trial could aid English reformers and it might even force England's government to remain neutral in the war. Buried in the address was a sentence that, in time, would cause trouble for Paine: "France is now a Republic; she has completed her revolution." Not all delegates thought the Revolution had ended.[53]

While the legislators wrangled, a collection of incriminating papers was discovered in the king's safe in the Tuileries Palace. The cache of documents—which included Louis's correspondence with foreign leaders—demonstrated the king's support for a counterrevolution and the reestablishment of the property and privileges of the church.[54] The eventual outcome in the Convention might have been the same even had that stash of papers not been found, but bringing them to light ended the debate. The angry delegates voted to try the former king. On December 10 the Convention charged him with having conspired to destroy the Revolution. The next day, one week before Paine was tried in London, Louis appeared before the legislators. He entered a plea of not guilty and answered questions. What one delegate called "stormy" debates over two questions continued for days. One issue involved the king's guilt or innocence. A second question, pushed by the Girondists, was whether to submit the Convention's verdict to the people in a national plebiscite.

Finally, on January 15, the delegates were ready to vote. Intermingled with considerable speechifying, four votes were taken over a period of five days. The first was on the issue of guilt or innocence. The outcome was never in doubt. The guilty verdict was unanimous. The Girondists' proposal to submit the verdict to a popular vote by the people was the next question to be decided. Paine had usually sided with Brissot and the Girondists, but on this question he voted against letting the people render the final verdict. Paine, who hoped to spare the king's life, was certain that if the people endorsed a guilty verdict—which was likely—nothing could prevent Louis's execution.[55] Once again, Paine was on the side of the majority. By nearly a two-to-one margin, the delegates rejected the proposal of a national vote.

The question of Louis's punishment resulted in an emotionally exhausting session that stretched for thirty-six hours and made clear that many delegates were deeply troubled and ambivalent. Each delegate stood before the assembly and orally cast his ballot. Many accompanied their vote with an explanation of their decision. Several confessed the pain they felt in reaching a judgment, and some admitted to having fallen ill as they wrestled with their choice. Some voted for death, others for death but with a plea that the Convention reprieve the ex-king. Paine did not waffle. From firsthand experience, he understood the value of second chances. Furthermore, compassion had always been among Paine's greatest virtues. He was a pragmatist as well, and given his lengthy activism Paine was more experienced in politics and statecraft than many of his colleagues. He saw things from a broad perspective.

Paine voted against a death sentence, explaining his decision in another translated address in which he pleaded that the king's life be spared. Capital punishment, he said, was part and parcel of the "abomination and perversity" of monarchy. A republic should be better than that. "As France has been the first of European nations to abolish royalty, let her also be the first to abolish the punishment of death," he implored. He argued, too, that Louis had not made himself a king. He was born into the position. Had Louis Capet enjoyed a normal life, "I cannot believe he would have shown himself destitute of social virtues."

Paine said that one great mistake had already been made with regard to the king. Louis should never have been put back on the throne following his aborted flight. It would have been better for France had the king's bid to escape been regarded as his abdication. Paine counseled against making a second mistake. He granted that the trial had "demonstrated in the face of the whole world, the intrigues, the cabals, the falsehood, the corruption, and rooted depravity" of Louis's reign. Nevertheless, it would be better for France to exile Louis than to execute him. Paine closed with an emotional appeal to send Louis to the United States. America could not have "shake[n] off the unjust and tyrannical yoke of Britain" without French assistance, and that aid would not have been forthcoming without Louis's sanction. A grateful America would provide asylum to the former king. Living where he would no longer be surrounded by "criminal" ultraroyalists, Louis might learn that "the true system of government consists not in kings, but in fair, equal and honorable representation."[56]

The king's sentence was not known until the very end of the voting. A majority of 361 votes were required for approval of the death sentence. Exactly 361 voted unconditionally for death. Thirty-four voted for death but with assorted conditions attached, such as permitting the citizenry to commute the sentence or to indefinitely postpone its being carried out. The 334 remaining delegates voted for life imprisonment or, like Paine, for exile. Immediately following the vote, the Girondins, desperately hoping to save the king, called for a fourth vote, this one on the issue of a reprieve. In this instance, Paine, accompanied by an interpreter, came before the Convention to appeal for clemency. He had barely begun speaking before Jean-Paul Marat, a militant newspaper editor and radical delegate, objected that Paine's Quakerism would prevent him from making a dispassionate judgment. Marat was shouted down by passionate cries of "free speech."

Calling again for Louis's exile to America, Paine said that his decision was based on "moral reasons" and what he truly believed would be in France's best interest. A danger existed that in time the Convention would come to be seen as having acted "from a spirit of revenge rather than a spirit of justice," a turn of events that could lead to Louis's martyrdom. In addition, he empha- sized that the United States was France's only ally and a major supplier of naval stores used in ship construction. Considerable sympathy for Louis existed in the United States, where the former king was remembered as its benefactor in the War of Independence. To carry out the death penalty was to run the risk of provoking such "heartfelt sorrow" in the United States that many of its citizens would turn against France. The greater hazard, however, was that Louis's execution would cause Great Britain to enter the war. The Convention, he counseled, should not take a step that seemed probable to "enlarge the number of our enemies" and "reduce . . . our friends."[57]

Paine's plea for the king's life failed. At three A.M. on Sunday, January 20, the Convention voted against mercy. Louis Capet's fate was sealed. His execu- tion was set for the following morning.

Thomas Paine wanted no part of it. Before departing England, Paine had vowed to leave France should the king be executed, declaring that he would "not abide among sanguinary men."[58] A gentle man, Paine had never thirsted for macabre events. Above all, he sincerely mourned for a man who had helped America defeat England.

Louis was awakened at five in the morning on January 21. He dressed, took Communion, received a final benediction, and said farewell to his family and most intimate attendants. Sometime after eight, he was taken from his prison home of the past five months to make the ninety-minute carriage ride through the damp, foggy streets of Paris to the Place de la Révolution. Louis climbed into a carriage owned by the mayor of Paris. Two hundred mounted soldiers— half in front of the conveyance and half at its rear—and twelve hundred foot soldiers were to accompany him, together with sixty drummers commanded by a drum major. These troops were but one-eightieth of the armed men mustered to preserve order on this day. At about eight thirty, the king began his final journey. All along the way, the shops were closed and every window and door of every residence was shut, according to the dictates of the Paris Commune. Block after block, armed guards stood four deep between the royal carriage and the estimated one hundred thousand Parisians who lined the streets or were perched on bridges and riverbanks hoping to a catch a glimpse of the somber procession. Eerily, the only sounds to be heard were those of horse hooves on cobblestones, the clanks and rattles of the carriage, and the mournful cadence of the drums.

It was nearly ten o'clock when the coach clattered to a stop at the scaffold. An equestrian statue of Louis XIV had once stood on this site. It had been demolished. A guillotine had been erected in its place. A large crowd, probably in the vicinity of twenty thousand, was present and remarkably quiet. Louis's coat was removed. His hands were bound and his hair closely cropped by the executioner's assistants. Wobbly and unsteady, Louis had to be helped up the steep steps by a priest, whose last words of solace were for Louis to remember that Jesus, too, had faced untold humiliations prior to his execution. Louis, wearing a white waistcoat, gray trousers, and white stockings, wished to speak to the crowd. He nodded at the drummers, who at his beckoning amazingly stopped their measured beat. "I die innocent, I pardon my enemies and I hope my blood will be useful to the French, that it will appease God's anger. . . ." Nothing else that he said could be heard, for the general in charge ordered a resumption of the drumbeat.

Once Louis was strapped to the plank and his head was braced, a hush fell over the throng. In his last moment of life, alone and terrified, Louis, according to a witness, "uttered a frightful scream, that was stifled only with the fall of the blade."[59]

CHAPTER 7

"ITCHING FOR CROWNS, CORONETS, AND MITRES"

THE RISE OF PARTISAN POLITICS

IN SEPTEMBER 1789, WHEN HE left France, Jefferson knew there was a possibility that Washington might offer him a position in his administration. Given his foreign experience, Jefferson also had to know that it was not improbable that he might be asked to be his nation's chief diplomat. Soon after landing at Norfolk in November—following a placid twenty-six day crossing—Jefferson learned that on the very day of his departure from Paris the president had named him to be the secretary of state. The Senate had already confirmed the appointment. If not stunned by the news, Jefferson was deeply conflicted. He was honored, and knew the office was certain to be crucially important during the new nation's founding years, but he longed to return to France. Jefferson was home for eighty-four days before he gave Washington his answer, dawdling that vexed the impatient president.[1]

Jefferson stopped in Hampton, Williamsburg, and Richmond, tending to business, shopping, seeing friends and relatives, but also speaking with old political allies in an effort to get a feel for things. While Paine had found that much had changed during his one-year absence from France before the fall of 1792, Jefferson, who was returning home after having been away for five years, would discover that the United States had undergone a political sea-change when he was abroad—a transformation so great that historian Joseph Ellis termed it a "second American Revolution."[2] The Articles of Confederation had been replaced by a new constitution that bore little resemblance to its predecessor. The weak central government had been supplanted by one that was immeasurably stronger. Where there had been neither a chief executive nor a Supreme Court under the Articles, both now existed. Congress had been transformed from a unicameral body in which each state had a single vote to a bicameral body in which the states were represented in one house, the people in the other. Some familiar figures held important positions: in addition to Washington, John Adams was the vice president, Henry Knox—who had commanded the Continental army's artillery corps—headed the Department of War, and James Madison was the leading figure in the House of Representatives. Jefferson knew a handful of congressmen, though many with whom he had been familiar during the American Revolution were no longer there, and not a few total strangers had emerged. No newcomer was more important than Alexander Hamilton, Washington's choice to be secretary of the Treasury. Without a doubt, Hamilton was the brightest star on the horizon and, next to Washington, the most influential figure in the new national government. At the time of his landing in Virginia, Jefferson did not know enough about Hamilton to make a perceptive judgment.

Three weeks after disembarking in Norfolk, and a week before he reached Monticello, Jefferson wrote to Washington that he wished to remain in his post in France, adding that he dreaded the public "criticisms and censures" he would face as secretary of state. However, he left open the door. He would serve if Washington thought it "best . . . for the public good."[3]

Jefferson finally reached Monticello two days before Christmas. Twenty years later, a visitor described Jefferson's hilltop as an "untamed woodland." But if Jefferson felt any consternation at returning to rusticity after Paris's glitter, glamour, and bustle, he never acknowledged it, though he redecorated his home with a multitude of pieces that he had acquired abroad and incorporated French cuisine and dining practices into his routine. A few weeks after his return, thirteen local residents—including James Monroe—came to Monticello to formally welcome him home. Jefferson was euphoric on that cold February day. Independence had been won and the Union appeared less fragile than it did when he left the country for Europe in 1784. He responded to his visitors by reminding them that "heaven has rewarded us," but he added that it "rests now with ourselves alone to enjoy in peace and concord the blessings of self-government, so long denied to mankind." The task that now faced Americans was to protect "the holy cause of freedom." But it was not solely America that was on his mind. He longed for the survival of freedom in America so that "it may flow thro' all times, gathering strength as it goes, and *spreading the happy influence of reason and liberty over the face of the earth.*"[4]

Jefferson remained at home for ten busy weeks. One objective in coming home had been his hope that Patsy would marry a Virginian. His wish was fulfilled. After a whirlwind courtship, Patsy in February married her third cousin, Thomas Mann Randolph Jr. Jefferson's other reason for returning home had been to cope with a personal crisis. He had long known that he was in debt, but it was only during his stay in France that he came to understand the magnitude of his problem. When his father-in-law died in 1773, Jefferson had accepted what had been bequeathed to Martha—eleven thousand acres, 135 slaves, and considerable debts owed to overseas creditors. Jefferson had understood the risk but thought it manageable, anticipating that he could sell some of the property, and that his thousands of acres of tobacco would produce a healthy income. But Jefferson had not foreseen an eight-year war with Great Britain that would cripple American commerce. His unrestrained spending habits exacerbated his problem, as did the damage inflicted on some of his property by the British army late in the Revolutionary War. Jefferson was already acutely worried before he left Paris, speaking of his "torment of mind" at the possibility in a worst-case scenario of losing everything. But he did not think it would come to that. In fact, he believed he could solve his problem during a short stay at home.

Jefferson underestimated the gravity of his situation, and he had not been home long before he understood that his dilemma was worse than he had imagined. He had begun to sell some of his property—land and slaves—four years before he left France and he sold still more after reaching home, but these steps raised barely enough money to service the interest on his debt. Soon, Jefferson knew that he could not return to France. It was imperative that his agricultural production be improved, a step that required some innovation and better management, including his occasional presence at Monticello. Two months after coming home, Jefferson formally accepted the president's offer to become the secretary of state. It is not inconceivable that Jefferson would have accepted the post even had he not faced a financial predicament. He had to know that it could be politically risky to spurn Washington. Even more, Jefferson was ambitious, and the office of secretary of state was certain to be crucial for the infant nation, especially as it was entirely possible that Europe's conservative powers would eventually band together in an effort to destroy the French Revolution. A European war would confront the United States with untold dangers.[5]

It was late March before Jefferson reached New York, the national capital. Washington immediately hosted a dinner for his cabinet officers and on two occasions during the ensuing months Jefferson invited Hamilton to his house for dinner. (There is no record of Hamilton having reciprocated.) Jefferson also renewed his friendship with John and Abigail Adams, and they spent many evenings together. Jefferson likely dressed casually when with old friends, but otherwise he initially comported himself as he had while conducting diplomacy in France, leading one somewhat surprised acquaintance to conclude that Jefferson was overdressed in his "suit of silk, ruffles, and an elegant topaz ring." Jefferson had an extremely busy social schedule that included numerous dinner parties with members of Congress.[6] One congressman left a vivid description of Jefferson as a "slender man" who

> has rather the air of stiffness in his manner; his clothes seem too small for him; he sits in a lounging manner, on one hip commonly, and with one of his shoulders elevated much above the other; his face has a sunny aspect; his whole figure has a loose, shackling air. He had a rambling, vacant look, and nothing of that firm, collected deportment which I expected would dignify the presence of a secretary or minister. I looked for gravity, but a laxity of manner seemed shed about him. He spoke almost without ceasing. But even his discourse partook of his personal demeanor. It was loose and rambling, and yet he scattered information wherever he went, and some even brilliant sentiments sparkled from him.[7]

Important New Yorkers also wanted to meet Jefferson, and he was a frequent guest at their dinner parties. Nights with the socially elite proved to be eye-opening experiences. Many of his hosts waxed on about their preference for monarchy, deploring America's newfound republican ways. Recoiling in "wonder and mortification," Jefferson immediately abandoned his courtly dress for a simpler "republican garb."[8]

Long before leaving France, Jefferson had learned from correspondents that some Americans pined for monarchy. During his stay at home, Monroe and Madison likely fleshed out the more conservative citizenry's distaste for the social and political changes unleashed by the American Revolution. Now that he was in New York, Jefferson encountered that antipathy on a firsthand basis, but everything and nearly everyone was new to him, and he wanted time and information before reaching any conclusions. Madison provided much of the information that he sought. He let Jefferson know that the tension between the supporters and foes of ratifying the Constitution had melted away once Congress in August 1789 adopted and sent to the states the Bill of Rights (which Madison had drafted). There were divisions between northern and southern states, however, which would not have surprised Jefferson, as sectional differences had existed since the first days of the Continental Congress in 1774. But the most important issue before Congress when Jefferson reached Manhattan was unlike anything that had surfaced during his two tenures as a congressman. Congress was debating Hamilton's initial economic report.[9]

As the country had been beleaguered by economic woes for more than a decade, every public figure in the capital fixated on Hamilton and the recommendations in his report. Jefferson, too, was anxious to learn what he could about his colleague in the cabinet. He had in all likelihood met Hamilton in Philadelphia seven years earlier, though it is doubtful that they spent much time in each other's company. The disparity in their ages—Jefferson was a dozen years older—could easily have posed an unbridgeable chasm. In addition, their personalities were strikingly dissimilar. Where Jefferson tended to be quiet, even withdrawn, around those he did not know well, Hamilton sought to dominate every room.

Even if they had not fraternized, Jefferson certainly would have been aware of Hamilton, who stood out in Congress as a leading player in the quest for a national impost. Indeed, when Jefferson was in Philadelphia early in 1783, Hamilton had been up to his neck in a plot to frighten Congress into passing an impost amendment to the Articles. The conspirators cloaked their skull-duggery in such deep secrecy that neither contemporaries nor historians ever fully understood all aspects of their intrigue. However, it is clear that Hamilton, together with some Continental army officers, northern merchants, and financiers—the list of those in on the intrigue included Henry Knox, Robert Morris, and Gouverneur Morris—were behind a warning that following the war's end the army would refuse to disband if an impost amendment had not been achieved. The implication of their threat was that the American Revolution would end in a military dictatorship. What Jefferson had known of the so-called Newburgh Conspiracy is unknown, but it is likely that he gathered some tidbits from members of Virginia's delegation. Arthur Lee, a Virginia congressman, had worried that the plotters were not beyond "subverting the Revolution" to gain their ends, while an alarmed Madison had been anxious that the "foundations of our Independence will be laid in injustice & dishonor," and the Union destroyed by the intrigue.[10]

What Jefferson knew about Hamilton when he reached Manhattan in 1790 is also unknown, but through his politically active friends he must have gleaned the broad outlines of the Treasury secretary's background and thinking. Born out of wedlock and abandoned by his father, Hamilton had been raised by his single mother in the West Indies. He had grown up in humble circumstances, enduring years of cruel barbs, slights, and discrimination, often the lot of those of illegitimate birth in the eighteenth century. These brutish experiences imprinted him with a hunger for acceptance, esteem, and deference. Hamilton had come to Britain's mainland colonies to attend college shortly before the outbreak of the War of Independence. While a student at what now is Columbia University—and yet an adolescent—he had authored two lengthy pamphlets defending the actions of the Continental Congress and assailing Great Britain's imperial policies.

Hamilton spent the war as a soldier, first in an artillery company, but mostly as an aide-de-camp to Washington. Hamilton had come under fire on more than one occasion and had won laurels for his valor at Yorktown. Furthermore, with the economy in tatters in 1780—more than a year before Yorktown—Hamilton had produced four perceptive newspaper essays. Writing as "The Continentalist," Hamilton had called for a strong national government with economic powers similar to those wielded by the rulers of the former mother country. It was next to impossible to "exhaust the resources of a nation . . . like that of Great Britain," he had written. Many had thought Hamilton, only twenty-five at the time, to be an economic genius. He was nominated as the country's superintendent of finance, a post that went instead to Robert Morris.[11]

While in France, Jefferson now and then heard about Hamilton from friends at home. They described him as "a federal man," the proponent of a stronger national government. By reading between the lines of Madison's opaque missives, Jefferson probably deduced that Hamilton wished to transfer "*essential* powers" from the states to the central government. He also knew that Hamilton had attended the Constitutional Convention and authored some of the *Federalist* essays. Jefferson had read those essays a year before departing Paris, and had not been especially impressed by the pieces written by Hamilton and John Jay, though he had praised Madison's contributions as "the best commentary on the principles of government which ever was written." Jefferson had learned from one acquaintance that Hamilton had been a "godlike figure" in the fight for ratification in New York, and that without his leadership the state's convention would never have ratified the Constitution.[12]

Jefferson, who had a way of getting information from the satellites around him, probably had not been in New York long before Madison provided greater details about Hamilton's postwar efforts to strengthen the central government. No one ever knew all the ins and outs of Hamilton's thinking, though in the troubled mid-1780s he may have shared some of his concerns with Madison, one of his closest confederates in the maneuvering to strengthen the central government. In the words of biographer Ron Chernow, Hamilton was gripped with "lurid visions that the have-nots would rise up and dispossess the haves." Aware that the American Revolution had elevated to positions of authority some who could never have gained important posts in the colonial period, Hamilton wrung his hands with worry that these "new men"—many of whom came from working-class backgrounds, not unlike Thomas Paine—were "the leveling kind." Many men of this ilk wanted to move beyond republicanism to democracy, which could well have terminated the elite's political supremacy and, among other things, led to alternative methods of taxation that would redistribute wealth. The solution embraced by Hamilton and not a few other nationalists was to make it more difficult for such men to rise to national offices, as well as to refashion the central government in such a way that change would be difficult to bring about. Madison assuredly was aware of some of this. In fact, his own *Federalist* number 10 was a defense of the proposed government for the very reason that effecting change would be an incredibly demanding undertaking.[13]

Madison was Hamilton's colleague for several weeks at the Constitutional Convention. Each sought a more powerful central government and both probably worried, as Hamilton confided to some, that "the Convention . . . will not go far enough" toward creating "a strong well mounted government."[14] At one point, Hamilton delivered a remarkable six-hour speech in that closed, stuffy room in the Pennsylvania State House. He lamented that the delegates had yet to consider a plan of government that would permit amassing adequate revenue, raising armies before war was declared, or satisfactorily checking democracy. These deficiencies would mean that neither "public strength" nor "individual security" could be achieved.

What should be done? Hamilton said that the thirteen states were outmoded and should be scrapped, though he acknowledged that such a recommendation would "shock public Opinion too much." He also "despair[ed] that a republican government [could] remove the difficulties" facing the new nation. The plan that he proposed was republican in only a narrow sense. Hamilton urged a national government drawn on the likeness of the British example, "the best model the world ever produced." The British government excelled because it both provided for national strength and inhibited change.

Hamilton told his colleagues that every society inevitably divided into "the few and the many." The few—the "rich and well born"—having already reached society's pinnacle, had no incentive to pursue radical change. In contrast, the many were "turbulent and changing," and could "seldom judge or determine right." Therefore, it was crucial that the Constitution be crafted to assure that the few would predominate. This was the only safe way to "check the imprudence of democracy."

Drawing on the British template, Hamilton recommended the creation of a bicameral congress consisting of a lower house elected for three-year terms by qualified voters and an upper house chosen for life by an electoral college. He additionally urged an executive chosen for life by an electoral college. Calling this official an "elective monarch," Hamilton said that a life term would place the executive "above temptation" while enabling him to act solely in the national interest. He urged that the executive be vested with extraordinary powers, including unalloyed control of the military, enormous authority in the realms of foreign policy and finance, and an ironclad veto of every act passed by Congress. In this layered structure of choosing the key officials, it went without saying that America's principal rulers would inevitably be drawn from society's elite. Most of those "trifling Characters" who tended to "obtrude" in republics would be screened out, he said.[15]

Hamilton did not get everything he had hoped for in the Constitution, but he signed it, believing that it would be ratified and that its acceptance would save the Union. In private, he said that one of the most beneficial aspects of the proposed structure of government was that it would keep in check "the democratic spirit" stalking the land. He left such thoughts under his hat in the fifty-one *Federalist* essays that he wrote, content to excoriate the Articles of Confederation, challenge some of the criticisms leveled by Anti-Federalists, and seek to convince his readers that the Constitutional Convention had produced the best document that a deliberative body consisting of conflicting interests could possibly piece together. Hamilton's *Federalist* essays were polemical. He cannily omitted much and abundantly shaded and misled in some areas that he addressed. For instance, Hamilton falsely portrayed the presidency as lacking powers given to many state governors. As an insider, he also knew that it was deceptive to assert that the Supreme Court would have "neither FORCE NOR WILL" and that federal judges would lack the "capacity to annoy or injure," or even to take any "active resolution whatever."[16]

Hamilton probably expected—and may in fact have known—that Washington would nominate him to be the Treasury secretary, although the president waited until Congress created the Treasury Department in September 1789 before acting. Washington had known Hamilton for more than a dozen years, going back to the day when the young artillerist joined his "family" as an aide. Of the nearly two dozen individuals who served him as aides, Washington appears to have believed that only Hamilton was indispensable. Washington found Hamilton to be extraordinarily bright, competent, dependable, persuasive, well informed, scrupulously loyal, and politically savvy. His outgoing, expansive, and animated manner won the affection and admiration of his fellow aides and the respect of most field-grade officers and politicians who came to headquarters. A good judge of character, Washington understood Hamilton through and through, admiring qualities in him that many found objectionable. Washington was aware that Hamilton's ambition knew no bounds and that he was cunning and given to intrigue. Having heard him speak at the Constitutional Convention, Washington was also fully aware of how Hamilton would have shaped the new nation had he had a free hand to do so. But he was not put off by what many others saw as danger signals in Hamilton's makeup. He had long believed in Hamilton. In fact, Washington had chosen Hamilton to lead the attack on Britain's last remaining redoubt at Yorktown, hoping to provide the young man with an opportunity to win laurels that would be useful in a postwar political career. Despite his awareness of Hamilton's role in the dangerous machinations of the Newburgh Conspiracy, Washington's admiration never flagged. On some level, Washington may have seen in Hamilton what he himself might have become if only he had been the beneficiary of a formal education. In turn, Hamilton, who was twenty-three years younger than the president, yearned to someday become an iconic figure like Washington, honored and revered by his countrymen.

Washington improbably claimed never to have discussed economics with Hamilton before appointing him to be the Treasury secretary. Even if that were true, the president had a sense of Hamilton's economic outlook and what might be achieved through the economic plans he would put forward. What Hamilton wanted was what Washington wanted: a strong and energetic central government capable of raising revenue and taking decisive action. Washington sought to increase America's military might as the means of opening the West for rapid settlement and to secure the nation against foreign predators. He also wished to assure that future generations of soldiers would never suffer the ghastly deprivations borne by the men in the Continental army. The president may not have known all the economic steps that had to be taken to get where he wanted to go, but he believed that Hamilton did.[17]

As Treasury secretary, Hamilton had the task of finding the means to resolve the nation's economic woes, which stretched back to the wartime collapse. Though hostilities had long since ended, the war's legacy included crushing debts, a situation eerily similar to that which in 1789 confronted France's ancien régime. America's national indebtedness had accrued from wartime loans made by foreign powers—chiefly France—as well as the costs incurred in waging war. So staggering was the debt, and so powerless to raise revenue was the government under the Articles, that payments on the annual interest alone exceeded the revenues of the United States government. The war had also left most states in debt, leading them to pile heavy taxes on their citizens in a largely futile quest for solvency. More than any other factor, this economic malaise was the root cause of the Constitutional Convention, and the document it produced vested the federal government with considerable revenue-raising powers. During the fight over ratification, Hamilton had artfully cautioned that the Constitution must be ratified or the fragile union would not survive. If the proposed Constitution was rejected, he added, the "universal disgust" that ensued might drive some states to rejoin the British Empire as colonies.[18]

The thirty-four-year-old Hamilton's appointment was approved by the Senate on the same day that it was submitted. A week later, the House gave him a January deadline—a bit over one hundred days away—for preparing a plan to resolve the nation's indebtedness. Hamilton worked daily throughout the autumn of 1789, often toiling deep into the night in his tiny, unadorned office, writing and rewriting, and sorting through mounds of material provided by his thirty-two assistants and clerks. His Report on Public Credit, a forty-thousand-word document, revealed a total indebtedness of $79 million, $52 million at the national level. If Hamilton's figures were not especially surprising, some were startled by two aspects of his plan for coping with the debt. Instead of proposing that all indebtedness be retired, Hamilton recommended that the new federal government "fund" it—what today would be called "refinancing." Hamilton had urged the creation of a new debt through which to pay off the existing debt. In addition, he called for the United States to assume the debts of the states. Both funding and assumption had been ideas that Robert Morris had mooted years earlier, though assumption had not received much public attention.[19]

Hamilton's funding plan called for new federal securities to be issued, replacing the total principal of all old securities. Investors would purchase these securities—they would become creditors making a loan to the United States—and the revenue raised from these sales would go toward retiring the old debt. The holders of the securities would receive from the Treasury a specified dollar amount annually, and this would be a secure and easily traded asset that would promote business activity. Hamilton sought two additional ends. Through the consolidation of national and state indebtedness, he wished to demonstrate the power of the central government. He also wanted to attach the wealthiest Americans—those who could afford to purchase Treasury securities—to the new national government. He knew that nothing would strengthen the government more than the loyalty of wealthy and propertied creditors. That, in turn, would enhance America's credit rating and entice European investors. Although Hamilton remained silent on this point, he saw consolidation and funding as merely the first step in a calibrated formula that would transform America into a powerful national state capable of defending itself and expanding its boundaries.

The battle in Congress over the funding and assumption bills had begun two months before Jefferson arrived in New York. Although Madison was leading the fight in the House against Hamilton's plan, Jefferson remained on the sidelines. He would say later that he had been "duped" by Hamilton and had "not . . . sufficiently understood" what the Treasury secretary was up to. That was hooey. Jefferson grasped then, as others did later, what he saw as the malignant implications of the program that Hamilton proposed. Like Madison, he, too, was vexed that a substantial portion of the beneficiaries would be the speculators who had purchased "Morris notes" from distressed veterans in 1783 and later, often for as little as ten cents on the dollar, and in some instances with reliable confidential information as to likely federal economic policies in the event that the consolidationist movement won out with a new constitution. Not only had the affluent speculators taken advantage of hard-pressed men who had risked life and limb in the Revolutionary War, but Jefferson believed that in many instances they had acquired their booty by "cozening" and "filching" the "poor and ignorant" former soldiers "by the most fraudulent practices."[20]

Nevertheless, Jefferson remained quiet. He was unfamiliar with the new political terrain and swamped by his own responsibilities in the State Department. In addition, soon after reaching Manhattan, Jefferson fell ill with one of his crippling headaches. It was his second within a year and one of the worst he ever experienced, leaving him incapacitated for a month. However, none of these factors fully explain why Jefferson—who had serious reservations about a permanent national debt—did not join the battle against Hamilton's plan.

Jefferson kept quiet because he knew full well the dangers of an unresolved national debt. He had watched as France's debt problem spiraled toward disaster for the ancien régime, and he feared that America's revenue quandary could also have tragic consequences for the new nation and the bright promise of the American Revolution. Jefferson thought the most immediate danger was the ruin of American credit in Europe, a turn of events that would bring on "the greatest of all calamities." Something else was at work too. Jefferson knew that Madison's opposition to Hamilton's plan was largely posturing. Madison was mending fences at home, for his leading role in strengthening the central government had cost him dearly in Virginia. Fighting Hamilton on this matter was Madison's act of atonement. A seasoned politician, Madison was also trolling for a compromise that would net something for Virginia. The prize that he sought was to bring the national capital to the Potomac.[21]

Jefferson additionally knew that Hamilton's plan was the only measure on the table that might resolve the debt crisis. Congress had enacted an impost in 1789—Madison had introduced it—but few believed it would generate sufficient revenue. It would be, as Robert Morris had said of the first proposed impost a decade earlier, "a Tub for the whale." The only viable alternative to Hamilton's plan was to secure revenue through the sale of federal land beyond the Appalachians, but there was a catch-22 at work. Before settlers could buy land across the mountains, a strong central government first had to pacify the frontier. Without revenue, the central government would lack the power to make the lands across the mountains safe for settlement. Besides, during Jefferson's second year in France, the Confederation Congress had passed legislation setting the terms for the acquisition of western lands at a staggering minimum purchase of 640 acres at one dollar per acre, an exorbitant price for the average citizen. Powerful interests wanted it that way so that land companies, in which they would invest and profit, would monopolize the sale of western lands.[22]

These assorted considerations led Jefferson to bring Madison and Hamilton together for dinner at his residence, hopeful they might hammer out a bargain. A deal was reached that was later widely known as the "Compromise of 1790." The three men present that evening agreed to lobby recalcitrant congressmen to agree to funding and assumption in return for locating the capital on the Potomac. Later, Jefferson contended that the agreement reached over the meal at his residence was the "real history" of how Hamilton's plan was realized. The story was more complicated than the tale Jefferson spread, but it was true that a swap had been agreed to, and by mid-summer Congress had enacted Hamilton's economic plan and the Residence Act, legislation that moved the capital temporarily to Philadelphia while the nation's permanent capital was under construction at a yet-to-be-determined site on the Potomac.[23]

In the long interim during which the government relocated to Philadelphia, Jefferson returned home. He stopped along the way at Mount Vernon, his first visit to the president's bucolic house. Once back at Monticello, where he stayed for nearly fifty days from September into November, Jefferson sold still more slaves and a thousand acres in his ongoing battle with the quagmire of indebtedness.[24] The trees had gone bare and a bitter late-autumn wind swept across Philadelphia by the time Jefferson returned. Nor was it only the weather that had changed, for he was now joined in the city by both Madison and Monroe, old friends whose once-warm relationship had been severely tested by the contentiousness of politics during Jefferson's absence abroad.

Monroe and Madison, both devotees of Jefferson's, had met early in the 1780s and were corresponding regularly when Monroe entered Congress in 1783. During his three years in Congress, Monroe took up many issues that Madison had sought to address earlier, especially those that would have strengthened the powers of the central government under the Articles of Confederation. They came to be so close that on his wedding day in 1786, Monroe took the time to write to Madison before going to the ceremony.[25]

When Monroe's term in Congress ended in 1786—at roughly the halfway point of Jefferson's stay in France—he and Elizabeth moved to Virginia. For the first time in years, Monroe held no office and he was at loose ends. Like Jefferson before him, Monroe found practicing law to be an unrewarding pursuit that led only to "excessive labor & fatigue & unprofitably so." But he stuck to it, as he had no ready alternative. He launched his practice in Fredericksburg, but on the side Monroe speculated in land and at one point he and Madison jointly invested in Genesee Valley property in New York. But Monroe was not terribly happy, which he disclosed to Jefferson, who responded from Paris with candor. Jefferson acknowledged his sorrow at learning of Monroe's departure from Congress, as he needed someone whose "discretion I can trust" to alert him to any "unjust designs of malevolence" toward him among the congressman. He advised Monroe to seek a seat on Virginia's council or in the judiciary—neither of which Monroe pursued—and Jefferson also counseled his young, newlywed friend to remember that nothing trumped the "tranquil happiness of domestic life." Enjoy life, marriage, and family, wrote Jefferson. Marriage was "not clear of inquietudes," but it could be filled with "more objects of contentment" than Monroe could ever find in public life or a profession.[26]

Monroe may have taken Jefferson's counsel to heart, but his thirst for office had hardly been quenched. Early in 1787 he won election to the Virginia assembly, though he had not yet taken his seat when the legislature chose the seven delegates to attend the Constitutional Convention. No one played greater roles in the selection process than Madison and Edmund Randolph, Virginia's governor. Needless to say, Madison and Randolph included themselves in the delegation. Three additional choices were without controversy: Washington, George Mason, who had done the lion's share of the work in writing Virginia's first constitution and its Declaration of Rights in 1776, and George Wythe, widely regarded as the state's foremost legal expert. The two remaining delegates were John Blair, who since 1766 had divided his time between the assembly and the judiciary, and Dr. James McClurg, who after earning a medical degree from the University of Edinburgh in 1770 had practiced medicine, taught at the College of William and Mary, and written numerous scientific papers.

Monroe was furious at not being selected, and much of his anger focused on Madison. Having been a stalwart advocate of strengthening the powers of the national government during the past half dozen years and far more experienced in public affairs than McClurg, Monroe felt that he deserved to be a member of the delegation. He was so irate that he fired off a letter to Jefferson, still in Paris, expressing his "great uneasiness" with what he saw as Madison's treachery, and implying that his supposed friend had been manipulated by Governor Randolph, who, he wrote, "I have reason to believe *is unfriendly to me.*" Monroe was not alone in thinking that Madison was easily manipulated. Hamilton, who in time came to think of him as Jefferson's puppet, once characterized Madison as unsophisticated—"very little Acquainted with the world," was how he put it—which rendered him pliable.[27]

In reality, Madison was not controlled by Randolph and the governor probably bore no ill will toward Monroe. This was politics. Neither Madison nor Randolph wanted Monroe in the delegation because he was a thoroughgoing Jeffersonian who was certain to balk at their well-laid plans for the constitution that they hoped would be drafted. Madison may have been naïve, but he was politically adroit and without a doubt better versed than Monroe in what was about to play out at the Constitutional Convention. The most conservative Americans—and this was to be a gathering of conservatives—were horrified by the political, social, and economic egalitarianism unleashed by the American Revolution, and they wanted a constitution that could curb the changes that threatened the social, political, and economic supremacy that wealth bestowed. There were other things, too, that Madison and Randolph, as southerners, wanted—the protection of slavery was a principal priority—and to accomplish their ends they were prepared for an exercise in giving and taking in Philadelphia. Madison, who had affiliated with Hamilton in the impost imbroglios years before, was an old and accomplished hand in the art of politics. Monroe was less practiced in such things and at times evinced a pronounced stubborn streak.

Madison was probably delighted that Jefferson was in France and he preferred that Monroe remain in Virginia. As it turned out, Randolph would kick off the convention with a keynote address contending that America faced a great "crisis" that threatened its "downfal." After ticking off numerous defects in the existing state and national constitutions, Randolph contended, "Our chief danger arises from the democratic parts of our constitutions. . . . None of the constitutions have provided sufficient checks against democracy." Steps must be taken, he added, to inhibit "the powers of government exercised by the people."[28] This sentiment would not have sat well with Jefferson or Monroe.

Monroe never confronted Madison about being omitted from Virginia's delegation. While the convention in Philadelphia was under way, Monroe wrote to him—somewhat cattily saying, "My leisure furnishes me with the opportunity" to correspond—to convey his wish for success in strengthening the central government. When the proposed Constitution was made public in September, Monroe confided to Madison that he objected to some of its contents, but his reservations were "overbalanc'd" by his concern for the "predicament in wh[ich] the Union now stands." The implication was that he would support the document's ratification and, indeed, he told others that his "wishes are of course for its success." However, during the winter Monroe changed course. He had been swayed by Anti-Federalist essays and by learning that Patrick Henry, George Mason, and his uncle Joseph Jones, among other influential Virginians, stood in opposition to ratification. Monroe nitpicked at this or that feature of the Constitution, but his primary objections boiled down to four major issues. First, the proposed document lacked a bill of rights. Second, he took exception to equal representation of the states in the Senate, urging apportionment according to population. Third, he thought senators should be directly elected rather than chosen by state assemblies. Finally, Monroe opposed granting Congress the authority to levy direct taxes, a step he feared would ultimately destroy the states. Although he believed the Constitution would "no where be rejected," Monroe stood for election to Virginia's ratification convention as an Anti-Federalist, pledging opposition unless the document was amended. He was defeated by a Federalist backed by General Washington. Monroe ran a second time in a different county. This time he sought election as an undeclared candidate, claiming that he had not yet examined the constitution "with the attention its importance required." His absurd stance notwithstanding, Monroe was elected.[29]

Monroe was a minor figure in Virginia's ratification convention. Madison and Governor Randolph led the fight for ratification, while Henry and Mason were in the vanguard of those who opposed the document. Only 23 of the 173 delegates spoke. Monroe was one of them, addressing the convention on four occasions. While acknowledging that the Articles of Confederation required changing, he thought the states had been stripped of too much of their authority and he was especially disturbed—as, unbeknownst to him, was Jefferson—by the structure of the presidency. Monroe assailed the electoral college, preferring the president's direct election; he denounced the president's lack of term limits, asserting that in time the office might evolve into a monarchy; and he doubted that any president would ever be removed from office through the procedure mandated by the Constitution. Monroe additionally urged the inclusion of a bill of rights and expressed concern at the provision that enabled two-thirds of senators "who may *happen* to be present" to ratify treaties. In a worst-case scenario, he cautioned, a bloc of northern states might consent to a treaty that was inimical to the interests of Virginia and the South. Finally, he stood in opposition to vesting Congress with the authority to levy direct taxes.[30] It will never be known what Jefferson might have said had he been a delegate to Virginia's ratification convention, but it is probable that his stance would have differed little from that of Monroe.

In the end, the convention ratified the Constitution, though it approved twenty amendments and a bill of rights for congressional consideration. The key to ratification, as Monroe and nearly all others recognized, had been Washington's support of the Constitution. Monroe still exuded "a boundless confidence" in the general's integrity, but he confided to Jefferson that he was not enthralled by the prospect of a Washington presidency. Washington, he said, was likely to be manipulated by the artful politicians "around him." It was a danger, he added, that would increase as Washington "advances in age."[31]

In November, following the ratification of the Constitution in June, a Patrick Henry–led Virginia legislature selected Richard Henry Lee and Richard Grayson as the state's two United States senators. Madison, who yearned to sit in the Senate, was slighted, punishment for his role in writing and supporting a constitution filled with what Henry called an "awful immensity of . . . dangers." Monroe had already decided to seek a House seat in the first federal Congress. Now Madison, with nothing else available and eager to get into the government he had helped create, jumped into the contest. They vied in Virginia's Fifth Congressional District, which included Orange County, home to Madison's estate, Montpellier, and Albemarle County, now Monroe's home. The odds favored Monroe, as the district had been gerrymandered by Patrick Henry— one historian said it had been "Henrymandered"—in that five of its seven counties had been Anti-Federalist strongholds. Henry was pulling out all stops to reduce the number of Federalists in Virginia's delegation in the House of Representatives.[32]

Madison and Monroe had remained on friendly terms despite the bruising events concerning the Constitution, in part because Monroe felt that Madison had displayed "great . . . propriety & respect" toward his opponents at the ratification convention.[33] Their friendship endured as well because each recognized that the other was close to Jefferson, and each knew that an angry break in their relationship might force Jefferson to choose between them. If that indeed was a restraining factor, it likely weighed more heavily on Monroe, who was aware of the length and depth of the bond between Jefferson and Madison.

Monroe and Madison corresponded through the summer and fall of 1788, their tones somewhat more formal than previously. During that winter's contest, a hard-fought three-week battle waged in the chill of January, each worked diligently, courting voters, making speeches, and issuing written statements, but refraining from attacking the other. Each stuck to the two dominant issues of the day. One was whether to amend the Constitution. Both favored the addition of a bill of rights, but Madison opposed—and Monroe favored—further amendments. The second burning question arose after Henry pushed a resolution through the autumn session of Virginia's legislature that urged Congress to call a second constitutional convention to revise the existing document. Monroe supported Henry's initiative. Madison and all Federalists were appalled by such a prospect. Fearing the destruction of the powerful national government before its birth, Washington labeled the prospect "mischievous" and "insidious."[34]

Madison and Monroe traveled, lodged, dined, and even worshipped together throughout the campaign. No two rival candidates in American political history ever appeared to be more dissimilar. At six feet in height, muscular with a rugged visage, Monroe looked every inch the proverbial man of action. Madison looked like the pensive sort who rarely got up from behind a desk; at five feet four, he was pale and anything but strapping, and on a good day he may have weighed all of 120 pounds. The two men rode through the bleak, wintry Virginia backcountry in search of votes, and on at least two occasions squared off in tactful debates. One lasted for hours on the snow-covered grounds of a Lutheran church in Culpepper County; the other took place before a large audience bathed in welcome sunshine on Court Day in Orange County. Though Madison would later speak of what he called the scar of battle, he also said that his friendship with Monroe endured without the "smallest diminution." In the end, Madison pulled off an electoral upset, winning by 336 votes out of the 2,280 cast, gaining victory largely because the Baptists in the district fondly remembered that he had been responsible for securing passage of the statute on religious freedom that Jefferson had originally drafted. Once the results were known, Monroe without conviction wrote to Jefferson that it "would have given [him] concern" to have denied Madison a seat in Congress, and he claimed to be untouched by his defeat.[35]

For nearly two years following his defeat, Monroe practiced law and worked his farm in Charlottesville. His chance to return to politics came when William Grayson, one of Henry's two handpicked senators, died during 1790. Choosing a temporary interim successor was left to the governor and council. Monroe was considered, but John Walker, another of Jefferson's neighbors, was chosen by one vote. An unhappy Jefferson, now back in the United States, made his feelings known about the outcome, and when the legislature convened for its customary autumn session, it elected Monroe. Throughout both contests, Monroe had adhered to the script that Washington habitually followed about holding office. Monroe insisted that he was uninterested in taking on public cares. But as decision time neared, Monroe allowed that after "the most mature reflection" he would "suffer" his "name to be mention'd." When chosen early in November, Monroe accepted the office only because it was his "duty to comply with the wishes of my country."[36]

In December, four months after Hamilton's funding and assumption plan had been approved, and some seventy-five days before Paine's *Rights of Man* was published, the thirty-two-year-old Senator Monroe arrived in Philadelphia. Jefferson and Madison had made their trek to the temporary capital a month earlier and had taken rooms at Mary House's boardinghouse at the corner of Fifth and Market Streets, where Jefferson had lodged during his residence in the city back in 1783 and 1784. They invited Monroe to move in as well, which he did in December, but by then Jefferson—needing space for the State Department—had rented two new adjoining four-story brick houses on Market near the intersection of Eighth Street. He would live on the ground floor of one of the houses and utilize the remaining space for State Department offices and functions. As remodeling was under way, Jefferson continued to take his meals in the boardinghouse through the first week of January, when he became a full-time resident at his State Department home. Jefferson invited Madison to move in with him, but he declined. He did not extend an invitation to Monroe, who remained with Madison as a lodger at Mary House's.[37]

Jefferson had returned to Philadelphia from his stay at Monticello expecting another economic report from Hamilton, though he was in the dark with regard to its contents. He did not have long to wait. In the last days of 1790, Hamilton sent to Congress his next slate of recommendations. Hamilton's Report on Public Credit the previous January had included a call for an excise tax on "every gallon" of spirits distilled in the United States, a duty that he said was necessary because the revenue produced by the impost would be insufficient. The "whiskey tax," as it was popularly known, had aroused such considerable opposition that Congress during the summer just past had turned down the Treasury secretary's proposal. Hamilton did not give up easily. In his latest report, he once again called for an excise on whiskey. Otherwise, he advised, the federal government would face a revenue shortfall of nearly one million dollars.[38]

Opposition was immediate, and the division was more along sectional lines than had been the case with funding and assumption. Farmers from Pennsylvania southward who distilled whiskey from the corn they raised— and especially those on the frontier whose primary income came from the whiskey they put in barrels and transported by mule across the mountains to markets in the eastern cities—were beside themselves with fury. The tax threatened to eviscerate their discretionary income. But there was support for Hamilton's levy. Merchants in the eastern portions of the northern states preferred a whiskey tax to a hike in the impost, and many southern land speculators thought it preferable to taxing the sale of western lands. After a tough fight, Hamilton won out. In the words of one historian, Hamilton was becoming "a mature politician" who knew how to get what he wanted from Congress. He had sown fears of the return of the crippling debt that had dogged the nation for nearly fifteen years. He had also encouraged his supporters to spread the word that Washington backed the bill. His strategy was sound. Anything "that can be fairly fixed on the President" will win support in Congress, one disgruntled senator groused. On the day the bill passed, the same senator added: "Mr. Hamilton is all-powerful, and fails in nothing he attempts." Despite considerable opposition to the levy within Virginia, Jefferson and Madison remained aloof from the battle, while Monroe voted for the bill.[39] The tax was a bitter pill, but Monroe, like Hamilton, understood political realities.

Jefferson did not stay on the sidelines when Hamilton, in the midst of the excise imbroglio, urged Congress to charter the Bank of the United States for twenty years "to be opened at the City of Philadelphia." Jefferson recognized immediately that the bank was the "engine" that would drive Hamilton's "machine." Whatever he had understood about funding and assumption, Jefferson now unmistakably grasped the meaning of Hamiltonianism and the Treasury secretary's design for the shape of the new American nation. Jefferson was correct in thinking the bank was to provide the thrust for the economic system that Hamilton envisaged. That in fact was how Hamilton saw it. By making credit available for businesses, the bank would stimulate investment, which in turn would power what for years had been a torpid economy.[40] The inspiration for Hamilton's economic thinking was the century-old British economic system and its triad of a funded debt, a central banking system, and a market in fruitful public securities. It was a system that had generated ample revenue for the British treasury and facilitated national expansion. In the course of a century or so, England had been transformed from a small backwater kingdom into the largest and most splendid empire since Rome.

Indisputably, the British economy had been good for some, but Jefferson discerned a dark side to what Hamilton saw as Britain's stunning success. Not only had propulsive growth been accompanied by resurgence in royal authority; commercialization changed the fabric of the country. Stock markets, speculation, banks, and trading companies had led to the rise of a new, moneyed class that wielded as much sway over Britain's public officials as the aristocracy had once exclusively exercised. Jefferson additionally believed that Britain's expansion abroad had fostered institutions and interests that craved further foreign growth, nourishing momentum for a standing army and frequent wars. In the past century, Britain had fought five major wars and two smaller ones. Paine had written about it in *Common Sense*, charging that the king had little to do but drag his country—and the colonists with it—into one war after another. Benjamin Franklin had reached the same conclusion. A year earlier than Paine, Franklin arraigned England for the "Injustice and Rapacity" that drove it inevitably into "plundering Wars." Jefferson, too, had long seen the malevolent side of Great Britain, thinking it a purveyor of violence and exploitation. He did not want the seeds sown that would start the United States down that same road.[41]

These were not the only dangers that Jefferson glimpsed in the path that Hamilton was paving. He saw that the bank was designed principally for the benefit of large northern merchants. Public resources were to be doled out to those who already were among the most affluent Americans. Here was a government entity that was designed to not only prevent wealthy investors from losing money but also see that they grew even wealthier. Given that wealth and power went hand in hand, Jefferson beheld the prospect of a merchant-financier dominated America, a turn of events that he saw as counter to the well-being of the new nation's newborn republicanism and destructive of the democratic forces unleashed by the American Revolution. All this was sufficient to make alarm bells ring in his mind.

That the architect of Hamiltonianism was Alexander Hamilton was in itself profoundly important to Jefferson. Not only was Hamilton noted for intrigue and hidden agendas, but at the Constitutional Convention he had candidly doubted the efficacy of republican governments, deplored democracy, championed rule by an elite class, and professed his affinity for monarchy and sundry other components of the British system. For Jefferson, Hamilton's bank proposal made the pieces of the puzzle come together. It explained much about the secret designs of many consolidationists during his absence in France, and it clarified why some of his countrymen—including his wealthy hosts at those Manhattan dinner parties a year earlier—ached for a monarchical America. Jefferson now believed that Hamiltonianism was a blueprint for the gradual transformation of America into the polar opposite of what the American Revolution had supposedly been about. Indeed, it would lead in time to an America strikingly akin to the country that most American revolutionaries had sought to escape.

Jefferson further believed that Hamiltonianism would put in motion the inexorable growth of industries and cities. Jefferson's residence in Paris and visits to other major European cities had led him to conclude that republicanism could not survive in a land in which most inhabitants were packed into cities and toiled in "work-shops." By the nature of economics, workers were inescapably the dependents of the shop owners. Jefferson knew that "Dependence begets subservience and . . . prepares fit tools for the designs" of their corrupt masters. "It is the manners and spirit of a people which preserve a republic in vigour. A degeneracy in these is a canker which soon eats to the heart of its laws and constitution." Compromised workers and the cities they inhabited were toxic to republics. An agrarian society was different and superior. Long before, Jefferson had written that those "who labour in the earth are the chosen people of God." Farmers were dependent only on themselves; their needs from government were minimal. But over time the society that Hamilton would put in place would eat away at the "genuine virtue" of husbandmen and extinguish the "sacred fire" of freedom that blazed within the agrarian United States.[42]

As Jefferson saw it, Hamiltonianism would be the death knell of the republican America that he and Paine and Monroe, among countless others, had fought so hard to create. Jefferson feared that the bank would not merely breed and sustain speculators and giant businesses; it would assure the sway of the "financial interest" over Congress. The bank would be like a mighty "engine in the hands of the Executive," adding to the unnerving surplus of powers the president already possessed. In time, presidential powers would be transformed into "a kingly authority." Jefferson foresaw government growing larger and less responsive to the people, as public officials carried out the wishes of their masters, a plutocracy spawned by commercialization. Republican America would become in fact, if not in name, royal America, as it would feature a dangerously powerful president and an all-controlling elite. Jefferson was certain in his convictions. The "natural progress of things is for liberty to yield and government to gain ground," he said, and through Hamiltonianism government would steadily gain more ground, slowly but surely eviscerating freedoms secured by the American Revolution.[43]

In his "holy cause of freedom" remarks to the well-wishers who had come up hill to Monticello, a year earlier almost to the day, to welcome home the soon-to-be secretary of state, Jefferson had cautioned that vigilance was essential if America's "general tide of happiness" was to survive and swell.[44] He had not foreseen that it would come under assault so soon, but Jefferson now realized that Hamiltonianism was nothing less than a full-blown onslaught against the deepest meaning of the American Revolution.

Despite all that Jefferson felt he now understood, he had to know that Congress would approve the bank. William Maclay, a Pennsylvania senator, instantly remarked that it was "totally vain to oppose this bill." He knew—as did Jefferson—that the bill would pass because the northern commercial states wanted it, had the votes to enact it, and were better organized than their counterparts. Indeed, Maclay, like Jefferson, believed this was part and parcel of what northern merchants and financiers had sought when they coalesced in the movement for the Constitutional Convention. Maclay also noted that the president had covertly joined in the lobbying for the legislation, and he thought that was crucial, as many congressmen were "borne down by . . . a fear of being charged with a want of respect to General Washington." As had Jefferson, Maclay, too, saw the bank as "an aristocratic engine" that would give the northern, urban elite—which he categorized as the "moneyed interests"—undue influence on public policies. Maclay shared Jefferson's suspicion of Hamilton, whom he called "a damnable villain." But after being lobbied by the president, and possibly intimidated by his monumental standing, Maclay voted for the bill.[45]

Monroe voted against it, basing his opposition in part on the premise that Congress lacked the constitutional authority to create a bank. Congress could tax, create an impost, and loan money, but it could not create a bank, he said. What next? Could Congress incorporate manufacturing companies? Could it give those companies monopoly powers? Could those companies loan money to Congress? "The government should rest on the people," he added, not on business enterprises and banks, though in time that would assuredly be the case if the bill passed. Monroe, like Jefferson, saw the bank as a component of Hamilton's master plan to "elevate the government above the people" and thwart further democratization. Monroe feared something else as well. His uncle, Joseph Jones, had schooled him to believe that "a great national bank can be only beneficially conducted in a great commercial city." Once the bank took root in Philadelphia, Monroe like Jefferson and Madison, feared that the national capital would never be moved to the Potomac. Monroe saw this as one more clever maneuver by Hamilton, the inveterate schemer. He was one of only six senators—all southerners—who voted against the measure.[46]

Following Congress's predictable passage of the Bank Bill, Jefferson myopically clutched at the hope that Washington would never sign it. After all, the president was a Virginian, his attorney general, Edmund Randolph, was a Virginian, and the fight against the bill in the House had been led by Washington's confidant, and fellow Virginian, James Madison. Randolph did advise Washington that Congress had acted unconstitutionally, but the president ignored his opinion and instead asked Jefferson and Hamilton to spell out their positions on the bank. Jefferson responded with a brief memorandum arguing that Congress lacked authority under the Constitution to create a bank. Hamilton, in a paper that was nearly ten times longer, took the position that the "necessary and proper" clause of the Constitution vested Congress with the authority to act; he added that a sovereign government always possessed the power to act, unless such action was immoral or explicitly prohibited by the Constitution. The president sided with Hamilton and signed the bill.[47]

Jefferson was astonished by Hamilton's political skills in getting the bank measure through Congress, but he was shocked when Washington signed the bill into law. Jefferson was not willing to believe, as some did, that Hamilton was manipulating the president. Instead, Jefferson now understood as never before the president's fierce commitment to centralized national power, which stemmed from Washington's wartime experiences. For the first time, too, Jefferson understood that he could never change the president's thinking. But he believed there was a way to stop Hamilton from realizing still more of his consolidationist designs. Jefferson reckoned that those who favored a decentralized political system and an agrarian America—and who, like himself, feared that Hamiltonianism threatened America's republican experiment—had to organize prior to the congressional elections that loomed a year or more down the road. He wrote to activists in several states seeking to learn if they shared his concerns about Hamiltonian speculative fever—what Jefferson called "scrip-pomany" and "stockjobbery"—and whether they were willing to "come forward and help" galvanize those who abhorred the policies of the Treasury secretary. Heartened by the responses that he received, Jefferson proceeded to cobble together a network of capital insiders and congressmen who could be trusted to report to him all that they learned about Hamilton or his plans.[48]

These were only his initial steps. Not only had America's newspapers overwhelmingly endorsed the bank, but for months Hamilton had utilized John Fenno's *Gazette of the United States* as a virtual house organ of the Treasury Department. Believing that the foes of Hamiltonianism required a journal of their own, Jefferson turned to Philip Freneau, a college chum of Madison's who, during his varied career, had been a poet, a ship captain, and an essayist noted for his antipathy to banks and speculators. As a writer, Freneau was in the same league as Paine, though his essays were more likely to display a taste for satire. To obtain his services, Jefferson had to put Freneau on the State Department payroll. Meanwhile, Madison set to work rounding up subscribers. The first issue of Freneau's *National Gazette* appeared that autumn.[49]

The last step was to organize those who were alarmed by Hamilton. Jefferson sensed that New York would provide fertile ground for this effort, as there was opposition to Hamilton within the state, and probably a majority of

New Yorkers had been Anti-Federalist during the ratification battle. Jefferson's plan was to travel to New York, accompanied by Madison, who was better connected there, and court potential allies. Jefferson's purpose was not to establish a political party, but to encourage those who opposed further Hamiltonian initiatives to seek seats in Congress. It would remain for Freneau to generate widespread resistance to Hamilton and those in his orbit. But Jefferson had to act surreptitiously, hiding his motives from Washington. After all, he was a member of the president's cabinet and the president had supported Hamilton's every step. Therefore, Jefferson and Madison claimed to be departing on a "botanizing tour," a vacation to study the flora and fauna in a part of the country far from their native Virginia. Their cover story was in fact partially true. Given his passion for science, Jefferson was eager to see the plants and animals in New York's backcountry and to bring back to Monticello cuttings of unfamiliar vegetation that caught his eye.

Their nine-hundred-mile excursion consumed thirty-three days. After reaching Manhattan, the party sailed up the Hudson—with stops along the way in Poughkeepsie and Albany—before ultimately reaching Lake George. The Virginians visited Revolutionary War sites, fished a little, inspected rock formations and waterfalls, dug up numerous plants for relocation back home, stayed on the lookout for unfamiliar animals, swatted hordes of mosquitoes and gnats, and watched as members of their party killed rattlesnakes. But they found time for politics. They met with Chancellor Robert Livingston, who in 1776 had served with Jefferson on the Committee of Five that drafted a declaration of independence. Livingston opposed Hamilton's economic initiatives, fearful that the state's long-dominant landed gentry—of which he was a part—would lose out to the merchants and financiers elevated by the Treasury secretary's programs. Jefferson and Madison also met with Governor George Clinton and Aaron Burr, whose antipathy to Hamilton had blossomed long before Washington's presidency. Much of the trip took them through small backcountry hamlets where the Anti-Federalists had predominated and suspicion of Hamilton and his designs flourished. They paused for talks with local officials in many villages and towns.[50]

Discreet as he may have been, it is doubtful that Jefferson ever believed that he could keep his political mission a secret. Given the stakes, he apparently decided that it was worthwhile to run the risk of discovery. He was persuaded after all that yet more alarming proposals from Hamilton were on the way. Obsessed with Hamilton, Jefferson saw red flags everywhere, some specious, some not, some from things he heard from Hamilton, some from the treasure trove of information passed along by his intelligence-gathering network. He appears to have given credence to tales such as that Hamilton, in

1776, had anonymously written a pamphlet assailing *Common Sense*, that at private dinner parties he raised toasts to George III, and that he had secretly drafted a blueprint for the establishment of an American monarchy. Jefferson's hackles were also raised by things he picked up on his own in conversations with Hamilton. For instance, once while dining with Jefferson and Adams, Hamilton pronounced that it was the combination of royal influence and financial interest that made Britain's government "the most perfect government which ever existed." On another occasion, Jefferson heard Hamilton remark that the Constitution was "a shilly shally thing, of mere milk and water, which could not last, and was only good as a step to something better."[51]

So troubled was Jefferson that early in 1792 he complained to Washington for the first time about Hamilton, and on three other occasions during the ensuing ten months he took his concerns to the president. Jefferson warned that Hamilton was seeking to make the "constitution . . . a very different thing from what the people thought they had submitted to." Hamilton's "ultimate object" was a monarchy in America. Already, said Jefferson, Hamilton's "system" of speculation had corroded Congress. A "corrupt squadron" of congressmen "devoted to the paper and stockjobbing interest" were "legislating for" financiers and speculators "in opposition to [the interests] of the people." Jefferson advised that this "corps of interested persons" took their marching orders from the Treasury secretary. Time after time, Jefferson reiterated the charge that Hamilton had already made great strides in laying the groundwork for "transforming the government into a monarchy." Washington remained unmoved. He told Jefferson that he approved of Hamilton's "treasury system," and he insisted that it was delusional to believe that monarchy could be reestablished in America. The only way it could happen would be if fanatics along the lines of Freneau provoked anarchy. In such an event, widespread disorders might fuel a movement for monarchy as the only means of regaining stability. (When Washington brought up the subject with his Treasury secretary, Hamilton retorted that only a "madman" would propose a monarchy for America. Not only would the citizenry never stand for it, but also generations would be required to bring it about. What politician, Hamilton asked, would seek something that could never be realized in his lifetime?)[52]

The last time that Jefferson brought up the subject with the president was during a visit to Mount Vernon in October 1792. After Washington and his guest had toured the gardens and walked over the dewy, green lawn in the chill of early morning, they retired to the mansion for breakfast. The two were barely seated before Jefferson turned the conversation to Hamilton's purported monarchical bent. Testily, Washington snapped that there were not "ten men in the U.S. whose opinions were worth attention who entertained . . . transforming this government into a monarchy." Jefferson laconically responded that there were "many more" monarchists than the president imagined, but sensitive to Washington's ire, the secretary of state dropped the subject and never again brought it up with the chief executive. Jefferson came away convinced that Washington was out of touch, as well as that he was inextricably bound to Hamilton.[53]

One of the "many more" monarchical-leaning Americans that Jefferson was thinking about during his discussion with Washington was Vice President Adams. In fact, Jefferson had already complained to the president of Adams's "apostacy to hereditary monarchy and nobility." With considerable time on his hands in his inconsequential office, Adams late in 1790 had produced a string of essays titled "Discourses on Davila." Adams was discoursing on political theory, not urging immediate constitutional reforms. Nevertheless, what he wrote sounded very much like what Jefferson imagined Hamilton to be thinking, as Adams's overriding theme was the necessity of safeguarding government from the influence of the people. Writing in the wake of the earliest bloody disorders of the French Revolution, Adams, much like Edmund Burke, defended monarchy and aristocracy as bulwarks of stability. One benefit of a government composed of a king and the "rich, the well-born, and the able" was that the bane of elections would be done away, saving society from the "slanders and libels" and all the other "hissing snakes" that were part of electoral campaigns.

Jefferson had been surprised by Hamilton, of whom he had known little before 1790, but he was aghast at what Adams had written, and during their frequent evenings together the two argued over "Davila." Jefferson privately predicted to Monroe that "Davila" would leave Adams's political future in "ruins." In the spring of 1791, in a private letter to a printer planning to publish a new edition of *Rights of Man*, Jefferson extolled the importance of Paine's work, adding indiscreetly, as it turned out, that *Rights of Man* was all the more crucial in light of the "political heresies which have sprung up among us." His casual remark was an obvious reference to Adams. To Jefferson's mortification, the printer published what he had written in the introduction to his edition of Paine's book. Enraged, John and Abigail Adams broke off ties with their old Virginia friend, and no amount of apologizing by Jefferson could undo the damage.[54]

Hamilton knew, of course, that Madison had opposed his funding and assumption plan and that both he and Jefferson had fought the creation of the bank. However, the Treasury secretary at first dismissed warnings about their hidden intentions on the "botanizing" tour. He only slowly came to understand what the Virginians were up to. It was not until the spring of 1792, a year after Jefferson and Madison traveled to New York, and months after Freneau picked up his poisonous pen, that Hamilton grasped what was afoot. Once he did, Hamilton's reaction mirrored that of Jefferson. Drawing on the tidbits provided by his informants, Hamilton's impression of Jefferson— like Jefferson's notions of him—was a tangle of truths, half-truths, and misconceptions. At bottom, he came to see Jefferson as a "man of profound ambition & violent passions" who embraced "unsound & dangerous" ideas about government. As Jefferson thought Hamilton a danger to the deepest meanings of the American Revolution, Hamilton saw Jefferson as a mortal threat to all the consolidationists had sought since the last years of the war.[55]

Each was consumed with the other. They were "daily pitted in the cabinet like two cocks," as Jefferson later put it.[56] Beyond that, each plotted the undoing of the other, Hamilton from fear that Jeffersonianism would result in a ruinous democratization and fatal weakening of America, and Jefferson from a foreboding that Hamiltonianism would ultimately restore the political and social evils that had been swept away after 1776. Jefferson knew, too, that if republicanism in America was undone by its domestic enemies, his hopes for the eviction of monarchs and their aristocratic allies throughout Europe would vanish like snow under a warm sun.

In June 1792, only weeks before Paine fled England for good, Jefferson wrote to him of the change in thinking of some old American revolutionaries: "We have a sect preaching up and panting after an English constitution of king, lords, and commons," but "our people . . . are firm and unanimous in their principles of republicanism, and there is no better proof of it than that they love what you write and read it with delight. Go on doing with your pen what in other times was done with the sword." In closing, Jefferson told Paine that there was no "more sincere votary, nor . . . a more ardent well-wisher than . . . Your friend & servt, Thomas Jefferson."[57]

On nearly the same day, Jefferson wrote to a friend in France that the monarchists' "heads among us [are] itching for crowns, coronets, and mitres." Considering what was on the horizon in France, he closed with an unfortunate flourish: "we shall sooner cut them off than gratify their itching."[58]

CHAPTER 8

"The Only Man Who Possessed the Confidence of the Whole"

Partisan America in a Predatory World

JEFFERSON AND HAMILTON CAME TO think that what the other stood for was misguided at best, exceedingly dangerous at worst. Initially, their most intense differences were over the long-term consequences of Hamilton's economic program, but in time their battlefield widened to include other concerns that troubled the new American nation.

American economic issues had been addressed by early 1791, but two menacing matters remained, and to some degree both arose from Britain's postwar policies toward the United States. In 1774, in reprisal for the Boston Tea Party, London had embargoed trade with Massachusetts. Once the Revolutionary War erupted a year later, Britain broke off trade with every colony, a boycott that most Americans believed would end when the war did. Instead, when peace came, the British ministry issued orders-in-council stipulating that Great Britain would sell to the United States, but it would permit only American tobacco and naval stores to enter ports in the home islands, and then only in British vessels. Britain additionally continued to close to United States trade its West Indian colonies, long the key market for American exports. London's actions amounted to a staggering economic blow for a wide swath of Americans, but the Middle Atlantic and New England states were hardest hit. Benjamin Franklin and Jefferson had worked long and hard throughout the 1780s to replace the lost British trade with exports to France, but neither envoy had succeeded. As prosperity and a thriving commerce went hand in glove, a resolution of America's commercial quandary was high on Washington's list of priorities when he took office.

The second matter dogging the Washington administration carried greater immediate dangers for the American union. The Treaty of Paris had specified that all British troops were to be removed from United States soil, and late in 1783 the British army departed from east of the Appalachians. But units of the army continued to garrison Britain's outposts in trans-Appalachia, a region the peace accord had awarded to the United States. The redcoats in those backcountry posts kept alive Britain's trade with the Indians, including a brisk traffic in firearms. Nevertheless, neither the presence of British soldiers nor armed Indians had prevented hordes of settlers from crossing the mountains in search of fertile farmland. Whereas virtually no colonists had put down roots west of the Appalachians before the war, by 1790 the population of Tennessee exceeded thirty-five thousand, Kentucky's was more than twice that number, and settlers were flooding into the region north of the Ohio River. The United States thought of the movement as a vast migration to territories won in the Revolutionary War. The Indian tribes looked on it as an invasion.

It was a volatile situation and there were bloody incidents, but it was not the only western problem. The Revolutionary War had hardly ended before Spain, a helpmate during the late hostilities, closed the Mississippi River and New Orleans—both of which it controlled—to American settlers. In these times when travel by road—if roads existed—was arduous and slow, the Mississippi was akin to an interstate highway for the farmers. Unable to profitably transport bulky shipments of grain across the mountains, western farmers desperately needed the Mississippi to reach markets in the eastern cities, West Indian islands, and Europe. If they could not get their goods to market, these frontier yeomen would remain dirt-poor subsistence farmers. Or, in order to become commercial farmers, they might break away from the United States and create their own separate nation, the very thing that Spanish agents were proposing they do in order to have the Mississippi reopened.

During the 1780s, the United States had been powerless to deal with these western issues. It had of course complained to London, but Britain answered that it would comply with the Treaty of Paris when Americans retired their prewar debts to British creditors, something that was also mandated by the treaty. In the wheezing postwar economy, those prewar debts were not being liquidated. Nor did America's weak central government have the muscle to force the British army from its posts, deal with the Indians, or compel Spain to open the Mississippi River. Farmers, merchants, and land speculators suffered economically, and nationalists seethed at the new nation's weakness.

No one was more troubled than George Washington. He had not been home from the war a month before he remarked that if the western predicament was not rectified, the American Revolution would have been "to very little purpose." What Washington found when he traveled to western Pennsylvania a bit later shook him to the core. He heard enough separatist talk to conclude that the "Western settlers stand as [if they] were upon a pivot—the touch of a feather, would turn them any way"—that is, into the arms of Spain or the British in Canada, or toward the creation of their own separate nation. Even before he returned home following the war, Washington had set to work to create a stronger central government that might, among other things, resolve both the western dilemmas and America's trade problems. Once he took office in 1789 as the chief executive in a more powerful national government, these issues moved front and center.[1]

The thorny matter of American trade came up first, a full year before Jefferson became secretary of state. The First Congress had hardly organized in 1789 before James Madison asked the House to enact the impost that twice had failed in the days of the Confederation. Congress unanimously consented, imposing a 5 percent duty on most imports. Madison additionally proposed discriminatory rates against Great Britain, which was responsible for 90 percent of all American imports. He saw discrimination as the only leverage available for compelling London to open its ports to American vessels. Madison lost that battle. Northern merchants feared that his plan would drive them out of business. Hamilton opposed the measure for additional reasons. Not only was revenue from the impost on British imports pivotal to the success of his funding system, but he feared that commercial discrimination would invite London to retaliate by cutting off its exports to America. Hamilton's solution was a commercial treaty with London, a step that at once would enhance American trade and rekindle a fondness for all things British.[2]

Six months into his presidency, and six months prior to Jefferson's arrival in New York, Washington learned that George Beckwith, a British envoy en route to his new post in Quebec, was in the capital. Washington was eager for talks and especially avid to have Beckwith pressed on the matter of the removal of British troops. Curiously, the president turned to Hamilton, who was totally lacking in diplomatic experience, to meet with the British emissary. Hamilton hardly broached the topic of Britain's frontier army in the West, though his misleading reports to Washington suggested that he was hammering away at the issue. Hamilton focused instead on laying the groundwork for a commercial treaty. Telling Beckwith that his sentiments reflected those of the president, which was patently untrue, Hamilton intimated that the United States "preferred a Connexion" with Great Britain. Indeed, he advised Beckwith that moving closer to Britain was "infinitely Important" to the United States. What Hamilton chiefly accomplished was to assure the failure of Gouverneur Morris, whom Washington had sent to London as a special envoy. It is not likely that Morris would have made much headway toward the removal of British troops or in modifying the orders-in-council, but Hamilton's submissive manner had sent signals of American desperation. Subsequently, Jefferson had only to read Morris's dispatches to confirm his belief that Great Britain was "averse to all arrangements with us" other than "on their . . . terms."[3]

Once he finally took office, Jefferson was not long in coming to the conclusion that neither was a satisfactory Anglo-American commercial accord in the cards nor that negotiations with Britain would resolve America's western problems. The best that could be hoped for was that in due course Revolutionary France would lift the ancien régime's trade restrictions, opening the door to a commercial pact with Paris. After George Hammond, Britain's first minister to the United States, arrived in Philadelphia toward the end of 1791, Jefferson played for time. With the practiced hand of a seasoned diplomat, he proceeded at an exaggeratedly leisurely pace. Sensing early on that he would get nowhere with Jefferson, Hammond—who had read Beckwith's reports that portrayed the Treasury secretary as desperately eager for a commercial treaty—turned to Hamilton and proposed that they engage in secret talks. Treacherously, Hamilton consented.[4]

With Washington apparently in the dark, Hamilton apologized to Hammond for Jefferson's foot-dragging and even falsely accused his cabinet colleague of having staked out positions that were contrary to what the president desired. Hamilton also communicated confidential information regarding the status of United States negotiations with Spain, divulged that the State Department was making no headway in concluding a new commercial agreement with France, and maintained that the United States was willing to accept many of the restrictions and regulations insisted on by Great Britain in order to reopen trade in the West Indies. Jefferson had an inkling that Hamilton was surreptitiously talking to Hammond, as the Treasury secretary on one or two occasions revealed things that the secretary of state knew he could have learned only from the British minister. These slips led Jefferson in his private notes to mention on one or two occasions "Another proof" of Hamilton's skullduggery. Even though he guessed that Hamilton had "communicated to Hammond all our views," Jefferson said nothing to Washington, possibly from a belief that Hamilton was acting on the president's secret orders.[5] If Hamilton was acting on his own, his conduct was indefensible; public knowledge of his behavior would in all likelihood have left the president with no choice but to cashier his Treasury secretary. In the end, Hamilton's clandestine diplomacy made little difference. Britain and the United States remained too far apart on most issues. Barring a total American capitulation, which was not going to happen under President Washington, no agreement on the outstanding issues with Great Britain could have been reached.

As to the western posts, Washington, like Jefferson, early on concluded that London would not budge on the matter. The president came to believe that the Northwest Territory could be opened only through the use of force. Jefferson fully supported such a course. While governor, Jefferson had prosecuted a war against the Indians in the Old Northwest, in 1780 even telling the commander of Virginia's army in that sector that he was content with the Indians "extermination or . . . removal beyond the [Great] lakes. . . . The same world will scarcely do for them and us." During Jefferson's four years as secretary of state, Washington dispatched two armies against the Indian tribes living in what now is the state of Ohio. Both American armies suffered humiliating defeats.[6]

Early in 1792, the president spoke privately of retiring when his term ended in March 1793. Only Washington knew whether he meant what he said, but it is easy to see why he would have hoped to go home for good. Washington would be sixty-five at the conclusion of a second term, more or less the average life expectancy in that day. He had suffered two life-threatening illnesses since taking office, afflictions that sapped his vigor and convinced him that his time was running out. He was additionally dismayed by the partisan bickering in the press and indignant that some criticism—quite ambiguous, to be sure— was directed at him. He called on Jefferson and Hamilton to do what they could to forestall further sniping. It is conceivable that his threat to step down after one term was merely a ploy to silence the vitriolic quarreling that Washington feared might threaten the stability of the Union.

Jefferson and Hamilton took the president's threat to retire seriously, and both agreed—it was about the only thing on which the two saw eye to eye— that it would be unfortunate should Washington step down. Both thought him the adhesive that held together the Union. Hamilton had an additional reason for keeping Washington in the presidency. His plans were unfulfilled and he knew that Washington's aegis would be crucial to their realization. Hamilton had been around Washington longer than Jefferson and had a better feel for what might persuade the president to stay on. Playing on the president's vanity, the Treasury secretary warned Washington that failing to serve a second term would be "critically hazardous" to his lasting reputation. Jefferson emphasized the fragility of the Union, an approach also taken by Hamilton, and told Washington that "North and South will hang together, if they have you to hang on." In October, with the leaves taking on their autumn hues and Washington still not committed to another term, Jefferson called on him at Mount Vernon, his fourth visit in thirty months. On this occasion, Jefferson told Washington he was "the only man in the U.S. who possessed the confidence of the whole." However, after one more term the people's habit of "submitting to the government and . . . thinking it a thing to be maintained" would be ingrained. Before Jefferson departed for Philadelphia, Washington consented to "make the sacrifice" should his "aid [be] thought necessary to save the cause."[7]

Jefferson and Hamilton had gotten what they wanted from Washington, and neither had pledged to abandon partisan fighting. In fact, during 1792, a congressional election year, the partisan warfare grew more heated. Hamilton and his faction were aroused by the venomous attacks that poured from Freneau's *National Gazette*. Freneau had started tepidly in the fall of 1790, as if some time was required for him to warm to the task. He hit stride the next year and, if possible, his assaults might have grown even more malicious throughout 1792. At times, Freneau utilized information that Jefferson had gained from his circle of informants. Jefferson also recruited writers, some of whom he assisted in framing arguments. Some of the recruits produced unfriendly essays aimed at President Washington.

Not everything that appeared in Freneau's paper was true. But not all of it was false, including his allegations that the wealthiest Americans—especially those in the northern cities—profited most from Hamiltonianism and that some of Hamilton's minions in Congress had gained personally through inside information. Those who were drawn to Hamilton, said Freneau, were mostly "Base, grasping souls" driven by avarice. Satirically, Freneau suggested that once the Hamiltonians succeeded in establishing a titled nobility, it might be christened "the order of the Leech" or the "Order of the Golden Fleece." The exalted noblemen might be furnished with titles such as "Their Rapacities" or "Their Hucksterships," and their coat of arms could include the motto "Cheating no felony."

Freneau equated Hamilton's style with that of British prime ministers who served their king, portrayed the Treasury secretary's satellites as "Noblesse and Courtiers," and lambasted Vice President Adams for his supposedly monarchist leanings. With a nod toward revolutionary France, where the new republican culture had supplanted the correct and formal customs that had prevailed under royalty, Freneau censured the "monarchical prettiness" of Washington's administration. He took swipes at the administration's stuffy old-world practices, such as levees, which according to Freneau resembled the ritualistic assemblies when Europe's kings met the public. Freneau additionally mocked the president's stiff and distant manner, including his habit of "*stately nods instead of shaking hands*," and lampooned Adams as the most pompous of the lot. Freneau also contended that unless Hamiltonianism was stopped, the United States would become little more than a client state of Great Britain. For the most part, however, he focused on how he—and Jefferson—thought Hamiltonianism would reshape domestic America. Hamilton's vision, Freneau contended, would lead to unlimited government, rising prices as monopolies were fashioned by northern manufacturers, and soaring taxes. In time, the legacy of Hamiltonianism would be a nation divided between pluto-crats who reveled in wealth and the great mass of people who were sunk in an "abyss of *discredit* and *poverty!*"[8]

Hamilton was outraged by the calumny flowing from the *National Gazette*, which hurt all the more as Freneau accompanied many of his fierce sorties on Hamiltonianism with what historian John Miller called "honeyed praise" for Jefferson, "that illustrious Patriot" and "Colossus of Liberty." Hamilton struck back starting in the summer of 1792. As always, he wrote at a pace that few could match—eleven essays in five months—each written in Hamilton's customary take-no-prisoners manner. All but one piece went into the *Gazette of the United States*, but somehow he managed, doubtless gleefully, to sneak one essay into Freneau's paper. As was true of Freneau, Hamilton wrote some things that were accurate and some that were not. He informed the public that Jefferson was responsible for the *National Gazette* and excoriated him for hiring its editor as a clerk in the State Department. He assailed Jefferson for seeking to create a political party and accused him of wishing to become the party's head. He contended that Jefferson in 1788 "had *strong objections* to the constitution—*so strong* that he was willing to risk *an ultimate dismember-ment*" of the Union if the proposed document was ratified. Charging that Jefferson believed that Washington had acted "injudiciously and wickedly" in signing the Bank Bill, Hamilton called on the secretary of state to resign his post. Jefferson, he went on, sought nothing less than to reduce the national government to "the skeleton of Power" with the states elevated "upon its ruins." If Jefferson succeeded, Hamilton warned, he would fatally weaken the United States, destroy the "reinvigoration" of the economy that had begun two years earlier, and leave in the place of a vibrant United States "National disunion, National insignificance, Public disorder and discredit."[9]

Hamilton expected a response from the secretary of state, but that was not Jefferson's style. Jefferson later claimed, apparently truthfully, that he had never written a partisan essay during the 1790s. He preferred to turn the task over to others, and in this instance he remained in the shadows while James Monroe and Madison put their pens to work. Jefferson had urged Madison to respond. The unblinkingly loyal Monroe acted on his own. Eager to win Jefferson's approval, Monroe was also a politician through and through. On a recent trip home, he had found that opinion in Virginia was overwhelmingly suspicious of the creep of monarchism and what he called the "corrupt influence" of Hamiltonianism. Monroe hoped to capitalize by broadcasting his republican credentials. In addition, he not only was convinced that many of his countrymen did not fully comprehend the dangers inherent in the Treasury secretary's schemes, but also believed that many feared to speak out. Whatever his shortcomings, a lack of courage never afflicted Monroe. He was avid to join this fight.[10]

It is not difficult to see why Jefferson wanted Madison to defend him, for his young friend had a proven record as an exemplary essayist. It is just as easy to see why Jefferson was not enthralled by Monroe's polemical skills. Monroe was industrious and trustworthy, and he exuded abilities that made him a political winner, but proficiency in crafting tracts that stirred passions was not his strong suit. Ill-equipped as a wordsmith, Monroe was not in the same league as Hamilton or Madison, and even further short of Paine and Freneau. In this instance, Monroe between September and December produced six essays titled "The Vindication of Mr. Jefferson." Madison supposedly collaborated on two of the pieces, but like Jefferson he must have done little more than furnish data. Monroe said up front that he was replying to two charges: that Jefferson "was always inimical to the present government" and that he had "abused the trust reposed in him" by putting Freneau on the State Department's payroll. He took some swipes at Hamilton, but for the most part, through several thousand words, he stuck to defending Jefferson against those two indictments, and not a little of what he wrote sounded like this thudding sentence: "The visionary danger which threatens in the minds of some men, the publick credit, has long been a theme for copious declamation."[11]

Madison meanwhile authored nineteen unsigned essays. His handiwork appeared in the *National Gazette* during the run-up to the congressional elections. Madison reframed the debate, so that thereafter most Jeffersonians who wrote in the popular press depicted the partisan battle as an epic contest between republicans and monarchists, and they cast Hamilton and his faction as favoring an elitist system in which the citizenry remained deferential and acquiescent in the face of the threatening revival of monarchism and hostility to America's new spirit of egalitarianism. Hamiltonianism, Madison wrote, was bottomed on the hope that control of the national government would "by degrees be narrowed into fewer hands" until it ultimately "approximated . . . an hereditary form." This, he said, was not what the American Revolution had been about. The Revolution had been a revolt against monarchical and aristocratic tyranny, and America's citizen-soldiers had fought and died in the Revolutionary War to escape a British state ruled from the top down by a small elite. In the course of his essays, Madison confirmed Hamilton's charge that a political party had come into being. Madison referred to the anti-Hamilton faction as the "Republican party," and the name stuck.[12]

Hamilton and his satellites countered by creating the Federalist Party, though neither his faction nor the Republicans did much in the way of actually organizing until the approach of the presidential election of 1796. Clearly, Washington's appeals for an end to partisanship had fallen on deaf ears, though the president kept trying. He asked both Jefferson and Hamilton for "forbearances and temporizing" and reiterated to his secretary of state that the Treasury secretary was a patriot motivated chiefly by a desire to do what was best for the United States.[13] Both brushed aside the president's pleas. A few weeks later the juiciest of juicy information, and the most tempting, fell into Jefferson's lap.

In the autumn of 1792, two scurrilous individuals, James Reynolds and Jacob Clingman, were arrested and incarcerated by federal authorities on charges of perjury and defrauding the government. Looking for a way to induce the government to abandon the case, Clingman—who once had served as a clerk to Pennsylvania's Frederick Muhlenberg, the Speaker of the House—made contact with his former boss and passed on the story that Reynolds and Hamilton had been partners in illegal speculation in Treasury securities. Clingman also helpfully passed along some correspondence between Hamilton and Reynolds, confiding to Muhlenberg that the missives contained sufficient evidence to "hang the secretary of the Treasury." This could not be ignored, but Muhlenberg first wished to conduct his own confidential investigation. He easily persuaded Abraham Venable, a fellow representative, and Senator James Monroe—both Virginians and, like Muhlenberg, opponents of Hamilton—to help him.

After speaking with Clingman and questioning Reynolds in his jail cell, the three sleuths confronted Hamilton at his home. The Treasury secretary denied the allegations of illegal behavior. Instead, he admitted to having had an extramarital affair throughout the summer with Reynolds's wife, Maria, after which the cuckolded husband had blackmailed him with threats of making public the news of Hamilton's infidelity. Hamilton confessed that he had already paid Reynolds about one thousand dollars, and he produced letters that convinced the congressmen of the truthfulness of his story. Indeed, according to Hamilton's subsequent account, the congressmen were not simply persuaded; they expressed their "perfect satisfaction" with his explanation and displayed "embarrassment" at having confronted him. At least Hamilton believed that Muhlenberg and Venable were fully swayed by his account, although he thought Monroe "was more cold." Nevertheless, at Hamilton's request, all three congressmen pledged to never reveal the story of what the Treasury secretary called "a plain case of private amour." However, the congressmen retained the letters that Clingman had turned over to Muhlenberg. Curiously for one as calculating as Hamilton, two days passed before he thought to ask that the documents be returned to him. Monroe, who possessed the documents, complied three days later. But sometime in the course of the five days between meeting with Hamilton and returning the missives, Monroe directed John Beckley—the clerk of the House and a Virginian who was a cog in Jefferson's machine of informants—to make duplicates of the documents.[14]

Despite the congressmen's vows of secrecy, Jefferson knew the sordid details of the story within forty-eight hours, though he may have been filled in by Beckley and not by one of the congressional gumshoes. As Hamilton had a reputation for philadering, Jefferson never for a moment doubted his confession of an extramarital tryst. However, he thought the extortion story spun by the Treasury secretary was bogus. Jefferson was persuaded that there was merit to the accusations made by Clingman, but his hands were tied. To have made an issue of it would have been to reveal that three Republican congressmen—including his protégé Monroe—had broken their covenant with Hamilton, branding them as dishonorable in an age when honor was thought to be an all-important virtue.[15]

If Jefferson did not feel that he could directly pursue Clingman's lead, he was active on other fronts. More convinced than ever that Hamilton was utterly corrupt, Jefferson was certain that a bit of digging would turn up solid evidence of his malfeasance. He worked behind the curtain with William Giles, a blindly loyal Virginia congressman, to search for financial improprieties that Hamilton might have committed. His plan was for Giles to introduce a set of resolutions designed to force Hamilton to do an accounting of the loans made by his department. He hoped the inquiry would produce evidence of Hamilton's outright misconduct or questionable behavior, either of which would compel him to resign. Even if it did not, Jefferson believed that Giles's hearings would awaken the citizenry to the "extent of [the] danger" it faced. Giles introduced the resolutions, which Jefferson had helped him prepare, but the scheme failed. Hamilton satisfactorily answered several of the resolutions while congressmen whom he tutored ran circles around Jefferson's less well-informed surrogates. Congress soon repudiated Giles's resolutions by heavy majorities. Jefferson had lost the battle, but he believed he had won the war. Several Republicans won election to Congress during 1792, leading him to conclude that the "Monocrats" were beaten and that the tide had turned in the House of Representatives. Given "faithful accounts of what

Thomas Jefferson by John Trumbull, 1788.
Jefferson during his residence in Paris.
THOMAS JEFFERSON FOUNDATION

Thomas Jefferson by Charles Willson
Peale, 1791. The painting was made while
Jefferson was secretary of state.
INDEPENDENCE NATIONAL HISTORICAL PARK

Thomas Jefferson by Rembrandt Peale,
1799–1800. A painting of Jefferson from
the time of the election of 1800.
WHITE HOUSE HISTORICAL ASSOCIATION

Thomas Paine engraving by William Sharp of a George Romney portrait. The original by Romney, on which Sharp based his engraving, was probably made of Paine during his residence in England between 1787 and 1792. LIBRARY OF CONGRESS PRINTS & PHOTOGRAPHS DIVISION, LC-USZC4-2542

Thomas Paine by John Trumbull, 1788. Jefferson commissioned Trumbull to paint Paine. It was rendered on the cusp of the French Revolution. © THOMAS JEFFERSON FOUNDATION AT MONTICELLO

Thomas Paine by John Wesley Jarvis, 1806–1807. Painted when Jarvis and Paine lived together during 1806–1807. NATIONAL PORTRAIT GALLERY, OBJECT NO. 1950.15.1 NGA

Thomas Paine bust by John Wesley Jarvis, 1809. Jarvis completed the sculpture immediately following Paine's death. PHOTOGRAPH © NEW-YORK HISTORICAL SOCIETY

James Monroe by J. Vanderlyn, 1784.
Monroe as he appeared while a young
lawyer and near the time of his marriage.
LIBRARY OF CONGRESS

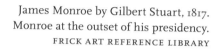

James Monroe by Sené, 1794.
Monroe during his initial year in
Paris as U.S. minister to France.
FRICK ART REFERENCE LIBRARY

James Monroe by Gilbert Stuart, 1817.
Monroe at the outset of his presidency.
FRICK ART REFERENCE LIBRARY

FACING PAGE: Emanuel Leutze, *Washington Crossing the Delaware*. Monroe is shown holding the flag, though in reality he did not cross the Delaware in the same boat with General Washington. LIBRARY OF CONGRESS *THIS PAGE*: John Trumbull, *Capture of the Hessians at Trenton*. The wounded Monroe is shown prostrate on the ground to Washington's right, cradled by Dr. John Riker. In actuality, there was not a formal surrender ceremony at Trenton. YALE UNIVERSITY ART GALLERY, TRUMBULL COLLECTION, 1832.5

John Trumbull, *The Declaration of Independence*. The members of the Committee of Five are, from left, John Adams, Roger Sherman, Robert R. Livingston, Thomas Jefferson (the tallest of the five), and Benjamin Franklin. YALE UNIVERSITY ART GALLERY, TRUMBULL COLLECTION, 1832.3

Benjamin West, *American Commissioners at the Preliminary Peace Negotiations.* From left to right: John Jay, John Adams, Benjamin Franklin, Henry Laurens, and William Temple Franklin, Secretary to the American Delegation. OIL PAINT ON CANVAS. COURTESY WINTERTHUR MUSEUM. GIFT OF HENRY FRANCIS DU PONT, 1957.856

John Trumbull, *General Washington Resigning His Commission*, 1824. Jefferson is seated and wearing the red coat. Monroe is the third person to his left. Madison is the shorter of the two men standing in front of the door in the rear. ARCHITECT OF THE CAPITOL

George Washington by Charles Willson
Peale, 1787, at the time of the Constitutional
Convention. COURTESY OF PENNSYLVANIA
ACADEMY OF THE FINE ARTS. GIFT OF MARIA
MCKEAN ALLEN AND PHEBE WARREN DOWNES
THROUGH THE BEQUEST OF THEIR MOTHER,
ELIZABETH WHARTON MCKEAN.

John Adams by Charles Willson Peale.
WIKIMEDIA COMMONS

James Madison by Charles Willson Peale,
1792. GILCREASE MUSEUM, ACCESSION NO.
0126.1006

Alexander Hamilton by John Trumbull, 1792.
GIFT OF THE AVALON FOUNDATION, NATIONAL
GALLERY OF ART, ACCESSION NO. 1952.1.1

Gouverneur Morris, left, and Robert Morris by James Sharples, 1783. COURTESY OF PENNSYLVANIA ACADEMY OF THE FINE ARTS. BEQUEST OF RICHARD ASHHURST

Marquis de Lafayette by Charles Willson Peale, 1779. GIFT OF GEORGE WASHINGTON CUSTIS LEE, WASHINGTON AND LEE UNIVERSITY, LEXINGTON, VIRGINIA. u1897.1.2

General Horatio Gates by Charles Willson Peale, 1782. COURTESY OF INDEPENDENCE NATIONAL HISTORICAL PARK

General Nathanael Greene by Charles Willson Peale, 1783. COURTESY OF INDEPENDENCE NATIONAL HISTORICAL PARK

Maria Cosway by Richard Cosway.

Edmund Burke by Sir Joshua Reynolds.

Maximilien Robespierre by Grevedon.

Jacques-Pierre Brissot.

LES PROMENADES DU LVXEMBOURG
Presenté a Son Altesse Serenissime Monseigneur le Prince de CONTY
Chez le Sr du Change Graueur du Roy Rüe St Jacques et chez l'Auteur dans la même Rüe

Luxembourg Palace [Prison].

"Union of the Two Great Republics," a pitcher crafted during the partisan 1790s. It celebrated the close ties between France and the United States.
NATIONAL MUSEUM OF AMERICAN HISTORY, ROBERT H. MCCAULEY COLLECTION

"Fashion before Ease," James Gillray. Thomas Paine, the former staymaker, is depicted with *Rights of Man* protruding from his pocket as he wrestles with Britannia's stays. The cartoon appeared in 1793, the year after Paine fled to France. Note that the cartoonist shows Paine's disfiguring rosacea.
LIBRARY OF CONGRESS

Wha WANTS ME

LEFT: "Wha Wants Me" [Paine Advertising His Services], 1792. An Isaac Cruikshank cartoon showing Paine holding a banner proclaiming "equality of property." In the background, Paine is accused of assorted crimes, including anarchy, murder, treason, and national ruin.

LIBRARY OF CONGRESS PRINTS & PHOTOGRAPHS DIVISION, LC-DIG-PPMSCA-19916

BELOW: "The Friends of the People," Isaac Cruikshank, 1792. The cartoon shows Joseph Priestley (LEFT) and Paine plotting revolution. They are surrounded by guns, gunpowder, swords, and hatchets. A winged putto looks on. Its inclusion is apparently meant to demonstrate God's displeasure at their actions. Paine's rosacea stands out.

WIKIMEDIA COMMONS

The FRIENDS of the PEOPLE

RIGHT: "The Providential
Detection." Vice President
Jefferson, the Mazzei Letter
in hand, is kneeling before
the French altar of despotism
and attempting to burn the
U.S. Constitution. An eagle is
attempting to thwart him.
AMERICAN ANTIQUARIAN
SOCIETY, WORCESTER,
MASSACHUSETTS/
THE BRIDGEMAN ART LIBRARY

BELOW: Jefferson Banner, 1801.
A banner celebrating Jefferson's
election as president and also
proclaiming, "JOHN ADAMS
is no MORE."
NATIONAL MUSEUM OF AMERICAN
HISTORY, SMITHSONIAN

"Mad Tom in a Rage." A Federalist cartoon, circa 1802–1803, depicting an alcohol-laced Tom Paine—note the liquor bottle at his feet—attempting to destroy the Constitution. Paine is assisted by a Satanic figure who is meant to be President Jefferson. As in the "Providential Detection" cartoon, an eagle defends the Constitution against the Jeffersonians. SHUTTERSTOCK is doing here," said Jefferson, the citizenry had made the right choices. After two tempestuous years, Jefferson was certain that Hamiltonianism had been stopped.[16]

Before 1792, the French Revolution had not been a matter for America's partisan warfare. Most Americans, like Jefferson and Paine, believed the French Revolution had been inspired by America. After all, during the searing summer of 1789 the Estates General limited monarchical authority, adopted the Declaration of the Rights of Man and of the Citizen—some of which bore a resemblance to parts of the Declaration of Independence—and had set about writing a constitution, just as the states and Continental Congress had done in the first blush of American independence. Those who cheered the French Revolution at its outset included a who's who of the Federalist Party. John Marshall, John Jay, and Timothy Pickering were among those who were swept up in the fervor, and the *Gazette of the United States*, the leading Federalist organ, proclaimed the Revolution "one of the most glorious" events in world history.

However, some conservatives were wary. From the very beginning, Hamilton was seized with a "foreboding of ill" given what he believed to be the passionate nature of the French, the possibility of a royalist-inspired counterrevolution, the "reveries" of the "philosophic politicians" who dominated the Estates General, and his own experiences in an American Revolution filled with unpleasant surprises. On the sly, Hamilton early on slipped items into the press that were designed to foster unfavorable sentiments toward the French Revolution (while Jefferson worked simultaneously to get favorable stories into newspapers). If Hamilton had always been chary, President Washington had been pleased by the French Revolution's good start, though he, too, brooded from the beginning that the "licentiousness of the People," royalist intrigue, or foreign intervention would cause trouble. Gouverneur Morris applauded the prospect of change in France in April 1789, but the earliest reforms—together with the initial mob activity in Paris in July—caused him to lose his appetite for the French Revolution. But until late 1792 the overwhelming majority of Americans, including most Federalists, hailed the stirring events in France. France had won American hearts during the Revolutionary War, and much of the French Revolution during its first couple of years seemed to be in step with the Spirit of 1776. It was so popular in America that here and there both Bastille Day and Independence Day were celebrated, and attendees at public commemorations of Washington's birthday sometimes also acclaimed Lafayette's role in the French Revolution. With gusto, taverngoers not infrequently sang French revolutionary songs. Only Washington was toasted more than Thomas Paine at public gatherings, and glasses were raised to Paine's support for the French Revolution: "Thomas Paine—May he open the eyes of the blind"; "Paine and friends of freedom throughout the world"; Paine and "all writers in defense of Liberty and the Rights of Man"; "The Clarion of Freedom, Thomas Paine"; and simply "Citizen Thomas Paine."

Some newspapers that would later be staunchly Federalist organs reacted viscerally to Burke's criticism of the French Revolution in 1791. Had they been aware of Jefferson's confidential sneer at "the rottenness of [Burke's] mind," not a few of Hamilton's adherents might have echoed his sentiment. When France went to war in the spring of 1792, most Americans fervently wished for the salvation of the French Revolution. So widespread was pro-French sentiment that General Henry Lee, a former Continental cavalry officer and unbending conservative, made plans to cross the Atlantic and fight for France. When word arrived that France's armies had stopped the Prussians and Austrians at Valmy, spontaneous celebrations erupted in many American cities and the revelry often measured up to that which had greeted the news of Cornwallis's surrender at Yorktown. The Tammany Society in New York erected a "liberty pole" crowned with a red hat akin to that worn by Parisian revolutionaries, and that evening those in attendance at a celebratory banquet drank to Paine and the destruction of "Kingcraft and . . . Priestcraft, the poisons of public happiness."[17]

John Adams had stood nearly alone among Americans in portraying the French Revolution as a catastrophe in the making. More than a year before the Estates General met, he and Jefferson had discussed the "Fermentation" throughout "All Europe." Jefferson had hoped change was on the way. Adams was fearful, especially if the reformers sought to establish republics, a move that could produce only "Confusion and Carnage" and "End in despotism." Adams characterized a string of French Enlightenment philosophers admired by Jefferson and Paine as "a liar," "a satyr," "a quack," "a fool," a "louse," and a "tick." Once the Revolution began—and well before Burke wrote critically of it—Adams predicted that France was on a path that led inescapably to "anarchy, licentiousness and despotism." Wiping out the titled nobility was a mistake, he thought, as an elite class provided a crucial source of stability in society. Adams was certain, too, that the French were playing with fire in tinkering with monarchical authority, for hereditary monarchy was attended with "fewer evils" than would be the case with republican chief executives.

Given his belief that it was "irrational and unpracticable" to think that pure republicanism could work in France, where some 98 percent of the citizenry was illiterate, Adams (like Hamilton) questioned the wisdom of aristocratic reformers such as Lafayette. The "Grossness of his Ignorance of Government and History" was remarkable, said Adams. As Parisian mobs became more commonplace, Adams railed at the idiocy of "exciting . . . Tumults among People who may be hired to [do] anything." After mobs stormed the Tuileries Palace and the assembly formally terminated the monarchy, Adams shook his head in disgust. A "democratical hurricane" was afoot and it could only have a bad end. He was one of the first to foresee what he called "King-killing." He thought it "astonishing" that Lafayette and his fellow aristocratic reformers had been so foolish as to put in motion "Furies" that had led to such a foreseeable end. "Dragon's Teeth have been sown in France and come up Monsters," Adams reflected. When word of Valmy arrived, he did not join in the merrymaking, in part because he had hoped the French Revolution would be rolled back, but also because he feared that France's victory would quicken "the Spirit of the Enemies of Government among us."[18]

Before 1792, few shared Adams's extreme views. Even those who worried the most about calamity in France appear to have remained hopeful for some thirty-six months after the electrifying start made by the Estates General. In Jefferson's opinion, it was not until Washington learned of the king's flight in 1791 that the president first seemed "dejected" and apprehensive that the constitutional monarchy might be doomed. During the following year, Washington grew more pessimistic in light of the turmoil and appalling incidents in Paris. Jefferson thought Washington's mind was being "poisoned" by Gouverneur Morris, a "high-flying Monarchy-man," who filed one glum dispatch after another that portrayed France as on the verge of being "plunged anew into the Horrors of Despotism." Six months before the September Massacres, Morris predicted, "Events seem fast ripening to . . . awful Catastrophe," and he advised that only a monarch could "succeed in saving" the country. Morris was not far off base, at least with regard to his forecasts of the coming cataclysm. Nevertheless, whereas Hamilton said the king's removal and the horrid bloodshed "cured" him of "goodwill for the French Revolution," Washington had not yet given up. He still said that "severe ills" were "inseparable from so important a Revolution." Washington, who had spilled blood to achieve American independence, understood that unpleasant things often happened in the course of bringing about radical change. Some other veterans of the American Revolution agreed with the president's thinking. Benjamin Franklin, for instance, defended the early carnage in Paris as "justifiable," for it was in pursuit of "future liberty."[19]

Jefferson shared the thinking of Washington and Franklin. He, too, contended that battling for liberty was worth a "little innocent blood." The struggle was monumental. At stake was liberty in France and throughout

Europe and England, but even more important Jefferson by 1791 or so believed that success in France would "serve to regenerate . . . the United States, whose principles were beginning to become corrupted." In a remark for which he has been savaged by critics ever since, Jefferson, with conviction and his penchant for rhetorical embroidery, went on to say that even if "half the earth [was] desolated" in quest of freedom, the destruction would be worth it. Indeed, "Were there but an Adam and Eve left in every country, and left free, it would be better than" for humankind to suffer under tyrannical oppression.[20]

Jefferson's belief was a variation of the widely held idea that some wars were "just wars," warranted because of the good they produced, even though many innocent civilians perished. Jefferson thought some revolutions were defensible. The American Revolution was one. So was the French Revolution. Jefferson unambiguously hoped the French Revolution would inspire others to launch their own revolutions against absolutist systems, spurred by the republican belief that "man can be governed by reason more effectually than by rods and chains." Jefferson additionally asserted that the success of the French Revolution was crucial to "the permanence of our" American Revolution. The failure of the French Revolution, he said, would provide American reactionaries with "a powerful argument to prove there must be a failure here."[21]

Toward the end of 1792, enthusiasm for the French Revolution rapidly waned among American conservatives. No one thing changed their outlook. The September Massacres and other bloody events throughout France were crucial. So, too, was the growing influence and popularity of Burke's critique, as his predictions of carnage had come true. The Revolution's onslaught against the church and clergy—including the occasional spoliation of naves and desecration of sacred relics—provoked a backlash. The most conservative shared Adams's misgivings about the elimination of France's aristocratic ruling class, but more probably agreed with the vice president that France's democratization would take the nation down nightmare alley. Apprehension that France's Revolution might spread to England—something that Paine had implicitly endorsed in *Rights of Man*—was also deeply alarming to America's Anglophiles.

Nothing unsettled American conservatives more than the rampant social changes within France. Their greatest concern appeared to be the disappearance of those highly visible pointers that had distinguished the privileged from commoners, especially as the badges of class differences persisted in post-Revolutionary America. They recoiled in horror at the thought that in place of titles all the French were now addressed simply as "citizen." Some found it disconcerting that powdered wigs had fallen out of favor and trousers, long the customary attire among artisans and laborers, were coming to replace knee britches and silk stockings among men of all classes. Some were appalled to learn that bowing had fallen out of favor, replaced by handshakes, a new form of greeting that traditionalists scorned as "hugging and rugging . . . addressing and caressing." Conservative elitists also derided the Parisian "contagion of levelism" that threatened to make the well-born and wealthy the "equal to French barbers." Even more were outraged that private property was no longer safe. Most disconcerting of all, of course, was the possibility that these French innovations portended their spread among American citizens enamored of the French Revolution.[22]

By early 1793 the most conservative Americans saw in the French Revolution a world of dark menace. Federalist essayists now pilloried the heroes of the French Revolution, defended a traditional society of the sort that Burke had lauded, portrayed Republicans as indistinguishable from the most radical revolutionaries in France, applauded Britain's quashing of republicanism in Ireland, and ridiculed as phonies and hypocrites elite Americans who—like elite French radicals—claimed to be egalitarians. Xenophobia became a staple of Federalist rhetoric. The French Revolution was depicted as a perversion, and those who continued to sympathize with it were branded as "foreign disorganizers" and purveyors of alien ideas and styles. The end result of such dangerous proclivities, it was said, would be the destruction of religious liberty and the United States Constitution. Federalist screeds also took pains to repudiate the conceit that America was committed to worldwide republican revolutions. For the first time, too, Paine was savaged in Federalist newspapers. He was targeted for having claimed that he was a "citizen of the world" and denounced as a firebrand who wished "to destroy all subordination in government." Paine, they charged, was committed only to "pull[ing] down empires."[23]

Throughout 1792 Federalists raised more questions than ever about the French Revolution, though the grave European situation gradually overshadowed all else in their thinking about France. Signs that England might join Austria and Prussia in the campaign to destroy the French Revolution grew following the collapse of the monarchy. Pitt's government recalled Britain's minister to France when the monarchy fell in late summer, and it warned that "all of Europe" would take offense should anything "happen to the King." Gouverneur Morris explained to the president that in "plain English," London was saying that it would "make War immediately" should the king be executed, and he added that he feared for Louis's life. "History informs us," Morris advised, "that the Passage of dethroned Monarchs is short from the Prison to the grave." As the trial of Louis XVI loomed, Morris reported to Washington that Britain would soon present France with an ultimatum that would make war unavoidable, for should the French acquiesce in London's demands "the Republic must be torne to Pieces by contending Factions." (Inexplicably, on nearly the same day Morris wrote to Jefferson that France wanted war, but he told Hamilton that France's rulers hoped to avoid war.)[24]

Though their perspectives differed, both Jefferson and Hamilton understood the enormity of troubles that would arise should Britain enter the war. An unrestrained Franco-British war on the high seas, with both sides blockading the other's ports, would play havoc with American trade and the flow of essential revenue. Of all the difficult questions that would be brought on by British belligerency, none would be greater than that of America's role in a widened European conflict. Would the United States remain neutral? Could it remain neutral in the face of depredations at sea? Would it join its French ally—the alliance of 1778 yet existed—and aid it in its struggle with Great Britain as France had come to the assistance of the United States in its conflict with London? Little imagination was required to foresee that Britain's entrance into the war would further inflame America's already torrid partisan politics. Throughout 1792, these possibilities added urgency to Jefferson's and Hamilton's efforts to persuade Washington to stay on for a second term.

"Gloomy indeed appears the situation," said Washington that fall. During the winter, with word expected of both Louis's execution and a British assault on France, the president prayed that his countrymen would have "too just a sense of our own interest" to become embroiled in Europe's war. In March, word at last reached Philadelphia that the king had gone to the scaffold. The response to the news revealed the hardened partisan divisions. Most Federalists would have agreed with the New England conservative who called the killing of the king "a wanton act of barbarity," or with Vice President Adams, who wondered, when "will these savages be satiated with blood?" Hamilton, who had not previously praised the king, now rhapsodized that he had been a good and benevolent man who "was not the enemy of liberty." On the other side, Philip Freneau in the *National Gazette* merrily announced that "Louis Capet has lost his Caput." The king's death, he added, "affects me no more than the execution of another malefactor." Madison and Monroe noted that Freneau's viewpoint reflected the sentiment of most Virginians. Jefferson's response was predictably the diametric opposite of Hamilton's. While in Paris, he had reproached the king's character, noting that he "hunts one half the day, is drunk the other, and signs whatever he is bid." When word of Louis's death reached Philadelphia, Jefferson observed that he hoped the king's fate might "soften" royal rule elsewhere by demonstrating that "monarchs [are] amenable to punishment like other criminals." If Hamilton saw virtue and right-mindedness in Louis XVI, Jefferson thought the king had "plunged the world into crimes and calamities which will forever stain the pages of modern history."[25]

The widening of Europe's war was now expected and, indeed, France had declared war on Great Britain eleven days after Louis climbed the steps to the guillotine.

CHAPTER 9

"I RELINQUISH HOPE"

THE FRENCH REVOLUTION
IN FRANCE AND AMERICA

WHEN THOMAS PAINE FLED ENGLAND four months before the execution of Louis XVI, he thought that not only would he find a sanctuary in France, but also that he could play an important role in the Revolution. Instead, as 1793 unfolded, Paine found himself faced with dangers as great, or greater, than those he would have faced in England.

Paine had opposed Louis's execution, but he supported going to war against England. Following the news of both events, Spain and Holland recalled their ambassadors, and France—aglow with a host of recent military victories in the Austrian Netherlands and Rhineland—declared war on them as well. Paine radiated optimism despite France's growing number of enemies. Although the "tyrants of the earth are leagued" against a France that stands "single-handed and alone," he said in mid-February, the Revolutionary nation was "unshaken, unsubdued, unsubdueable, and undaunted," and only poor generalship could cause its defeat.[1]

This would have been a good time for Paine to take his leave of France and sail for America. In fact, before taking flight from England he had said that he would quit France if the king was executed. Paine stayed on, however, thinking he could still play a substantive role in the Convention, especially as during the previous autumn the Girondin-dominated assembly had chosen him and eight others to draft France's first republican constitution. Paine had made progress in reading French, if not in speaking it, and he made some contributions to the document produced by the committee and submitted in April 1793.[2] But nothing came of the committee's work. By the time spring settled over Paris, another faction controlled the Convention.

Paine was never a hard-and-fast member of any bloc, though he usually voted with the Girondins, or Brissotins as they were sometimes called. The faction was dominated by Jacques Brissot de Warville, who had left his law practice in 1789 to become the editor of a democratic and abolitionist newspaper, *Patriote Français*. Paine and Brissot were friends and one-time collaborators. As Brissot was fluent in English, the two could also readily converse, and both were writers and republicans who abhorred slavery and dreamed somewhat the same dream for a post–ancien régime France. Both also harbored deep feelings for America. Brissot had visited America in 1788, a year after Paine sailed for France and while Jefferson was still living in Paris. Brissot had made the journey in hopes of learning why the American Revolution had succeeded and to "study the effects of liberty on the development of man, society, and government."

After landing in Boston, he traveled through several states, along the way meeting seemingly every important American. His thumbnail sketches of those he called on are intriguing, sometimes quite accurate, sometimes not. Madison had "the thoughtful look of a wise statesman" and evinced the "meditative air of a profound politician"; Hamilton had "a resolute, frank, soldierly appearance" as well as "the determined appearance of a republican"; John Adams (whom he encountered during the harvest on his farm) had "retired to the obscurity of the country life" and was "oblivious of the time when he struck down the pride of his king"; Samuel Adams embodied "all the republican virtues almost to a fault," including "complete honesty, simplicity, modesty, and above all sternness"; Washington was "astonishing . . . amazing," incredibly modest—"especially to a Frenchman"—and "the kindness of his heart shines in his eyes." Aside from the scourge of slavery, Brissot loved America, perhaps even more than did Paine, and before the French Revolution changed everything he decided that someday soon he would move to Pennsylvania, a province that he believed was blessed with a good climate, low taxes, fertile land, and a humane citizenry.[3]

The Girondins had been the dominant element within the Convention since its inception in the late summer of 1792, but by the following April the Montagnards—or "the Mountain," an amalgam of several groups, but a faction dominated by Parisian radicals—had gained control. Both Girondins and Montagnards had supported the abolition of the monarchy, but since the previous autumn several issues had divided the two. Girondins had hoped to spare the king's life; Montagnards had sought his execution. Girondins had been in the forefront of the campaign for going to war in 1792 and for declaring war on England in 1793; in both instances, the Montagnards—who feared France's generals more than its foreign adversaries—had been less eager for hostilities. Girondins wished to vest provincial governments with greater measures of autonomy; Montagnards abhorred decentralization. The two clashed over the role of the people, an issue that became paramount in the aftermath of the September Massacres. From that tragic event onward, the Girondins feared that the Mountain's close ties to Parisian extremists would result in anarchy and the destruction of the Revolution. Girondin dominance eroded starting in midwinter 1793. Opposition to Louis's execution cost them dearly, but growing economic distress during that winter—and their opposition to price controls and other government regulations—may have been more important in the unraveling of Girondin supremacy. As spring took hold in Paris, the Montagnards had the wind in their sails. Soon they controlled the Convention, and in the weeks that followed, the Montagnards consolidated their domination.[4]

That juncture would have been the next best time—in fact, very nearly the last possible time—for Paine to leave France, and in April he wrote to Jefferson that he was contemplating "returning home" to America. One line in his missive suggests that, however nebulously, Paine already foresaw what he feared would be the betrayal of the Revolution. He confided to Jefferson: "Had this Revolution been conducted consistently with its principles, there was once a good prospect of extending liberty through the greatest part of Europe; but I now relinquish that hope."[5]

But Paine did not leave. Seventeen years earlier he had written about standing fast in the midst of times that tried men's souls, and he was not about to decamp while the French Revolution faced what he saw as an "extraordinary crisis." An abundance of additional reasons might also explain why he remained in France. Paine may have sensed a gathering calamity, but at that moment neither he nor anyone else could imagine the panoply of horrors that lay down a very short road. Even after the atrocities began to unfold, Paine thought he was safe because of his American citizenship. He had to know, too, that it might be dangerous to try to leave. Many a Frenchman who tried to get out had been apprehended and incarcerated, or worse, after being brought before a merciless revolutionary tribunal on a charge of being an enemy of the Revolution. Even if Paine made it out of France, he would have to cross an Atlantic thick with British warships. To be captured would result in his imprisonment, and possibly his execution in England. There was also the matter of Paine's vanity. He was a celebrity in France. People wanted to see and meet him. For the past six months, he had lived happily at White's Hotel, an enclave for Americans, but in the spring the crush of the curious and starstruck knocking on his door led him to move to a more remote residence on the Rue de Richelieu. That did not solve his problem. Throngs of admirers soon found him. To have any time to himself, Paine set aside a portion of two mornings a week for what a friend called his "levee days," periods when he met those who came calling. He delighted in the recognition, but at the same time he found it annoying. In April, he moved again, settling on the Rue Faubourg Saint-Denis, a mile and a half from White's and some seven miles from the center of the city, an area heavily populated by workers in the construction trades.[6]

He found this residence to be the "most agreeable" of the many he occupied while in France, for he enjoyed a "tranquility" that he had never known downtown. Characterizing his abode as "an old mansion farm-house," Paine had an upstairs apartment that consisted of three rooms—a storage room crowded with firewood, a bedroom, and a sitting room. The latter, which he used as a study, included a glass door that let the sun pour in and through which he could see the surrounding grounds. During good weather, Paine could descend a narrow outside stairway "almost hidden by the vines that grew over it," and alight in a one-acre garden flush with flowers, assorted fruit trees, several varieties of fowl, rabbits, and two pigs, all of which he enjoyed feeding. Still an inveterate walker, Paine could saunter to his heart's content, including "walking alone in the garden at night," relaxing strolls in the moonlight that were helpful for collecting his thoughts for his compositions. Several others lived in the immense house, but he was closest to two Englishmen, William Choppin and William Johnson, whom he had known previously, and M. La Borde, once an officer in the French army who shared Paine's interest in math and mechanics. An acquaintance, who thought La Borde "an intolerable aristocrat," remarked that Paine—given his "unbounded liberality" toward others with different ideas and disagreeable bearings— never let class differences impede his relationships.[7]

Paine was not a recluse in Saint-Denis. He occasionally accepted dinner invitations, and one of his hosts later gushed that for four hours Paine had kept the others at the table on the edge of their seats with observations and stories about the American Revolution and its leading participants. Sadly, the "several curious facts of humour" and "numberless anecdotes" that could "never be forgotten" by his dinner companions were not recorded and preserved. From time to time he made the long walk to White's to call on friends, and several of them, in turn, dropped in on him. None came more often than Joel Barlow, a New Englander noted for his social charm as well as for his republican activism. Seventeen years younger than Paine, Barlow was a Yale graduate who had served as a chaplain in a Massachusetts brigade during the war. A year after Paine first arrived in France, Barlow crossed to Paris as a representative of an American land company. In short order, his life in Europe came to bear some resemblance to Paine's. Barlow remained abroad for years and he, too, shuttled between Paris and London. He made acquaintances with many of the same people with whom Paine kept company, among them Mary Wollstonecraft and Jefferson. (Barlow had attended Jefferson's final Independence Day bash in Paris in 1789 and signed the lavish tribute to him as the author of the Declaration of Independence.) Like Paine, Barlow was a writer; he turned out poetry and essays. One of Barlow's tracts, *Advice to the Privileged Orders*, was comparable in tone to *The Rights of Man* and appeared in London just ten days before the publication of Paine's *Part the Second.*[8]

English and French acquaintances visited Paine, keen to see him and looking forward to lively conversation accompanied by flowing spirits. Brissot was an occasional visitor, and Paine also spent frequent evenings at his residence, which was not far away. Wollstonecraft was back in France and enjoyed talking with Paine, as did Jean-Henri Bancal, a Brissotin deputy and secretary of the Convention whom he had met years before through Benjamin Franklin. But Paine was not overrun with visitors, which was fine with him, and he rapidly slipped into a regimen that one observer described as "a life of retirement and philosophical ease." He rose around seven A.M., breakfasted with the "little happy circle" of fellow boarders with whom he was closest, enjoyed a table game or two with them, and took a solitary walk for one or two hours. Midmorning found Paine back in his study, where he remained, absorbed by his writing and correspondence until the second and final meal of the day late in the afternoon. He spent most evenings conversing with a handful of other residents of Saint-Denis, exchanges that one described as "often witty and cheerful, always acute and improving, but never frivolous."[9]

Paine's only complaint about his residence in Saint-Denis was that it was "too remote from the Convention," but that was a short-term problem. Paine largely stopped attending the Convention sessions late in the spring and— happy to be far from "the alarms and confusion" of center-city Paris—after early summer never returned to the assembly.[10]

A series of events starting early in 1793 plunged France into the grave crisis that Paine had reported to Jefferson. Wars—foreign and domestic—were the root causes of the trouble. Faced with a swelling number of enemies, the Convention in February voted to double the number of men under arms, calling for three hundred thousand new recruits. The prospect of military service in support of the Revolution touched off riots in several provinces, and by the second week in March the disorders had grown into full-blown insurrections in some sectors. Some uprisings began among peasants long since roiled by heavy taxes, the Revolution's religious policies, and the removal and killing of their king. Food shortages brought on by the war stoked the fire in many provinces.

In some instances, the rebellions were encouraged, even directed, by royalist aristocrats and priests. Since the king's flight, there had been endless talk among the revolutionaries about the threat of a "grand conspiracy." Its day appeared to have come. Indeed, it seemed evident to many in the Convention that the long-feared counterrevolution and civil war had commenced. The government fought back by establishing revolutionary tribunals in the provinces. Blood literally flowed in the streets of Nantes as the authorities suppressed the insurgency with a heavy hand, but in the Vendée, a largely rural region in western France, the rebels appeared to be unstoppable. Vendée armies and guerrilla fighters emerged, winning a string of victories in clashes with Revolutionary armies. Soon, with nearly the entire Vendée under their control, emboldened rebels paraded with flags that bore Christian symbols and tore down visible signs of the Revolution, such as liberty trees.

At the same moment, bad news arrived from the war zones. While Britain blockaded the coasts, disasters occurred at the front. General Charles-François Dumouriez—once the Girondin-backed foreign minister who had successfully led France's armies in 1792, winning laurels at Valmy—ordered a retreat following a defeat in an engagement at Neerwinden. Soon, the French army in Germany was falling back as well. Like Lafayette before him, Dumouriez early in April sought to lead his army into Paris, destroy the Convention, and restore monarchy by placing Louis XVI's young son on the throne. The army had refused to follow Lafayette and it rebuffed Dumouriez, who, like his predecessor, fled into enemy territory. Little now stood between the foreign armies and Paris, causing panic not unlike that of the previous summer.

The Convention took several steps to deal with the emergencies. It stepped up military recruiting, sent reinforcements to the front, rushed troops into the provinces—some fifty thousand were sent to the Vendée alone—vested local administrators with nearly dictatorial powers for coping with the rebel "brigands," placed foreigners under surveillance, and created a Revolutionary Tribunal to try suspected counterrevolutionaries without appeal. The Girondins initially opposed the creation of the tribunal, but in March, swept up by the crisis confronting the *patrie*, they joined the Montagnards and other delegates in supporting many of the emergency measures. The Convention, a body that from the outset had been designed for revolutionary action unimpeded by gridlock, was rushing toward cataclysm. (Years later, John Adams wrote that the lack of a second house that might have served as a safeguard against unbridled emotionalism had been the Revolutionaries' "fatal" blunder.) Even as radicals in the assembly lashed out at the "villainous Brissotins" as *veritables traîtres*" to the Revolution, Bertrand Barère, a leading Girondin, urged the death penalty for counterrevolutionaries, prompting the deputies to leap to their feet and shout, "Death! Death! Death!" Soon thereafter, the Convention decreed that all foreigners be placed under strict oversight, a step that quickly led to surveillance of some who aroused suspicion. In April, again with the support of most Girondins, the Committee of Public Safety was created and in no time it grew to be the Convention's twelve-member executive wing.

By mid-spring, the Girondins at last awoke to the danger inherent in the measures they had endorsed. Among other things, they resisted demands that the Committee of Public Safety be vested with unlimited power, including the authority to arrest and bring to trial suspects who had not been indicted by the Convention. Brissot, in his newspaper, warned that the Montagnards planned to liquidate rival delegates and establish a dictatorship.

It was too late. The Montagnards had been strengthened by the crisis and aided by radicals in Paris, especially the Jacobins, a club in Paris that grew steadily more prestigious, and more extreme, in the face of the many crises of 1792 and 1793. The Jacobins organized protests that vilified Brissot, once the hero of the people, and demanded action against the Girondins. Both Jacobins and Montagnards asked: Had not Brissot and his followers cried the loudest for war? Had not Maximilien Robespierre, a Montagnard leader, warned of the danger that war posed to the spread of republicanism? Had not Robespierre said at the time that to "want to give liberty to others before conquering it ourselves is to assure our own enslavement and that of the whole world?"[11] Had not Brissot and his followers opposed the execution of the king? Had not he and his followers sought greater self-rule for the provinces, some of which had now taken up arms against the Revolution. Had not the traitor Dumouriez been allied with the Girondins? Despite the peril that the Revolution now faced, were not the Brissotins opposing measures that were needed for saving the Republic?

In April, the most radical sections in Paris petitioned the Convention to arrest twenty-two leading Girondins. The public galleries in the assembly erupted with cries of "to the guillotine!" but no action was taken. The pot boiled for a month, until early in June the militant Paris Commune organized a march on the Convention by the National Guard and a surging crowd estimated at eighty thousand. The mob screamed for the arrest of specified Girondins who had allegedly plotted to destroy the Revolution. While crowds outdoors demonstrated against Girondin "crimes"— including the preposterous charge that they had instigated the Vendée uprising—Robespierre called on the people of Paris "to place themselves in insurrection against the corrupt deputies." Montagnards took the floor and demanded the arrest of the twenty-two previously accused Girondin deputies, including Brissot. One said: "Such is the terrible compromise we must make in order to preserve our Revolution.... Only thus will the fatherland be saved and our cowardly enemies struck down and defeated." Deputies who tried to leave were forced at gunpoint back into the hall. After hours of inflamed oratory, the Convention ordered the arrest of those Brissotins on the Montagnard's list of the Revolution's presumed enemies.

French authorities had started into the vortex that the citizenry would come to refer to as "the Terror." The ultimate fate of the Brissotins was not difficult to imagine in this frenzied atmosphere, especially when newspapers committed to repression urged "let blood flow" and "let it be the blood" of those who had betrayed the Revolution. Virtually all aristocrats, clergy, royalist soldiers, foreigners in France, and now the members of what once had been the leading political faction in Revolutionary France were suspected of seeking the destruction of the Revolution.[12]

Paine had arrived late for the Convention session on the fateful June 2 when the Girondins were arrested. Despite the whiff of doom in the air outside the Manège, he tried to push his way into the assembly hall. While trying to gain entrance, Paine encountered Georges Danton, a fellow assemblyman. Once thought of as a flaming radical, Danton had come to be seen as a moderate as the Convention grew more extreme. When Paine appealed to him for assistance in entering the Manège, Danton warned that Paine would be risking his life should he go inside. Paine took his advice and returned home. Paine had taken a backseat in the six months since the battles over the king's fate, partly because of the language barrier, but also because he feared where events were headed. Back on March 13, his friend Pierre Vergniaud, a leading Girondin, had warned the Convention that the growing hysteria might result in the Revolution "devouring its children" and bringing on "despotism with the calamities that accompany it." Not long thereafter, Paine, filled with foreboding, had written to Danton predicting that "internal contentions" would destroy the Republic, an outcome he had understatedly hinted at in his April letter to Jefferson.[13] The events of June 2 confirmed his fears. A foreigner who had usually voted with the Girondins, Paine knew that the time had come for him to stay out of sight.[14]

Confirmation that France and England were at war reached the United States early in April. President Washington was in the ninth day of a vacation at Mount Vernon when he received the news. He left the next morning for Philadelphia. As word of the widening European war spread, a Virginia Federalist wrote to the president that the "considerate part of society," by which he meant the socially elite and most conservative, hoped the United States would not aid France. In fact, most Americans, regardless of their social class, wanted to stay of out of Europe's conflict. Jefferson said at the time, "No country perhaps was ever so thoroughly disposed against war, as ours." When Washington met with his cabinet on April 19 "it was agreed by all" that the nation's neutrality must be proclaimed, a policy the president formally announced three days later. The major players in the Washington administration had experienced the travail of the Revolutionary War, and none was eager for another round of conflict. Each realized how perilous and uncertain wars could be, and each knew that hostilities with either France or England would sow deep and possibly fatal divisions within America. The nation's interest—not merely the well-being of the American economy, but perhaps the very survival of the fragile new republic—required that it avoid what Jefferson called "the calamities of a war."[15]

While Jefferson and Hamilton were of like mind on American neutrality, they skirmished over whether the 1778 Treaties of Alliance and Commerce with France remained in effect. Hamilton, the Anglophile, feared that a rigid adherence to the accord might aid France in its war against Great Britain; Jefferson, the Anglophobe, valued the treaties for exactly this reason. In private, Jefferson characterized the Federalists in the cabinet as desiring what he called a "sneaking neutrality." He believed they hoped to covertly aid Britain to a degree that would "astonish mr Pitt himself." But Jefferson made what Washington thought was the best legal case for the treaties and the president backed him against Hamilton. The country "shall be indebted for it to the President," Jefferson exclaimed. The cabinet also unanimously agreed that the United States should receive the new French minister, Citizen Edmond-Charles-Edouard Genêt, who was known to be crossing the Atlantic that spring. Appointed during the winter, Genêt was the choice of the Girondin-controlled foreign ministry, and it was Brissot who introduced him to Paine and his circle of American friends so that the diplomat could gain insights into the United States and its leaders. (All that is known of their conversations is that when Genêt asked how Americans would respond to the king's execution, Paine responded: "Bad, very bad.") Paine in turn introduced the envoy to Gouverneur Morris, who subsequently advised Washington that Genêt's character and ability were questionable.[16]

Morris's misgivings were well founded, although one of Genêt's handicaps was his mistaken belief that America so fervently embraced the French Revolution that he would be given a free hand. He and his Girondin backers undoubtedly got the idea in part from the initial reaction to the Revolution within the United States. They also reached that conclusion after talking to the Americans in Paris, including Paine, who in turn got much of his information on American attitudes from Jefferson. It was not so much that Jefferson misled Paine. The conservative reaction in America against the horrors of the Revolution gathered steam only late in 1792; given the lag in trans-Atlantic communication, the shifting attitudes in some quarters of America were unknown in France before Genêt sailed.

If Genêt had two strikes against him before he departed France, his instructions assured the failure of his mission. He was directed to use propaganda, secret agents, and American adventurers to make trouble for Spain in Florida and Louisiana, and Great Britain in Canada—initiatives designed to compel France's enemies to divert some resources from the war in Europe. Genêt was also to do everything possible to facilitate the privateering war on British shipping, including demanding that the privateers be outfitted in American ports and permitted to sell their prizes in those havens. For the United States to permit Genêt to do as he wished would be to run the risk of provoking a British declaration of war. Therefore, Genêt was to offer a pot-sweetener. He was to reveal that France would open its ports and those of its colonies to American commerce—the very thing that Franklin and Jefferson had unsuccessfully sought throughout the 1780s. Even so, there was a hitch. In return, the United States must discriminate against any nation (such as Great Britain) that did not extend free trade rights to America.[17]

By the time Genêt landed in Charleston in April, Washington's attitude toward the French Revolution had soured badly. The French in their "paroxysm of disorder" were about to "tare each other to pieces," he said, and the president additionally believed that France's leaders would in time become America's "worst enemies." With uncanny accuracy, he also expected France to face "sad confusion" that would ultimately bring on an "entire change in [its] political system."[18] Having already tilted in his views toward the French Revolution, the president was appalled by the ecstatic greetings lavished on Genêt. Large and enthusiastic crowds welcomed the envoy at every stop during his unhurried monthlong tour of cities and villages from South Carolina to Philadelphia. Both Washington and Genêt now understood that a great many Americans looked with favor on the French Revolution. For Genêt, it confirmed all that he had heard before sailing regarding the American public's pulsating infatuation with the French Revolution. For Washington, it was recognition that maintaining American neutrality might pose a growing challenge.

On May 16, Genêt reached Philadelphia, which also greeted him with open arms. Thirty days of rousing welcomes prompted Genêt to remark, "I live in the midst of perpetual festivals." But when he was received by Washington, Genêt was not hailed as a friend. The president's demeanor was one of icy formality, even disdain. Stories soon circulated that Washington greeted Citizen Genêt while standing beside a bust of Louis XVI. Jefferson's successor as secretary of state said that such tales were "notoriously untrue." Jefferson did not say.[19]

While Washington girded for trouble and Hamilton was, in Jefferson's words, "panick struck" by the fervor displayed toward this French revolutionary, the secretary of state saw hope. Negotiations with a minister sent by the revolutionary government in Paris seemingly held great promise. There was a very real possibility, Jefferson believed, that the two republics could agree to a commercial accord that would be beneficial to the Americans. It might also have the ancillary benefit of inducing London both to rethink its harsh trade policies and to reevaluate remaining at war with France. Jefferson knew that the war had already caused English bankruptcies to climb, stock prices to fall, and unemployment to rise. In his most rapturous moments, Jefferson even imagined that England's financial woes might set in motion the death rattle of the British monarchy.

Jefferson's exuberance only increased when he learned that thousands of Philadelphians had crowded the city docks and burst "into peals of exultation" when a French frigate arrived with a captured British prize in tow. That spectacle, as well as the effusive greetings that Genêt had received, convinced Jefferson that "the old spirit of 1776 is rekindling." More than ever, he was persuaded that the populace still wished for the birthday of the new world that Paine had promised. Jefferson also interpreted what he saw in partisan terms. All signs, he believed, pointed toward a growing sentiment that was detrimental to nearly all that the Federalist Party stood for. Even "the Monocrat papers are obliged to publish the most furious Philippics against England," he chortled. James Monroe, who had returned home following Congress's adjournment in March, reported to Jefferson that Virginians were steadfast in their support of the French Revolution. Monroe mentioned, too, that Genêt had made "a most favorable impression" during his passage through Virginia.[20]

Monroe applauded the neutrality proclamation, as in his estimation it did more to ensure the "success of the French Revolution" than would have resulted from openly aiding the French as an ally. He naively reasoned that Britain would permit the neutral United States to trade with France, providing great "support" for France's cause. Monroe did not think it imprudent for Genêt to assist American privateers or to do what he could to stir up enough trouble on the frontier to make Britain and Spain "desperate & raving mad." Monroe insisted that he hoped war could be avoided, though he also said: "There is no sacrifice I would not be willing to make for the sake of France &

her cause." He cautioned Jefferson to be aware that the goal of the Federalists was "to separate us from France & ultimately unite us with England."[21]

As secretary of state, Jefferson could not concur with Monroe in his openly pro-French stance, but from the outset his warm manner toward Genêt contrasted with the frostiness he had steadfastly shown the British minister. He and Genêt met frequently in cordial sessions. Initially, Jefferson acted as something of a mentor, seeking to convince Genêt that if he went too far, too fast, he would stir up a backlash and earn the president's enmity. Jefferson made it clear that the United States would not allow French agents to arm and outfit privateers in American ports, nor would it permit Genêt to raise and arm American mercenaries to strike against Spanish and British provinces along the frontier. But Genêt stuck to his orders, refusing to desist. The final straw came when Hamilton leaked to the press that Genêt had privately threatened to go over Washington's head and solicit public support for his initiatives. An exasperated Jefferson had already quietly condemned Genêt, calling him "Hotheaded . . . disrespectful and even indecent." Jefferson added that he was left with no choice but "quitting a wreck which could not but sink all who should cling to" him. In August, Jefferson agreed with Washington and Hamilton that the administration must demand Genêt's recall.[22]

Jefferson saw the sorry episode as a missed opportunity, perhaps the best that would ever exist, to secure better and closer economic ties with France. Nevertheless, he argued in cabinet meetings for Washington to direct Gouverneur Morris "not to lose the chance of obtaining so advantageous a treaty." Washington consented, perhaps buying into Jefferson's rosy prediction that the "present struggles in France would end in a free government of some sort" that would abide by the treaties agreed to by its revolutionary predecessors.[23] Genêt's mission had stirred passions, but it was two other factors that brought domestic partisan politics to an unprecedented fever pitch: the chaos and atrocities unfolding in France, and Britain's entrance into the widening European war.

The early salvos of partisan warfare that would consume the remainder of the decade appeared in the Republican press in the wake of the administration's announcement that it would not take sides in the European war. Republican essayists laid down a barrage against the Federalists and, for the first time, Washington as well. They questioned the constitutionality of a presidential proclamation of neutrality; censured Washington for his "cold indifference" toward a Revolutionary War ally that now faced a life-or-death struggle against monarchical tyrants; and intimated that Washington was being manipulated by some members of his cabinet who were indistinguishable from the

Tories of 1776. The thin-skinned chief executive recoiled in anger at the criticism directed toward him. Soon after the publication of a tasteless piece on the guillotining of "King Washington," the president's volcanic temper erupted at a cabinet meeting. According to Jefferson, Washington "got into one of those passions when he cannot command himself." Railing about the "personal abuse which had been bestowed on him," the president declared that "*by god* he had rather be in his grave than in his present situation. That he had rather be on his farm than to be made *emperor of the world.*" His life was being made miserable, he added, by "that *rascal Freneau*" and other Republican polemicists.[24]

The Federalists wasted no time in firing back at the Republicans. Hamilton led the pack. He might not have panicked at the news of Genêt's ebullient reception, as Jefferson had alleged, but for the first time he openly proclaimed his "*abhorrence*" of the French Revolution. During the summer of 1793, Hamilton dashed off sixteen newspaper essays in eight weeks. In some he assailed Genêt, in others he defended American neutrality, but along the way he drifted into other territory. He charged that the foes of neutrality were inspired by one objective: to bring the United States into war on the side of France. That would be madness, he wrote. France "has but *one enemy* and that is ALL EUROPE." The United States is "a young nation . . . without armies, without fleets." It would be folly to enter the war. Yes, France aided the United States during the Revolutionary War, but "the interest of France had been the governing motive of the aid afforded us." Now peace was in the best interest of the United States. Many of the Treasury secretary's arguments were well founded, but Hamilton being Hamilton, he could not refrain from wild swings at the opposition. He alleged that Washington's critics were subversives not unlike the most radical Jacobins in France, and that the end game of their "insidious and ruinous machinations" was the "overturning" of the "Government of the Union." His dubious claim made Hamilton the first in a long line of right-wing politicos to impugn the loyalty of those who questioned American foreign policy.[25]

When the Federalists arranged several public meetings across the nation for the purpose of adopting resolutions that supported a strict neutrality, Jefferson pressed a reluctant Madison to respond to Hamilton's avalanche of essays. Though unwilling, Madison wrote five pieces under the pen name "Helvidius." With greater enthusiasm, he and Monroe collaborated on drafting a series of resolutions to counter those adopted by Federalist-orchestrated meetings. The counterbalancing resolutions penned by Madison and Monroe acknowledged "with gratitude" France's "generous aids" during the American Revolution, portrayed the Federalists as striving to undermine support for a French Revolution that sought "to open the eyes of all mankind to their natural and political Rights," and charged that the ultimate objective of a Federalist Party "disaffected to the American Revolution" was "toward assimilating our Government to the form & spirit of the British Monarchy." Four public meetings in western Virginia, including one in Charlottesville, adopted the resolutions drafted by Madison and Monroe.[26]

Jefferson had not asked Monroe to answer Hamilton's polemics. But calling himself "Agricola," Monroe did so anyway in five essays that he turned out between September and December. Much that Monroe wrote rehashed his earlier resolutions, though he also hammered away at the notion that the American Revolution had inspired the French Revolution and that at bottom the two shared the same "great principles." Each "exclude[d] the idea of hereditary distinctions, and rest[ed] on the same basis of equality." He warned, too, that Great Britain's entrance into the European war would provoke the Federalists to move mountains to bring the United States into London's orbit and deal a death blow to the French Revolution.[27]

Given his political savvy and genuine commitment to neutrality, Jefferson soon realized that the Republican Party was risking a public backlash in openly defending France. It was clear to him that his countrymen over-whelmingly wanted peace and trusted Washington's judgment. In addition, he may also have been influenced by Paine's disconsolate April letter announcing his dwindling faith in the French Revolution. If Paine, the great enthusiast of revolution, was so dismayed by the turn of events, Jefferson could only wonder whether the French Revolution had a future. Jefferson was not ready to abandon hope for France, but he saw the need to recalibrate the Republican message. The safer line would be to emphasize that the Federal-ists pulsated with fervor for the monarchy everywhere, including its restora-tion in France.

Jefferson had in fact been moving in this direction for some time. Writing to Brissot back in May—a note penned a month prior to the Girondin leader's arrest—Jefferson acknowledged the presence of American royalists who, "as they float on the surface," can be seen in their true light as "zealous apostles of English demi-despotism." To Monroe, Jefferson now declared that Hamilton and his adherents were a malevolent combination of "old tories, joined by our merchants who trade on British capital, paper dealers, [and] the idle rich of the great commercial towns." Stating the party line in this manner was an oblique way of defending the French Revolution without sounding too pro-French or too hawkish.[28]

Jefferson may have grown more disheartened than he cared to acknowl-edge. He badly wanted to leave the State Department and go home, though his longing for Monticello stemmed from more than disillusionment. Not only had eleven years had passed since he had spent a full year at home, but his initiatives to extricate himself from debt were not working. He now believed that his full-time attention to his property was essential. Early in 1792, Jefferson informed Washington of his plans to retire within a year, but when the time neared and he told the president that he would be leaving office in six weeks, Washington pleaded with him to stay on. Reluctantly, Jefferson consented to stay on until late summer 1793. As summer's end approached, Jefferson wrote to Washington that September 30 would be a "convenient" moment for him to retire. Washington responded in an extraordinary fashion. He called on the secretary of state at his residence, possibly the only time during his presidency that Washington visited the home of one of his cabinet officers, and yet again asked Jefferson to stay on longer. This time, Washington pleaded with Jefferson to remain at his post through the end of the year, by which time the "affairs of Europe would be settled." Jefferson pondered the request for five days before consenting.[29]

One major item remained on Jefferson's agenda before leaving Philadelphia. Britain's trade policies toward the United States stuck in his craw. He had opposed Parliament's restrictions on colonial America's trade before 1776 and Britain's self-serving commercial policies since the end of the war caused him to seethe with indignation. He longed for Congress to adopt bold measures aimed at gaining commercial reciprocity with London. In December, in his final substantive act as secretary of state, Jefferson handed Congress a lengthy report on American commerce, an accounting that Congress had requested nearly three years before. His report was laden with statistical data calculated to show the dangerous degree to which Britain dominated American commerce. Greater trade with others, he contended, was crucial for the American economy and American defense. It would lead not just to America's economic independence, but to its actual independence from Great Britain. He chose this moment to divulge that France was ready to negotiate a commercial treaty "on liberal principles," and he urged economic retaliation against any nation that discriminated against American commerce. With very nearly his last words as a cabinet official, Jefferson appealed to Congress to impose punishing taxes on English imports or to forbid altogether the importation of British commodities until London agreed to commercial reciprocity.[30] A few days later, on January 5, 1794, Jefferson set off for Monticello and what he said would be his permanent retirement.

Paine had likely moved to Saint-Denis in April 1793, six weeks or so before Brissot and twenty-one other Girondins were arrested. Previously, Paine had not been reclusive, but with high-placed friends in custody he stayed closer than ever to his residence.[31] He was badly frightened, and he had good reason to be.

Crisis after crisis racked the French Revolution that summer, creating an atmosphere not unlike that which had prevailed at the time of the September Massacres a year earlier. The economy, not in good shape to begin with, was pinched by the British blockade and the prowess of the Royal Navy on the high seas. France's up-and-down fortunes in the war deteriorated, as the Germans and Austrians continued their painstaking advance toward Paris. In addition, the insurgents in the Vendée seemed unstoppable. In fact, uprisings had occurred in sixty departments, though none approached the intensity of that in western France.[32]

In this hour of crisis, Bertrand Barère, the Girondin deputy who in the spring had whipped the Convention into a frenzy by urging death for those who betrayed the Revolution, sought out Paine. Barère, for the most part a somewhat moderate deputy who had served with Paine on the abortive committee to draft a constitution and had been the presiding officer in the trial of the king, had by September become a member of the Committee of Public Safety. It was in that role that he approached Paine and asked his counsel concerning the wisdom of appealing to the United States for help. Barère mooted the idea of sending commissioners to Philadelphia to appeal for American aid, including upwards of one hundred shiploads of flour. Paine endorsed the idea, adding that the timing was perfect in as much as Secretary of State Jefferson was "an ardent defender of the interests of France." Paine further advised that the foreign ministry would be wise to bypass Gouverneur Morris, who was "badly disposed towards you" and "not popular in America." Barère also proposed Paine's inclusion on the commission, or at least his affiliation with it, given that he knew key figures in the American government and could use his pen to arouse support for assisting France. Paine was wary. He declined to serve on the commission, though he initially agreed to accompany the French commissioners and provide whatever help he could. He was driven both by the hope of saving the French Revolution and himself, for the undertaking would provide a relatively safe means of escaping France. Paine suggested that the commissioners cross the Atlantic in a convoy consisting of French warships and some forty-five American vessels currently anchored in Bordeaux, merchant ships that could return with the much-needed flour. Little imagination is required to see that Paine hoped to be aboard one of those vessels.

Ultimately, Paine concluded that it was too dangerous to cross the war-torn Atlantic, even in a convoy. But he helped Barère and later, in his memoirs, the Frenchman said that Paine had "worked long hours . . . to bring about this massive purchase of provisions" without which "our armies and the departments would have been menaced with a terrible famine." Exactly what Paine did is unknown, though he likely served as a go-between in Barère's discussions with American ship captains and merchants in French ports.[33]

Curiously, Paine never informed Jefferson of Barère's proposal, though in two letters he pleaded with the secretary of state to send an American commission to join with Europe's neutral countries in mediating the European war, which he portrayed as hopelessly stalemated. Paine included a long memorandum on the European situation, leaving it to Jefferson to determine whether it would be useful for it to be published. Paine argued that Britain's objectives in entering the European war had been to restore a chastened Bourbon monarchy with limited naval capacities or to partition France so that it could never again threaten England. If successful, Great Britain's prowess on the continent would increase and it would become an even greater maritime power. The piece tacitly implied that the interest of the United States would best be served if Britain was denied victory and a republican government of some sort survived in a unified France. In the end, France never sent commissioners to America, Jefferson had retired by the time Paine's letters reached Philadelphia, and the essay on Europe's affairs was never published.[34]

During the three months that followed his collaboration with Barère, Paine seldom left Saint-Denis, though he tried to convince himself that he was safe. In light of his caustic writings about his homeland in *Common Sense* and *Rights of Man,* Paine reckoned that his English background would be overlooked. Given that he had never been required to take an oath of allegiance to France, he also felt that he would be seen by all as an American who was nothing more than an honorary French citizen.[35] That nearly everyone in France regarded him as an American citizen seemed apparent to him. After all, why else would an important official such as Barère have turned to him for assistance with the United States? Reason was Paine's lodestar, and each of his deductions seemed rational. Paine thought he was out of danger, but he could never be sure, and throughout the autumn of 1793 he lived with fear every day.

His apprehension grew throughout the summer and into the fall as more unnerving news reached his ears. Paris was swept with rumors of homicidal conspiracies and plots to liberate Marie Antoinette. A steady diet of bad news from the front lines only increased his anxieties. Although March's *levée en masse* had brought the number of soldiers in France's army to several times the size of its pre-Revolutionary army, frontier fortresses were lost, French forces on the Rhine were in retreat, an English army was advancing on Dunkirk from the Netherlands, and a Spanish army was on French soil and menacing Perpignan on the Mediterranean.[36] The setbacks led many in Paris to believe that France's top generals were traitors. Playing on France's growing troubles, the Montagnards repeatedly accused the Girondins of royalism and insisted that they had aided and abetted the provincial rebellions.

Increasing calls were heard for vengeance against those who supposedly imperiled the Revolution. Some openly argued that the Revolution could be saved only through the harshest repression. There were those, too, who wished to take the Revolution in new directions, proposing to institute direct democracy, de-Christianization, celebrations honoring a God of nature, a new calendar, and the creation of a utopia of virtue. On July 10, the Convention expelled those members of the Committee of Public Safety who had argued for reconciliation with the Girondins. Danton was among those who were gone. Included among those elected in their stead was Maximilien Robespierre, the Jacobin, who did not shrink from pitiless means to stabilize the Revolution. His hard-line views won adherents in the face of growing troubles.

Unease mounted in late summer in the face of food shortages—the crisis that had roused Barère to consult with Paine—and word that Toulon had surrendered to the British navy. Not long passed before news arrived that Toulon had proclaimed its support for putting the son of Louis XVI on the throne as France's new monarch. In response to Toulon's sudden royalist proclivities, Barère demanded of the Convention: "Let us make terror the order of the day" in the fight against all counterrevolutionaries. The Convention rapidly created a national conscript army, and it additionally enacted the Law of Suspects, legislation that vested the Committee of Public Safety with blanket powers to arrest and punish those it branded as enemies of the Revolution. At the same moment, the Convention enlarged the Revolutionary Tribunal so that it could do its work more expeditiously.

The hammer came down early in October, shortly after Paine helped Barère. The first sitting deputy in any Revolutionary assembly was executed, convicted of disloyalty for having attempted to flee the country. Soon, more Girondins were arrested, including two who were still serving as deputies. During the last week of the month, Brissot and his fellow Girondin deputies who had been arrested in June were put on trial and charged with having conspired to foment rebellion in the provinces. All were sentenced to death, the verdict read late at night in a torchlit room. On their last night, the condemned partook of a solemn final supper in the prison chapel. The next day, a rainy October 30, they were transported to the guillotine in three tumbrels, all singing "La Marseillaise" throughout their journey. One by one in a harrowing span of forty minutes, the victims were executed, until only one prisoner was left to valiantly sing the anthem in his final moments on earth. And then he, too, was beheaded. The Girondins had ascended the stairs to the same scaffold that they had sought to spare Louis XVI from having to climb nine months earlier, and the very steps that Marie Antoinette—her "eyes ... bent on vacancy," her "cheeks ... streaked with red" and "overspread with deadly paleness"—had mounted two weeks before. Some had grieved when the former king was executed, but virtually no one, save perhaps for Edmund Burke, mourned the fate of the widow Capet. Popular sentiment may have been expressed by the journalist who thought good riddance to the "fucking tart."

The lion's share of the Terror during the autumn was visited on those in the provinces who were openly part of the insurgency. Republican troops fanned out through the hinterland, first securing the Atlantic ports, then moving with brutal force against rebels throughout the countryside. Order was quickly restored in some areas, but only after prolonged sieges in Toulon and Lyon. The fighting was often bloody and the justice meted out to real or suspected rebels was ferocious. Some were guillotined. Others faced firing squads. Hideously, some were bound and loaded in groups aboard boats that were sunk. That the tribunals' bloodthirstiness knew no bounds was apparent when large numbers were harnessed together in open fields and slaughtered by artillery fire. Nearly 2,000 were executed in Lyon alone, and altogether as many as 250,000 supposed counterrevolutionaries may have perished throughout France in battles and executions. Many who died had once fervidly supported the Revolution, but in this new, ghastly phase, revolutionaries had begun to devour one another. Condorcet was one who was cut down. A friend of Paine's and Jefferson's, Condorcet, together with the duc de la Roche-foucauld (who had been killed by a revolutionary mob a year earlier), had been Jefferson's final dinner guests before he departed Paris. Condorcet's fate was the same as five others among the eight who with Paine had served on the committee that drafted the so-called Girondin constitution eighteen months earlier. Death in the Terror was the destiny of some 65 percent of those who had composed the Girondin leadership back in the spring. Fear begat the killing, and the killing touched off panic among the killers, who intensified the Terror lest they too become its victims.[37]

As jails filled up that autumn, Paine knew many who had fallen into the clutches of the police. William Choppin and William Johnson, the two English boarders at Saint-Denis who had become Paine's close companions, had come within a whisker of being arrested. Agents arrived at the front door of the château late into a November night bitter with a whisper of the winter that was to come. A warrant had been issued for the arrest of the two Englishmen, suspects because they were English. But they were gone. Alerted a few days earlier that they were in the authorities' crosshairs, Paine had pulled strings at the Foreign Ministry to secure passports for his friends, and they had gotten away. Once Brissot and other old friends from better days had been carted to the scaffold, Paine was haunted by the fear that he might be next. "I saw my life in continual danger," he said later. "My friends were falling as fast as the guillotine could cut their heads off, and I every day expected the same fate." His nerves frayed, Paine may have tipped the bottle with more than customary gusto. Gouverneur Morris claimed that Paine was "besotted from morning till night," but it was an allegation based on hearsay. He had not seen Paine in weeks.[38]

Paine had played with fire in undertaking a visible role in the French Revolution. He was not alone in having run the risk. All who had chosen activism were imperiled in 1793. They could never be certain that their ideas and their faction would prevail tomorrow. They never knew whether today's friend would be tomorrow's comrade or foe. In the vertiginous world of the French Revolution, there was always the possibility that demagogic leaders who played on people's fears would turn the existing world upside down. The French Revolution, in the long-ago words of historian R. R. Palmer, had become "a thing in itself, an uncontrollable force that might eventually spend itself but which no one could direct or guide."[39] All who had ridden in this whirlwind faced uncertainty, but few were more vulnerable than Paine. An outsider who was not adequately acquainted with French history, culture, politics, or the language, Paine faced severe impediments in fully under-standing the people and events of the Revolution, and it put him at grave risk.

No one can know how he would respond if faced with a plight akin to Paine's. Thinking he was on his "death-bed, for death was on every side of me," and that he "had no time to lose," Paine chose to write another book. As he seldom left Saint-Denis during the seven months after early June, Paine had time on his hands. He also may have hoped that if the book made him an even greater celebrity, the authorities would not dare touch him. What is known is that the book Paine had in mind—ruminations on religion, faith, and the church—was something he had long intended to write. He had contemplated tackling the subject as early as 1776, though at that time he had said he preferred to wait until the "latter part of life." Given his quandary in the fall of 1793, and that he now was fifty-six years old, Paine must have thought that if the book was to be written, it was now or never. At first blush, the topic that Paine chose was an unlikely one. Over the years, Paine had taken on myriad subjects, but he had never troubled with religion. The only explanation he offered for selecting his subject matter was that he was drawn to it because "France was running headlong into atheism."[40] But France was not veering toward atheism. Robespierre and his fellow Jacobins had indeed undertaken a campaign of de-Christianization, but like Paine they were Deists, not atheists. Deists believed that God was the creator of the universe and life, but thereafter the inventor never again intruded, leaving it to humankind to do good or evil, to improve or worsen what had been provided.[41]

If Paine's stated reason for turning to the subject of religion was unconvincing, there were valid rationales behind his choice. The hold that the church and clergy exerted had been a crucial factor in leading many to oppose the Revolution. Furthermore, the church throughout Europe not only had a long history of indifference to the woeful circumstances of the masses, but it also had steadfastly bolstered royalist absolutism, defending its tyranny and justifying its rapacious wars. Paine had grown despondent about the French Revolution, but as never before he had come to understand that if someday there was to be a successful revolution, it was imperative that this solid pillar of royalty and aristocracy be weakened. In *Common Sense*, Paine had taught his American readers that their problems grew not just from their colonial status, but from the implacably hurtful governance system in the mother country. In *The Age of Reason*, as he would title his book on religion, Paine hoped to make his readers see that the church and clergy had utilized superstition and ritual to keep those on the bottom rung torpid in the face of exploitation, not to mention condoning of wars and persecutions.

Paine told his readers that he believed in God and an afterlife. A good and just life on earth, he added, consisted in behavior exemplified by "doing justice, [displaying] loving mercy, and endeavoring to make our fellow creatures happy." He did not believe in the "creed professed" by any religion, whether Christian, Jewish, or Islamic; each propounded doctrines that were "no other than human inventions, set up to terrify and enslave mankind." "My own mind is my own church," he insisted. Jesus, he went on, "was a virtuous and an amiable man" who had lived a moral life and preached love and benevolence toward others. But much about him that had been passed down to succeeding generations was purely mythological, including the "strange fable" of his divinity. The Old Testament was a dreary collection of "obscene stories" of "voluptuous debaucheries," "cruel and torturous executions," and "unrelenting vindictiveness" more likely inspired by a "demon" than by God. The New Testament's Gospel stories were a jumble of contradictions, though that mattered little as the Christian church "set up a system of religion very contradictory to the character of the person whose name it bears." The church's "fabrications" underscored its "contempt for human reason." The "Christian system of faith" was "a species of Atheism" in that it "professes to believe in a man rather than in God." The world could not be understood through the "fraud" and "fables" put forth in the Bible. It could be comprehended only through science. At the outset of *The Age of Reason*, and again in its conclusion, Paine ruminated on a future life. He said that he was content in the belief that "the Power that gave me existence is able to continue it, in any form and manner He pleases, with or without this body; and it appears more probable to me that I shall continue to exist hereafter, than that I should have had existence, as I now have."[42]

What Paine wrote was hardly original, and it led some to accuse him of plagiarism, though that charge was without foundation. Paine had drawn on ideas that he had read and heard in countless lectures and spirited conversations. He had also thought things through on his own. The Enlightenment was about scrutinizing conventional thought, and nothing had come under greater examination than religious beliefs. Science, not faith, was the new guiding light. It was the personification of reason, and rationalism lay at the heart of the Enlightenment. The pursuit of science led intellectuals to rethink nearly everything in a grand search for the betterment of life on earth. Joseph Priestley, the scientist and liberal philosopher who had influenced young Paine's thinking, had foreseen how science would "overturn . . . error and superstition," prove fatal to "prejudice," and bring to an end "all undue and usurped authority." Priestly and Paine's friend Condorcet were certain that science would make people's lives "more easy and comfortable," even "glorious and paradisiacal."[43] For a hundred years before Paine, faith-based ways of thinking had shuddered before the onslaught of Enlightenment thinkers. They and their disciples had hoped for the termination of militant religious dogmatism and the torments that had gone hand in hand with it. As a young man who frequented London's intellectually invigorating clubs, Paine had been introduced to rationalism and its assault on religion's mythology. As was true of so many like-minded others, Paine's discoveries led him down the well-traveled road of those who—in the words of historian Peter Gay—"hated priests and priestcraft, mystery-mongering, and assaults on common sense."[44] For many, Deism lay at the end of that road. It was where Paine landed in his thinking, as did nearly every American Founder, including Jefferson, Washington, Madison, Franklin, Hamilton, and, though problematical, probably Monroe.[45]

Throughout the autumn, anxiety was Paine's daily companion, though he was spared the dreaded arrival of the police on his doorstep. Sometime on Christmas Day, however, Paine learned that hours earlier the Convention, at Robespierre's behest, had expelled all foreign-born members. "There were but two in it, Anacharsis Cloots and myself," Paine later wrote, and he may have been aware that Robespierre had recently denounced Cloots (who was still attending the Convention) as "a traitor" who spent his time "with our enemies." Certain that his expulsion from the legislature was preparatory to his arrest, Paine suspected that he had "but a few days of liberty left." His doom seemed all the more assured when he learned that he had been singled out for a venomous attack on the Convention floor by François Bourdon, a Montagnard. After reminding his listeners of Paine's English background, Bourdon preposterously claimed that he had "intrigued with a former agent of the bureau of Foreign Affairs" to betray the Revolution by aiding Great Britain. A day or two later, and unbeknownst to Paine at the time, it was Barère, who only recently had sought Paine's aid in obtaining American grain, who made the speech that sealed his fate. Barère portrayed Paine as of dubious loyalty to the Revolution, indicting him for having wished to spare the king's life. Robespierre once remarked that Bourdon enjoyed "killing with his own hand. He combines perfidy with fury," and that may have been the best accounting for the deputy's wildly implausible accusation. Years later Barère provided the reason for his betrayal of Paine, saying "he felt himself in danger and was obliged to do it." Whatever Paine thought at the time, he later came to believe that Gouverneur Morris and unnamed "Terrorists in America" had conspired with the French government to bring about "my destruction." It was, he reasoned, a confederacy born of a desire to silence an influential penman. He believed that one party to the presumed conspiracy wished to prevent him from thwarting the Tory counter-revolution in America while the other wanted to keep him from impeding the course of the French Revolution.[46]

Paine's immediate response to the danger that was upon him was to prevail on Joel Barlow, his close American friend, to take about half his handwritten manuscript to John Hurford Stone, an English coal merchant who had established an English-language press in Paris. Barlow also agreed to pick up batches of the proof sheets as they were ready and deliver them to Paine for proofreading. While Stone set the print for the portion of *The Age of Reason* that he had been given, Paine wrapped up his tract in a marathon of urgent and purposeful writing.

Finished at last, Paine arranged to meet with several American acquaintances at the Hôtel de Philadelphie on the evening of December 27. He had long been in the habit of enjoying a night of celebration once a manuscript was completed. Dining, drinking, and conversing with friends was a joy following his self-imposed isolation. This night must have been special for

Paine. He celebrated having finished another book as well as the freedom that he still enjoyed.

The merrymaking ended at midnight. Paine said goodbye to his friends and went to the room he had reserved in the hotel. He got less than three hours' sleep. Deep in the night he was awakened by a loud pounding on his door. He unlatched it to find five policemen, two agents of the Committee of General Surety, and the hotel manager, who translated what the authorities said. Paine was told that he was to be arrested and his papers were to be examined, with anything that appeared "suspicious" to be "put under seal" and brought before the authorities. Though groggy from a night of little sleep, Paine thought fast. He asked that Achille Audibert, who had accompanied him on the voyage from England to Calais fifteen months earlier and was also a guest in the hotel, be brought to his room for a brief consultation. The police agreed, unaware that what Paine sought was for Audibert to hurry to Saint-Denis and remove anything that appeared to be incriminating. Playing for time to ensure Audibert's success, Paine next told the officers that Barlow had all his remaining papers. After a thorough search of Paine's room at the hotel, the police, with Paine in tow, set off for Barlow's residence in the Hôtel Grande Bretagne. If the police suspected duplicity on Paine's part, it did not stir them to act any faster. Pausing for a leisurely breakfast, the party finally reached Barlow's apartment at eleven A.M., eight hours after they had entered Paine's hotel room.

Barlow acknowledged that he had one proof sheet and thirty-one handwritten pages of *The Age of Reason* manuscript, but nothing more of Paine's. Thinking it was not "right to rely on what he said," the constables searched Barlow's quarters. Nothing else that belonged to Paine was found. At this point, apparently for the first time, the authorities suspected "a subterfuge on the part of Citizen Thomas Paine" and asked where was "his usual place of abode." At last, they heard the words "Saint-Denis." Paine, accompanied by Barlow, was taken to his residence. It was now early afternoon. Audibert had been given ample time to remove anything that might have seemed compromising. Paine showed the police the final forty-four pages of the manuscript. If they had questioned Barlow's veracity, the police certainly did not trust Paine. They combed every inch of his lodging and "gathered in the Sitting-room all the papers found in the other rooms." These they subjected to the "most scrupulous examination." In their official report, the police acknowledged that "none of [the papers] has been found suspicious" and it was decided that "no seal should be placed" on anything found at Saint-Denis. Paine was permitted to hand over his entire manuscript to Barlow for transmittal to the printer. Paine later claimed that one of the policemen commented that *The Age of Reason* "is an interesting work; it will do much good."

At four P.M., thirteen hours after their arrival at Paine's hotel room, the police began the cheerless drive back to the center of Paris, slowly clattering past barely lit houses and trees that stood stark and bare on this early-winter afternoon. Along the way, the police stopped and arrested Cloots, whose principal crime appeared to be that he was a German nobleman known to have been friendly with supposed enemies of the Revolution.[47]

Night had long since fallen by the time Paine and Cloots were led into the Luxembourg prison. About a mile away stood the guillotine that had disposed of Louis XVI, Brissot, and so many others.

CHAPTER 10

"A CONTINUED SCENE OF HORROR"

PAINE, MONROE, AND THE LUXEMBOURG

THE LUXEMBOURG, ONCE A GRAND royal palace, had been transformed by the Revolutionary authorities into a prison capable of housing upwards of one thousand inmates. Its architecture aside, nothing of its former splendor remained, though lovingly tended gardens and magnificent trees still dotted the grounds. The spacious ballrooms, halls, and bedchambers had been carved into small cells shared by up to four detainees. Some official with an organizational bent had thought to name the cells, mostly designating them after a figure from antiquity—Cincinnatus, Brutus, Socrates—but some were given incongruous tags, such as "Liberty." Until the jailers were overwhelmed by the daily influx of new prisoners, an attempt was even made to house those who were incarcerated in a room that bore a name matching the supposed offense. For instance, one accused of "federalism" (advocating greater autonomy for provincial departments) was sent to an "Indivisibility" cell.

Paine was finally processed and taken to his cell at nine P.M. on December 28, eighteen long, stressful hours after the authorities had pounded on his door. His new home was an eight-by-ten-foot chamber that he shared with three others. It was furnished with a straw sleeping pallet for each man, one chair, and one wooden storage box. Located on the ground floor, his cell's brick floor and walls remained damp and moldy much of the time, especially during Paris's wet winter and spring. The room's only window had been boarded up, so only a thin strip of winsome daylight ever shined through. By the time of Paine's detention, the prison officials had evidently run out of erudite names for each cell. His simply had a chalked number on its door.

The prisoners were assigned morning tasks, including sweeping, cleaning, and looking after the fireplaces. When their duties were completed, the inmates had considerable freedom to move about the section of the Luxembourg in which they were housed. Paine spent substantial time drinking tea with Anacharsis Cloots. The two rehashed the Revolution and discussed politics, but as Cloots was an atheist, a substantial portion of each visit was given over to wrangling about religion. In the early phase of his incarceration, Paine devoted some time to writing. In what he called an "Autobiographical Interlude," Paine composed an account of his arrest and the preservation of his manuscript, a short piece that he hoped would eventually be included in a future edition of *The Age of Reason*. He also composed essays on Robespierre and aristocracy, though neither has survived. During this more casual phase of his imprisonment, Paine was permitted visitors, and was even allowed to meet some of them in the outdoor gardens. Inmates formed singing groups and were permitted to rehearse and perform until early evening, when each prisoner was to return to his cell. Prisoners with money, and that included Paine, could buy candles, newspapers, and even meals from nearby taverns.

Paine's first warden in the Luxembourg was an avuncular elderly man who was assisted by members of his family. He treated the prisoners with what Paine described as "civility" and "respect." Another inmate lauded his "compassion and gentleness" and his refusal to "be intimidated into cruelty" by the "implacable monsters" above him. Late that winter, in the delirium of the Terror, the warden was arrested and hauled before the Tribunal. Though acquitted, he was relieved of his duties. His successor was cut from different cloth. A hard taskmaster, he restricted or discontinued the liberties the prisoners had enjoyed, and he read all letters to the inmates before they were delivered. The scuttlebutt was that the new warden had been "an executioner" during the suppression of the insurgency in Lyon, and at least one internee thought he "looked as if he were prepared for a massacre." Conditions steadily deteriorated. Inmates, including even prisoners of war housed in the Luxembourg, were allotted only one meal per day, a repast prepared by the prison's cook that seemed to vary from "too scanty" to inedible. The warden eventually terminated all communication between the inmates and the outside world, leading Paine to later remark that from March onward he did not receive "a single line or word" from anyone.

Following the clampdown, the police made routine inspections to determine whether the prison continued to be "well regulated." They also asked "if the prisoners had any subject of complaint." Few dared to speak their mind. The appearances by François Hanriot, the son of a peasant who had risen to be the head of the Paris National Guard, were fearful events. One inmate later recalled that he brandished his sword and bellowed "oaths and imprecations" as he walked the halls and entered cells, a look of "ferocity" in his eyes. He delighted in telling the English captives, who in the eyes of the authorities included Paine, that specially designed guillotines were being constructed for use on them.[1]

Paine entered the Luxembourg confident that his confinement would be brief. He had American friends in Paris who were prepared to do all in their power on his behalf, just as they had already done in successfully liberating two Americans taken into custody earlier in the fall. Paine also hoped that Gouverneur Morris would leave no stone unturned to secure his release, for a minister's duties included assisting Americans who were in France. Three weeks after his arrest, eighteen members of the American community in Paris, including Joel Barlow, were permitted to approach the Convention about setting Paine free. They reminded the delegates that England looked on Paine as an enemy and "your American allies . . . your brothers" regarded him as a citizen of the United States. They pointed out, too, that the police who searched Paine's residence had found nothing incriminating. His American friends characterized Paine as "the apostle of liberty in America," a "citizen renowned for his virtue," and an advocate of principles that "earned him the hatred of kings." If released, they added, Paine would leave France and return to America. With many deputies hissing as the Americans read their statement, the petitioners must have known that theirs was a lost cause. The Convention wasted no time in spurning their appeal.[2]

Immediately after his friends' petition was rejected, Paine wrote to Gouverneur Morris to request that he remind the French foreign ministry of his American citizenship. Morris did so, but was told that France regarded Paine as a French citizen, because of both his acceptance of France's offer of citizenship and his service in the Convention.[3] Paine quickly responded to Morris, his desperation evident in every word he wrote: "You must not leave me in [this] situation. . . . You know I do not deserve it. . . . They have nothing against me—except that they do not choose I should be in a state of freedom to write my mind freely upon things I have seen. . . . A reply to the Minister's letter is absolutely necessary. . . . Otherwise your silence will be a sort of consent to his observations." Paine acknowledged that he and Morris were "not on terms of the best harmony," but he appealed to the American minister's sense of decency and morality, as well as to the fulfillment of his obligations as America's official representative in France.[4]

Paine may as well have pleaded to his prison guards for help in gaining his freedom. Morris never again approached the foreign ministry about Paine, though he left the erroneous impression with his own government in Philadelphia that "as Mr. Paine's friend" he had moved mountains in a futile effort to secure his release. Shortly after Paine's incarceration, Morris informed Jefferson, whom he presumed was still the secretary of state, that if Paine remained "quiet in prison," he might survive, but as "he has a larger share of every other sense . . . than common sense," there was a real likelihood that "the long suspended axe might fall on him."[5]

Morris callously abandoned Paine to languish in the potential death trap that was the Luxembourg, and possibly to face the all-too-likely fate of hordes of his fellow prisoners, a death sentence handed down by the Revolutionary Tribunal. Perhaps his antipathy for Paine was such that Morris was unmoved by his suffering. He might possibly have accepted Paine's demise with equanimity. Morris had long been contemptuous of Paine, and atop that he had in recent months come to believe that Paine had sought his recall as America's minister to France. Six months prior to Paine's arrest, Morris had remarked that he regarded Paine as an enemy who was "intriguing against me." His conjecture was not misplaced. In fact, Paine, not the least sheepishly, had earlier told Morris straightaway that his "appointment . . . was the most unfortunate and the most injudicious . . . that could ever be made." In addition, Morris suspected—again probably accurately—that Paine had a hand in writing a summer 1793 message sent to Philadelphia by American ship captains trapped in French ports. The desperate seafarers complained of Morris's inattentiveness and disinterest. In addition to his loathing for the prisoner, the minister knew that if released from prison, Paine was expected to return to America, and once there he could be counted on to seek Morris's recall as well as to marshal his unequaled writing skills on behalf of the Republicans. An arch-Federalist, Morris would not have been happy with such an occurrence.

Subsequently, when Robespierre's papers were made public, Paine discovered that the leading Montagnards had wanted him imprisoned for what they said was "the interest of America, as well as of France." Paine had told Morris in his plaintive letter that he suspected that leaders of the Convention wished to silence him, but Robespierre's notes—and Morris's striking indifference to his dilemma—led Paine to ultimately conclude that there were high officials in Philadelphia who were equally interested in seeing that he "should be continued in arrestation," and in silence. There is no evidence that the Washington administration played any role in Paine's arrest, and, to be sure, Jefferson—who remained secretary of state until one week following Paine's arrest—would never have countenanced such conduct.[6]

Month after month, Paine languished in the Luxembourg. Yet, according to a fellow inmate he somehow managed to maintain a cheerful and hopeful demeanor that bolstered others. His "brilliant powers of conversation" and "sportive wit," as well as his willingness to listen to others who despaired, made Paine "a very general favourite" among the prisoners. "He was the confidant of the unhappy, the counselor of the perplexed," many of whom were within "the hour of death." One person Paine helped was General Charles O'Hara, the British officer who had served as Earl Cornwallis's stand-in during the surrender ceremony at Yorktown thirteen years earlier and now was confined in the Luxembourg as a prisoner of war. When O'Hara was released, Paine gave him two hundred pounds to facilitate his return to England. Paine's empathetic response toward O'Hara was not untypical. A few months before his arrest, Paine had spent an evening at White's Hotel, dining and drinking with acquaintances, one of whom was Captain Grimstone, an English aristocrat and archconservative, half Paine's age. Grimstone became so angry with Paine's political comments that he "struck him a violent blow." At the time, Paine was still a member of the Convention, and it was a capital crime to assault an assemblyman. Grimstone was taken into custody, but Paine saved his assailant from the guillotine, pulled strings to secure a passport for him, and gave him money to make the trip back to England.[7]

Paine knew from the outset of his confinement that he was in a world of trouble. The Terror had at first been directed largely against proven counterrevolutionaries, but during Paine's last weeks of freedom the government earnestly went after the Revolution's previous leaders, especially those who had once supported a constitutional monarchy. By the spring of 1794, eightyeight former members of the Convention had perished, most either on the guillotine, by suicide, or from the rigors of prison life, though some had been murdered. On March 24, Cloots, the only other foreigner to serve in the Convention after being awarded French citizenship, was taken from his cell and dispatched on the lonely ride that ended at the scaffold. (Some awaited their fate silently, but shortly before the blade fell, Cloots screamed: "Hurrah for the fraternity of nations! Long live the Republic of the world!") By then, Montagnards were dooming other Montagnards, and some members of the faction found themselves subject to the Terror they had once supported. During the week of Cloots's demise, Paine stumbled on Georges Danton, once one of the most powerful members of the assembly and the individual who may have saved Paine's life by warning him not to enter the Convention on the spring day that the Montagnards and their allies set on the Girondins. Danton was now a prisoner. Seeing Paine, Danton took his hand and said: "That which you did for the happiness and liberty of your country, I tried in vain to do for mine. I have been less fortunate, but not less innocent." Now his doom was sealed, he told Paine. Danton was executed early in April.[8]

In the nine months before mid-summer 1794, more than 300,000 throughout France had been arrested and some 17,000 had been executed following a trial. Many others were killed without having gone through the judicial process, and still others died in prison or by their own hand.

Somewhere in the vicinity of 40,000 are believed to have died in the Terror. Altogether, 9,249 were imprisoned in Paris alone between August 1792 and July 1794. There is no way to know what percentage of those who were jailed survived their ordeal. It is known that the overwhelming majority of executions in Paris occurred in the spring and summer of 1794, the very period of Paine's confinement. In March and early April an average of 5 executions occurred daily in the Place de la Révolution. Thereafter, the rate of deaths intensified into the summer, reaching a gory zenith between July 18 and 26, when on average 38 executions were carried out each day. So many people were being put to death so quickly that the bodies could not be disposed of with adequate speed, leading the citizenry to complain of the "mephitic odors" that pervaded sections of summertime Paris. The total number guillotined in Paris between March 20 and July 28 approached 2,000.[9]

Caught in this macabre orgy of death, Paine had "little expectation of surviving." Later, he described his ordeal as "a continued scene of horror. No man could count upon life for twenty-four hours." Night after night—it was always in the dead of night—agents came and took away prisoners to "a pretended tribunal" that nearly always handed down a sentence of death to be carried out before the next sunset. Paine later said that each night "every man went to bed with the apprehension of never seeing his friends or the world again." He recalled many instances of having conversed with a fellow inmate who, an hour later, was "seen marching to his destruction." During that appalling spring and summer hardly "a night passed in which ten, twenty, thirty, forty, fifty or more were not taken" to be tried. Paine later recalled a night in July when three score or more were taken from the Luxembourg and all but eight were dead within eighteen hours. He added: "There seemed to be a determination to destroy all the Prisoners without regard to merit, character, or any thing else."[10]

Twice, Paine came to death's door. His first close brush was when he fell desperately sick. An eighteenth-century prison was a breeding ground for dangerous illnesses, and the conditions that Paine endured—inadequate diet, little exercise, a damp and unhealthy cell, incredible stress, and confinement in close proximity with other sickly inmates—eventually caught up with him. He collapsed that summer, probably in July, with what he later variously called a "violent" and a "malignant" fever. It is likely that he suffered from typhoid fever, a bacterial infection that is most commonly spread by the ingestion of food or water contaminated by feces from an infected person. Symptoms may include weakness, abdominal pain, headache, and loss of appetite, and some victims exhibit rose-colored spots. Paine was so sick that for several days he was "insensible of my own existence," as he later said. He survived through the help of his cellmates and aid provided by two physicians who were internees, the prison doctor and General O'Hara's surgeon, all of whom tried to keep him hydrated and to get food into him. His life hung in the balance for two weeks, and his recovery thereafter was slow and unsteady. Ten weeks after first falling ill, Paine remained "too weak . . . to sit up."[11]

Paine came equally close to dying on the scaffold. On July 24 the public prosecutor listed his name among those who were to be taken before the dreaded Revolutionary Tribunal. His illness may have saved him, as at the time he was likely comatose or too weak and muddled to respond in court. That was the explanation he offered a year later. In 1802, Paine provided a rather fanciful account of how he had dodged the executioner. His new story was that each morning, while the prisoners were away from their cells tending their chores, a guard with the death list in hand secretly put a chalk mark on the cell door of each intended victim, signaling which prisoners were to be taken by the police during the coming night. On the morning of July 25, the jailer supposedly made the mark of condemnation on Paine's door, but as the portal stood open, he chalked the inside of the door. By happenstance, that night turned cool and Paine and his cellmates were given permission to close their door. The police who came to collect their victims on the evening of July 25–26 did not see the mark. That, according to Paine's later, and most likely embroidered, story was how "the destroying angel passed by" his cell.[12]

Paine clung to two hopes throughout his months of tribulation in the Luxembourg. One was that the Montagnard rulers—they were referred to by another inmate as "Robespierre and his jury of assassins"—would fall from power. The other was that Gouverneur Morris would be recalled and replaced with someone more conscientious and compassionate. As far as Paine was concerned, so long as Morris remained America's envoy to France, there was "no Minister" in Paris.[13]

Both of Paine's fervent wishes came true, the former just in the nick of time. Robespierre's fall came on July 27, seventy-two hours after Paine had been ticketed to appear before the Revolutionary Tribunal. In an environment in which no one was safe, frightened and desperate assemblymen organized a coup that resulted in the arrest of Robespierre and several confederates. Robespierre was taken to the Luxembourg, though the terrified guards refused to process him. They sent him to the mayor's office, but the equally panicked officials there sped him to the city hall. Robespierre's allies tried to mobilize the Paris Commune to wrest him from custody, but in the confused fighting that followed in the wee hours of July 28 the prisoner was badly wounded, shot through the jaw. Robespierre remained in custody. Bleeding profusely and in great agony, he was taken before the Revolutionary Tribunal around midday and condemned to death. At seven thirty P.M. that same day, seventeen excruciating hours after being wounded, Robespierre perished on the scaffold to which he and his fanatical accomplices had sent so many others.[14]

Paine quickly learned of Robespierre's fate, but thereafter long weeks elapsed before he became aware that his second wish—the replacement of Morris—had also come true. In mid-autumn of 1793, weeks before Paine's arrest, France learned that America had asked that Citizen Genêt be recalled. The French government acted quickly in choosing his successor, but it also demanded Morris's recall, a step taken partly because of the minister's enmity toward the Revolution and partly in retaliation for Genêt's fate. The new French minister to the United States arrived in Philadelphia late in February, at almost the precise moment that Paine wrote his plaintive letter to Morris beseeching help. That French minister advised Washington that France wished the recall of Morris.[15]

Naming Morris's replacement was the least pressing of Washington's problems, for just then the United States faced its most serious foreign policy crisis since the Revolutionary War. Not long after entering the war against France, Great Britain had not only blockaded its enemy's coastline; it broadened its definition of "contraband" to include foodstuffs, a move sure to have a crippling impact on American exports. In one of his last acts as secretary of state, Jefferson persuaded Washington to include passages in his State of the Union message that censured London's more inclusive definition of contraband and its discriminatory trade practices. Washington's tart remarks were fruitless, and worse, in March 1794, the president learned that a new British order-in-council had blockaded all trade to the French West Indies. Before the close of the month, Philadelphia newspapers were filled with lists of American ships and cargoes that had been seized by the Royal Navy. In addition, stories abounded of sailors aboard American ships who had been impressed into Britain's navy on the pretense that they were British citizens who had deserted. The toll of plundered American vessels mounted until, in no time, it was known that nearly four hundred ships had fallen victim to Britain's war policy. Docks in every port city were idled and farmers watched their grain go into storage rather than into the cargo holds of ships bound for markets. War fever swept the country.[16]

Since January, James Madison in the House and James Monroe in the Senate had led their party's fight in Congress to pressure Washington to take a stronger stand against Britain's many injurious policies. Some Republicans privately complained of the president's "supiness & negligence" and wanted their party to call on the president to issue a proclamation terminating the payment of all debts to British creditors. Some Republicans were alarmed solely by the deleterious economic impact of Britain's policies. Many also feared that the stricter British blockade would prove fatal to France and the French Revolution. Constituents wrote to Monroe reminding him that America could not have won the Revolutionary War without French aid, informing him that in Virginia the "Cause of France is almost universally admired," and beseeching action to assure that the French Revolution was not destroyed by the Federalist "Band of Patriots whose Idols are paper [securities] & autocratic principles." Newspapers, too, ran attacks on Washington, a relatively uncommon occurrence before this crisis. Essayists complained of the president's "pusillanimous disposition" and portrayed him as akin to the "grand Sultan of Constantinople, shut up in his apartment and unacquainted" with the suffering spawned by British policies.[17]

The last thing that Hamilton and northern merchants and investors wanted was war with Britain or retaliation against London's policies. American revenue would run dry in a minute, and the national economy would sink back into the doldrums, where it had remained throughout the 1780s. The Federalists fought back with a shrewd campaign that was conceived in part, if not wholly, by Hamilton. The party's speaker of the house, Theodore Sedgwick, introduced a "national defense" plan that called for the creation of a fifteen-thousand-man army to guard against a British invasion. The prospect of such a force caused as much anxiety among the Republicans as had London's orders-in-council. No one was more alarmed than Monroe. That it would be a standing army was bad enough. Even worse, in Monroe's estimation, was the certainty that the army's corps of field officers would be composed almost entirely of Federalists and the "generalissimo" might be Hamilton himself. The "whole force of the country will be in the hands of the enemy of publick liberty," Monroe declared, adding that the threat it posed was "more dangerous than any now menac'd" by Great Britain. He told Livingston: "Of Britain I have no fear. The danger is not an external one," but an internal one.[18]

The Federalists also let it be known that they wanted the president to dispatch an envoy extraordinary to London to negotiate a settlement of differences between the two nations. Word quickly circulated that Washington was considering Hamilton as his choice to cross to London and conduct the negotiations. Jefferson responded that the mere thought of sending Hamilton was "degrading." Senator Monroe was so distrustful of Hamilton that he protested directly to Washington, among other things spelling out for the president the Treasury secretary's "constant & systematic enmity to the French nation & revolution" and his unadulterated Anglophilia. A Hamilton mission,

Monroe added, would in the long run be dangerous to America's republicanism. The president, unaccustomed to having his judgment questioned, fired back a cold and hostile note: "I alone am responsible for a proper nomination" and it "behooves me to name such a one as in my judgment combines the requisites to the peace & happiness of this country." Monroe wrote a second time. Washington did not answer.[19]

Washington had long done what he could to facilitate Hamilton's political fortunes, and he knew that a successful mission in London would enhance the Treasury secretary's chances of someday becoming the secretary of state, possibly even of ascending to the presidency. But the outcry against Hamilton was so great that the Treasury secretary withdrew his name. Washington then chose Hamilton's fellow New Yorker John Jay for the mission, a move that was no more popular with the Republicans. Many in the party suspected that Jay's Anglophilia was on par with Hamilton's. Monroe, among others, feared that a Jay mission would guarantee Britain's "conquest of the French & perhaps afterwards of the Spanish Islands" in the Caribbean and, in time, it might fulfill the Federalist dream of allying with London and "detaching us from France." A bruising fight over Jay's confirmation occurred in the Senate, with Monroe taking a leading role in opposing the president's choice. But the Federalists enjoyed a numerical majority and confirmed Jay's nomination. Even so, at least in Madison's judgment, naming Jay as the envoy caused Washington to suffer the "most powerful blow" to his popularity that he experienced during his presidency.[20]

Once Jay's appointment was out of the way, Washington turned to finding a successor to Gouverneur Morris in Paris. He first thought of moving Thomas Pinckney, America's minister to Great Britain, to Paris and replacing him in London with Jay. But Jay demurred, not wishing a lengthy stay abroad. The president next offered the post in France to Madison, but the latter's fear of sailing led him to decline the offer. Washington then turned to Livingston, but he, too, spurned the post. Writing more candidly to Monroe, his friend, than he had to the chief executive, Livingston confided that he had refused the tender because Washington's antipathy to the French Revolution would have confronted him with the choice of saying and doing things that "violate my own principles" or of "risk[ing] my reputation" by flouting the president's wishes. At this juncture, several Republicans, including Madison and Monroe, urged the president to consider Aaron Burr, a Republican senator from New York. Washington would not listen. Monroe attributed the president's rebuff to "objections of a personal nature." Others thought the same thing, and some said they believed the president questioned Burr's "integrity." In fact,

Washington barely knew Burr. More likely, he was swayed by Hamilton, long Burr's political adversary in New York.[21]

Monroe was Washington's next choice. He had been recommended by Edmund Randolph, the secretary of state, the very man whom Monroe back in 1787 had suspected of disliking him. Though both Washington and Monroe were Virginians and former soldiers, the two had never been close. Age was a factor—Washington was twenty-five years older—but in addition Monroe time and again had opposed matters that were dear to Washington: ratification of the original Constitution, Hamilton's economic program, and most recently the appointment of both Hamilton and Jay for the mission to London. On May 26, five months almost to the day since Paine's incarceration, Randolph approached Monroe with the president's offer. Inexplicably, Randolph gave Monroe only one hour to make up his mind. He also told him that if he accepted, he was to "embark immediately."

Monroe could not have been more surprised. Only moments before Randolph knocked on his door, Monroe had written to Jefferson that "appearances authorize the belief that [Burr] will be appointed." Monroe believed he was "among the last" that Washington would consider. He was startled and had next to no time to think through what he might be getting into. He of course saw the same dangers in accepting the post that Livingston had discerned. If he would have had the opportunity to speak with Jefferson, who saw another danger, his decision might have been different. Jefferson, at Monticello, immediately concluded that Washington had turned to Monroe "merely to get him out of the Senate and with an intention to seize the first pretext for exercising the pleasure of recalling him" and ruining his career. Monroe might not have listened to Jefferson's advice had he been aware of it. He was terribly ambitious and found the prospect of occupying the very office that Jefferson had once filled to be exhilarating. Nevertheless, before making a decision, Monroe used the hour he had been allotted to consult with Madison, who in turn spoke with several Republicans senators to gauge their support. Confident that his party was behind him, Monroe accepted the president's tender. Two days later the Senate confirmed his appointment.[22]

Given little time to put his personal affairs in order, Monroe left the matter of selecting the spot for the house that he planned to build near Monticello in the hands of Jefferson, Madison, and his uncle, Joseph Jones. Furthermore, compelled to pay out of pocket the seven-hundred-dollar charge for his Atlantic crossing, Monroe lacked the additional funds to meet a note due on a five-thousand-acre tract of land in Loudoun County, losing what he believed to be an extraordinary investment. He booked passage on a ship set to leave

Baltimore in mid-June for himself, his wife, Elizabeth, and Eliza, his seven-year-old daughter.[23]

While Elizabeth shopped for items such as ham and sugar, thought to be in short supply in Paris, Monroe received the president's instructions, which opened with a statement declaring Washington's friendship for the French Revolution and his "immutable" wish for its success. Monroe was told to avoid ties with any political faction in France, strictly adhere to America's policy of neutrality and the terms of the Franco-American Treaty of Alliance, and seek to allay French fears and "suspicions" occasioned by Jay's mission to London. "You go, Sir . . . to strengthen our Friendship with that country," said the president, after which he ordered Monroe not to evince "undue complaisance" toward France.[24]

Finally, all preparations were completed. Monroe and his family set off for Baltimore thirteen days after Randolph had approached him with the president's offer. On June 18, a warm, sultry day, the *Cincinnatus* weighed anchor and began its voyage for France.[25]

Monroe departed with little knowledge of what had transpired in France during recent months. He had some idea of what he called "the terror of the revolutionary Tribune," for American newspapers had reported the arrest of Brissot and other Girondin leaders, but Monroe was unaware of their fate. (He had been instructed to report to the president on whether the Girondins had been "extinguished" and Danton and his followers "overwhelmed," and if "Robespierre's party [was] firmly fixed.") He had no idea of what had become of Thomas Paine. Morris had sent word that Paine had been arrested, but the executive branch had curiously kept a lid on the news, neither revealing it to the public nor to Monroe. In fact, Paine was not mentioned in the directive given to Monroe by the secretary of state. About all that Monroe did know when he sailed was that whatever sympathy President Washington once had for the French Revolution had vanished, and that conservative Federalists—the ruling party—had long since recoiled in fear and horror at its excesses. Perhaps John Adams best expressed the conservatives' revulsion when he remarked that democratic "Majorities . . . banishing, confiscating, massacring, guillotining Minorities, has been the whole History of the French Revolution."[26]

When the *Cincinnatus* docked in Le Havre near the end of July, Monroe got his first real news about recent events in France. He was told that "another great convulsion had shaken & torn Paris to pieces," one in which Robespierre had been toppled and executed. Monroe reached Paris on August 3, six days after Robespierre's fall. During his dusty, sun-seared carriage ride to the metropolis, Monroe found that "perfect tranquility" prevailed in the countryside. Paris was quiet too, though many told him without hesitation that so long as the war continued the danger remained that France could slide back into disorder and terror. Soon after his arrival, Monroe met with Gouverneur Morris, who escorted him to the foreign ministry. But because of what ministerial officials referred to as the "moment of commotion" brought on by the coup against Robespierre, no official with an executive title was available to receive him. Days passed. After languishing for nearly two weeks, Monroe—almost certainly following the advice of Morris—requested that he be received by the Convention. Finally, on August 15, Citizen Monroe, as Parisians called him, appeared before the deputies in the same hall where Paine had once sat. He received an ecstatic welcome unlike anything ever bestowed on Morris. In his formal address, Monroe said that the world's two republics, the United States and France, clung to similar principles and shared a common cornerstone: "the equal and unalienable rights of man." He hoped for perpetual harmony between the two nations and vowed to "promote the interest of both." Much that he said would anger officials in the executive branch in Philadelphia, particularly his promise to "pursue the dictates of my own heart" when dealing with America's ally. However, the delegates loved what he said, and the assembly's journal noted that the legislators listened "with a lively sensibility" and responded to Monroe's speech "with applause." The moment that Monroe completed his remarks, the president of the Convention leaped forward and gave the Minister "the *accolade*," a warm embrace that signified "the fraternity which unites these two peoples."[27]

Two days later a Paris newspaper that reported on Monroe's speech found its way into the now more-relaxed confines of the Luxembourg. Paine saw the story. It was the first word he had received that Morris—from whom he had heard nothing in seven months—was no longer the American minister to France. Grabbing pen and paper, Paine wrote immediately to the new minister. He persuaded the prison lamplighter, who had always displayed an "unabated friendship," to deliver the missive. Paine did not know Monroe or anything about him, but the news that Morris was gone "is joy to me and will be to every American in France," he exclaimed. Paine related that he had been imprisoned since December and had nearly died during his confinement. He did not know why he had been jailed, though the order said it was because he was "a Foreigner." As Morris, his "inveterate enemy," had stood by idly throughout his detention, Monroe was now his sole hope "of delivery."[28]

Paine wrote to Monroe again the next day—altogether, he sent him nine letters in eleven weeks—this time pleading his case of American citizenship. France had conferred citizenship on him, as it had on President Washington, he wrote; but just as Washington surely had never thought of renouncing his American citizenship to become a French citizen, Paine said that he had never relinquished his American citizenship. He again recounted the suffering he had endured in the Luxembourg, where he had always been in a "precarious situation," his life "suspended as it were by a single thread of accident." He exhorted Monroe to use his authority to "release me from this unjust imprisonment." Paine did not stop with an appeal to Monroe. He also petitioned the Convention, telling the deputies that eight months in confinement "seems almost a life-time," and it should never have occurred in the first place. His incarceration had been due to Robespierre, "my inveterate enemy," a tyrant who struck against all who resisted tyranny. All along, said Paine, he had planned to return to America, where he was a citizen, but his "heart was devoted to all France" and he had sacrificed "private tranquility" in "the hope of seeing a Revolution happily established."[29]

Meanwhile, Achille Audibert and other friends urged the authorities to release Paine. They acted in vain. Nor did the Convention respond to Paine's entreaty. It merely forwarded his letter to the Committee of General Surety. Monroe waited a month before answering Paine's two initial letters, though in the interim it appears that he ascertained that Paine was no longer in danger of having to stand trial. Monroe moved slowly: He wished to investigate the reasons behind Paine's arrest and incarceration, but in addition he could do nothing until his credentials were approved, a process that dragged on for weeks. All the while, Paine waited impatiently, uneasily. Lamenting that he had "nothing to do but to sit and think," Paine wrote to Monroe again and again. He asked the new minister if it would not be more desirable for America—and Monroe—to receive credit for his liberation than for him to someday "glide out of prison" through what was seen as the act of a kindly French official? He reminded Monroe that all the Revolution's great changes "have been sudden." Today's "calm" could turn to horror tomorrow. In a flash, his safety could once more be jeopardized. He reiterated the question of his citizenship in a turgid forty-three-page letter that might have been boiled down to one sentence: Though born in England, he was no more an English citizen than was any American colonist who had been English before July 4, 1776. Now and then Paine excoriated Gouverneur Morris, confiding to Monroe that his predecessor had left him to rot in jail from fear that he would return to America and "expose his misconduct."[30]

Forty-six days after reaching Paris, Monroe finally responded with a letter that Paine thought was "very friendly and affectionate," and that "relieved my mind from a load of disquietude." Monroe said that he would do all that he could to secure Paine's release. He added, "your countrymen ... are interested in your welfare."[31]

Thereafter, forty-six excruciating days passed while Paine sat in his cell watching as many of his fellow inmates were set free. Growing increasingly peevish, he told Monroe that "my patience is exhausted." Paine added that he had never imagined he would "remain in prison two months after the arrival of a new Minister." Finally, on November 4, the Committee of General Surety responded to Monroe's appeal and ordered Paine's release. Monroe personally rode to the Luxembourg to witness Paine's liberation and to offer him a home in his residence. Always thin, Paine was now thinner than normal and afflicted with a bad cough. After ten months and eight days, Paine once again was free and in "good spirits," and he thought it likely that his freedom had been gained just in the nick of time, for his frail health required "liberty and a better air."[32]

Monroe revered Paine. He was familiar with Paine's major publications, including *Common Sense*, which he likely read before enlisting in the Continental army. He knew of Paine's service in the American Revolution and was aware that Jefferson admired him. But Monroe knew little of Paine's private side. Above all, he did not know that once Paine was offered a place to stay, he often stayed indefinitely. Paine initially told Monroe that he planned to return to the United States before the end of the year. Weeks later, he intimated that he would depart within the next three or four months. Paine was still residing with the Monroes after eighteen months. That Paine stayed on in Paris was due in part to his fear of a making a wartime Atlantic crossing, an endeavor that might be even more dangerous given his lingering health issues. There was also the matter of where he might live in America, for the farmhouse that New York had awarded him in New Rochelle had burned a couple of years earlier. Unwilling to live in out-of-the-way Bordentown, where he owned a small house, Paine more or less faced a choice of Philadelphia or Paris. He preferred the latter, partly because it was more cosmopolitan and partly because he now had more close acquaintances in the French capital than in the temporary capital of the United States.

Before long, Monroe discovered that Paine was a ticking time bomb. Paine was embittered by his arrest, as he had a right to be, and justifiably incensed that Morris had left him to his fate in the Luxembourg. During the first ninety days of his freedom, Paine additionally came to believe that Washington, too, had "winked at his imprisonment and even wished he might die in jail."[33] Paine's conviction that the president was part of grand conspiracy to do him harm arose from piecing together what he had known prior to his imprisonment and information that he gleaned thereafter. That Washington had appointed Morris to succeed the Francophiles Franklin and Jefferson was in itself enough to cause Paine to question the president's intentions. Even more troubling to Paine was Washington's embrace of neutrality during France's hour of maximum peril. What he must have learned from Monroe about the Federalist Party—which the minister was given to calling "the B[ritis]h faction" in America—and Washington's habitual approval of Federalist policies added to Paine's growing suspicion, as did his discovery that the president had sent an Anglophile, John Jay, to London to negotiate with France's enemy. If Monroe divulged that the French foreign ministry was extremely apprehensive about what Jay might agree to in London, Paine's misgivings about Washington as a neutralist would only have increased.[34] Already seething, Paine by February 1795 had become convinced that Washington and Morris had acted in concert to silence his pen. To Paine's way of thinking, each wished to shield the Federalist Party. Morris also feared savage attacks by Paine, while Washington sought to prevent him from stoking the fires of hostility toward American neutrality.

Given his irrepressible rage, it is not difficult to see how Paine could conclude the worst with regard to Washington, though he was wrong to think that the president had connived to have him locked up. It was a theory for which there is no evidence. But whether Washington knowingly let Paine sit in his French jail cell is another matter. Morris notified Jefferson of Paine's imprisonment in two letters, one written in January and the other in March 1794, though the missives arrived in Philadelphia following the former secretary of state's resignation and return to Monticello. Nonetheless, as Morris typically sent the State Department duplicates or even triplicates of his correspondence—and as Jefferson forwarded the official mail that he received unopened, merrily remarking "from all such reading good lord deliver me!"— Secretary of State Randolph must have known of Paine's incarceration within seventy-five days at most of his entering the Luxembourg. It boggles the mind to think that Randolph did not immediately inform Washington of Paine's plight. In fact, on receiving Morris's second communication, Randolph rapidly notified the president that "another letter" from Morris had arrived, wording that points to Washington's familiarity with the envoy's initial letter. Washington received Morris's second letter concerning Paine's imprisonment on June 30, twelve days after Monroe sailed for France, and he waited a month before providing direction to Randolph with regard to those Americans who were incarcerated in France.

Washington's response, as conveyed to Monroe by Randolph, was that the president was aware that "several of our *citizens*" were jailed in France because of "a suspicion of criminal attempts against the government. If they are guilty, we are extremely sorry for it; if innocent, we must protect them." Washington named two Americans that "ought to be immediately assisted." He did not name Paine, though Monroe was told to "collect intelligence of every American *citizen* under confinement" and to do "whatsoever ought and can be done" on their behalf. Washington's directive could be read as authorizing Monroe, if warranted, to seek Paine's release—which is how the minister interpreted it—or it could be construed as indicating that the president accepted France's, and Morris's, viewpoint that Paine was not an American citizen and that nothing should be done to help him. Washington's thinking is far from evident. But that he likely waited more than four months after learning of Paine's plight before acting, and that he did not rally to Paine's claim of American citizenship, lends credence to Paine's suspicion that the president either wanted Paine silenced or, no longer finding him of any use, had callously relegated him to his discard pile.[35]

There can be little doubt that Paine told Monroe of his hunch that Washington and Morris had conspired to silence him. Monroe never said what he thought of Paine's theory, though he asked his guest not to publicly assail the president while living under his roof. In fact, Monroe went further. He told Paine to "write nothing for the publick, either of Europe or America," while a guest in his house. The "injury such essays would do me" could be colossal, Monroe said.[36] Paine assented, giving his word he would comply with Monroe's wishes. But obsessed with Washington, Paine soon betrayed his liberator. In a frenzy of passion, Paine secretly drafted an acrimonious private letter to the president—he later acknowledged that "it was not written in very good temper"—and on Washington's birthday in 1795 entrusted its delivery to a French diplomat about to sail for Philadelphia. Paine opened with the accusation that Washington knew of the danger he had faced from the spring of 1793 onward, yet he had responded with a "guarded silence." He went on to charge Washington with never having "directed any inquiry to be made whether I was in prison or at liberty, dead or alive." Paine said that he expected more from his friend and president, especially considering that "everything I have been doing in Europe was connected with my wishes for the prosperity of America." He took some swipes at Washington's willingness to negotiate with England, calling it "a satire upon the Declaration of Independence," and at American neutrality, a stance that only encouraged London's "insults and depredations." He also carped about Washington's choice of Morris to represent the United States in Paris. Morris's "total neglect of all business" had alienated every American in Paris, his "prating" and "pomposity" had made him "offensive" to all that he encountered, and his anti-republicanism had threatened a rupture in Franco-American relations.[37]

A few days later Paine, not particularly sheepishly, confessed to Monroe what he had done and showed him a copy of the letter. Appalled, Monroe succeeded in retrieving the letter before the envoy sailed. Thinking that was the end of it, Monroe naively breathed a sigh of relief, confident that Paine would not again "disquiet . . . me." Monroe also permitted his disloyal guest to remain in his house.[38]

Paine set aside his grudge against Washington for a considerable time. A month after his release from prison, the Convention not only reinstated the seventy-three living deputies that had been ousted during the Terror, but it also awarded them back pay—more than eleven months' compensation in Paine's case. Paine did not attend any session of the Convention for well over half a year. He returned only when the Convention debated yet another constitution, what was to become the Constitution of the Year III. Paine wished to question the restrictions on universal manhood suffrage in the proposed document. Rising to speak, he was greeted warmly, though the assemblymen listened to his address in silence.[39] Undeterred, Paine declared that voting restrictions would breach the "grand object of the Revolution" as pledged in the Declaration of Rights of 1789. The proposed constitution was for "the good only of a *few*" rather than "the good of *all*," he added. His speech having fallen on deaf ears, Paine immediately rushed into print a short essay, "Dissertation on First Principles of Government." His tract dwelled on the evils of the "inequality of rights" and how such discrimination enabled "one part of the community to exclude another part from its rights." In practice, he wrote, it almost always was the rich that took away the rights of the poor. In closing, Paine asserted that the "protection of a man's rights is more sacred than the protection of property."[40]

Aside from this one instance, Paine remained aloof from politics for the longest time. Instead, he sought out old friends and resumed former habits, especially long nights given over to socializing in taverns. One observer thought prison had aged Paine. After listening to him pontificate for a spell, that same onlooker concluded that Paine was a "professed revolutionary, naïf, fanatic, monomaniac, full of candour . . . a man of virtue, bold in doctrine, cautious in practice; likely to deliver himself instantaneously to revolutions, but incapable of accepting their dangerous consequences." An individual who encountered Paine several months later described him as "a well-dressed and most gentlemanly man, of sound and orthodox republican principles, of a good heart

[and] strong intellect." He added, as had so many others, that Paine was a "fascinating" conversationalist. Katherine Wilmot, an Irish devotee of Mary Wollstonecraft, met Paine while touring Europe. "In spite of his surprisingly ugliness," she found "his manners easy and benevolent, and his conversation remarkably entertaining." She added that he was "guileless and good natured." None of these observers hinted that Paine had a drinking problem, though Joel Barlow, who saw Paine often and still liked him, suggested otherwise. Barlow considered Paine "among the brightest and most undeviating luminaries of the age," and praised both his charity toward the poor and his ever-present willingness to aid Americans in France. But he had grown less tolerant of his friend's overweening vanity and inability to accept criticism. Finding that many of Paine's old friends wanted little to do with him, Barlow came to look on his old comrade as a sad case, a stranger to a new generation, a lonely man who sought "refuge in low company" and "compassion in the sordid, solitary bottle."[41]

Paine struggled with poor health throughout the first year of his freedom from the Luxembourg. He suffered from gout and thought he had contracted tuberculosis. That was not the case, though the lingering effects of the prison-born fever and of nearly a year's stay in a dank cell had left him with pulmonary problems. During the summer of 1795 Paine also fell victim to what was variously described as an "abscess in his side" and an "open wound in the side." Paine likely had incurred a large infected boil, an affliction that can be caused by bacteria; in an age long before the advent of modern antibiotics, curing such a malady was challenging. Monroe thought Paine was dying and could not survive longer than a month, but a Paris surgeon was called in to treat the wound, probably by lancing the abscess and allowing it to heal while open. In September, with the abscess presumably healing, Paine was laid low again by an unrelated ailment. He thought it a recurrence of the prison fever. He was probably wrong on that count. Whatever the disorder, he was bedfast for days and faced a protracted convalescence.[42]

Since at least the early 1790s, Paine had also been afflicted with a pronounced case of rosacea, a chronic inflammatory skin condition that had provoked Katherine Wilmot to describe him as homely. (English political cartoonists had cruelly depicted it in their artwork on him as early as 1792.) When untreated, rosacea worsens over time. It causes redness, usually beneath the eyes, that appears similar to blushing or sunburn. Constant inflammation, which seems to have been the case with Paine, can cause small red pimples to appear. Phymatous rosacea, which without a doubt afflicted Paine, centers on the nose, causing it to appear swollen, grotesquely so in some cases. Countless observers commented on his misshapen nose during the last twenty-five years of his life. Numerous things can cause or aggravate rosacea, including weather and certain foods, but Paine's condition most likely was brought on and exacerbated by stress and the consumption of alcohol.

Health issues or not, Paine turned to writing soon after he left the Luxembourg. He had originally planned a much larger version of *The Age of Reason* than the one Barlow succeeded in shepherding into print early in 1794, and once Paine was free, he rapidly turned to completing his book. Within six months of walking out of prison, he delivered to his publisher what he would title *Part the Second*. What Paine had written prior to being jailed dealt generally with faith-based celestial revelation. He took up the Bible in his sequel. Paine set forth where he was going in his opening sentence: "if the Bible be not true . . . it ceases to have authority, and cannot be admitted as proof of anything." After that introductory pronouncement, he went on to point out numerous biblical contradictions, inconsistencies, historical inaccuracies, and fables that were drawn from other sources. The result of centuries of "Christian priests and preachers . . . impos[ing] the Bible on the world as a mass of truth and as the Word of God," he charged, was that humanity had embraced a "system of falsehood, idolatry, and pretended revelation." That, in turn, had led to "habits of superstition" and incalculable "wickedness." According to one scholar, the "remarkable thing about his conclusions is that in so many cases they anticipated those of modern theologians."[43]

Sales of the initial installment of *The Age of Reason* had boomed in 1794, outpacing the breathtakingly successful *Rights of Man*. *The Age of Reason, Part the Second* sold equally well in England and colossally in America, where seventeen editions were published in two years. Paine anticipated fevered criticism, and it was immediately forthcoming. Militant atheists challenged him to prove that there was one God, in which he had said he believed. Christians defended their faith and also derided Deism as faith-based and irrational, the same reasoning—they pointed out—that Paine had utilized in assailing Christianity. Some critics resorted to ad hominem assaults. Mason Locke Weems, an Episcopalian priest who later gained fame as "Parson Weems," author of a fable-laden biography of Washington, charged that the dissolute Paine had "no other church but the alehouse" and that a lifetime of intemperance had left him with "palsied legs [that] can scarce bear him to that sink of vomiting and filth."[44]

Perhaps puffed up by the astounding success of yet another book, and incapable of suppressing his long-simmering anger toward Washington, Paine struck again in September 1795, seven months after Monroe foiled the delivery of his initial letter to the president. Although he admired Monroe as an "open-hearted man," and looked on him with "respect and gratitude" for his help and generosity, Paine deliberately betrayed him yet again by sending another private missive to Washington. This time, Monroe was unaware of what Paine had done.

Paine opened his dispatch by telling the president that once he had been informed of his onetime friend's imprisonment, it had been "incumbent on [him] to have made some inquiry" into the cause of Paine's jailing. Lecturing Washington was risky enough, but Paine immediately thereafter charged that he could attribute the president's silence only to "*connivance* at my imprisonment." As Paine now knew that Robespierre had stated in writing that he was to be jailed in order to protect both American and French interests, Paine said that he suspected Washington of "treachery" in wishing to mute him. Paine added that he would "continue to think you treacherous, till you give me cause to think otherwise."[45]

Washington never answered Paine's intemperate letter, a snub that only fueled his anger. An incandescent passion had driven Paine to produce his best essays, whether from a pent-up fury toward Britain's monarchy and aristocracy or from a zeal to liberate humankind everywhere from those same malign elements and their priestly allies. But if hatred can open one's eyes, it can also blur one's vision. It did both in the case of Paine's thinking toward Washington. He saw flaws in Washington's character and performance as a public official that only became apparent to dispassionate historians writing generations later. Yet Paine's reason was so clouded by bitterness and loathing that he could not see Washington clearly. He was blind to the adversities and confounding perplexities with which Washington—like any leader—had been forced to contend. Nor did Paine realize the risk that his attack would pose to his own standing.

Having not heard from the president by the spring of 1796, Paine opted to publicly air his feelings. He authored a long, malice-laced tract that he titled *Letter to George Washington*. Parts of it were published in a Philadelphia newspaper later in the year—during the presidential election of 1796—and the entire essay appeared as pamphlet in 1797.[46] Until its publication, Paine had remained exceedingly popular in America. To be sure, *The Age of Reason* had given birth to many detractors, but what Paine had done for the American Revolution was still fondly remembered. Even many who came to hate the French Revolution applauded Paine's vote to spare the life of Louis XVI and empathized with his suffering at the hands of Jacobin extremists. But with his assault on Washington, Paine threw away the solicitude and fervid admiration that he had earned through his writings and years of service and sacrifice for America.

Perhaps he had been away too long and failed to understand how iconic Washington had come to be. More likely, Paine's grandiose—and not entirely unmerited—sense of self-importance skewed his judgment. He was convinced that what he had done for the American Revolution was on a par with Washington's contributions. In his unsent letter to Washington, Paine had written: "I do not hesitate to say that you have not served America with more disinterestedness, or greater zeal, or more fidelity, than myself, and I know not if with better effect." He further believed that his labors to spread the American Revolution and liberate humankind far exceeded anything that Washington had done. While he had risked his life by "ventur[ing] into the new scenes of difficulties," Paine had written in his first missive, "you rested at home."[47] The fire that burned within Paine blazed not only because of his conviction that much of the reverence and honor heaped on General Washington for having won the war was undeserved, but also from his belief that President Washington and those surrounding him were bent on overturning the new republican era brought into being by the American Revolution.

In his *Letter to George Washington*, Paine portrayed the president as a man with an oversize ego that habitually required "the grossest adulation," a blemish that led him to surround himself with sycophants. Washington, he said, "has no friendships" and was "incapable of forming any." He used people and when they no longer were of use, he cast them aside "with constitutional indifference." Like Gouverneur Morris, he wrote, Washington could be shockingly unmoved by human suffering. "The chief difference" between the two was that Morris "is profligate enough to profess an indifference about *moral* principles, and [Washington] is prudent enough to conceal the want of them." He added, "Errors or caprices of the temper can be pardoned and forgotten; but a . . . crime of the heart . . . is not to be washed away."

Paine's excoriation of Washington as a public official took up the largest portion of the essay. He thought little of Washington's generalship, writing that veneration of him for having won the Revolutionary War was "fraudulent." The virtue most often attributed to the general was his "constancy," but "constancy was the common virtue of the Revolution. Who was there that was inconstant? I know but of one military defection, that of [Benedict] Arnold," and none among the members of Congress who voted for independence. Paine grudgingly acknowledged Washington's heroics at Trenton and Princeton, though he added that those victories "would scarcely be noticed" had the general not conducted such a "gloomy campaign" in New York during the preceding summer.

For the most part, he continued, Washington's generalship had been distinguished by "little enterprise." "Nothing was done in the campaigns of 1778, 1779, 1780, in the part where General Washington commanded. . . . The Southern States in the meantime were over-run by the enemy." The war, said

Paine, had three turning points. The first was Horatio Gates's victory over John Burgoyne at Saratoga, of which Washington had no part. That cataclysmic British defeat brought the French into the conflict, and "had it not been for the aid received from France," Washington's "cold and unmilitary conduct . . . would in all probability have lost America." The second was Nathanael Greene's brilliant campaign that "accomplished the recovery" of the South. The third was the victory at Yorktown, a triumph due largely to the French and in which Washington "had little share." The truth, wrote Paine, was that "You slept away your time in the field, till the finances of the country were completely exhausted," all the while leaving it to others to carry the burden of winning the war. Gates and Greene, in fact, were the real heroes among America's general officers. Indeed, discontent with Washington's leadership was so widespread that Congress would have removed him in 1778 had it not been for France's pending entry into the war and the political fallout that would have ensued.

If possible, Paine thought even less of Washington's presidency. The American Revolution had elevated the "fame of America, moral and political" to new heights, but the "Washington of politics . . . appeared" and the "lustre" vanished. At home, Washington's "imbecile administration" had with "treachery and ingratitude" disregarded the common soldiers who fought and gained America's victory, turning over to wealthy speculators the western lands the soldiery had sacrificed to win. In a reference to Washington's practice of holding weekly levees at the President's House, Paine wrote that "the levee-room is [the speculators'] place of rendezvous." Abroad, Washington had utilized Gouverneur Morris and John Jay to cuddle up to England, a policy that had alienated France, once America's benefactor, but now a nation that viewed the United States as "a treacherous friend."

As scathing as was everything that preceded his closing paragraph, Paine finished with a bilious flourish: "And as to you, Sir, treacherous in private friendship (for so you have been to me, and that in the day of danger) and a hypocrite in public life, the world will be puzzled to decide whether you are an apostate or an imposter; whether you have abandoned good principles, or whether you ever had any."[48]

Paine's condemnation of Washington's generalship and distaste for the president's imperious manner were shared by many who had served since 1776 in important capacities. Jefferson, Hamilton, and John Adams had all remarked in private about Washington's limitations and flaws, and numerous others noted his off-putting demeanor. Hamilton blamed Washington in part for the war's having dragged on so long after 1778; thought him petty, vain, ill-tempered, inconsiderate, insecure, and unoriginal in his thinking; and once remarked, "I have felt no friendship for him." While Adams praised Washington as a soldier, he thought him only a "viceroy under Hamilton" when it came to politics, and to that he added that Washington "loved Adulation and could not resist her Charms. The real Friends of the Country are deluded and ruined in Such extravagant Hozannas to his Name."[49]

From the Valley Forge winter onward, virtually no one had dared to publicly reproach Washington. Intriguingly, neither Hamilton nor Adams joined their Federalist brethren in showering Paine with invective once *Letter to George Washington* appeared. (Hamilton did not even respond to a close associate who wrote privately complaining of Paine's "most infamous calumnies.") But Federalist newspapers were filled with attacks on Paine. He was called an "ingrate" and "Judas" for having authored a "base, malignant, treacherous, unnatural, and blasphemous" essay. "These sweepings from Tom's brain," one writer contended, had been emptied onto the public at the direction of France's government. Paine had been corrupted by his residence in France, it was said. "The touch of France is pollution. Her embrace is death."[50]

Paine would have been wise to seek Jefferson's counsel before he publicly assailed Washington. As Jefferson had on more than one occasion cautioned Monroe not to write an inflammatory piece, and given his understanding of Washington's symbolic status, he would surely have sought to stay Paine's hand. While Jefferson did not comment on Paine's handiwork, shortly after excerpts appeared in the press in 1796 he remarked: "Such is the popularity of the President that the people will support him in whatever he will do, or will not do, without appealing to their own reason or to any thing but their feelings towards him. . . . I have long thought therefore it was best for the republican interest to soothe him by flattery where they could approve his measures, and to be silent where they disapprove. . . . In short, to lie on their oars while he remains at the helm."[51]

Even had Paine turned to Jefferson for advice, he might not have listened. His rage toward Washington, and his all-consuming belief that the president and Gouvernor Morris had conspired to cause him harm, was so great that Paine seemed inexorably driven to share with the public his caustic assessment of America's most revered individual. Paine, standing on principles that were crucial to him, had burned his bridges in England and come close to paying with his life in France. His *Letter to George Washington* sprang from a less idealistic source, and it would severely damage—and in some circles, destroy—his reputation in America.

CHAPTER 11

"THE FEDERALIST TIDE IS STRONG"

GLOOMY YEARS FOR THE APOSTLES OF REVOLUTION

ONE WEEK AFTER PAINE WAS jailed, Jefferson arrived at Monticello to begin his retirement. He received little news that he trusted about the French Revolution during the next two years, describing most that he read as an "ocean of lies" floated by English newspapers. In his more candid moments, Jefferson acknowledged that France was passing through a "severe revolution." Yet he clung unwaveringly to the hope that in the end France would enjoy "some form of government favorable to liberty and tranquility" while England, inspired by America and France, would experience the "dawn of liberty and republicanism."[1]

Washington had hoped that Jefferson would not retire, as did many others. None lamented his departure more movingly than Horatio Gates, the once-revered general. Jefferson, he wrote, had returned home "covered with Glory," and quickly added that he was "wanted at philadelphia." Gates persisted: "If the best Seamen abandon the Ship in a Storm, she must Founder; and if all Human means are neglected, Providence will not Care for The Vessel; She must Perish." Jefferson answered with his own nautical metaphor: "In storms . . . all hands must be aloft. But calm is now restored." He was "fixed for life" at Monticello, he told Gates. The disbelieving aged soldier responded that the day would come when the "Voice of a great Nation" would summon Jefferson back to office, and on that day he must return, answering the people's call with his "Great Talents, Joined to Great Integrity."[2]

Having been "liberated from the hated occupations of politics," Jefferson told several correspondents that the "length of my tether is now fixed for life from Monticello to Richmond." True to his word, Jefferson's longest journey during the next three years was to Richmond, and he appears to have gone there to tend to business, not politics. Jefferson told many correspondents that he had come home to stay, intending to "sink into the bosom of my family, my farm, and my books." He may have meant it. Now in his early fifties and having served continuously in public office for the past eleven years, Jefferson assured others that the "little spice of ambition, which I had in my younger days, has long since evaporated."[3] Whether or not true, he indisputably had no interest in returning to Europe to fill any diplomatic post, and in fact eight months into his retirement he declined Washington's request that he serve as envoy extraordinary to Spain. Serving yet again in the cabinet was unappealing, as was the thought of returning to Congress.[4] Only Jefferson knew whether he dreamed of someday becoming president. If so, remaining silent was the judicious course. Washington had three years to go in his second term, and it was possible, though unlikely, that his acolytes might persuade him to serve a third term. Even if Washington stepped down in 1797, the feeling was widespread that Vice President Adams was next in line.

Besides, there were compelling reasons for Jefferson to remain at home. His oldest daughter, Martha, lived nearby, and she and the grandchildren were frequent visitors. Fifteen-year-old Maria resided with him at Monticello, almost the first time since his wife's death more than eleven years earlier that he and his daughter had lived together. As never before, Jefferson said, he wished for serenity and to be the "Master of my own time," and his habits bore out what he said. Months passed before he read a Philadelphia newspaper. He had been home for nearly one hundred days before he wrote to Washington, and when he did so he stuck mostly to matters of farming. In fact, Jefferson no longer spent much time on his correspondence. Averaging only six letters a month during his first year at home, a fraction of the number he had written previously, Jefferson claimed that he wrote letters only on rainy days when he was prevented from doing something more alluring.[5] The focus of his daily routine was superintending operations at Monticello and his neighboring lands. "I live on my horse," he said without much exaggeration. He rose before sunrise. Following a light breakfast and a couple of hours alone in his library, he saddled up to make the rounds, inspect his property and oversee his laborers. He returned to the mansion in mid to late afternoon for his second and final meal of the day, like his breakfast a nourishing but not a gluttonous repast that was long on vegetables, short on meat, and prepared in accordance with his newly acquired preference for French cuisine. Jefferson clearly followed a healthy regimen. He neither smoked nor used hard liquor, though he enjoyed a glass or two of wine—French, of course—with his evening meal, and he remained physically active, daily walking considerable distances and, if the weather obliged, riding a couple of hours purely for exercise.[6]

Jefferson had left France so that he could tend more closely to his financial predicament, but after four years he had made little headway. In fact, since coming back to the United States his indebtedness had increased by more than 15 percent. At a time when the annual income of a journeyman artisan in, say, Philadelphia, might with luck be about £150, Jefferson's debt exceeded £8,500. Selling land and slaves had not solved his problem. Exuding optimism, Jefferson thought he could resolve matters through hands-on management, and he resourcefully attempted numerous expedients. He moved some field hands into other pursuits as he transformed his plantation into a small industrial village where nails, textiles, and charcoal were produced and shipped to market. He also largely replaced tobacco with grains that could be sold in America's growing urban markets; devised an innovative crop-rotation system; instituted an assortment of incentives to get more out of his laborers; and carefully managed the workers during the annual harvest. His nailery was a moneymaker, but, like all farmers, he suffered losses from droughts, floods, and ill-timed freezes, and his wheat production was crippled by the Hessian fly, a devastating blight that plagued farmers from New England southward. By the end of the decade, if not earlier, he came to the realization that slavery was such an inefficient system of labor that it was fundamental to his plight, but he shrank from liberating his chattel, a step that would have compelled him to abandon Monticello. Had he lived more frugally, Jefferson might have made greater progress in his debt campaign, but "frugality" was not a word in his vocabulary. At least a year before he left Philadelphia, Jefferson decided to reconstruct Monticello in the Palladian architectural style with which he had become acquainted while in Europe. His tiny grandchildren would be adults before building was completed, if it ever was fully completed.[7]

Jefferson had put Maria Cosway behind him long before he left Washington's cabinet. He had last seen her more than six years before and had not heard from her since about the time he became secretary of state. On that occasion, in 1790, Jefferson not only had written back to her immediately but also told her that should she come to Monticello it would be "all I could desire in the world." When he next heard from her, in 1795, she spoke of coming to be with him. Now, however, he did not respond for nine months, and when he did write, he did not invite her to Monticello. She wrote to him again, expressing pleasure at the receipt of his letter, urging him to write more often, revealing that she kept his picture "on the side of my Chimney always before me," and closing with "What would I give to surprise you on your Monticello!" He did not answer her letter and never again wrote to her.[8]

By 1795 Jefferson was deep into an intimate relationship with Sally Hemings, one of his slaves. Born in 1773, she was the child of John Wayles—Jefferson's father-in-law—and Betty Hemings, a slave at the Forest. Sometime around 1776, Jefferson brought Betty and her six children to Monticello. Sally was nine when her half-sister, Jefferson's wife, Martha, died. (Sally and Martha were both children of John Wayles's.) At age fourteen in 1787, Sally accompanied Maria on her Atlantic crossing to join her father in Paris. Sally and her brother James, who had crossed with Jefferson three years earlier, lived off and on with the Jeffersons in Paris until they made the return crossing with them in the autumn of 1789.

Sally grew from an adolescent to a young woman of seventeen while in Paris. By all accounts she was strikingly attractive and bore a decided resemblance to Jefferson's late wife. She was described as having long, flowing black hair and, according to one observer, was "mighty near white." In fact, some of her siblings are believed to have passed as white when set free. Others spoke of her as diligent, efficient, and personable. Sally later said that she had been Jefferson's "concubine" while in Paris, but there is no concrete evidence to support her allegation.[9] There can be no doubt, however, that she became pregnant in 1795, and that altogether she gave birth to six children between that autumn and 1808. DNA testing conducted in 1998 confirmed that someone in the Jefferson bloodline sired her children, and circumstantial evidence points toward Thomas Jefferson as the most plausible father of Sally's children. He owned her, she lived at Monticello, he was home nine months before the birth of each of her children, and late in life he freed all her children, though the liberation of chattel was the rarest of acts on Jefferson's part.[10]

Throughout most of 1794, Jefferson said next to nothing about public affairs, though the war scare brought on by Britain's interference with America's trade with France drew his attention. He was gratified to discover that most of his countrymen still felt "their ancient hatred of Gr. Britain." Yet, despite London's "kicks and cuffs," he did not wish for war. Peace was preferable, if it could be preserved with honor. But if war came, he declared, "we will meet it like men." The country would march to war more unified than it had been during the Revolutionary War, given that Britain "has conducted itself so atrociously." Deep down, Jefferson thought war unlikely. The "mass of thinking men" were opposed to war, and that included most Federalists, who feared the ruination of the economy that would result from hostilities with Great Britain. What they wanted, said Jefferson, were "armies and debts" from which the "Monocrats and Papermen" could reap gains.[11]

Confident the crisis would go away peacefully, Jefferson for the most part appeared to be largely disinterested in public affairs. However, a series of actions by the president, the first of which occurred during Jefferson's initial year at home, transformed his outlook. The Washington administration had not succeeded in resolving the nation's western problems during Jefferson's four years in the cabinet. Those living along the frontier from Pennsylvania southward had waited impatiently since 1789 for the removal of the British army from trans-Appalachia and for steps to be taken to compel Spain to open the Mississippi River to American commerce. Until the redcoats were gone and the Mississippi opened, yeomen who ventured into the fertile region won by the United States in the Treaty of Paris were doomed to live in fear of the Indians while hacking out an existence as dirt-poor subsistence farmers. By 1794 many on the frontier had lost confidence in Washington. But their disaffection was not due solely to the failure to secure the frontier in trans-Appalachia. They hated the administration's 1791 excise tax on whiskey, a levy that fell hardest on them. By the time Jefferson came home, many small back-country farmers were convinced that Washington's government was dominated by wealthy northeastern merchants and speculators who were indifferent to the plight of those who lived on the frontier.

Jefferson did not blame Washington for having failed to resolve the western problem. He knew that no one was more troubled than the president by the western quandary; twice already Washington had resorted to force, with no success. In 1791, and again the following year, the president had dispatched armies to deal with the Native Americans. Both armies suffered mortifying defeats, but Jefferson did not condemn Washington for their failures. A third army, this under the command of General Anthony Wayne, formerly of the Continental army, was being raised in 1794. Jefferson was not a member of the cabinet when the decision was made to dispatch Wayne with yet another army, but he would not have objected.

The excise on whiskey, however, was another matter. After Hamilton urged its adoption in 1791, Jefferson had warned the president that the levy was discriminatory and would cause trouble. Not only would it wipe out all profits that farmers might realize from the sale of their corn whiskey, it was also an unfair tax in that large commercial distillers—who soon included Washington himself—were assessed a lower rate per gallon than were farmers who made whiskey in their small backyard stills. Furthermore, Jefferson as much as told Washington that small farmers would understand that the real beneficiaries of the duty would be wealthy easterners who owned the federal securities sold to pay for funding and assumption. Jefferson correctly saw Hamilton's plan as, at least in part, a scheme for transferring wealth from the least to the most affluent in America, and he cautioned Washington that Hamilton's "odious" plan would produce "clamour [and] evasion." Its collection, he added, would require "arbitrary and vexatious means," including possibly making "war on our own citizens." Five state legislatures told Congress more or less the same thing, and some congressmen predicted that any attempt to collect the duty would result in "war and bloodshed." Washington was unmoved. The whiskey tax became law.[12]

The naysayers were prescient. Trouble flared immediately. Federal revenue agents faced widespread resistance, including violence in the South, western Pennsylvania, and the Kentucky territory. Rumors buzzed in the hollows of Pennsylvania that Hamilton hoped the tax would provoke defiance—a notion that not a few historians subsequently believed to be true—so that the federal government could demonstrate its might and its overarching superiority by crushing the insurgents. Washington initially temporized. He persuaded Congress to lower the duty on whiskey and sent emissaries to the frontier both to reason with the farmers and to cajole them. The West cooled down for a spell, but by 1794 it was again aflame. No revenue was collected in western Pennsylvania during the twelve months prior to mid-1794, leading Hamilton and Henry Knox, the secretary of war, to implore the president to suppress the dissidents. Raise and dispatch an army of 12,000 men to enforce the law, they counseled. Arguing that the farmers were engaged in a "dark conspiracy" that aimed at nothing less that forcing the United States into war with Great Britain, Hamilton said the rebellion must be crushed in order to save the "very existence" of the national government. As usual, he won over Washington. Nine months after Jefferson's departure from the cabinet, the president issued a proclamation that bore an uncanny resemblance to George III's 1775 declaration that the colonists were rebels who must be brought to heel through the use of force. His order additionally called for raising an army of 12,950 men. He appointed Henry Lee, formerly a Continental army cavalry officer, to command the force.[13]

Washington was too shrewd—and too committed to preserving his exalted standing—to accompany the army on its march across Pennsylvania. However, Hamilton dug out his old uniform and rode west with the soldiery in October, pausing now and then to unsparingly flay the foes of the tax as "madmen" and "wicked insurgents" who must be "skewered, shot, or hanged." If Hamilton thought he would win laurels from this enterprise, he was mistaken. Indeed, in the end even he considered the campaign an embarrassing fiasco. The rebel farmers disappeared into the hills and forests. Meanwhile, the poorly supplied troops endured hunger and cold, and for all their hardships rounded up only twenty "traitors." Those gaunt victims faced appalling suffering, as they were made to walk in the gloom of winter from western Pennsylvania to Philadelphia to face trial. Only two were convicted. Washington, bent on damage control, pardoned both.[14]

Jefferson was appalled, as much by Washington's use of force against the citizenry as by the seeming ease with which Hamilton had coaxed him into taking such an approach. Jefferson may even have reflected on Monroe's 1787 cautionary prophecy that as Washington aged he would be susceptible to manipulation by malefactors in his midst. Jefferson said nothing publicly, though in private he labeled Washington's dispatch of a huge army "against people at their ploughs" to have been "an inexcusable aggression." He knew that the president had been persuaded to take the step by those in his circle who were bent on "strengthening government and increasing the public debt." He thought Washington's portrayal of a dangerous and widespread insurrection in western Pennsylvania was untrue. The president might as well have offered "shreds of stuff from Aesop's fables and Tom Thumb," he said. The only good thing about the affair, Jefferson added, was that Hamilton had pompously gone to battle an "insurrection" that "was announced and proclaimed and armed against, and marched against, but could never be found."[15]

Shortly after the farmers were paraded under guard to and through the capital, Washington denounced the Democratic-Republican Societies, remarks that further disillusioned Jefferson. The Democratic-Republican Societies had sprung into being during 1793, and before the year ended some fifty chapters were scattered through several states. Hamilton thought Edmond Genêt was responsible for their creation, but that was untrue. Britain's entrance into the war against France was the spark that brought the societies into being among Americans who hated England and wanted the French Revolution to succeed. Those drawn to the societies were inspired by France's embrace of the egalitarian and natural rights principles that had been part and parcel of the American Revolution, but they were additionally enthralled by France's democracy, which many believed would be the catalyst for the "regeneration" of society within the United States. In many cases, the outlook of those who joined a Democratic-Republican chapter had been shaped by reading Paine's *Rights of Man*. Most longed for the democratization of American politics, and most were also alarmed by the growing reach and power of the national government, including what many thought were the monarchical overtones of Washington's presidency. Society members wore red, white, and blue cockades in imitation of the revolutionaries in France, addressed one another as "fellow citizen" rather than with the class-imbued "sir," and not infrequently thought of themselves as adherents of the nascent Republican Party. Society orators and publications levied withering attacks on Washington and the policies of his administration.[16]

Federalists had assailed the Democratic-Republican Societies from the outset, branding them "Jacobin Clubs" financed by "French gold" and characterizing the local chapters as secret bodies. None of the charges were true. Calling the Whiskey Rebellion "the first *fruits* of [the Society's] blessed *harvest*," Federalists also contended that the movement was responsible for the farmers' insurgency.[17] Though this charge was a fabrication, Washington was convinced of its truthfulness, and it was that belief that led him to publicly deprecate the Societies. Speaking out in November 1794, what the president said sounded remarkably similar to what had been promulgated by Federalist writers. Washington contended that the Societies' "arts of delusion" had "fomented" the Whiskey Rebellion. Dangerous "combinations of men," the president added, had "disseminated . . . suspicions [and] jealousies," embittering and arousing previously peaceful citizens to break the law and defy "the whole Government."[18]

Jefferson was outraged by the president's remarks. Washington had assailed "the freedom of discussion, the freedom of writing, printing, and publication," he said privately. The "incredible fact," said Jefferson in a hyperbolic statement of his own, was that Washington had more "boldly" assailed "freedom of association, of conversation, and of the press" than had England's repressive government under Pitt the Elder. Both Jefferson and Madison had come to believe that Washington was under the thumb of Hamilton, whom Jefferson characterized as the "servile copyist of Mr. Pitt." For the first time, too, both now concluded that Washington was not above partisan politics, as he had steadfastly postured. He was a Federalist in fact if not in name. Later, Jefferson said that once he had left the cabinet, "the federalists got unchecked hold of Genl. Washington." However, unlike Paine, who had been driven by sizzling rage when he wrote his public letter to the president, Jefferson still respected Washington. He was aware of the pressures that Washington faced and grateful that the president had accepted a second term, which he presumably had not wanted. Disappointment, not enmity, shaped Jefferson's feelings, and he held to the hope that Washington would step down at the end of his second term. Jefferson was convinced that in time the Republican Party would be the majority party. The Federalist "tide . . . is unquestionably strong but it will turn," he said, and he advised a follower: "Hold on then like a good and faithful seaman till our brother-sailors can rouse from their intoxication and right the vessel." What he meant was that when Washington retired, or once the citizenry no longer was misled by its adulation of the president, the

Federalist Party was doomed. Jefferson was convinced that the Federalists' commitment to a powerful government and growing indebtedness, and their propensity for violence and repression, were at variance with American traditions and the essence of the American Revolution. As black as things looked, he told Monroe in the spring of 1795, "the public sense is coming right."[19]

Early in Jefferson's second year at home, Hamilton left the cabinet and returned to Manhattan to practice law. Jefferson did not comment on his departure. His correspondence during that year mostly concerned farming. He went on about fertilizers, plows, breeds of livestock, and crop rotation. He confessed that he was "more interested and engrossed" than ever by "the concerns of a farmer," and lamented the "useless waste of time" that he had once devoted to other pursuits, implying even that the "public gridiron" had been among his misplaced activities.[20] It was not a long-lived feeling.

Washington had proclaimed a Thanksgiving Day in February 1795 to honor both the suppression of the whiskey rebels and a pivotal victory won by General Wayne's army. So complete was Wayne's conquest in the one-hour Battle of Fallen Timbers in August 1794 that Indian resistance in the Ohio Country was broken. The triumph of arms would be a crucial step in opening the region to settlement and reducing the likelihood that western settlers might turn away from the United States and into the arms of Spain. Before the decade ended, the population of the Ohio territory would reach forty-five thousand, more people than had inhabited many of the colonies in 1776.[21] Washington's jubilation lasted only for a moment. He soon faced a new problem. John Jay's treaty with Britain reached his desk in March 1795.

Jay had departed for London shortly before Monroe sailed for Paris, and he had spent more than half a year negotiating what would be popularly known as the Jay Treaty. Washington despaired when he read the text of the accord. Aside from agreeing to pay compensation for damages inflicted on American shipping since 1793, Britain conceded nothing that it had not already agreed to in the treaty ending the Revolutionary War, including the removal of its army from United States soil. In addition, the treaty not only placed restrictions on America's European trade, but its definition of "contraband" would acutely limit the goods that America as a neutral nation could carry.[22] It was not a good treaty, but as the president feared that war with Britain would be the result of spurning it, he opted to submit the Jay Treaty to the Senate for ratification. Washington summoned Congress to a special session in June. In the meantime, he sequestered the treaty, hoping that when it was released, the Senate would ratify it quickly before critics filled the press with hostile essays. It was a savvy stroke by a seasoned politician. The Senate rapidly ratified the treaty in a vote along party and sectional lines. All twenty Federalists voted for ratification, all ten Republicans against; eighteen of the twenty who supported the treaty were northerners and seven of the ten who voted against it were southerners.

Washington next told the public that he was going to Mount Vernon, where he would deliberate over signing the treaty, all the while listening to "dispassionate" advisors. Six or so weeks elapsed before the president acted, an interval in which Washington listened only to Hamilton. In fact, during his supposedly methodical contemplation, the president encouraged Hamilton to write newspaper essays in defense of the treaty, pieces that would prepare the public for his signature. Hamilton obliged, grinding out twenty-eight installments in what he called "The Defence." Soon after Hamilton's tracts began rolling off the press, Washington signed Jay's treaty.[23]

Hamilton's essays on the treaty were among the first to appear, but they were hardly the last. Nothing since Hamilton's economic program five years earlier had caused a stir to equal the Jay Treaty. It drove partisan warfare to a new level and was crucial in the formation of true political parties, as both Federalists and Republicans fashioned the machinery necessary for running candidates and winning elections. The treaty was savaged by the Republican press. Jay fared even worse. He was repeatedly portrayed as either incompetent or a British lackey. (Jay himself remarked that he could have walked across the country at night in the illumination cast by his burning effigies.) Hamilton fought back, speaking and writing on behalf of the treaty. Once, while defending the unpopular accord before a rowdy gathering of some five hundred New Yorkers, Hamilton was hooted, jeered, and struck in the head by a rock thrown from the crowd.[24]

Jefferson claimed that "no man in the US," with the exception of Hamilton, thought it a good treaty. He even tipped his hat to Hamilton's persuasive and polemical skills. "Hamilton is really a colossus to the antirepublican party. Without numbers, he is an host within himself." It was not in Jefferson's makeup to answer Hamilton. Instead, he tried in vain to persuade Madison to take up his pen. He needed someone with the talent of Paine. Whether or not Jefferson knew it, Paine had written an anonymous piece on the treaty that appeared in the *Philadelphia Aurora* on very nearly the day Washington revealed its contents. Obviously, Paine had written his essay months earlier when he could have had no knowledge of the actual accord. His piece bore the stamp of something the French government might have paid him to write in hopes of covering all bases should Jay "do anything reprehensible." With clairvoyance, Paine predicted the Federalists—taking a line from Monroe, he, too, called them "the British party in America"—would support any treaty that Jay negotiated, but that the American people would not. Through thick and thin, Americans would remain attached to France. "All the American hearts will be French," was how he put it.[25]

Jefferson never said anything along those lines, but he saw a rainbow in the imbroglio over the treaty. The "public pulse," he said, had not "beat so full and in such universal unison on any subject since the declaration of Independence." By supporting a dreadful and unpopular treaty, the Federalists had "got themselves into a defile" that would jolt the party with "the most radical shock."[26]

In the meantime, more disturbing news reached Philadelphia. By early July, three weeks before Washington signed the treaty, word abounded that Great Britain was once again plundering American shipping bound for French ports. It had been going on for a spell. Washington knew in April—some sixty days before the Senate took up the treaty—that Britain had taken its first prize. Jefferson thought Washington's action in signing the treaty in the face of British pillaging was "incomprehensible," even more so as the president was "the only honest man who has assented to" the accord. Soon, word reached Monticello that was still more bewildering. Washington had in effect fired Secretary of State Randolph, Jefferson's successor and fellow Virginian. In August, two other cabinet members, Timothy Pickering and Oliver Wolcott—the successors of Knox and Hamilton, a duo that historian William Hogeland piquantly characterized as "third-string functionaries of high federalism"—had confronted Washington with a questionable document that insinuated Randolph had sought to extort money from France and might have passed along state secrets to the French minister in Philadelphia.

Although Randolph had served as a loyal cabinet officer for six years, never betraying the slightest hint of impropriety, Washington immediately embraced the uncertain and unauthenticated allegation that his secretary of state had acted treasonously. In retrospect, Randolph appears to have been the victim of devious—and vengeful—cabinet officials bent on ousting a colleague who had opposed Hamilton's bank and had neither wholeheartedly supported using force against the whiskey rebels nor of sending Jay to London. Washington named Pickering as his new secretary of state, a man some thought even more Hamiltonian than Hamilton. The president appointed James McHenry, who had been close to Hamilton since their days together as aides to Washington during the war, to replace Pickering as secretary of war. Together with Treasury Secretary Wolcott, who had served as comptroller under Hamilton, Washington's cabinet was now thoroughly dominated by extreme Federalists who were unswervingly loyal to Hamilton.[27]

Less than a year later, the last official in an important post who was out of step with the Hamiltonians was dealt with. That official was James Monroe.

* * *

Monroe had gone to Paris fully aware that he would face trials and tribulations. He doubtless thought it inevitable that he would have to make painful choices in complying with the president's wishes. He knew, too, that the French would present difficulties. He sailed during the aftermath of the Genêt affair and at a time when France, fighting for its life, was seizing American grain shipments bound for enemy ports. Monroe was charged with seeking an end to the provocations and securing indemnification for the losses already suffered by American merchants. Furthermore, there was a very real potential that Jay's mission to London might stir adverse repercussions in Paris.

From the start, Washington was uncomfortable with Monroe's performance. The minister's speech to the National Convention, ringing with elation at French military victories and fervent for restoring and sealing the bond between France and the United States, had not been well received by the president. Washington, through Randolph, reprimanded Monroe for not having insisted on a private reception where he could have made innocuous remarks "so framed, as to leave heart-burning no where." Monroe's "extreme glow" toward France, the president continued, was unworthy of the representative of a neutral nation, and it had provoked displeasure among France's enemies, including in London. (Washington showed a different face to John Jay, telling him that while Monroe had "stepped beyond the true line," his comments might prove useful by arousing sufficient fear in London of an American rapprochement with France that the treaty negotiations with Great Britain would be brought to "a happy & speedy result.")

Monroe's initial speech was not the only instance in which he displayed diplomatic inexperience. In his first discussions regarding French restrictions on America's trade, Monroe bizarrely remarked that if France indeed benefited from preying on American commerce, the American government and its citizenry would understand and endure the consequences "not only . . . with patience but with pleasure." (Gouverneur Morris, aware of Monroe's sympathy for the French Revolution, pitched in by telling Washington that it was fortunate his successor had not arrived at the height of the Terror, for he doubtless "would have been a little too well" disposed toward Robespierre and his bloody confederates.)[28]

Monroe had been in Paris for six months before the president's rebuke reached him. At the same moment, he heard from Randolph—in his last weeks as secretary of state—who wrote privately to mollify Monroe. Indeed, what Randolph said could not have been more dissimilar to the president's words. Randolph stressed the "importance of the friendship of the French republic" and urged Monroe to "Cultivate it with zeal." Randolph went on to say that he did not prefer "a connection with Great Britain" and objected to any steps that would weaken "our old attachment to France."[29] Unseasoned and alone, Monroe may have thought that he had a friend in Randolph, someone with whom he could be quite candid.

Nevertheless, Monroe worried that assorted observations in his earlier reports would further irritate Washington. For instance, he had expressed embarrassment at having to dwell on France's obstruction of American trade, even suggesting that the "most safe and sound policy" was not to raise the matter. Monroe had also led authorities in Paris to believe that the United States might loan France several million dollars—though nothing along those lines had been mentioned to him by the administration—and he had continued to speak of America's "attachment" to France's welfare and its "solicitude for their [military] success." In November, he had written an exultant letter to Washington about "the storm that is gathering" within England as a result of French victories. He was even more candid in his correspondence with the secretary of state, unaware that Randolph no longer occupied the post. Monroe had not hidden his jubilation that French military success would likely "excite disturbances" in England. He proposed that the United States could assure the ruin of that "proud & insolent nation" by launching military attacks on England's western posts and its colonies in Canada and Bermuda. These strikes would be "decisive," he said, adding that "Britain is certainly not in a condition to embark in a war against us." Monroe additionally insisted that a "strong union" with France was crucial for the United States, especially as "we are not cordial with England."

In December 1794, four months after his arrival in Paris, the French confronted Monroe with newspaper reports that Jay had been sent to conclude a commercial pact with England. Unbeknownst to Monroe, who had been kept in the dark with regard to Jay's instructions, the minister insisted to French officials that the press stories were untrue. With "unshaken confidence in the integrity of the President," as he put it, Monroe pledged to French officials that Washington would never have directed Jay to do such a thing that would "stain our national character" and "weaken our connection with France." Those in the Federalist administration in Philadelphia must have thought that Citizen Monroe was the mirror image of Citizen Genêt. Whereas that French envoy had done everything within his power to steer the United States away from its policy of neutrality, Washington and his advisors may have wondered if Monroe was bent on demonstrating to France that in reality the United States was not neutral, but a crypto-ally.[30]

Taken to task once again, Monroe thereafter tempered his reports. However, he was less chary in his private correspondence, especially once the terms of the Jay Treaty were known. Among other things, Monroe blasted away at the treaty and the mischief it was causing in Paris. He made clear that outraged French officials, fearful that the United States was reuniting with its former mother country, had retaliated by refusing to carry through with commercial concessions that they had been close to accepting. The Jay Treaty, he went on, might even provoke France to declare war on the United States, an eventuality that would force America into Britain's arms and prepare the way for aristocratic rule in what once had been Revolutionary America. He continued to advocate attacks on the British and reiterated that the best interests of the United States would be served by maintaining close ties with France. He spoke of the sad state of affairs in America, an allusion to both the crushing of the whiskey rebels and the assault on the Democratic-Republican Societies, and expressed hope that Jefferson would be elected president in 1796. He waxed on about the pro–French Revolution sympathies of virtually all Americans living in Paris, noting that at the latest Independence Day party at his residence many toasts had been raised to the "gallant armies of France" and perpetuation of close Franco-American ties. Despite Jefferson's repeated misfortunes with his private utterances, Monroe expected what he wrote in his private correspondence to remain private. But that is not always the way of the world. Somehow, some of his messages found their way into the hands of high administrative officials.[31]

The best diplomats that America had sent abroad since 1776 had on occasion blundered because of inexperience. Monroe was not the most adroit of the bunch, and his callowness led him to err often and badly. At times, circumspection seemed to him an unknown art, as he appeared to be intrinsically incapable of separating his partisan desires from his diplomatic responsibilities. Naïveté aside, the heart of Monroe's problem stemmed from his unwavering hope that the French Revolution would succeed, spreading change across Europe and bolstering those in America who struggled against all the Federalist Party stood for. But some of Monroe's slips came about as a result of his mistaken belief that the thinking of Secretary of State Randolph, with whom he had spoken at length before sailing, tallied with that of the president. In actuality, whereas Monroe and Randolph more or less thought alike, Washington—while favoring neutrality above all else—leaned as Hamilton did, and possibly because of Hamilton, more toward Britain than toward France. Robert R. Livingston was aware of that when he declined the offer to go to Paris, and in effect advised Monroe to think twice before accepting the assignment. Monroe, who was heavily influenced by the thinking of Jefferson and Madison, both of whom only later came to a better understanding of the president's mind-set, embarked on his mission under a cloud of delusion.

Though Monroe often erred, he was not a disaster. Quite in contrast to Gouverneur Morris, Monroe developed a harmonious relationship with French officials, who appeared to genuinely like him. America was still only a minor player on the world stage, and neither Monroe nor any other American envoy could have moved mountains. Nevertheless, during his first eighteen months in Paris, relations improved between the two countries, highlighted by France's 1794 revocation of its restrictions on American grain shipments to enemy ports.

But whatever progress Monroe thought he was making was stopped in its tracks by the Jay Treaty. When Monroe at last saw the terms of the accord, he knew immediately that what Jay had agreed to—and what Washington and the Senate had concurred in—would arouse profound indignation in Paris. Jay had acquiesced to British maritime law on the matter of the wartime commerce of neutrals, which meant that his treaty "was helpful to England and harmful to France, our ally," as Monroe put it. He correctly anticipated France's response that the Jay Treaty was "an outright betrayal of the . . . alliance." French officials informed Monroe that the treaty had shattered the "good harmony that should exist between old allies." As the pact was but the latest in a series of "lapses of a friend," the French foreign minister informed Monroe that his government "considered the alliance between us as ceasing to exist."[32]

No one was more disappointed than Monroe by this dark turn in Franco-American relations. As Jefferson had come to see Washington in a different light during 1794 and 1795, the Jay Treaty—together possibly with the contents of Paine's *Letter to Washington*—opened Monroe's eyes. "I think myself ill treated" by Washington, he confided to a friend, for he now believed that the president's "many professions of . . . attachment to French revolution," even to genuine American neutrality, had never been true.[33]

Monroe stayed on, however, happy to be living in Paris and taking pride in his work. After initially residing in the huge country mansion that Morris had occupied, the Monroes—with Paine in tow—had moved to a small, but elegant, one-story house on the hilly north side of the city. Beginning what was to be their lifelong taste for French furniture and decorative arts, the couple lovingly filled their home with Louis XIV pieces and luxuriated in the carefully maintained formal gardens. They sent Eliza to a fashionable girls' school and before long she and her parents spoke French so fluently that Monroe disposed of a translator. The family entertained frequently, hosting French officials, numerous English and Americans living in Paris, several friends that Jefferson had made during the previous decade, and even Irish revolutionaries who were in town lobbying France to invade their island and set it free from English domination. (Monroe coached them on what approach to take and which officials to see.) Wolfe Tone, a leader in the Catholic emancipation movement, was among the Irish whom Monroe invited to the embassy. As Tone had just come from a stay in the United States, Monroe questioned him at length about Washington and his cabinet, both of which, according to Tone, were viewed by the citizenry as "mere puppets, danced by Mr. Hamilton." Monroe was not lumped in that group, Tone added. Indeed, insiders thought that Hamilton and the cabinet hoped to make Monroe's "situation unpleasant." "No," Monroe responded. They hope to "cut my throat."[34]

Monroe found that one of the satisfactions provided by his job was in helping the distraught. He succeeded in winning the freedom of all the Americans who were incarcerated in France. He also worked diligently to set free Adrienne Lafayette, the wife of the general, who had been arrested and released in 1792 and arrested again during the Terror. Her stay in a Paris prison was twice the length of Paine's, and while she was confined, her mother and grandmother, who were fellow inmates, were guillotined. Monroe's efforts to free her were at first met with intransigence, but in the spring of 1795 she was released. As with Paine, her health had also suffered given the prison conditions. The Monroes took her in and nursed her, and gave her financial assistance when she was well. Monroe secured a passport for her, and as soon as her health permitted, she left the country to join her husband in an Austrian prison. Once in Austria, she wrote to Monroe to thank him for "having given me the sweetest taste of happiness . . . so dear and sacred to me—which is also to savor the feeling of gratitude I owe you, and that I shall retain all my life."[35]

Washington was not happy to learn of Monroe's association with Irish rebels, one of whom had been convicted of sedition in England, and in private he speculated as to whether Monroe's conduct was "part of a premeditated system to embarrass" the English government.[36] But he did not raise the issue with Monroe and never questioned his minister about having taken in Paine, who also had been convicted in England of sedition. But if Washington displayed restraint, his cabinet—as Monroe had surmised and confided to Wolfe Tone, and as Jefferson had warned when the appointment was offered to his young friend—had their knives out for him, and sought to have him recalled. Yet, as Oliver Wolcott acknowledged, while Monroe had at times stumbled, there was no "demonstrable" reason for his recall. He had done nothing that seriously injured the interests of the United States, though perhaps he had too exuberantly complied with his orders to do nothing that would alienate France, "our first and natural ally" in the event "of war with any nation."

Still, those around the president wanted Monroe out of Paris. In a note to Hamilton, Wolcott let slip the real reason: "we must stop the channels by which foreign poison is introduced into our Country or suffer the [Federalist] government to be overturned."[37] In his private correspondence—some of which had fallen into the hands of cabinet members—Monroe had communicated France's side of the story at every turn, information that, suggested Wolcott, could be used by the Republicans. In a worst-case scenario, what Monroe was imparting might be wielded to impede Federalist foreign policy or to aid Republicans in the coming elections in 1796. In short, the impetus for ousting Monroe had more to do with domestic politics than with American diplomacy.

The acerbic Timothy Pickering, the new secretary of state, directed his mean tongue toward Monroe in several letters. (Monroe compared the timbre of Pickering's correspondence to what might be heard in the orders "from an overseer to the foreman of his gang.")[38] Throughout late 1795 and into the next year, Pickering and Wolcott combed through Monroe's reports, searching for any nugget that might persuade the president to recall him. They ran to Washington—and to Hamilton, who stood ready to provide guidance—with each supposedly incriminating morsel that was uncovered. The president was not swayed. Washington may not have always been entirely happy with Monroe, but he thought him "a man of honour" and wanted no part of a witch hunt against him. But it may have been Hamilton's counsel that stayed the president's hand, as he advised that there were "weighty reasons against" recalling Monroe, chiefly that it would provoke a political firestorm.[39]

If restraint characterized the president's conduct, the break the conspirators awaited finally came when France terminated its alliance with the United States and resumed raiding American vessels. Washington needed no coaching to discern the gravity of the situation. He himself said: "These are serious things; they may be productive of serious consequences; and therefore require very serious & cool deliberation." Apparently on his own, the president decided that it might be best to send a new minister to France, one who would be seen in Paris as the personal representative of the chief executive, a step that might possibly open the door to fruitful negotiations. The always-helpful Hamilton had a candidate in mind. He suggested Charles Cotesworth Pinckney, a South Carolina Federalist and a former general in the Continental army. "What shall be done with Mr. M," the president asked. The answer was clear: Monroe was to be recalled.[40]

Whatever Washington's true feelings, Pickering told Monroe that the president had acted because of his "uneasiness & dissatisfaction" with his minister's performance.[41] Though hardly surprised, Monroe was beside himself with fury at this "unprecedented outrage." He expected the public to interpret his recall as a presidential "censure." A disgrace of that magnitude, together with the scorn certain to follow from being seen as having lost Washington's confidence, could be politically ruinous. Despite the tumult within him, Monroe at first said that he yet felt "some tenderness towards General Washington," certain that the president had been manipulated with incredible virtuosity by his cabinet. The actions of Washington's advisors, he added, bore the "marks equally [of] the violence" of the extreme Federalist mentality and their "desperation" in the face of the approaching elections of 1796.

Monroe's tender feelings toward Washington were not evident, however, in a rage-filled letter that he immediately drafted to Pickering. After first demanding to know what "pernicious error" on his part had accounted for the president's action, Monroe hit his stride. He had done nothing wrong. Washington had acted on trumped-up charges that were merely a "pretext" for his starkly political step. The president's partisanship in this matter "corresponds with the general political conduct of the administration." Despite the pretense of being above politics, Washington was a Federalist president, and in this instance he had "abuse[d] the trust reposed in him."[42] Monroe wrote the letter just days after an abbreviated version of Paine's Letter to Washington hit the streets in Philadelphia. After thirty months of serving Washington in Paris, Monroe had reached largely the same conclusions about the president as had Paine and Jefferson. Scant weeks before, Monroe had received a letter from Monticello that portrayed Washington as a Federalist and lamented the public's blindness in supporting "his judgment against their own." But Jefferson had counseled that his fellow Republicans must not reproach the revered president. To do so would be counterproductive. Besides, he soon would be gone. Jefferson was sure that Washington would step down at the conclusion of his second term.[43] Paine, a hot mass of feelings, had aired his bitter loathing in public. Jefferson had not. Wisely, Monroe waited before sending his furious letter to Pickering. On reflection, he chose to leave it in his desk.

Long before Monroe learned that he had been recalled, Paine had moved out of the minister's home. He left in the spring of 1796, not without a shove from Monroe, who had learned of Paine's private letter to Washington and of his plans to "compromit [sic] me" by publishing a "virulent" attack on the president. Monroe simply said that Paine had departed because he knew "it was inconvenient for me to keep him longer in my family" given his wish "to treat on our politicks." Paine first moved to Versailles, where he lived throughout that summer as the guest of an English banker who had renounced his aristo-cratic title and settled in France. After a time, he moved to a country home outside Paris that had been rented by Fulwar Skipwith, the American consul general and member of a Virginia family with close ties to Jefferson. Paine was not there long before he moved again, this time to a suburb six miles from downtown Paris, where he remained for another several months.[44]

When Paine learned of Monroe's recall, he decided to return with him to America. He was eager to turn loose his pen against the Federalists and to defend Monroe. Paine proclaimed that America was "the country of my heart," though at the same moment he confessed that he "should blush to call myself a citizen of America." Thanks to Washington's "malignant and blundering" presidency, "its character . . . is sunk" among the enlightened throughout Europe. France, he added, was "enraged at [America's] ingrati-tude, and sly treachery!" Paine may have been dispirited toward America, but he had nowhere else to turn. Going back to England was out of the question, as was moving to almost anyplace on the continent, nearly all of which was at war with France. He could remain in France, but he was thoroughly disen-chanted with his adopted country, calling it "the promised land but not the land of promise." He had experienced "a thousand dangers" in France, he said, and feared that the future might be just as precarious. He was at last ready to depart France and, by default, sail for America. However, crossing with Paine was not what Monroe wanted. Alighting in America arm in arm with Paine might complete the ruin of Monroe's political career, if indeed it had any life after the humiliation of being recalled by Washington. In gentle terms, Monroe made clear that they must sail on separate vessels, and Paine understood.[45]

In March 1797, ten years after he had sailed from the United States to France, Paine traveled to Le Havre-de-Grâce to book his return passage. But fear got the best of him, and with good reason. With entire squadrons of British warships prowling the Atlantic and stopping and searching American ships, an ocean crossing was more risky than ever.[46] In April, he returned to Paris and moved in with the family of Nicolas de Bonneville, an old friend with whom Paine—along with Brissot and Condorcet—had started the Republican Club in the aftermath of the king's flight six years earlier. A printer and bookstore owner who was twenty-three years younger than Paine and who harbored similar religious and republican views, Bonneville in 1792 had published Paine's letter to the people of France, and two years later he issued a French edition of *The Age of Reason*. Bonneville and his wife, Margue-rite, and their three sons lived near the center of Paris in a two-story house that included a print shop on the ground floor and what must have been congested living quarters above. They took in Paine for what was supposed to be a few days. He stayed for five years. The Bonnevilles seem not to have minded. Filled with admiration for their guest, they provided him with a study and bedroom.

Paine turned sixty about the time that he moved in with the Bonnevilles. At this point in his life, Paine might have been drinking heavily, as around this time an acquaintance said that he "drinks like a fish." That Paine was a drinker is undeniable, but whether he was an alcoholic, as many contemporaries alleged, is uncertain. Most who characterized him as an alcoholic were political foes. With the exception of Joel Barlow, virtually no friend or admirer said any such thing until the last three or four years of Paine's life. Furthermore, some rumors about his drinking were surely exaggerated or based on hearsay. For instance, tales had long circulated that Paine could write only if he was intoxicated. John Adams, who knew next to nothing of Paine's private side, bought into the speculation and announced that "Tom Paine could never write without . . . Alcohol, Rum, or Brandy, in his Stomach."[47] It was a regrettable comment that influenced both popular and scholarly images of Paine. In fact, Paine appears to have mostly written during daytime hours, after which he laid aside his pen and relaxed, including in the alehouse. But when rushing to get out a piece, as when he hurried to answer Edmund Burke, Paine sequestered himself and spent long, frenetic, and solitary hours at his desk, drinking little, if at all. It is not inconceivable that Paine was a functioning alcoholic. What seems beyond dispute is that in times of great stress he suffered bouts of depression, desolate stretches brought on by the loss of jobs, penury, slights by those who saw him as a social inferior, the dangers inherent in revolutionary politics, and the pressures that are often the handmaiden of writers. It might have been that when he was most miserable, he sought solace in the bottle. Indeed, Paine admitted as much, once confiding to his closest friend that "sometimes, borne down by public and private affliction," he was "driven to excesses."[48]

If Paine was in the grip of alcoholism in the late 1790s, he somehow managed not to be a burden to the Bonnevilles. He rose late in the morning, read the newspapers, went for a walk, and napped for up to three hours before taking his late-afternoon meal. According to Madame Bonneville, Paine for the most part stayed inside her dwelling throughout each day. He passed some days in writing, others in tinkering with a "mechanical invention," and on many days patiently receiving visitors. But if they made "mere chit-chat," Paine retired to another room, "leaving them to entertain themselves." He went out frequently in the evenings, visiting friends such as Barlow or seeking an outlet at the Irish Coffeehouse, a gathering place for those who spoke English.[49]

During the five years following the completion of *The Age of Reason* and *Letter to Washington*, Paine published less than he had in any other comparable period after 1775. However, he still had one important essay left in him, a piece that he titled *Agrarian Justice*. It was published near the beginning of 1796, about fifteen months before he settled in with the Bonnevilles. Paine drafted the tract in a mood of pervasive disillusionment with the French Revolution. Not only was misery widespread in France after the fall of the monarchy and aristocracy, but the recent abandonment of universal manhood suffrage jeopardized those reforms already accomplished. Nor was it merely the French Revolution that had gone off the tracks. The English people had never risen up against their oppressors, and might never do so. Then there was America. Paine was apprehensive that the American Revolution, the one successful model for others, was fatally threatened by a strong conservative reaction. Probably from his conversations with Monroe, Paine had come to believe that a coterie of conservatives had secured a Constitution that impeded the popular sovereignty many Americans had fought to secure in the long Revolutionary War. What was more, he understood that artful, well-organized financiers had found ways—and would always find the means—to sway public officials to advance their interests at the expense of the majority of the citizenry. Some in the United States had already come to the same conclusion. Philip Freneau's *National Gazette* and other Republican journals had been arguing for some time that the former emphasis on laying all blame on monarchies and aristocracies was obsolete. Even in a republic, they insisted, the "corrupt influence" of special interests could succeed in bringing about "a real domination" by "the few" that would frustrate "the will of society."[50] The tangled aftermath of the two great revolutions of which Paine had been a part was the catalyzing agent for his last truly significant essay.

Paine never repudiated revolution. In fact, he believed the program he outlined in *Agrarian Justice* was crucial in order to "give perfection to the Revolution of France." In many respects, though, it was England that was on his mind. Where he had once urged revolutionary changes in England, he now proposed nonrevolutionary reforms aimed at instituting social and economic benefits for the downtrodden. In *Rights of Man*, Paine had touched on aids that resembled what future generations would come to call the "welfare state." In *Agrarian Justice*, he rounded out his thinking. Paine, like Freneau and others in America, had come to see that even if kings were driven from their thrones and titled nobilities were stripped of their privileges, societies would inevitably remain divided between the haves and the have-nots, or what he called the "extremes of affluence and want." Inevitably, he said, some in every society would be "more affluent" and some "more wretched." Hence, instead of sounding the trumpet once again against autocratic monarchies, Paine focused on the causes of poverty and its amelioration. He did not blame poverty on kingship and he took pains to assert that indigence was not due to individual failure. Rather, Paine asserted that the impoverished class was trapped in a self-perpetuating state. Once a person was enmeshed in poverty, the condition was nearly inescapable, and the penurious nearly always passed along an even worse state of wretchedness to their descendants. "The great mass of the poor," wrote Paine, "are become an hereditary race, and it is next to impossible for them to get out of that state of themselves." It is "necessary that a revolution should be made"—he clung tenaciously to the term "revolution"—so that those on the bottom rung could have an opportunity to escape hopeless misery.

In both *Common Sense* and *Rights of Man*, Paine had argued that substituting republicanism for monarchy and nobility would pave the road to widespread prosperity and happiness. He never abandoned the notion that republicanism was superior to the royal governance that had prevailed before 1776 and which yet persisted in England and throughout Europe. But in *Agrarian Justice* his emphasis took a dramatic turn. Whereas previously he had equated oppression with governmental tyranny, he now emphasized that maldistribution of wealth was as merciless as political despotism, possibly more so. He called income inequality intolerable, writing that it was "unjust that some should enjoy abundance while others are impoverished." He had come to believe that if the downtrodden were to have any chance of escaping the bequeathed hopelessness in which they were ensnared, they required help from those who flourished. Paine was not a leveler, and he did not advocate an equal distribution of wealth, but the refinement he now urged was for the government to lend a helping hand to extricate the bulk of society from its crippling poverty.

Envisioning something akin to Franklin Roosevelt's New Deal make-work programs, Paine proposed "employment buildings." These were to be erected by the government and were to provide temporary jobs, food, and comfortable lodgings for those who could not find work. In addition, every person, rich or poor, was to receive from the government a stipend of fifteen pounds on their twenty-first birthday, an amount that was close to the annual income of most English craftsmen. On turning fifty, every person was to begin drawing an annual pension of ten pounds. Revenue for the employment projects, public welfare, and social security would come from an inheritance tax, the beauty of which was that it would not diminish "the property of any of the present [living] possessors." It was a plan, wrote Paine, that "will benefit all, without injuring any."

Paine, of course, knew that without universal manhood suffrage there was no chance that these reforms could be achieved, and he also understood that enfranchising the poorest in society would be crucial for sustaining such improvements. Once again, he called for the right of all adult males to vote. "The right of voting . . . is inherent in the word liberty." It and it alone "constitutes the equality of personal rights." The "first principle of civilization," he emphasized, is that "the condition of every person born into the world after a state of civilization commences, ought not to be worse" than it was prior to the advent of civilization. Yet, "the condition of millions, in every country in Europe, is far worse than if they had been born before civilization began." Paine had once seen the form of government as the most important factor in determining the quality of life of most of humanity. He never turned his back on that belief, but he now understood that without access to capital, the great mass of humanity would remain intractably mired in "the long and dense night" of destitution. He had additionally come to believe that while peace, a flourishing commerce, education, science, and escape from the destructive superstitions peddled by the priesthood were all crucial in the production of affluence, only some—and a small portion of the citizenry at that—would achieve prosperity through the marketplace alone. Only government, he now believed, could create the conditions for achieving a more equitable and ethical distribution of wealth and opportunities. Paine was far ahead of his time. Next to none of Paine's contemporaries displayed his grasp of poverty's gravitational pull or had contemplated state-funded welfare entitlements. What he mooted was ultimately realized by Europe's social democrats three-quarters of a century later, and still later by the adherents of progressivism in America.[51]

Jefferson's thinking had at times paralleled that of Paine. Although subsidies and pensions had not crossed Jefferson's mind, he had much earlier urged giving land to every free man in Virginia and providing free education for those with merit. His object, like Paine's, had been to help the less fortunate rise from poverty and grasp otherwise nonexistent opportunities, though Jefferson also sought to create conditions in which republicanism could flourish and survive. Jefferson had been shocked during his residence in France by the enormously "unequal division" of wealth throughout Europe, and he like Paine thought it produced "so much misery to the bulk of mankind." Jefferson's proposed land and economic reforms had not gained traction in Virginia, though so much land was available in America that he looked with optimism toward an American future of nearly universal property ownership among those who were free. And Jefferson, as early as 1785, had advocated exempting the poor from taxation and imposing the heaviest burdens on the affluent through the system known to the twentieth century as graduated taxation. To this he added: "No other sure foundation can be devised for the preservation of freedom, and happiness." Jefferson, however, never radiated Paine's optimism that social and economic reform was feasible in heavily populated Europe. A thousand years from now, said Jefferson, the "mass of the people" in Europe would continue to suffer from "poverty and oppression of body and mind."[52]

Insiders knew early in 1796 that Washington planned to retire at the end of his second term, a step that assured the presidential election of 1796 would for the first time be a contest between the candidates offered by the two parties. Pressure built on Jefferson to enter the race. Yet, during his three years at Monticello, Jefferson had said nothing that indicated he was equivocating in the least on his vow to never again hold public office. Even in his private correspondence, Jefferson seldom alluded to politics, and when he did it was to encourage Madison to seek the presidency should Washington step down. Madison responded by asking Jefferson to run, urging him not to "abandon your historical task. You owe it to yourself, to truth, to the world," he pleaded. Republicans appealed to Madison to continue prodding Jefferson. He did so, but he was never certain what his friend would do. Early in 1796, however, Madison confided to Monroe that the "republicans . . . mean to push him"—that is, to nominate Jefferson—whether or not he wanted to take on the presidency.[53]

The inscrutable Jefferson may not have wanted to become president, at least not in 1797. He was preoccupied with his debts and must have additionally understood that following an icon like Washington would not be easy. Furthermore, he had to know that defeating John Adams would be an uphill battle, as the vice president was certain to capture all the electoral votes from New England, many from the mid-Atlantic states, and possibly a handful in the South, especially in Maryland and South Carolina, where the Federalist Party had enjoyed some success. The prospect of an Adams presidency did not especially trouble Jefferson. His supposedly monarchical bent notwithstanding, Adams was neither a military adventurer nor an Anglophile. Above all, he was so fiercely independent that Jefferson could not imagine him being dominated by Hamilton or anyone else.

Jefferson never announced his candidacy, but he never unconditionally refused to run, and ultimately a caucus of congressional Republicans chose him and Aaron Burr as the party's nominees. Two candidates were necessary, as the Constitution mandated that each member of the electoral college was to "vote by Ballot for two Persons" for the presidency. As expected, the Federalists selected Adams and South Carolina's Thomas Pinckney.

Jefferson had followed the precedent set by Washington. Not wishing to appear to have lusted for the presidency, Jefferson wanted to be seen as having been summoned to the office. He did not leave home during the autumn campaign. In fact, he did nothing to win the election and, for that matter, neither did Adams and Pinckney. Only Burr actively campaigned. While most of the candidates were inactive, others were busy on their behalf. Party activists courted the 60 percent or so of all adult white males who could vote, furnishing them with liquor and food at banquets and rallies, making speeches, and turning out innumerable pamphlets, newspaper essays, and broadsides. One who was active behind the scenes—or at least he was suspected by many of playing a covert role—was Hamilton. There was widespread conjecture that Hamilton believed his fortunes would be better served by the election of Pinckney; Hamilton's presumed reasoning was that Adams was not susceptible to manipulation, but the less experienced Pinckney could be easily controlled. Not a few were convinced that Hamilton surreptitiously conspired to persuade some Federalist electors in the South to cast one of their votes for Pinckney and their second vote for someone, anyone, other than Adams.[54]

Recognizing that his economic policies would not be a winner at the polls, Hamilton advised Federalist activists to appeal to the "passions of the people." The result was a negative campaign aimed at smearing Jefferson. He was portrayed as an impractical, philosophical sort—"visionary" was the word used most often—who perhaps was suited to be a college president, but was too "weak, wavering, indecisive" to be the nation's chief executive. Focusing on Jefferson's record as a war governor, the Federalists portrayed him as timid, indecisive, and inept. Some partisan essayists also twisted what Jefferson had written about religious freedom to depict him as an atheist. The Republicans gave as good as they got, but in the end the outcome was close to what Jefferson likely all along thought it would be. Adams won the presidency by a margin of three electoral votes, pushed over the top by having received one electoral college vote in Virginia and one in South Carolina. Had Jefferson—who received all the other electoral votes cast below the Potomac—captured those two southern votes, he would have nipped Adams by one vote. If Adams's victory was not startling, this election came with a surprise. New Englanders had heard the rumors about Hamilton's machinations, and to assure Adams's victory, eighteen Yankee electors had cast their second vote for assorted Federalists other than Pinckney. Because of that,

Jefferson polled the second-largest number of electoral votes. Finishing second meant that Jefferson had been elected as vice president.[55]

Jefferson appeared to be happy with the outcome, remarking that he would miss "Neither the splendor, nor the power, nor the difficulties, nor the fame, or [the] defamation" of the presidency.[56] In reality, he must have been torn with mixed emotions, though he most assuredly was happy to escape the overabundance of troubles that awaited Adams. The Jay Treaty had made an enemy of France, and that ensured a grave foreign policy crisis. In addition, there was much about the vice presidency that Jefferson found attractive. Like Adams before him, he would stay in the capital while Congress met, which was ordinarily only about four months annually. He planned to spend the rest of each year at Monticello. Above all, Jefferson had always felt that the Federalists would self-destruct. Now that Washington was gone, Jefferson was all the more certain of such an outcome. Should that in fact occur, the presidency at some point down the road would become a much more valuable— and attainable—prize.

Jefferson wrote to congratulate Adams, but also to warm him about Hamilton, a man given to intrigue, whose "spies and sycophants" abounded, and who would try to control the new administration.[57] In the end, Jefferson never sent the letter. It might have done Adams a world of good had he been able to read Jefferson's warning.

CHAPTER 12

"THE REIGN OF WITCHES"

THE HIGH FEDERALISTS
TAKE CHARGE

JEFFERSON WAS IN PHILADELPHIA for John Adams's inauguration. He saw Washington, who also attended the festivities, and their encounter was harmonious. That was about to change. A year earlier, Jefferson had written to his former neighbor, Philip Mazzei, now a resident of Pisa. After a lengthy discourse on Mazzei's ongoing business affairs in Virginia, Jefferson turned to politics and told his friend that in "place of that noble love of liberty and republican government" that once had predominated in America, "a monarchical and aristocratical party has sprung up, whose avowed object is to draw over us the substance" of the British government.

Jefferson's views along these lines were well known, but as this was a private letter he also expounded on an idea he had not shared publicly. Many officials, he wrote, "all timid men who prefer the calm of despotism to the boisterous sea of liberty," were enthralled by "the rotten as well as the sound parts of the British model. It would give you a fever were I to name to you the apostates who have gone over to these heresies, men who were Samsons in the field and Solomons in the council, but have had their heads shorn by the harlot England."[1] The scornful allusions to Washington and Adams, respectively, were unmistakable.

Jefferson was prone to exaggeration, but what he told Mazzei was a fairly accurate statement of his feelings. Although he had been burned before, he naively thought that his private reflections would remain private. He was wrong. Mazzei passed along the letter to three friends, one of whom published it in a Paris newspaper about six weeks before Adams's inauguration. Several weeks later, a Federalist editor printed the missive in his New York newspaper. Soon, it was splashed in newspapers throughout the United States.[2] All now knew that Jefferson accused Washington and Adams of indifference to absolutism. Indeed, he had as much as charged that they wished to see American republicanism supplanted by England's wicked system.

Hamilton and other Federalists had long embraced stories of Jefferson's alleged duplicity toward Washington, and the previous spring a Philadelphia newspaper had published a hostile piece about the president that many wrongly attributed to Jefferson. On that occasion, Jefferson wrote to Washington truthfully denying authorship and contending that there were those who wished "to sow tares between you and me."[3] Washington accepted his explanation and that was the end of it—until Jefferson's Mazzei letter hit the streets. A bitter Washington, in retirement at Mount Vernon, broke off his relationship with Jefferson. He never wrote to him again, never invited him to Mount Vernon, and never called on Jefferson during his lone visit to Philadelphia late in 1798. Following the ex-president's death late in 1799, Martha Washington—who had come to think that Jefferson was "one of the most detestable of mankind"—made it clear that he was not welcome at Mount Vernon.[4]

A decade and a half later, with the benefit of distance, Jefferson reappraised Washington more charitably. In another private letter—one that was not made public—he declared that "Washington did not harbour one principle of federalism" and "he was neither an Angloman [nor] a monarchist." The following year he more fully reconsidered Washington, and what he produced was nothing like the vitriolic piece that Paine had written. Intriguingly, too, it was more positive than anything ever served up by Adams or Hamilton. Jefferson mentioned only three flaws: "His heart was not warm in it's affections," Washington had a volcanic temper, and he was at best a mediocre conversationalist. Jefferson noted abundant strengths in Washington. His mind was "great and powerful," though not "so acute as that of Newton, Bacon, or Locke." He was unequaled as a decision maker, slow to decide, "but sure." He was also honest and virtuous. However, Washington's strongest feature had been his "prudence." He never permitted self-interest, friendship, or enmity to "bias his decision." He was "in every sense of the words, a wise, a good, & a great man." Revisiting what he had said in the Mazzei letter, Jefferson added that Washington was "no monarchist," but he was filled with "gloomy apprehensions" about the long-term survival of America's republican experiment, and he believed that in time the United States would move toward "something like a British constitution."[5]

Jefferson's candor in the 1796 letter to Mazzei was not the only instance of a private letter coming back to haunt him. His once-close relationship with Adams had been ruined in 1791 by things he had said that were made public.[6] Since that time, the two had exchanged a few formal letters, but following Adams's victory in the recent election both seemed eager for reconciliation. Jefferson wrote a warm letter of congratulations, the one in which he cautioned Adams that Hamilton would seek to control his presidency. One had only to read between the lines to see that Jefferson, who hinted that most in Washington's final cabinet were intensely loyal to Hamilton, was advising the incoming president to stay clear of these men. Adams never saw the letter. James Madison had gotten in the way. An obsessive political operative who was already looking toward the election of 1800, Madison feared that the rekindling of the Jefferson-Adams friendship would inhibit Jefferson from speaking out against the policies of the new president's administration. He had advised against sending the letter and Jefferson had taken his advice.

Meanwhile, using his old friend Elbridge Gerry as a conduit, Adams let Jefferson know that he had always looked on him as a man of honor and integrity. But when Adams sought to go further in courting Jefferson, his cabinet thwarted his initiative. Indeed, Adams had made his first profound mistake even before his inauguration. He retained Washington's cabinet, a misstep that would have fatal implications for his presidency. By Inauguration Day everyone in Philadelphia aside from Adams appears to have been aware that three members of his cabinet—Timothy Pickering (State), Oliver Wolcott (Treasury), and James McHenry (War)—were toadies of Hamilton's. Soon enough, the new president would discover that his cabinet was intransigently opposed to any Republican involvement in the Adams administration. Aside from two cordial meetings shortly before Adams was sworn in, the president and vice president were hardly ever together during the next four years.[7]

Three problems that Washington had faced at the outset of his presidency had been resolved by 1797. The economy was on its feet again; Great Britain had removed its troops from the posts in trans-Appalachia; and Spain had agreed not only to America's demands concerning the boundary between the United States and Spanish Florida, but it had also opened the Mississippi River and New Orleans to traffic. Resolution of the latter issue virtually eliminated the threat that settlers in the newly acquired trans-Appalachian West would break away from the United States. Other problems remained, including Great Britain's refusal to open its ports to American shipping. Without a doubt, however, the deterioration in relations with France would be Adams's most pressing quandary. Britain and France were waging all-out war on the high seas, each seeking to block the other's trade, whether with belligerents or neutrals. The United States was victimized by the navies and privateers of both powers, but Washington and the Federalists, and now Adams, focused more on the property and human damages that resulted from French depredations, and with some justification. In 1795 alone French vessels had seized 316 American ships, mostly in the Caribbean, and by Inauguration Day in 1797 the number of captures was on the increase. In fact, just days earlier news broke of an incident in which a French privateer had fired on a vessel out of Newburyport, Massachusetts, wounding four American citizens.[8]

Washington had sought to open talks leading to a normalization of relations with France when he replaced Monroe with Charles Cotesworth Pinckney. The new American minister arrived in Paris early in December 1796 and was introduced to the French foreign minister by his predecessor. Pinckney's welcome was the antithesis of what Monroe had experienced a couple of years earlier. To describe it as chilly hardly begins to depict the icy atmosphere that day in the French Foreign Ministry. Monroe knew that the unfriendly greeting accorded Pinckney arose from a deeply held sense of betrayal among French officials. Less than twenty years after France had made enormous sacrifices to help the infant United States in the Revolutionary War, its ally had agreed to the Jay Treaty, which the French saw as America's abandonment of neutrality in favor of a pro-British policy. Monroe was angry too. His fury was directed toward those "vain, superficial blunderers" surrounding Washington, men who so hated the French Revolution that in their wrongheadedness they threatened to "plunge our affairs" into calamity.[9]

When Adams took office, he had not yet heard from Pinckney, but he was already considering sending a plenipotentiary to Paris. Prior to his inauguration, Adams approached Jefferson about returning to France, but the incoming vice president thought it inappropriate for the second official in the executive branch to be out of the country for months on end. Before going further, Adams told his Treasury secretary that he planned to approach Madison about undertaking a mission to France. Wolcott exploded. He and his confederates had just rid themselves of Monroe, and he suspected that Madison would be his facsimile. Wolcott threatened to resign should Adams appoint any Republican for such a vital assignment, and he informed the president that the entire cabinet would join him in quitting. The president backed down, but this was the tip of the iceberg for the new chief executive. Adams's steadfast interest was in finding an honorable and peaceful solution to Franco-American discord. That, however, was not the agenda of his supposedly trusted advisors.[10]

Most within the Federalist Party were anti-French and pro-British, but there was a divide within the party. There were those like Adams and there were those like Hamilton and his three minions in the cabinet, ultra-nationalists who saw the crisis with France in partisan terms. For the first time in America's political history, but not the last, a party glimpsed the opportunity of increasing its strength through a foreign crisis. Since World War II, it has most often been extremists on the political right that have sought the partisan prizes to be won through taking a hard-line approach, and that was the case in 1797. Hamilton, the pivotal figure within the extremist wing of the Federalist Party, hoped to prolong the crisis. His immediate goal was the creation of a large American army. Hamilton wanted a force that could be used for military adventures in the borderlands of the United States, and possibly in the Caribbean, adding territory to the United States and distracting and weakening France, which would help assure the safety of Great Britain.

Hamilton also pursued a personal agenda. Extraordinarily ambitious, he envisaged a leading role for himself in that army. It is not too much to say that Hamilton secretly yearned to be another George Washington, attaining a revered status through his military service. In the earliest letter that he is known to have written, at age fourteen, Hamilton had said: "I wish there was a War." He was spinning "Castles in the Air," as he put it, looking to soldiering as his means of escaping a hopelessly dead-end condition on St. Croix and rising to prominence.[11] He had soldiered when the opportunity arose in the Revolutionary War, and in 1797 he still cherished the hope that through soldiering again he might win more glory and an ever more exalted status. But Hamilton wanted no part of the European war in 1797. He believed that if war came prematurely, America's citizenry would be fatally divided. He did not wish to bring about an American defeat or to jeopardize the existence of the Union that he had worked so hard to sustain. However, a long, unresolved crisis, replete with damaging incidents that could be stoked by writers with a keen eye for galvanizing public opinion, would serve his purposes.

After capitulating to his cabinet on the matter of sending Madison to France, Adams suggested dispatching a three-member commission. Pickering, Wolcott, and McHenry—displaying the canine subservience that would be their hallmark—immediately sought Hamilton's guidance. To their surprise, he consented to the notion of a commission and even said that he was fine with the inclusion of Madison, so long as Federalist domination was assured. He also directed them to urge the president to call for the augmentation of the navy and the expansion of America's tiny army to twenty-five thousand men. He even coached the cabinet officers on how to explain this course of action to Adams. The president was to be told that these steps were not designed "to *provoke* a war," but to prevent one. Hamilton instructed his allies to assert that France, driven by "a spirit of *domination* and *Revenge*," planned to invade the United States. Hamilton additionally confided to Federalists in Congress that should President Adams resist the wishes of his party, "a *plot* has been laid to take hold" of the presidency. What Hamilton had in mind is not clear, but he spoke in private of "the President's Administration" and the "actual administration." His remark suggests that he envisaged formulating policy behind the throne that would be forced on the president by extreme Federalists in Congress and the cabinet.[12]

While Adams mulled over his choices, word arrived toward the end of his second week in office that France had refused to accept Charles Cotesworth Pinckney as minister and ordered him out of the country. The courier who brought that news also reported on recent French seizures of American vessels in the Caribbean. These tidings deepened the crisis and led the president to summon Congress to a special session in May. No one was more worried than Jefferson by this "awful crisis." While unaware of what had transpired within the cabinet, Jefferson had already divined Hamilton's influence over those around the president. Fearing that Adams might not be capable of withstanding those in his party that would push him toward war, Jefferson met on several occasions with the French consul general in Philadelphia, always counseling that France must be patient. The Federalists would be out of power after 1800, he insisted, and prudence would be restored. When that occurred, "all will return to order."[13]

When the congressmen gathered for the special session, Adams greeted them with such a strident speech that Madison called him "our hot-headed Executive." The president urged a major augmentation of the navy, as it was the country's "natural defense," but he only asked Congress to "seriously deliberate" strengthening the army's cavalry and artillery branches and making arrangements for forming an additional "provisional army." (Congress eventually approved the expansion of the navy, but none of the changes to the army put forward by the president.) Adams additionally announced his intention of sending a three-member diplomatic commission to Paris, in one additional effort at accommodation. The cabinet was livid when Adams revealed that he intended to include Elbridge Gerry, a Republican who had opposed the ratification of the Constitution, on the delegation to be sent to France. However, in a rare instance of defiance, Adams stuck to his guns and Gerry was added to the delegation, which included Pinckney, still in Europe, and John Marshall, the Virginia Federalist. Jefferson immediately told Gerry that "peace even at the expense of spoliations past and future" was essential. He also explained his views on America's foreign relations, a perspective that was the diametric opposite of Hamilton's. "Our countrymen have divided themselves by such strong affections to the French and the English, that nothing will secure us internally but a divorce from both nations." When the session ended and the congressmen returned home, there was nothing to do but wait. Nine long months would pass before the nation learned of France's response to the three American envoys.[14]

* * *

On June 27, while Congress was still meeting, the *Amity* completed a sixty-nine-day Atlantic crossing and docked in Philadelphia. James Monroe and his family were among its passengers. Monroe had closed his mission to France on New Year's Day in a formal ceremony. In his final remarks, Monroe remained true to his principles and impressively indifferent with regard to the enmity his words would arouse among the Federalists. He had been "deeply penetrated" by the principles of the American Revolution, he said, adding that they were "the same with those of your revolution." When he returned home, he would inform his countrymen of France's victories, prosperity, and "excellent constitution," tidings that would be greeted with "joy" by all Americans who longed for "a close union and perfect harmony" between France and America.[15]

Monroe had thought it best not to risk an ocean crossing in winter, so from January into March he and his family toured Holland and Switzerland. In almost thirty months abroad, Monroe had done remarkably little sightseeing. The one trip he and his wife had planned, back in the summer of 1795, had been cut short when they hurried back to the embassy to tend to Paine, whom they believed to be at death's door. When Monroe returned to Paris from his wintertime trek through the countries near France, he faced a wait of several weeks for the arrival of the *Amity*. He used the time to see what he might dig up on Hamilton, convinced that the latter was the sorcerer behind his recall. Monroe's detective work grew out of a tip from Paine, who claimed that not long after the conclusion of the Revolutionary War, Hamilton and Henry Knox had entered into secret talks with William Pitt, Britain's prime minister, to furnish New England soldiers for a clandestine British operation to liberate Spain's South American colonies. The scheme allegedly involved General Francisco de Miranda, a South American adventurer active in the Latin American independence movement. Always on the lookout for excitement, Miranda had soldiered for France after 1792, and that was when he met Paine. The two had mingled socially and Paine had even entertained him at Saint-Denis. When Miranda was arrested and tried following military defeats in 1794, Paine had testified on his behalf. His helping hand was important in saving Miranda from the guillotine. Now Paine wished to help Monroe. He confided that Miranda had documents in his possession that showed Hamilton's undercover ties to the British government. Monroe set about getting his hands on those documents. But Miranda was not about to jeopardize his campaign for Latin American independence. He acknowledged that Paine had been in his home and had seen some papers, but the general claimed that Paine was mistaken about their contents. Monroe's sleuthing had failed.[16]

When the *Amity* docked in Philadelphia, Jefferson, Aaron Burr, and Albert Gallatin, a Swiss-born immigrant and Republican congressman who was a rising star politically, came aboard to greet Monroe. Four days later the governor of Pennsylvania, Thomas McKean, hosted a banquet—which Monroe habitually referred to as "the feast"—to honor the diplomat's home-coming. Jefferson was in the sizable audience and he heard McKean lavish praise on Monroe and denounce the "machinations of the invidious, and the slanders of the profligate" who had engineered his recall. Monroe responded that with "fervent zeal" he had sought to "promote harmony between the two republics." During the toasts, some hissed at the mention of Washington's name, an incident that was immediately reported in the Federalist press.[17]

Myriad individuals within the Republican Party would have relished the opportunity to inflict mortal political harm on Hamilton, and on the day before the *Amity* arrived in Philadelphia a publication containing the most damaging material ever published about the former Treasury secretary appeared in the press. It was the work of James Callender, a Scotsman who, like Paine, had been forced to flee England because of his inflammatory essays. Since arriving in America four years earlier, Callender had produced pieces for Republican publications. Heretofore, nothing that he had written had drawn much attention, but Callender hit the jackpot in June 1797. He broke the news not only about Hamilton's tryst years before with Maria Reynolds, but also that the Treasury secretary had paid hush money to her husband, James. Back in 1792, the three congressmen—Frederick Muhlenberg, Abraham Venable, and Monroe—had investigated the matter and accepted Hamilton's explanation of marital infidelity and blackmail, clearing him of suspicion of the criminal misuse of federal money. Following the congressional detectives' interviews with Hamilton—and their solemn pledge that the papers in their possession would never see the light of day—Monroe had asked John Beckley, the clerk of the House, to make copies of all the documents.

Now, five years later, someone had turned over those documents to Callender. It was never entirely clear who had possessed these explosive mate-rials since 1792, much less who passed along to Callender the treasure trove of ruinous particulars. The list of those eager to smear Hamilton was endless. Jefferson might have been responsible. He knew Callender, who had visited his home in Philadelphia, and the vice president had subsidized some of his previous writing. In addition, Callender likely got his hands on these mouth-watering items at the very moment that the Federalists were making hay from Jefferson's Mazzei letter. Or Monroe might have been complicit in unleashing the bundle of documents. He had an ax to grind, as he blamed what might be his career-ending recall on Hamilton's machinations. At the same moment that he was seeking to dig up dirt on Hamilton through Miranda, Monroe may have seen to it that the mother lode of defamatory information found its way into Callender's hands. Or it may have been that neither Jefferson nor Monroe was the culprit. Both Venable and Wolcott told Hamilton that they believed Beckley was responsible for leaking the material, and many historians have concurred.

However, it was Hamilton's fierce conviction that Monroe was the guilty party, and he confronted him face-to-face. Monroe and his wife were in Manhattan to visit her friends and relatives when a "very much agitated" Hamilton arrived at their residence and, in front of in-laws and acquaintances, angrily accused Monroe of having given the documents to Callender. When Monroe denied the charge, Hamilton called him a liar and challenged him to a duel. Hamilton had a long track record of issuing challenges, though no duels had ever materialized. In Monroe, however, Hamilton had assailed a tough Virginian who had often risked his life in combat, Monroe responded by calling Hamilton a "Scoundrel." The flinty Monroe—whom one witness described as "quite cool"—said to his accuser: "I am ready get your pistols." Hamilton appears to have been startled that Monroe, unlike so many others, had not quaked. In fact, Monroe may have given the impression that he would have relished the opportunity to shoot Hamilton. Put off his stride, Hamilton retreated. He simply asked Monroe to publish a repudiation of the allegation that the Treasury secretary had committed a criminal offense.

Hamilton had such a letter from Monroe within a week, but he was irritated by its tone and thought it insufficient. Unfriendly letters followed and for a time a duel seemed inevitable. Honor was crucial to Monroe, and he was not about to be humiliated by Hamilton, but he did not seek to spill blood. He clearly hoped to avoid a duel. He had a wife and daughter, and in the aftermath of his festive welcome home by Philadelphia's leading Republicans—not to mention Jefferson's counsel that the Federalist Party was in decline— Monroe once again believed that he had a political future. Monroe may have been entirely innocent of having passed on the discrediting materials to Callender, and if that was true, he hardly wished to die for something he had not done. He told friends that he "had no hand" in releasing the letters and "was sorry" that they had been made public. He added that years before he, Venable, and Muhlenberg had left the letters with a friend in Virginia. That friend was probably Beckley, as Monroe told close associates that he believed the former clerk of the House was responsible for having provided the particulars to Callender.

The prudent Monroe may have wished to avoid risking his life, but he never flinched in the face of Hamilton's provocations. He retained Aaron

Burr as his second and told him that he would fight if an honorable solution could not be found. He also confided that he did not wish to harm Hamilton, "tho' he merits it highly." Burr thought a duel pointless, and he told Monroe that he doubted Hamilton would go through with it. He never does, Burr counseled. "You may put this business wholly out of your Mind," he advised, and in time Burr succeeded in defusing matters, thanks in large measure to both men's eagerness to find an honorable way out of the dilemma.

At one point in the sizzling war of words, Hamilton had charged that Monroe's endgame was to "drive me to the necessity of a formal defense." If that was what Monroe sought, he got what he wanted. That summer, Hamilton published his confession, contending that he was compelled to answer the "Jacobin Scandal-Club." He stuck to the story of an extramarital affair and blackmail, acknowledging a restless libido but denying corruption in office. Neither Callender nor Jefferson believed his version, and had they known that he came to Philadelphia to write his account, they might have been even more skeptical. It had never been Hamilton's practice to leave home to draft his essays and pamphlets, and had Jefferson and Callendar been aware of the departure from his conventional behavior, it likely would have led them to raise additional questions. Hamilton's best biographer attributed his uncustomary conduct to an unwillingness to "face his family" as he "confessed his sins." A better explanation might be that Hamilton, for whatever reason, wished to peruse the Treasury department's ledgers, a step the slavish Wolcott would have permitted.[18]

While the possible duel with Hamilton awaited resolution, Monroe had sought to wring from Pickering an explanation for his recall. As the secretary of state had written the previous summer that "concurring circumstances" led Washington to change ministers in Paris, Monroe asked him to explain those circumstances. Pickering was not about to indulge Monroe, and he wrote coldly that neither he nor Washington were under any obligation to discuss the "expediency" of presidential decisions. Monroe tried again. After working hard to gain "an honest fame," he said, he felt that he now was being "robbed of it" by a secret cabinet decision leading to his censure. In the public's mind, his recall was due to "some act of misconduct." Pickering superciliously replied that sometimes an official was recalled not because of any impropriety, but due to "want of ability." Though Monroe felt that Pickering was bent on the "disguise of the real motive," he tried yet again. Pickering never answered.[19]

Monroe was already being vilified in the Federalist press. Neither Hamilton nor Pickering had penned any of the attacks, though Monroe likely saw their fingerprints in what he called "the infinitude of calumnies" heaped on him. One Federalist accused Monroe of treason for supposedly having shaped

France's hostility to the Jay Treaty. Others charged that he had misused public money by speculating in Parisian property. Both charges were ludicrous. As Monroe probably anticipated, he was also assailed for sheltering Paine while the writer penned his savage attack on Washington. He was additionally accused of not having been wary of the French Revolution from its inception and of continuing to support it in the wake of its many bloody excesses.[20] Monroe's initial inclination was to answer his critics. Jefferson and Madison wisely counseled that a war of words in the press would gain him nothing, and Monroe listened. However, when Monroe proposed authoring a pamphlet to defend his behavior in Paris, and also to publish documents concerning his mission, both approved on the grounds that he not attack Washington. He consented and his friends read early drafts of what would appear in December as a 407-page tract.[21]

Monroe's lengthy pamphlet also had such a lengthy title—it consisted of thirty-three words—that it was popularly called A View. Monroe's effort exuded earnestness, but he had never been a scintillating writer and this tract was turgid and stultifying. Outside of Virginia—where those obsessed with politics "scrambled" to get a copy—few read it. Jefferson, alluding to Monroe's defense of his diplomacy and not to the publication's literary qualities, called it "masterly" and "unanswerable," though James McHenry was more nearly accurate when he said A View "has been little read and has made no converts to his party." Wolcott was correct, too, when he declared that it "will make no impression beyond the circle of Tom Paine's admirers." One who did read it closely was the former president. Washington immediately purchased a copy and wrote numerous letters seeking to learn the public's reaction to Monroe's pamphlet. Pickering told him that the publication would lead to Monroe's "own condemnation." McHenry concurred, adding that Monroe "has . . . sunk in public opinion." For his part, Washington pored over the tract, making copious marginal notations, something he seldom did. "Curious and laughable," "impudent," "unfounded," "a striking instance of his folly," a "mistake in toto," and "Self importance appears here" were typical Washington comments. To these comments, Washington praised Gouverneur Morris as a diplomat, adding that had Monroe possessed his "zeal and ability . . . we should not have been in the situation we now are."[22]

Monroe had included his correspondence with administration officials in A View, and in his narrative he sought to demonstrate that he had done his best to preserve good relations with France. The Franco-American relationship had soured, he argued, because he had received next to no guidance from a State Department that was more interested in fostering a bond with England than in maintaining America's essential ties with France. In the final pages, Monroe charged that the Washington administration's pro-monarchical bent had angered France, as had its continual efforts to sow discontent toward the French Revolution. "We might have stood well with France" and "preserved our ancient renown" as a "defender of liberty." Instead, "Our national honor is in the dust." Furthermore, a continued good relationship with France would have been "highly advantageous." It would have led to greater protection for American commerce, the hopeful promise of a beneficial economic accord with France, and most of all it would have provided the United States with the leverage needed to engage in truly fruitful negotiations with Great Britain. Sadly, Monroe wrote in closing, Washington's administration had turned its back on republicanism and chosen instead to become bedfellows with "monarchy and our late most deadly foe."[23]

Aside from taking swipes at administration policies, Monroe had heeded Jefferson's and Madison's advice concerning attacking the former president. But his simmering rage toward Washington was the equal of Paine's, and it drove Monroe to draft a separate essay in which he poured out his feelings. Unlike Paine, he did not criticize Washington's generalship, but he charged that the mission of Washington's presidency had been to "wrest the government from the people" and place it in the hands of an oligarchic faction. No one had done more harm to the country during the past decade, Monroe wrote. Washington had gathered the "spiritual rays" of America's worst reactionaries and turned them loose "against the best interests of society." Like Paine, Monroe addressed Washington's character. Washington had postured as the embodiment of unselfish sacrifice in answering the call of his countrymen, but in fact the former president had always been consumed with "low ambition" and his own "personal aggrandizement." Perhaps unleashing his venom on paper was cathartic, or maybe in the end he saw that he would be the one who suffered most from its publication. Monroe never published his diatribe.[24]

Nor did he answer the critics of *A View*. He had planned to, but when Jefferson, early in 1798, urged him to remain silent, Monroe heeded him.[25] By then, Monroe had long since returned to Virginia. After having spent most of the previous summer in Philadelphia and New York, he sped to Charlottesville. Along the way, he passed through Alexandria without stopping. He "did not honor me by a call," an irritated Washington reflected glumly at nearby Mount Vernon, realizing for perhaps the first time since surrendering power that the day had come when not everyone would pay obeisance to him. Reaching Albemarle County, Monroe at last saw the site selected for his residence by Jefferson, Madison, and Joseph Jones. It was a rolling 3,500-acre spread only three miles from Monticello, and when the foliage disappeared,

Jefferson's capacious residence could easily be seen on a taller hill. Monroe immediately began construction of his home, a project that would require twenty-eight months. In the meantime, the family lived in the cramped confines of the house he had purchased years before on the edge of town. The house that he was building, which he named "Highlands," was modest for someone of his stature, a six-room, one-story clapboard dwelling, but it was the best he could do. Like Jefferson, Monroe was deeply in debt, the legacy of his public service and the consumerism that he and Elizabeth had found irresistible—also like Jefferson—while in Paris. Monroe wasted no time getting crops in on both of his Charlottesville properties and soon, with great reluctance, returned to his legal practice, though he remained on the lookout for a suitable public office.[26]

Monroe also watched throughout that bitter winter as tension mounted with every French seizure of an American ship. When Congress debated arming American merchant ships, which Adams had urged, Monroe warned the Republicans that "there is a systematic scheme on foot to involve us in a war with France."[27] In fact, by the time he issued the warning, the crisis had taken a dangerous new turn.

Expecting to hear any day from the three envoys he had sent to Paris during the previous summer, President Adams in January 1798 asked his cabinet to consider what steps he should take if the news from the three was bad. Hamilton gave the cabinet secretaries their marching orders. They, in turn, passed along their leader's recommendation that the unsuspecting chief executive must ask Congress to increase the regular army to twenty thousand men and create a *provisional* army" of thirty thousand. Hamilton had additionally advised that Adams should proclaim a national day of prayer, as it would be "very expedient" politically.[28]

During the first week in March, Adams finally heard from Pinckney, Marshall, and Gerry. The news was worse than disappointing. The diplomats had been met by agents, identified only as "X, Y, and Z," who demanded that the United States apologize for Adams's truculent speech to the special session of Congress, abandon claims for damages suffered at the hands of French vessels on the high seas, and pay bribes to leading officials. Only after these conditions were met would France open talks. Outraged by the affront, Adams consulted his cabinet, which again secretly touched base with Hamilton. Still hopeful of avoiding hostilities, the former Treasury secretary's advice remained the same as it had a month earlier, save for his recommendation that the president make a "*temperate,* but *grave solemn* and *firm* communication" to Congress. When the cabinet covertly passed along Hamilton's suggestions, Adams softened the vehement speech he had planned to deliver. He again asked that the navy be strengthened, but unlike his message to the special session of Congress a year earlier, Adams said nothing about expanding the army or creating a provisional army. (In private, he remarked that there was "no more prospect of seeing a french Army here, than there is in Heaven.") Wanting neither war nor a wave of war hysteria that might tie his hands, Adams merely told the public that France had refused to receive his envoys.[29]

Adams may have moderated his speech, but the Republicans were shocked by its harshness. Monroe believed Adams was "wild" and driven by a "passion . . . to out-do" Washington in the hope that he, too, would be exalted as a hero. Jefferson thought Adams's remarks were "insane." He told friends that the president had become the "stalking horse" of the "war gentlemen" within the "war-party."[30] Having originally thought that Adams was trustworthy, Jefferson had changed his mind, though his view of the president was not as jaded as that of Paine.

Adams and Paine had once enjoyed a cordial, though not close, relationship. On one occasion in 1776, Paine "spent an Evening" in Adams's apartment at Mrs. Yard's boardinghouse discussing the best form of government. They disagreed and Adams told Paine that his preferences were too "democratical" and would lead to chaos. Adams later described their conversation as having been conducted in "good humour," and it probably had been, for a couple of years later Adams was instrumental in securing the congressional secretarial position that Paine held for a time. Their friendship, such as it was, turned bumpy when Adams with insufficient evidence came to suspect that Paine spread the "scandalous Lye that I was one of a Faction . . . against General Washington" during the Valley Forge winter. They were never in one another's presence after 1777 and neither appears to have given much thought to the other until each was aroused by what the other wrote during the 1790s. Adams was appalled by *Rights of Man* and *The Age of Reason*. Paine was disgusted by the cozy feelings toward monarchy that stood out in Adams's "Davila" essays. Adams expected that "Mad Tom"—as he now called him—would come to a bad end in the Terror, and he might not have been deeply saddened had that been Paine's fate. With apparent glee, Adams ruminated on the likelihood that Paine had been "roasted or broild or fryed" by the bad crowd with whom he had been keeping company in Paris. Paine of course lived through it and went on to publish his *Letter to Washington*, an essay that Adams called the work of a "Lunatick." For his part, Paine thought Adams was jealous of his success as a writer, and he may have been correct. Not long before he became president, Adams said: "I shall never be so popular as Tom Paine, but I believe the time will come, when more Men will think as I do than as he does."[31]

Once Paine learned the outcome of the 1796 election, he had nothing good to say about the incoming president. Paine feared the worst, in part because he thought Adams owed his victory to the "mercantile wise-acres of America." In addition, Paine exclaimed to Jefferson, "Adams has not character to do any good." He thought Adams a man with a "fractious untractable disposition" who "mistakes Arrogance for greatness, and sullenness for wisdom." Sensing correctly that the second president would be "entirely under the government of a bad" faction within the Federalist Party, Paine urged Jefferson to "keep an eye upon John Adams, or he will commit some blunder that will make matters worse. He has a natural disposition to blunder and to offend. . . . John Adams can do nothing but harm." To make matters worse, Paine added, Adams's chief foreign policy advisor was to be "the clownish" Pickering.[32]

Jefferson was unaware of what was transpiring inside Adams's administration, but a year after Paine's cautionary note, the vice president was certain that the Federalist extremists alluded to by Paine were manufacturing a crisis for their own ends. Jefferson's strategy was for the Republicans to play for time. If Congress could be prevented from taking bellicose actions until its next session commenced in December, Jefferson thought war could be avoided. By then, he reasoned, France would be victorious, or on the cusp of victory, and the "Hamilton party" would not dare go to war against a powerful adversary that was no longer fighting nearly all of Europe. But the misplaced skepticism of some members of his own party sabotaged Jefferson's grand design. Some Republican congressmen, suspecting that Adams was concocting a greater crisis with France, demanded the release of the communiqués sent by Pinckney, Marshall, and Gerry. When Adams complied, the nation learned of France's provocative actions in what would become known as the "XYZ Affair." Outrage—and war fever—swept the land. Even Jefferson condemned the French behavior as "very unworthy of a great nation," though he did not think it cause for war. At times, it must have seemed to Jefferson that he alone opposed hostilities, as many Republicans jumped on the bandwagon for war. More than ever, the disconsolate Jefferson was certain that the Hamilton wing among the Federalists—the so-called High Federalists—was soon to be the predominant faction within a party committed to bringing the United States into the European conflict to save Great Britain from being "blown up."[33]

Jefferson was wrong in thinking that Hamilton wanted war with France. All along, Hamilton's hope had been to capitalize on America's troubles with France, and now his wish had come true. The Federalist press unleashed an anti-French campaign. With his sure instinct for arousing and exploiting fear, Hamilton joined in with several squibs of his own. He contended that American "independence is menaced" by France. Ominously, Hamilton added that France could not harm the United States unless internal enemies provoked an "abject submission to their will." He called those who questioned the president's hard line "tools of France" and French "satellites" who hoped "their country should become a province to France."[34]

Hamilton attained what he was after. With much of the country thirsting for war that spring and summer—Jefferson called it a moment of "unguarded passion" arising from the "XYZ dish cooked up" by the Federalists—congressional Federalists took steps they could have taken only in an atmosphere of delirium.[35] Congress more than doubled the existing army, increasing it to twelve thousand men. Now popularly called the "New Army," it immediately began to recruit. Congress additionally authorized a Provisional Army of ten thousand men. This was the army that Hamilton had sought for more than a year, though by now he was calling for a force of fifty thousand. Given that there was already an "old" army on the frontier and that Congress had additionally provided for what some called an "Eventual Army" of twenty-eight regiments, the total number of men under arms could soar in the event of "imminent danger" to forty-four hundred—considerably more than the United States had fielded in any year during the long, desperate Revolutionary War.[36]

The High Federalists did not stop there. Following up on Hamilton's warning about internal threats to American security, Congress enacted the repressive Alien and Sedition Acts during that torrid summer. The exigencies of war necessitated the restriction of civil liberties, they maintained. One of the acts was not unlike the draconian law through which Pitt's government had brought charges against Paine. The Sedition Act made it a crime to "write, print, utter or publish" anything "scandalous, and malicious" about the United States government, or to bring into "contempt or disrepute" the Congress or the president. The remaining acts were directed against immigrants. The time of residency before an immigrant could become a citizen was tripled and resident aliens could be deported.

The Federalist-dominated Congress embraced the legislation for partisan reasons. Conservative extremists who feared domestic change exploited the presumptive foreign threat as the means through which, in the words of historian James Roger Sharp, "to consolidate their strength and destroy their political opposition." As the lion's share of immigrants voted Republican upon attaining citizenship, the Federalists were seeking to shrink the numbers available to the competing party. The Sedition Act was hatched for the stark purpose of intimidating Republican journalists. As historian Ron Chernow has written, its design was "to muzzle dissent and browbeat the Republicans into submission."[37] Once Republicans were silenced, said Hamilton, *national unanimity*" would be realized. That would make all things possible. The Federalist Speaker of the House and other party stalwarts thought now that the "Spirit of the People is roused," a "wise policy required a declaration of war" against France. But Hamilton still did not favor that course. He had other things in mind.[38]

First, Hamilton had to secure a leading position in the Provisional Army. Washington got it for him. Feeling that he had no choice, Adams had first asked Washington to command the new army. To the president's astonishment, Washington dictated his terms: The old general demanded that he must be permitted to remain at Mount Vernon until a French invasion was imminent, and Hamilton must be named inspector general, the second-highest-ranking post. As virtually no one—including Washington—thought a French invasion was likely, this would make Hamilton the day-to-day commander of the army. Adams was enraged, but not even the president of the United States could defy George Washington. The former chief executive continued to believe in Hamilton, and now he had delivered an army to him. Hamilton was two years younger than Washington had been at the time of his appointment to command the Continental army. Washington was doing what he could to position Hamilton to follow in his footsteps.[39]

Jefferson was no less appalled than Adams by what had occurred. He shared Adams's concerns with regard to what Hamilton might attempt with his army, but as frightening as that was, Jefferson was plunged into gloom by the entire train of swiftly moving events. In the spring, Jefferson had thought the tide had turned against the Federalist Party. Now the Federalists were demonstrably in control, and the most extreme wing of the party at that. Jefferson was convinced that like the masters of England whom they revered, the Federalists were bent on snuffing out free speech and waging war, and this atop an economic system they had copied from London's playbook. The "reign of witches" had taken root in America, said Jefferson. Now anything and everything could be expected, including the possibility of the most "atrocious" actions. Jefferson worried mostly about Hamilton's army. As "nobody pretends . . . there is . . . the least *real* danger of invasion," Jefferson could only wonder what Hamilton had in mind. Whatever it was, Jefferson feared he could get away with it, for the Federalist Party was in the driver's seat and the party "is in truth the Hamilton party."

But what did Hamilton want with his army? Some believed—almost certainly correctly—that he saw the army as the means of building the Federalist base. Hamilton could appoint his subordinate officers from every nook and cranny throughout the land, and thereafter those men would not only be fervid Federalists, but they would be loyal to him, much as most within the officer corps had been ardently devoted to General Washington during and after the Revolutionary War. Some feared that Hamilton intended to seize on some incident, some latter-day Whiskey Rebellion, as the pretext for invading a Republican state and crushing his enemies.

Jefferson did not go that far, but he worried that Hamilton would make a war somewhere. That, in fact, was the most widely held supposition with regard to Hamilton's intent. A war with France may have been Jefferson's worst nightmare, but it was not his only concern. Many Republicans— credibly, it now appears—thought the most plausible explanation for Hamilton's machinations was that the army was to be used against the Spanish in Louisiana or Florida. To Jefferson, war in the borderlands would be as terrible as hostilities with France. "If war takes place, republicanism has every thing to fear," he remarked. Jefferson saw Hamiltonianism, from its economic program to its army, as a threat to the essential principles of the American Revolution. But war would pose the greatest threat of all. Just as France's decision to go to war in 1792 had unleashed forces that eviscerated the early promise of the French Revolution, a war provoked by the Federalists well might destroy Jefferson's—and Paine's and Monroe's—dreams for the American Revolution. Though uneasy at what might be in the offing, Jefferson acknowledged Hamilton's political adroitness. Washington's "irresistible influence" could not be discounted in the Federalist string of successes, but Jefferson felt that for the most part the party's triumphs were due to "the cunning of Hamilton." In private, Jefferson took to referring to Hamilton as "our Buonaparte," alluding to the upstart general who made himself ruler of France. The vice president was not aware that nearly simultaneously the First Lady, Abigail Adams, likewise labeled Hamilton "a second Buonaparty."[40]

The army belonged to Hamilton, and not long passed before it was clear that the inspector general did not wish to share his army with anyone, even Washington. After having been kept in the dark for four months—not even his demand that he be told "*at once* and *precisely*" what was being done with the army produced any results—an irritated Washington rode to Philadelphia late in 1798 for a firsthand look. His presence changed nothing. He was still ignored, including by Pickering and McHenry, his former cabinet officials. Their master now was Hamilton. "My opinions and inclinations are not consulted," Washington raged, and when that did no good he threatened to resign.[41] That, too, was unavailing. In fact, his resignation might have been welcomed, for if the old general quit, no officer would outrank Hamilton. Soon, Washington went home for good. When Washington's presidency was drawing to an end, Jefferson had predicted that his "bubble is bursting."[42] Washington had gotten an inkling of his shrinking influence when Monroe shunned him during his transit through nearby Alexandria. Now Washington knew for sure that he had served his purpose and been jettisoned, much as he had discarded so many others throughout his long career.

During that black autumn, Jefferson conceded that things were going from "bad to worse." However, his steadfast faith in the people remained solid. They "are essentially republican" and "retain unadulterated the principles" of 1776, he declared. But peace was the key. If war could be avoided, the people would in time "see through the delusions of the moment, and republicanism will be saved in this country." Somehow, the people had to come out from under the "powerful sedatives" of what he variously called "the XYZ inflammation," the "XYZ fever," the "XYZ delusion," and the "XYZ romance." Toward the end of the year, Jefferson saw a ray of hope. He glimpsed a turn in public opinion brought on by Federalist excesses. There had been popular support for preparing America's defenses, but only extremists had actually favored war or supported the assault on civil liberties in the name of defense. The steady rise of Republican newspapers—which Jefferson had long preached was essential—had helped awaken the public to the dangers that lurked. The "American mind" was breaking "through the mist under which it has been clouded," said Jefferson at the dawning of 1799. He was more certain than ever that "the tide . . . will sweep before it all" that Hamiltonianism embodied.[43]

Jefferson may have been correct that his countrymen were incorrigibly republican, and he may also have been accurate in his late-autumn prediction that "the Doctor is now on his way to cure" the war fever, for he "comes in the guise of a taxgatherer" to collect the taxes levied to pay for the Federalists' defense establishment.[44] But nothing was more crucial in defusing the crisis than the resolve, and prudence, of John Adams. The scales had begun to fall from the president's eyes when he had been compelled to name Hamilton as inspector general. Adams had wanted to name Henry Knox to be Washington's second in command; he had no desire to put the army in Hamilton's hands. The jarring episode awakened Adams to the possibility that a faction within his party had exaggerated the French threat. Adams had always looked on Hamilton as dangerously ambitious and impulsive for glory, and he knew full well of the inspector general's penchant for intrigue. Even so, he had discounted the rumors that Hamilton had plotted to deprive him of the presidency in 1796. Now he doubted nothing about Hamilton's designs, and no longer questioned the whispers about Hamilton's sway over the High Federalists. As his second year in office was drawing to a close, Adams at last was coming to understand that Hamilton had operated "underground and in darkness" first to prevent him from being elected, and next to manipulate his cabinet. Like Paine and Monroe before him, Adams now concluded that

"Washington . . . was only [the] viceroy under Hamilton." At last, the shaken and angry president saw that through his disloyal cabinet officials he, too, had been "the dupe" of Hamilton's machinations. If his wife—and Jefferson—saw a parallel between Hamilton and Napoleon, Adams took to privately referring to Hamilton as "Caesar."[45]

When several Federalists in Congress not only advocated an even larger army but also urged jingoistic policies, the president concluded that Hamilton was behind their initiatives. Philadelphia was buzzing with rumors that Hamilton was preparing to take his army into Spanish Florida or that he was about to join with Britain's armed forces to liberate Spain's colonies in South and Central America. Adams immediately vowed not to lead his country into any such "hazardous and expensive and bloody experiments." About the same time, someone—maybe a Virginian or possibly an alarmed Federalist who thought Hamilton dangerously delusional—showed Adams a letter that the inspector general had written about invading Virginia. Waxing on about Virginia's supposedly "insidious plan" to break up the American union, Hamilton appeared to propose that he march his army into Virginia to suppress supposed "internal disorders" raging within the state. To Adams, there seemed little doubt that Hamilton's ultimate objective was an invasion of Virginia. "The man is stark mad," said Adams.[46]

But more than Adams's bitterness toward Hamilton led him to reassess the Franco-American crisis. Information passed along by American envoys and private citizens in Europe—including Paine's friend Joel Barlow—led the president to believe that a rapprochement with France was possible. In December 1798, in his annual address, Adams said that he remained committed to a peaceful settlement. Jefferson did not believe him. A worried Hamilton did, however, and he encouraged the High Federalists to be on guard. When January and February brought additional evidence that France was willing to reach an accommodation, Adams without warning delivered to Congress a message announcing that he was sending a new team of envoys to Paris. High Federalist congressmen were apoplectic and confronted Adams in a stormy, closed-door meeting. Meanwhile, Pickering, Wolcott, and McHenry fought the president in tense cabinet meetings. But Adams stood his ground.

With all else failing, General Hamilton saddled up and rode to meet the president face-to-face. While Adams sat smoking a cigar, Hamilton initially exhibited his customary overweening manner as he offered every possible argument against sending the envoys to Paris. Hamilton had nearly always had his way with Washington. Not with Adams. Vexed to the core and relentlessly pacing the floor as he spoke, Hamilton grew more frenzied and agitated as he sensed that his was a losing cause. Adams played him with virtuosity, enjoying watching this "[over]wrought . . . little man" make an "impertinent ignoramus" of himself. With the sloping black shadows of late day creeping across the landscape, Adams at last tired of sporting with Hamilton and dismissed his general. Hamilton was left to face a long, cold, lonely ride back to an army that he now knew was doomed to extinction. The president, bent on diplomacy, never bowed to his party's pressure and in time his team of envoys sailed for Paris. Within the next few weeks, Adams cleaned house, dismissing Pickering and McHenry from his cabinet.[47]

Jefferson immediately saw that the course chartered by Adams in defying his party and renewing the search for an honorable peace was a great event, as he put it. Adams had silenced "all arguments against the sincerity of France" and rendered the Federalists' "efforts for war desperate." Jefferson believed the president's diplomatic initiative would bring about reconciliation with France, an event "so hateful & so fatal" to the Federalists, as it would spell their downfall and banish from America the "Gothic idea that we are to look backwards instead of forwards for the improvement" of humankind.[48]

The dark days of witches seemed to be ending, and the ideals of the American Revolution that Jefferson had coveted in 1776 might yet survive and flourish. But he knew that such an outcome to this turbulent decade would be assured only if the Republicans won the 1800 presidential election. Jefferson had been a reluctant candidate in 1796. His unwillingness diminished as he considered the stakes in 1800.

CHAPTER 13

"I KNOW OF NO REPUBLIC
EXCEPT AMERICA"

ENDGAME

JAMES MONROE HARDLY SEEMED to notice what Jefferson had called "the reign of witches." He continued to obsess over his treatment by Washington and how to set the record straight with regard to his conduct in Paris. He was also absorbed with getting his personal affairs in order. In addition to having resumed his legal practice, he was building his house, and in the spring of 1799 Elizabeth gave birth to the couple's second child, a son they named James Spence. (Monroe wished to name him after Jefferson, but his wife insisted on naming him for members of her family.)[1] Monroe was "embarrassed" by having fallen into debt. Calling his situation a "heavy business," he devoted considerable time to selling land, looking after farming operations on three properties—Highlands, Oak Hill in Loudoun County, and Monroe Hill, his original Charlottesville property situated on what now is the campus of the University of Virginia—and successfully seeking a land grant for his service in the Continental army. He received 3,100 acres in Kentucky, which he immediately put on the market, though it did not sell quickly. His struggles led Monroe into corners where he would have preferred not to go. He had to borrow money from his wife's relatives, mortgage some of his property at disadvantageous rates, and sell his first tobacco crop so early that it fetched a lower price than that of his neighbors who had the luxury of selling later. But after a year at home, Monroe said that his financial situation was "sound in the main" and that he would be completely "at ease" once his western properties were sold.[2]

Returning to his legal practice was a major initiative toward getting his financial affairs back in order. As was customary with nearly every important decision he confronted, Monroe went to Jefferson for advice. Jefferson blithely told him that resuming his legal practice was a good idea. The law "business is very profitable," and was likely to become even more rewarding now that some influential Richmond attorneys, including John Marshall, had closed their law offices after agreeing to serve under Washington or Adams. Besides, said Jefferson, practicing law would "shield" Monroe from the intolerable "languor of ennui" that accompanied the full-time pursuit of farming—an eye-opening remark from the nation's most renowned exponent of husbandry. Early in the spring of 1798, nine months after returning from Paris, Monroe was once again riding the legal circuit through Virginia's drowsy countryside.[3]

What Monroe really longed for was an important public office, but nothing was available aside from seeking reelection to the House of Representatives. Jefferson and Madison both encouraged him to take that step. Jefferson advised that any public statements that Monroe made as a congressman would be viewed as offered from the "high ground" in contrast to saying the same thing in a pamphlet. Winning election to Congress, Jefferson added, would also demonstrate that Monroe had regained the public's confidence. Samuel Cabell, who held the seat for the Albemarle County district, indicated a willingness to step down should Monroe wish to run. But Monroe declined the opportunity, fearing the economic consequences to his family, and also conscious that he could accomplish little in a chamber under Federalist control. Jefferson sought to persuade him that the Federalists were nearly finished and the Republicans would be in control before his first term ended. Monroe responded that to achieve nothing would "hurt my credit not advance it." In actuality, Monroe had set his sights on becoming the governor of Virginia. He believed that to be chosen the chief executive of a state, rather than a representative of a small congressional district, would constitute a more pronounced vote of confidence.[4]

But the governor's chair was not available. It had become customary in Virginia for the incumbent to serve three one-year terms. Monroe faced a wait of thirty long months. He marked time, often working more or less covertly with Jefferson and Madison on internal affairs within the Republican Party, seeking to hold the party together for the next presidential election. Reluctant to commit anything to paper, they huddled when Madison came down from Montpelier, a bit over twenty miles away, to meet with his two friends. Between meetings, Monroe and Jefferson communicated by having slaves carry their messages from one residence to the other.[5]

Since returning home, Monroe had published *A View* and written several essays that never went to press, and during 1798 yet another matter prompted him to write yet again. At the height of that summer's furor over the XYZ Affair, President Adams was flooded with patriotic messages sent by towns, organizations, and even grand juries. The president answered each with a brief and usually truculent address. In his reply to the statement sent by Lancaster, Pennsylvania, Adams referred to Monroe as the "disgrac'd minister" who had been "dismissed in displeasure for misconduct." (Even Hamilton thought some of Adams's messages were "intemperate" and "very indiscreet," though he was not critical of what the president said about Monroe.) In a less harsh but nonetheless condemnatory manner, Adams a year earlier had suggested to Congress that Monroe bore responsibility for the deterioration in Franco-American relations. Monroe read Adams's assorted remarks and bristled. He worked briefly on a rejoinder to the president's "low spleen & malice," but in the end Monroe never got past the bare bones of a draft.[6] Perhaps he decided that one defense of his conduct in France was sufficient. Or maybe he had learned something from Paine's misstep in publicly assailing a president.

Word made the rounds in 1798 that Virginia's Republicans would dump Governor James Wood for his lame response to the Alien and Sedition Acts, but nothing came of it. However, when Wood made clear that he would step down at the end of his third term late in 1799, the party coalesced around Monroe as his successor. Since 1776, Virginia's governors had been elected by the legislature and, early in December, Monroe's name was placed in nomination. Federalist assemblymen demanded a formal investigation of Monroe's mission to France, but they were easily brushed aside. On December 6, nearly three years to the day since Pinckney had arrived in Paris to replace him, Monroe was elected governor, winning 111 of 177 votes.[7] The order differed, but Monroe's career path was following that of Jefferson step for step: state legislator, congressman, diplomat, governor.

While Monroe marked time in Virginia, Paine was doing the same in France. During his first two years out of prison Paine had published three of his most important works, *The Age of Reason*, *Agrarian Justice*, and *Letter to George Washington*. Each was more memorable than anything published in America during the 1790s, and for a very long time thereafter. But in the five years that followed 1797, Paine's literary production was scanty and circumspect, owing less to fecklessness than to his ardent wish to avoid yet again being cast into harm's way. He waited impatiently for the peace that would end France's seemingly endless war with England and allow him to sail for America. Paine may have been more eager to escape France than to come home to America, though he still believed deeply in the American Revolution and the ideals he had written about in *Common Sense*. Paine had grown disillusioned with the French Revolution, and his last years in France—in the insightful remark of biographer Christopher Hitchens—"give the impression of the sour aftermath of a love affair."[8]

It is easy to see why "caution" would have been the watchword for the battle-scarred Paine. What remained of the decade after Robespierre's fall was filled with frightening uncertainty. It was a time, as one historian described it, of struggles among numerous factions "for the Revolution's soul," and the outcome was far from clear.[9] All that seemed apparent in the wake of the Terror was that new winds were blowing. Culturally, the revolution was thought to be at an end, as many returned to the couture fashionable under the ancien régime and revolutionary forms of address gave way to the traditional "Monsieur" and "Madame." Some royalists took heart, thinking the time ripe for a restoration of a constitutional monarchy or, perhaps, a return to all that had existed under the ancien régime. In 1795, about a year after Paine's liberation from the Luxembourg, the Directory—the executive under the Constitution of the Year III—faced a royalist insurrection. It was crushed by a military force led by Napoleon Bonaparte.

The one bright spot for France was that the war took a favorable turn, due largely to the brilliant generalship of Napoleon, who had been made commander of the Army of the Interior in 1795. In a series of campaigns during the next two years, Napoleon knocked Austria out of the war and made France dominant in Europe. (It was this turnabout that had led Jefferson in 1798 to conclude that peace in Europe was at hand and that the Federalists would not go to war against a victorious France.) But in 1799, Great Britain cobbled together a "Second Coalition" that included Russia, Austria, and several minor Italian and German states. Once again, France faced war with most of Europe. By then, too, restless domestic disturbances were mushrooming, spurred by opposition to compulsory conscription and despair over mounting economic woes. Unemployment was high in some sectors and many farmers were reduced to bartering for goods. A panicky element in French ruling circles, fearful that conditions were ripe for Jacobinism and another Terror, plotted a coup that would bring into the government a "Grand Elector," a military man who was to occupy an essentially ceremonial position. The assorted collaborators focused on Napoleon, who would prove to be more difficult to control than they imagined. The "Revisionists," as they were called, successfully brought off their coup in November 1799 (18–19 Brumaire) and installed Napoleon, supposedly the first step toward another constitution. They then announced: "Citizens, the Revolution is established upon the principles which began it: it is ended."[10]

Throughout the tumult, Paine averaged only about one publication every twelve months. *The Decline and Fall of the English System of Finance* was his most consequential. It aimed at exploiting dissent within England, though he may also have hoped that his swipe at English profligacy and habitual warfare would awaken Americans to what he saw as similarly noxious proclivities among the Federalists. Paine took on what historians today refer to as the fiscal-military state that had emerged in England nearly a century earlier. For all that time, said Paine, England's ruling structure had labored under the delusion that its funding system enabled it to wage war after war without reaping serious internal harm. He countered that Britain's six major wars during the past one hundred years had produced skyrocketing indebtedness. By his calculation, Britain's debt had climbed from about £21 million in the late seventeenth century to a figure likely to be fifty times greater by the end of its current war with France. Marshaling earlier works by Richard Price and Adam Smith, Paine argued that no government could survive such escalating obligations, and he predicted national bankruptcy for Great Britain within the next twenty years.[11]

Paine also authored a short defense of Monroe, describing him as a "worthy, enlightened" republican and challenging the belief among some that his supposed bungling had caused France's rupture with the United States. The damage, said Paine, had been done by an American government under Washington that had been "sold to the enemies of freedom."[12] Soon thereafter Paine turned out a pamphlet that over the years has often been censured by scholars. He defended the Directory's repression of royalists. Paine was a visionary, though he could be pragmatic. During America's desperate war, he had supported General Washington despite what he believed to be dangerous shortcomings; silence, he had thought, was preferable to the dangers that would follow Washington's removal. In the face of the royalist threat in 1797, Paine concluded that what France most needed was stability. Since the day of the king's flight six years earlier, recurrent turbulence had caused enormous harm. The greatest wrong turn of all, he wrote in *The Eighteenth Fructidor: To the People of France and the French Armies*, had been the ascendancy of the Montagnards. Under their rule, "Security succeeded to terror, prosperity to distress, plenty to famine. . . . It was the real republicans who suffered most during the time of Robespierre." Now those real republicans, the surviving remnants of the Girondins, were back in power and responsible for the suppression of the reactionaries, steps dictated by what Paine called the "supreme law of absolute necessity" to prevent a royalist counterrevolution. "Everything was at stake," he went on, and he urged citizens and soldiers to see the course of action taken by the rulers as a "matter of joy," for it had saved the Revolution.[13]

Paine knew instinctively that the once glorious promise of the French Revolution had vanished with the onset of the Terror. The Directory's late-1799 proclamation that the Revolution was over was merely confirmation of what had long since been reality. As the 1790s drew to a close, Paine and Jefferson lost hope in the possibility of a revival of the exuberant republican spirit of the first years of the French Revolution. Their erstwhile dream for the spread of the Revolution had been dashed as well. As America's presidential election of 1800 approached, Jefferson, Paine, and Monroe believed that the fulfillment of the American Revolution—and with it the hope that a republican beacon of light might shine toward the rest of the world—rode on the coming canvass.

Paine was too far removed from America to write an informed piece on its domestic partisanship, though he could not resist an occasional swipe at the "wrong-headed, tumultuous Administration of John Adams."[14] But his principal focus was on France's never-ending hostilities, in particular its naval war with Great Britain, and he wrote several essays on the topic for Nicolas de Bonneville's paper. The articles had not gained much attention, but sometime, most likely in 1798, a man who had read them appeared at Nicholas de Bonneville's door and asked to see Paine. The man was Napoleon Bonaparte. The previous year, the Directory had pressed him to invade England, and for some time Napoleon had been studying its chances of success. Ushered in, Napoleon laid on the treacle, telling Paine that he slept with *Rights of Man* under his pillow every night. A statue of Paine ought to be erected in every city on earth, he added. Once Paine's capacious vanity had been properly massaged, Napoleon pumped this disaffected Englishman for information about his native land. Napoleon also asked Paine to accompany the invading army, hopeful the writer with the golden pen could persuade sufficient numbers of Englishmen to rise up against Britain's rulers. When the talk turned to whether an invasion of England could possibly succeed, Paine assured the general that it could, so long as the French did not make the mistake the English had made in the Revolutionary War. Britain's redcoats had plundered the southern countryside, driving southerners to wage a guerrilla war that sapped British strength. Paine also advised that the best site for an invasion would be on the North Sea beaches, where the English were the least prepared. He contended that a flotilla of gunboats could cause major disruptions in English commerce. It was a revolutionary idea, Paine conceded, "but we live in an age of revolution." Paine asserted that the invasion itself would play havoc with England's food supply and economy. Given the English government's "want of popularity," said Paine, an invading army need seize only a small amount of territory in order to spark an insurgency that would knock England out of the war. Later, Paine elaborated on his thoughts at a meeting of the Military Council of Paris, which had convened to discuss with Napoleon the wisdom of invading England.[15]

A skeptical Napoleon eventually told the government that an invasion of England was unlikely to succeed. "The right time to prepare ourselves for this expedition has been lost, perhaps forever," he said late in 1798. Wisely, he ignored Paine, though two years later Napoleon dispatched an aide to confer with him on an array of matters ranging from an invasion of Ireland—which Paine had publicly urged—to peace negotiations with London. Once again, Napoleon paid scant attention to Paine's advice.[16]

During 1798, Paine was interrogated by the police concerning his relationship with an Irish priest who was suspected of spying for England. Police thinking does not change much over the centuries. The presence of one English spy in France aroused suspicion that a hive of spies must exist among the British natives living in France, and it led the Paris constabulary to keep a watchful eye on Paine. The police knew of Paine's English background, though it seems wildly improbable that they could have seriously thought that he posed a danger. It may be that they never thought him a threat, and that they leaned on Paine in the hope of persuading him to become an informant. If so, there is no evidence that such a strategy succeeded. Whatever the authorities believed, Paine worried constantly, and with good reason. Once, at a dinner celebrating Napoleon's early victories, the general looked directly at Paine— or so Paine thought—and announced in a loud and threatening voice: "The English are all alike; in every country, they are rascals."

Paine was aware that the police were watching him, and he remembered all too well the outcome of their scrutiny a few years earlier. The anxiety provoked by their investigation was doubtless a major factor in what he wrote and did not write, and it might explain his puzzling decision to publish recommendations for attacking the United States. Mostly, Paine abandoned writing. Instead, for the first time in years he turned his attention back to bridge building. It was a departure due to numerous factors, including his need for money and the realization that he had little left to say that was likely to produce another bestseller. Paine's interest in bridges was reawakened, too, when he learned that an iron bridge recently erected over the Wear River in Durham County, England, had been modeled on the design he had exhibited at Paddington nearly a decade earlier. Feeling both cheated and vindicated, Paine set about casting in metal a five-foot-long-model of his earlier design, though he told Jefferson that his new conception was stronger and more elegant than anything he had previously built. Paine being Paine, he also said that it was "the opinion of every person who has seen it" that his new bridge was "one of the most beautiful objects the eye can behold."[17] He further told Jefferson that he had invented a new and superior carriage wheel. But selling either the bridge or the wheel in wartime France was out of the question. That would have to wait until he returned to America, which—though he did not say so to Jefferson—enjoyed a better economy than had existed back in the 1780s when he had sought sponsors for his first bridge.

Despite having abandoned publishing, Paine was spooked by the police surveillance. He was so apprehensive that he left Paris for six months or more beginning in the fall of 1799. He first moved in with a friend in Dieppe, a port city in upper Normandy. Later he pushed on to Bruges, a canal-laced town in what now is Belgium, where he resided with a former Luxembourg cellmate. When he returned to his apartment in Bonneville's Paris home sometime in 1800, Paine found that his movements had only quickened the authorities' suspicion. During another visit by the police, Paine was told that his slightest misstep would result in his deportation to the United States, a punishment that could be fatal when crossing the war-torn Atlantic.

When Paine dropped anchor yet again with Bonneville's family, he was nearly broke. Unable to pay the rent, he cut a deal with Bonneville, who like-wise planned to move to America if and when the war with England finally ended. Paine not only promised that the Bonnevilles could reside with him when they arrived in America, but he also pledged that on his demise he would leave to Mme Bonneville and her children the lion's share of his property. Paine stayed on with the Bonneville family for the duration of his time in France, reading and tinkering in his apartment by day, socializing at night. If an English newspaper is to be believed—and there is reason both to accept its veracity and to suspect a degree of hyperbole—Paine nightly drank "brandy in such profusion, as to reduce him nearly to a state of insensibility."[18]

An Englishman who had last seen Paine seven years earlier, during his days in Saint-Denis, visited him around 1800. He was startled by the clutter and disarray in which Paine lived, but more shocked by his appearance. Now sixty-three, Paine's visitor thought, "Time seemed to have made dreadful ravages over his whole frame, and a settled melancholy was visible on his coun-tenance." Paine was listless until their conversation turned to politics. Suddenly energized, he raged against the French: "This is not a country for an honest man to live in; they do not understand any thing at all of the principles of free government, and the best way is to leave them to themselves." When his visitor referred to France as a republic, Paine burst forth, "Republic! Do you call this a Republic? . . . I know of no Republic in the world except America." He was "done with Europe, and its slavish politics," Paine roared.[19]

During 1800, Paine wrote to Jefferson that he was in "exceeding good health." At last, he said, his vexatious abscess had "entirely healed" after nearly five worrisome years. He yearned to return to America, he added, something he had also mentioned in his last letter to Jefferson, written forty-two months earlier. Paine had meant it in 1797 and he meant it in 1800. He closed by asking Jefferson to pull some strings and send an American frigate on which he might secure passage for his Atlantic crossing. He really wanted to come home.[20]

By the time Jefferson received Paine's missive, he was deep into the electoral campaign of 1800. His talk of retiring forever from public office had abated well before he was nominated by the Republican Party during the previous election. Throughout his vice presidency, Jefferson had remained silent about his future plans, though on occasion he had hinted that he might like a second term in that office. However, it is likely that at the latest he made the decision to once again seek the presidency during the tumultuous summer of 1798. He thought the Alien and Sedition Acts, the expanded army, and Hamilton's ascent to the inspector generalship had not just "dishonored our country" but could be an augury of even worse to come if the Federalists remained in control for four more years. Something else influenced Jefferson's thinking. Where he had expected Adams to win in 1796, Jefferson had come to think that a backlash against Federalist rule was "fast ripening" that would open the door for the Republicans to win the presidency and control of Congress.[21]

Crucial events in the 1800 election occurred in April, even before the two parties selected their candidates. The most pivotal was the stunning triumph by the Republicans in New York's assembly elections. The victory was engineered by Aaron Burr, who was nearly unrivaled in his understanding of the emerging politics of democracy. As New York's presidential electors would be chosen by the state assembly, and as the assembly would now be in the hands of the Republicans, Adams—who had won all twelve of New York's electoral votes four years earlier—was not going to garner a single electoral vote in that state in 1800. As Adams had squeaked by with three votes to spare in 1796, the odds against his reelection were suddenly much longer. The icing on the cake for the Republicans was what transpired that spring in Virginia. The state dropped its procedure of electing presidential electors by district, going instead to a winner-take-all system. In 1796, Adams had won one crucial electoral vote in Virginia. However, it now was clear that the president would be shut out in solidly Republican Virginia in 1800. As the Federalists were expected to carry New England and the Republicans appeared certain to do very well in the southern and western states, most observers thought the outcome in 1800 would hinge on Pennsylvania and South Carolina, states in which both parties were strong.[22]

Soon after the critical New York elections, Federalist and Republican congressmen caucused and selected their party's nominees. The Federalists chose Adams and Charles Cotesworth Pinckney. The Republicans picked

Jefferson and Burr, as they had four years before. But as a safeguard against unforeseen machinations, congressional Republicans stipulated that Jefferson was their first choice for the presidency. Soon after the caucuses, Jefferson, Adams, and Pinckney returned to their homes. None engaged in open electioneering. Burr, however, headed off to New England, and later to New Jersey, in hopes of garnering one or two electoral votes in those Federalist strongholds. Burr was not alone on the campaign trail. Hamilton embarked on a three-week tour of New England. Supposedly, he was in the field to disband his army, but no one was fooled. From the president on down, all who followed politics assumed that Hamilton was searching for Federalist electors whom he could persuade not to vote for Adams.[23]

Though Jefferson did not stump for votes, he wrote a campaign autobiography, the first presidential candidate to do so. It was so gloomily unenthusiastic that today no campaign manager would permit such a thing to see the light of day. Jefferson began by remarking that the United States and its people might not be any better off as a result of his years of public service. When he cataloged his achievements, he added that sooner or later everything he had done "would have been done by others." Nevertheless, he listed numerous accomplishments, including the revelation that he had been the principal author of the Declaration of Independence. During the campaign, Jefferson also wrote to several influential party members spelling out his convictions, letters that in a sense constituted a party platform. He articulated his belief in reserving to the states those powers not expressly given to the national government, and added that he wished to retire the national debt, limit the president's encroachment on congressional authority, eliminate the standing army, keep the navy small, rely on the militia to safeguard national security, and avoid foreign alliances.[24]

All the while, officeholders and workers from both parties made speeches, wrote pamphlets, and scribbled short essays for newspapers on behalf of their nominees. The vitriol may have been more pronounced than in the previous election, but the arguments put forward were largely a rehash of those in 1796. While each party defended its record and candidates, much of what was said and written would today be called "attack ads" and "negative campaigning." Republicans portrayed Adams as a monarchist and Pinckney as a mediocrity. They savaged the Federalists for Hamiltonian economics, the recently created army, the taxes it necessitated, and the Alien and Sedition Acts. The Federalists limned Burr as unprincipled, but they expended most of their energy in beating up Jefferson. He was accused of having lived sumptuously while others sacrificed during the Revolutionary War, of having been an ineffectual chief executive of Virginia, of cowardice in running from the British soldiers that descended on Monticello in June 1781, and of hating George Washington. It was said that Jefferson's stay in France had transformed him into a dangerous radical whose head was filled with a "stock of visionary nonsense." Federalists belittled his contribution to the Declaration of Independence, contending that the document was the work of a committee that had included Adams. A Federalist newspaper in Virginia alleged that Jefferson had a slave mistress, though nothing was said along those lines outside the state. Pouncing on the religious views that he had expressed in *Notes on the State of Virginia*, Federalists repeatedly branded Jefferson an atheist. They even exhorted New Englanders to hide their Bibles in the event of his election, lest Jefferson confiscate them. The voters' choice was clear, said a Federalist: "A RELIGIOUS PRESIDENT or . . . JEFFERSON AND NO GOD."[25]

Of all that was published, nothing had a longer-lasting impact than a tract written by Hamilton. Driven by a blinding rage at the way Adams had treated him, and the realization that he would have no influence should Adams be reelected, Hamilton came unhinged. During the summer, he wrote to Adams an extraordinary letter, worded along the lines of a first communiqué leading to a challenge to a duel. When Adams did not respond, Hamilton fired off a second letter in which he maintained that the president had said things that were indicative of a depraved mind. Adams did not respond to that letter either.[26] Soon thereafter Hamilton published an open attack on his party's president. Throughout America's long political history, few have been willing to take on an incumbent president of their own party, even when that leader was less popular than Adams in 1800. Hamilton gambled that he could so frighten a handful of electors that they would turn away from Adams. It was a desperate stab at keeping the executive branch in Federalist hands and in electing Pinckney, whom Hamilton appears to have seen as weak and easily manipulated. Hamilton would be badly damaged by the pamphlet. As his leading biographer noted, it "made Hamilton look hypocritical and woefully indiscreet, especially when combined with the Maria Reynolds pamphlet." In addition, it ruined him with many New England Federalists, who respected Adams, leaving in shambles whatever lingering aspirations Hamilton yet harbored for someday becoming president.[27]

In his fifty-four-page *Letter from Alexander Hamilton, Concerning the Public Conduct and Character of John Adams, Esq. President of the United States*, Hamilton assailed Adams's allegedly wrongheaded behavior as a congressman, diplomat, and chief executive. Adams's failings, wrote Hamilton, arose from his "distempered jealousy," "extreme egotism," "vanity without bounds," "ungovernable indiscretion," and "ungovernable temper." He implied that Adams was emotionally troubled, perhaps even mentally unbalanced. Given four more years in the presidency, he concluded, Adams might bring the Union to the brink of doom.[28]

As informed observers had suspected all along, the election hung on the outcomes in Pennsylvania and South Carolina. In Pennsylvania, the two parties divided the vote. The two Federalist candidates won seven electoral votes, the two Republicans eight. That meant the issue would be decided by South Carolina, which was exactly what Hamilton had hoped for, as Pinckney was a native son. No one knew for sure how matters would play out in the electoral college, but it was a good bet that each of the four candidates would net about sixty-five votes exclusive of South Carolina. Theoretically, Adams still could win reelection, though Pinckney's chances were better. Jefferson had won all eight of South Carolina's votes in 1796 and he might do so again, but as he remarked: "considering local & personal interests & prejudices," it "is impossible to foresee how the juggle will work." There was no uniform manner of choosing electors in 1800. South Carolina gave the choice to the state assembly, and that meant the legislative elections in mid-October were crucial.

As expected, the Federalists piled up votes in Charleston, a shipping and mercantile center. All hinged on the outcome of numerous contests in the backcountry, a region inhabited largely by yeomen who had never cottoned to a strong national government and were roiled by the taxes levied in 1798 to pay for the recently expanded army. The western farmers turned out in suffi- cient numbers to hand control of the assembly to the Republicans. Even so, given that Pinckney was a South Carolinian, some expected the assembly to command each elector to give one of his votes to Jefferson and one to Pinckney. But that was not the course taken by the Republican assemblymen. They directed the electors to vote for "republican *candidates only.*" It appeared that Jefferson and Burr would each receive eight votes from South Carolina, and that Adams and Pinckney would come up empty-handed. A Federalist could not be elected president in 1800. (Had Pinckney and Jefferson divided South Carolina's vote, Pinckney would have come up one short of capturing the presidency, for a Federalist elector in Rhode Island had balloted for John Jay rather the South Carolinian. Had the Federalists captured control of the South Carolina assembly, and had Adams and Pinckney equally divided that state's electoral votes, Adams would have been reelected by a single vote.)[29]

Once Jefferson learned that the South Carolina assembly had directed the state's electors not to vote for Pinckney, he was certain that he had won the presidency. Not only had he been his party's first choice for the presidency, but in confidence he had been informed that one or two southern electors would not cast their second vote for Burr. Jefferson believed the final tally would show that he had reaped seventy-one or more electoral votes and "Burr about 70." In this frame of mind, Jefferson wrote to Burr in December to explain how he planned "to compose an administration." Burr's electoral calculations were more or less the same as Jefferson's, and he responded with a letter that alluded to "your administration." However, to the surprise of both candidates, just before Christmas several newspapers published electoral results showing that Jefferson and Burr had each received seventy-three votes, Adams sixty-five, and Pinckney sixty-four. There was not a clear winner. Under the Constitution, if two candidates tied with a majority of the electoral votes, the House was to choose between them.[30]

Jefferson had been his party's first choice and his election by the House should have been a formality. But nothing about this election was that simple. Once Burr discovered that he was a whisker away from the presidency, he refused to concede, a decision that opened a Pandora's box of intrigue. In the electoral deadlock, each state would have one vote in the House's balloting to determine who was to be the president. The Republicans controlled eight delegations and the Federalists seven, while Vermont's two-member delegation consisted of one Federalist and one Republican. As there were with sixteen states, nine votes were needed for a majority, and victory. The Republicans were one vote shy of being able to elect one of their candidates, presumably Jefferson. Despite having lost the election, the Federalists immediately saw the glittering opportunities before them if they could persuade a congressman here and there to change his likely vote. Schemes and plots of every conceivable form became the order of the day, prompting Jefferson to lament that "we remain in the hands of our enemies by the want of foresight" by those at the Constitutional Convention who had conceived of such a flawed manner of electing presidents.[31]

Some Jeffersonians, including Governor Monroe, initially thought it unlikely that the Federalists would make a serious attempt to deny Jefferson the presidency. They would probably seek to "irritate" him, Monroe predicted toward the end of December, but eventually "more correct views" would dominate within the "Tory party" and it would accept Jefferson's victory. Within a week Monroe had changed his tune. Stories of Federalist machinations swirled in Washington, and soon reports of an assortment of Federalist ploys reached Richmond. As it turned out, each rumored gambit that came to Monroe's attention had indeed been proposed and considered in the supposedly secret Federalist caucuses. Several Federalist schemes involved stringing out the decision in the House past noon on March 4, the moment that Adams's term was to end. If no decision had been reached by that time, the country would be without a chief executive. In that event the Federalist-dominated Congress might call for a second presidential election or—after a supposedly objective investigation—invalidate the outcomes in Georgia and South Carolina on the grounds of voting irregularities, giving Adams a majority of the electoral vote. Still another idea was for President Adams, during his last minute in office, to appoint a federal official—almost certainly the chief justice of the United States—to be president during the next four years; that artful plan, as Monroe was aware, was the brainchild of John Marshall, who happened to be the chief justice of the United States. The Federalists also considered having Congress elect either the president of the Senate or the Speaker of the House, both of whom were Federalists, to serve as the nation's executive until December—nine long months away—when the newly elected Republican-dominated Congress would at last take office. The most straight-forward stratagem that the Federalists contemplated was to offer Burr the presidency in exchange for his pledge to support parts of the Federalist program, a bargain that would produce sufficient ripples in enough congressional delegations to make Burr the winner. This latter option gained momentum when Burr, in what one scholar has characterized as a "stealth campaign," encouraged the Federalists to open negotiations.[32]

Having at first thought the Federalists incapable of such "a degree of . . . wickedness" as to deny Jefferson and his followers "the success we have merited," Governor Monroe by February was convinced that this "desperate party" was neck-deep in "intrigue" to maintain Adams's presidency or to put Burr into the President's House. But Monroe clung to two hopes. One was that the northern states—the Federalist stronghold—would not push things so far as to risk breaking up the Union over this election. They "only mean to bully us," he predicted, convinced that the North would never "giv[e] up the hold they have on the valuable productions of the south." Monroe also hoped against hope that Burr, his longtime friend, would "have more firmness than to become their dupe."[33]

By February, the Federalists were mostly fighting among themselves over which Republican, Jefferson or Burr, was the lesser evil. Hamilton and his satellites, once unremitting critics of Jefferson, now displayed a sudden affinity for him. Long Burr's rival in Manhattan's politics, Hamilton contended that his old adversary was not merely an untrustworthy and "unprincipled . . . voluptuary"; he was the "most dangerous man of the Community." Jefferson, he said, was a hypocrite whose "politics are tinctured with fanaticism," but he was "*able* and *wise*." Hamilton remained in New York throughout the campaign, while Gouverneur Morris, who seemed to be everywhere—he was now a Federalist senator from New York—was on hand in Washington to relay information and pass along directives. Some northeastern Federalists preferred Burr, seeing him as one who understood the needs of their region while Jefferson, a rural southerner, might cause "the roots of our Society [to be] pulled up & a new course of cultivation substituted." Hamilton countered that it would be "political suicide" for the Federalist Party should Burr be elected, for in that event sufficient numbers in the northern states would drift to the Republican Party, making it the permanently dominant faction.[34]

While a driving snow fell outside, the House began voting on Wednesday, February 11, three weeks prior to Inauguration Day. On the first vote, Jefferson garnered eight states to Burr's six, but the Maryland and Vermont delegations deadlocked and neither state cast a vote. Jefferson was one vote short of victory. The House voted time and again that day and on subsequent days, sometimes quitting when darkness gripped the village of Washington, sometimes persisting throughout the night, stopping only at the break of dawn. By the time it adjourned late on a chilly Saturday afternoon, the House had voted thirty-three times in four days. The tally had never changed. Jefferson remained one vote short. New rumors now coursed through the capital: Virginia would secede if Jefferson was denied his victory; several northern states would leave the Union if Burr did not win; militiamen from Pennsylvania and Virginia would march on Washington to force the House to elect Jefferson; New England would raise an army of sixty thousand and march it south across the sodden winter landscape to resist those Jeffersonian militiamen. No one has ever known whether the talk of secession was serious, nor can it be known how close this disputed election came to producing a military confrontation. What is certain, however, is that Governor Monroe took preparatory steps toward using force.

Fearing that some "plan of usurpation" might be attempted by Federalists who had for "so long convulsed & disgrac'd this country," Monroe on the eve on the House's initial vote called the Virginia assembly into session. He vowed to the legislators that "should anything occur which requires" action on his part, "be assured" he would meet the challenge. In mid-February, he learned that a caucus of Republican legislators in Pennsylvania had "resolved to put every thing to the hazard" to ensure Jefferson's victory and had endorsed putting twenty-two thousand militiamen under arms. Monroe immediately swung into action. With the "State of things so critical and alarming," he announced the creation of a "chain of expresses" between Washington and Richmond. If a military showdown was in the offing, time would be of the essence. Monroe alerted authorities to prepare for the possibility that he might summon the militia to duty and he took steps to have the arms that the militiamen would need moved from armories in the isolated west to more central distribution points. Furthermore, acting on intelligence that the federal government was about to confiscate some four thousand muskets and bayonets from the arsenal in New London, Virginia, Monroe dispatched a militia unit to guard the precious weapons.[35]

Meanwhile, the steely Monroe urged Jefferson to neither compromise with the Federalists nor "yield the ground after gaining the victory." Since the fights in the Constitutional Convention and over ratification, he went on, his side and Jefferson's had "been . . . long accustomed to render & they [the Federalists] to conquer." That must stop. He urged "firmness," insisting from the start that the Federalists were bluffing in the hope of yet another capitulation by their weak-kneed adversaries that would "preserve [the Federalist] ascendancy, and improve their profits." Should the Republicans compromise yet again, this time with an electoral victory in hand, it would "shake the republican ranks" and ruin "the republican interest." Federalists and Republicans were too far apart ideologically to allow for a judicious bargain. "Either democracy . . . or royalty must prevail."

Monroe loved and admired Jefferson and had long looked toward his presidency, and he hated the Federalists and those in the party who had done all within their power to humiliate and destroy him. Even when imploring Jefferson not to bend, Monroe's obsessive rancor toward Washington shined through. He advised Jefferson not to be like General Washington, who by his "pusillanimous and temporizing policy" during the war had "suffered our people to perish in the jails & prison ships" of the enemy. Instead, Monroe appealed to Jefferson to be as you were as Virginia's governor when your "firmness and decision . . . advanc'd yr fame & served the cause." Jefferson, in response, declared "unequivocally that I would not receive the government on capitulation, that I would not go into it with my hands tied." He let pass Monroe's swipe at Washington, but concurred that at least some Federalists—the "incurables" among the High Federalists—were comparable to the Tories of 1776 who had opposed the American Revolution.[36]

Monroe and Virginia were poised for action, though the governor had always expected the Federalists to yield in the face of an unflinching stand by Jefferson. That, however, was not exactly how the crisis ended. The tipping point came when the Republicans floated the warning that if Jefferson's election was prevented, they would demand another convention to "re-organize the government, & to amend" the present Constitution to guarantee that it reflected the "democratical spirit of America." Whether or not a deception, the threat worked. As Jefferson remarked, the pledge to rewrite the Constitution "shook" the Federalists and gave "them the horrors."[37]

Suddenly, there was movement among the Federalists. James Bayard, Delaware's lone congressman who hitherto had cast every ballot for Burr, announced in a caucus that he would switch his vote, a move that would give

Jefferson the ninth state he needed for victory. Bayard subsequently said that he made the decision after Jefferson had been offered, and accepted, a deal. Jefferson always denied having agreed to a bargain of any sort. (He told Samuel Adams that he wanted to "see harmony restored among our citizens," but he would not "sacrifice . . . principle to procure it.") No concrete evidence substantiates Bayard's claim of a bargain, but there was a ring of truth to it. For instance, Jefferson supposedly consented to leave Hamilton's economic system intact, which in fact he would do throughout his presidency. The one thing that is clear is that the Federalists persuaded Bayard to delay switching sides while a last-ditch bargain of some sort was extended to Burr, who was in New York. On Monday, while awaiting Burr's decision, the House voted twice. It remained deadlocked. But in the pale pink-blue light of morning on Tuesday, February 17, word arrived from Burr before the House was gaveled into session. He had spurned the final Federalist offer. The recipient of Burr's letter, the Federalist Speaker of the House, Theodore Sedgwick, destroyed the missive, denying posterity the opportunity to learn what the Federalists had offered and Burr had demanded. Sedgwick then sighed: "the gig is up." When the House reassembled, it voted a thirty-sixth time. It was the magic ballot. With Jefferson's election now assured, more than one Federalist changed his vote. Jefferson received ten votes. He was over the top. Jefferson had been elected president of the United States.[38]

Monroe's dreams had come true. "We are safe in port," he exclaimed. Obviously more optimistic than Paine and Jefferson about the situation in France, he added: "unless Bounaparte turns royalist & villain, the commenc'ment of the 19th century will be more favorable to the causes of liberty, than any former epoch of time. America & France in republican hands can advance the cause with effect."[39]

The news of Jefferson's election triggered celebrations in every section of the land, including here and there in the Federalist-dominated Northeast. Some breathed a sigh of relief that power would be peacefully transferred from one party to another. For many, Jefferson's election meant that what he once had called the holy cause of freedom had been rescued from the hands of those who had sought to curb it. Monroe saw it as the "overthrow of the royalist party," and he and not a few others interpreted Jefferson's triumph as nothing less than the consummation of the American Revolution. Indeed, Jefferson in the glow of victory referred to his electoral triumph as a second Revolution, the "Revolution of 1800."[40]

Inauguration Day, March 4, arrived gray and cold. Around eleven o'clock Jefferson left his boardinghouse. Wearing a plain suit and joined by a covey of

United States marshals and members of the Alexandria, Virginia, militia, the incoming president made a mud-splattered walk up the gently sloping hill to the Capitol. When he reached the summit, artillery rang out and the militiamen saluted and stood at attention. The incoming president passed through a scrum of curious onlookers and hearty well-wishers as he proceeded slowly toward the Senate chamber. He found that some Federalist congressmen had stayed away. John Adams was absent as well. At dawn, the outgoing president had caught the stage for Massachusetts, refusing to honor his onetime friend. But some twelve hundred people were crowded into the tiny chamber. The room was called to order by Burr, who already had taken the oath of office as vice president and was now officially the Senate's presiding officer. He introduced Jefferson. The new president came to the podium to read the inaugural address that he himself had written. Jefferson began to read his speech in what one observer described as an "almost femininely soft" voice.[41]

Neither Washington nor Adams had delivered memorable inaugural addresses, but Jefferson's was noteworthy. He gently sought to defuse the passion and anger in the fractured land, mostly by reassuring his political foes. "We are all republicans: we are all federalists," he said. He was not referring to political parties. Jefferson meant that most in both parties believed that power came from the people, embraced an "attachment to the union and representative government," and accepted that the national government possessed some powers while the states were endowed with others.

Much of Jefferson's speech was a lyrical paean to his belief that America's revolutionary heritage had at last been fulfilled. He spoke of "this blessed country," this "chosen country," that had been shaped "through an age of revolution and reformation." Having survived the tempest of war and a stormy foundation, it now was a "rising nation . . . advancing rapidly to destinies beyond the reach of mortal eye." His administration would embody the "bright constellation" of "sacred" republican ideals that embodied the American Revolution: "a jealous care of the right of election by the people"; the "absolute acquiescence in the decisions of the majority"; "equal rights" for the minority; "equal and exact justice to all men"; and "the sacred preservation of the public faith."

However, he did not ignore the tenets of his party. While pleading for the restoration of "harmony and affection," he urged the abandonment of "religious intolerance," low taxes so as "not [to] take from the mouth of labor the bread it has earned," "freedom of the press," "freedom of person under the protection of the habeas corpus," and the "honest payment of our debts." He reminded his listeners that America's revolutionary precepts had included resistance to standing armies, and vowed that henceforth "a well disciplined militia [is] our best reliance in peace, and for the first moments of war, till regulars may relieve them." Since 1776, the "wisdom of our sages, and blood of our heroes have been devoted" to attaining all the goals that he had broached, and they were the objects sought by George Washington, "our first and greatest revolutionary character." These abundant ideals of the American Revolution will be the "creed of our political faith [and] . . . touchstone by which to try the services of those we trust."

He never mentioned France or the French Revolution, though he alluded to the "throes & convulsions of the ancient world, during the agonizing spasms of infuriated man, seeking through blood & slaughter his long lost liberty." Those gory events had been "more felt & feared by some [Americans] and less by others." He also mentioned that for nearly a decade Europe had been snared in the seemingly inescapable web of the "exterminating havoc" of war. Given that this "troubled world" was filled with "nations who feel power and forget right," the means through which "to make us a happy and prosperous people" was to strive for "peace, commerce, and honest friendship with all nations, entangling alliances with none." As he had so often in the past, Jefferson proclaimed that republican America remained "the world's best hope." It was the new president's sole testimony to his indefatigable belief that the success of republicanism in an amicable, religiously tolerant United States would be a beacon to the world, an inspiration for others longing to escape "angels in the form of kings" who offered only despotism and war.

Much of Jefferson's inaugural address spoke to the same linchpin themes that had rung out in *Common Sense* a quarter century before. Nevertheless, there was a difference. Thomas Paine in 1776 had dreamed of an as yet unrealized American Revolution. His hope was for a revolution that would deliver the colonists from the "crowned ruffians" of Europe and give birth to an America that would be the "lone spot of the . . . world" where liberty prevailed and stood as "an asylum for mankind." Jefferson believed that the American world Paine had envisaged had been realized, only to be imperiled by those who had never embraced the full meaning of the American Revolution. But the election of 1800 had fashioned the "surest bulwarks against antirepublican tendencies." A blissful America had "regain[ed] the road which alone leads to peace, liberty and safety."[42]

In the first days following his inauguration, Jefferson wrote letters to several friends. Each seemed to contain things that he had wanted to say in his formal address but, for one reason or another, had omitted. We have "done our part," he wrote, to save liberty by defeating America's extremists and reactionaries. We "deserve the embraces of our fathers" now that the "storm is over." Turning to a nautical metaphor, as he did so often, Jefferson declared that the American Revolution, after being tossed on rough seas during the Federalists' rule, had arrived safely "in port." In a sentence that carried much the same meaning as Paine's declaration in 1776 that the American Revolution was the birthday of a new world, Jefferson reflected that now a "new chapter in the history of man" was beginning. Guided by the spirit of the American Revolution, America in this new epoch would continue to inspire the oppressed around the globe. Just as the American Revolution had been the stimulus for the French Revolution, America's example of a "democratical spirit" would stir the hearts of the downtrodden everywhere.[43]

Paine was among the old friends to whom Jefferson wrote. The new president underscored that it was America and the American Revolution alone that could rouse hope among faraway peoples. America, Jefferson began, had avoided "wasting the energies of our people in war & destruction, [and] we shall avoid implicating ourselves with the powers of Europe, even in support of principles which we mean to pursue." The European nations have "so many other interests different from ours, that we must avoid being entangled in them. We believe we can enforce those principles as to ourselves by peaceable means, now that we are likely to have our public councils detached from foreign views."

He closed by telling Paine of his "high esteem & affectionate attachment" for him, and added that the ship he had requested for safe passage to America was about to sail from Maryland. He hoped that Paine would come home to America, and Jefferson hoped too that he would "find us returned generally to sentiments worthy of former times. In these it will be your glory to have steadily labored & with as much effect as any man living. That you may long live to continue your useful labours & to reap the rewards in the thankfulness of nations is my sincere prayer."[44]

CHAPTER 14

"DEATH HAS NO
TERRORS FOR ME"

CLOSING THE AGE OF PAINE

SIXTY-FIVE-YEAR-OLD Thomas Paine returned to America as he said he would, but not on the ship that President Jefferson provided. Paine steadfastly refused to risk an ocean crossing while France and Great Britain were at war, and negotiations for the Treaty of Amiens, which laid the groundwork for peace, were not concluded until late March 1802, a year after Jefferson had written his welcoming letter. Even then, Paine waited a bit, unwilling to make a voyage until the definitive treaty was signed and spring's "equinoxial gales are over." In late summer, he was at last ready. English friends in Paris helped settle his debts, and Clio Rickman, an old and constant friend from his days in Lewes, crossed the Channel to assist Paine in putting his affairs in order and accompany him to the coast. Paine insisted that no liquor go into his luggage. The two said their sad goodbyes in Le Havre knowing they would never see each other again, and early in September Paine embarked for America. Fifteen years had passed since Paine, his bridge in tow, left the United States for Paris, and as Rickman noted, ten years almost to the day had gone by since Paine had fled England for the supposed safety of France. As the vessel bearing Paine disappeared over the horizon, the melancholy Rickman composed a little poem about his friend who was leaving a France "unworthy [of] thy talents" and "hastening to join the happy and free" in America.[1]

The crossing consumed nine restless weeks, but it was a safe voyage, and Paine disembarked in Baltimore early in November in good health. He never said what kind of reception he expected, though a portion of Rickman's poem must have captured Paine's aspirations and uncertainty. Rickman had written that if the Americans were "fill'd . . . with reason and light," they would see Paine as a hero of their Revolution and the "champion of all that is glorious and good."[2]

As it turned out, not all Americans were filled with goodwill toward Paine. Many conservatives had long been contemptuous of him. For some time he had been vilified in the Federalist press, and at party gatherings the faithful had toasted sending *"Tom Paine* to the devil" or celebrated his incarceration in the Luxembourg prison. Some conservatives had first soured on Paine because the radical bent of *Rights of Man*, but many Americans—whatever their politics—were put off by his assault on Christianity and the Bible in *The Age of Reason.* Thereafter, he was often denounced as a "monster of impiety." Many, again regardless of party affiliation, were embittered by Paine's later attack on what one scribe called "the holy character of Washington."[3] By the time Paine returned to the United States, Federalists loathed him as they "would a scourge of scorpions," in the words of Levi Lincoln, Jefferson's attorney general. But they did not merely hate Paine; they feared him, living in "dread" of anything he wrote, for according to Lincoln they knew that the public found his persuasive writings to be "irresistible." Indeed, once the Federalists learned that he was returning to America—the news got out because Paine, his monumental vanity unchecked, leaked word of Jefferson's offer of a ship to the Parisian press—party scribblers laid down a thunderous barrage of invective. Paine was labeled a "lying, drunken, brutal infidel" and equated with Benedict Arnold as a traitor to America. He was called a "scavenger of faction" who delighted in "basking and wallowing in . . . confusion, devastation, bloodshed, rapine, and murder." Some assaults were painfully personal, such as those that depicted him as homely, playing on his disfiguring rosacea. "His nose is a blazing star," said one writer, and another wrote that his carbuncled nose sagged "nearly as low as his mouth."[4]

No political conservative hated Paine more than did John Adams. Now at home in Quincy, Massachusetts, Adams spoke of being exiled in "an enemies' Country," a fate that he attributed mostly to Hamilton. His bitterness toward the backstabbing Hamilton was boundless, but it was nearly equaled by his loathing for Paine, who he thought had been responsible for evil on a grand scale. Although he conceded that "Without the pen of the author of *Common Sense,* the sword of Washington would have been raised in vain," Adams blamed Paine for nearly all that he believed had gone wrong since July 1776. Aside from its contribution to the war effort, Adams thought *Common Sense* a "Malicious, short-sighted, Crapulous Mass." Variously characterizing him as "*a Star of Disaster*" and a "Dangerous Meteor," Adams concluded that he knew "not whether any Man in the World has had more influence on its inhabitants or affairs for the last thirty years than Tom Paine." Given his extraordinary "Career of Mischief," Adams thought the period beginning in 1776 should be called by historians the "Age of Paine." Fully wound up, Adams added one of his better-remembered lines. Paine, he wrote, was "a mongrel between Pigg and Puppy, begotten by a wild Boar on a Bitch Wolf."[5]

Much of the Federalist abuse was directed at Paine and Jefferson together, "affectionate friend[s]" whose "united exertions" had sought nothing less than the destruction of "the reputation of Washington and with it" the national government. It was said to be deplorable that President Jefferson looked on this "most inveterate hater of Christ and his religion" as a confidant or that he was chummy with "that living opprobrium of humanity, TOM PAINE." A Federalist political cartoon showed Paine acting in concert with the Devil— who clearly was Jefferson—to pull down the sturdy pillars of the American republic. A liquor bottle stood at Paine's feet while he tugged on a rope to dismantle the federal government. Jefferson urges him not to give up. "Pull away Pull away my Son dont fear I will give you my assistance."[6]

Paine might have thought he had landed in enemy territory or—as his friend Rickman subsequently put it—in "a country abounding in fanatics." His reception in Baltimore was anything but warm. He was turned away by two innkeepers before he found what one observer called a "paltry" tavern that agreed to rent him a room and serve the thirsty traveler. In time, Paine discovered that not everyone was so unkind. Some Republican newspapers defended him, prompting Paine to write to Rickman and claim hyperbolically that every newspaper in every state "was filled with applause or abuse" for him. Nor were all the descriptions of him laced with vitriol. A New Englander who saw him shortly after his arrival thought he looked older than his age and added that he "bends a little forward" cupping his hands behind his back when walking. He went on to say that Paine "dresses plain like a farmer, and appears cleanly . . . in his person," aside from the "snuff which he uses in profusion." That same observer made a point of disclosing that Paine ate and drank in moderation, and that neither age nor habits had dulled the famous author's keen intellect. His "memory preserves its full capacity, and his mind is irresistible," so that his "conversation is uncommonly interesting; he is gay, humorous, and full of anecdote."[7]

Paine did not linger in Baltimore. He was eager to reach nearby Washington and meet with the president. If he expected Jefferson to put him up in the President's House, as James Monroe had billeted him in Paris, Paine was disappointed. Nevertheless, the president frequently invited Paine to dinner during the one hundred or so days that he spent in the capital. His decision to host Paine required fortitude on Jefferson's part, given the ongoing torrent of venom by the Federalists. Once Federalists learned that the "two Toms" often dined together, the president was roasted for keeping such company; "our stomachs . . . nauseate" at the thought "of their affectionate embraces," wrote one polemicist. According to one of the more scurrilous pieces, the two were so close that Paine asked the president to share Sally Hemings with him. A fellow guest at one of the dinners noted that Paine "conversed and behaved towards [the president] with the familiarity of an intimate and an equal."[8] In some respects, Paine considered himself the equal of the president—egalitarianism was his abiding principle—and having spent time in the presence of important men such as Washington, Franklin, Lafayette, and Napoleon, he was not intimidated by prominent figures.

After a few weeks, Paine understood that he was an outsider in the capital, much as had been the case during his later years in Paris. When Congress assembled in December for its annual session, many Republican delegates seemed wary of his company. Thereafter, too, Jefferson's invitations arrived less frequently, partly because of the press of business, partly from political considerations. Paine was miffed that the president had not taken the time to speak with him about the bridge models and designs for carriage wheels that he had brought from France, and he churlishly told Jefferson of his displeasure. Paine was no less disappointed by the president's indifference toward his advice. When Paine urged Jefferson to offer to purchase Louisiana from France—which it had regained from Spain—the president turned the conversation in another direction. Paine dropped by the President's House the following day to raise the matter again. This time Jefferson (who had learned of the change in Louisiana's status a year or more before Paine had heard of it) cut off his visitor with the cryptic remark that "measures were already taken in that business." The president was referring to the orders he had long since given to America's minister to France, Robert R. Livingston, to explore the purchase of southern and southwestern borderlands. If Paine broached the notion that Louisiana might become a homeland for free blacks and newly liberated slaves—something he proposed in a missive to Jefferson two years later—the president was uninterested.[9]

Paine had not planned to remain in Washington for long. He was eager to travel to Bordentown, New Jersey, where he had owned a small house since 1783. He expected to return to the capital later in 1803, though the return trip never materialized and he never again saw Jefferson. Paine set off for New Jersey in February. He had looked forward to pausing along the way in Philadelphia to renew old acquaintances, but his brief stay was disheartening. Several former friends, including Benjamin Rush, refused to meet with him, and some Philadelphians were conspicuously rude and insulting. Paine departed after only three days in the city, more eager than ever to reach Bordentown and see his old friends, Colonel and Mary Kirkbride, and John Hall, his former bridge-building assistant. But Paine had not come solely to see them. He knew that Marguerite Bonneville and her three sons had planned to sail for the United States shortly after his departure from Le Havre, and in the deal he made with the Bonnevilles back in 1800, Paine had offered to help them when they came to America. Paine was also aware that the French government had refused to permit Nicolas Bonneville to leave the country, though Mme Bonneville—and perhaps Paine as well—believed the ban would be of short duration. Sometime after Paine's vessel made port in Baltimore, Marguerite, now thirty-five years old, and her three boys disembarked in Norfolk. Paine had provided her with directions to Bordentown and, the language barrier notwithstanding, she and her sons—Louis, Benjamin, and Thomas (Thomas Paine Bonneville, in fact)—found their way. Paine had told her that she would "receive every friendship" from the Kirkbrides, who lived near his cottage, and that had proven to be true. She arrived in Bordentown before Paine, and the Kirkbrides had cared for her and the boys following their move into Paine's house.[10]

When Paine reached Bordentown in February, Hall noted that he looked good and thought him "jollier than I have ever known him." Paine paused there for only a week. Not only was he anxious to get a look at his property in New Rochelle, but also he likely learned that James Monroe was in New York for a brief stay and he hoped not to miss seeing him.[11] His journey to the city did not get off to a good start. The proprietor of the express stage from nearby Trenton to Manhattan cursed Paine and refused to sell him a ticket, and another man who rented coaches also declined his business. Hours passed before Paine found someone who was willing to lease him a carriage, but by then a large crowd described by the local newspaper as consisting mostly of young and affluent Federalists had gathered. One in the throng played the "rogue's march" on a drum while others showered the carriage with rocks. Despite the danger it posed for the passenger, one hooligan sought to spook the horse. The newspaper account said that Paine displayed no sign of fear, and that he stepped from the carriage and told the assemblage that their hostility did not "hurt his feelings or injure his fame." The mob backed off and Paine at last departed.[12]

On arriving in New York City, Paine was briefly reunited with Monroe, their first—and last—meeting since Monroe's departure from France nearly six years earlier. Paine remained in the city for several days, finding the New Yorkers friendlier than the Philadelphians or Trentonians. He was the guest of honor at a dinner at the City Hotel, at which the large audience sang "The Fourth of July," a ditty that Paine composed for the occasion and mischievously set to the tune of "Rule Britannia." Many called on him at his lodging, including a part-time clerk at a Presbyterian church who was subsequently fired for having shaken Paine's hand. The clerk seemed to think that meeting Paine was ample compensation for being sacked by the church. "I have seen Thomas Paine," he exulted, and he left a description of his hero as "long, lank, coarse-looking," and cordial.[13]

At length, Paine made the excursion to New Rochelle. The house given to him by New York had been struck by lightning and burned several years before, but a smaller dwelling—originally for use by a tenant or hired hand—remained. Paine was satisfied with what he found, and his thoughts immediately turned to how to make his property profitable. He could sell some of his considerable acreage, but more immediately the estate could be timbered for firewood that would be sold in New York City. Paine reckoned that during the first winter he could sell upwards of three thousand cords of wood at $3.50 per cord.[14] Plotting his finances was a departure for Paine, who had usually seemed strikingly indifferent to pecuniary matters. Age certainly had something to do with it, as did his responsibilities toward Marguerite Bonneville and her sons. Otherwise, his changed outlook probably signaled a painful awareness that he was unlikely to ever again write a book that would sell as well as his famous earlier ones.

By early April, Paine was back in Bordentown, staying with the Kirkbrides while Mme Bonneville and her boys occupied his cottage. Save for a brief return trip to Manhattan for a gala Independence Day celebration, Paine remained in Bordentown for four months. He lived quietly, rising late and reading and writing during the day. At the same time late every afternoon he walked into town for an evening of conversation at the Washington House Tavern. He was open and accessible, willing to talk with anyone who was thoughtful and informed. He usually attracted a crowd. Before summer ended it was said that as a result of his discourses on religion, "several members of the church were turned from their faith." The locals were puzzled by his eccentricities. On his walks to town Paine was "generally absorbed in deep thought" so that he "seldom noticed any one as he passed, unless spoken to." On his nighttime return home he "was frequently observed to cross the street several times."[15]

Though generally happy, Paine was disappointed by the failure of his bridge-building dreams. Hall had noted in February that Paine was "full of whims and schemes and mechanical inventions." He had previously sought Jefferson's help in speaking with members of Congress about obtaining a federal subsidy to get the bridge project off the ground, and while in Washington, he lobbied congressmen personally. Later, he appealed to them in writing and courted potential investors in Philadelphia and New York. Paine also persuaded the artist Charles Willson Peale to display his model bridge in his Philadelphia museum. It was all to no avail. By the fall of 1803 Paine appeared to realize once and for all that the bridge to which he had devoted so much thought and energy for nearly twenty years would never be built. As autumn settled in, his thoughts turned in another direction. He conceived the idea of reissuing his most popular works in a five-volume set, each piece introduced by an original introductory essay explaining "the state of affairs . . . at the time it was written." He never got around to the project.[16]

Late that summer Paine traveled to Stonington, Connecticut, for what was planned to be a three-week sojourn with a ship owner and longtime friend. As was Paine's custom, he overstayed his visit by nearly two months, though in this instance his tarrying arose from his warm welcome in the busy little fishing community. The residents, mostly farmers, artisans, mariners, and fishermen, were unaccustomed to having a celebrity in their midst. Some called on Paine and others crowded into the tavern he frequented each evening, hanging on his every word. He had plenty to say. He regaled them with stories and recollections, read aloud newly received letters from President Jefferson and Secretary of State James Madison, discoursed on the rights of man, and expanded on the major issues of the day such as the acquisition of Louisiana, the renewal of war between Britain and Napoleonic France, and the upcoming presidential election of 1804. When asked about his faith and views on Christianity and the Bible, he did not hold back. These were heady days for Paine. Reveling in the attention and adulation, he came away convinced that many New Englanders shared his hostility toward the Federalist Party.[17]

The approach of autumn's inclement weather finally uprooted Paine, and he scurried to New Rochelle to look after his plans for vending firewood. Health issues frustrated his entrepreneurial venture. Paine had hardly arrived before suffering a debilitating affliction of gout, his first since shortly after his release from prison eight years earlier. Soon after recovering, he took a nasty fall on the ice, which laid him up for a month. A local store clerk took him in during his convalescence. He found Paine to be affable and cheerful, "careless in his dress and prodigal of his snuff," but "always clean and well-clothed." Seeing no sign of his guest's rumored alcoholism, the clerk characterized Paine as "abstemious."

With his wood-selling scheme aborted, and finding his ramshackle little cabin painfully uncomfortable in a harsh New Rochelle winter, Paine moved to the City Hotel in New York early in 1804. The hotelier could not have been more pleased with his guest. He, too, said that Paine drank little—less than any other lodger, he said—and he was impressed by the frequent dinner invitations that Paine received from local luminaries.[18]

Paine was a New Yorker for the remainder of his life, dividing his time—at least at first—between the city and his rural estate. Sometime after leaving Stonington, Paine learned that Colonel Kirkbride had died. He never returned to Bordentown. Nor did Marguerite Bonneville linger there. Unable to adjust to a tiny farming community after a lifetime in bustling Paris, she packed up her children and moved to a New York City rooming house sometime during the first months of 1804. Paine found a room for himself in the same facility, though he was soon unhappy with the arrangement. The rent was steep and Mme Bonneville was hardly frugal in her habits, at least from Paine's perspective. With a nudge from him, she soon found a job teaching French.[19]

When warmer days arrived in late spring, Paine returned to his rural cottage in New Rochelle, leaving Mme Bonneville in the city. His estate was substantial, consisting of 360 acres in an oblong parcel that extended nearly one and a half miles. Roughly one-third of his farm was meadowland, another third pastureland, and the remainder woodland. Paine lived simply, as he had during most of his adult life. The cabin was small and rustic, and came with six chairs and a table, two beds—one a feather bed, the other "a bag of straw"—a tea kettle, a pot, two pans, a gridiron for grilling food over an open fire, assorted tableware, and two candlesticks and snuffers. In addition, he had two small wagons, a pair of oxen and an oxcart, a horse, a cow, and a sow and nine piglings. During his first full year of residence, Paine sold sixty acres for $4,020, a considerable sum in that day, so much in fact that he put his notion of selling firewood on a back burner and never got around to it. Not only did he think he was fixed for life, but he also considered renovating his residence. His plan was to make the necessary repairs to the existing dwelling and build a one-story addition consisting of several rooms and a workshop. He contemplated a deck atop the addition that would serve as an observatory and outdoor living space in the summer months. He sought the opinion of Jefferson, a compulsive remodeler, who advised that Paine's plan to live outdoors was impractical. It mattered little, for like so much that Paine contemplated, he never embarked on his projected upgrades.[20]

Mme Bonneville's teaching career was short-lived. "She has not the least talent of managing affairs for herself," Paine grumbled, and he advised that she move in with an affluent family and serve as a tutor to their children. Instead, she and two of her children—Louis had returned to France—moved in with Paine. Not long passed before he was unhappy. He found Marguerite "an encumbrance . . . all the while," unwilling to "do anything," he said, "not even make an apple-dumpling for her own children." By late summer 1805 the experiment in living together had ended and she was back in the city. But Paine took responsibility for her children's education, and he was willing to have nine-year-old Benjamin—whom he called "Bebee"—live with him.

Paine's ties with Mme Bonneville provoked gossip, tattle that endured after a posthumous early biography portrayed the couple as lovers and hinted that Paine was the father of at least one of her children. There is no way of knowing whether theirs was an amorous or merely friendly relationship, or whether Paine simply felt honor bound to abide by the commitment he had made in 1800 to care for all the Bonnevilles following their crossing to America. For that matter, nothing is known about Paine's sex life, including whether he had one. When a friend probed with regard to the devotion and care he lavished on Bebee, Paine enigmatically responded: "I will take care of him for his own sake and his fathers, but this is all I have to say."[21] The best bet is that Paine's fidelity to her and the two boys sprang from amiability, gratitude for the kindness the Bonnevilles had bestowed on him in Paris, and the deep streak of humanitarianism in Paine's character.

Paine made an abundance of enemies during his lifetime, but in 1804 a run-in with one aggrieved individual very nearly resulted in more harm than even Gouverneur Morris had visited on him. Sometime after settling down in New Rochelle, Paine hired Christopher Derrick to work on the farm. It was not a good choice, and Paine fired him. Unhappy with his dismissal, Derrick's anger grew when Paine pressed him for the repayment of a not-inconsequential loan. Rage and the consumption of a large amount of rum got the best of Derrick on Christmas Eve. Paine was entertaining neighboring friends that cold December night when Derrick crept up near the house armed with a musket. He could see Paine seated at the window. Taking aim, Derrick fired, intent on killing his former employer. Only Derrick's impaired condition, and the notorious inaccuracy of muskets, saved Paine. The ball narrowly missed its target. Derrick was arrested on a charge of attempted murder, but Paine refused to press charges and his assailant was set free.[22]

Paine found another incident to be almost as disturbing. In 1806 the local election supervisor—a Federalist and descendant of Loyalists—declared Paine ineligible to vote in that year's congressional election. His reasoning was that Paine was not a United States citizen. As if to rub salt in Paine's wounds, the official grounded his decision on Gouverneur Morris's refusal in 1794 to acknowledge Paine's American citizenship. Paine argued and protested, but to no avail.[23]

Paine had once spoken of retiring when he returned to America. If he ever actually contemplated calling it quits, his was one of the shortest retirements in history. Sixteen days after disembarking in Baltimore, Paine broke his five-year semi-drought as a writer. That was only the beginning. Over the next six years Paine published some thirty-five additional essays. He also wrote frequently to Jefferson offering advice, which the president generally ignored. Once, he offered to sail to France and serve as the president's special envoy to meet with Napoleon, but Jefferson did not respond. In fact, having been burned more than once by his private letters being made public—in one instance by Paine—Jefferson seldom replied to Paine's missives. Paine contemplated a trip to Washington in 1805, but it was canceled given the severity of the winter weather, and he never again visited the capital.[24]

Nothing that Paine wrote during this period even remotely approached the significance or influence of his most important earlier works. As had been the case when he first came to America in the 1770s, Paine wrote on a wide variety of subjects, including religion. Although he believed that America's evangelicals would largely ignore him if he said nothing more on religion, he evidently did not mind being troubled by them. In 1804, he wrote several essays for the *Prospect*, the monthly publication of the Theistic Society, a deistical organization. Three years later he produced *Examination of the Prophecies*, one of three pamphlets he authored after returning to America. Paine sometimes referred to these compositions as part three of *The Age of Reason*, and taken together they were comparable in length to that popular book. What he turned out were variations on themes he had treated earlier, though all were written in his customarily inflammatory style, guaranteed to arouse indignation in some quarters. For instance: the Bible bore "no evidence of being the work of any other power than man"; the notion of forgiveness of sins encouraged wickedness, making it "dangerous to morals in this world" and to the chances of "happiness in the next world"; the "Christian system of religion is an outrage on common sense"; prophecies were "insulting nonsense" through which the "priestcraft . . . gain their living" by exclaiming against faithlessness, though actual infidelity was the belief "IN THE STORY OF CHRIST."[25]

Paine occasionally turned to events in Europe and hot-button political issues in America. He blamed Great Britain for ending the fourteen-month-old Peace of Amiens and plunging the continent back into war. He predicted in one article that Napoleon would invade England and touch off a revolution. In another, he argued that England was in more desperate straits than at any time since the Anglo-French warfare commenced in 1793. Calls for an expanded United States navy in 1807 led Paine to churn out an essay counseling that the Royal Navy was bankrupting England while contributing little to the nation's defense, a fate that could haunt America as well should it create a huge fleet. He wrote on political and constitutional issues in Pennsylvania and New York, lashed out at Federalist polemicists in Massachusetts and Virginia, and dished up a tract on the liberty of the press. In an important essay that went unheeded, Paine in 1804 urged the prohibition of slavery in the soon-to-be-organized Louisiana territory. In another composition that same year—one that he must have especially relished writing—he took apart the effusive eulogy that Gouverneur Morris delivered at the funeral of Alexander Hamilton, who had died that summer in a duel with Aaron Burr. Paine sought to demonstrate that Morris had exaggerated Hamilton's role during the American Revolution, its war, and the siege of Yorktown, and he informed his readers that at the Constitutional Convention Hamilton had sought a monarchy and an upper house of Congress in which members held their seats for life. Paine devoted more space to assailing Washington than Hamilton, charging that Washington had packed his cabinet with those who at the Constitutional Convention had supported an arbitrary, undemocratic system.[26]

In 1803, Paine came out with a long essay on building iron bridges and another on dreams. Later, he wrote on freemasonry, gunships, the causes of yellow fever, the possibility of war with Britain, and a piece claiming to show that Napoleonic France had "always behaved in a civil and friendly manner to the United States.[27]

Paine's earliest essay, the one that appeared within days of his arrival in Washington, was the first in what ultimately became an eight-part series that appeared over thirty months. Titling these essays "To the Citizens of the United States," Paine hoped the series would be a blockbuster along the lines of his string of *American Crisis* pieces. But unlike America in 1776, the nation in 1802 was neither in dire straits nor facing an emergency. Much of the sense of peril unleashed by the XYZ Affair had vanished, thanks both to a negotiated settlement with Napoleon in the final days of Adams's presidency and the peaceful resolution of the turbulent election of 1800. The crisis mentality that had prevailed prior to Paine's return had been replaced by a sense of national tranquility. Furthermore, little was new in "To the Citizens." Much that he wrote covered ground plowed in the previous decade by numerous Republican polemicists while Paine was abroad. In addition, some readers must have been put off by Paine's palpable self-regard. He had barely gotten rolling in the inaugural essay before he bragged about the astronomical sales of his previous works and reminded readers of his "established fame in the literary world." In a subsequent piece, he came close to suggesting that the role he had played in the American Revolution was as crucial as that of General Washington. He may have been correct in boasting that his arrival in America had afflicted Federalists with a deadly malady akin to "canine madness," but many readers likely found his egotism off-putting.[28]

Throughout the string of "To the Citizens" essays, Paine focused almost entirely on what he saw as the Federalist menace. As that party had not come into existence until years after he left the United States, his knowledge of American partisanship must have been derived in large measure from conversations with Monroe in Paris and, possibly, through discussions with Jefferson during visits to the President's House. Monroe may have provided insights about Hamilton, about whom Paine knew little, if anything, before he sailed for France in 1787. Jefferson may have fleshed out the ramifications of Hamiltonian economics. Paine might additionally have gleaned much about the Federalist mind-set from his exchanges in London and Paris with Gouverneur Morris, a party stalwart. In any case, Paine was a seasoned thinker who needed little tutoring.

At one time, much of Paine's thinking had tallied with that of Hamilton. Both were urbanites who in the 1780s advocated a strong commercial republic, and each supported manufacturing, a national bank, and a stronger central government than existed under the Articles of Confederation. Like Hamilton, Paine had supported national indebtedness, writing in *Common Sense*, "No nation ought to be without a debt. A national debt is a national bond." Hamilton could not have put it better. But Paine found many features of Hamiltonianism repugnant, including the Federalists' compulsive belligerence, affinity for the rich and influential, transparent Anglophilia, hostility toward the French Revolution, and what he saw as a Burkean veneration for monarchy and aristocracy.[29]

Paine, like Jefferson, believed that Hamiltonianism contained the seeds of a growing and sustainable concentration of wealth and inequality. He was certain, too, that what the Federalists stood for would in time leave power in the hands of a small elite, robbing much of the citizenry of hope for a better life, as England's oligarchy had. Paine aspired to a more virtuous world characterized by ideals such as kindness, love, charity, goodness, gentleness, and happiness, and in which popular self-rule prevailed. Long before his return to America, Paine's ethos was antithetical to that of the Federalist Party, and it was hardly surprising that he saw the Federalists as arch-conservative Tories who wished to undo as much as possible of the new world ushered in by the American Revolution.

As the Federalists' true designs would inevitably be injurious to the common people, said Paine in these essays, party spokesmen concealed the party's real intentions. As the "Feds do not declare what their principles are," he contended, "we may infer, that either they have no principles, and are mere *snarlers*, or that their principles are too bad to be told." The latter was the case, Paine said. They deliberately obscured their actual agenda. Paine advised that the Federalists' gambit in public presentations was fearmongering, spreading fallacies about the menace of disloyal immigrants, and peddling absurdly lurid allegations about the Jeffersonians' atheism and subservience to France. He saw Federalist tactics in the same light that many on the American left in modern times have seen their right-wing foes. Federalists, he wrote, camouflaged their genuine aims by ginning up foreign crises. The Federalists' stock in trade was to ramp up anxiety about national security, after which they donned "the garb of patriotism" and postured as America's defenders against the imagined threat. They manufactured a war scare with France, a deception that enabled them to institute a "Reign of Terror" through which they succeeded in curtailing natural rights with the Alien and Sedition Acts. Their most coveted prize, won by deceit during the contrived hysteria provoked by claims of an imminent French invasion, had been the creation of a standing army. But their overarching "aim has been and still is, to involve the United States in a war with France." Paine's divination of Federalist strategy was uncannily accurate, almost as if he had been reading Hamilton's letters to his flunkies in Adams's cabinet.

Paine's scrutiny of what the conservatives had achieved—the emasculation of the authority of the states, putting in place Hamiltonian economics, and turning much of the once pro-French citizenry against the nation's only ally—led him to conclude that chief among their "sinister designs" was oligarchical rule, the reestablishment of royalty, the undoing of the American Revolution, and a foreign policy based on nothing less than the eternal "English scheme" of concocting disputes "to provoke France to hostilities." Labeling the Federalists apostates to the true principles of the American Revolution, Paine charged that they had come close to taking the sheen off the "lustre" of liberty in America. He warned that should they ever regain power, they would once again implement the makeover of the United States on the template of England. Fortunately, he added, these "war-whoop politicians" had been denied the war they coveted by an awakened citizenry that elected Jefferson in 1800.[30]

Curiously, Paine said next to nothing about Hamilton. He took a few swipes at "surly" Timothy Pickering and Washington, who had died three years earlier. He mentioned Washington, he said, only because the Federalists continued to utilize him "as their stalking horse." He took no notice of Washington's presidency, centering instead on his Revolutionary War generalship, which Paine yet again characterized as a "series of blunders" that "nearly ruined the country." To a public that knew little or nothing of Washington's private side, Paine divulged the "icy and death-like constitution" of the Olympian former president. Most of Paine's vitriol was reserved for John Adams. Paine called him vain, arrogant, and lacking in good judgment. Adams postured as a republican, but in reality he was a monarchist "whose brain was teeming with projects to overturn the liberties of America." Ordinarily,

Adams would never have risen so high politically, but "the accidents of the times rendered [him] visible on the political horizon." Adams's one book had "descended to the tomb of forgetfulness," wrote Paine. Adding that "John was not born for immortality," Paine predicted that subsequent generations would not remember the second president.[31]

Two or three years earlier, wrote Paine, the promise of the American Revolution had been in doubt. "But a spark from the altar of *Seventy-Six*, unextinguished and unextinguishable through the long night of error, is again lighting up, in every part of the Union, the genuine name of rational liberty." That spark had resulted in the election of Jefferson and for the first time given the Republican Party control of Congress. America's revolution had spawned the French Revolution, Paine went on, which at its outset had held the promise of "the dawn of liberty rising in Europe." The principles of the French Revolution "were copied from America" and those responsible for launching it had been "honest" men. But the French Revolution had been destroyed by the "fury of faction," as one grouping "sent the other to the scaffold." Of those who had played a substantive role in the events in France between 1791 and 1794, "I am almost the only survivor," he added without much exaggeration. Now, said Paine, the hopes of humankind everywhere rested on the survival of the guiding principles of the American Revolution, "for it is through the New World [that] the Old must be regenerated." His radiant dream in 1776 had been the birthday of a new world. At the dawning of the nineteenth century, all hope of starting the world anew lay with the United States and its preservation of the "first principles" of the American Revolution.[32]

During the thirty months that he spent on his "To the Citizens" series, Paine enjoyed good health and appeared to be more contented than during his final years in France. What would have made Paine even happier would have been to write another hugely successful book, but that dream eluded him. It was not that he had lost his touch as a writer. The times had changed, and he seems to have known it. Paine understood that the French Revolution was over and the chance of other uprisings sweeping across Europe and in England were unrealistic in his lifetime. However dimly, he had probably begun to understand this during France's descent into the Terror in 1793. In addition, before Paine sailed for America, Napoleon had been made consul for life; two years after Paine landed in Baltimore, the coronation of Napoleon as emperor was staged. Beyond a doubt, the French Revolution that Paine had defended in *Rights of Man* was gone forever, replaced by an empire led by a man whom he now called "the completest charlatan that ever existed."[33] Nor was there the slightest prospect of a sweeping revolution in England. Not only had England's government taken draconian steps to thwart radicalism, but the bloody excesses in France had left many would-be English reformers wary. With each year, the American Revolution seemed safer, and while Paine rejoiced in that, its safety gave him less and less to write about.

Paine still clung to the belief that the success of the American Revolution would be a blazing light to illumine and inspire change elsewhere. Long before, Paine had said that his country was wherever humankind was downtrodden, but by early in the nineteenth century Paine understood that America was special for him. It "is the place of my political and literary birth," he said, but it meant more to him than that. It was the place where the age of revolutions had begun, and the one place where a revolution had truly succeeded. "America . . . is the country of my heart," an earnest Paine remarked shortly after crossing to the United States.[34]

A few years after returning to the United States, Paine slipped into the grasp of melancholia. His "To the Citizens" essays had aroused little interest, and Jefferson and other important Republicans had distanced themselves from him. Paine's rise had been phenomenal. Much has been made—and rightly so—of the spectacular ascent of Hamilton, but Paine's had been no less spectacular. At age thirty-seven—ten years older than Hamilton had been when he was elected to Congress—Paine at rock bottom had come to America to start anew, and within a few years he was hailed on two continents as the most important political writer of his day. But now, with his seventieth birthday approaching, Paine knew that the sensational writing that had earned him fame and respect was behind him. Though he continued to turn out an essay now and then, he was aware that he had no more thunderbolts left in his quiver.

The "Age of Paine," as John Adams had christened the period from 1776 onward, was winding down as was Paine himself. As much as he disliked Adams, Paine would have cherished the appellation "Age of Paine" had he been aware of it, and he would have believed that it was true. And, to a degree, it was. Of course, no one person could possibly have been responsible for the colossal upheavals and changes in the late eighteenth century, but Paine's writings—more so than those of any other individual—had stirred great numbers on two continents to rethink their world and welcome its transformation.

Since early adulthood, Paine had lived something of a peripatetic life, and things were no different after he returned to America. He lived longer on his farm in New Rochelle than anywhere, about two years altogether. Early in 1805, however, after Derrick tried to kill him, Paine moved in for several weeks with William Carver in Manhattan. A native of Lewes, Carver had long venerated Paine and, like his idol, he, too, had immigrated to America, where he became a blacksmith and veterinarian. Once Paine felt that it was safe to return to New Rochelle, he went back to his farm. A gregarious sort who craved companionship, Paine grew ever more lonely, and in his solitude he felt a mounting sense of abandonment and rejection. As Paine slipped deeper into the valley of despair, whatever battles for sobriety that he fought were lost. When Carver looked in on him in the spring of 1806—nine months or more after the two men had last been together—he found Paine drunk in a tavern. Paine had not bathed or shaved in ages, his clothing was in tatters, and his toenails had grown around his toes. Carver brought him back to Manhattan and for five months Paine once again lived with the Carver family.

With Carver keeping an eye on him, Paine drank little, if at all. Late on a warm July evening, as he was climbing the stairs to retire for the night, Paine collapsed with what was diagnosed as a "fit of an apoplexy"—a stroke. He was insensible for a time and the Carvers, who rushed to his side upon hearing him fall down the stairs, could detect neither a pulse nor any sign that he was breathing, probably because of a precipitous drop in his blood pressure. In a short while, Paine became aware of his surroundings and began to feel "tolerably well." The Carvers hired a nurse to look after him, as Paine remained bedfast for three weeks, in part given the soreness he experienced from his tumble, but more alarmingly because of a "want of strength" in one leg.[35] It would be a life-altering experience for him in many ways.

Thereafter, Paine's despondency intensified. Irascibility is sometimes the legacy of a stroke. It became Paine's hallmark. He grew short-tempered and disagreeable, and mired in an inescapable black depression. By late 1806, he had returned to the bottle. If Carver is to be believed, Paine each week consumed nearly one hundred fluid ounces of rum, roughly one and one-half gallons. Driven more by his unchecked irritability than alcohol, Paine broke his ties with the Carvers, who had done so much for him, but not before he complained of what he imagined to be their incivility.

A friend arranged for Paine to move in with John Wesley Jarvis, a twenty-five-year-old emerging artist who lived with two large hounds. They got along well, but Jarvis was a heavy drinker himself, which did nothing toward keeping Paine sober. After five months, Jarvis moved out. Acquaintances secured a nice two-room apartment for Paine in a house owned by a hospitable baker, but the accommodations were on the outskirts of the city and far from his remaining friends. Few old companions took the trouble to make the long trek to see him and, increasingly disabled, he could not travel to see them. The one benefit to his isolation was that Paine devoted much of his time to writing, and he produced more than he had in any comparable period following his return point to America.

Though remarkably productive, Paine was agitated and fearful. Over the years, he had often said that he did not fear dying. "Death has no terrors for me," he said. The "key of heaven," he had told Samuel Adams four years before, is "Our relation to each other in this world." He did not believe a future life hinged on prayer, asking for forgiveness, or belonging to any sect. It would come from extending "the right hand of fellowship" to others, to helping those who needed help, and that was the life that Paine believed he had lived.[36] It was not death that made Paine anxious after the summer of 1806; it was the haunting fear that he would suffer another stroke, one that would leave him utterly helpless. Such anxiety is not abnormal among victims of a stroke, and today it is widely believed by medical specialists that nearly a quarter of stroke victims do in fact suffer a second stroke. Indeed, one New York newspaper reported that Paine did suffer a second stroke, probably fifteen to eighteen months after the first. Paine never mentioned it, but the journalist was probably accurate.

Soon after his initial stroke in 1806, Paine began a frantic search for money. He tried without success to sell the farm in New Rochelle. He wrote to Congress asking to be compensated for his service in accompanying John Laurens to France early in 1781, where money and supplies had been procured that were crucial for the Yorktown campaign. He additionally reminded the legislators that he had never received a penny of the three thousand dollars that Congress had resolved to pay him following the war. "All the civilized world know[s] I have been of great service to the United States," he pleaded, but Congress never responded to his entreaties. He wrote to Jefferson asking for his intervention—it is the last letter that Paine is known to have written—but it, too, was unavailing.[37]

When Paine's landlord, the baker, raised the rent early in 1808, the nearly destitute Paine moved to a room above a tavern near Wall Street. He remained in that unwholesome environment for several weeks until he sold his Bordentown property. Obtaining eight hundred dollars from the sale, Paine moved to nicer—though more remote—accommodations in Greenwich, several blocks to the north, where he remained for ten mostly lonely months. By late 1808 or early the next year, Paine had entirely lost the use of his legs, due either to the two strokes or to atrophy from his immobility. Enfeebled, Paine knew for certain that the end was approaching. As is true of perhaps most who understand the reality of impending death, Paine entered a twilight period devoid of ambition. He now inhabited an unfulfilling and purposeless present in which the affairs of this world faded from his consciousness and concern. Some among the few friends who visited thought he was in good spirits, but his landlord, who saw the real Paine, often found him weeping.

Paine's last one hundred days were filled with cascading distress. Marguerite Bonneville called regularly throughout his ordeal, and as the end neared she moved to Greenwich to care for him. Paine was immediately carried to her residence on Grove Street. It was his final stop. During his last month, old friends, aware that he was dying, visited. One who came was William Carver, and he and the dying Paine reconciled. Christian zealots also found his door. They were uninvited and unwanted, and their importuning that he accept Jesus Christ as his savior fell on deaf ears.

Paine lingered until June 8, 1809, dying peacefully that morning at age seventy-two. John Wesley Jarvis came to make a death mask and later sculptured a bust. Paine left $1,500 to Marguerite Bonneville and directed his executors to rent or sell his New Rochelle estate, dividing whatever was netted between Clio Rickman, Nicolas Bonneville, and the three Bonneville boys.[38]

On the day following his death, Paine's body was taken for burial to the farm in New Rochelle. The mahogany coffin was loaded into a carriage. Fourteen people, including Mme Bonneville and her son Benjamin, accompanied the vehicle on the long, slow ride. An unadorned green field near the property's entrance was selected for a grave site. In the day's last wedges of sunlight, American soil was shoveled onto the casket. Marguerite Bonneville stood at one end of the grave, Benjamin at the other. She uttered the last words of the informal ceremony: "Oh! Mr. Paine! My son stands here as testimony of the gratitude of America, and I, for France!"[39]

Much that Paine had written in his last years had been ignored, and similarly, the American public took little notice of his passing. Hundreds of funerary services for Washington had been conducted throughout the country. New York City had declared a day of mourning following Alexander Hamilton's death, and an overflow crowd packed Trinity Church for his funeral. Housetops and streets "were covered with spectators" (including "weeping females") who had gathered to pay homage to the former Treasury secretary and soldier as the funeral procession made its measured way up Broadway. Newspapers would be filled with eulogies for every other major Founder, but none who had been close to Paine—not Jefferson, not Monroe— took the trouble to write a tribute. If Paine's death was mentioned in newspapers, it was mostly without comment.

Old acquaintances were hardly grief stricken. On hearing the news, Dr. Rush, his onetime friend, reacted by deploring Paine's vanity and "intemperate and otherwise debauched" lifestyle, though he praised his talent as a writer. Monroe never took notice of Paine's demise. Perhaps his political ambition was so immense that he would not risk the taint of guilt by association that might accompany praise of the writer he had once esteemed. No issues of the sort vexed Jefferson, but he, too, said nothing publicly about Paine. (In 1822, at age seventy-nine, he even refused to sanction the publication of one of his letters to Paine, pleading: "Into what a hornet's nest would it thrust my head.") Yet at the same moment, Jefferson privately reflected that Paine had been honest and committed to liberty, and a writer whose literary skills were unmatched, even by the likes of Benjamin Franklin.[40]

Paine might have expected Jefferson and Monroe to mourn his passing, but he likely suspected that most Americans would be indifferent. Around the time of the thirtieth anniversary of independence, Paine had noted that "a new generation . . . has risen up" since 1776 that knew little about the American Revolution and its perilous times.[41] Many young Americans in 1809 believed that the world they inhabited had begun not in 1776, but with the implementation of the Constitution in 1789 or Jefferson's election in 1800. Paine was a vestige of another time. Worse, he was a relic who had had the temerity to express very radical, even heretical ideas that made some Americans exceedingly uncomfortable.

The fires of aspiration had yet raged in Paine's heart when he returned to America, and at the same moment a similar fire blazed no less intensely within James Monroe. He had retired after three years as Virginia's governor, stepping down a month after Paine landed in Baltimore. Throughout his tenure, Monroe had preached that as a result of the American Revolution "our lot may justly be considered the happiest among nations." Unlike the excesses in France's revolution, he claimed (in an amnesia-clouded remark) that America's rebellion had witnessed "No strife, no unbecoming violence, no popular tumult." What he really meant, he said in an additional comment, was that the American citizenry had demonstrated "how competent the people are to self government." Monroe shared Paine's—and Jefferson's—conviction that America remained "an instructive, an illustrious example, to nations," demonstrating that "liberty so long the idol of Mankind" could be attained and preserved. But Monroe warned that if Americans somehow lost the liberty they had won by "heroic exertion" in the Revolutionary War, the American people would deserve "the reproach and scorn of the World."[42]

Once he left the governor's office, Monroe's future in public life was only briefly uncertain. Within a month Jefferson asked him to return to Paris as an envoy extraordinary to seek a settlement to the gathering muddle brought on by France's reacquisition of Louisiana. He told Monroe that the "future destinies of this Republic" hinged on a satisfactory resolution of the matter. Both knew that possession of New Orleans was vital for the trade of settlers in trans-Appalachia, both understood that custody of Louisiana was impera- tive if the United States was to someday expand beyond the Mississippi River. Employing his inimitable arts of persuasion, Jefferson added: "All eyes, all hopes, are now fixed on you. . . . Some men are born for the public. Nature by fitting them for the service of the human race on a broad scale, has stamped with the evidences of her destination and their duty." Monroe was such a man, said the president, and as a result he had "unlimited confidence" in him and his diplomatic skills. Monroe hardly needed coaxing. He readily accepted the appointment.[43]

Monroe's instructions went beyond those given to Robert R. Livingston eighteen months earlier. He, together with Livingston, was authorized to offer up to ten million dollars for New Orleans and whatever else they could get, and to make clear that the United States would not tolerate France's pres- ence at the mouth of the Mississippi. By the time Monroe arrived in Paris— six years after having been recalled by Washington—Napoleon had decided to sell Louisiana, which Paine had long before told Jefferson would be the case. The two American envoys concluded a treaty that resulted in perhaps the greatest real estate transaction in history—sixteen million dollars for the vast domain of Louisiana. For barely more than ten cents an acre, the United States peacefully acquired 828,000 square miles from which fifteen states would eventually be carved.[44]

After dining with Napoleon, Monroe hurried to London. He had crossed the Atlantic knowing that Jefferson had named him America's minister to Great Britain. Following negotiations in Paris, he was to seek a treaty with the British in which the United States secured "commercial advantages," London agreed to abandon its policy of impressment, and America's rights as a neutral were satisfactorily acknowledged.[45] Monroe welcomed the chal- lenge, hopeful that he could achieve for his country what John Jay had failed to gain a decade earlier. His guiding light, Monroe said later, was "to make an accommodation with England, the great maritime power . . . rather than hazard war, or any other alternative."[46] But there was more. Monroe hungered for a great and memorable achievement that would enable him to reap acco- lades such as Jefferson had realized for the Declaration of Independence and Paine had won from his most successful publications.

The highlight of Monroe's first year in London was his meeting with George III, who received him warmly and spoke of improving relations with the United States.[47] But after months of difficult negotiations, Monroe had nothing to show for his efforts. Twenty years earlier, John Adams had found that British officials were "high against America." Monroe discovered that not much had changed.[48] As directed, Monroe's next stop was Madrid, where he was to seek to resolve Spanish-American differences over East and West Florida. That mission was unproductive as well, and after six months Monroe returned to London, where he learned that he would be joined by William Pinckney, whom Jefferson had appointed as an envoy extraordinary. Eighteen months of arduous negotiation finally produced a treaty. Monroe and Pinckney had succeeded in resolving some of the commercial discord that had dogged Anglo-American relations since before Washington's presidency, but the British would not budge on the issue of impressment. The two American diplomats had faced a difficult choice: consent to an accord that would be commercially advantageous but that failed to heal the shattered national self-esteem brought on by submitting to Britain's seizure of American sailors.[49] The envoys chose commerce and what they believed would be increased prosperity. When Jefferson and Secretary of State Madison read the terms of the treaty, they, too, had to make a choice. Unlike Washington, they were unwilling to accept an unsatisfactory treaty with London. They rejected the pact. Monroe first learned of Jefferson's decision from others who wrote of the president's "disappointment & astonishment" that his diplomats had consented to what he thought was a flawed accord.[50]

Monroe was disconsolate and embittered, and he simmered with anger for a very long time. Monroe had a proclivity for suspecting hostility on the part of others, even of imagining dark and crafty intrigues against him. Earlier, his paranoia operating in overdrive, Monroe had convinced himself that Jefferson and Madison had sent Pinckney to London to join in the negotiations so that he would not reap full credit for any treaty that resulted. Their motive, Monroe believed, was to deny him the standing that would enable him to successfully challenge Madison for the Republican Party's nomination in the 1808 presidential contest. Now he was certain that the only credible explanation for Jefferson's and Madison's rejection of the treaty was to blacken his reputation and thwart his presidential aspirations. Monroe could never have too much praise heaped on him, and in this instance when Jefferson and Madison finally wrote, neither said anything laudatory about his toils in London. The president did offer him the post of governor of the Louisiana territory, but Monroe saw such a position as the equivalent of exile to Siberia.[51] The blow to Monroe's oversize pride was so great that it nearly destroyed the close ties with Jefferson that he had so long cultivated.

Monroe read too much into Jefferson's and Madison's decision not to support the treaty. Nevertheless, his suspicion that Jefferson preferred that Madison succeed him in the presidency was doubtless true. The president's relationship with Madison was longer, closer, and more paternal, and Jefferson was dependent on Madison in ways that he never was with Monroe.[52] There can be little question that Jefferson thought Madison was the more talented of the two. That is not to say that Jefferson shared the feelings of those who disparaged Monroe's abilities. For instance, John Armstrong, long a confederate, thought Monroe only "ordinarily gifted," while Aaron Burr, supposedly his friend, said that Monroe was "Naturally dull & stupid . . . indecisive . . . [and] pusillanimous." On the other hand, John Quincy Adams, an excellent judge of character, later spoke of Monroe's "pure and gallant spirit" and "distinguished ability," and John Marshall, though a political rival, thought him talented and accomplished, viewpoints that Jefferson unquestionably shared.[53]

But Monroe was a long way from home, and it had been ages since he last spoke with either Jefferson or Madison, and he had worked himself into one of his inflammatory moods. Monroe's acrimony poured out in a choleric note to the president that laid bare his sense of betrayal. He had thought a "perfect understanding, personal as well as political," had existed between himself and Jefferson and Madison, and after four painful years of diplomacy he had concluded what he thought was the best possible treaty.[54] In the end, Monroe decided not to mail his angry letter. He remained in London for an additional six months before sailing for home. During that time, he never received another letter from Jefferson.

Monroe did not linger long at home before he called on Jefferson and Madison early in 1808. In his judgment, they received him coldly and, despite his years in London, neither sought his counsel on relations with Great Britain. Growing more resentful by the minute, Monroe was receptive toward Virginia dissidents who, in their dissatisfaction with the administration's foreign policy, courted him as the antidote to Madison succeeding Jefferson as president in 1809. Although Monroe did not openly challenge Madison, he permitted the "Old Republican" faction in Virginia to push his candidacy. Seeing what was afoot, Jefferson at last wrote in his best guarded manner, though a cryptographer was not needed to divine that he wanted Monroe to step aside. Jefferson expressed his "infinite grief" at the possibility of a rift between Monroe and Madison, and voiced his "sincere friendship for both of you." He added: "I have ever viewed mr Madison and yourself as two principal pillars of my happiness." To lose Monroe's friendship, he went on, would be "among the greatest calamities which could assail my future peace of mind." Jefferson's missive—and the fizzling of the challenge to Madison's candidacy—was sufficient to heal the breach. Once the air was somewhat cleared, Monroe unburdened himself to the president, confessing that he had interpreted

Jefferson's response to the treaty as nothing less than a ruinous condemnation of his character, service, and dexterity. Jefferson appeared shocked and surprised to learn of Monroe's feelings, and responded that it was "the most sacred of truths that I never one instant lost sight of your reputation."[55]

Monroe had patched up his relations with Jefferson, but the bruising events of 1807 and 1808 corroded his ties with Madison, and their relationship deteriorated even more when Monroe was not offered an important post following Madison's victory in the presidential election of 1808. For the next three years Monroe held no public office. Visitors found him gloomy and despondent and convinced that he would never again hold a major position. Madison ignored him, never writing and never calling on him during visits to nearby Monticello. Monroe also studiously avoided dropping in on Jefferson while Madison was his guest. Month after month, year after year, Monroe tended to his farm, though he utilized his considerable spare time to write his version of his failed diplomatic mission to London. He never finished that endeavor. Holding office remained his passion, and in 1810 Monroe took the first step toward healing the breach with Madison. He made a long speech in Charlottesville in which for the first time—but not the last—he condemned the dissidents within the Republican Party and avowed his loyalty to Madison. He also traveled to Washington in May and called on the president, and somewhat to his surprise found that Madison was "kind and friendly."[56] But the president offered him no office. Later that year, when the governor's chair in Virginia unexpectedly came open, Monroe successfully sought it. He did not occupy the post for long. Some sixty days after Monroe returned to the governorship, Madison asked him to be his secretary of state. As had been Washington's and Jefferson's habit when an office was tendered, Monroe said things such as his "mind is against it" and the "time is past when my counsel" might be important. But it was a glittering opportunity for one so ambitious as Monroe, and to no one's surprise he accepted the tender.[57]

All along, Monroe had followed in Jefferson's footsteps. While little in politics is preordained, the post of secretary of state had come to be seen as a stepping stone to the presidency. Not every previous secretary of state had become the chief executive, but both Jefferson and Madison had, and Monroe knew that the post could be the crucial ingredient in completing his arc of ascent.

Monroe was secretary of state when the United States went to war with Great Britain. Later in the War of 1812, he became the secretary of war, and he briefly held both offices simultaneously. When a British military force of some 4,500 came after the capital late in the summer of 1814, Secretary Monroe valorously took to the field and redeployed militia units in a futile effort to prevent widespread destruction. Following the debacle, he remained on his mount helping with the soldiers' retreat. Throughout the war, Monroe, as the nation's chief diplomat, dealt with proposals from abroad for mediation, and he directed Joel Barlow, Paine's old friend who now was the United States minister to France, in his negotiations with officials in Paris. Monroe also coped with Federalist New England, much of which refused to furnish militia for America's defense or to make loans to the hard-pressed United States, and he simmered with rage while his former nemesis Timothy Pickering openly called for the region's secession. Together with Madison, Monroe in 1814 drafted instructions for America's peace commissioners, guidelines that abandoned the demand that Britain disavow its policy of impressment. Their supple direction paved the way for the quite satisfactory Treaty of Ghent that ended the war. A century would pass before another administration faced the challenge of a European-wide war.

Although contemporaries did not know it during the ecstatic celebration of peace in 1815, a new era was settling in. Albert Gallatin, who had been Jefferson's Treasury secretary and more recently a peace commissioner, perceptively noted that the War of 1812 "has renewed and reinstated the national feelings which the Revolution had given."[58] In his final annual message, President Madison voiced the new Republican nationalism by urging the creation of a national bank, the fear of which had been the impetus behind the launch of the Republican Party twenty-three years before. A time of one-party politics had also begun. The so-called Era of Good Feelings—a term that has given many historians heartburn—was dawning. The Federalist Party had dwindled in influence since its nail-biting defeat in 1800, and its stance during the war was its death knell. New figures who had not been born in 1776, or who were young children when independence was declared, had emerged and would dominate American politics for the next generation or more. As the Founders died or retired, the likes of Henry Clay, Daniel Webster, John C. Calhoun, John Quincy Adams, and Andrew Jackson succeeded them and wrestled with new and different matters. After 1815, politicians grappled with tariffs, economic panics, industrialization, the construction of turnpikes, canals, and railroads, and slavery's expansion.

Along with much that was new, vestiges of older ways remained. The Republicans used the outdated and soon to be discarded congressional caucus method when choosing their presidential nominee in 1816. In something of a paradox, the new breed of congressmen chose one of the last remnants of the Revolutionary era to preside over the inception of what was to be a new age. They nominated Monroe, who had faced combat as a Continental soldier before some who selected him were born. In the fall election, Monroe outpaced the last real Federalist presidential candidate by a margin of 183 to 34. (The Federalists had carried seven of the sixteen states and won electoral votes in three others in 1800, but in 1816 the forlorn party—ruined, said John Adams, by its "Selfishness, Exclusion, and Intolerance"—captured only three of nineteen states.) Monroe was inaugurated as president in March 1817, and as if to underscore that he hailed from another time, he dressed in the manner of gentlemen of the era of the American Revolution. He wore knee-length pants and silk stockings, and his hair was powdered and tied in a queue at the back. Throughout his presidency, Monroe eschewed the new, modern styles of dress adopted by those surrounding him, marking himself as the last president to stick compulsively to the old-fashioned attire.[59]

Forty years beyond 1776 found America in a "happy state," Monroe said in his inaugural address, and he pointed out that the new nation's good fortune was due to what "we accomplish[ed]" in the American Revolution. The revolutionaries' dream of starting the world anew—the yearning that Monroe himself had shared when he journeyed to France for the first time in 1794—had not been realized. By the time of his inauguration, a Bourbon— Louis XVIII, the nephew of the ill-fated Louis XVI—was once again the monarch in France, and kings reigned throughout Europe. But the republican aspirations of America's Revolutionary generation had been fulfilled in the United States. Much that had existed in colonial Anglo-America had been transformed. Monarchy was gone, titled nobility never came into being, free men enjoyed greater freedom and more substantial opportunities than had their predecessors before 1776, and a quantum leap in the numbers possessing suffrage rights had occurred since independence. "Never . . . was success so complete," said the new president. Never had any country grown so rapidly, and never had any people been "so prosperous and happy" within forty years of a nation's founding.[60]

Jefferson had been back at Monticello for eight years when Monroe began his presidency, having completed his presidency and returned home in 1809, fifty-three days prior to Paine's death. In his first year at home, Jefferson said— as he had many times before—that he did not miss politics and its often ugly "scenes of difficulty, anxiety & of contending passions." He added that he was "constantly in my garden or farm, as exclusively employed out of doors as I was within doors when at Washington, and I find myself infinitely happier in my new mode of life."[61] Jefferson never said that he was unhappy in retirement, though in his seventh year at home he confessed that were it not for his family and property, he would spend the remainder of his life in France.

There, he added, one with time on his hands "will always find something amusing to do. Here," he continued, "the man who has nothing to do is the prey of ennui." But he quickly added that he had plenty to do, and that Martha, his sole surviving daughter, his grandchildren, books, and correspondence provided all that was "indispensable for happiness."[62] Actually, so many visitors came up the hill to Monticello—as many as fifty at one time were guests—that Jefferson hardly had time for loneliness. They came out of curiosity and to pay homage to him, and the numbers swelled to such proportions that his grandson once remarked that Jefferson was "hunted down by the reputation he had won in the service of his country."[63]

Jefferson was overjoyed that he had been succeeded as president first by his longtime collaborator and next by his long-standing acolyte. As the years unfolded, Jefferson was no less elated that his hopes for the American Revolution had been realized. When he had told Paine in 1801 that the American Revolution had survived the tempestuous seas of the 1790s, he sensed that he stood on the cusp of what Monroe fifteen years later in his inaugural address would refer to as the fulfillment of the American Revolution.

Like a torrent that bursts a sturdy dam, forces brought to the fore by the Revolution, or bred by it, swept over America during the early years of the nineteenth century. Paine and Jefferson had seen it coming, and so, too, had others. The Revolutionary War had hardly ended when the reflective Benjamin Rush noted that Europeans thought "the American Revolution is *over*. This is . . . far from being the case. . . . We have only finished the first act of the great drama." The second act came largely after 1800, and when its day arrived it brought about the "revolution in our principles, opinions, and manners" that Rush had also forecast.[64] The birthday of the new world that Paine and Jefferson had envisaged with American independence had at last come, flowing over the new nation and transforming it into a more egalitarian and democratic country than most who were living in 1776 could ever have imagined. By the time Monroe took the oath of office as president, America was very different from what it had been when Paine landed in Philadelphia and Jefferson drafted the Declaration of Independence, and it was strikingly unlike the country over which Washington had presided in the 1790s. President Monroe's clothing styles may have reflected an earlier age, but almost everything else about his nation was changing dramatically, for in the words of historian Gordon Wood, America had become "a bustling democratic world that required new thoughts and new behavior."[65]

As proud as Jefferson was about the changes in America, he now and then lamented the "dreadful catastrophe" of the French Revolution. France's slide toward the abyss of "horrors" and "depravity" had come about because the "honest & enlightened patriots" of the earliest phase of the Revolution—he specified Lafayette and the "Brissotines," of whom Paine had been a member—had been undercut by "closet politicians . . . unpracticed in the knolege of man." The "fatal error" of the misguided activists "of the Mountain" had been that they knew not when to stop pushing for ever greater change. Somewhat stunningly, though perhaps with uncanny accuracy, Jefferson maintained that had they been willing to accept "the certainty of . . . a degree of liberty, under a limited monarchy" rather than to seek "a little more [liberty] under the form of a republic," the French Revolution might have succeeded, and its success might have spawned other liberating revolutions throughout Europe. Instead, in their quest for a "second change," a more radical transformation than had been realized in 1789, these imprudent "daemons of human liberty" had "murdered their king" and "Septemberized the nation, . . . demolishing liberty, and government with it," catastrophes that in the long run had paved the road for Napoleon's rise. Those who had destroyed the Girondins were the very "genii of despotism," for they had "thrown back" the "moral world" of 1790 "to the point from which it had departed 300 years before," remaking France and with it "Europe entire" into a "Bastille."[66]

But "the pure spirit of the principles of our revolution" had survived and endured, an exultant Jefferson announced on numerous occasions in his last years. He radiated confidence that 1776's "precious work" of winning and safeguarding the "natural rights of man" had first triumphed over Tory England and later over those in America who "were warring against the liberty of [their] own country and [the] independence of others." As Jefferson in 1813 approached his seventieth birthday, the proverbial limit of life expectancy in his time, he rejoiced in the "political conduct by my republican countrymen." Their commitment to the new world that he, Thomas Paine, and James Monroe had fought to win was nothing less than "a pillow of sweet repose to me."[67]

Paine had not lived long beyond his seventieth birthday. Jefferson squeezed in an additional thirteen busy years. He gardened, looked after his properties (aided after 1815 by a farm manager), tended to his correspondence, worked on his memoirs, largely remained aloof from politics, and most assuredly ignored the pleas of those who beseeched him to speak out against slavery. Slavery deserves "our . . . moral and political reprobation," he said privately. But he refused to condemn it publicly. What is more, unlike Washington—who had provided for the liberation of his chattel following his and Martha's demise—Jefferson declined to emancipate his slaves, aside from members of the Hemings family. No one can fathom Jefferson's heart with regard to the slavery issue, though there can little doubt that he feared anti-slavery rhetoric might trigger slave insurrections, and he was no less anxious that abolition-ism's intrusion into politics could destroy the American Union.[68]

Although Jefferson largely avoided public issues during his retirement, he sought to persuade the Virginia assembly to institute a state system of educa-tion. He failed in that endeavor, as he had forty years earlier, but succeeded in his campaign to create a university in Charlottesville, and he lived to see students taking classes at the University of Virginia. Jefferson offered little advice to his successors, though he kept a wary eye on the Federalists until he was certain that the party and its "gangrene" were fading away forever. The "Anglomen" and the "sickly, weakly, timid" elitists who "fear[ed] the people" had flocked to the Federalist banner, he said, but in time the people had seen through the Tory party's intentions and cast them into oblivion. He was overjoyed by Monroe's victory in 1816 over the lingering vestiges of Federalists, not just for the sake of his disciple, but as it meant twenty-four unbroken years of Republican domination, a span sufficient to "so conse-crate" the party "in the eyes of the people as to secure them" from any future danger of a Federalist resurrection.[69]

Jefferson by and large adhered to his stated objective in leaving the presi-dency. In 1809 he had said that he was returning home to a retirement that he hoped would be crowned with tranquility. For the most part, his wish came true. The one dark shadow that hung over his mountain residence was the indebtedness he could never shake. He tried numerous expedients, including the sale of his library to the federal government and putting more of his land and slaves on the market. At best, he marked time, and at the end he was one hundred thousand dollars in debt.[70]

Otherwise, his retirement years were quiet and restful, and he appeared to be happy. However, when asked if he would like to relive his life, Jefferson said he would repeat the years between ages twenty and sixty, but nothing before or after. Once past sixty—he had been sixty-six when he left the presidency—"faculty after faculty quits us" and "debility creeps on," he said. In his early seventies, he mentioned that his eyesight and hearing were not what they once had been, he suffered aches and pains where none had previously existed, and he had grown more forgetful. But he never suffered from dementia, which he feared more than death. When Jefferson was seventy-five, a visitor found him "stooping and lean with old age," but all in all in good shape, an assessment confirmed two years later by another guest who thought him "strong, active, and in full possession of a sound mind." Two travelers who called on Jefferson after he reached octogenarian status remarked that they would have guessed his age at about sixty. But by that time Jefferson privately complained that arthritis in his wrist made writing difficult and he was exasperated by his inability to stay warm. As he grew less active physically, Jefferson carped for the first time about the "heavy hours" he sometimes faced.[71]

He not only lived longer than Paine, but whereas Paine endured three years of steep decline, Jefferson's health remained remarkably good until his final months. Jefferson thought his good fortune came from having "lived temperately," and indeed he was the very model of self-restraint. Jefferson drank two or three glasses of wine daily, but eschewed what he called "ardent spirits." He was not a vegetarian, but many of his meals bordered on those of a vegan. He ate lightly, exercised regularly, and tried to get seven to eight hours of sleep each night.[72]

At age seventy-six Jefferson pronounced that he had "one foot in the grave," though he lived another seven years and remained sufficiently active that he did not discourage visitors who wished to make the trek up the hill to Monticello. To his disappointment, however, he rarely saw James Monroe, who now lived exclusively at Oak Hill, in Loudon County, some one hundred miles away.

Once he entered his eighties, Jefferson complained of the heavy hand of old age. He found walking to be arduous, though for another year or two he was still able to ride, and on occasion even to stay aboard a horse for twenty miles or more. But his maladies were piling up, and as they did his despair was evident. He was "oppressed with disease, debility, age," he said at the outset of his last year, and as with Paine's toward the end, his interest waned in many worldly things. As the road ahead offered nothing but "gloom," he spoke increasingly of welcoming the "friendly hand of death."[73] His religious outlook appeared to be somewhat similar to that of Paine. Jefferson, too, believed that what was most important was to be honorable, virtuous, philanthropic, and principled in one's relationship with others. Like Paine, Jefferson believed in an afterlife, one in which he anticipated meeting old friends and reuniting with loved ones "whom we shall still love and never lose again." He differed from Paine in that he devoted some time to meditation and the study of Jesus's moral teachings, and in his final years he appears to have said "daily prayers." As the end neared, Jefferson like Paine, was comfortable with the life he had lived. His core belief, he said, had been to "Adore God . . . love your neighbor as yourself, and your country more than life." Jefferson felt that he had been "honest and dutiful to society," and also to the "sublime morality" that Jesus had taught, especially practicing "the duties and charities we owe to others."[74]

Throughout 1826, Jefferson knew that he was fading away. He was mostly confined to his house, new afflictions cropped up, and his correspondence declined to a fraction of what it once had been.[75] His last letter was penned ten days prior to his death. Aware that it would be his final missive, Jefferson summoned the energy to expand one more time on the theme of revolution. What he wrote was the quintessence of what the American Revolution, and the Age of Revolution, had meant to him. While it was purely Jeffersonian, it might as easily have been Thomas Paine's last epistle had he possessed the wherewithal at the end to put pen to paper. Jefferson wrote that he continued to believe that the American Revolution would be "the signal of arousing men to burst the chains" that bound them, and to inspire people everywhere to understand that they, too, possessed "the free right to the unbounded exercise of reason and freedom of opinion." Once armed with the power of reasoning, people could unshackle the restraints "under which monkish ignorance and superstition had persuaded them to bind themselves." Like Paine and Monroe, Jefferson never abandoned his belief that American independence had been the birthday of a new world. "All eyes are opened, or opening, to the rights of man," and thanks to the American Revolution the "mass of mankind" now understood they had "not been born with saddles on their backs, nor a favored few booted and spurred, to ride them." Revolutions to secure the rights of man will come "finally to all."[76]

Jefferson fought to stay alive until July 4, the fiftieth anniversary of independence. He died during that day, as did John Adams, who had also clung to life until Independence Day.[77]

Jefferson was laid to rest in the family burial plot at Monticello. Students and faculty from the university, many neighbors and residents of Charlottesville, and some of Jefferson's slaves—who faced a very uncertain future in the aftermath of their owner's demise—stood in the rain to pay their respects and listen to the rector of the local Episcopal church. When it was done, the coffin that had been made by the half-brother of Sally Hemings was lowered into a sodden grave next to that of Jefferson's late wife.[78]

James Monroe was at Oak Hill and did not learn of Jefferson's passing until after the funeral. Monroe had rarely returned to Albemarle County after becoming president. In 1794, he and his uncle, Joseph Jones, had jointly purchased land in Loudoun County. Jones constructed a six-room house on his portion, which Monroe inherited in 1808. The estate, containing two thousand acres and worked by some twenty-five slaves, was situated only thirty miles from Washington.[79] Monroe had used it as a convenient getaway during his presidency. Health issues that made travel difficult for him and his wife, as well as Monroe's desire to remain close to the capital, led him to choose to retire at Oak Hill in 1825. While Washington and Jefferson had been true celebrities receiving a stream of visitors, few callers appeared at Monroe's door. However, when the Marquis de Lafayette came for a fifteen-month tour of America near the conclusion of Monroe's presidency, he visited Oak Hill to see the friend he had made in the Continental army and the man who had been so gracious toward his wife nearly thirty years before.

Lafayette's visit was one of the few high points of Monroe's last years, for there was little serenity in his retirement. As Jefferson had been, Monroe was so vexed with debts that his future seemed to hang precariously in the balance. In letter after letter to Jefferson and Madison, and others, he bemoaned his plight, not infrequently in terms that resembled the distress that Paine had expressed in his last years. Monroe feared his "absolute ruin," adding that all he wished after his "long and laborious service" was "to cherish tranquility." Instead, his situation was "very difficult" and it caused him to anguish constantly over whether in the end his staggering indebtedness would "leave me enough to exist in tolerable comfort with my family." He had once told Jefferson that his preference had been to live out his life in Albemarle County, but circumstances necessitated the sale of that property and the slaves that lived and worked there. In fact, he kept his creditors at bay for a time by selling both his Albemarle property and his Kentucky holdings during his first two years at home.[80] But it was not long before bankers laid siege to him once again. Lafayette, learning of Monroe's troubles, offered money that would have immediately freed him from his dire straits. But Monroe refused, writing to Lafayette that it would be "an outrage to my feelings" to "take anything from" one who had suffered so much from his public service and given so much to the "friends of liberty everywhere."[81]

Ultimately, a Republican-dominated Congress came to Monroe's rescue on two separate occasions. First, in 1828, it revisited his claims for reimbursement from his first mission to Paris thirty years before and awarded him nearly twenty-four thousand dollars. That reduced his debt by two-thirds. In 1831, with Monroe in ill health and faced with destitution, a Congress that could not bear the sight of an indigent former president yet again provided for his deliverance. It awarded him thirty thousand dollars for his years of public service, a gratuity that liquidated his debt.

Monroe was on the eve of his sixty-seventh birthday when he left the White House in 1825. He remained in generally good health during his initial three years at home. That first summer he traveled to Albemarle County to be part of the festivities at the University of Virginia when Lafayette called on Jefferson. It was the last time that Monroe and Jefferson saw each other, and it came at a time when Jefferson felt "sorely and deeply wounded" by Monroe's behavior. In 1824, Jefferson had asked President Monroe to appoint a business associate who had fallen on hard times to be the postmaster in Richmond. Monroe not only had failed to do so, but had offered an excuse that Jefferson did not believe.[82] During those first years following his presidency, Monroe devoted considerable time and energy to managing farm operations at Oak Hill, and he worked on his memoirs, though he did not get past his second mission to Europe. The time he gave over to his autobiography was largely wasted. What he produced paled in comparison to the memoirs left by Franklin, John Adams, and Jefferson. Monroe's was a dry third-person recitation of facts that was devoid of anecdotes, character appraisals, or insights.

He and Madison drew closer than ever during these years. They corresponded and visited each other, and in 1828, two years after Jefferson's death and a year after all of his 130 slaves and farm equipment had been sold at auction, the two made a sojourn to Monticello—which itself was for sale—for one last look. Visitors in Jefferson's last years were already describing the house as "rather old and going to decay," and by the time of Madison's and Monroe's pilgrimage the mansion was "dark & much dilapidated with age & neglect," and the once-resplendent grounds and gardens were shabby and unkempt.[83] It was a sad experience, but also a joyous one, for in Madison's presence Monroe came alive. The two talked, and laughed, at countless reminiscences of bygone days. But the string was running out for Monroe. In the wake of his last tramp to Monticello, he suffered a series of misfortunes that sapped his strength. He fell from his horse on two occasions. He was so badly injured in the second fall that he lay alone and unable to move for hours before a neighbor found him. Thereafter, he was bedridden for three weeks and confined to the house for several additional weeks. In 1829, barely a year after he and Madison trekked the grounds at Monticello, Monroe tried to attend Virginia's constitutional convention, but he was so feeble that he stayed only briefly. Colds and influenza struck him, and by 1830 he was in the grip of a pulmonary disorder that left him "too weak" for much exertion and wracked by chronic coughing. Within a year, Monroe acknowledged that "the restoration of my health [is] very uncertain" and the likelihood of "any favorable change in it" was not expected.[84]

The worst blow had already come. At summer's end in 1830, Elizabeth—his wife of forty-four years—died. Monroe was inconsolable and unable to care for himself, and months later his daughters moved him to New York, where he lived his last six months with the family of his youngest daughter, Maria, at her residence at Prince and Marion streets, only a short walk from where Thomas Paine had spent his final days.[85] Monroe's last letter, written three months before his death, was to Madison. Mentioning his "ill health &

advanced years," Monroe closed: "I deeply regret that there is no prospect of our ever meeting again."[86]

From the moment that James Monroe set out on his career path, he had steadfastly followed in Jefferson's footsteps, and like his lodestar Monroe held on until July 4. As his countrymen celebrated the fifty-fifth anniversary of the Declaration of Independence in 1831, Monroe died at age seventy-three.

AFTERWORD

Thomas Paine, in one of his last letters, summed up what he had stood for:

> My motive and object in all my political works . . . [has] been to rescue man from tyranny and false systems and false principles of government, and enable him to be free and establish government for himself.[1]

Had Jefferson and Monroe been privy to Paine's letter, they would have said that those had been their goals in the American Revolution and their hope for England and Europe as well. When Paine wrote that valedictory in 1806, he, together with Jefferson and Monroe, believed that at least in America their struggles had been crowned with success—Americans lived under republican governments, society was far more egalitarian than in the colonial era, and a discernible democratic tidal wave was gathering that would sweep away the deferential politics that had mostly carried the day before 1776.

These three apostles of revolution were pleased that Revolutionary America had taken on a cast unlike the British prototype cherished by the most conservative of their countrymen. They had vanquished the Tories, the sobriquet that these three hung on their political foes. Alexander Hamilton, in many ways America's Edmund Burke, had in his final letter lamented that "our real Disease . . . is DEMOCRACY." Hamilton's bête noire John Adams similarly scorned democracy. Adams wrote that "democracy never lasts long. It soon wastes, exhausts, and murders itself. There never was a democracy that did not commit suicide." But Jefferson, Paine, and Monroe believed passionately in democracy and exulted in the new nation's democratization. Among other things, democracy to them meant that the earth belonged to the living, as Jefferson had told James Madison. Paine, in *Rights of Man,* had proclaimed the same ideal, writing that as the "circumstances of the world are continually changing, and the opinions of men change also . . . government is for the living, and not for the dead." These three aspired to a governmental system in which

the voices of a living, broadly representative electorate—not an oligarchy—
would chart the nation's course.[2]

They were true radicals whose belief in democracy and egalitarianism was
exceptional in their time—and not only in 1776, but throughout the 1790s
when the dominant Federalist Party sought to preserve as much as possible of
the political and social system of pre-Revolutionary America. Paine's radicalism, nourished by the personal scars that he bore from living in oligarchic
England and the misery and hopelessness he had seen in France, surpassed
that of Jefferson and Monroe. His ideas were far ahead of their time. Paine's
understanding of the destructive consequences of inequality—in particular
the unequal distribution of wealth—and his accompanying critique of existing
economic arrangements went well beyond what even other contemporary
radicals recognized.

Radicals often pay a price for their convictions. Of the three, Paine suffered
the most, for his reputation has been sullied by generations of conservatives
that assailed him, less by confronting his ideas than by besmirching his character, and in particular by branding him a drunken wastrel. To be sure, Paine
had his foibles, but his character flaws did not prevent him from becoming
the most influential writer of his age, the espouser of many ideas that have
resonated with generations of readers. Whatever his blemishes, Paine was
compassionate and charitable, and his bountiful empathy was a virtue hardly
matched by his most notable contemporaries.

Jefferson, Paine, and Monroe went to their graves confident that the threat
posed by America's British-loving Tories had been forestalled, and not merely
for the immediate future. For generations to come, possibly for centuries,
successive frontiers of new farmlands stretching toward the Pacific Ocean
would open at a leisurely pace. After all, it had taken 150 years for the colonists to settle the lands between the Atlantic seaboard and the mountains, a
distance of some 125 miles. The Pacific Ocean, where presumably America's
frontier would someday close, was 3,000 miles away. The immense realm
between the Appalachians and the Pacific coast would ever so gradually be
filled by the measured migration of new generations of republican and democratic farmers. They believed these yeoman would be passionately dedicated
to the ideals that governments derived their authority from the people, were
accountable to the people, were based on the principle of political equality, and
existed to protect the life, liberty, happiness, and property of the citizenry.

Jefferson, Paine, and Monroe never expected history to stop. There would
be new problems, new ways of thinking, and future changes. "We might as
well require a man to wear still the coat which fitted him when a boy, as civilized society to remain" static, was how Jefferson put it.[3] Dramatic changes

had already occurred by the fiftieth anniversary of independence. Whereas hardly a cotton mill had been built when Jefferson was elected president, hundreds dotted the landscapes of New England, Pennsylvania, and New York in 1826; by then, one-fourth of the Yankee and mid-Atlantic labor force already worked in factories. In his last years, Jefferson grew uneasy at the sight of the burgeoning world of banks, paper money, and rampant speculation that was part and parcel of the business culture north of the Potomac. That was not all that troubled him. Jefferson lived long enough to know that new political winds were blowing. John Quincy Adams, elected as Monroe's successor in 1824, opened his presidency by advocating a federal role in the construction of roads and canals, a step that an apprehensive Jefferson saw as a renewal of Hamiltonianism and consolidation.[4] That, it turned out, was merely the tip of the iceberg. Following Jefferson's passing, America's transformation continued at an accelerated rate. Half a century after the jubilee of independence, the Northeast was heavily industrialized and the Midwest was headed in that direction; by the late nineteenth century, industry and finance were nearly dominant in American politics. In another fifty years, corporate America was indisputably the commanding force economically and politically. By then, too, the Census Bureau reported that a majority of Americans lived in urban areas and farmers were a disappearing breed.

Jefferson, Paine, and Monroe might have lacked the capability to fully divine the future. But the three shared the belief that if history demonstrated anything, it was that there would always be the wealthy and the poor, and further that it was an implacable law that some among the rich would utilize their wealth—and the power that came with it—to seek to control society and government. If successful, some with fortunes would use their vast personal resources and the mechanisms of the state to see that the people were shepherded "blindfold into the snare"—so said Jefferson—that would perpetuate oligarchy's rule.[5]

These three thought that people could be led astray in myriad ways, but two means were crucial. Oligarchies always exerted a powerful sway over the communication of ideas, and in their unremitting campaign to shape the people's outlook and cultivate docility, oligarchs sowed false principles and assailed reason and rationalism. Oligarchies solidified their hold on power through repeated warfare. War, Paine wrote, was fundamentally "the art of conquering at home." War "furnishes the pretense of necessity for taxes and appointments to places and offices," paving the way for the oligarchs to place their satraps in positions of authority from the top of the structure to the very bottom. A "principal part of the system of [oligarchical] governments," Paine added, was what he called the "system of war"—the practice of ginning up fear of some foreign enemy. Once the warlords attired society in "the garb of patriotism," Paine wrote, dissent was seen as dangerous and the path was cleared for the "torch of [war]" to extinguish the "flame of liberty."[6]

The fights that Paine, Jefferson, and Monroe waged against the Hamiltonian Federalists were in large measure to prevent the establishment of oligarchical rule. They saw Toryism as bent on reestablishing in America the wicked stew of oligarchical structure and networks that had been swept away in 1776. The three believed, as Paine put it in 1805, that the Tories they battled stood for a credo that "was a great departure from the principles of the Revolution," for to their mind Hamiltonian Toryism wished nothing less than to reshape the new United States "on the *corrupt models of the old world.*" The three apostles of "*beginning the world anew,*" as Paine yet again remarked following his final return to the United States, knew that unrelenting vigilance was essential to prevent oligarchical rule and the despotism to which it could lead.[7]

If Paine, Jefferson, and Monroe could observe modern America from the afterlife that each believed was coming, the three surely would be delighted to find a citizenry that was less constrained and more free than the inhabitants of eighteenth-century America. It is probable, too, that these three would be pleased by the breadth of today's democracy. As Paine's long, winding road in search of a solution to the destitution and despair faced by the poor, elderly, and ill ultimately led him to the notion of government-funded assistance, he almost certainly would approve of today's multifarious social safety net. One can only guess whether Jefferson and Monroe, who in their day were stalwarts of minimalist government, would see things in the same light as Paine. But as both Jefferson and Monroe were caring and altruistic, and as Jefferson sought state help for the landless and freemen blocked from receiving a formal education, it is a good bet that they, too, would applaud the belief that government should lend a helping hand to those willing to help themselves, providing relief for the indigent and balms against catastrophic economic and health calamities. Beyond a doubt, Jefferson would take pride in learning that the Declaration of Independence isn't just read; it remains what one historian has called the "American Scripture."[8] Paine would relish finding that his greatest writings are still read today, and that they might, in fact, be more widely read than anything else published in America in his lifetime.

Nevertheless, much that the three would find would come as a shock, beginning perhaps with the discovery of the lionization of Alexander Hamilton in the greatest hit show on Broadway in years, a hip-hop musical that scorned Jefferson and ignored Paine. That would be but a prelude to a series of unpleasant revelations, paramount among which would be the realization that modern America is more the country of which Hamilton dreamed than the nation that Jefferson imagined might remain intact for ages to come. The threesome would come upon a political system deluged with money and politicians beholden to those capable of financing election campaigns, a nation that seemed frequently to be waging war, that maintained a large standing army and provided seemingly limitless assets for the military, an economy underpinned by a federal banking system and a permanent national debt, and a presidency so powerful that it resembled the eighteenth-century English monarchy. They would find that wealth in the United States was in about the same percentage of hands as had been the case in England in 1776. The three might see modern America as oligarchical. Like Paine, in 1805, they might think today's elites resembled those of his day in that they used the politicians in their service to "disguise and conceal sinister designs" that they sought "to impose on the nation by clamorous and false pretenses."[9]

If this was what they believed they found, the three apostles of revolution might conclude that much in modern America mirrored what they had thought was despicable in the England of the late eighteenth century.

Jefferson, Paine, and Monroe might welcome another Age of Paine.

ABBREVIATIONS

AA	Abigail Adams
AFC	L. H. Butterfield et al., eds. *Adams Family Correspondence.* Cambridge, Mass: Harvard University Press, 1963–.
AH	Alexander Hamilton
AJL	Lestor J. Cappon, ed. *The Adams-Jefferson Letters: The Complete Correspondence Between Thomas Jefferson and Abigail and John Adams.* 2 vols. Chapel Hill, N.C.: University of North Carolina Press, 1959.
AJM	Stuart Gerry Brown. *The Autobiography of James Monroe.* Syracuse, N.Y.: Syracuse University Press, 1959.
BF	Benjamin Franklin
CTJ	Saul K. Padover, ed. *The Complete Jefferson: Containing His Major Writings, Published and Unpublished, Except His Letters.* Freeport, N.Y.: Books for Libraries, 1969.
CWTP	Philip Foner, ed. *The Complete Writings of Thomas Paine.* 2 vols. New York: Citadel Press, 1945.
DAJA	L. H. Butterfield et al., eds. *The Diary and Autobiography of John Adams.* 4 vols. Cambridge, Mass.: Harvard University Press, 1961.
Ford, *WTJ*	Paul Leicester Ford, ed., *The Writings of Thomas Jefferson* 10 vols. New York: G. P. Putnam's, 1892–99.
GW	George Washington
JA	John Adams
JM	James Monroe
JMB	James A. Bear and Lucia Stanton, eds., *Jefferson's Memorandum Books: Accounts, with Legal Records and Miscellany, 1767–1826.* 2 vols. Princeton, N.J.: Princeton University Press, 1997.
L&B, *WTJ*	A. A. Lipscomb and A. E. Bergh, eds., *The Writings of Thomas Jefferson.* 20 vols. Washington, D.C.: Thomas Jefferson Memorial Association of the United States, 1900–1904.
LDC	Paul H. Smith, ed., *Letters of Delegates to Congress, 1774–1789.* 29 vols. Washington, D.C.: Library of Congress, 1976–2000.

LLP	Stanley J. Idzerda et al., eds., *Lafayette in the Age of the American Revolution: Selected Letters and Papers.* 5 vols. Ithaca, N.Y.: Cornell University Press, 1977–83.
LP	*Lee Papers, Collections of the New-York Historical Society for the Year 1871, . . . 1872, . . . 1873, . . . 1874.* New York: New-York Historical Society, 1872–1875.
NG	Nathanael Greene
PAH	Harold C. Syrett and Jacob E. Cooke, eds., *The Papers of Alexander Hamilton.* 27 vols. New York: Columbia University Press, 1961–87.
PBF	Leonard W. Labaree et al., eds. *The Papers of Benjamin Franklin.* New Haven, Conn.: Yale University Press, 1959–.
PGWC	W. W. Abbot et al., eds. *The Papers of George Washington: Confederation Series.* 6 vols. Charlottesville, Va.: University Press of Virginia, 1985–97.
PGWP	Dorothy Twohig et al., eds. *The Papers of George Washington: Presidential Series.* Charlottesville, Va.: University Press of Virginia, 1987–.
PGWR	Philander Chase et al., eds. *The Papers of George Washington: Revolutionary War Series.* Charlottesville, Va.: University Press of Virginia, 1985–.
PGWRet	Dorothy Twohig et al., eds. *The Papers of George Washington: Retirement Series.* 4 vols. Charlottesville, Va.: University Press of Virginia, 1998–99.
PH	T. C. Hansard, ed. *The Parliamentary History of England . . . The Parliamentary Debates.* London, 1806–20.
PJA	Robert J. Taylor et al., eds. *Papers of John Adams.* Cambridge, Mass.: Harvard University Press, 1977–.
PJM	Daniel Preston et al., eds. *The Papers of James Monroe.* Westport, Conn.: Greenwood Press, 2003–.
PNG	Richard K. Showman et al., eds. *The Papers of General Nathanael Greene.* Chapel Hill, N.C.: University of North Carolina Press, 1976–2005.
PTJ	Julian P. Boyd et al., eds. *The Papers of Thomas Jefferson.* Princeton, N.J.: Princeton University Press, 1950–.
PTJ: Ret.Ser.	J. Jefferson Looney et al., eds. *The Papers of Thomas Jefferson: Retirement Series.* Princeton, N.J.: Princeton University Press, 2004–.
TJ	Thomas Jefferson
TP	Thomas Paine
WJM	Stanislaus Murray Hamilton, ed. *The Writings of James Monroe.* 7 vols. New York: G. P. Putnam's Sons, 1898–1903.
WMQ	*William and Mary Quarterly*

Works   Charles F. Adams, ed. *The Works of John Adams, Second President of the United States.* 10 vols. Boston, 1850–56.
WW   John C. Fitzpatrick, ed. *The Writings of Washington.* 39 vols. Washington, D.C.: U.S. Government Printing Office, 1931–44.

SELECT BIBLIOGRAPHY

PRIMARY SOURCE MATERIALS

The voluminous correspondence and writings of Thomas Jefferson, Thomas Paine, and James Monroe are available in published editions.

The modern edition of Jefferson's papers has been dribbling out since 1950, and at the completion of this manuscript had reached roughly the midpoint of his presidency. One should see Julian P. Boyd et al., eds., *The Papers of Thomas Jefferson* (Princeton, N.J., 1950–). Fortunately, in 2004 a second Jefferson papers project commenced that will span his seventeen-year retirement following his presidency. See J. Jefferson Looney et al., eds., *The Papers of Thomas Jefferson: Retirement Series* (Princeton, N.J., 2004–). Two older multivolume series are useful in filling in the gaps during Jefferson's final years. These are Paul Leicester Ford, ed., *The Writings of Thomas Jefferson* (New York, 1892–99) and A. A. Lipscomb and A. E. Bergh, eds., *The Writings of Thomas Jefferson* (Washington, D.C., 1900–1904).

An additional gap is closed by Lester J. Cappon, ed., *The Adams-Jefferson Letters: The Complete Correspondence Between Thomas Jefferson and Abigail and John Adams* (2 vols., Chapel Hill, N.C., 1959). Jefferson's letters to and from his daughters and other family members can be found in E. M. Betts and J. A. Bear Jr., eds., *The Family Letters of Thomas Jefferson* (Columbia, Mo., 1966). The financial record books that Jefferson kept are available. See James A. Bear and Lucia Stanton, eds., *Jefferson's Memorandum Books: Accounts, with Legal Records and Miscellany, 1767–1826* (2 vols., Princeton, N.J., 1997).

A massive single-volume compilation of Jefferson's letters and writings can be found in Saul K. Padover, ed., *The Complete Jefferson: Containing His Major Writings, Published and Unpublished, Except His Letters* (Freeport, N.Y., 1969). While not as complete as its title suggests, it contains Jefferson's autobiography and other materials not yet available in the modern editions of his papers. Single-volume editions of Jefferson's most important letters and writings have been edited by Merrill D. Peterson. See *The Portable Thomas Jefferson* (New York, 1977) and *Thomas Jefferson, Writings* (New York, 1984).

For the best collection of Paine's writings and correspondence, see Philip Foner, ed., *The Complete Works of Thomas Paine* (2 vols., New York, 1945). For two single-volume editions containing Paine's principal publications, see Eric Foner, ed., *Thomas Paine: Collected Writings* (New York, 1995) and Ian Shapiro and Jane E. Calvert, eds., *Selected Writings of Thomas Paine* (New Haven, Conn., 2014).

The modern edition of James Monroe's papers will not be completed for years. At the time of the completion of this manuscript it had spanned the period to the War of 1812. See Daniel Preston et al. eds., *The Papers of James Monroe* (Westport, Conn., 2003–). The older, original edition of his papers therefore still serves a purpose. See Stanislaus Murray Hamilton, ed., *The Writings of James Monroe* (7 vols., New York, 1898–1903). Monroe's memoirs were long ago published separately. See Stuart Gerry Brown, ed., *The Autobiography of James Monroe* (Syracuse, N.Y., 1959).

SECONDARY SOURCE MATERIALS

Thomas Jefferson

The most comprehensive life of Jefferson is the six-volume encyclopedic work by Dumas Malone. It was collectively published as *Jefferson and His Time* (6 vols., Boston, 1948–81). Alf J. Mapp Jr. covered Jefferson's life in two volumes, *Thomas Jefferson: A Strange Case of Mistaken Identity* (Lanham, Md., 1987) and *Thomas Jefferson Passionate Pilgrim: The Presidency, the Founding of the University, and the Private Battle* (Lanham, Md., 1993). For longer single-volume treatments, I recommend the following (which are listed chronologically): Merrill D. Peterson, *Thomas Jefferson and the New Nation* (New York, 1970); Fawn Brodie, *Thomas Jefferson: An Intimate History* (New York, 1974); Noble Cunningham, *In Pursuit of Reason: The Life of Thomas Jefferson* (Baton Rouge, La., 1987); Willard Sterne Randall, *Thomas Jefferson: A Life* (New York, 1992); and Jon Meacham, *Thomas Jefferson: The Art of Power* (New York, 2012).

The following are excellent short biographies: Page Smith, *Thomas Jefferson, A Revealing Biography* (New York, 1976); Norman K. Risjord, *Thomas Jefferson* (Lanham, Md., 2002); Richard Bernstein, *Thomas Jefferson* (New York, 2003); and Francis D. Cogliano, *Thomas Jefferson: Reputation and Legacy* (Charlottesville, Va., 2006). Joseph Ellis's, *American Sphinx: The Character of Thomas Jefferson* (New York, 1997) is an important semi-biographical character study.

A noteworthy study of Jefferson's life, character, and thought is that of Annette Gordon-Reed and Peter S. Onuf, *"Most Blessed of the Patriarchs": Thomas Jefferson and the Empire of the Imagination* (New York, 2016).

Though neither are biographical, anyone interested in Jefferson must become familiar with two books by Annette Gordon-Reed, *Thomas Jefferson and Sally Hemings: An American Controversy* (Charlottesville, Va., 1997) and *The Hemingses of Monticello: An American Family* (2008). John C. Miller's volume *The Wolf by the Ears: Thomas Jefferson and Slavery* (New York, 1977) is also crucial reading for students of Jefferson. Andrew Burstein has done a better job than most in penetrating the impenetrable inner Jefferson. See his two books *The Inner Jefferson: Portrait of a Grieving Optimist* (Charlottesville, Va., 1995) and *Jefferson's Secrets: Death and Desire at Monticello* (New York, 2005).

Two important books treat how others saw Jefferson. For how he has been viewed by subsequent generations, see Merrill D. Peterson, *The Jeffersonian Image in the American Mind* (New York, 1960). For how he was seen by his contemporaries, see Robert M. S. McDonald, *Confounding Father: Thomas Jefferson's Image in His Own Time* (Charlottesville, Va., 2016).

I also recommend four estimable collections of essays on Jefferson. Peter Onuf has edited two collections of original essays. One is *Jeffersonian Legacies* (Charlottesville, Va., 1993). The other, on which Onuf collaborated as an editor with Simon P. Newman, is *Paine and Jefferson in the Age of Revolutions* (Charlottesville, Va., 2013). One should also see Darren Staloff, *Hamilton, Adams, Jefferson: The Politics of Enlightenment and the American Founding* (New York, 2005), a study that emphasizes how the Enlightenment guided and transformed these Founders. Finally, valuable essays and a bibliography can be found in Francis D. Cogliano, ed., *A Companion to Thomas Jefferson* (Chichester, England, 2012).

The literature on Jefferson is vast and those who wish to delve deeply into it would be well served by looking into two exhaustive lists of books and articles published prior to 1992 that were compiled by Frank Shuffelton: *Thomas Jefferson: A Comprehensive Annotated Bibliography of Writings About Him* (New York, 1983) and *Thomas Jefferson: An Annotated Bibliography* (New York, 1992).

Scores of additional secondary works on assorted aspects of Jefferson's time can be found in the notes of this book.

Thomas Paine

Paine has been the subject of numerous biographies, some lengthy and some brief, and some that are particularly insightful. The following, listed alphabetically by author, is a comprehensive list of Paine biographies: Alfred Owen Aldridge, *Man of Reason: The Life of Thomas Paine* (Philadelphia, 1959); A. J. Ayer, *Thomas Paine* (Chicago, 1988); Jack Fruchtman, *Thomas Paine: Apostle of Freedom* (New York, 1994); David Freeman Hawke, *Paine* (New York, 1974); Christopher Hitchens, *Thomas Paine's "Rights of Man": A Biography* (New York, 2006); Harvey J. Kaye, *Thomas Paine and the Promise of America* (New York, 2005); John Keane, *Tom Paine: A Political Life* (Boston, 1995); Craig Nelson, *Thomas Paine: Enlightenment, Revolution, and the Birth of Modern Nations* (New York, 2006); Mark Philp, *Paine* (Oxford, England, 1989); and Audrey Williamson, *Thomas Paine: His Life, Works and Times* (London, 1973).

The pioneering two-volume biography by Moncure Daniel Conway, *The Life of Thomas Paine* (2 vols., New York, 1892), has been eclipsed by recent works, yet it remains important as a repository of documentary materials related to Paine.

Three contemporary biographies written by Paine's enemies must be handled with care. These are James Cheetham, *Life of Thomas Paine* (New York, 1809), William Cobbett, *Cobbett's Review of the Life of Thomas Paine* (London, n.d.), and Francis Oldys [George Chalmers], *The Life of Thomas Paine, The Author of the Seditious Writing, Entitled The Rights of Man* (London, 1792).

Thomas Clio Rickman's *The Life of Thomas Paine* (London, 1819) is also a contemporary biography, but one that was written by a friend who knew, and wrote of, the private Thomas Paine, including his habits and character.

Although none are biographies, the following are useful for understanding Paine and his thinking and times: Gregory Claeys, *Thomas Paine: Social and Political Thought* (Boston, 1989); Seth Cotlar, *Tom Paine's America: The Rise and Fall of Transatlantic Radicalism in the Early Republic* (Charlottesville, Va., 2011); Clement Fatovic, *America's Founding and the Struggle Over Economic Inequality* (Lawrence, Kans., 2015); R. R. Fennessy, *Burke, Paine and the Rights of Man* (London, 1963); Jack Fruchtman Jr., *Thomas Paine and the Religion of Nature* (Baltimore, 1993); Jack Fruchtman Jr., *The Political Philosophy of Thomas Paine* (Baltimore, 2009); Eric Foner, *Tom Paine and Revolutionary America* (New York, 1976); and Edward Larkin, *Thomas Paine and the Literature of Revolution* (Cambridge, England, 2005). Sara Rosenfeld's *Common Sense: A Political History* (Cambridge, Mass., 2011) is wide ranging and includes an important analysis of Paine and his first great pamphlet.

For important essays on assorted aspects of Paine's life and thought, see William Christian, "The Moral Economics of Tom Paine," *Journal of the History of Ideas* 34 (1973): 367–80; Joseph Dorfman, "The Economic Philosophy of Thomas Paine," *Political Science Quarterly*

53 (1938): 372–86; Robert A. Ferguson, "The Commonalities of *Common Sense*," *William and Mary Quarterly* 57 (2000): 465–504; Jill Lepore, "A World of Paine," in Alfred F. Young, Gary B. Nash, and Ray Raphael, eds., *Revolutionary Founders: Rebels, Radicals, and Reformers in the Making of the Nation* (New York, 2011), 87–96; Gordon S. Wood, "The Radicalism of Thomas Jefferson and Thomas Paine Considered," in Gordon S. Wood, *The Idea of America: Reflections on the Birth of the United States* (New York, 2011), 213–228; and Gordon S. Wood, "Thomas Paine: America's First Public Intellectual," in Gordon S. Wood, *Revolutionary Characters: What Made the Founders Different* (New York, 2006), 203–222. Several insightful original essays on Paine's life and thought can be found in two volumes previously cited: Simon P. Newman and Peter S. Onuf, eds., *Paine and Jefferson in the Age of Revolutions* (Charlottesville, Va., 2013), and Ian Shapiro and Jane E. Calvert, eds., *Selected Writings of Thomas Paine* (New Haven, Conn., 2014).

For a quirky, sometimes hilarious, account of the search for Paine's remains, see Paul Collins, *The Trouble with Tom: The Strange Afterlife and Times of Thomas Paine* (New York, 2005).

A crucial study for understanding Paine and his bridge is that of Edward G. Gray, *Tom Paine's Iron Bridge: Building a United States* (New York, 2016).

James Monroe

Much less has been written on Monroe, but the following biographies should be consulted: W. P. Cresson, *James Monroe* (Chapel Hill, N.C., 1946); Harry Ammon, *James Monroe: The Quest for National Identity* (New York, 1971); Gary Hart, *James Monroe* (New York, 2005); and Harlow Unger, *The Last Founding Father: James Monroe and a Nation's Call to Greatness* (Cambridge, Mass., 2009).

Given the paucity of biographies of Monroe, readers interested in his life and times after 1800 would be well served by Noble E. Cunningham, *The Presidency of James Monroe* (Lawrence, Kans., 1996); George Dangerfield, *The Awakening of American Nationalism, 1815–1828* (New York, 1965); Marshall Smelser, *The Democratic Republic, 1801–1815* (New York, 1968); and Gordon S. Wood, *Empire of Liberty: A History of the Early Republic, 1789–1815* (New York, 2009).

NOTES

PREFACE

1. TP, *Rights of Man* (1791), *CWTP*, 1:344; TJ, Inaugural Address, March 4, 1801, *PTJ* 33:151.

2. JA to TJ and Thomas McKean, July 30, 1815, in *AJL* 2:451; TJ to JA, August 10[–11], 1815, ibid., 452.

3. Quoted in Kevin Phillips, *1775: A Good Year for Revolution* (New York, 2012), ix.

PROLOGUE

1. Howard C. Rice Jr., *Thomas Jefferson's Paris* (Princeton, N.J., 1976), 27–31.

2. Alistair Horne, *Seven Ages of Paris* (New York, 2003), 151.

3. Kenneth L. Sokoloff and George C. Villaflor, "The Early Achievement of Modern Stature in America," *Social Science History* 6 (1982): 435–81.

4. JM to Secretary of State, August 15, 1794, *PJM* 3:24.

5. Owen Connelly, *The French Revolution and Napoleonic Era* (New York, 1991), 108–59.

6. Harry Ammon, *James Monroe: The Quest for National Identity* (New York, 1971), 87–88, 98.

7. JM, Address to the National Convention, August 15, 1794, *PJM* 3:30–31; JM to James Madison, September 2, 1794, ibid., 3:48.

8. Ammon, *James Monroe*, 120–21; JM to Madison, September 2, 1794, *PJM* 3:48; Remarks of Philippe Merlin de Douai, August 15, 1794, ibid., 3:31–32.

9. JM to TJ, September 7, 1794, *PJM* 3:59.

10. JM to Madison, September 2, 1794, ibid., 3:49; JM to the Committee of Public Safety, September 3, 1794, ibid., 2:52.

11. Thomas Paine, *Common Sense* (1776), in *CWTP* 1:16, 29, 45–46; TP to Anonymous, March 16, 1789, ibid., 2:1286.

12. TP to GW, July 21, 1791, *PGWP* 8:362.

13. Alfred Owen Aldridge, *Man of Reason: The Life of Thomas Paine* (Philadelphia, 1959), 147; Thomas Paine, "Address to the People of France," September 25, 1792, *CWTP* 2:538.

14. TJ to William Temple Franklin, May 7, 1786, *PTJ* 9:466.

15. Rice, *Thomas Jefferson's Paris*, 30.

16. TJ to Madison, October 28, 1785, *PTJ* 8:681–82; TJ to TP, July 11, 1789, ibid., 15:269.

17. TJ to TP, July 29, 1791, ibid., 20:308.

CHAPTER 1: "THE DESTINIES OF LIFE":
ON THE ROAD TO BIGGER THINGS

1. Susan Kern, *The Jeffersons at Shadwell* (New Haven, Conn., 2010), 1–40; David Freeman Hawke, *Paine* (New York, 1974), 8. Some details on Monroe's youth can be found in *AJM*, 21–22. On JM, see also W. P. Cresson, *James Monroe* (Chapel Hill, N.C., 1946), 7.

2. Dumas Malone, *Jefferson and His Time* (Boston, 1948–81), 1:1012; TJ, Autobiography, *CTJ*, 1119.

3. TJ to Joseph Priestley, January 27, 1800, *PTJ* 31:340; TJ, Autobiography, *CTJ*, 1120.

4. TJ to John Harvie, January 14, 1760, *PTJ* 31:340; TJ to John Page, December 25, 1762, ibid., 1:5; TJ to Vine Utley, March 21, 1819, Ford, *WTJ* 9:126; Malone, *Jefferson and His Time*, 1:56–57. The "high standing" quotation can be found in Trevor Colbourn, ed., *Fame and the Founding Fathers: Essays by Douglass Adair* (New York, 1974), 7. The figures on landowning and slave owning can be found in Jackson Turner Main, *The Social Structure of Revolutionary America* (Princeton, N.J., 1965), 44–46; Sylvia Frey, *Water from the Rock: Black Resistance in a Revolutionary Age* (Princeton, N.J., 1991), 9.

5. Edward Dumbauld, *Thomas Jefferson and the Law* (Norman, Okla., 1978), 66–83; Frank L. Dewey, *Thomas Jefferson, Lawyer* (Charlottesville, Va., 1986), 9–14; Edmund Randolph, "Essay on the Revolutionary History of Virginia," *Virginia Magazine of History and Biography* 43 (1953): 123. The "monastic" quote can be found in Peter S. Onuf, "Making Sense of Jefferson," in Peter S. Onuf, ed., *The Mind of Thomas Jefferson* (Charlottesville, Va., 2007), 28.

6. TJ to John Page, December 25, 1762, July 15, October 7, 1763, January 19, 1764, February 21, 1770, *PTJ* 1:11, 13–14, 34–35; Jon Kukla, *Mr. Jefferson's Women* (New York, 2007), 41–63.

7. TJ to Maria Cosway, January 30, 1787, *PTJ* 11:509; TJ to William Fleming, March 20, 1764, ibid., 1:16; Thomas Jefferson, *Notes on the State of Virginia*, ed. William Peden (Chapel Hill, N.C., 1955), 18–20; Charles A. Miller, *Jefferson and Nature: An Interpretation* (Baltimore, 1988), 102; Rhys Isaac, "The First Monticello," in Peter S. Onuf, ed., *Jeffersonian Legacies* (Charlottesville, Va., 1993), 77–108. Details on the construction of Monticello can be found scattered throughout Jack McLaughlin, *Jefferson and Monticello: The Biography of a Builder* (New York, 1988), beginning on page 33. The "rather look at . . . than live at" quotation can be found in Merrill D. Peterson, ed., *Visitors to Monticello* (Charlottesville, Va., 1989), 35.

8. Malone, *Jefferson and His Time*, 1:129.

9. On electioneering in colonial Virginia, see Charles S. Sydnor, *Gentlemen Freeholders: Political Practices in Washington's Virginia* (Chapel Hill, N.C., 1952), 11–59.

10. Harry S. Randall, *The Life of Thomas Jefferson* (New York, 1858), 1:62–64; Fawn M. Brodie, *Thomas Jefferson: An Intimate History* (New York, 1974), 88.

11. For the two preceding quotations, see TJ to James Ogilvie, February 20, 1771, *PTJ* 1:63; TJ to Robert Skipwith, August 3, 1771, ibid., 1:78.

12. TJ to Elizabeth Wales Eppes, October 3[?], 1782, ibid., 6:198; TJ, Autobiography, *CTJ*, 1151.

13. TJ to Page, December 25, 1776, *PTJ* 1:5; TJ to Fleming, [October 1763], ibid., 1:13; Randall, *Life of Jefferson*, 98, 109; Marie Kimball, *Jefferson: The Road to Glory, 1743–1776* (New York, 1943), 134; Dewey, *Thomas Jefferson, Lawyer*, 83–93; John W. Davis, "Thomas Jefferson: Attorney at Law," *Proceedings, Virginia State Bar Association*, 38 (1926): 369.

14. TJ to Utley, March 21, 1819, Ford, *WTJ* 9:126. On TJ's early years, see Malone, *Jefferson and His Time*, 1:3–109. Malone is good on TJ's property holdings in 1774; see ibid., 1:439–45.

For more on TJ down to 1774, see Merrill D. Peterson, *Thomas Jefferson and the New Nation: A Biography* (New York, 1970), 3–31; Fawn M. Brodie, *Thomas Jefferson: An Intimate History* (New York, 1974), 19–38.

15. Quoted in Bernard Bailyn, *The Ordeal of Thomas Hutchinson* (Cambridge, Mass., 1974), 169.

16. Merrill Jensen, *The Founding of a Nation: A History of the American Revolution, 1763–1776* (New York, 1968), 430–31; Samuel Adams to Richard Henry Lee, April 10, 1773, in Harry Alonzo Cushing, *The Writings of Samuel Adams* (New York, 1968), 3:25; Peterson, *Thomas Jefferson and the New Nation*, 69.

17. For a history of the coming of the American Revolution, see John Ferling, *Whirlwind: The American Revolution and the War That Won It* (New York, 2015), 12–98.

18. T. H. Breen, *Tobacco Culture: The Mentality of the Great Tidewater Planters on the Eve of Revolution* (Princeton, N.J., 1985), 175–78; Woody Holton, *Forced Founders: Indians, Debtors, Slaves, and the Making of the American Revolution in Virginia* (Chapel Hill, N.C., 1999), 49, 53, 57. GW's quote can be found in Kevin Phillips, *1775: A Good Year for Revolution* (New York, 2012), 108. The TJ quotation is in Peterson, *Thomas Jefferson and the New Nation*, 40.

19. Joseph Albert Ernst, *Money and Politics in America, 1755–1775* (Chapel Hill, N.C., 1973), 3–88, 353–62; Jensen, *Founding of a Nation*, 51–55; Holton, *Forced Founders*, 62.

20. Holton, *Forced Founders*, 3–32, 62, 66–73; Jensen, *Founding of a Nation*, 386–93; Thomas P. Abernethy, *Western Lands and the American Revolution* (Charlottesville, Va., 1937), 1–58.

21. Noble E. Cunningham, *In Pursuit of Reason: The Life of Thomas Jefferson* (Baton Rouge, La., 1987), 28–31; Norman K. Risjord, *Thomas Jefferson* (Lanham, Md., 1994), 21–23; Ari Helo, "Jefferson's Conception of Republican Government," in Frank Shuffelton, comp., *The Cambridge Companion to Thomas Jefferson* (Cambridge, England, 2009, 35–38; Kristofer Ray, "Thomas Jefferson and *A Summary View of the Rights of British North America*," in Francis D. Cogliano, ed., *A Companion to Thomas Jefferson* (New York, 2012), 34; Gordon S. Wood, *The American Revolution: A History* (New York, 2003), 28–29, 58–60, 102–3; Joyce Appleby, *Capitalism and a New Social Order: The Republican Vision of the 1790s* (New York, 1984), 18–23; Gordon S. Wood, *Liberalism and Republicanism in the Historical Imagination* (Cambridge, Mass., 1992), 4–5, 8, 13, 15, 20, 25, 299.

22. The "place for every man" quote is in Clarence L. Ver Steeg, *The Formative Years, 1607–1763* (New York, 1964), 129. The additional quotations in the paragraph are drawn from Gordon S. Wood, *The Radicalism of the American Revolution* (New York, 1992), 11–42, and Main, *Social Structure of Revolutionary America*, 198–242.

23. *DAJA* 3:326; JA to TJ, July 13, 1813, *AJL* 2:355.

24. TJ, Autobiography, *CTJ*, 1122; [Thomas Jefferson], *A Summary View of the Rights of British America* (Williamsburg, Va., 1775), *PTJ* 1:122, 135.

25. On the Coercive Acts and the colonists' response, see Ferling, *Whirlwind*, 81–98.

26. TP, *The Rights of Man* (1792), in *CWTP* 1:405.

27. Roy Porter, *English Society in the Eighteenth Century* (London, 1982), 52–53.

28. J. H. Plumb, *England in the Eighteenth Century* (Baltimore, 1950), 15, 19.

29. John F. C. Harrison, *The Birth and Growth of Industrial England* (New York, 1973), 4–11.

30. Porter, *English Society in the Eighteenth Century*, 52–53.

31. TP, *The Rights of Man* (1792), in *CWTP* 1:405. The "every person of learning" and "seldom passed five minutes" quotes are in *CWTP*, 1:ix.

32. Craig Nelson, *Thomas Paine: Enlightenment, Revolution, and the Birth of Modern Nations* (New York, 2006), 20.

33. For descriptions of TP, see Alfred Owen Aldridge, *Man of Reason: The Life of Thomas Paine* (Philadelphia, 1959), 45; Hawke, *Paine*, 14; Audrey Williamson, *Thomas Paine: His Life, Work and Times* (New York, 1973), 48, 126, 167; Moncure Daniel Conway, *The Life of Thomas Paine* (London, 1909), 131; Nelson, *Thomas Paine*, 21. On how he was addressed, see Jill Lepore, "A World of Paine," in Alfred F. Young, Gary B. Nash, and Ray Raphael, eds., *Revolutionary Founders: Rebels, Radicals, and Reformers in the Making of the Nation* (New York, 2011), 87.

34. TP to the Chairman of the Society for Promoting Constitutional Knowledge, May 1792, *CWTP* 2:1325–26; Thomas Clio Rickman, *The Life of Thomas Paine* (reprint, Cambridge, England, 2014), 38. On TP sitting on the Lewes town council, see Jack Fruchtman Jr., "Thomas Paine's Early Radicalism, 1768–1783," in Simon P. Newman and Peter S. Onuf, eds., *Paine and Jefferson in the Age of Revolutions* (Charlottesville, Va., 2013), 53.

35. Rickman, *Life of Thomas Paine*, 39.

36. On the shop's inventory, see Nelson, *Thomas Paine*, 42.

37. TP to Oliver Goldsmith, December 21, 1772, *CWTP* 1:1129.

38. TP, *Case of the Officers of Excise* (1772), ibid., 2:1–15. The tract was printed for Parliament but not reprinted and published as a pamphlet for public consumption until 1793.

39. Jonathan Israel, *A Revolution of the Mind: Radical Enlightenment and the Intellectual Origins of Modern Democracy* (Princeton, N.J., 2010). The foregoing section draws on pages vii–ix, xi, and 48.

40. Eric Foner, *Tom Paine and Revolutionary America* (New York, 2005), 7–17; Esmond Wright, *Franklin of Philadelphia* (Cambridge, Mass., 1986), 115.

41. On oligarchical rule in Thetford, as well as its violence and poverty, see John Keane, *Tom Paine: A Political Life* (New York, 2003), 3–12.

42. H. T. Dickinson, *British Radicalism and the French Revolution, 1789–1815* (Oxford, England, 1985), 1–8; H. T Dickinson, *Liberty and Property: Political Ideology in Eighteenth-Century Britain* (New York, 1977), 195–208.

43. Peter D. G. Thomas, *John Wilkes: A Friend to Liberty* (Oxford, England, 1996), 25–108; *PBF* 16:xxiii. On the percentage that could vote in Thetford, see Nelson, *Thomas Paine*, 16.

44. Ian R. Christie, *Wilkes, Wyvill and Reform: The Parliamentary Reform Movement in British Politics, 1760–1785* (London, 1962), 1–52.

45. BF to Richard Bache, September 30, 1774, *PBF* 21:325–26; TP to Henry Laurens, January 14, 1779, *CWTP* 2:1162; Philipp Ziesche, "Thomas Paine and Benjamin Franklin's French Circle," in Newman and Onuf, *Paine and Jefferson in the Age of Revolutions*, 122.

46. BF, "A Letter from London" (printed in the *Boston Gazette*, April 25, 1774), *PBF* 21:83; BF to Thomas Cushing, September 15, 1774, ibid., 21:306; BF to Jonathan Williams Sr., September 28, 1774, ibid., 21:324.

47. The foregoing on Paine's life down to 1774 draws on Hawke, *Paine*, 7–25; Williamson, *Thomas Paine*, 19–64; Aldridge, *Man of Reason*, 13–32; Jack Fruchtman Jr., *Thomas Paine: Apostle of Freedom* (New York, 1994), 15–39; Nelson, *Thomas Paine*, 12–50; A. J. Ayer, *Thomas Paine* (New York, 1988), 1–7; and Harvey J. Kaye, *Thomas Paine and the Promise of America* (New York, 2005), 3–34.

48. Thomas Jefferson, *Notes on the State of Virginia*, ed., William Peden (Chapel Hill, N.C., 1955), 153.

49. *AJM*, 22. On JM's preparatory education, see Harry Ammon, *James Monroe: The Quest for National Identity* (New York, 1971), 3; Cresson, *James Monroe*, 7–8; and Jean Edward Smith, *John Marshall: Definer of a Nation* (New York, 1996), 21–22, 35.

50. Cunningham, *In Pursuit of Reason*, 25–26.

CHAPTER 2: "THE BIRTHDAY OF A NEW WORLD IS AT HAND": REVOLUTIONARIES

1. TJ, Autobiography, *CTJ* 1124.

2. For an intriguing analysis of TJ's views of monarchial authority, see Eric Nelson, *The Royalist Revolution: Monarchy and the American Founding* (Cambridge, Mass., 2014), 58–60.

3. TJ, *A Summary View of the Rights of British America* (Williamsburg, Va., 1774), in *PTJ* 1:121–35.

4. Ibid., 1:127, 134.

5. John Ferling, *Whirlwind: The American Revolution and the War That Won It* (New York, 2015), 86–98; Report of Committee to Prepare a Plan for Militia, March 25, 1775, *PTJ* 1:160–62; Dumas Malone, *Jefferson and His Time* (Boston, 1948–81), 1:199–201.

6. David Hackett Fischer, *Paul Revere's Ride* (New York, 1994), 184–260.

7. *JMB* 1:396; TJ to William Small, May 7, 1775, *PTJ* 1:165–66.

8. TP to BF, March 4, 1775, *CWTP* 2:1130.

9. TP, "A Dialogue between General Wolfe and General Gage in a Wood near Boston" (1775), ibid., 2:47–49.

10. TP, "African Slavery in America" (1775), ibid., 2:16–19; David Brion Davis, *Inhuman Bondage: The Rise and Fall of Slavery in the New World* (New York, 2006), 146; Gary B. Nash, *Race and Revolution* (Madison, Wisc., 1990), 7–10. Rush is quoted in David Freeman Hawke, *Benjamin Rush: Revolutionary Gadfly* (Indianapolis, Ind., 1971), 108.

11. David Freeman Hawke, *Paine* (New York, 1974), 29; TP, "Duelling" (1775) *CWTP* 2:28–32; TP, "Reflections on Titles" (1775) ibid., 2:33–34; TP, "Reflections on Unhappy Marriages" (1775) ibid., 2:1118–20; TP, "Reflections on the Life and Death of Lord Clive" (1775) 2:22–27. On the abolitionist society, see Craig Nelson, *Thomas Paine: Enlightenment, Revolution, and the Birth of Modern Nations* (New York, 2006), 65.

12. TP, "Liberty Tree" (1775), *CWTP* 2:1091–92.

13. TP, "The Dream Interpreted" (1775), ibid., 2:50–52.

14. TP, "Thoughts on Defensive War" (1775), ibid., 2:52–55. For the speech by Sandwich, see PH 18:446–48.

15. For a cogent summary of the classical republican ideal, see Gordon S. Wood, *The American Revolution: A History* (New York, 2003), 91–95.

16. Hawke, *Paine*, 34–39; George W. Corner, ed., *The Autobiography of Benjamin Rush: His "Travels Through Life" together with His Commonplace Book for 1789–1813* (Princeton, N.J., 1948), 113.

17. *JMB* 1:399, 409n.

18. Samuel Ward to Henry Ward, June 22, 1776, *LDC* 1:535; JA, Autobiography, *DAJA* 3:335–36; JA to Timothy Pickering, August 6, 1822, *Works*, 2:512.

19. The quotations are scattered through Malone, *Jefferson*, 1:203, 295, 392, 420; John Ferling, *Setting the World Ablaze: Washington, Adams, Jefferson, and the American Revolution* (New York, 2000), 49; and Merrill D. Peterson, ed., *Visitors to Monticello* (Charlottesville, Va.,

1989), 28, 42, 57, 62, 98. See also James Bear, ed., *Jefferson at Monticello* (Charlottesville, Va., 1967), 11, 13, 18, 71–73; JA, Autobiography, *DAJA* 3:335–36; JA to Pickering, August 6, 1822, *Works*, 2:513–14. The "sensible spirited fine Fellow" quote can be found in Samuel Ward to Henry Ward, June 22, 1776, *LDC* 1:535.

20. Diary of Silas Deane, *LDC* 1:351.

21. Dickinson, "Notes for a Speech in Congress," [May 23–25?], 1775, ibid., 1:371–82.

22. JA to Hezekiah Niles, February 13, 1818, *Works* 10:282.

23. Quoted in Nick Bunker, *An Empire on the Edge: How Britain Came to Fight America* (New York, 2014), 213.

24. Eliphalet Dyer to Joseph Trumbull, July 10, 1775, *LDC* 1:620; *DAJA* 2:140; JA to AA, June 17, 1775, *AFC* 1:216; JA to James Warren, July 6, 1775, *PJA* 3:61; JA to Josiah Quincy, October 6, 1775, ibid., 3:187; JA to Moses Gill, June 10, 1775, ibid., 3:21; John Hazleton, *The Declaration of Independence: Its History* (New York, 1906), 161–62.

25. *JMB* 1:400; JA to Joseph Palmer, July 5, 1775, *PJA* 3:55. For TJ's and Dickinson's drafts of the Declaration of the Causes and Necessity for Taking Up Arms and for the declaration as finally adopted by Congress on July 6, 1775, see *PTJ* 1:187–218. For TJ's draft of the response to Lord North's peace plan and for the congressional resolution on the first minister's conciliatory proposal adopted on July 25, 1775, see ibid., 1:225–33.

26. *JMB* 1:403, 406, 411, 417–18.

27. TJ to Page, May 17, 1776, *PTJ* 1:293; TJ to John Randolph, November 29, 1775, ibid., 1:269.

28. For the two preceding paragraphs, see GW to George William Fairfax, May 31, 1775, *PGWC* 10:368; GW to Richard Henry Lee, December 26, 1775, *PGWR* 2:611; GW to Joseph Reed, December 15, 1775, ibid., 2:553; and Edward Rutledge to Ralph Izard, December 8, 1775, *LDC* 2:462. See also Gary B. Nash, *The Forgotten Fifth: African Americans in the Age of Revolution* (Cambridge, Mass., 2006), 28–29; Alan Gilbert, *Black Patriots and Loyalists: Fighting for Emancipation in the War for Independence* (Chicago, 2012), 21–28; Douglas R. Egerton, *Death or Liberty: African Americans and Revolutionary America* (New York, 2009), 70–71.

29. The King's Speech to Parliament, October 26, 1775, in David C. Douglas et al., eds., *English Historical Documents* (London, 1953–70), 9:851–52.

30. TP, "A Serious Thought" (1775), *CWTP* 2:20; Alfred Owen Aldridge, *Man of Reason: The Life of Thomas Paine* (Philadelphia, 1959), 33, 36.

31. Corner, *Autobiography of Benjamin Rush*, 114; Aldridge, *Man of Reason*, 326; Hawke, *Paine*, 40–41.

32. Corner, *Autobiography of Benjamin Rush*, 113–14, 323.

33. Eric Foner, *Tom Paine and Revolutionary America* (New York, 2005), 75–76.

34. TP, *Common Sense* (1776), *CWTP* 1:4–46. The quotations in the foregoing paragraphs can be found on pages 4, 5, 6, 8, 9, 12, 13, 16, 17, 20, 21, 23, 26, 29, 30–31, and 45.

35. Sophia Rosenfeld, *Common Sense: A Political History* (Cambridge, Mass., 2011), 143; TJ to Francis Eppes, January 19, 1821, L&B, *WTJ* 15:305.

36. Corner, *Autobiography of Benjamin Rush*, 323; TP to Henry Laurens, January 14, 1779, *CWTP* 2:1162. Hereafter, all references to Henry Laurens are cited as "H. Laurens."

37. Josiah Bartlett to John Langdon, January 13, 1776, *LDC* 3:88; GW to Joseph Reed, April 1, 1776, *PGWR* 4:11. For the sales figures for *Common Sense*, see TP to H. Laurens, January 14, 1779, *CWTP* 2:1163; Wood, *American Revolution*, 55; Gordon S. Wood, "Thomas Paine, America's First Public Intellectual," in Gordon S. Wood, *Revolutionary Characters: What Made the Founders Different* (New York, 2006), 209; Thomas Paine, *Common Sense*, ed. Isaac Kramnick (New York, 1986), 8–9; Nelson, *Thomas Paine*, 92; and Nicole Eustace, *Passion Is the Gale:*

Emotion, Power, and the Coming of the American Revolution (Chapel Hill, N.C., 2008), 441. Historian Trish Loughran, in *The Republic in Print: Print Culture in the Age of U.S. Nation Building, 1770–1870* (New York, 2009), questioned the commonly accepted sales figures. Her argument can be found on pages 57–58. On pastors reading *Common Sense* to their congregations, see Douglas Bradburn, *The Citizenship Revolution: Politics and the Creation of the American Union, 1774–1804* (Charlottesville, Va., 2009), 39. For information on European editions of *Common Sense*, see Nelson, *Thomas Paine*, 82, 91. On Paine's lack of earnings, also see Nelson, page 91, and Aldridge, *Man of Reason*, 42. The quotations by BF and Rush can be found in Robert A. Ferguson, "The Commonalities of *Common Sense*," *WMQ* 57 (2000): 57:466. On TP's arguments having been used by local bodies in addresses, instructions, and resolutions, see David Armitage, *The Declaration of Independence: A Global History* (Cambridge, Mass., 2007), 37. On congressional aid in calling attention to the pamphlet, see Robert G. Parkinson, *The Common Cause: Creating Race and Nation in the American Revolution* (Chapel Hill, N.C., 2016), 188–92.

38. GW to Reed, January 31, 1776, *PGWR* 3:228; Charles Lee to GW, January 24, 1776, ibid., 3:183. The quotations other than those of GW and Lee can be found in Nelson, *Thomas Paine*, 92–93. Lee's remark about TP having "genius in his eyes" is in Ferguson, "The Commonalities of *Common Sense*," *WMQ* 57 (2000): 474n.

39. JA to AA, February 18, 1776, *AFC* 1:348; JA to William Tudor, April 12, 1776, *PJA* 4:118; JA to TJ, June 22, 1819, *AJL* 2:542. On the eighteenth-century view of democracy, see Bernard Bailyn, *The Ideological Origins of the American Revolution* (Cambridge, Mass., 1967), 70, 282.

40. TP to H. Laurens, January 14, 1779, *CWTP* 2:1163.

41. JA to AA, February 18, 1776, *AFC* 1:348.

42. Joseph Hewes to Samuel Johnston, June 4, 1776, *LDC* 4:139; Commissioners to Canada to John Hancock, May 10, 17, 27, 1776, ibid., 3:646–47; 4:22–24, 80–82; Hancock to Certain Colonies, June 4, 1776, ibid., 4:136. On the Canadian debacles and Congress's response, and on the events that helped shift opinion toward independence in several colonies, see John Ferling, *Independence: The Struggle to Set America Free* (New York, 2011), 170–293, and Ferling, *Whirlwind*, 117–57.

43. On how TJ came to be chosen to write the draft, see Ferling, *Independence*, 299–300.

44. The literature on the ideas that influenced TJ is enormous. I was especially influenced by Armitage, *Declaration of Independence*, 49–50, and Pauline Maier, *American Scripture: Making the Declaration of Independence* (New York, 1997), 104, 126–27. But also see Carl Becker, *The Declaration of Independence: A Study in the History of Political Ideas* (New York, 1942), and Gary Wills, *Inventing America: Jefferson's Declaration of Independence* (New York, 1978). For TJ's draft of a constitution for Virginia, see Third Draft by Jefferson, (Before June, 13, 1776), *PTJ* 1:356–64. The quotation can be found on page 357. For a good treatment of George Mason's draft of the Virginia Declaration of Rights, see John E. Selby, *The Revolution in Virginia, 1775–1783* (Williamsburg, Va., 1988), 100–104. On the inclusion of "war crimes," see Parkinson, *The Common Cause*, 123–24.

45. For TJ's draft in various stages, the alterations recommended by JA and BF, and the important editorial note by the first modern editor of TJ's papers, see *PTJ* 1:413–28. See also Becker, *Declaration of Independence*, 135–52. The language and spelling in the Declaration that follows is that adopted by Congress on July 4. See *PTJ* 1:429–30.

46. TJ to Henry Lee, May 8, 1825, L&B, *WTJ* 7:407; JA to Pickering, August 6, 1822, *Works*, 2:514n; Maier, *American Scripture*, xvii.

47. Jay Fliegelman, *Declaring Independence: Jefferson, Natural Language, and the Culture of Performance* (Stanford, Calif., 1993), 4–28. Armitage's comment can be found in Armitage, *Declaration of Independence*, 140. Lincoln is quoted by Armitage on page 97.

48. TJ to Lee, July 8, 1776, *PTJ* 1:456; Lee to TJ, July 21, 1776, ibid., 1:471; Ferling, *Independence*, 318–41; Maier, *American Scripture*, 143–53.

49. Richard R. Beeman, *Our Lives, Our Fortunes and Our Sacred Honor: The Forging of American Independence, 1774–1776* (New York, 2013), 418; Maier, *American Scripture*, 157–58. The "IMAGE of the BEAST" quotation can be found in Maier.

CHAPTER 3: "THESE ARE THE TIMES THAT TRY MEN'S SOULS": PAINE AND MONROE GO TO WAR

1. TP, "A Dialogue between the Ghost of General Montgomery and an American Delegate" (1776), *CWTP* 2:88–93; TP, "The Forester's Letters" (1776), ibid., 2:61–87; JA to AA, April 28, 1776, *AFC* 1:401. The "bored" quote is in David Freeman Hawke, *Paine* (New York, 1974), 56.

2. GW to Hugh Mercer, July 27, 1776, *PGWR* 5:483, 484n; TP to Laurens, January 14, 1779, *CWTP* 2:1163.

3. *PNG* 1:lvi. On the campaign for New York, see John Ferling, *Almost a Miracle: The American Victory in the War of Independence* (New York, 2007), 120–48, and Ferling, *Whirlwind: The American Revolution and the War That Won It* (New York, 2015), 166–78.

4. Craig Nelson, *Thomas Paine: Enlightenment, Revolution, and the Birth of Modern Nations* (New York, 2006), 102–104.

5. On the military events in October and November 1776, see Ferling, *Almost a Miracle*, 145–55.

6. NG to Governor Nicholas Cooke, December 4, 1776, *PNG* 1:362; TP, "Retreat Across the Delaware" (1777), *CWTP* 2:93–94; TP, "To the Citizens of the United States" (1803), ibid., 2:922; TP to Samuel Adams, January 1, 1803, ibid., 2:1434. GW did not attempt to deceive Congress regarding the loss of weaponry and baggage at Fort Lee. See GW to John Hancock, November 19[–21], 1776, *PGWR* 7:183.

7. GW to Hancock, November 23, 1776, *PGWR* 7:197n; TP, "Retreat Across the Delaware," *CWTP* 2:94–95.

8. Harry Ammon, *James Monroe: The Quest for National Identity* (New York, 1971), 1–7; John E. Selby, *The Revolution in Virginia, 1775–1783* (Williamsburg, Va., 1988), 1–89; John Richard Alden, *General Charles Lee: Traitor or Patriot?* (Baton Rouge, La., 1951), 108–13.

9. Half a century later, in his memoirs, JM said that he abandoned his studies in January 1776, but he likely remained as a student for several weeks longer than he recalled. See *AJM*, 22.

10. Harry M. Ward, *Duty, Honor or Country: General George Weedon and the American Revolution* (Philadelphia, 1979), 45–56. On the supposed "germ warfare," see Robert G. Parkinson, *The Common Cause: Creating Race and Nation in the American Revolution* (Chapel Hill, N.C., 2016), 246.

11. Robert K. Wright, *The Continental Army* (Washington, D.C., 1983), 283–93; John Hancock to GW, September 3, 1776, *PGWR* 6:207, 207n.

12. TJ to Page, August 20, 1776, *PTJ* 1:500; John Chilton to Joseph Blackwell, September 13, 1776, in Michael Cecere, ed., *They Behaved like Soldiers: Captain John Chilton and the Third Virginia Regiment, 1775–1778* (Bowie, Md., 2004), 79; Ammon, *Monroe*, 7–9; Ward, *Duty, Honor or Country*, 57–58.

13. GW, General Orders, September 17, 1776, *PGWR* 6:320; GW to Hancock, September 18, 1776, ibid., 6:333; Editor's Note, ibid., 6:334–36n; *AJM*, 23; Chilton to Blackwell, September 13, 1776, Cecere, *They Behaved Like Soldiers*, 79–80; Chilton to Martin Pickett, Thomas Keith, or Charles Chilton, September 17, 1776, ibid., 81–83; Chilton to Friends, October 4, 1776, ibid., 84. Weedon's quote is in Ward, *Duty, Honor or Country*, 62.

14. Ward, *Duty, Honor or Country*, 65–66; Chilton to friends, October 4, 1776, Cecere, *They Behaved like Soldiers*, 84.

15. Ward, *Duty, Honor or Country*, 66–68.

16. *AJM*, 24; David Hackett Fischer, *Washington's Crossing* (New York, 2004), 129; GW to Hancock, December 16, 1776, *PGWR* 7:352; ibid., 7:197n; Chilton to Charles Chilton, November 30, 1776, Cecere, *They Behaved Like Soldiers*, 87–88. Weedon's "uncommonly hard" quote is in *They Behaved Like Soldiers*, 23. The "scarecrows" quote is in Richard Ketchum, *The Winter Soldiers* (Garden City, N.J., 1973), 279. The "disfigured" faces quote is in William M. Dwyer, *The Day Is Ours! An Inside View of the Battles of Trenton and Princeton* (New York, 1983), 105. GW and JM were the two future presidents; the three cabinet officials were Henry Knox, AH, and JM; and the three future governors were Joseph Reed and Thomas Mifflin in Pennsylvania and JM in Virginia.

17. GW to Hancock, November 30, 1776, *PGWR* 7:233; Fischer, *Washington's Crossing*, 128–31; TP, *The American Crisis* II (1777), in *CWTP* 1:63. On AH's soldiering in 1776, see John Ferling, *Jefferson and Hamilton: The Rivalry That Forged a Nation* (New York, 2013), 60–64.

18. Ward, *Duty, Honor or Country*, 72.

19. GW to Hancock, December 5, 1776, *PGWR* 7:262; also see ibid., 7:274–75n and 292n.

20. TP to Samuel Adams, January 1, 1803, *CWTP* 2:1434; TP, "Messrs. Deane, Jay, and Gérard," *Pennsylvania Packet*, September 14, 1779, ibid., 2:186; Fischer, *Washington's Crossing*, 140; Hawke, *Paine*, 59.

21. TP, *The American Crisis* I (1776), in *CWTP* 1:50–57. The quotations can be found on pages 50, 53, 54, 55, 56, and 57. On the criticism of GW as indecisive, see John Ferling, *The Ascent of George Washington: The Hidden Political Genius of an American Icon* (New York, 2009), 119–20.

22. Quoted in Hawke, *Paine*, 61.

23. *PGWR* 7:431n.

24. TP, *Letter to the Abbé Raynal, on the Affairs of North America, in which the Mistakes in the Abbes Account of the Revolution of America are Corrected and Cleared up* (1782), in *CWTP* 2:222.

25. The best account of the Trenton operation can be found in Fischer, *Washington's Crossing*, 206–54. For JM's account, see *AJM*, 25–27. On Dr. Cochran, see *PGWR* 7:279–80n.

26. GW to Hancock, December 27, 1776, *PGWR* 7:454; ibid. 7:460n; Fischer, *Washington's Crossing*, 405–6; Howard H. Peckham, ed. *The Toll of Independence* (Chicago, 1974), 27. The "eagle upon a hen" quote can be found in Cresson, *James Monroe* (Chapel Hill, N.C., 1946), 30.

27. *PGWR* 13:611n; *AJM*, 26.

28. Fischer, *Washington's Crossing*, 412–15; TP, *Letter to the Abbé Raynal*, in *CWTP* 2:226.

29. TP, "Retreat Across the Delaware," *CWTP* 2:93–96; TP, *The American Crisis* II (1777), ibid., 1:58–72. The quotes can be found in "Retreat," page 95, and *American Crisis* II, pages 67 and 69.

30. GW to William Shippen Jr., May 3, 1777, *PGWR* 9:340, 340n; Joseph Jones to GW, August 11, 1777, ibid., 10:586; GW, General Orders, November 20, 1777, ibid., 12:327.

31. For the evolution of Britain's campaign plans, see Ferling, *Whirlwind*, 185–86, 195–96.

32. On Stirling's background and character, see Alan Valentine, *Lord Stirling* (New York, 1969), 3–205. See also Charles Carroll of Carrollton to GW, September 27, 1777, *PGWR* 11:330; ibid., 2:81n; Stephen R. Taaffe, *The Philadelphia Campaign, 1777–1778* (Lawrence, Kans., 2003), 7.

33. Laura Auricchio, *The Marquis: Lafayette Reconsidered* (New York, 2015), 32–49. The "Secure to us" comment was made by a member of Congress. The quotation is on page 47. The relationship between GW and Lafayette was complex. A good starting point for understanding their association is Stuart Leibiger, "George Washington and Lafayette: Father and Son of the Revolution," in Robert M. S. McDonald, ed., *Sons of the Father: George Washington and His Protégés* (Charlottesville, Va., 2013), 210–31.

34. The quotations can be found in Taaffe, *Philadelphia Campaign*, 73; Charles Royster, *A Revolutionary People at War: The Continental Army and American Character, 1775–1783* (Chapel Hill, N.C., 1979), 225; Caroline Cox, *A Proper Sense of Honor: Service and Sacrifice in George Washington's Army* (Chapel Hill, N.C., 2004), 163.

35. Quoted in Valentine, *Lord Stirling*, 209–10. See also *AJM*, 28.

36. For Lafayette's account of the engagement, see "Lafayette Memoir" in Stanley J. Idzerda et al., eds., *Lafayette in the Age of the American Revolution: Selected Letters and Papers, 1776–1790* (Ithaca, N.Y., 1977), 1:94. For a good account of the battle, see Taaffe, *Philadelphia Campaign*, 63–76.

37. GW to Hancock, September 13, 15, 17, 18, 19, 23, 1777, *PGWR* 11:213, 237, 247, 253, 262, 268, 301; *AJM*, 28.

38. GW, General Orders for Attacking Germantown, October 3, 1777, *PGWR* 11:375; GW to Hancock, October 5, 1777, ibid., 11:393–94; Valentine, *Lord Stirling*, 211. Good accounts of the battle can be found in Taaffe, *Philadelphia Campaign*, 93–107, and in Christopher Ward, *The War of the Revolution* (New York, 1952), 1:362–71.

39. H. Laurens to John Laurens, October 16, 1777, January 8, 1778, in Philip M. Hamer et al., eds., *The Papers of Henry Laurens* (Columbia, S.C., 1968–2002), 11:554–55; 12:275. On the purported conspiracy, see Ferling, *Ascent of George Washington*, 140–64. TP was mistakenly convinced that JA was part of the cabal to remove GW. See TP, "To the Citizens of the United States," Letter III (1802), *CWTP* 2:922.

40. *AJM*, 24. Stirling is quoted in Wayne Bodle, *The Valley Forge Winter: Civilians and Soldiers in War* (University Park, Pa., 2003), 41. JA's assessment can be found in JA to James Lovell, July 26, 1778, *PJA* 6:318–19.

41. TP, "To the Citizens of the United States," Letter III (1802), *CWTP* 2:922; TP, *The American Crisis* IV (1777), ibid., 1:102–5; TP, *The American Crisis* V (1778), ibid., 1:111, 115, 122; TP to BF, May 16, 1778, ibid., 2:1143, 1147.

42. On the Valley Forge winter, see Ferling, *Almost a Miracle*, 274–82, and Bodle, *The Valley Forge Winter*, especially pages 103–42.

43. JM to John Thornton, November 21, 1777, *PJM* 2:7.

44. TP to BF, May 16, 1778, *CWTP* 2:1150.

45. Nelson, *Thomas Paine*, 164; Alfred Owen Aldridge, *Man of Reason: The Life of Thomas Paine* (Philadelphia, 1959), 56; Hawke, *Paine*, 69; TP to Elihu Palmer, *CWTP* 2:1426; TP to BF, May 16, 1778, ibid., 2:1145; TP, "To the Citizens of the United States," Letter III, ibid., 2:923; *PGWR* 13:137n.

46. Hawke, *Paine*, 71; Rush to Elizabeth Graeme Ferguson [?], July 16, 1782, in L.H. Butterfield, ed., *The Letters of Benjamin Rush* (Princeton, N.J., 1951), 1:280. The description of TP's daily regimen while in Lancaster can be found in Aldridge, *Man of Reason*, 56–57.

47. GW, General Orders, May 5, 7, 1778, *PGWR* 15:38–40, 68–70; ibid., 15:40–41n; JM to Peter Duponceau, May 7, 1778, *PJM* 2:9; Ferling, *Almost a Miracle*, 293–94; Royster, *A Revolutionary People at War*, 250–54.

48. Aldridge, *Man of Reason*, 59; Ferling, *Whirlwind*, 205–12. Joseph Galloway, an American Tory, urged North's government in 1778 to utilize the "800,000 Negroes" who might be receptive to serving the British army; see Parkinson, *The Common Cause*, 364.

49. JM to GW, June 28, 1778, *PJM* 2:10.

50. Valentine, *Lord Stirling*, 226–32; Ammon, *Monroe*, 23–24; Nancy Isenberg, *Fallen Founder: The Life of Aaron Burr* (New York, 2007), 37, 45. The best, and most detailed, study of the engagement at Monmouth is Mark Edward Lender and Gary Wheeler Stone, *Fatal Sunday: George Washington, the Monmouth Campaign, and the Politics of Battle* (Norman, Okla., 2017).

51. *PGWR* 20:575n.

52. JM to Thornton, July 3, 1777, *PJM* 2:4; *AJM*, 29; GW to Archibald Cary, May [22], 1779, ibid., 20:574–75.

53. Ammon, *Monroe*, 26; AH to John Laurens, May 22, 1779, *PAH* 2:52; *PGWR* 20:575n.

54. JM to TJ, September 9, 1780, *PJM* 1:8; Ammon, *Monroe*, 583.

55. Cresson, *James Monroe*, 47.

56. Ammon, *Monroe*, 17–18.

57. TP, *The American Crisis* VI (1778), *CWTP* 1:132, 136, 137, 138; GW, Circular to the States, December 29, 1777, *PGWR* 13:36–37. On the Carlisle Commission and its possibilities, see Parkinson, *The Common Cause*, 384–99.

58. TP to BF, October 24, 1778, *CWTP* 2:1153; TP, *The American Crisis* VII (1778), ibid., 1:140–57. The "American Crisis" quotations can be found on pages 150, 153, and 155.

59. Eric Foner, *Tom Paine and Revolutionary America* (New York, 2005), 131–32, 135.

60. TP, "To the People" (1777), *CWTP* 2:269–72. The quote is on page 270.

61. TP, "A Serious Address to the People of Pennsylvania on the Present Situation of Their Affairs" (1778), ibid., 2:278–302. The quotations are on pages 286 and 287. This passage draws on Foner, *Tom Paine and Revolutionary America*, 144.

62. GW to George Mason, March 27, 1779, *PGWR* 19:627; GW to Benjamin Harrison, December 18[–30], 1778, ibid., 18:449–50.

63. The discussion of corruption draws on Gordon S. Wood, *The Creation of the American Republic, 1776–1787* (Chapel Hill, N.C., 1969), 32–36, 107–17, 414–25. See also Zephyr Teachout, *Corruption in America: From Benjamin Franklin's Snuff Box to Citizens United* (Cambridge, Mass., 2014), 17–80. The quotations are in Wood, page 420.

64. TP, "The Affair of Silas Deane" (1778–79), *CWTP* 2:97–188. The quotations are on pages 104, 117, 118, 136, and 137.

65. Ibid., 2:112.

66. Hawke, *Paine*, 80–91. See also TP to Henry Laurens, December 15, 1778, January 14, 17, 1779, *CWTP* 2:1154–55, 1160–66; TP to Congress, January 6, 7, 8, 1779, ibid., 2:1156–60. Gouverneur Morris's quote can be found in William Howard Adams, *Gouverneur Morris: An Independent Life* (New Haven, Conn., 2003), 117.

67. TP to Congress, January 7, 1779, *CWTP* 2:1158.

68. TP to GW, January 31, 1779, ibid., 2:1167; TP to BF, March 4, 1779, ibid., 2:1167–68; TP to Jonathan Williams, November 26, 1781, ibid., 2:1200.

69. TP to Laurens, September 14, 1779, ibid., 2:1178; Hawke, *Paine*, 101.

70. GW to George Mason, March 27, 1779, *PGWR* 19:628.

CHAPTER 4: "DEFENDING OUR FANES AND FIRE-SIDES":
WINNING THE REVOLUTIONARY WAR

1. Gordon S. Wood, *The American Revolution: A History* (New York, 2003), 65–106; Jackson Turner Main, "The American Revolution and the Democratization of the Legislatures," *WMQ* 23 (1966): 391–406; idem., *The Sovereign States, 1775–1783* (New York, 1973), 143–221.

2. JA to AA, July 3, 1776, *AFC* 2:28.

3. TJ remarked that he "saw . . . that the laboring oar was really at home." TJ, Autobiography, *CTJ*, 1151. For JA's comment, see JA to Richard Cranch, August 2, 1776, *AFC* 2:74. JA was applauding the eradication of "Idolatry to Monarchs, and servility" to aristocracies.

4. TJ, "Third Draft by Jefferson" [before June 13, 1776], *PTJ* 1:356–65. See also Francis D. Cogliano, "'The Whole Object of the Present Controversy': The Early Constitutionalism of Paine and Jefferson," in Simon P. Newman and Peter S. Onuf, eds., *Paine and Jefferson in the Age of Revolutions* (Charlottesville, Va., 2013), 34–36.

5. Merrill D. Peterson, *Thomas Jefferson and the New Nation* (New York, 1970), 45.

6. TJ to JA, October 28, 1813, *AJL* 2:391. TJ's "more good sense" quotation can be found in Peterson, *Thomas Jefferson*, 14.

7. TJ, Autobiography, *CTJ*, 1119; Henry S. Randall, *The Life of Thomas Jefferson* (New York, 1858), 1:13.

8. The TJ quotes can be found in [Thomas Jefferson], *A Summary View of the Rights of British America* (Williamsburg, Va., 1774), 122, 123, 124, 124, 127. Wood's quote is in Gordon S. Wood, "The Radicalism of Thomas Jefferson and Thomas Paine Considered," in Newman and Onuf, *Paine and Jefferson in the Age of Revolutions*, 15.

9. The foregoing draws on Thomas Jefferson, *Notes on the State of Virginia*, ed. William Peden (Chapel Hill, N.C., 1955), 128; TJ to Samuel Kercheval, July 12, 1816, in Ford, *WTJ* 12:4; TJ, Autobiography, *CTJ*, 1139–40; TJ to JA, October 28, 1813, *AJL* 2:388–89; Wood, *American Revolution*, 91–93.

10. Hancock to TJ, September 30, 1776, *PTJ* 1:523–24; Lee to TJ, September 27, November 3, 1776, ibid., 1:522–23, 590; TJ to Hancock, October 11, 1776, ibid., 1:524.

11. Lee to TJ, August 25, 1777, ibid., 2:29.

12. TJ to Lee, April 21, 1779, ibid., 2:255; TJ to William Phillips, [April ?, 1779], ibid., 2:261; TJ to Henry, March 27, 1779, ibid., 2:237–44.

13. TJ to Lee, August 30, 1778, ibid., 2:210–11; Edmund Pendleton to TJ, May 11, 1779, ibid., 2:266.

14. Fawn M. Brodie, *Thomas Jefferson: An Intimate History* (New York, 1974), 152–53, 159; Annette Gordon-Reed, *The Hemingses of Monticello: An American Family* (New York, 2008), 129–30, 132. On claims that Martha Jefferson may have fought for her life in these two pregnancies, see Virginia Scharff, *The Women Jefferson Loved* (New York, 2010), 118–20.

15. TJ, Autobiography, *CTJ*, 1144–46.

16. TJ to Wythe, November 1, 1778, *PTJ* 1:230; TJ, Bill Nos. 64–76, ibid., 2:492–522, 505–6n; TJ, Bill Nos. 51, 53, ibid., 2:2:470–72, 475–76; TJ, *Notes on the State of Virginia*, 137–45; TJ, Autobiography, *CTJ*, 1140, 1144–47, 1149–50; John Selby, *The Revolution in Virginia* (Charlottesville, Va., 1980), 160; R. B. Bernstein, *Thomas Jefferson* (New York, 2003), 38–40; Paul Finkelman, "Jefferson and Slavery: 'Treason Against the Hopes of the World,'" in Peter S. Onuf, ed., *Jeffersonian Legacies* (Charlottesville, Va., 1993), 196; John Chester Miller, *The Wolf by the Ears: Thomas Jefferson and Slavery* (New York, 1977), 20–21; Robert McColley, *Slavery and Jeffersonian Virginia* (Urbana, Ill., 1973), 2–3, 72, 115–16, 120, 132–35, 143–59.

17. TJ, Bills Nos. 79, 80, 81, *PTJ* 2:526-45; TJ to Edward Carrington, January 16, 1787, ibid., 11:49; TJ to Wythe, August 13, 1786, ibid., 10:244; TJ, *Notes on the State of Virginia*, 146-49; TJ, Autobiography, *CTJ*, 1149, 1150; TJ to JA, October 28, 1813, *AJL* 2:389; Garrett Ward Shelton, *The Political Philosophy of Thomas Jefferson* (Baltimore, 1991), 65.

18. TJ, Third Draft by Jefferson of a Constitution, [Before June 13, 1776], *PTJ* 1:362; TJ to JA, October 28, 1813, *AJL* 2:389.

19. TJ, Bill No. 20, *PTJ* 2:391-93, 393n. On entail in practice, see Holly Brewer, "Entailing Aristocracy in Colonial Virginia: 'Ancient Feudal Restraints' and Revolutionary Reform," *WMQ* 54 (1997): 307-46.

20. TJ, *Notes on the State of Virginia*, 164-65.

21. TJ to GW, August 14, 1787, *PTJ* 12:38; TJ to JA, October 28, 1813, *AJL* 2:391. For good succinct essays—or portions thereof—on TJ's agrarianism, see Richard K. Matthews, *The Radical Politics of Thomas Jefferson: A Revisionist View* (Lawrence, Kans., 1984), 31-52; John Howe, "Republicanism," in Merrill D. Peterson, ed., *Thomas Jefferson: A Reference Biography* (New York, 1986), 73-74; and Robert Shalhope, "Agriculture," ibid., 393-94. For the classical sources of TJ's agrarian philosophy, see Caroline Winterer, "Thomas Jefferson and the Ancient World," in Francis D. Cogliano, ed., *A Companion to Thomas Jefferson* (Chichester, England, 2012), 380-94.

22. TJ, Bill No. 82, *PTJ* 2:545-47 and 547-53n; TJ to JM, December 16, 1786, ibid., 10:603-4; TJ to Wythe, August 13, 1786, ibid., 10:244; TJ, *Notes on the State of Virginia*, 159; Merrill D. Peterson, "Jefferson and Religious Freedom," *Atlantic Monthly* 272 (December 1994): 113-24. See also the two following important essays: John A. Ragosta, "The Virginia Statute for Establishing Religious Freedom," in Cogliano, *A Companion to Thomas Jefferson*, 75-90; and Johann N. Neem, "A Republican Reformation: Thomas Jefferson's Civil Religion and the Separation of Church and State," ibid., 91-109.

23. TJ, "Jefferson's Services to His Country," [1800?], *CTJ*, 1288. On the link between what TJ sought after 1776 and the philosophy he articulated in the Declaration of Independence, see Cogliano, "'The Whole Object of the Present Controversy,'" in Newman and Onuf, *Paine and Jefferson in the Age of Revolutions*, 36.

24. TJ, *Notes on the State of Virginia*, 87, 137-40. See Casandra Pybus, "Thomas Jefferson and Slavery," in Cogliano, *A Companion to Thomas Jefferson*, 271-83; TP, "African Slavery in America" (1775), *CWTP* 2:17.

25. Lee to TJ, May 3, 1779, *PTJ* 2:263; Pendleton to TJ, May 11, 1779, ibid., 2:266; Fleming to TJ, May 10, 11, 22, 1779, ibid., 2:264, 265, 267-69; TJ to Lee, June 17, 1779, ibid., 2:298; TJ to William Phillips, June 25, 1779, ibid., 3:15. On Collier's raid, see Michael Kranish, *Flight from Monticello: Thomas Jefferson at War* (New York, 2010), 114-17, and Michael A. McDonnell, *The Politics of War: Race, Class, and Conflict in Revolutionary Virginia* (Chapel Hill, N.C., 2007), 343-44.

26. TJ to Phillips, June 25, 1779, *PTJ* 3:15.

27. McDonnell, *Politics of War*, 277, 393-94, 411-19; L. Scott Philyaw, "A Slave for Every Soldier: The Strange History of Virginia's Forgotten Recruitment Act of 1 January 1781," *Virginia Magazine of History and Biography* 109 (2001): 367-86; Kranish, *Flight from Monticello*, 130; TJ to GW, December 16, 1779, *PTJ* 3:228; TJ, Form of Recruiting Commission, [November 28, 1780], ibid., 3:330; Henry to TJ, February 15, 1780, ibid., 3:293.

28. E. James Ferguson, *The Power of the Purse* (Chapel Hill, N.C., 1961), 25-100; GW to John Jay, April 23, 1779, *PGWR* 20:176.

29. John Ferling, *Whirlwind: The American Revolution and the War That Won It* (New York, 2015), 256–62.

30. TJ to JM, June 16, 1780, *PJM* 2:18; JM to TJ, June 26, September 9, 1780, ibid., 2:20–21, 26–27; TJ to Samuel Huntington, June 15, 28, 1780, ibid., 3:446, 468.

31. Gates to TJ, August 3, 1780, 3:524–25; TJ to Gates, August 4, September 3, 1780, ibid., 3:526, 588; TJ to George Rogers Clark, September 29, 1780, ibid., 3:670; TJ to GW, July 2, 1780, ibid., 3:478.

32. JM to TJ, June 26, 1780, ibid., 3:465.

33. Edward Stevens to TJ, August 20, 27, 30, 1780, ibid., 3:559, 563–64, 576–77; TJ to GW, September 3, 1780, ibid., 3:594–97; Paul David Nelson, *General Horatio Gates: A Biography* (Baton Rouge, La., 1976), 229–39; John Buchanan, *The Road to Guilford Courthouse: The American Revolution in the Carolinas* (New York, 1997), 161–72; John Pancake, *This Destructive War: The British Campaign in the Carolinas* (Tuscaloosa, Ala., 1985), 103–6; Ferling, *Whirlwind*, 264–66. The quotations can be found in *PTJ* 3:559, 596–96.

34. TJ to Huntington, September 3, 1780, *PTJ* 3:589.

35. GW to TJ, September 11, October 10, 1780, ibid., 3:639; 4:27; TJ to GW, October 22, 1780, ibid., 4:59–60; TJ to Huntington, October 22, 25, November 3, 19, 1780, ibid., 4:58, 67–68, 92–93, 128; TJ, Steps to Be Taken to Repel General Leslie's Army, October [22?], 1780, ibid., 4:61–63. On JM's military service during this emergency, see *AJM*, 32. The "canvass wings" remark was made by General Charles Lee and can be found in Eric Robson, *The American Revolution: In Its Political and Military Aspects, 1763–1783* (Hamden, Conn., 1965), 107.

36. TJ to Philip Mazzei, May 31, 1780, *PTJ* 3:405; TJ to GW, July 2, 1780, ibid., 3:478; TJ to Huntington, September 3, 14, 1780, ibid., 3:589, 648.

37. John Keane, *Tom Paine: A Political Life* (London, 1995), 188; TP, "A Serious Address to the People of Pennsylvania on the Present Situation of Their Affairs" (1778), *CWTP* 2:283.

38. The foregoing draws on Eric Foner, *Tom Paine and Revolutionary America* (rev. ed., New York, 2005), 145–82. On GW, see GW to Benjamin Harrison, December 18[–30], 1778, *PGWR* 18:447–50; GW to Mason, March 27, 1779, ibid., 19:626–28; GW to Burwell Bassett, April 22, 1779, ibid., 20:160–61; GW to Gouverneur Morris, May 8, 1779, ibid., 20:385–86. The Armstrong quote can be found in Keane, *Tom Paine*, 182.

39. Keane, *Tom Paine*, 183–85. The quotes can be found on page 185.

40. On the congressional battles over peace terms, see John Ferling, *A Leap in the Dark: The Struggle to Create the American Republic* (New York, 2003), 210–13.

41. TP to H. Laurens, September 14, 1779, *CWTP* 2:1178–80; TP to Supreme Executive Council, September 28, October 11, 1779, ibid., 2:1181–82, 1182–83; Keane, *Tom Paine*, 188, 192–93; Alfred Owen Aldridge, *Man of Reason: The Life of Thomas Paine* (Philadelphia, 1959), 80.

42. TP, *American Crisis* VIII (1780), in *CWTP* 1:158–64. The quotes are on pages 158 and 162.

43. GW to Joseph Reed, May 28, 1780, *WW* 18:434–40.

44. Reed to GW, June 5, 1780, ibid., 18:439n.

45. TP to Blair McClenaghan, May [?], 1780, *CWTP* 2:1183–85; TP to Reed, June 4, 1780, ibid., 2:1186–88. The quotations are pages 1186 and 1187.

46. TP, *American Crisis* IX (1780), ibid., 1:166–70.

47. Keane, *Tom Paine*, 199; Elizabeth Cometti, "Women in the American Revolution," *New England Quarterly* 20 (1947): 329–46; Linda Grant DePauw and Conover Hunt, *Remember the Ladies: Women in America, 1750–1815* (New York, 1976), 86.

48. TP, *The Crisis Extraordinary* (1780), in *CWTP* 2:171–85. The quotation is on page 185. At the last moment, TP learned of Arnold's treason and added a postscript about what he called "this black business." It can be found on pages 185–88. See also Keane, *Tom Paine*, 203.

49. TP to NG, September 9, 1780, *CWTP* 2:1188–90.

50. TP to a Committee of the Continental Congress, October [?], 1783, ibid., 2:1233; *PNG* 6:407n.

51. James Lovell to JA, January 2, 1781, *LDC* 16:537; John Ferling, *Almost a Miracle: The American Victory in the War of Independence* (New York, 2007), 472.

52. TP to a Committee of the Continental Congress, October [?], 1783, *CWTP* 2:1234; Sarah Bache to BF, January 14, 1781, *PBF* 34:272.

53. TP to a Committee of the Continental Congress, October [?], 1783, *CWTP* 2:1233–34; TP to NG, January 10, 1781, ibid., 2:1191; David Freeman Hawke, *Paine* (New York, 1974), 114; Marquis de Chastellux, *Travels in North America in the Years 1780, 1781, and 1782* (Chapel Hill, N.C., 1963), 1:175–76; GW to John Laurens, January 15, 1781, *WW* 21:107, 108, 110.

54. General Greene's Requisition for the Southern Army, November 20, 1780, *PTJ* 4:133–34; NG to TJ, November 20, 1780, ibid., 4:130–32; TJ to Steuben, December 21, 1780, *PTJ* 4:219.

55. Cornwallis to Clinton, August 6, 1780, in Charles Ross, ed., *Correspondence of Charles, First Marquis Cornwallis* (London, 1859), 1:54; Walter Edgar, *Partisans and Redcoats: The Southern Conflict That Turned the Tide of the American Revolution* (New York, 2001), 73–90, 97–106; Robert D. Bass, *The Green Dragoon: The Lives of Banastre Tarleton and Mary Robinson* (New York, 1957), 84–94, 104–26; Buchanan, *Road to Guilford Courthouse*, 131–41, 173–86. On the partisan warfare, see also Russell F. Weigley, *The Partisan War: The South Carolina Campaign of 1780–1782* (Columbia, S.C., 1970); the essays in Ronald Hoffman, Thad Tate, and Peter J. Albert, eds., *An Uncivil War: The Southern Backcountry During the American Revolution* (Charlottesville, Va., 1985); Christopher Ward, *The War of the Revolution* (New York, 1952), 2:739–45; and Hank Messick, *King's Mountain: The Epic of the Blue Ridge "Mountain Men" in the American Revolution* (Boston, 1976), 107–55.

56. TJ to Benjamin Harrison, November 24, 1780, *PTJ* 4:150; GW to TJ, November 8, December 9, 1780, ibid., 4:105, 195; TJ, Diary of Arnold's Invasion [The 1796? version], December 31, 1780, January 1, 1781, ibid., 4:258; Arnold's Invasion as Reported by TJ in the *Virginia Gazette*, January 13, 1781, ibid., 4:269.

57. TJ, Diary of Arnold's Invasion, January 2–5, 1781, ibid., 4:258–59; Benedict Arnold to Sir Henry Clinton, January 21, 1781, in Ian Saberton, ed., *The Cornwallis Papers: The Campaigns of 1780 and 1781* (Uckfield, England, 2010), 5:81–83; TJ, *Virginia Gazette*, January 13, 1781, ibid., 4:269–70; Depositions of Archibald Blair, Daniel Hylton, and James Currie, October 12, 1796, ibid., 4:271–72; TJ to GW, January 10, 1781, ibid., 4:333–35; TJ to George Weedon, January 10, 1781, ibid., 4:335–36; Kranish, *Flight from Monticello*, 167–99; Selby, *Revolution in Virginia*, 222–25; Willard M. Wallace, *Traitorous Hero: The Life and Fortunes of Benedict Arnold* (New York, 1954), 274.

58. Quoted in McDonnell, *Politics of War*, 402; Selby, *Revolution in Virginia*, 223–24; John Ferling, *Setting the World Ablaze: Washington, Adams, Jefferson and the American Revolution* (New York, 2000), 232. The Pendleton quote can be found in Kranish, *Flight from Monticello*, 203–4.

59. TJ to Phillips, June 25, 1779, *PTJ* 3:15; NG to TJ, February 15, 1781, *PTJ* 4:615.

60. NG to TJ, February 15, 28, March 10, 1781, ibid., 4:615–16; 5:23, 111–12; TJ to Steuben, January 14, February 7, 12, 16, March 10, 1781, ibid., 4:357–58, 555, 592–93, 633; 5:117–20; GW to TJ, February 6, 1781, ibid., 4:543–44.

61. TJ to Huntington, January 15, 1781, ibid., 4:370.

62. On the Battle of Cowpens, see Lawrence E. Babits, *A Devil of a Whipping: The Battle of Cowpens* (Chapel Hill, N.C., 1998). On Cornwallis's pursuit of the rebels and the engagement at Guilford Courthouse, see Lawrence E. Babits and Joshua B. Howard, *Long, Obstinate, and Bloody: The Battle of Guilford Courthouse* (Chapel Hill, N.C., 2009).

63. NG to TJ, March 23, 31, 1781, *PTJ* 5:215, 301–2.

64. The foregoing draws on Steuben, Proposal for an Expedition against Cornwallis, March 27, 1781, in Stanley J. Idzerda et al., eds., *Lafayette in the Age of the American Revolution: Selected Letters and Papers, 1776–1790* (Ithaca, N.Y., 1976–83), 3:419–20; Lafayette on Steuben's Proposed Expedition, March 27, 1781, ibid., 420–21; Lafayette to GW, September 8, 1781, ibid., 4:392; Lee to TJ, March 27, 1781, *PTJ* 5:252; Weedon to TJ, March 27, 1781, ibid., 5:267; NG to TJ, April 6, 1781, ibid. 5:361; NG to William Smallwood, June 9, 1781, *PNG* 8:371; NG to Samuel Huntington, June 9, 1781, ibid., 8:363; Harry M. Ward, *Duty, Honor or Country: General George Weedon and the American Revolution* (Philadelphia, 1979), 177–82. The Weedon quotation is in Peterson, *Thomas Jefferson*, 226.

65. TJ to Chevalier de La Luzerne, April 12, 1781, *PTJ* 5:421–22; Lee to the Virginia Delegates in Congress, June 12, 1781, ibid., 6:91; Jones to GW, June 20, July 3, 1781, *LDC* 17:337–38, 372.

66. TJ to Speaker of the House of Delegates, May 10, 1781, ibid., 5:626; Selby, *Revolution in Virginia*, 272–74; Kranish, *Flight from Monticello*, 233, 240–51.

67. TJ to James Wood, October 5, 1780, *PTJ* 4:14–15; TJ to the Virginia Delegates to Congress, October 27, 1780, ibid., 4:76–77; TJ to Lee, September 13, 1780, ibid., 3:642; TJ to de La Luzerne, April 12, 1781, ibid., 5:421; TJ to GW, May 28, 1781, ibid., 6:33.

68. Earl Cornwallis to Clinton, May 26, 1781, in Saberton, *Cornwallis Papers*, 5:89.

69. TJ, Diary of Arnold's Invasion, ibid., 4:261; James Madison to Philip Mazzei, July 7, 1781, *LDC* 17:383.

70. Kranish, *Flight from Monticello*, 283–84.

71. *JMB* 1:510–11n; Kranish, *Flight from Monticello*, 286; Cornwallis to Clinton, June 30, 1781, in Saberton, *Cornwallis Papers*, 5:104–5.

72. TJ to William Gordon, July 16, 1788, *PTJ* 13:363; TJ to Edmund Randolph, September 16, 1781, ibid., 6:118.

73. John Beckley to TJ [Enclosing a Resolution of the House of Delegates], June 12, 1781, ibid., 6:88; Archibald Cary to TJ, June 19, 1781, ibid., 6:97; TJ to George Nicholas, July 28, 1781, ibid., 6:105; Charges Advanced . . . with Jefferson's Answers [After July 31, 1781], ibid., 6:106–8; TJ to Lafayette, August 4, 1781, ibid., 6:111–12; TJ to Isaac Zane, December 24, 1781, ibid., 6:143; Resolution of Thanks to Jefferson by the Virginia General Assembly, December 12, 1781, ibid., 6:135–36.

74. TP to James Hutchinson, March 11, 1781, *CWTP* 2:1192.

75. Winslow C. Watson, ed., *Men and Times of the Revolution, or Memoirs of Elkanah Watson* (New York, 1856), 108–10; Jonathan Williams Jr. to BF, April 18, 1781, *PBF* 34:558. JA is quoted in Craig Nelson, *Thomas Paine: Enlightenment, Revolution, and the Birth of Modern Nations* (New York, 2006), 90.

76. TP to Robert Morris, February 20, 1782, *CWTP* 2:1206, 1208; TP to a Committee of the Continental Congress, October 1783, ibid., 2:1233–34.

77. TP to NG, September 10, 1781, *PNG* 9:317; TP to a Committee of the Continental Congress, October 1783, *CWTP* 2:1234; *PBF* 35:28n; BF to William Jackson, July 6, 1781, ibid., 35:224; James Madison to Edmund Pendleton, September 3, 1781, *LDC* 18:5.

78. TP to NG, September 10, 1781, *PNG* 9:317–18.

79. Ferling, *Almost a Miracle*, 504–5.

80. Cornwallis to Clinton, June 30, 1781, Saberton, *Cornwallis Papers*, 5:106.

81. GW to Lafayette, August 15, 1781, *WW* 22:502.

82. The soldiers' quotations and an extended narrative of the Yorktown campaign can be found in Ferling, *Whirlwind*, 293–309. The soldiers' quotes are on page 304. For TP's comment, see TP to Jonathan Williams, November 26, 1781, *CWTP* 2:1201.

83. TJ to Randolph, September 16, 1781, *PTJ* 6:118; TJ to Lafayette, August 4, 1781, ibid., 6:112; TJ, Autobiography, *CTJ*, 1150.

84. TJ, Autobiography, *CTJ*, 1139, 1150, 1151; TJ to JM, October 5, 1781, *PTJ* 6:127. The "tone and spirit" quotation alluding to the Declaration of Independence is in Robert G. Parkinson, "The Declaration of Independence," in Cogliano, *Companion to Thomas Jefferson*, 48.

85. TP to Thomas McKean, [August or September, 1781], *CWTP* 2:1196–97; TP to a Committee of the Continental Congress, October 1783, ibid., 2:1234; TP to GW, November 30, 1781, ibid., 2:1203–4.

CHAPTER 5: "THE TIMES THAT TRIED MEN'S SOULS, ARE OVER": PEACE AND NEW DEPARTURES

1. JM to Lafayette, September 27, 1781, *PJM* 2:30; JM to TJ, October 1, 1781, ibid., 2:31–32; Harry Ammon, *James Monroe: The Quest for National Identity* (New York, 1971), 33.

2. Robert Morris's ongoing accounts of the talks with GW and TP can be found in E. James Ferguson et al., eds., *The Papers of Robert Morris* (Pittsburgh, 1973–99), 4:111–12, 115–16, 139, 142, 143, 259, 262, 281–82, 327–28. See also Robert Morris, Agreement with Robert R. Livingston and George Washington, February 10, 1782, ibid., 4:201–2. See, too, John Keane, *Tom Paine: A Political Life* (New York, 1995), 217–18. The term "hireling writer" was Joseph Reed's disparaging description of TP. See *Papers of Robert Morris*, 4:202n. The sixty-five-thousand-dollar estimate is that of Craig Nelson, *Thomas Paine: Enlightenment, Revolution, and the Birth of Modern Nations* (New York, 2006), 159.

3. Morris, Memorandum on Thomas Paine (February 1782), *Papers of Robert Morris*, 4:327–28; William Hogeland, *Founding Finance: How Debt, Speculation, Foreclosures, Protests, and Crackdowns Made Us a Nation* (Austin, 2012), 84–86.

4. TP, *Common Sense* (1776), *CWTP* 1:26, 29; TP, *Public Good* (1781), ibid., 2:303–33; TP to Robert Morris, February 20, November 20, 1782, ibid., 2:1207, 1214–15. The quotations from *Public Good* are on pages 304–5, 329, and 332–33.

5. TP, *The American Crisis* X (1782), ibid., 1:189–207; TP, *The American Crisis* XI (1782), ibid., 208–16. The quotes can be found on pages 191, 194, 198, 201, 204, and 214. Historian John Keane has pointed out that Paine's earliest essays, often misidentified as *The American Crisis* X, were in actuality a two-part essay that appeared in a Philadelphia newspaper. For his clarification, see Keane, *Tom Paine*, 578–79n. On TP being in the pay of the French, see Alfred Owen Aldridge, *Man of Reason: The Life of Thomas Paine* (Philadelphia, 1959), 93–94.

6. TP, *Letter to the Abbé Raynal, on the Affairs of North America, in which the Mistakes in the Abbes Account of the Revolution of America are Corrected and Cleared up* (1782), *CWTP* 2:211–63. The quotes can be found on pages 217, 230, 243, 247, 254, 255, and 256. Philip S. Foner, editor of the *CWTP*, noted that Paine evidently looked on the *Letter* with great

pride inasmuch as after 1782 he often referred to himself as the author of *Common Sense* and the *Letter to the Abbé Raynal*. See ibid., 212n.

7. TP to GW, March 17, 1782, ibid., 2:1209; TP to Robert Morris, March 17, 1782, ibid., 2:1210.

8. TP, *The American Crisis*, XII (1782), ibid., 1:221–29. The quotations can be found on pages 223 and 225. The reaction of BF, of which TP likely remained unaware, can be found in David Freeman Hawke, *Paine* (New York, 1974), 132. For NG's comment, see NG to TP, November 18, 1782, *PNG* 12:206.

9. TP's several essays are lumped together in his collected works as "Six Letters to Rhode Island" (1782–83), *CWTP* 2:333–66. See also TP to Robert Morris, November 20, December 7, 1782, January 23, 1783, ibid., 2:1213–15, 1216; TP to a Committee of the Continental Congress, October 1783, ibid., 2:1237–40. The "mercenary writer" quote is in Hawke, *Paine*, 134. TP's quote on "regulation and protection" can be found in *CWTP* 2:350. On the impost and its failure, see E. James Ferguson, *The Power of the Purse: A History of American Finance, 1776–1790* (Chapel Hill, N.C., 1961), 116–18, 152–53. On TP's newspaper campaign in support of the impost, see Alfred Owen Aldridge, "Some Writings of Thomas Paine in Pennsylvania Newspapers," *American Historical Review* 56 (1951): 832–38.

10. TP to Elias Boudinot, June 7, 1783, *CWTP* 2:1217.

11. For the three preceding paragraphs, see TP, *The American Crisis* XIII (1783), ibid., 1:230–35. The quote from *Common Sense* can be found ibid., 1:45.

12. TJ to McKean, August 4, 1781, *PTJ* 6:113; TJ to the Speaker of the House of Delegates, May 6, 1782, ibid., 6:179; TJ to JM, May 20, 1782, ibid., 6:184–86.

13. Howard C. Rice Jr., ed., *Travels in North America in the Years 1780, 1781 and 1782 by the Marquis de Chastellux* (Chapel Hill, N.C., 1963), 1:2–24; 2:389–96.

14. TJ to JM, May 20, 1782, *PTJ* 6:186; TJ to Chastellux, November 26, 1782, ibid., 6:203; TJ to Elizabeth Wayles Eppes, October 3[?], 1782, *PTJ* 6:198. For accounts by friends and TJ's daughter Martha, see ibid., 6:186–87n. On TJ's wife's health and final illness, see Jon Kukla, *Mr. Jefferson's Women* (New York, 2007), 78–85, and Virginia Scharff, *The Women Jefferson Loved* (New York, 2010), 142–50. For the inscription on the tombstone, see Andrew Burstein and Nancy Isenberg, *Madison and Jefferson* (New York, 2010), 93.

15. *JMB* 1:524–32; Keane, *Tom Paine*, 240.

16. *JMB* 1:xlviii, 536–40; TJ to Madison, August 31, 1783, *PTJ* 6:336; Dumas Malone, *Jefferson and His Time* (Boston, 1948–81), 1:403–4.

17. For the tense period following Yorktown, see William M. Fowler Jr., *American Crisis: George Washington and the Dangerous Two Years After Yorktown, 1781–1783* (New York, 2011).

18. TP to GW, October 13, 1783, *CWTP* 2:1243; Keane, *Tom Paine*, 246, 249. TP's essay appeared in the December 9, 1783, issue of the *Pennsylvania Gazette*. The TP quotes are in Keane, *Tom Paine*, 249.

19. TP to James Duane, December 3, 1783, *CWTP* 2:1244–45; TP to GW, September 21, 1783, April 28, 1784, ibid., 2:1223–24, 1248–49; TP to a Committee of the Continental Congress, [October 1783], ibid., 2:1228; TJ to Madison, May 25, 1784, *PTJ* 7:289; GW to Madison, June 12, 1784, *PGWC* 1:445; GW to Henry, June 12, 1784, ibid., 1:443; Keane, *Tom Paine*, 242, 251–53; Hawke, *Paine*, 144, 393. TP's quotes are in his appeal to Congress, *CWTP* 2:1228, and Keane, *Tom Paine*, 242. The French minister awarded Paine 2,400 livres, which was worth about $800. On the livres' value, see Ferguson, *Power of the Purse*, 41n.

20. TP to Boudinot, June 7, 1783, *CWTP* 2:1217–18; TP to A Committee of the Continental Congress, [October 1783], ibid., 2:1229, 1241; Keane, *Tom Paine*, 253.

21. Hawke, *Paine*, 147.

22. GW to TP, September 10, 1783, *WW* 27:146–47; John Ferling, *The First of Men: A Life of George Washington* (reprint, New York, 2010), 315–16.

23. Fowler, *American Crisis*, 227–33.

24. TJ, Report of a Committee on the Response by the President of Congress, December 22, 1783, *PTJ* 6:412–14, and editor's note, 402–9n; GW, Address to Congress, December 23, 1783, *WW* 27:284–85.

25. Jefferson's Notes on Coinage, *PTJ* 7:175–85, 150–60n; TJ, Report of the Committee, March 1, 1784, ibid., 6:603–5. See also the editorial note in *PTJ*, 6:581–600n; TJ, Observations on [Jean Nicolas] Démeunier's Manuscript, June 26, 1786, ibid., 10:58. See also the editorial note on TJ's plans for the West, ibid., 6:581–600n.

26. *JMB* 1:554–57, 556–57n.

27. *AJM*, 38.

28. JM to John Francis Mercer, March 14, October 4, 1783, *PJM* 2:55, 64.

29. JM to R. H. Lee, December 16, 1783, ibid., 2:71; JM to TJ, May 14, June 1, 1784, ibid., 2:98, 106; *JMB* 1:541n.

30. AA to John Thaxter, March 20, 1785, in *AFC* 6:80; AA to Cotton Tufts, March 8, 1785, ibid., 6:78; AA to Mary Smith Cranch, May 8, 1785, ibid., 6:119; AA to TJ, June 6, 1785, *AJL* 1:28; TJ to Madison, January 30, 1787, *PTJ* 11:94–95; Edith B. Gelles, *Abigail and John: Portrait of a Marriage* (New York, 2009), 165–74. On TJ's indifference to salons, see Conor Cruise O'Brien, *The Long Affair: Thomas Jefferson and the French Revolution, 1785–1800* (Chicago, 1996), 35, and Annette Gordon-Reed and Peter S. Onuf, *"Most Blessed of the Patriarchs": Thomas Jefferson and the Empire of the Imagination* (New York, 2016), 98. Gordon-Reed and Onuf contend that TJ shunned Parisian salons because "he could not count on being the smartest person in the room" and he soon found that the aristocrats in attendance did not defer to him as did the bumpkins in Virginia.

31. TJ to John Jay, February 1, 1787, *PTJ* 11:101; TJ to Madison, January 30, 1787, ibid., 11:96.

32. Malone, *Jefferson and His Time*, 2:112–28, 147–49.

33. TJ to Page, May 4, 1786, *PTJ* 9:445–46; TJ to William Stephens Smith, September 28, 1787, ibid., 12:193; Malone, *Jefferson and His Time*, 2:51–63.

34. TJ to Maria Cosway, October 5, 12, 1786, April 24, 1788, *PTJ* 10:393, 431–32, 443–53; 13:104; Maria Cosway to TJ, September 20, October 5, 1786, ibid., 10:393–94, 433; Kukla, *Mr. Jefferson's Women*, 86–92.

35. TJ to Maria Cosway, October 12, November 29, December 24, 1786, July 1, 1787, *PTJ* 10:443–53, 555, 627; 11:520; Maria Cosway to TJ, February 15, 1787, ibid., 11:148. On Trumbull as a courier, see Andrew Burstein, *The Inner Jefferson: Portrait of a Grieving Optimist* (Charlottesville, Va., 1996), 76–79.

36. Maria Cosway to TJ, December 10, 25, 1787, *PTJ* 12:415, 459–60.

37. Maria Cosway to TJ, November 13, 24, 1794, December 4, 1795, ibid., 28:201, 209–10, 543–44; TJ to Maria Cosway, January 31, April 24, 1788, May 21, 1789, June 23, 1790, ibid., 12:540; 13:103–4; 15:143; 16:551.

38. A Fourth of July Tribute to Jefferson, July 4, 1789, ibid., 15:239; Anne Cary Morris, ed., *The Diary and Letters of Gouverneur Morris, Minister of the United States to France* (New York, 1888), 1:94, 138; Gouverneur Morris to GW, November 12, 1788, ibid., 1:xxxii; *JMB* 1:726;

Malone, *Jefferson and His Time*, 2:140–41, 143, 145. Gouverneur Morris's quotes concerning how French officials saw TJ can be found in Max M. Mintz, *Gouverneur Morris and the American Revolution* (Norman, Okla., 1970), 207. Shippen is quoted in John P. Kaminski, ed., *The Founders on the Founders: Word Portraits from the Revolutionary Era* (Charlottesville, Va., 2008), 295.

39. TJ to Eliza House Trust, December 15, 1786, *PTJ* 10:600.

40. TP to GW, April 28, 1784, *CWTP* 2:1248; TJ to GW, November 14, 1786, *PTJ* 10:532–33. Which of TP's several songs was composed for the Society is uncertain, but the editors of *PGWC* believed it was named "Columbia" and sung to the tune of "Anacreon in Heaven." The lyrics began: "Ye Sons of Columbia, then join hand in hand / Divided we fall, but united we stand." See *PGWC* 1:321n. On TP's support of the Society as a body that could aid widows and orphans, see Keane, *Tom Paine*, 254.

41. The "foul play" quote is in the diary of John Hall, a portion of which is reprinted in Moncure Daniel Conway, *The Life of Thomas Paine* (New York, 1892), 2:462. See also Hawke, *Paine*, 149–59; Keane, *Tom Paine*, 254–63; Eric Foner, *Tom Paine and Revolutionary America* (New York, 2005), 192–203. The additional quotations in this paragraph can be found in Foner, 203; Hawke, 159; and Keane, 262.

42. TP, *Letter to the Abbé Raynal, on the Affairs of North America, in which the Mistakes in the Abbes Account of the Revolution of America are Corrected and Cleared up* (1782), *CWTP* 2:241. The Descartes quotation can be found in Peter Gay, *The Enlightenment: An Interpretation* (New York, 1969), 6.

43. Edward G. Gray, *Tom Paine's Iron Bridge: Building a United States* (New York, 2016), 84–98.

44. Ibid., 99–108; John Hall Diary, in Conway, *Life of Thomas Paine*, 2:461–62, 465–67; TP to BF, June 6, 1786, *CWTP* 2:1026–28; TP to John Hall, September 22, 1786, ibid., 2:1257; TP to George Clymer, November 19, 1786, ibid., 2:1258; TP to Thomas Fitzsimmons, November 19, 1786, ibid., 2:1259–60.

45. TP to BF, March 31, June 22, 1787, *CWTP* 2:1260–61, 1262; BF to TJ, April 19, 1787, *PTJ* 11:301–2; Philipp Ziesche, "Thomas Paine and Benjamin Franklin's French Circle," in Simon P. Newman and Peter S. Onuf, eds., *Paine and Jefferson in the Age of Revolutions* (Charlottesville, Va., 2013), 124. On TP and the bridge, see Keane, *Tom Paine*, 267–70; Hawke, *Paine*, 160–70; Aldridge, *Man of Reason*, 108–17; Nelson, *Thomas Paine*, 171–75. BF's descriptions of TP can be found in Keane on page 271, and Ziesche on page 124.

46. TP to BF, June 22, 1787, *CWTP* 2:1262; Aldridge, *Man of Reason*, 111.

47. TP to the Royal Academy of Sciences, July 21, 1787, *CWTP* 2:1263–64; TP to Clymer, August 15, December 29, 1787, ibid., 2:1264, 1267; Keane, *Tom Paine*, 273; Nelson, *Thomas Paine*, 181; Gray, *Tom Paine's Iron Bridge*, 116.

48. For TP in Thetford, see Keane, *Tom Paine*, 281. For the two descriptions, see Royall Taylor, *The Algerine Captive, or the Life and Adventures of Doctor Updike Underhill: Six Years a Prisoner among the Algerines* (Hartford, Conn., 1816), 90–91, and Thomas Rickman's description reprinted in Conway, *Life of Thomas Paine*, 1:321–22. The "idle chatter" comment can be found in Andrew Burstein and Nancy Isenberg, *Madison and Jefferson* (New York, 2010), 104.

49. Gaye Wilson, "Thomas Jefferson's Portrait of Thomas Paine," in Newman and Onuf, *Paine and Jefferson in the Age of Revolutions*, 229–51.

50. Gray, *Tom Paine's Iron Bridge*, 1–2, 125–35.

51. TP to Hall, November 25, 1791, *CWTP* 2:1321–22.

52. TP to TJ, September 9, 1788, February 26, July 13, September 15, 1789, ibid., 2:1268–69, 1281, 1294, 1295; TP to TJ, August 18, 1787, PTJ 12:45. For detailed accounts of TP's frustrating years chasing his bridge dreams in France and England, see Gray, *Tom Paine's Iron Bridge*, 111–35; Keane, *Tom Paine*, 272–82; Aldridge, *Man of Reason*, 111–16; and Nelson, *Thomas Paine*, 176–80. The quote of the president of the American Society of Civil Engineers can be found in Audrey Williamson, *Thomas Paine: His Life, Work and Times* (New York, 1973), 106. On bridge construction in England after 1791, and on TP's legacy, see Gray, *Tom Paine's Bridge*, 153–97.

53. TJ to Madison, July 1, 1784, *PTJ* 7:356.

54. Madison to TJ, March 18, May 12, June 19, December 4, 1786, March 19, 1787, ibid., 9:334–35, 519, 660; 10:574; 11:219–20. For the formulation of Madison's thinking, see John Ferling, *A Leap in the Dark: The Struggle to Create the American Republic* (New York, 2003), 268–73.

55. JM to TJ, December 14, 1784, April 12, June 16, July 15, 1785, *PJM* 2:149, 198, 225–26, 239; JM to Madison, February 11, 1786, October 26, 1788, ibid., 2:277, 457; JM to Joseph Jones, March 2, 1786, ibid., 2:279; *AJM*, 36–49; Ammon, *James Monroe*, 41–62, 74. The female acquaintance's description of JM can be found in Ammon, page 46. The quotations about the expedition to Niagara Falls are in *AJM*, 39–40.

56. JM to TJ, July 27, 1787, *PJM* 2:391.

57. TJ to Madison, June 20, 1787, *PTJ* 11:480; TJ to Edward Carrington, August 4, 1787, ibid., 11:678; TJ to JA, August 30, 1787, *AJL* 1:196.

58. TP, *Common Sense* (1776), in *CWTP* 1:4–5.

59. TJ to Madison, June 20, 1787, *PTJ* 11:481; TJ to Jean-Nicolas Demeunier, June 24, 1786, ibid., 10:14; TJ to Carrington, January 16, 1787, ibid., 11:49; TJ to AA, February 22, 1787, *AJL* 1:173. The section on TJ's philosophy of government draws on John Howe, "Republicanism," in Merrill D. Peterson, ed. *Thomas Jefferson: A Reference Biography* (New York, 1986), 59–79.

60. For the foregoing paragraphs, see TJ to JA, November 13, 1787, *AJL* 1:212; TJ to Lafayette, February 28, 1787, *PTJ* 11:186; TJ to Madison, June 20, December 20, 1787, ibid., 11:480; 12:439–42; TJ to Smith, November 13, 1787, February 2, 1788, ibid., 12:356–57; TJ to John Rutledge Jr., February 2, 1788, ibid., 12:557; TJ to Francis Hopkinson, March 13, 1789, ibid., 14:650; TJ to Edward Carrington, December 21, 1787, May 27, 1788, ibid., 12:446; 13:208; TJ to William Carmichael, June 3, 1788, ibid., 13:232; TJ to GW, May 2, 1788, ibid., 13:128; GW to TJ, August 31, 1788, ibid., 13:556; TJ to Francis Hopkinson, March 13, 1789, ibid., 14:650; Madison to TJ, December 8, 1788, ibid., 14:339; TP to TJ[?], ibid., 13:4–5, 6–8n; Lafayette to GW, January 1, 1788, *PGWC* 6:5; Laura Auricchio, *The Marquis: Lafayette Reconsidered* (New York, 2014), 165–66. The "energetic government is always oppressive" quotation is in Malone, *Jefferson and His Time*, 2:169.

61. These two paragraphs draw on TJ to Charles Bellini, September 20, 1785, *PTJ* 8:569; TJ to GW, December 4, 1788, ibid., 14:330; TJ to Madison, January 30, 1787, ibid., 11:96; TJ to Baron Geismar, September 6, 1785, ibid., 8:500; TJ to AA, June 21, 1785, *AJL* 1:34; William Howard Adams, *The Paris Years of Thomas Jefferson* (New Haven, Conn., 1997), 9–11, 43, 59, 227–32; James C. Thompson, *Thomas Jefferson's Enlightenment* (Alexandria, Va., 2013), 87–91; Annette Gordon-Reed and Peter S. Onuf, *"Most Blessed of the Patriarchs": Thomas Jefferson and the Empire of the Imagination* (New York, 2016), 154–59, 163.

62. Good starting points for French society under the ancien régime are William Doyle, *The Oxford History of the French Revolution* (New York, 1989), 7–43; Peter McPhee, *Liberty or*

Death: The French Revolution (New Haven, Conn., 2016), 1–22; John Shovlin, "Nobility," in William Doyle, ed., *The Oxford Handbook of The Ancien Régime* (New York, 2012), 111–26; Sarah Maza, "Bourgeoisie," ibid., 127–40; and Alan Forrest, "Poverty," ibid., 167–82.

63. TJ to Charles Bellini, September 30, 1785, *PTJ* 8:568; TJ to Madison, October 28, 1785, ibid., 8:681–82; TJ to Eliza House Trist, August 18, 1785, ibid., 8:404; TJ, Notes of a Tour into the Southern Parts of France, &c. (1787), ibid., 11:414, 420, 424, 458; TJ to William Short, March 15, 1787, ibid., 11:214; TJ to Lafayette, April 11, 1787, ibid., 11:285. Figures on the Duc d'Orleans annual rent can be found in George Armstrong Kelly, *Victims, Authority, and Terror: The Parallel Deaths of d'Orleans, Custine, Bailly, and Malesherbes* (Chapel Hill, N.C., 1982), 29.

64. For the two foregoing paragraphs, see TJ to Bellini, September 30, 1785, *PTJ* 8:568–69; TJ to Madison, October 28, 1785, January 30, 1787, ibid., 8:681–82; 11:92–93; TJ to Lafayette, April 11, 1787, ibid., 11:285; TJ to Eliza House Trist, August 18, 1785, ibid., 8:440; TJ to Joseph Jones, August 14, 1787, ibid., 12:34; TJ to Wythe, August 13, 1786, ibid., 10:244; TJ to GW, May 2, 1788, ibid., 13:128; Jefferson's Observations on Demeunier's Manuscript, [February [?]–June 22, 1786], ibid., 10:52; TJ to David Ramsay, August 4, 1787, ibid., 11:687; TJ to Carrington, January 16, 1787, ibid., 11:49; TJ to JM, June 17, 1785, ibid., 8:233.

65. TJ to Madison, October 28, 1785, ibid., 8:681–82.

66. TJ to AA, February 22, 1787, *AJL* 1:173; TJ to Madison, January 30, 1787, September 6, 1789, *PTJ* 15:392–97; 11:93; TJ to Ezra Stiles, December 24, 1786, ibid., 10:629; TJ to Smith, November 13, 1787, ibid., 12:356.

67. TP to GW, October 16, 1789, *PGWP* 4:197.

68. TJ, Autobiography, *CTJ*, 1164, 1176–77. On the forecast that the American Revolution would inspire significant change in France, see Janet Polasky, *Revolutions Without Borders: The Call to Liberty in the Atlantic World* (New Haven, Conn., 2015), 24, 44. The quote by BF is in Polasky, page 44. For the Boston Club and Condorcet's quote, see Susan Dunn, *Sister Revolutions: French Lightning, American Light* (New York, 1999), 9.

69. TJ to John de Crevecoeur, August 6, 1787, *PTJ* 11:692; TJ to Jay, June 21, 1787, ibid., 11:489; TJ to JM, August 9, 1788, ibid., 13:489; TJ to JA, August 30, 1787, *AJL* 1:196. On France's troubles, see Owen Connelly, *The French Revolution and Napoleonic Era* (New York, 1991), 56–62; Georges Lefebvre, *The French Revolution* (London, 1962), 102–19; and Jonathan Israel, *Revolutionary Ideas: An Intellectual History of the French Revolution from the Rights of Man to Robespierre* (Princeton, N.J., 2014), 40–43. The "politicization" quote is in Israel, page 43.

70. TJ to Jay, May 23, August 3, 1788, *PTJ* 13:190, 464; TJ to Anne Willing Bingham, May 11, 1788, ibid., 13:151; TJ to GW, December 4, 1788, ibid., 14:330.

71. TJ to Madison, January 30, 1787, ibid., 11:95; Lafayette to GW, January 1, 1788, *PGWC* 6:6. On Lafayette's town house in Paris, see Laura Auricchio, *The Marquis: Lafayette Reconsidered* (New York, 2015), 131–35.

72. TJ to Lafayette, May 6, June 3, 1789, ibid., 15:97, 165–66; TJ to Rabaut de St. Etienne, June 3, 1789, ibid., 15:166–67; TJ, Draft of a Charter of Rights, [June 3, 1789], ibid., 15:167–68; Lafayette's Draft of a Declaration of Rights, ibid., 15:230–31; TJ, Autobiography, *CTJ*, 1177, 1182; Peter Bruckman, *Lafayette: A Biography* (New York, 1977), 143–44. For accounts of TJ's activities, see Philipp Ziesche, "Exporting American Revolutions: Gouverneur Morris, Thomas Jefferson, and the National Struggle for Universal Rights in Revolutionary France," *Journal of the Early Republic* 26 (2006): 437–40, and Adams, *Paris Years of Thomas Jefferson*, 251–95. The "school of Revolution" quote is in Timothy Tackett, *The Coming of the Terror in the French Revolution* (Cambridge, Mass., 2015), 48. On GW and Lafayette, see Stuart Leibiger, "George

Washington and Lafayette: Father and Son of the Revolution," in Robert M. S. McDonald, ed., *Sons of the Father: George Washington and His Protégés* (Charlottesville, Va., 2013), 210–31.

73. Israel, *Revolutionary Ideas*, 60, 78–79, 84; Bailey Stone, *Reinterpreting the French Revolution: A Global-Historical Perspective* (Cambridge, England, 2002), 88, 105. The "electric whirlwind" quote is in Tackett, *Coming of the Terror*, 60.

74. These three paragraphs draw on TJ to Lafayette, June 3, 1789, *PTJ* 15:165–66; TJ, Draft of a Charter of Rights [June 3, 1789], ibid., 15:167–68; TJ to Jay, May 9, July 19, 1789, ibid., 15:110, 289–90; TJ to Madison, May 11, 1789, ibid., 15:121; TJ to TP, July 11, 13, 17, 1789, ibid., 15:268–69, 273, 279; TJ to Countess de Diodati, August 3, 1789, ibid., 15:325–26; TJ, Autobiography, *CTJ*, 1183, 1185, 1188; Tackett, *Coming of the Terror*, 65. The king's comment can be found in John Hardman, *Louis XVI* (New Haven, Conn., 1993), 158. La Rochefoucauld-Liancourt's comment to the king can be found in Simon Schama, *Citizens: A Chronicle of the French Revolution* (New York, 1989), 8. Lafayette's quote is in Auricchio, *The Marquis*, 195.

75. TJ to Jay, August 13, 27, September 19, 1789, *PTJ* 15:340, 358, 458–60; TJ to Madison, August 28, 1789, ibid., 15:366–67.

76. TJ to TP, September 13, 1789, ibid., 15:424; TJ to George Mason, February 4, 1791, ibid., 19:241; TJ to Diodati, August 3, 1789, ibid., 15:326.

77. TJ to Jay, November 19, 1788, ibid., 4:214–15; TJ to Elizabeth Wayles Eppes, December 15, 1788, ibid., 14:355; TJ to JM, August 28, 1789, ibid., 15:368–69; TJ to Nicholas Lewis, July 29, 1787, ibid., 11:640; Madison to TJ, May 27, 1789, ibid., 15:153.

78. Robert M. S. McDonald, *Confounding Father: Thomas Jefferson's Image in His Own Time* (Charlottesville, Va., 2016), 14, 19, 20; TJ, Answers to [Francois] Soulés' Queries [September 13–18, 1786], ibid., 10:380; TJ, To the Editor of *Journal de Paris*, August 29, 1787, ibid., 12:61–65.

79. A Fourth of July Tribute to Jefferson, July 4, 1789, ibid., 15:239–40.

80. *JMB* 1:743–48.

81. TP to TJ, February 19, 1788, *CWTP* 2:1267.

82. TP to Kitty Nicholson Few, January 6, 1789, ibid., 2:1274–78; TP to TJ, February 26, September 18, 1789, ibid., 2:1281–82, 1296.

CHAPTER 6: "MY COUNTRY IS THE WORLD": PAINE AND THE EARLY YEARS OF THE FRENCH REVOLUTION

1. Owen Connelly, *The French Revolution and Napoleonic Era* (New York, 1991), 78, 84–86; Simon Schama, *Citizens: A Chronicle of the French Revolution* (New York, 1989), 428–70; Peter McPhee, *Liberty or Death: The French Revolution* (New Haven, Conn., 2016), 2.

2. TP to GW, May 1, 1790, *CWTP* 2:1302–3. TP's quote on the Bastille is in TP, *The Rights of Man* (1791), ibid., 1:264.

3. TP to TJ, January 15, 1789, *PTJ* 14:454; David Freeman Hawke, *Paine* (New York, 1974), 190. Burke is quoted in Carl B. Cone, *Burke and the Nature of Politics: The Age of the French Revolution* (Lexington, Ky., 1964), 293. The "friend to mankind" quotation can be found in R. R. Fennessy, *Burke, Paine and the Rights of Man* (The Hague, 1963), 45.

4. TP to Edmund Burke, January 17, 1790, Thomas W. Copeland et al., eds., *The Correspondence of Edmund Burke* (Chicago, 1958–78), 6:67–75. Charles James Fox is quoted in Yuval Levin, *The Great Debate: Edmund Burke, Thomas Paine, and the Birth of Right and Left* (New York, 2014), 24.

5. Jonathan Israel, *Revolutionary Ideas: An Intellectual History of the French Revolution from The Rights of Man to Robespierre* (Princeton, N.J., 2014), 84, 110.

6. Lafayette to GW, March 17, 1790, *PGWP* 5:242.

7. TP to GW, May 1, 1790, *CWTP* 2:1303; TP to William Short, June 1, 1790, ibid., 2:1306; TP to Burke, January 17, 1790, in Copeland, *Correspondence of Edmund Burke*, 6:69.

8. Cone, *Burke and the Nature of Politics*, 295–96.

9. Dumas Malone, *Jefferson and His Time* (Boston, 1948–81), 2:55; Cone, *Burke and the Nature of Politics*, 300–304; John Keane, *Tom Paine: A Political Life* (New York, 1995), 287.

10. Edmund Burke, Speech in the House of Commons (February 7, 1790) in PH 28:351–63. The quotes can be found on columns 354, 355, 358, and 359. The statement by Burke's publisher is in Keane, *Tom Paine*, 288.

11. TJ to TP, March 17, 1789, *PTJ* 14:671–72.

12. Lafayette to GW, January 12, 1790, *PGWP* 4:567; Keane, *Tom Paine*, 288; Fennessy, *Burke, Paine and the Rights of Man*, 10.

13. Alfred Owen Aldridge, *Man of Reason: The Life of Thomas Paine* (Philadelphia, 1959), 131; W. Clark Durant, ed., William Godwin, *Memoirs of Mary Wollstonecraft* (reprint, New York, 1969), 62–63.

14. The two paragraphs draw on Gouverneur Morris, *A Diary of the French Revolution*, ed., by Beatrix Cary Davenport (Boston, 1939), 1:197, 315, 331, 358, 360, 367, 369, 374, 375, 407, 486, 487, 488, 507, 516, 517, 531, 533, 540, 546, 549, 552, 553, 554, 559, 560, 562, 563, 568, 570, 571, 572, 577, 579, 580, 589, 607; 2:159. The quotes can be found on 1:197, 487, 488, 573, 589, and 2:159. Morris's disdainful quote about Paine's humble background was first mentioned in chapter 3. It was taken from William Howard Adams, *Gouverneur Morris: An Independent Life* (New Haven, Conn., 2003), 117.

15. Paine to Anonymous, April 16, 1790, *CWTP* 2:1300–1302; TP to GW, May 1, 1790, ibid., 2:1303; Janet Polasky, *Revolutions Without Borders: The Call to Liberty in the Atlantic World* (New Haven, Conn., 2015), 67; Keane, *Tom Paine*, 290–91; Craig Nelson, *Thomas Paine: Enlightenment, Revolution, and the Birth of Modern Nations* (New York, 2006), 193.

16. Keane, *Tom Paine*, 291.

17. Edmund Burke, *Reflections on the Revolution in France* (1790). Edited by J. C. D. Clark (Stanford, Calif., 2001). The quotations can be found on pages 189, 192, 205, 211, 212, 228, 239, 242, 261, 290, 339, 345, 383, and 385. This edition includes an insightful introductory essay by the editor and more than seven hundred helpful explanatory notes. The appraisal of Burke's views on government and society draws on Levin, *The Great Debate*, a notably perceptive work, and the older, but still useful, Fennessy, *Burke, Paine and the Rights of Man*.

18. Burke, *Reflections*, 232, 237, 238.

19. TP to GW, May 1, 1790, *CWTP* 2:1303; TP, *Rights of Man*, ibid., 1:260; TJ, Autobiography, *CTJ*, 1188; TJ to JA, August 30, 1787, *AJL* 1:195; Morris, *Diary of the French Revolution* 1:67, 130–31, 246.

20. TJ to Madison, October 28, 1785, *PTJ* 8:68–69; TP, *Rights of Man*, *CWTP* 1:258; Fennessy, *Burke, Paine and the Rights of Man*, 3–5, 181, 183, 196. Some in England thought the French insurgents in 1789 had gone no further than the English in their Glorious Revolution in 1688.

21. TP, *Rights of Man*, *CWTP* 1:244. GW waited nearly a year before answering TP and offering "thanks . . . for the token of your remembrance" in sending the fifty copies of *Rights of Man*. GW said nothing of the contents of TP's tract aside. He said simply that "no one can

feel a greater interest in the happiness of mankind than I do." See GW to TP, May 6, 1792, *PGWP* 10:357.

22. On TP's troubles in finding a publisher and for sales figures, see Keane, *Tom Paine*, 305, 307, 333; Hawke, *Paine*, 223–24, 230; Seth Cotlar, *Tom Paine's America: The Rise and Fall of Transatlantic Radicalism in the Early Republic* (Charlottesville, Va., 2011), 39, 44. For *Reflections'* sales figures, see Keane, 289, and Cone, *Burke and the Nature of Politics*, 341–42. For TP on his plans for a "cheap edition," see TP to GW, July 21, 1791, *CWTP* 2:1319.

23. H. T. Dickinson, *Liberty and Property: Political Ideology in Eighteenth-Century Britain* (New York, 1977), 195–241. TP's "in all cases" quote is in TP, *Rights of Man, CWTP* 1:251.

24. TP, *Rights of Man, CWTP* 1:244–344. The quotes can be found on pages 245, 246, 251, 252, 254, 257, 259, 266, 272, 286, 287, 288, 300, 320, 325, 326, 337, and 338.

25. Morris, *Diary of the French Revolution*, 2:163; Cone, *Burke and the Nature of Politics*, 349–50.

26. Quoted in Moncure Daniel Conway, *The Life of Thomas Paine* (New York, 1892), 1:306.

27. Hawke, *Paine*, 227; Keane, *Tom Paine*, 313–14; Francis Oldys [George Chalmers], *The Life of Thomas Paine* (London, 1791), 127–28. For the allusion to the "For Rent" sign, see Nelson, *Thomas Paine*, 211.

28. Timothy Tackett, *When the King Took Flight* (Cambridge, Mass., 2003), 3–9, 41–85; Schama, *Citizens*, 549–59. The quote in the king's declaration can be found in McPhee, *Liberty or Death*, 132.

29. TP to Antoine-Nicholas de Condorcet, Nicholas de Bonneville, and François Lanthenas, June 1791, *CWTP* 2:1315–18. Aside from Condorcet, TP's letter was actually addressed to republicans with whom he was better acquainted.

30. TP, "To the Abbé Sieyès" (July 1791), ibid., 2:519–20; TP, "A Republican Manifesto" (July 1, 1791), ibid., 2:517–19; TP, "Answer to Four Questions on the Legislative and Executive Powers" (June–July 1792), ibid., 2:521–34; Aldridge, *Man of Reason*, 147; Hawke, *Paine*, 228; Connelly, *The French Revolution and Napoleonic Era*, 105.

31. TP to TJ, February 13, 1792, *CWTP* 2:1323; Morris, *Diary of the French Revolution*, 2:212–13. The "drunk with vanity" characterization is quoted in Keane, *Tom Paine*, 311. On seeing Morris as an "Aristocrat," see Philipp Ziesche, "Exporting American Revolutions: Gouverneur Morris, Thomas Jefferson, and the National Struggle for Universal Rights in Revolutionary France," *Journal of the Early Republic* 26 (2006): 424. On Morris's habit of sheltering aristocrats, see Richard Brookhiser, *Gentleman Revolutionary: Gouverneur Morris—The Rake Who Wrote the Constitution* (New York, 2003), 137, and James J. Kirschke, *Gouverneur Morris* (New York, 2005), 237.

32. TJ to TP, July 29, 1791, *PTJ* 20:308; TP to GW, July 21, 1791, *CWTP* 2:1318–19; John Hall's London Journal (April 20, 1792) can be found in Conway, *Life of Thomas Paine* 2:472.

33. The quotes on the "moral obligation" to help children, the elderly, and the impoverished can be found in Keane, *Tom Paine*, 323. The "REVOLUTION OF ALL THE WORLD" quote can be found in Cotlar, *Tom Paine's America*, 73.

34. Mary Beth Norton, *The British-Americans: The Loyalist Exiles in England, 1774–1789* (Boston, 1972), 131, 236; Hawke, *Paine*, 231–32; Oldys [George Chalmers], *Life of Thomas Paine*.

35. TP, *Rights of Man. Part the Second* (1792), *CWTP* 1:346–458. The quotes are on pages 347 and 348.

36. Cone, *Burke and the Nature of Politics*, 359–66; Morris, *Diary of the French Revolution*, 2:174.

37. TP, *Rights of Man. Part the Second*, *CWTP* 1:346–458. The quotations can be found on pages 351, 356, 383, 385, 398, 400, 411, 412, 413, 421, 423, 437, 439, 444, and 449. For an excellent brief analysis of TP's thoughts on social rights, see Jack Fruchtman Jr., *The Political Philosophy of Thomas Paine* (Baltimore, 2009), 119–27.

38. Fruchtman, *Political Philosophy of Thomas Paine* 1:413–14.

39. Morris, *Diary of the French Revolution*, 2:368, 370. For the sales figures, see Keane, *Tom Paine*, 333, and Fennessy, *Burke, Paine and the Rights of Man*, 229.

40. The quotes can be found in Fennessy, *Burke, Paine and the Rights of Man*, pages 94, 187, 214–15, 242, and 246. See also Jill Lepore, "A World of Paine," in Alfred F. Young, Gary B. Nash, and Ray Raphael, eds., *Revolutionary Founders: Rebels, Radicals, and Reformers in the Making of the Nation* (New York, 2011), 91.

41. Keane, *Tom Paine*, 334–43.

42. TP to the Attorney-General, n.d., *CWTP* 2:443–45; TP to Henry Dundas, June 6, September 15, 1792, ibid., 2:446–57, 466–69; TP to Onslow Cranley, June 17, 21, 1792, ibid., 2:457–66; TP, *Letter Addressed to the Addressers on the Late Proclamation* (1792), ibid., 470–511. The quotes can be found on pages 446, 448, 470, and 479.

43. Hawke, *Paine*, 254–55; TP to Dundas, September 15, 1792, *CWTP* 2:466–69. The story of Blake warning Paine is in Christopher Hitchens, *Thomas Paine's Rights of Man: A Biography* (London, 2006), 53.

44. The quotes can be found in R. R. Palmer, *The Age of the Democratic Revolution: A Political History of Europe and America, 1760–1800* (Princeton, N.J., 1964), 2:38.

45. Alexis de Tocqueville, *The Old Regime and the French Revolution* (1856; reprint, Garden City, N.Y., 1955), 207–208. The "Down with the fat-head" quote is in Palmer, *Age of the Democratic Revolution*, 2:41.

46. This lengthy section that begins with TP's return to France draws on Timothy Tackett, *The Coming of the Terror in the French Revolution* (Cambridge, Mass., 2015), 113–20, 165–227; George Lefebvre, *The French Revolution* (London, 1962), 1:179–256; Israel, *Revolutionary Ideas*, 237–77, 316–44; Schama, *Citizens*, 573–639; Polasky, *Revolutions Without Borders*, 234; Jean-Paul Bertaud, *The Army of the French Revolution: From Citizen-Soldiers to Instrument of Power* (Princeton, N.J., 1988), 77, 81; and McPhee, *Liberty or Death*, 150, 162. On Brissot's "new republicanism," see George Armstrong Kelly, *Victims, Authority, and Terror: The Parallel Deaths of d'Orleans, Custine, Bailly, and Malesherbes* (Chapel Hill, N.C., 1982), 77. The quotes can be found in Tackett on pages 167, 168, 183, 192, and 227, and in Schama on pages 628 and 630. The "first link in the chain" quote is in Palmer, *Age of the Democratic Revolution*, 2:39. On the downfall of Lafayette, see Laura Auricchio, *The Marquis: Lafayette Reconsidered* (New York, 2014), 212, 222–62, 265. For the comparison of GW and Lafayette in their respective crises, see Auricchio, 227.

47. Hawke, *Paine*, 256–58.

48. David P. Jordan, *The King's Trial: The French Revolution vs. Louis XVI* (Berkeley, Calif., 1979), 44–46.

49. TP, *Address to the People of France* (1792), *CWTP* 2:538–40. The quotes are on pages 538–39. On republican revolutions and the elimination of the cause of war, see TP, *Rights of Man. Part the Second*, ibid., 1:355–56.

50. TP, *An Essay for the Use of New Republicans in their Opposition to Monarchy* (1792), ibid., 2:541–47. The quotes are on pages 542 and 543.

51. Hawke, *Paine*, 265; Godwin, *Memoirs of Mary Wollstonecraft*, 225; Patrick Byrne, *Lord Edward Fitzgerald* (Dublin, 1955), 20–24, 112.

52. Nelson, *Thomas Paine*, 244–47. The quote is on page 247.

53. TP, "On the Propriety of Bringing Louis XVI to Trial" (November 20, 1792), *CWTP* 2:548–51.

54. Bailey Stone, *Reinterpreting the French Revolution: A Global-Historical Perspective* (Cambridge, England, 2002), 195.

55. Keane, *Tom Paine*, 366.

56. TP, "Reasons for Preserving the Life of Louis Capet" (January 15, 1793), *CWTP* 2:551–55. The quotes are on pages 554 and 555.

57. TP, "Shall Louis XVI be Respited" (January 19, 1793), ibid., 2:556–58.

58. Quoted in Hawke, *Paine*, 277.

59. The paragraphs on the trial and execution of Louis draw on Tackett, *Coming of the Terror in the French Revolution*, 233–42; Schama, *Citizens*, 655–70; Dan Edelstein, *The Terror of Natural Right: Republicanism, the Cult of Nature, and the French Revolution* (Chicago, 2009), 146–58; Jordan, *The King's Trial*, 101–207; Susan Dunn, *The Deaths of Louis XVI: Regicide and the French Political Imagination* (Princeton, N.J., 1994), 3. The "frightful scream" quotation is in Tackett, 241.

CHAPTER 7: "ITCHING FOR CROWNS, CORONETS, AND MITRES": THE RISE OF PARTISAN POLITICS

1. GW to TJ, October 13, November 30, 1789, January 21, 1790, *PTJ* 15:519–20; 16:8–9, 116–18.

2. Joseph J. Ellis, *The Quartet: Orchestrating the Second American Revolution, 1783–1789* (New York, 2015).

3. TJ to GW, December 15, 1789, *PTJ* 16:34–35.

4. TJ, Address to the Residents of Albemarle County, February 12, 1790, ibid., 16:178–79; Editor's Note, ibid., 16:167; Annette Gordon-Reed and Peter S. Onuf, *"Most Blessed of the Patriarchs": Thomas Jefferson and the Empire of the Imagination* (New York, 2016), 2, 103. Italics added by the author.

5. *JMB* 1:749–50; TJ to GW, February 14, 1790, *PTJ* 16:184; Dumas Malone, *Jefferson and His Time* (Boston, 1948–1981), 1:441–46.

6. TJ to Rush, January 16, 1811, *PTJ:Ret.Ser.* 3:305; Deborah Norris Logan, ed., *Memoir of Dr. George Logan of Stanton* (Philadelphia, 1899), 50.

7. William Maclay, *The Journal of William Maclay: United States Senator from Pennsylvania, 1789–1791* (New York, 1927), 265–66.

8. Logan, *Memoir of Dr. George Logan*, 50.

9. Chris DeRose, *Founding Rivals: Madison vs. Monroe, the Bill of Rights, and the Election that Saved a Nation* (Washington, D.C., 2011), 248.

10. Arthur Lee to Samuel Adams, January 29, 1783, *LDC* 19:639; Madison to Edmund Randolph, January 28, 1783, ibid., 19:632. On the conspiracy, see Richard H. Kohn, "The Inside History of the Newburgh Conspiracy: America and the Coup d'État," *WMQ* 27 (1970): 187–220.

11. AH, "The Continentalist," Parts I, II, III, and IV [July–August 1781], *PAH* 2:649–52, 654–57, 660–65, 669–74.

12. Short to TJ, April 6, 1788, *PTJ* 13:42; Madison to TJ, August 10, 1788, ibid., 13:498; Thomas Lee Shippen to TJ, February 5, 1789, ibid., 14:519; TJ to Madison, November 18, 1788, ibid., 14:188.

13. Ron Chernow, *Alexander Hamilton* (New York, 2004), 219; AH to Robert Livingston, April 15, 1785, *PAH* 3:609.

14. AH to GW, July 3, 1787, *PAH* 4:224.

15. Four delegates at the Philadelphia Convention took notes during AH's presentation: Madison, Robert Yates, John Lansing, and Rufus King. Though varying in detail, the four sets of notes are in general agreement on what AH said. See *PAH* 4:187–207. Outlines that AH prepared to guide him in making his remarks can be found ibid., 4:178–87, 207–209.

16. For an excellent short essay on AH and the *Federalist Papers*, see Chernow, *Alexander Hamilton*, 243–69. On AH and the judiciary, see AH, *The Federalist*, nos. 27, 66, 78. See also Gottfried Dietze, *The Federalist: A Classic on Federalism and Free Government* (Baltimore, Md., 1960), 141–75, and Jill Lepore, "Benched," *New Yorker* (June 18, 2012): 77–82, especially page 79.

17. On AH's youth, wartime service, and relationship with GW, see Chernow, *Alexander Hamilton*.

18. AH, Conjectures about the New Constitution, [September 17–30, 1787], *PAH* 4:276.

19. AH, Report on Public Credit, January 9, 1790 [submitted on January 14, 1790], ibid., 6:65–168; Thomas K. McCraw, *The Founders and Finance: How Hamilton, Gallatin, and Other Immigrants Forged a New Economy* (Cambridge, Mass., 2012), 95. Robert Morris endorsed the assumption of state debts in February 1783. See Clarence L. Ver Steeg, *Robert Morris: Revolutionary Financier* (reprint, New York, 1972), 175.

20. TJ to GW, September 9, 1792, *PTJ* 24:352. The TJ quote about "cozening" and "filching" is in Mike Wallace, "That Hamilton Man," *New York Review of Books*, February 10, 2005, 30.

21. "Jefferson's Account of the Bargain on the Assumption and Residence Bills," [1792], *PTJ* 17:205–207; TJ to John Harvie Jr., July 25, 1790, ibid., 17:271; TJ to JM, June 20, 1790, ibid., 16:537; Madison to Edmund Pendleton, June 22, 1790, in William T. Hutchinson et al., eds., *The Papers of James Madison* (Chicago and Charlottesville, Va., 1962–), 13:252–53.

22. On federal land policy, see Gordon S. Wood, *Empire of Liberty: A History of the Early Republic, 1789–1815* (New York, 2009), 114–23. The "Tub for the whale" remark by Morris can be found in John C. Miller, *Alexander Hamilton: Portrait in Paradox* (New York, 1959), 87. On Madison leading the fight for the impost, see Stanley Elkins and Eric McKitrick, *The Age of Federalism* (New York, 1993), 65–74.

23. "Jefferson's Account of the Bargain on the Assumption and Residence Bills," [1792], *PTJ* 17:205–207. The literature on the Compromise of 1790 is considerable. For a good starting point, see Jacob E. Cooke, "The Compromise of 1790," *WMQ* 27 (1970): 524–45, and Kenneth R. Bowling, "Dinner at Jefferson's: A Note on Jacob E. Cooke's 'The Compromise of 1790,'" ibid., 28 (1971): 629–48.

24. *JMB* 1:766–68, 766–67n; Henry Wiencek, *Master of the Mountain: Thomas Jefferson and His Slaves* (New York, 2012), 89–90.

25. JM to Madison, February 11, 1786, *PJM* 2:277; Harry Ammon, *James Monroe: The Quest for National Identity* (New York, 1971), 41–60; DeRose, *Founding Rivals*, 89–126.

26. JM to TJ, October 12, 1786, *PJM* 2:364; TJ to JM, December 18, 1786, ibid., 2:369; JM to Madison, October 2, 7, 1786, ibid., 2:361, 362; Ammon, *James Monroe*, 63, 65, 74, 78.

27. JM to TJ, July 27, 1787, *PJM* 2:391; AH, Conversation with George Beckwith, [October 1789], *PAH* 5:488. For succinct sketches of those elected to attend the Constitutional Convention from Virginia, see Clinton Rossiter, *1787: The Grand Convention* (New York, 1966), 119–25.

28. Max Farrand, ed., *The Records of the Federal Convention of 1787* (rev. ed., New Haven, Conn., 1966), 1:26–27.

29. JM to Madison, May 23, October 13, 1787, *PJM* 2:384, 397; JM to Lambert Cadwalader, October 15, 1787, ibid., 2:398; JM to TJ, April 10, 1788, ibid., 2:405; JM, Some Observations on the Constitution, [May 1788], ibid., 2:408–27; Ammon, *James Monroe*, 67–70.

30. JM, Some Observations, *PJM* 2:415; JM, Speech in the Virginia Constitutional Convention, June 10, 13, 18, 1788, ibid., 2:428–42; DeRose, *Founding Rivals* 167–201; Ammon, *James Monroe*, 70–73. The quotations from JM's ratification constitution speeches can be found in *PJM* 2:432, 433, 436. On JM's fear that the presidency might evolve into a monarchy, see JM, "Some Hints Directing the Measures To Be Taken To Form A Monarchy Out of Several Confederate Democracies," [June 1788], *PJM* 2:443–47.

31. JM to TJ, July 12, 1788, *PJM* 2:448–49.

32. The quotes can be found in DeRose, *Founding Rivals*, 197, 214.

33. JM to TJ, February 15, 1789, *PJM* 2:461.

34. The quotes can be found in Robert Douthat Meade, *Patrick Henry: Practical Revolutionary* (Philadelphia, 1969), 375, 377.

35. Ammon, *James Monroe*, 73–77; DeRose, *Founding Rivals*, 220–47. Madison's comment on his relationship with JM can be found in Irving Brant, *James Madison* (Indianapolis, Ind., 1950), 3:241. The description of Madison draws on that provided in Ellis, *The Quartet*, 115.

36. JM to TJ, October 20, 1790, *PJM* 2:487; JM to James Lyle, November 19, 1790, ibid., 2:488; Ammon, *James Monroe*, 81–82.

37. *JMB* 1:527n, 770n; 2:808; Malone, *Jefferson and His Time*, 2:319–25; Ammon, *James Monroe*, 82.

38. TJ, The Anas, February 4, 1818, Padover, *CTJ* 1209, 1211; AH, Report on Public Credit, January 9, 1790, *PAH* 6:102–3; AH, First Report on the Further Provision Necessary for Establishing Public Credit, December 13, 1790, ibid., 7:210–36. Thomas P. Slaughter, *The Whiskey Rebellion: Frontier Epilogue to the American Revolution* (New York, 1986), 95–97.

39. Maclay, *Journal of William Maclay*, 375, 376, 379, 387; JM to Zachariah Johnston, February 11, 1791, *PJM* 2:497; Slaughter, *Whiskey Rebellion*, 96–105. The "mature politician" notion can be found in William Hogeland, *The Whiskey Rebellion: George Washington, Alexander Hamilton, and the Frontier Rebels Who Challenged America's Newfound Sovereignty* (New York, 2006), 62–63.

40. AH, Final Version of the Second Report on the Further Provision Necessary for Establishing Public Credit (Report on a National Bank), December 13, 1790, *PAH* 7:305–42; AH, Draft of an Act to Incorporate the Bank of the United States, [December 1790], ibid., 7:399–406; McCraw, *The Founders and Finance*, 115.

41. Wood, *Empire of Liberty*, 93–94; Gordon S. Wood, "Illusions of Power in the Awkward Era of Federalism," in Gordon S. Wood, *The Idea of America: Reflections on the Birth of the United States* (New York, 2011), 257–59; TP, *Common Sense* (1776), *CWTP* 1:20–21; BF to Joseph Galloway, February 25, 1775, *PBF* 21:509. On the changes wrought in England, including the levels of taxation, see John Brewer, *The Sinews of Power: War, Money and the English State, 1688–1783* (New York, 1989), 29, 89, 118, 175, 193–96, 199, 200, 203.

42. TJ, *Notes on the State of Virginia* (1785), edited by William Peden (Chapel Hill, N.C., 1955), 164–65.

43. TJ, Notes on the Letter of Christoph Daniel Ebeling, [after October 15, 1795], *PTJ* 28:507; TJ to Edward Carrington, May 27, 1788, ibid., 13:208-209.

44. TJ, Address to the Residents of Albemarle County, February 12, 1790, *PTJ* 16:179.

45. Maclay, *Journal of William Maclay*, 242, 243, 249, 341, 345-62. The quotations can be found on pages 341, 353, 358, 361, and 362.

46. JM to Johnston, February 11, 1791, *PJM* 2:497; Jones to JM, January 27, 1791, ibid., 2:495; JM to TJ, June 17, 1791, ibid., 2:505; Ammon, *James Monroe*, 83.

47. TJ, Opinion on the Constitutionality of the Bill for Establishing a National Bank, February 15, 1791, *PTJ* 19:275-80; AH, Draft of an Opinion on the Constitutionality of an Act to Establish a Bank [n.d.], *PAH* 8:64-97; AH, Final Version of an Opinion on the Constitutionality of an Act to Establish a Bank, February 23, 1791, ibid., 8:97-134.

48. TJ to George Mason, February 4, 1791, *PTJ* 19:242; TJ to Edward Rutledge, August 25, 1791, ibid., 22:74; TJ to Robert R. Livingston, February 7, 1791, ibid., 19:241; TJ to Henry Innes, March 13, 1791, ibid., 19:542-43; Livingston to TJ, February 20, 1791, ibid., 19:296; TJ, The Anas, February 4, 1818, and July 10, 1792, Padover, *CTJ*, 1211, 1224-25.

49. TJ to Philip Freneau, February 28, 1791, *PTJ* 19:351; TJ to JM, May 9, July 21, 1791, ibid., 20:293, 657; Noble E. Cunningham, *The Jeffersonian Republicans: The Formation of Party Organization, 1789-1801* (Chapel Hill, N.C., 1957), 17; Jeffrey L. Pasley, *"The Tyranny of Printers": Newspaper Politics in the Early Republic* (Charlottesville, Va., 2001), 64; James Roger Sharp, *American Politics in the Early Republic: The New Nation in Crisis* (New Haven, Conn., 1993), 43. See the editorial note in *PTJ* 20:718-53.

50. TJ, Journal of the Tour, May 21-June 10, 1791, *PTJ* 20:453-56; TJ, Notes on the Hessian Fly, May 24-June 18, 1791, ibid., 20:456-62; TJ to Martha Jefferson Randolph, May 31, 1791, ibid., 20:463-64; TJ to GW, June 5, 1791, ibid., 20:466-67; TJ, Table of Distances and Rating of Inns, May 17-June 19, 1791, ibid., 20:471-73; *JMB* 2:818-23; Nancy Isenberg, *Fallen Founder: The Life of Aaron Burr* (New York, 2007), 105-7; Todd Estes, "Jefferson as Party Leader," in *A Companion to Thomas Jefferson*, ed. Francis D. Cogliano (Chichester, England, 2011), 128-44.

51. TJ, The Anas, March 11, 12, September 30, October 1, November 19, 1792, June 7, 12, 1793, Padover, *CTJ*, 1220, 1221, 1226, 1227, 1228, 1231, 1244, 1245, 1246; TJ to Rush, January 16, 1811, *PTJ:Ret.Ser.* 3:305.

52. TJ, Memoranda of Conversations with the President, March 1, 1792, *PTJ* 23:186-87; TJ, Notes of a Conversation with George Washington, July 10, 1792, ibid., 24:210-11; TJ, Notes of a Conversation with George Washington, October 1, 1792, ibid., 24:433-36; TJ to GW, May 23, September 9, 1792, ibid., 23:537; 24:352-59; TJ, The Anas, February 7, 1793, Padover, *CTJ*, 1234-35; AH to GW, August 18, 1792, *PAH* 12:228-58.

53. TJ, Notes of a Conversation with George Washington, October 1, 1792, *PTJ* 24:433-35.

54. [John Adams], "Discourses on Davila, A Series of Papers on Political History, in *Works* 6:223-404; TJ to GW, May 8, 1791, *PTJ* 20:291-92, 284-87n; TJ to JM, July 10, 1791, ibid., 20:297; TJ to Jonathan B. Smith, April 26, 1791, ibid., 20:290. See also the analysis in John Howe, *The Changing Political Thought of John Adams* (Princeton, N.J., 1966), 156-92. The "rich, the well-born, and the able" quote can be found in Howe, page 169.

55. AH to Carrington, May 26, 1792, *PAH* 11:426-45.

56. TJ to Walter Jones, March 5, 1810, *PTJ:Ret.Ser.* 2:272.

57. TJ to TP, June 19, 1792, *PTJ* 20:312.

58. TJ to Jean Antoine Gautier, June 8, 1792, ibid., 24:42.

CHAPTER 8: "THE ONLY MAN WHO POSSESSED
THE CONFIDENCE OF THE WHOLE": PARTISAN AMERICA
IN A PREDATORY WORLD

1. GW to TJ, March 29, 1784, *PGWC* 1:237, 239; GW to Benjamin Harrison, January 18, October 10, 1784, ibid., 1:56; 2:92; GW to Henry Knox, December 5, 1784, ibid., 2:171–72. For the western population figures, see Gordon S. Wood, *Empire of Liberty: A History of the Early Republic, 1789–1815* (New York, 2009), 115.

2. Stanley Elkins and Eric McKitrick, *The Age of Federalism* (New York, 1993), 65–74, 124.

3. Conversation with George Beckwith, [October 1789], *PAH* 5:482–90; Conversation with George Beckwith, [July 15, 1790], August 7–12, 8–12, ibid., 6:497–98, 546–48, 6:550–51; TJ to GW, December 15, 1790, *PTJ* 18:301–3; Editor's Note, ibid., 18:220–83; Elkins and McKitrick, *Age of Federalism*, 212–21. Morris's reports of April 7, May 29, July 3, August 16, and September 18, 1790, can be found in *PTJ* 18:285–300. The surviving notes of the discussion between AH and Beckwith are those of Beckwith.

4. TJ to George Hammond, October 26, November 29, December 5, 12, 13, 15, 28, 1791, January 28, February 2, 25, March 30, 31, April 12, 13, May 29, June 2, 6, July 6, 9, 12, 1792, February 16, April 18, May 3, 15, June 5, 13, 19, 25, 26, August 1, 4, 7, 8, September 5, 10, 11, 12, 13, 22, November 13, 14, December 26, 1793, *PTJ* 22:234, 352–53, 378–79, 394, 399, 409–11, 467; 23:82, 97, 148–49, 352–53, 357, 406, 417, 551–602; 24:18–19, 37, 164, 202–3, 221; 25:206–7, 563–64, 644; 26:38–40, 197–98, 290–91, 321, 322, 361–62, 375–76, 378, 596, 612–13, 634–35, 639–40; 27:35–37, 82–83, 89, 99–100, 106, 143, 353, 368–71, 620–22; Memorandum of Conversation between Philemon Dickinson and George Hammond, March 26, 1792, ibid., 23:344–45; S. W. Jackman, "A Young Englishman Reports on the New Nation: Edward Thornton to James Bland Burges, 1791–93," *WMQ* 18 (1961): 85–121; Elkins and McKitrick, *Age of Federalism*, 244–56.

5. Conversations with George Hammond, December 15–16, 1791, January 1–8, 2–9, March 31, April 30–July 3, May 28–29, May 29–June 2, July 1–2, 1792, *PAH* 10:373–76, 493–96, 498–99; 11:212–14, 347–48, 446–49, 454–55; 12:1–3; ibid., 10:350–51n; *CTJ* 1219–20; *PGWP* 10:73n.

6. TJ to George Rogers Clark, January 1, 1780, *PTJ* 3:259; *PGWP* 6:245n; John Ferling, *The Ascent of George Washington: The Hidden Political Genius of an American Icon* (New York, 2009), 317–23.

7. AH to GW, July 30[–August 3], 1792, *PAH* 12:137–38; TJ, Memoranda of Conversations with the President, March 1, 1792, *PTJ* 23:185–86; TJ to GW, May 23, 1792, ibid., 23:535–40; TJ to GW, September 9, 1792, ibid., 24:358; TJ, Notes of a Conversation with George Washington, October 1, 1792, ibid., 24:434.

8. Lewis Leary, *That Rascal Freneau: A Study in Literary Failure* (reprint, New York, 1964), 196–223; Steven Watts, *The Republic Reborn: War and the Making of Liberal America, 1790–1820* (Baltimore, 1987), 78–86. The quotations can be found in Leary on pages 203 and 223, and in Watts on page 82. On the newspaper warfare of the period, see Jeffrey L. Pasley, *"The Tyranny of Printers": Newspaper Politics in the Early Republic* (Charlottesville, Va., 2001), 48–78, and Joanne Freeman, *Affairs of Honor: National Politics in the New Republic* (New Haven, Conn., 2001), 105–58.

9. John C. Miller, *The Federalist Era, 1789–1801* (New York, 1960), 91; AH in the *Gazette of the United States*, July 25, August 4, 11, 18, September 19, 29, October 17, 24, November 24,

December 22, 1792, and in the *National Gazette*, September 11, 1792, *PAH* 12:107, 157–64, 188–93, 193–94, 224, 361–65, 393–401, 498–506, 578–87, 613–17; 13:229–31, 348–56. The quotations can be found in volume 12, on pages 159, 161, 162, 163, 362, and 394.

10. TJ to GW, October 17, 1792, *PTJ* 24:494 and 495n; JM to TJ, June 17, July 17, 1792, *PJM* 2:549, 554–55.

11. JM, "The Vindication of Mr. Jefferson," September 22, October 10, 20, 30, December 3, 31, 1792, *PJM* 2:559–61, 564–66, 569–72, 574–76, 581–83, 591–94. The quotes can be found on pages 559 and 576.

12. Madison's series of *National Gazette* essays are interspersed throughout volume 14 of William T. Hutchinson et al., eds., *The Papers of James Madison* (Chicago and Charlottesville, Va., 1962–). The quotes can be found in 14:370–72. TJ later told GW that he could pledge, "in the presence of heaven, that I never did by myself, or any other, directly or indirectly, say a syllable" in Freneau's newspaper, "nor attempt any kind of influence" over the editor. See TJ to GW, September 9, 1792, *PTJ* 24:356. For other items in this paragraph, see Conor Cruise O'Brien, *The Long Affair: Thomas Jefferson and the French Revolution, 1785–1800* (Chicago, 1996), 119; Joyce Appleby, *Capitalism and the New Social Order: The Republican Vision of the 1790s* (New York, 1984), 73–74; Wood, *Empire of Liberty*, 148–51.

13. GW to TJ, August 23, 1792, *PTJ* 24:317; GW to AH, August 26, 1792, *PAH* 12:276–77.

14. Alexander Hamilton, *Observations on Certain Documents Contained in No. V & VI of "The History of the United States for the Year 1796," In Which the Charge of Speculation Against Alexander Hamilton, Late Secretary of the Treasury, is Fully Refuted, Written by Himself* (Philadelphia, 1797), in *PAH* 21:257–59; AH to JM, Frederick A. C. Muhlenberg, and Abraham B. Venable, December 17, 1792, ibid., 13:330; JM to AH, December 20, 1792, ibid., 13:344; Muhlenberg to AH, July 10, 1797, ibid., 21:158; Venable to AH, July 10, 1792, ibid., 21:159. In their letters to AH cited above, Muhlenberg and Venable said that they never saw the documents again following their meeting with AH and that JM had possession of the documents. For a list of the documents given to Muhlenberg by Clingman, see *PAH* 21:131n.

15. AH, *Observations on Certain Documents*, ibid., 21:238–85; TJ, Notes on the Reynolds Affair, December 17, 1792, *PTJ* 24:751; TJ to John Taylor, October 8, 1797, ibid., 29:546; Muhlenberg, Venable, and JM to GW [with enclosures containing the text of assorted interviews], December 13, 1792, *PJM* 2:584–88; Muhlenberg, Venable, and JM interview with AH, December 16, 1792, ibid., 2:589; AH to Muhlenberg, Venable, and JM, December 17, 1792, ibid., 2:590.

16. TJ to GW, May 23, 1792, *PTJ* 23:537; TJ to Thomas Mann Randolph Jr., November 2, 16, 1792, March 3, 1793, *PTJ* 24:556, 623; 25:314; TJ to Thomas Pinckney, December 3, 1792, ibid., 24:696; JM and John Beckley, An Examination of the Late Proceedings in Congress, Respecting the Official Conduct of the Secretary of the Treasury, March 8, 1793, *PJM* 2:601–15.

17. Elkins and McKitrick, *Age of Federalism*, 308–11; Seth Cotlar, *Tom Paine's America: The Rise and Fall of Transatlantic Radicalism in the Early Republic* (Charlottesville, Va., 2011), 53, 71; Conor Cruise O'Brien, *The Long Affair*, 79–81, 85–86; Charles Downer Hazen, *Contemporary American Opinion of the French Revolution* (Baltimore, 1897), 164, 182; TJ to Benjamin Vaughn, May 11, 1791, *PTJ* 20:391; AH to Lafayette, October 6, 1789, *PAH* 5:425; GW to Gouverneur Morris, October 13, 1789, *PGWP* 4:180–81; Philipp Ziesche, "Exporting American Revolutions: Gouverneur Morris, Thomas Jefferson, and the National Struggle for Universal Rights in Revolutionary France," *Journal of the Early Republic* 26

(2006): 426, 435, 437. The newspaper quotation is in Elkins and McKitrick, page 310, and the Tammany quotation can be found in *AFC* 9:372n. The toasts to TP in the preceding paragraph are in Cotlar, *Tom Paine's America*, 73-75. On General Lee's plans to fight for France, see Andrew Burstein and Nancy Isenberg, *Madison and Jefferson* (New York, 2010), 254.

18. JA to TJ, December 10, 1787, *PTJ* 12:413; JA, "Discourses on Davila, A Series of Papers on Political History," *Works* 6:232, 236-42, 251-56; JA to Charles Adams, October 12, 1792, March 18, 1793, *AFC* 9:314, 419; JA to Abigail Adams Smith, October 29, 1792, ibid., 9:318; JA to John Quincy Adams, January 2, 1793, ibid., 9:369; JA to AA, January 2, 14, 1793, ibid., 9:367, 378; Zoltan Haraszti, *John Adams and the Prophets of Progress* (Cambridge, Mass., 1952), 30, 165-70; John R. Howe Jr., *The Changing Political Thought of John Adams* (Princeton, N.J., 1966), 170-73. JA's "liar," "satry," "quack," "fool," "louse," and "tick" quotations, as well as his belief that Lafayette was ignorant of government and history, can be found in Susan Dunn, *Sister Revolutions: French Lightning, American Light* (New York, 1999), 40-41.

19. TJ, Memorandum of Conversations with the President, April 9, 1791, *PTJ* 23:260-61; Morris to GW, December 27-31, 1791, *PGWP* 9:335-37; GW to Morris, October 20, 1792, ibid., 11:245; AH to Lafayette, April 28, 1798, *PAH* 21:450. BF is quoted in H. W. Brands, *The First American: The Life and Times of Benjamin Franklin* (New York, 2000), 705-706. Morris's "awful Catastrophe" quotation can be found in O'Brien, *The Long Affair*, 130.

20. TJ to William Short, January 3, 1793, *PTJ* 25:14; TJ to Mason, February 4, 1791, ibid., 19:241. The "regenerate" quotation can be found in O'Brien, *The Long Affair*, 114.

21. TJ to Joseph Fay, August 30, 1791, ibid., 22:103; TJ to Edward Rutledge, August 25, 1791, ibid., 22:75.

22. AH, "The French Revolution" (1794), *PAH* 17:586; Fisher Ames, "[Untitled] Against Jacobins," [1794?], *Works of Fisher Ames: As Published by Seth Ames*, edited and enlarged by W. B. Allen (Indianapolis, Ind., 1983), 2:974-84; Ames to Theodore Dwight, August [?], 1793, ibid., 2:964; David Waldstreicher, "Federalism, the Style of Politics, and the Politics of Style," in Doran Ben-Atar and Barbara B. Oberg, eds., *Federalists Reconsidered* (Charlottesville, Va., 1998), 115-16; Chauncey Goodrich to Oliver Wolcott, February 17, 1793, in George Gibbs, ed., *Memoirs of the Administrations of Washington and Adams, Edited from the Papers of Oliver Wolcott* (New York, 1946), 1:88.

23. Cotlar, *Tom Paine's America*, 82-97. The "destroy all subordination" and "pull[ing] down empires" quotations can be found in Simon P. Newman, "Paine, Jefferson, and Revolutionary Radicalism in Early National America," in Simon P. Newman and Peter S. Onuf, eds., *Paine and Jefferson in the Age of Revolutions* (Charlottesville, Va., 2013), 79. See also Alan Taylor, *American Revolutions: A Continental History, 1750-1804* (New York, 2016), 416-17; Waldstreicher, "Federalism, the Styles of Politics, and Politics of Style," in Ben-Atar and Oberg, eds., *Federalists Reconsidered*, 107-08, 114.

24. Morris to TJ, August 22, December 21, 1792, *PTJ* 24:314, 773; Morris to GW, October 23, December 28, 1792, *PGWP* 11:256, 560; Morris to AH, December 24, 1792, *PAH* 13:376.

25. GW to Morris, October 20, 1792, *PGWP* 11:245; GW to David Humphreys, March 23, 1793, ibid., 12:363; AH to [?], May 18, 1793, *PAH* 14:475; JM to TJ, May 9, 1793, *PTJ* 25:697; Madison to TJ, April 12, 1793, ibid., 25:533; TJ to Fay, March 18, 1793, ibid., 25:402; TJ, Autobiography, *CTJ*, 1188; Hazen, *Contemporary American Opinion of the French Revolution*, 254-57.

CHAPTER 9: "I RELINQUISH HOPE": THE FRENCH REVOLUTION
IN FRANCE AND AMERICA

1. TP to James O'Fallon, February 17, 1793, *CWTP* 2:1330; TP to TJ, April 20, 1793, ibid., 2:1331–32.

2. John Keane, *Tom Paine: A Political Life* (New York, 1995), 370; Letter of Marguerite Bonneville, n.d., in Moncure Daniel Conway, *The Life of Thomas Paine* (New York, 1892), 2:443.

3. J. P. Brissot de Warville, *New Travels in the United States of America*, ed. Durand Echeverria (Cambridge, Mass., 1964), 77–78, 101–104, 145–46, 237–38, 343–44. For Brissot's life history, see Eloise Ellery, *Brissot de Warville: A Study in the History of the French Revolution* (reprint, New York, 1970). See page 84 for his plan to move to Pennsylvania. On the Girondin faction, see M. J. Sydenham, *The Girondins* (London, 1961). For more on Brissot's newspaper, see Hugh Gough, *The Newspaper Press in the French Revolution* (Chicago, 1988).

4. Timothy Tackett, *The Coming of the Terror in the French Revolution* (Cambridge, Mass., 2015), 228–33, 245–48; Jonathan Israel, *Revolutionary Ideas: An Intellectual History of the French Revolution from the Rights of Man to Robespierre* (Princeton, N.J., 2014), 310; David Freeman Hawke, *Paine* (New York, 1974), 262–64.

5. TP to TJ, April 20, 1793, *CWTP* 2:1331.

6. Thomas Clio Rickman, *The Life of Thomas Paine* (reprint, Cambridge, England, 2014), 129–30; Emmet Kennedy, *A Cultural History of the French Revolution* (New Haven, Conn., 1989), 6. TP in December 1793 said that he had resided at Saint-Denis for "about nine months." See TP, *The Age of Reason* (1794), *CWTP* 1:512.

7. TP, "Forgetfulness: From the Castle in the Air to the Little Corner of the World" (1794[?]), *CWTP* 2:1123–24.

8. On Barlow's life, see Richard Buel Jr., *Joel Barlow: American Citizen in a Revolutionary World* (Baltimore, 2011). On his activities in France and England, and his relationship with TP, see pages 140–81.

9. For TP's routine at Saint-Denis, see Rickman, *Life of Thomas Paine*, 130–37.

10. TP, "Forgetfulness," *CWTP* 2:1123.

11. Quoted in R. R. Palmer, *The Age of the Democratic Revolution: A Political History of Europe and America, 1760–1800* (Princeton, N.J., 1964), 2:13.

12. Tackett, *Coming of the Terror in the French Revolution*, 245–7; Simon Schama, *Citizens: A Chronicle of the French Revolution* (New York, 1989), 678–725; Israel, *Revolutionary Ideas*, 316–44, 420–49. The quotations can be found in Tackett, 268, 278–79, Israel, 423, 426, 444, 446, and Schama, 722, with the exception of JA's "fatal" remark, which is in Susan Dunn, *Sister Revolutions: French Lightning, American Light* (New York, 1999), 73.

13. TP to Georges Danton (1793), *CWTP* 2:135–38.

14. Alfred Owen Aldridge, *Man of Reason: The Life of Thomas Paine* (Philadelphia, 1959), 201. Pierre Vergniaud is quoted in Schama, *Citizens*, 714.

15. AH to GW, April 8, 1793, *PGWP* 12:424; GW to AH, April 12, 1793, ibid., 12:447; Henry Lee to GW, April 29, 1793, ibid., 12:494; Minutes of a Cabinet Meeting, April 19, 1793, ibid., 12:459; GW, Neutrality Proclamation, April 22, 1793, ibid., 12:472–73; TJ to Morris, April 20, 1793, *PTJ* 25:576; TJ to Madison, April 28, 1793, ibid., 25:619.

16. TJ, Opinions on the Treaties with France, April 28, 1793, *PTJ* 25:597–602n, 608–18; TJ to Madison, April 28, 1793, ibid., 25:619; TJ to JM, May 5, 1793, ibid., 25:661; TJ, The Anas (April 18, May 6, 1793), *CTJ*, 1242–43; Morris to GW, December 28, 1792, January 6, 1793,

PGWP 11:561–62, 593; Hawke, *Paine*, 266; Stanley Elkins and Eric McKitrick, *The Age of Federalism* (New York, 1993), 340–41. TP is quoted in Keane, *Tom Paine*, 364.

17. Elkins and McKitrick, *Age of Federalism*, 332–34.

18. GW to Henry Lee, May 6, 1793, *PGWP* 12:533–34.

19. Elkins and McKitrick, *Age of Federalism*, 330–36, 341; Edmund Randolph to JM, June 10, 1794, *PJM* 3:8. Genêt's "perpetual festivals" comment can be found in Merrill D. Peterson, *Thomas Jefferson and the New Nation: A Biography* (New York, 1970), 487.

20. TJ to JM, May 5, 1793, *PTJ* 25:661; JM to TJ, May 28, 1793, *PJM* 2:623–24.

21. JM to TJ, May 28, June 27, August 21, September 3, 1793, *PJM* 2:623, 627, 635, 640.

22. TJ to Madison, April 28, July 7, August 11, 1793, *PTJ* 25:619; 26:444, 652; TJ to JM, May 5, 1793, ibid., 25:660–62; Christopher J. Young, "Connecting the President and the People: Washington's Neutrality, Genêt's Challenge, and Hamilton's Fight for Public Support," *Journal of the Early Republic* 31 (2011): 454; Elkins and McKitrick, *Age of Federalism*, 341–54.

23. TJ, Notes of Cabinet Meeting on a Commercial Treaty with France, August 23, 1793, *PTJ* 26:749–50.

24. TJ, Notes of Cabinet Meeting on Edmond Charles Genêt, August 2, 1793, ibid., 26:602–3. The "cold indifference" quotation is in Ron Chernow, *Washington: A Life* (New York, 2010), 693.

25. TJ, Notes on Alexander Hamilton and the French Revolution, November 15, 1793, *PTJ* 27:384; AH, "Defense of the President's Neutrality Proclamation," May 1793, *PAH* 14:503; Elkins and McKitrick, *Age of Federalism*, 360. AH's sixteen "No Jacobin" and "Pacificus" essays run throughout volume 15 of *PAH*. The quotes can be found in that volume on pages 103 and 105.

26. Resolutions on Neutrality and Relations with France, August 27, 1793, *PJM* 2:637–38, 638n.

27. JM, "Agricola," September 4, October 8, 30, November 13, December 4, 1793, ibid., 2:641–643, 646–50, 652–54, 659–62, 665–667. The quotes can be found on pages 642 and 647.

28. TJ to Brissot de Warville, May 8, 1793, *PTJ* 25:679; TJ to JM, June 4, 1793, ibid., 26:190; Elkins and McKitrick, *Age of Federalism*, 363–64.

29. TJ, Notes of Conversations with George Washington, March 1, October 1, 1792, February 7, August 6, 1793, *PTJ* 23:184–87; 24:434; 25:154; 26:627–30; TJ to GW, May 23, September 9, 1792, July 31, August 11, 1793, ibid., 23:539; 24:358; 26:593, 659–60.

30. TJ, First, Second, and Final State of the Report on Commerce, [August 23, 1791–April 13, 1792, February 5–23, 1793, December 16, 1793], ibid., 27:535–78. See also the Editor's Note, ibid., 27:532–35; Elkins and McKitrick, *Age of Federalism*, 378–81; Doran S. Ben-Atar, *The Origins of Jeffersonian Commercial Policy and Diplomacy* (New York, 1993), 17–133.

31. TP to Madison, September 24, 1795, *CWTP* 2:1378.

32. Tackett, *Coming of the Terror in the French Revolution*, 280–89.

33. TP to JM, October 20, 1794, *CWTP* 2:1365–66; TP to Citizen Barère, September 5, 1793, ibid., 2:1332–33; Alfred Owen Aldridge, *Man of Reason: The Life of Thomas Paine* (Philadelphia, 1959), 203–4; Hawke, *Paine*, 289; Keane, *Tom Paine*, 384–86. Barère is quoted in Aldridge, page 204.

34. TP to TJ, October 10, 20, 1793, *PTJ* 27:226–27, 227n, 258–59; TP, "A Citizen of America to the Citizens of Europe," [Autumn 1793?], *CWTP* 2:561–65.

35. TP to Madison, September 24, 1795, *CWTP* 2:1378.

36. Jean-Paul Bertaud, *The Army of the French Revolution: From Citizen-Soldiers to Instrument of Power* (Princeton, N.J., 1988), 100, 102; Peter McPhee, *Liberty or Death: The French Revolution* (New Haven, Conn., 2016), 210–11.

37. The foregoing paragraphs on the reasons for the Terror, its bloody excesses, and the execution of the Girondins and Marie Antoinette, draw on Tackett, *Coming of the Terror in the French Revolution*, 299–327; Israel, *Revolutionary Ideas*, 503–44; Schama, *Citizens*, 726–805; M. J. Sydenham, *The Girondins* (London, 1961), 121, 130, 136–37, 138, 209; Dumas Malone, *Jefferson and His Time* (Boston, 1948–81), 2:235. The "terror the order of the day" quote is from Tackett, page 301. The description of Marie Antoinette at the scaffold is that of Helen Maria Williams, who was present at the execution. See Jack Fruchtman Jr., ed., *An Eye-Witness Account of the French Revolution by Helen Maria Williams: Letters Containing a Sketch of the Politics of France* (reprint, New York, 1997), 101. The execution of the Girondins draws on Tackett, 514–15; Dunn, *Sister Revolutions*, 89–90; and Eloise Ellery, *Brissot de Warville: A Study in the History of the French Revolution* (Boston, 1915), 385–86. The "tart" quote can be found in Richard Brookhiser, *Gentleman Revolutionary: Gouverneur Morris— The Rake Who Wrote the Constitution* (New York, 2003), 138.

38. Keane, *Tom Paine*, 401; TP to Samuel Adams, January 1, 1803, *CWTP* 2:1436; Anne Cary Morris, ed., *The Diary and Letters of Gouverneur Morris* (New York, 1888), 2:48.

39. Palmer, *Age of the Democratic Revolution*, 2:35.

40. TP to Samuel Adams, January 1, 1803, *CWTP* 2:1436; Adams to TP, November 30, 1802, ibid., 2:1433.

41. For an excellent appraisal of TP's religious beliefs and thought, see Jack Fruchtman Jr., *Thomas Paine and the Religion of Nature* (Baltimore, 1993).

42. TP, *The Age of Reason, Being An Investigation of True and Fabulous Theology, Part First*, in *CWTP*, 1:463–512.

43. Quoted in Isaac Kramnick, ed., *The Portable Enlightenment Reader* (New York, 1995), xiii.

44. Peter Gay, ed., *Deism: An Anthology* (Princeton, N.J., 1968), 13.

45. On JM and religion, see David L. Holmes, *Faith and the Founding Fathers* (New York, 2006), 79–85.

46. TP, *The Age of Reason, Part First*, in *CWTP* 1:514–15; Eli Sagan, *Citizens and Cannibals: The French Revolution, The Struggle for Modernity, and the Origins of Ideological Terror* (Lanham, Md., 2001), 369; Buel, *Joel Barlow*, 179. Bourdon is quoted in Conway, *Life of Thomas Paine*, 2:95. Robespierre's quote on Bourdon is in Peter McPhee, *Robespierre: A Revolutionary Life* (New Haven, Conn., 2012), 204. TP's quote on the motives of Barère and his thinking that "terrorists" in America and France were implicated in his imprisonment can be found in TP, "To the Citizens of the United States," Letter III (1802), *CWTP* 2:919–20.

47. TP, *The Age of Reason, Part the First*, in *CWTP* 1:512–14; TP, *The Age of Reason, Part the Second*, ibid., 1:514–15. The police report and the arrest warrant can be found in Conway, *Life of Thomas Paine*, 2:104–107. See also Hawke, *Paine*, 295–96. On Cloots, see McPhee, *Liberty or Death*, 235–36, and Sagan, *Citizens and Cannibals*, 369.

CHAPTER 10: "A CONTINUED SCENE OF HORROR":
PAINE, MONROE, AND THE LUXEMBOURG

1. TP, *The Age of Reason, Part the Second* (1795), in *CWTP* 1:515–16; TP to JM, August 18, 1794, ibid., 2:1343; Jack Fruchtman Jr., ed., *An Eye-Witness Account of the French Revolution by Helen Maria Williams: Letters Containing a Sketch of the Politics of France* (reprint, New York, 1997), 56–68, 121, 127, 174–75, 176, 199; John Keane, *Tom Paine: A Political Life* (New York, 1995), 402–9; David Freeman Hawke, *Paine* (New York, 1974), 301–302.

2. The quotations can be found in Keane, *Tom Paine*, 404–5. See also Richard Buel Jr., *Joel Barlow: American Citizen in a Revolutionary World* (Baltimore, 2011), 180–81.

3. Morris to Francois Louis Michel Deforgues, February 14, 1974, in Moncure Daniel Conway, *The Life of Thomas Paine* (New York, 1892), 2:120; Deforgues to Morris, February 19, 1794, ibid., 2:120.

4. TP to Morris, February 24, 1794, *CWTP* 2:1338–39.

5. Morris to TJ, January 21, March 6, 1794, in Jared Sparks, *The Life of Gouverneur Morris* (New York, 1832), 2:393, 408–409.

6. TP, *The Age of Reason, Part the Second*, in *CWTP* 1:516; TP to JM, September 10, 1794, ibid., 2:1349; TP to Samuel Adams, March 6, 1795, ibid., 2:1375; Ann Cary Morris, ed., *The Diary and Letters of Gouverneur Morris* (New York, 1888), 2:48; William Howard Adams, *Gouverneur Morris: An Independent Life* (New Haven, Conn., 2003), 245. Morris's comments on TP were in a June 25, 1793, letter to Robert Morris that is printed in Ann Cary Morris, 2:47–49.

7. Helen Maria Williams, *Letters Containing a Sketch of the Politics of France* (London, 1796), 4:55–56; Thomas Clio Rickman, *The Life of Thomas Paine* (reprint, Cambridge, England, 2014), 151–53. The edition of Williams's letters edited by Fruchtman, and cited elsewhere in these notes, contains only volumes 1 and 2 of her essays published in 1796. Volumes 3 and 4 can be found in the original edition of her work. Volume 4 contains the section on TP's kindness and compassion toward his fellow prisoners. On TP helping General O'Hara, see *CWTP* 1:516n.

8. Timothy Tackett, *The Coming of the Terror in the French Revolution* (Cambridge, Mass., 2015), 327–30; Hawke, *Paine*, 300. Danton is quoted in Conway, *Life of Thomas Paine*, 2:129. The Cloots quote can be found in Janet Polasky, *Revolutions Without Borders: The Call to Liberty in the Atlantic World* (New Haven, Conn., 2015), 269.

9. These statistics draw on Tackett, *The Coming of the Terror in the French Revolution*, 330–34; Jonathan Israel, *Revolutionary Ideas: An Intellectual History of the French Revolution from the Rights of Man to Robespierre* (Princeton, N.J., 2014), 569; and Simon Schama, *Citizens: A Chronicle of the French Revolution* (New York, 1989), 836–39. The "mephitic odors" quote can be found in Schama, page 836.

10. TP, *Letter to George Washington* (1796), in *CWTP* 2:699; TP to JM, August 18, 25, 1794, ibid., 2:1343, 1344; TP, *The Age of Reason, Part the Second*, ibid., 1:515–16.

11. TP, To the French National Convention, August 7, 1794, ibid., 2:1339; TP to JM, August 17, 1794, ibid., 2:1341; TP to Madison, September 24, 1795, ibid., 2:1379; Keane, *Tom Paine*, 412–13; Audrey Williamson, *Thomas Paine: His Life, Work and Times* (New York, 1973), 218.

12. TP, *The Age of Reason, Part the Second*, *CWTP* 1:516; TP, "To the Citizens of the United States" (November 15, 1802), ibid., 2:921.

13. Fruchtman, *An Eye-Witness Account of the French Revolution by Helen Maria Williams*, 173; TP to JM, October [?], 1794, *CWTP* 2:1364.

14. Peter McPhee, *Robespierre: A Revolutionary Life* (New Haven, Conn., 2012), 213–20.

15. Edmund Randolph to GW, February 21, 1794, *PGWP* 15:255.

16. Stanley Elkins and Eric McKitrick, *The Age of Federalism* (New York, 1993), 353, 365, 377, 389.

17. JM to TJ, March 3, 1794, *PJM* 2:690; Robert R. Livingston to JM, March 13, 1794, ibid., 2:695; Jones to JM, March 14, 1794, ibid., 2:697; Henry Tazewell to JM, March 14, 1794, ibid., 2:698; Philip S. Foner, ed., *The Democratic-Republican Societies, 1790–1800: A Documentary Sourcebook* (Westport, Conn., 1976), 75, 134.

18. JM to TJ, March 16, 1794, *PJM* 2:699; JM to Livingston, March 17, 1794, ibid., 2:701.

19. JM to GW, April 8, 11, 1794, ibid., 2:710, 711; GW to JM, April 9, 1794, ibid., 2:710–11; TJ to JM, April 24, 1794, ibid., 2:717.

20. JM to TJ, May 4, 1794, ibid., 2:720–21; Ron Chernow, *Washington: A Life* (New York, 2010), 715–16. JM's quote can be found in Chernow, page 716.

21. Livingston to JM, May 16, 1794, *PJM* 2:724; JM to TJ, May 26, 1794, ibid., 2:725; Milton Lomask, *Aaron Burr* (New York, 1970–82), 1:183; Nancy Isenberg, *Fallen Founder: The Life of Aaron Burr* (New York, 2007), 125–27; Irving Brant, *James Madison* (New York, 1941–56), 3:400; W. P. Cresson, *James Monroe* (Chapel Hill, N.C., 1946), 127. AH's characterization of Burr can be found in John Ferling, *Jefferson and Hamilton: The Rivalry That Forged a Nation* (New York, 2013), 326.

22. JM to TJ, May 26, 27, 1794, *PJM* 2:725; 3:1–2; TJ to Enoch Edwards, January 22, 1797, *PTJ* 29:269; Harry Ammon, *James Monroe: The Quest for National Identity* (New York, 1971), 112–13; *PGWP* 16:135n. For the argument that GW may have turned to Monroe in order to seem evenhanded, see Conor Cruise O'Brien, *The Long Affair: Thomas Jefferson and the French Revolution, 1785–1800* (Chicago, 1996), 202. O'Brien contends that GW wished to balance the appointment of Jay, an Anglophile, with the selection of a Francophile.

23. Ammon, *James Monroe*, 114–16; JM to TJ, June 18, 1794, *PJM* 3:16.

24. Ammon, *James Monroe*, 116; Randolph to JM, June 10, 1794, *PJM* 3:6–10.

25. Ammon, *James Monroe*, 116.

26. Randolph to JM, June 10, 1794, *PJM* 3:8; JA to Charles Adams, May 17, 1794, *AFC* 10:183. The quotes in the instructions given to JM can be found in *PJM* 3:8.

27. JM, Journal, [July 31, August 15, 1794], ibid., 3:23, 32–33; JM to Randolph, August 15, 1794, ibid., 3:24–29; JM, To the French Convention, August 15, 1794, ibid., 3:30–31; O'Brien, *The Long Affair*, 131, 207–8.

28. Conway, *Life of Thomas Paine*, 2:142; TP to JM, August 17, 1794, *CWTP* 2:1341–42.

29. TP to JM, August 18, 1794, *CWTP* 2:1342–43; TP to the French National Convention, August 7, 1794, ibid., 2:1339–40.

30. TP to JM, August 25, September 10, 1794, ibid., 2:143–44, 1344–54; JM to TP, September 18, 1794, *PJM* 3:82; Keane, *Tom Paine*, 414–15, 417.

31. TP to JM, October 4, 1794, *CWTP* 2:1355–56; JM to TP, September 18, 1794, *PJM* 3:81–82.

32. TP to JM, October 13, November 2, 1794, *CWTP* 2:1357, 1374–75; JM to the Committee of General Security, November 1, 1794, *PJM* 3:138–39; JM to Randolph, November 7, 1794, ibid., 3:143–44.

33. These were JM's words, not TP's. See JM to Madison, July 5, 1796, *PJM* 4:39.

34. JM to Randolph, December 18, 1794, ibid., 3:189; JM to John Jay, January 17, 1795, ibid., 3:207; JM to Jones, February 1, 1795, ibid., 3:217; JM to Livingston, February 23, 1795, ibid., 3:243.

35. Morris to TJ, January 21, March 6, 1794, Sparks, *Life of Gouverneur Morris*, 2:393, 408; Randolph to GW, February 21, March 19, June 25, 1794, *PGWP* 15:255, 414–15, 415n; ibid., 16:277–78, and 278n; GW to Randolph, June 30, 1794, ibid., 16:300; Randolph to JM, July 30, 1794, *PJM* 3:20; TJ to Randolph, February 3, May 14, 1794, 28:15, 74. The "lord deliver me" quotation can be found in *PTJ* 28:74. GW's use of the word "citizen" has been italicized by the author.

36. JM to Madison, January 20, 1796, *PJM* 3:573; JM to Thomas Pinckney, January 7, 1796, ibid., 3:559.

37. TP to GW, February 22, 1795, *CWTP* 2:706–9.

38. JM to Madison, November 30, 1794, January 20, *PJM* 3:164, 573.

39. Jack Fruchtman Jr., *The Political Philosophy of Thomas Paine* (Baltimore, 2009), 143–44.

40. TP, *Dissertation on First Principles of Government* (1795), *CWTP* 2:570–88; TP, Speech in the National Convention, July 7, 1795, ibid., 2:588–94. The quotations from his essay can be found on pages 578 and 580, while the quotes from his speech can be found on pages 590 and 594. See also Keane, *Tom Paine*, 422–24, and Hawke, *Paine*, 310–12.

41. Buel, *Joel Barlow*, 278–79; Williamson, *Thomas Paine*, 245. The "professed revolutionary" quote is in Williamson, page 226. The "well-dressed" quote can be found in Alfred Owen Aldridge, *Man of Reason: The Life of Thomas Paine* (Philadelphia, 1959), 258. Katherine Wilmot is quoted in Craig Nelson, *Thomas Paine: Enlightenment, Revolution, and the Birth of Modern Nations* (New York, 2006), 297.

42. JM to Jones, September 15, 1795, *PJM* 3:456. The "open wound" quote can be found in Keane, *Tom Paine*, 425.

43. TP, *The Age of Reason, Part the Second* (1795), *CWTP* 1:514–604. The quotations can be found on pages 517, 529, and 537. The "remarkable thing" quotation can be found in Williamson, *Thomas Paine*, 228.

44. Keane, *Tom Paine*, 396–400; Jill Lepore, "A World of Paine," in Alfred F. Young, Gary B. Nash, and Ray Raphael, eds., *Revolutionary Founders: Rebels, Radicals, and Reformers in the Making of the Nation* (New York, 2011), 93. The quotation is in Keane, page 398.

45. TP to GW, September 20, 1795, *CWTP* 2:705–6. This letter can be found within TP's *Letter to George Washington*, which was published in Philadelphia nine months after the previously unpublished September 20 letter was drafted and sent. TP's characterization of JM is also in his published essay on GW. See ibid., 2:703.

46. TP sent his essay to Benjamin Franklin Bache, the grandson of BF and the son of Richard Bache, to whom BF had written his letter of introduction when TP prepared to sail from England to Philadelphia in 1774. Bache published excerpts from the *Letter to George Washington* during the fall elections and issued the entire essay as a pamphlet in 1797. See Aldridge, *Man of Reason*, 245–46.

47. TP to GW, February 22, 1795, *CWTP* 2:707.

48. TP, *Letter to George Washington*, in *CWTP* 2:691–723. The quotations can be found on pages 691, 693, 695, 698, 703, 704, 710, 711, 713, 715, 718, 719, 720, and 723.

49. AH to Philip Schuyler, February 18, 1781, *PAH* 2:565–67; AH to James McHenry, February 18, 1781, ibid., 2:569; JA to Benjamin Waterhouse, May 9, 1813, in Worthington C. Ford, ed., *Statesman and Friend: Correspondence of John Adams with Benjamin Waterhouse, 1784–1822* (Boston, 1927), 98; John Ferling, *John Adams: A Life* (reprint, New York, 2010), 424.

50. Hawke, *Paine*, 321; Donald H. Stewart, *The Opposition Press of the Federalist Period* (Albany, N.Y., 1969), 398, 528; Aldridge, *Man of Reason*, 246; Oliver Wolcott to AH, December 8, 1796, *PAH* 20:436.

51. TJ to Archibald Stuart, January 4, 1797, *PTJ* 29:252.

CHAPTER 11: "THE FEDERALIST TIDE IS STRONG": GLOOMY YEARS FOR THE APOSTLES OF REVOLUTION

1. TJ to Samuel Blackden, December 11, 1794, *PTJ* 28:216; TJ to Madame de Tessé, September 6, 1795, ibid., 28:452; TJ to Constantin Volney, December 9, 1795, ibid., 28:551; TJ to William Branch Giles, April 27, 1795, ibid., 28:337.

2. Horatio Gates to TJ, January 5, March 14, 1794, ibid., 28:6–7, 37; TJ to Gates, February 3, 1794, ibid., 28:14.

3. *JMB* 2:910–12; TJ to Angelica Schuyler Church, November 27, 1793, *PTJ* 27:449; TJ to Madison, April 27, 1795, ibid., 28:339; TJ to Gates, February 3, 1794, ibid., 28:14.

4. Edmund Randolph to TJ, August 28, 1794, *PTJ* 28:117–19; TJ to Randolph, September 7, 1794, ibid., 28:148.

5. TJ to JM, April 3, October 30, 1794, ibid., 28:50, 337; TJ to JA, April 25, 1794, February 6, 1795, ibid., 28:57, 261; TJ to GW, May 14, 1794, ibid., 28:74–75; TJ to Robert Morris, February 19, 1795, ibid., 28:268.

6. Jack McLaughlin, *Jefferson and Monticello: The Biography of a Builder* (New York, 1988), 9–10, 20–25, 162–63, 228–34, 356–59, 361–68; Annette Gordon-Reed and Peter S. Onuf, *"Most Blessed of the Patriarchs": Thomas Jefferson and the Empire of the Imagination* (New York, 2016), 195; Margaret Bayard Smith in Merrill D. Peterson, ed., *Visitors to Monticello* (Charlottesville, Va., 1989), 49.

7. TJ to John Bolling, October 7, 1791, *PTJ* 22:198–99; TJ to Thomas Mann Randolph, January 8, 1792, January 24, 1793, ibid., 23:33; 24:91; TJ to Stevens Thomson Mason, October 27, 1799, ibid., 31:222; TJ to James Lyle, April 15, 1793, July 10, 1795, ibid., 25:550–51; 28:405–6; TJ to Jean Nicolas Démeunier, April 29, 1795, ibid., 28:341; TJ to Volney, April 10, 1796, ibid., 29:61; TJ to Wythe, October 23, 1794, ibid., 28:181. On TJ's farming plan, see the account of the duc de La Rochefoucauld-Liancourt, who visited Monticello in 1796. It can be found in Peterson, *Visitors to Monticello*, 23–27. See also Lucia Stanton, "Thomas Jefferson: Planter and Farmer," in Francis D. Cogliano, ed., *A Companion to Thomas Jefferson* (Chichester, England, 2011), 253–70; Lucia Stanton, "'Those Who Labor for My Happiness': Thomas Jefferson and His Slaves," in Peter S. Onuf, ed., *Jeffersonian Legacies* (Charlottesville, Va., 1993), 147–80; Henry Wiencek, *Master of the Mountain: Thomas Jefferson and His Slaves* (New York, 2012), 92–93, 113, 149; Stephen B. Hodin, "The Mechanisms of Monticello: Saving Labor in Jefferson's America," *Journal of the Early Republic* 26 (2006): 377–418; McLaughlin, *Jefferson and Monticello*, 239–338. On the earnings of craftsmen in Philadelphia in the 1790s, see Billy G. Smith, *The "Lower Sort": Philadelphia's Laboring People, 1750–1800* (Ithaca, N.Y., 1990), 92–125, 230–37.

8. Cosway to TJ, April 6, 1790, November 13, 24, 1794, December 4, 1795, *PTJ* 16:312–13; 28:201, 209–11, 543–44; TJ to Cosway, June 23, 1790, September 8, 1795, ibid., 16:550–51; 28:455–56.

9. "The Memoirs of Madison Hemings" (March 13, 1873), in Annette Gordon-Reed, *Thomas Jefferson and Sally Hemings: An American Controversy* (Charlottesville, Va., 1997), 245–48. For Heming's appearance and character, see Gordon-Reed and Onuf, *"Most Blessed of the Patriarchs,"* 129.

10. For the best secondary sources on TJ and Sally Hemings, see ibid.; Annette Gordon-Reed, *The Hemingses of Monticello: An American Family* (New York, 2008); and Fawn M. Brodie, *Thomas Jefferson: An Intimate History* (New York, 1974). On DNA testing to determine the possibility of TJ's paternity of at least one of Hemings's children, see Eugene Foster, "Jefferson Fathered Slave's Last Child," *Nature* 396 (November 5, 1998): 27–28, and Foster's response to letters in *Nature*, 397 (January 7, 1999): 32. The DNA tests were conducted on male-line descendants of two sons of Field Jefferson, TJ's paternal uncle, a male line descendant of Eston Hemings's, Sally Hemings's last child, and others. The tests divulged a link with the male descendants of Field Jefferson, meaning that one of the eight Jeffersons alive in 1808 could have been the father of Sally's last child. The eight were TJ, his brother Randolph, the five sons of Randolph, and a cousin, George Jefferson. There are skeptics with

regard to TJ's paternity. For a collection of essays by doubters, see Eyler Robert Coates Jr., ed., *The Jefferson-Hemings Myth: An American Travesty* (Charlottesville, Va., 2001).

11. TJ to Madison, April 3, 1794, *PTJ* 28:49–50; TJ to JM, April 24, 1794, ibid., 28:55; TJ to Tench Coxe, May 1, 1794, ibid., 28:67.

12. TJ to GW, May 23, 1792, ibid., 23:536; TJ, "Notes of Agenda to Reduce the Government to True Principles," [ca. July 11, 1792), ibid., 24:215; Thomas P. Slaughter, *The Whiskey Rebellion: Frontier Epilogue to the American Revolution* (New York, 1986), 95–105, 113–14; William Hogeland, *The Whiskey Rebellion: George Washington, Alexander Hamilton, and the Frontier Rebels Who Challenged America's Newfound Sovereignty* (New York, 2006), 62–69; Terry Bouton, "William Findley, David Bradford, and the Pennsylvania Regulation of 1794," in Alfred F. Young, Gary B. Nash, and Ray Raphael, eds., *Revolutionary Founders: Rebels, Radicals, and Reformers in the Making of the Nation* (New York, 2011), 233–51.

13. Bouton, "William Findley, David Bradford, and the Pennsylvania Regulation of 1794," Young, et al., *Revolutionary Founders*, 243; Conference Concerning the Insurrection in Western Pennsylvania, August 2, 1794, *PAH* 17:9–13; AH to GW, August 2, 5, 1794, ibid., 17:15–19, 24–58; GW, Proclamation, August 7, 1794, *PGWP* 16:531–34. AH's conspiracy theory was aired in a series of "Tully" essays. See *PAH* 17:132–35, 148–50, 159–61, and 178–80.

14. AH to Angelica Church, October 23, 1794, *PAH* 17:340; AH to Rufus King, October 30, 1794, ibid., 17:348; AH to Samuel Hodgdon, October 7, 1794, ibid., 17:309, 310; AH to Knox, October 8, 1794, ibid., 17:312–13; AH to Mifflin, October 17, 1794, ibid., 17:327; AH to GW, October 29, November 8, 15, 1794, ibid., 17:347, 361, 372; Slaughter, *Whiskey Rebellion*, 217–20. AH's comments about skewering and hanging insurgents can be found in Ron Chernow, *Alexander Hamilton* (New York, 2004), 475.

15. TJ to Madison, October 30, December 28, 1794, *PTJ* 28:182, 229; TJ to JM, May 26, 1795, ibid., 28:359.

16. Eugene Link, *Democratic-Republican Societies, 1790–1800* (New York, 1942), 44–70; Matthew Schoenbachler, "Republicanism in the Age of Democratic Revolution: The Democratic-Republican Societies of the 1790s," *Journal of the Early American Republic* 18 (1998): 237–61; Matthew Rainbow Hale, "Regenerating the World: The French Revolution, Civic Festivals, and the Forging of Modern American Democracy, 1973–1795," *Journal of American History* 103 (2017): 891–920. See also Philip S. Foner, ed., *The Democratic-Republican Societies, 1790–1820: A Documentary Sourcebook* (Westport, Conn., 1976).

17. Link, *Democratic-Republican Societies*, 12, 19, 115; Donald H. Stewart, *The Opposition Press of the Federalist Period* (Albany, N.Y., 1969), 87.

18. GW, State of the Union Message, November 19, 1794, *PGWP* 17:181–88. The quotes are on pages 181 and 186.

19. TJ to Giles, December 17, 1794, *PTJ* 28:219; TJ to Madison, December 28, 1794, ibid., 28:228–29; TJ to JM, May 26, 1795, ibid., 28:359–60; Madison to TJ, November 30, 1994, ibid., 28:211. GW's "federalists got unchecked hold" comment can be found in Brian Steele, " 'General Washington Did Not Harbor One Principle of Federalism': Thomas Jefferson Remembers George Washington," in Robert M. S. McDonald, ed., *Sons of the Father: George Washington and His Protégés* (Charlottesville, Va., 2013), 77.

20. TJ to David Rittenhouse, February 24, 1795, ibid., 28:279; TJ to Robert Morris, February 19, 1795, ibid., 28:268.

21. For an excellent account of GW's Indian warfare and his hidden motives in pursuing such a course, see William Hogeland, *Autumn of the Black Snake: The Creation of the U.S. Army and the Invasion That Opened the West* (New York, 2017). On Ohio's population,

see Gordon S. Wood, *Empire of Liberty: A History of the Early Republic, 1789–1815* (New York, 2009), 2, 316.

22. For an excellent brief summation of the Jay Treaty's provisions, see Amanda C. Demmer, "Trick or Constitutional Treaty?: The Jay Treaty and the Quarrel Over the Diplomatic Separation of Powers," *Journal of the Early Republic* 35 (Winter 2015): 583–84.

23. GW to AH, July 3, 13, 29, August 31, 1795, *PAH* 18:398–400, 461–63, 524; 19:205; AH to GW, Remarks on the Treaty of Amity Commerce and Navigation lately made between the United States and Great Britain, [July 9–11, 1795], ibid., 18:404–54. AH's "Defence" series can be found ibid., volumes 18, 19, and 20. The publication date for each essay can be found in "Editor's Note," ibid., 18:476. See also John Ferling, *The Ascent of George Washington: The Hidden Political Genius of an American Icon* (New York, 2009), 341–44.

24. Richard Buel, *Securing the Revolution: Ideology in American Politics* (Ithaca, N.Y., 1972), 52; Walter Stahr, *John Jay: Founding Father* (New York, 2005), 334–38. On AH being struck, see Joanne B. Freeman, *Affairs of Honor: National Politics in the New Republic* (New Haven, Conn., 2001), xiii. For an excellent analysis of the political fallout from the accord, see Todd Estes, *The Jay Treaty Debate, Public Opinion, and the Evolution of Early American Political Culture* (Amherst, Mass., 2006).

25. TJ to Madison, September 21, 1795, *PTJ* 28:475; TP, "Observations on Jay's Treaty (1795), *CWTP* 2:568–69.

26. TJ to JM, March 2, July 10, 1796, *PTJ* 29:4, 147.

27. TJ to Madison, ibid., March 27, 1796, 29:51; Hogeland, *Whiskey Rebellion*, 240. On the Randolph episode and his resignation, see the assorted interpretations and Randolph's defense in Irving Brant, "Edmund Randolph Not Guilty!," *William and Mary Quarterly* 7 (1950): 179–98; Mary K. Bonsteel Tachau, "George Washington and the Reputation of Edmund Randolph," *Journal of American History* 73 (1986): 15–34; Stanley Elkins and Eric McKitrick, *The Age of Federalism* (New York, 1993), 424–31, 505; Edmund Randolph, *A Vindication of Mr. Randolph's Resignation* (Philadelphia, 1795); John Ferling, *The First of Men: A Life of George Washington* (reprint, New York, 2010), 458–60; Ron Chernow, *Washington: A Life* (New York, 2010), 732–36.

28. Randolph to JM, December 2, 1794, *PJM* 3:172; JM to the Committee of Public Safety, September 3, 1794, ibid., 3:52; Morris to GW, December 30, 1794, *PGWP* 17:340; GW to Jay, December 18, 1794, ibid., 17:286.

29. Randolph to JM, December 5, 1794, *PJM* 3:186.

30. The two foregoing paragraphs draw on JM to GW, November 19, 1794, ibid., 3:132; JM to Randolph, November 7, 20, December 2, 18, 1794, ibid., 3:141, 155, 177, 189; and Elkins and McKitrick, *The Age of Federalism*, 498–502.

31. JM to Short, May 30, 1795, *PJM* 3:316; JM to Madison, June 13, 30, September 8, October 23, 24, 29, 1795, July 5, 1796, ibid., 3:353, 385, 439, 495, 497, 502; 4:41; JM to John Beckley, June 23, 1795, ibid., 3:371; JM to Livingston, June 23, 1795, ibid., 3:372; JM to Samuel Bayard, September 18, 1795, ibid., 3:457; Independence Day Toasts (July 4, 1795), ibid., 3:395–96; Elkins and McKitrick, *The Age of Federalism*, 502–3.

32. JM to Livingston, June 23, 1795, *PJM* 3:372; JM to Madison, October 25, 1795, July 5, 1796, ibid., 3:497–98; 4:39; Charles Delacroix to JM, February 20, 1796, ibid., 3:593–94; Harry Ammon, *James Monroe: The Quest for National Identity* (New York, 1971), 117–56. The "helpful to England" quotation is the conclusion of diplomatic historian Samuel Flagg Bemis. See Bemis's *Jay's Treaty: A Study in Commerce and Diplomacy* (New Haven, Conn.,

1962), 367. That Jay's treaty was seen in Paris as an "outright betrayal" was the judgment of historian Jerald A. Combs in *The Jay Treaty: Political Battleground of the Founding Fathers* (Berkeley, Calif., 1970), 153.

33. JM to Madison, July 5, 1796, *PJM* 4:38–40.

34. Theobald Wolfe Tone, Journal [February 15, 23, 1796], ibid., 3:589, 599–600; Ammon, *James Monroe*, 133–37; *PJM* 3:49n.

35. JM to Randolph, February 12, 1795, *PJM* 3:228; Adrienne Lafayette to JM, [February 1795], ibid., 3:249; *AJM*, 70–71; Olivier Bernier, *Lafayette: Hero of Two Worlds* (New York, 1983), 247–62; Ammon, *James Monroe*, 137–38.

36. GW to Randolph, July 24, 1795, *PGWP* 18:413.

37. Randolph to JM, June 10, 1794, *PJM* 3:10; Wolcott to AH, June 17, 1796, *PAH* 20:231.

38. Pickering to JM, June 13, 1796, *PJM* 4:36; JM to Madison, September 1, 1796, ibid., 4:85.

39. AH to GW, July 5, 1796, *PAH* 20:246–47; Enoch Edwards to JM, April 20, 1798, *PJM* 4:267.

40. AH to GW, July 5, 1796, *PAH* 20:246–47; GW to AH, June 26, 1796, *PAH* 20:238–39.

41. Pickering to JM, August 22, September 9, 1796, *PJM* 4:81, 88–89; GW to the Directory of France, September 9, 1796, ibid., 4:89; Ammon, *James Monroe*, 150–52.

42. JM to Madison, November 13, 1796, *PJM* 4:117; JM to Pickering, November [?], 1796, ibid., 4:118–30. The quotes in JM's letter to Pickering are on pages 118, 120, and 123. The letter to Pickering was never sent.

43. TJ to JM, June 12, 1796, ibid., 4:34.

44. Madison to JM, April 7, 1796, ibid., 4:2; JM to Madison, July 5, 1796, ibid., 4:41; David Freeman Hawke, *Paine* (New York, 1974), 319, 323; Audrey Williamson, *Thomas Paine: His Life, Work and Times* (New York, 1973), 245; Alfred Owen Aldridge, *Man of Reason: The Life of Thomas Paine* (Philadelphia, 1959), 261.

45. TP to Anonymous, March 4, 1797, *CWTP* 2:1385; TP to Madison, April 27, 1797, ibid., 2:1395; TP to Fulwar Skipwith, April 26, 1797, ibid., 2:1392; TP to TJ, April 1, 1797, ibid., 2:1387. The "promised land" quotation is in Thomas Clio Rickman, *The Life of Thomas Paine* (reprint, Cambridge, England, 2014), 166.

46. TP to Madison, April 27, 1797, *CWTP* 2:1394.

47. JA to Benjamin Waterhouse, May 21, 1821, in Worthington C. Ford, ed., *Statesman and Friend: Correspondence of John Adams with Benjamin Waterhouse, 1784–1822* (Boston, 1927), 157. The "drinks like a fish" quote can be found in Hawke, *Paine*, 323.

48. Thomas Clio Rickman, *The Life of Thomas Paine* (reprint, Cambridge, England, 2014), 11–12. Rickman, TP's longest and closest friend, authored his biography in 1819.

49. Letter of Marguerite Bonneville, n.d., in Moncure Daniel Conway, *The Life of Thomas Paine* (New York, 1892), 2:443–44.

50. Seth Cotlar, *Tom Paine's America: The Rise and Fall of Transatlantic Radicalism in the Early Republic* (Charlottesville, N.C., 2011), 132, 179.

51. For the entire pamphlet, see TP, *Agrarian Justice* (1797), *CWTP* 1:606–23. The quotations can be found on pages 606, 607, 609, 610, 618, 619, and 621. For excellent analyses of the pamphlet, see Eric Foner, *Tom Paine and the Revolutionary America* (New York, 2005), 249–53; Adrian Little, "The Politics of Compensation: Tom Paine's Agrarian Justice and Liberal Egalitarianism," *Contemporary Politics* 5 (1999): 63–73; Judith Buber Agassi, "The Rise of the Ideas of the Welfare State," *Philosophy of the Social Sciences* 21 (1991): 444–57; Jack

Fruchtman Jr., *Thomas Paine: Apostle of Freedom* (New York, 1994), 355–62; and Jack Fruchtman Jr., *The Political Philosophy of Thomas Paine* (Baltimore, 2009), 119–33.

52. TJ to Madison, October 28, 1785, *PTJ* 8:681–2; TJ to George Wythe, August 13, 1786, ibid., 10:244.

53. TJ to Madison, December 28, 1794, April 27, 1795, *PTJ* 28:230, 338–39; Madison to TJ, March 23, 1795, February 7, 1796, ibid., 28:315, 607; TJ to Constantin Volney, December 9, 1795, *PTJ* 28:551; TJ to JM, July 10, 1796, ibid., 29:147; Madison to JM, February 26, 1796, *PJM* 3:602; Jeffrey L. Pasley, *The First Presidential Contest: 1796 and the Founding of American Democracy* (Lawrence, Kans., 2013), 188; Dumas Malone, *Jefferson and His Time* (Boston, 1948–81), 2:273–74.

54. John Ferling, *Adams vs. Jefferson: The Tumultuous Election of 1800* (New York, 2004), 87–89.

55. Pasley, *The First Presidential Contest*, 224–406. The AH quote is in Pasley, page 245.

56. TJ to James Sullivan, February 9, 1797, *PTJ* 29:289.

57. TJ to JA, December 28, 1796, ibid., 29:235; TJ to JM, January 1, 1797, ibid., 29:247–48.

CHAPTER 12: "THE REIGN OF WITCHES": THE HIGH FEDERALISTS TAKE CHARGE

1. TJ to Philip Mazzei, April 24, 1796, *PTJ* 29:82.

2. See the editor's lengthy note in *PTJ*, 29:73–81.

3. TJ to GW, June 19, 1796, ibid., 29:127.

4. Martha Washington is quoted in Robert M. S. McDonald, *Confounding Father: Thomas Jefferson's Image in His Own Time* (Charlottesville, Va., 2016), 1.

5. TJ to John Melish, January 13, 1813, *PTJ:Ret.Ser.* 5:565; TJ to Walter Jones, January 2, 1814, ibid., 7:101–3. See also Brian Steele, "'General Washington Did Not Harbor One Principle of Federalism': Thomas Jefferson Remembers George Washington," in Robert M. S. McDonald, ed., *Sons of the Father: George Washington and His Protégés* (Charlottesville, Va., 2013), 72–98.

6. See chapter 7. For a more detailed account of the damage to the relationship between TJ and JA, see John Ferling, *John Adams: A Life* (reprint, New York, 2010), 287–91, 306–309.

7. Ferling, *John Adams*, 333, 341.

8. Alexander DeConde, *The Quasi-War: The Politics and Diplomacy of the Undeclared War with France, 1797–1801* (New York, 1966), 8–9. For a useful account of the U.S.-Florida border differences, and the survey of the boundary, see William J. Morton, *The Stargazer Who Defined America* (Atlanta, 2015).

9. JM to Madison, January 1, 1797, *PJM* 4:140.

10. TJ, Notes on Conversations with John Adams and George Washington [after October 13, 1797] *PTJ* 29:551–53; JA, "Correspondence Originally Published in the *Boston Patriot*," *Works* 9:285; Oliver Wolcott to AH, March 31, 1797, *PAH* 20:571.

11. AH to Edward Stevens, November 11, 1769, *PAH* 1:4.

12. AH to Pickering, March 26, 29, May 11, 1797, ibid., 20:549, 557; 21:81–84; AH to William L. Smith, April 10, 1797, ibid., 21:29–41; AH to Wolcott, March 30, 1797, ibid., 20:567–68; AH to Rufus King, February 15, 1797, ibid., 20:515–16; AH to James McHenry, March [?], 1797, ibid., 20:574–75. Italics added by the author to the word "plot."

13. TJ to Elbridge Gerry, May 13, 1797, *PTJ* 29:363–64. TJ's remarks to the French consul general are quoted in Stanley Elkins and Eric McKitrick, *The Age of Federalism* (New York, 1993), 566.

14. Madison to TJ, February 18 or 19, 1798, *PTJ* 30:116–17; TJ to Elbridge Gerry, June 21, 1797, ibid., 29:448; JA, "Message to Congress," May 16, 1797, in James D. Richardson, ed., *A Compilation of the Messages and Papers of the Presidents* (New York, 1897–1917), 1:233–39; DeConde, *Quasi-War*, 25–35. The quotes in JA's speech to Congress are in Richardson, 1:237 and 238. For the suggestion that JA was not entirely subservient to his cabinet, see Nathan Perl-Rosenthal, "Private Letters and Public Diplomacy: The Adams Network and the Quasi-War, 1797–1798," *Journal of the Early Republic* 31 (2011): 283–311.

15. JM, Address to the Executive Directory, January 1, 1797, *PJM* 4:138.

16. Harry Ammon, *James Monroe: The Quest for National Identity* (New York, 1971), 157; John Keane, *Tom Paine: A Political Life* (New York, 1995), 371, 378–79; JM to Madison, January 1, 1797, *PJM* 4:140; Francisco de Miranda to JM, April 2, 1797, ibid., 4:152, 4:155n.

17. Thomas McKean Address, July 1, 1797, *PJM* 4:154–55; JM, Philadelphia Speech, July 5, 1797, ibid., 4:155–56; JM to John Dawson, March 26, 1798, ibid., 4:257.

18. AH to John Fenno, [July 17–22, 1797], *PAH* 21:167; Wolcott to AH, July 3, 1797, ibid., 21:144–45; AH to Jeremiah Wadsworth, July 28, 1797, ibid., 21:187; Abraham Venable to AH, July 9, 10, 1797, ibid., 21:153–54, 159; "David Gelsen's Account of an Interview between Alexander Hamilton and James Monroe," July 11, 1797, ibid., 21:159–62; JM and Muhlenberg to AH, July 17, 1797, ibid., 21:168–70; AH to JM, July 17, 18, 20, 22, 28, August 4, 9, January [?], 1797, ibid., 21:172–73, 174–75, 176–77, 180–81, 186, 200, 208, 346; AH, *Observations on Certain Documents Contained . . . In Which the Charge of Speculation Against Alexander Hamilton . . . is Fully Refuted, Written by Himself* (Philadelphia, 1797), ibid., 21:238–85; Editor's Note, ibid., 20:121–44n; JM to AH, July 17, 18, 21, 25, 31, August 6, December 2, 1797, *PJM* 4:164, 165, 167–68, 171, 173, 178–79, 192–93; JM to Aaron Burr, August 6, December 1, 1797, ibid., 4:177–78, 191–92; Burr to JM, August 9, 1797, ibid., 4:179; James Callender to TJ, September 28, 1797, *PTJ* 29:536–37; TJ to John Taylor, October 8, 1797, ibid., 29:546; Ron Chernow, *Alexander Hamilton* (New York, 2004), 533.

19. JM to Pickering, July 6, 19, 31, 1797, *PJM* 4:157–58, 165–66, 173–76; Pickering to JM, July 17, 24, 1797, ibid., 4:164–65, 170–71.

20. Ammon, *James Monroe*, 165; JM to Dawson, March 26, 1798, *PJM* 4:257; JM to Madison, June 8, 1798, ibid., 4:272; Joseph W. Cox, *Robert Goodloe Harper: Champion of Southern Federalism* (Port Washington, N.Y., 1972), 106; Donald H. Stewart, *The Opposition Press of the Federalist Period* (Albany, N.Y., 1969), 284.

21. JM, Speech at Richmond, January 26, 1798, *PJM* 4:239; TJ to JM, September 7, October 25, 1797, ibid., 4:184–85, 189; Madison to JM, October 19, 1797, ibid., 4:186.

22. TJ to JM, December 27, 1797, ibid., 4:234; John Taylor to JM, March 25, 1798, ibid., 4:256; TJ to Madison, January 3, 1798, *PTJ* 30:11; McHenry to GW, February 1, 1798, *PGWRet* 2:66; GW, Comments on JM's *A View* [March 1798], ibid., 2:170–214. GW's quoted comments can be found on pages 180, 184, 186, 192, 196, 202, and 208. Pickering's "condemnation" comment and McHenry's "sunk" prediction can be found in William M. Ferraro, "George Washington and James Monroe: Military Compatriots, Political Adversaries, and Nationalist Visionaries," in McDonald, *Sons of the Father*, 110.

23. JM, *A View of the Conduct of the Executive, in the Foreign Affairs of the United States, Connected with the Mission to the French Republic, During the Years 1794, 5, & 6*

(Philadelphia 1797), *PJM* 4:195–227. The quotations can be found on pages 226 and 227. For TJ's comments, see TJ to JM, December 27, 1797, ibid., 4:234, and TJ to Madison, January 3, 1798, *PTJ* 30:11. See also McHenry to GW, February 1, 1798, *PGWRet* 2:66; Wolcott to GW, January 30, 1798, ibid., 2:61.

24. JM, Essay: To George Washington (1798), *PJM* 4:301–4.

25. JM, A View of the Political Situation of the United States in the Commencement of the French Revolution (1798), ibid., 4:304–308; JM, War with France (1798), ibid., 4:30813; JM, Liberty and Tyranny (1798), ibid., 4:313–20. None of these tracts were published. The first two focused on the benefits to the United States from a French victory in the European war and argued that had GW pursued an astute foreign policy, the United States could have secured an excellent trade agreement with France and won other concessions. The latter dealt with the kindred ideologies of the American Revolution and the French Revolution, and how America would benefit from a French victory in the European war.

26. TJ to JM, February 8, 1798, ibid., 4:245; JM to TJ, February 25, 1798, ibid., 4:249; Randolph to JM, March 11, 1798, ibid., 254; GW to Pickering, August 29, 1797, *PGWRet* 2:327; Ammon, *James Monroe*, 163–64, 170.

27. JM, To the Republican Members of Congress, [February 1798], *PJM* 4:251.

28. JA to His Cabinet, January 24, 1798, *PAH* 21:339–40; McHenry to AH, January 26, 1798, ibid., 21:339; AH to McHenry, [January 27–February 11], 1798, ibid., 21:341–46.

29. AH to Pickering, March 17, 1798, ibid., 21:364–66; JA, "Message to Congress," March 19, 1798, in Richardson, *Compilation of the Messages and Papers of the Presidents* 1:264–65. For JA's original version of the speech before it was softened, see Message, *Adams Papers*, 1639–1889, microfilm edition, 608 reels (Boston: Massachusetts Historical Society, 1954–59), reel 387, and JA to McHenry, October 22, 1798, ibid., reel 391.

30. TJ to Madison, March 21, April 5, 1798, *PTJ* 30:189, 245.

31. *DAJA* 3:333; 4:5; JA to AA, January 14, 1793, January 2, December 8, 1796, *AFC* 9:378; 11:119, 440; JA to Charles Adams, May 17, 1794, ibid., 10:183.

32. TP to TJ, April 1, 1797, *CWTP* 2:1386–90; TP to Madison, April 27, 1797, ibid., 2:1394. TP's characterization of JA as "fractious" and arrogant was in TP to TJ, October 1, 1800, *PTJ* 31:193n. Probably recalling that the last time he saw TJ back in 1789 when TJ and JA had been good friends; TP had second thoughts and excised his comment about JA before dispatching the letter to the vice president.

33. JM to TJ, April 8, 1798, *PJM* 4:265; TJ to Madison, April 5, 6, 1798, *PTJ* 30: 244–45, 250–51.

34. AH, "The Stand," nos. I–VII [March 30–April 21, 1798], *PAH* 21:381–87, 390–96, 402–8, 412–18, 418–32, 434–440, 441–47; AH, "A French Faction," [April 1798], ibid., 21:452–53. The quotations are on pages 383–84, 446, and 452.

35. TJ to Madison, April 26, 1798, *PTJ* 30:299; TJ to Edmund Pendleton, January 29, 1799, ibid., 30:661.

36. Gordon S. Wood, *Empire of Liberty: A History of the Early Republic, 1789–1815* (New York, 2009), 245–46, 263–64; Richard H. Kohn, *Eagle and Sword: The Federalists and the Creation of the Military Establishment in America, 1783–1802* (New York, 1975), 224–29, 229n. Kohn is the best available source on the armies, but see also TJ to Madison, February 5, 11, 1799, *PTJ* 31:9, 23.

37. James Roger Sharp, *American Politics in the Early Republic: The New Nation in Crisis* (New Haven, Conn., 1993), 176; Chernow, *Alexander Hamilton*, 570.

38. AH to Rufus King, June 6, 1798, *PAH* 21:490. The "Spirit of the People" and the "wise policy" quotes can be found in Sharp, *American Politics in the Early Republic*, 176, 180.

39. GW to JA, July 13, September 25, 1798, *PGWRet* 2:402–4; 3:36–43; GW, Suggestions for Military Appointments, July 14, 1798, ibid., 2:414–15; JA to McHenry, August 29, September 30, 1798, *PAH* 22:8n, 16; AH to GW, May 19, June 2, 1798, ibid., 21:466–68, 479–80; GW to AH, May 27, 1798, ibid., 21:470–74.

40. TJ to John Taylor, June 4, November 26, 1798, *PTJ* 30:388, 389, 589; TJ to William Strickland, March 23, 1798, ibid., 30:212–13; TJ to Samuel Smith, August 22, 1798, ibid., 30:484–85; TJ to Stevens Thomson Mason, October 11, 1798, ibid., 30:560; TJ to Tadeusz Kosciuszko, June 18, 1798, February 21, 1799, ibid., 30:416; 31:52–53; TJ to Thomas M. Randolph, February 2, 1800, ibid., 31:358. AA's "second Buonaparty" quote can be found in DeConde, *Quasi-War*, 97.

41. GW to James McHenry, August 10, September 14, 16, October 1, 23, 1798, February 10, March 25, May 13, July 7, 1799, *PGWRet* 2:509–10, 610–12; 3:4–5, 65, 132, 342–43, 364–65, 437–43; 4:70–72, 177–79; GW to Pickering, September 9, 1798, ibid., 2:596–99; GW to James McAlpin, May 12, 1799, ibid., 4:67.

42. TJ to Madison, January 8, 1797, *PTJ* 29:255.

43. TJ to Mason, October 11, 1798, ibid., 30:559; TJ to Taylor, November 26, 1798, ibid., 30:588; TJ to JM, January 23, 1799, ibid., 30:635; TJ to Gerry, January 26, 1799, ibid., 30:649; TJ to Nicholas Lewis, January 30, 1799, ibid., 30:664; TJ to Madison, January 30, 1799, ibid., 30:665; TJ to Edmund Pendleton, April 22, 1799, ibid., 31:97.

44. TJ to Taylor, November 26, 1798, ibid., 30:588.

45. JA to McHenry, August 29, September 13, 1798, *Works* 8:588, 594; JA to John Trumbull, July 23, November [?], 1805, *Adams Papers*, microfilm edition, 608 reels (Boston: Massachusetts Historical Society, 1954–59), reel 118; JA to F. A. Vanderkemp, August 23, 1806, April 3, 1815, Simon Gratz Collection, Historical Society of Pennsylvania; JA to Rush, August 23, September 30, December 4, 1805, January 25, 1806, September 2, November 11, 1807, April 18, 1808, August 28, 1811, in John A. Schutz and Douglass Adair, eds., *The Spur of Fame: Dialogues of John Adams and Benjamin Rush, 1805–1813* (San Marino, Calif., 1966), 35, 42, 45, 47–48, 94–95, 98–99, 113, 192; JA to Benjamin Waterhouse, July 12, 1811, in Worthington C. Ford, ed., *Statesman and Friend: Correspondence of John Adams and Benjamin Waterhouse, 1784–1822* (Boston, 1927), 65; JA to William Cunningham, October 15, 1808, in *Correspondence between the Hon. John Adams . . . and the Late William Cunningham* (Boston, 1823), 44.

46. Chernow, *Alexander Hamilton*, 567–68; DeConde, *Quasi-War*, 119; David McCullough, *John Adams* (New York, 2001), 518; AH to Harrison Gray Otis, December 28, 1798, *PAH* 22:394.

47. JA, Second Annual Address, December 8, 1798, Richardson, *Messages of the Presidents*, 1:261–65; AH to Otis, December 27, 1798, *PAH* 22:393–404; AH to James Gunn, December 22, 1798, ibid., 22:388–89; Barlow to GW, October 2, 1798, *PGWRet* 3:68–72; GW to JA, February 1, 1799, ibid., 3:350–51; JA to GW, February 19, 1799, ibid., 3:387–89; DeConde, *Quasi-War*, 162–222; Elkins and McKitrick, *Age of Federalism*, 615–41. On JA's account of his meeting with AH, see *PAH* 23:546–47n. On JA and his cabinet, see Ferling, *John Adams*, 390–95. The "impertinent ignoramus" quote can be found in John Ferling, *Adams vs. Jefferson: The Tumultuous Election of 1800* (New York, 2004), 124.

48. TJ to JM, February 19, 1799, *PTJ* 31:47–48; TJ to Pendleton, February 19, 1799, ibid., 31:49; TJ to Madison, February 26, 1799, ibid., 31:64; TJ to Joseph Priestley, January 27, 1800, ibid., 31:341.

CHAPTER 13: "I KNOW OF NO REPUBLIC EXCEPT AMERICA":
ENDGAME

1. TJ to JM, May 13, 1799, *PJM* 4:329; JM to Janet Montgomery, May 6, 1800, ibid., 4:368.

2. JM to TJ, January 27, June 10, 1798, ibid., 4:240, 277; JM to Dawson, December 25, 1797, ibid., 4:232; Dawson to JM, March 5, 1798, ibid., 251; JM to John Breckenridge, June 12, 1798, ibid., 4:278; ibid., 4:68n; Harry Ammon, *James Monroe: The Quest for National Identity* (New York, 1971), 157; John Keane, *Tom Paine: A Political Life* (New York, 1995), 164.

3. JM to TJ, January 27, February 25, 1798, *PJM* 4:240; TJ to JM, February 8, March 8, 1798, ibid., 4:245-46, 253; JM to Dawson, April 8, 1798, ibid., 4:263.

4. TJ to JM, May 21, 1798, ibid., 4:270; Madison to JM, June 9, 1798, ibid., 4:273-74; JM to TJ, June 10, 1798, ibid., 4:275-76.

5. Ammon, *James Monroe*, 169-72.

6. JM, Response to Speech by John Adams, [June 1798], *PJM* 4:283-85, 285n. On JA's addresses, see John Ferling, *John Adams: A Life* (reprint, New York, 2010), 357. On AH's criticism, see AH to Wolcott, June 5, 1798, *PAH* 21:485.

7. *PJM* 4:336n; Ammon, *James Monroe*, 173.

8. Christopher Hitchens, *Thomas Paine's Rights of Man: A Biography* (London, 2006), 63.

9. Jonathan Israel, *Revolutionary Ideas: An Intellectual History of the French Revolution from the Rights of Man to Robespierre* (Princeton, N.J., 2014), 615.

10. The foregoing draws on Israel, *Revolutionary Ideas*, 615-34, 670-94; Peter McPhee, *The French Revolution, 1789-1799* (New York, 2002), 332-41; Owen Connelly, *The French Revolution and Napoleonic Era* (New York, 1991), 160-201; Denis Woronoff, *The Thermidorean Regime and the Directory, 1794-1799* (Cambridge, England, 1984), 1-61, 168-91.

11. Thomas Paine, *The Decline and Fall of the English System of Finance* (1796), *CWTP* 2:652-74, 2:651-52n.

12. Thomas Paine, "The Recall of Monroe" (1797), ibid., 2:613-15. The quotations can be found on page 614.

13. Thomas Paine, *The Eighteenth Fructidor: To the People of France and the French Armies* (1797), ibid., 2:594-613. The quotations can be found on pages 599, 600, and 605.

14. TP, *To the People of England on the Invasion of England* (1804), ibid., 2:683.

15. Ibid., 333; TP to Napoleon Bonaparte, October 1, 1800, *CWTP* 2:1413-16. TP's letter to Napoleon is misidentified in *CWTP* as a letter to TJ. For TP's ideas concerning an invasion of England, see TP, "To the People of England on the Invasion of England" (1804), an essay that was not published until years later but likely consisted of the advice that he gave Napoleon in 1799. See ibid., 2:675-83. The "age of revolution" quote can be found ibid., 2:681.

16. See Patrice Gueniffey, *Bonaparte, 1769-1802* (Cambridge, Mass., 2015), 378-81, 400-402. The quote can be found on page 402. On Napoleon subsequently seeking TP's advice, see TP to TJ, October 1, 1800, *CWTP* 2:1409. On TP's call for an invasion of Ireland, see Alfred Owen Aldridge, *Man of Reason: The Life of Thomas Paine* (Philadelphia, 1959), 262-63. On TP's speaking at the Military Council of Paris, see Henry Redhead York, *France in Eighteen Hundred and Two*, J. A. C. Sykes, ed. (London, 1906), 241.

17. TP to TJ, October 1, 1800, *CWTP* 2:1411-12. Napoleon's comment on the rascality of the English can be found in Craig Nelson, *Thomas Paine: Enlightenment, Revolution, and the Birth of Modern Nations* (New York, 2006), 300.

18. On TP's private life in these years, see Aldridge, *Man of Reason*, 263-72, and Keane, *Tom Paine*, 443-47. The newspaper account of his excessive drinking is in Hawke, *Paine*, 336.

19. York, *France in Eighteen Hundred and Two*, 230–40.

20. TP to TJ, October 1, 1800, *CWTP* 2:1412. See also this letter in *PTJ* 32:185–91 and 191–93n, as a portion of the letter as shown in *CWTP* had been excised by TP before it was dispatched.

21. TJ to Joseph Priestley, January 27, 1800, *PTJ* 31:341.

22. Burr to TJ, May 5, 1800, ibid., 31:557. On the contest in New York, see Alfred Young, *The Democratic Republicans of New York, the Origins: 1763–1797* (Chapel Hill, N.C., 1967), 474–76; Gordon Wood, "The Enemy Is Us: Democratic Capitalism in the Early Republic," *Journal of the Early Republic* 16 (1996): 293–308; David Waldstreicher, "Federalism, the Style of Politics, and the Politics of Style," in Doran Ben-Atar and Barbara B. Oberg, eds., *Federalists Reconsidered* (Charlottesville, Va., 1998), 99–117; John Ferling, *Adams vs. Jefferson: The Tumultuous Election of 1800* (New York, 2004), 128–31; Nancy Isenberg, *Fallen Founder: The Life of Aaron Burr* (New York, 2007), 196–200. On Virginia, see Ammon, *James Monroe*, 183.

23. JA to Thomas Boylston Adams, July 14, 1800, *PAH* 24:574n; Abigail Adams to Thomas B. Adams, July 16, 1800, ibid., 24:575–76n; AH to King, January 5, 1800, ibid., 24:168; AH to Sedgwick, May 10, 1800, ibid., 24:475; AH to McHenry, June 6, 1800, ibid., 24:573; Joseph Hale to King, July 9, 1800, ibid., 24:577n; John Rutledge Jr. to AH, July 17, 1800, ibid., 25:30.

24. TJ, "Summary of Public Service," [after September 2, 1800], *PTJ* 32:122–24; TJ to Gerry, January 26, 1799, ibid., 30:645–50; TJ to Amos Alexander, June 13, 1800, ibid., 32:6; TJ to Gideon Granger, August 13, 1800, ibid., 32:95–97; TJ to Jeremiah Moore, August 14, 1800, ibid., 32:102–3; TJ to Caesar A. Rodney, December 21, 1800, ibid., 32:336–37; TJ to John Vanmetre, September 4, 1800, ibid., 32:136; TJ to Samuel Smith, October 17, 1800, ibid., 32:227; Cunningham, "Election of 1800," in Arthur M. Schlesinger Jr., Fred L. Israel, and William A. Hansen, eds., *History of American Presidential Elections, 1789–1968* (New York, 1971), 1:114, 118–19.

25. For an expanded treatment of the campaign rhetoric in 1800, see Ferling, *Adams vs. Jefferson*, 144–56. On the steps taken by the Republicans to organize for the election, see Noble E. Cunningham, *The Jeffersonian Republicans: The Formation of Party Organization, 1789–1801* (Chapel Hill, N.C., 1957), 153–60. On the press in the campaign, see Jeffrey L. Pasley, *"The Tyranny of Printers": Newspaper Politics in the Early Republic* (Charlottesville, Va., 2001).

26. AH to JA, August 1, October 1, 1800, *PAH* 25:51, 125–26.

27. Ron Chernow, *Alexander Hamilton* (New York, 2004), 624.

28. AH, *Letter from Alexander Hamilton, Concerning the Public Conduct and Character of John Adams, Esq. President of the United States* (1800), *PAH* 25:186–234. The quotations are on pages 190, 192, 196, 210, 214, 226, 222, and 233.

29. TJ to Madison, November 9, 1800, *PTJ* 32:250; TJ to Thomas Mann Randolph, December 5, 12, 1800, ibid., 32:271, 300; Charles Pinckney to TJ, December 6, 1800, ibid., 32:279–80; Peter Freneau to TJ, December 2, 1800, ibid., 32:265–66.

30. TJ to Thomas Mann Randolph, December 12, 1800, ibid., 32:300; TJ to Burr, December 15, 1800, ibid., 32:307; Burr to TJ, December 23, 1800, ibid., 32:342–43.

31. TJ to JM, December 20, 1800, *PJM* 4:453.

32. On Burr's "stealth" campaign, and attempts by the Federalists to negotiate with him, see Thomas N. Baker, "'An Attack Well Directed': Aaron Burr Intrigues for the Presidency," *Journal of the Early Republic* 31 (2011): 553–98.

33. JM to Jones, January 27, 1801, *PJM* 4:467; JM to TJ, December 30, January 6, 18, March 3, 1801, ibid., 4:456, 458, 460, 489; JM to Unknown, February 12, 1800, ibid., 4:479; Ferling, *Adams vs. Jefferson*, 175–76; Bruce Ackerman, *The Failure of the Founding Fathers: Jefferson, Marshall, and the Rise of Presidential Democracy* (Cambridge, Mass., 2005), 42–45.

34. AH to Wolcott, December 16, 1800, *PAH* 25:257; AH to James Bayard, December 27, 1800, January 16, 1801, April 6, 1802, ibid., 25:276–77, 319–24; 25:588; AH to John Rutledge Jr., January 4, 1801, ibid., 25:293–98; AH to James Ross, December 29, 1800, ibid., 25:280–81; AH to McHenry, January 4, 1801, ibid., 25:292; George Cabot to AH, August 10, 1800, ibid., 25:64; Baker, "'An Attack Well Directed,'" *Journal of the Early Republic* 31 (2011): 564–67.

35. JM to John Hoomes, February 14, 1801, *PJM* 4:480; JM to Alexander Quarrier, February 10, 1801, ibid., 4:476–77; Samuel Tyler to JM, February 9, 1801, ibid., 4:475; Thomas Mann Randolph to JM, February 14, 1801, ibid., 4:480; Michael A. Bellesiles, "'The Soil Will Be Soaked with Blood': Taking the Revolution of 1800 Seriously," in James Horn et al., eds., *The Revolution of 1800: Democracy, Race, and the New Republic* (Charlottesville, Va., 2002), 78; Bernard A. Weisberger, *America Afire: Jefferson, Adams, and the Revolutionary Election of 1800* (New York, 2000), 271.

36. These two paragraphs draw on JM to TJ, December 30, 1800, January 6, March 3, 1801, *PJM* 4:456, 458–59, 489; TJ to JM, February 15, March 7, 1801, ibid., 4:482, 490.

37. TJ to JM, February 15, 1801, *PTJ* 32:594; TJ to Madison, February 18, 1801, ibid., 33:16; TJ, Anas (April 15, 1806), *CTJ*, 1286–87; JM to TJ, January 6, 1801, *PJM* 4:459; Ackerman, *Failure of the Founding Fathers*, 87–88; James E. Lewis Jr., "'What Is to Become of Our Government': The Revolutionary Potential of the Election of 1800," in Horn, *The Revolution of 1800*, 20; Bellesiles, "'The Soil Will Be Soaked with Blood': Taking the Revolution of 1800 Seriously," ibid., 65; James Roger Sharp, *American Politics in the Early Republic: The New Nation in Crisis* (New Haven, Conn., 1993), 267–71.

38. "Deposition of James A. Bayard," April 3, 1806, in *Memoirs of Aaron Burr: With Miscellaneous Selections from His Correspondence*, Matthew L. David, ed. (New York, 1971), 2:122–33; John S. Pancake, *Samuel Smith and the Politics of Business, 1752–1839* (Tuscaloosa, Ala., 1972), 57; Frank A. Cassell, *Merchant Congressman in the Young Republic: Samuel Smith of Maryland, 1752–1839* (Madison, Wisc., 1971), 99–101; Bayard to Richard Bassett, February 16, 1801, *Annual Report of the American Historical Association for the Year 1913* (Washington, 1915), 126; Bayard to Samuel Bayard, February 22, 1801, ibid., 131–32; Morton Borden, *The Federalism of James Bayard* (New York, 1955), 84–93; Bayard to AH, March 8, 1801, *PAH* 25:344; TJ to Samuel Adams, March 29, 1801, *PTJ* 33:487–88. On the battles within the House, see Ferling, *Adams vs. Jefferson*, 175–96.

39. JM to Unknown, February 12, 1801, *PJM* 4:479.

40. JM to TJ, March 12, 1801, ibid., 4:494; Ferling, *Adams vs. Jefferson*, 201–2.

41. Ferling, *John Adams*, 413; Editor's Note, *PTJ* 33:134. The "femininely soft voice" quote is in Margaret Bayard Smith, *The First Forty Years of Washington*, ed., Gaillard Hunt (New York, 1906), 26.

42. TJ, First Inaugural Address, March 4, 1801, *PTJ* 33:148–52; Thomas Paine, *Common Sense* (1776), *CWTP* 1:16, 17, 30–31, 45. Two earlier drafts of TJ's inaugural address can be found *PTJ* 33:139–47. In outlining the ideals that his administration would embrace, TJ in private referred to them not as republican precepts but as "antient whig principles." See TJ to Knox, March 27, 1801, ibid., 3:466.

43. TJ to John Dickinson, March 6, 1801, *PTJ* 33:196–97; TJ to Priestley, March 21, 1801, ibid., 33:393–95; TJ to Samuel Adams, March 29, 1801, ibid., 33:487–88; TJ to JM, February 15, 1801, ibid., 32:594.

44. TJ to TP, March 18, 1801, ibid., 33:358–59.

CHAPTER 14: "DEATH HAS NO TERRORS FOR ME": CLOSING
THE AGE OF PAINE

1. TP to TJ, March 17, 1802, *CWTP* 2:1427; John Keane, *Tom Paine: A Political Life* (London, 1995), 452; Thomas Clio Rickman, "Stanzas, Written on the Beach at Havre de Grace and Addressed to the Sea" (1802), in Thomas Clio Rickman, *The Life of Thomas Paine* (London, 1819), 170, 172.

2. Rickman, Stanzas," in *Life of Thomas Paine*, 171.

3. The quotes can be found in Simon P. Newman, "Paine, Jefferson, and Revolutionary Radicalism in Early National America," in Simon P. Newman and Peter S. Onuf, eds., *Paine and Jefferson in the Age of Revolutions* (Charlottesville, Va., 2013), 81.

4. Levi Lincoln to TJ, December 6, 1802, *PTJ* 39:116. The quotations can be found ibid., 39:l–li; Gordon S. Wood, "Thomas Paine: America's First Public Intellectual," in Gordon S. Wood, *Revolutionary Characters: What Made the Founders Different* (New York, 2006), 222; Keane, *Tom Paine*, 457–58; David Freeman Hawke, *Paine* (New York, 1974), 354.

5. JA to TJ, June 22, 1819, *AJL* 2:542; *DAJA* 3:330; JA to Benjamin Waterhouse, March 11, 1812, October 29, 1805, in Worthington Chauncey Ford, ed., *Statesman and Friend: Correspondence of John Adams with Benjamin Waterhouse* (Boston, 1927), 78, 31. JA's remark about living in an "enemies' Country" can be found in Fred Anderson, "The Lost Founders," *New York Review of Books*, September 21, 2006, 58. JA's "Without the pen" quotation can be found in Paul Collins, *The Trouble with Tom: The Strange Afterlife and Times of Thomas Paine* (New York, 2005), 22.

6. *PTJ* 39:l–li. The "opprobrium of humanity quote can be found in Newman, "Paine, Jefferson, and Revolutionary Radicalism in Early National America," in Newman and Onuf, *Paine and Jefferson in the Age of Revolutions*, 87.

7. Rickman, *Life of Thomas Paine*, 5; Seth Cotlar, *Tom Paine's America: The Rise and Fall of Transatlantic Radicalism in the Early Republic* (Charlottesville, Va., 2011), 1; TP to Rickman, March 8, 1803, *CWTP* 2:1439. The description of TP is quoted in Keane, *Tom Paine*, 467.

8. Quoted in Keane, *Tom Paine*, 470–71; Hawke, *Paine*, 356; *PTJ* 39:331n.

9. Hawke, *Paine*, 359; Keane, *Tom Paine*, 508–9; TP to TJ, December 25, 1802, January 12, 1803, January 25, 1805, *CWTP* 2:1431–32, 1439, 1457–58, 1462.

10. TP to Madame Bonneville, November 15, 1802, *CWTP* 2:1430–31; Hawke, *Paine*, 365; Keane, *Tom Paine*, 451, 480; Audrey Williamson, *Thomas Paine: His Life, Work, and Times* (New York, 1973), 266.

11. John Hall's London Journal, in Moncure Daniel Conway, *The Life of Thomas Paine* (New York, 1892), 2:472; TP to Rickman, March 8, 1803, *CWTP* 2:1439.

12. Conway, *Life of Thomas Paine*, 2:327n.

13. *CWTP* 2:1502n; Keane, *Tom Paine*, 480–82.

14. TP to TJ, September 23, 1803, *CWTP* 2:1449.

15. Quoted in Conway, *Life of Thomas Paine*, 2:325.

16. John Hall's London Journal, ibid., 2:472; TP "The Construction of Iron Bridges," June 1803, *CWTP* 2:1051–57; TP to TJ, September 23, 1803, ibid., 2:1449; Keane, *Tom Paine*, 482–83.

17. TP to TJ, September 23, 1803, *CWTP* 2:1450; Hawke, *Paine*, 370–71.

18. TP to Mr. Hyer, March 24, 1804, ibid., 2:1452. The clerk is quoted in Hawke, *Paine*, 372, which is also the source for the hotelier's observation. On TP's abstinence during his ten-week ocean crossing, see Conway, *Life of Thomas Paine*, 304–305.

19. TP to Hyer, March 24, 1804, *CWTP* 2:1452; TP to Skipwith, March 1, 1804, ibid., 2:1451; Hawke, *Paine*, 372.

20. TP to John Fellows, July 31, 1805, *CWTP* 2:1471; TP to TJ, April 20, 1805, ibid., 2:1057–58; TJ to TP, June 5, 1805, ibid., 2:1057n.

21. TP to Fellows, July 31, 1805, ibid., 2:1471.

22. TP to William Carver, January 16, 1806, ibid., 2:1455–56; Hawke, *Paine*, 376–77.

23. TP to Madison, May 3, 1807, *CWTP* 2:1486–87.

24. TP to TJ, January 1, April 20, 1805, January 30, 1806, ibid., 2:1453, 1465, 1475–76.

25. TP's essays in *The Prospect* (1804–5) can be found ibid., 2:788–830. TP's *Examination of the Prophecies* (1807) is ibid., 2:848–93. The quotations can be found on pages 791, 793, 801, 853, 857, and 890.

26. TP, "Remarks on the Political and Military Affairs of Europe" (1806), ibid., 2:615–17; TP, "To the People of England on the Invasion of England" (1804), ibid., 2:675–83; TP, "Remarks on English Affairs" (1805), ibid., 2:684–87; TP, "Of the English Navy" (1807), ibid., 2:687–88; TP, "To the People of New York" (1807), ibid., 2:1077–79; TP, "Three Letters to Morgan Lewis" (1807), ibid., 2:968–75; TP, "To Mr. Hurlbert" (1805), ibid., 2:975–79; TP, "Another Callender— Thomas Turner of Virginia" (1805); TP, "Constitutions, Governments, and Charters" (1805), ibid., 2:989–92; TP, "Constitutional Reform" (1805), ibid., 2:992–1007; TP, "Liberty of the Press" (1806), ibid., 2:1010–11; TP, "To the French Inhabitants of Louisiana" (1804), ibid., 2:963–68; TP, "Remarks on Gouverneur Morris's Funeral Oration on General Hamilton" (1804), ibid., 2:958–62.

27. TP, "The Construction of Iron Bridges" (1803), ibid., 2:1051–57; TP, "An Essay on Dream" (1803), ibid., 2:841–48; TP, "Origin of Freemasonry," ibid., 2:830–41; TP, "Of Gunboats" (1807), ibid., 2:1067–72; TP, "Of the Comparative Powers and Expense of Ships of War, Gun-Boats, and Fortifications" (1807), ibid., 2:1072–77; TP, "On the Question, Will There Be War?" (1807), ibid., 2:1012–17; TP, "Cheetham and His Tory Paper" (1807), ibid., 2:1017–18; TP to TJ, January 25, 1805, ibid., 2:1460. The quotations are on pages 1018 and 1460. TP's essay on freemasonry was written in 1805. A fragment was published in 1810 and the entire piece appeared posthumously in 1819.

28. TP, "To the Citizens of the United States," Letters I (1802), III (1802), ibid., 2:910–11, 922.

29. TP, *Common Sense* (1776), ibid., 1:32. See Jack Fruchtman Jr., *The Political Philosophy of Thomas Paine* (Baltimore, 2009), 107–15.

30. TP, "To the Citizens of the United States," Letters I, II (1802), III, IV (1802), VI (1803), VIII (1805), *CWTP* 2:911, 915, 917, 918–19, 928, 931, 934, 935, 936, 949. TP's elaboration on Federalist secrecy was not in the "To the Citizens" essays. See TP, "A Challenge to the Federalists to Declare their Principles" (1806), ibid., 2:1007–10.

31. Ibid., Letters II, III, VI, ibid., 2:913, 915–16, 922–23, 936–37.

32. Ibid., Letters I, II, ibid., 2:909, 910, 912.

33. Quoted in Christopher Hitchens, *Thomas Paine's Rights of Man: A Biography* (London, 2006), 67.

34. TP, "To the Citizens of the United States," Letter IV, *CWTP* 2:926.

35. TP to Andrew Dean, August 15, 1806, ibid., 2:1483, 1485.

36. TP to Samuel Adams, January 1, 1803, ibid., 2:1438; TP to Dean, August 15, 1806, ibid., 2:1483.

37. TP to the Honorable Senate of the United States, January 21, 1808, ibid., 2:1489–92; TP to the Committee of Claims of the House of Representatives, February 14, 1808, ibid.,

2:1492–94; TP to the Speaker of the House of Representatives, February 28, March 7, 1808, ibid., 2:1494–96; TP to TJ, July 8, 1808, ibid., 2:1496–98.

38. "The Will of Thomas Paine," ibid., 2:1498–1501. The will stipulated that Rickman and Nicolas Bonneville were each to receive a quarter, while the boys were to divide the remaining 50 percent of the net.

39. For Paine's final years, I drew on Hawke, *Paine*, 373–401; Keane, *Tom Paine*, 515–36; Alfred Owen Aldridge, *Man of Reason: The Life of Thomas Paine* (Philadelphia, 1959), 273–316; Craig Nelson, *Thomas Paine: Enlightenment, Revolution, and the Birth of Modern Nations* (New York, 2006), 305–25; and Jack Fruchtman Jr., *Thomas Paine: Apostle of Freedom* (New York, 1994), 389–435. Much of the account is based on the memoirs of Mme Bonneville, which can be found in Conway, *Life of Thomas Paine*, 2:449–55.

40. *PAH* 26:323; Richard Brookhiser, *Alexander Hamilton: American* (New York, 1999), 214; George W. Corner, ed., *The Autobiography of Benjamin Rush: His "Travels Through Life" together with his Commonplace Book for 1789–1813* (Princeton, N.J., 1948), 323; TJ to Francis Eppes, January 19, 1821, in John P. Kaminski, ed., *The Founders on the Founders: Word Portraits from the American Revolutionary Era* (Charlottesville, Va., 2008), 459. TJ's "Into what a hornet's nest" quote is in Conway, *Life of Thomas Paine*, 2:310n.

41. TP to George Clinton, May 4, 1807, *CWTP* 2:1488.

42. JM to Larkin Smith and Richard Kennon, December 7, 1801, *PJM* 4:544–51.

43. TJ to JM, January 10, 13, 1803, ibid., 5:1, 2.

44. TP to TJ, December 25, 1802, *CWTP* 2:1431–32; JM to Madison, May 14, 1803, *PJM* 5:65–68, JM, Memorandum of the Negotiations for the Cession of Louisiana, May 1, 1803, ibid., 5:49–53; A Convention Between the United States of America and the French Republic, May 2, 1803, ibid., 5:53–54. For details of JM's mission, see Dumas Malone, *Jefferson and His Time* (Boston, 1948–81), 4:239–310, and Harry Ammon, *James Monroe: The Quest for National Identity* (New York, 1971), 203–24.

45. JM, Memorandum of the Negotiations for the Cession of Louisiana, May 1, 1803, *PJM* 5:49; Madison to JM and Robert Livingston, April 18, 1803, ibid., 5:31–34.

46. JM to Madison, March 23, 1811, ibid., 5:802.

47. JM to Madison, August 31, 1803, ibid., 5:114.

48. John Ferling, *John Adams: A Life* (reprint, New York, 2010), 266–86.

49. JM and William Pinckney to Madison, January 3, 1807, *PJM* 5:562–72. The quote is on page 567.

50. John Purviance to JM, March 20, 1807, ibid., 5:586–87; William Branch Giles to JM, March 4, 1807, ibid., 5:587n. The quotation is on page 587n.

51. TJ to JM, March 21, 1807, ibid., 5:588; Madison to JM and William Pinckney, March 18, 31, 1807, ibid., 5:585–86, 589–90.

52. The best source on TJ's relationship with Madison, the source on which I draw, is Andrew Burstein and Nancy Isenberg, *Madison and Jefferson* (New York, 2010).

53. The quotes can be found in William M. Ferraro, "George Washington and James Monroe: Military Compatriots, Political Adversaries, and Nationalist Visionaries," in Robert M. S. McDonald, ed., *Sons of the Father: George Washington and His Protégés* (Charlottesville, Va., 2013), 113–14.

54. JM to TJ, May 1807, *PJM* 5:622–24.

55. JM to TJ, February 27, 1808, ibid., 5:674–75; TJ to JM, March 10, 1808, ibid., 5:694–96.

56. JM, Speech, April 10, 1810, ibid., 5:762–64; JM to John Taylor, September 10, 1810, ibid., 5:766–75. The quote is on page 772.

57. Richard Brent to JM, March 8–12, 1811, ibid., 5:797; JM to Littleton W. Tazewell, March 14, 1811, ibid., 5:797–98; Madison to JM, March 20, 1811, ibid., 5:801–802; JM to Madison, March 23, 1811, ibid., 5:802. The quote is on page 798.

58. Quoted in George Dangerfield, *The Awakening of American Nationalism, 1815–1828* (New York, 1965), 3.

59. The foregoing paragraphs on politics and diplomacy after 1801 draw on Marshall Smelser, *The Democratic Republic, 1801–1815* (New York, 1968); Gordon S. Wood, *Empire of Liberty: A History of the Early Republic, 1789–1815* (New York, 2009), 276–314, 620–738; and Dangerfield, *Awakening of American Nationalism*, 1–35. JA's comment on Federalist "Intolerance" is in JA to Waterhouse, March 11, 1812, Ford, *Statesman and Friend*, 80.

60. JM, First Inaugural Address, March 4, 1817, in James D. Richardson, comp., *A Compilation of the Messages and Papers of the Presidents, 1789–1908* (Washington, 1899–1908), 2:4–10. The quotes can be found on pages 6 and 10. On JM's presidency, see Noble E. Cunningham, *The Presidency of James Monroe* (Lawrence, Kans., 1996); Dangerfield, *Awakening of American Nationalism*, 36–211; and Gary Hart, *James Monroe* (New York, 2005), 57–150. That the Federalist Party was not doomed to extinction before 1812 is the subject of Philip J. Lampi, "The Federalist Party Resurgence, 1808–1816: Evidence from the New Nation Votes Database," *Journal of the Early Republic* 33 (2013): 255–81.

61. TJ to Etienne Lemaire, April 25, 1809, *PTJ:Ret.Ser.* 1:162; TJ to John Armstrong, March 6, 1809, ibid., 1:20.

62. TJ to Short, March 25, 1815, ibid., 8:382.

63. Annette Gordon-Reed and Peter S. Onuf, *"Most Blessed of the Patriarchs": Thomas Jefferson and the Empire of the Imagination* (New York, 2016), 237–64. The "hunted down" quote is on pages 263–64.

64. Benjamin Rush to Richard Price, May 25, 1786, in L. H. Butterfield, ed., *Letters of Benjamin Rush* (Princeton, N.J., 1951), 1:388–90.

65. The quotation can be found in Wood, *Empire of Liberty*, 736.

66. TJ to William Plumer, January 31, 1815, *PTJ:Ret.Ser.* 8:230; TJ to Benjamin Galloway, February 2, 1812, ibid., 4:471; TJ to Lafayette, February 14, 1815, ibid., 8:262; TJ to Pierre Paganel, April 15, 1811, ibid., 3:562; TJ to Madame de Tessé, March 27, 1811, ibid., 3:504; TJ to JA, January 16, 1816, *AJL* 2:459.

67. TJ to John Langdon, March 5, 1810, *PTJ* 2:274; TJ to William Plumer, July 12, 1810, ibid., 2:505; TJ to William Lambert, July 16, 1810, ibid., 2:541.

68. Edward Coles to TJ, July 31, 1814, ibid., 7:503–4; TJ to Coles, August 25, 1814, ibid., 7:603–5; TJ to Coles, August 25, 1814, ibid., 7:603; JA to TJ, December 21, 1818, February 3, 1821, *AJL* 2:551, 571; TJ to Lafayette, December 26, 1820, November 4, 1823, Ford, *WTJ* 10:181, 281; Gordon-Reed and Onuf, *"Most Blessed of the Patriarchs,"* 54, 271. See also Joseph J. Ellis, *American Sphinx: The Character of Thomas Jefferson* (New York, 1997), 144–52; Ari Helo and Peter S. Onuf, "Jefferson, Morality, and the Problem of Slavery," *WMQ* 60 (2003): 583–614; Peter S. Onuf, "'To Declare Them a Free and Independent People': Race, Slavery and National Identity in Jefferson's Thought," *Journal of the Early Republic* 18 (1998): 1–46; Henry Wiencek, *Master of the Mountain: Thomas Jefferson and His Slaves* (New York, 2012).

69. TJ to Lafayette, May 14, 1817, November 4, 1823, Ford, *WTJ* 10:83–84, 281.

70. Jack McLaughlin, *Jefferson and Monticello: The Biography of a Builder* (New York, 1988), 376–78.

71. TJ to JA, August 1, 1816, October 12, 1823, *AJL* 2:483–84, 599; TJ to Lafayette, December 26, 1820, Ford, *WTJ* 10:179; TJ to William Gordon, January 1, 1826, ibid., 10:358. For the

descriptions of TJ, see Merrill D. Peterson, ed., *Visitors to Monticello* (Charlottesville, Va., 1989), 74, 90, 95, 105.

72. TJ to Vine Utley, March 21, 1819, Ford, *WTJ* 10:125.

73. TJ to Short, October 31, 1819, ibid., 10:145; TJ to Thomas Jefferson Randolph, February 8, 1826, ibid., 10:374; TJ to JA, October 12, 1823, *AJL* 2:599.

74. TJ to JA, November 13, 1818, April 11, 1823, *AJL* 2:529, 592; TJ to Charles Thomson, January 29, 1817, Ford, *WTJ* 10:76; TJ to Short, October 31, 1819, ibid., 10:144; TJ to Thomas Jefferson Grotjan, January 10, 1824, ibid., 12:331. On TJ's thought on life in the hereafter, see Andrew Burstein, *Jefferson's Secrets: Death and Desire at Monticello* (New York, 2005), 257–63, and Gordon-Reed and Onuf, "*Most Blessed of the Patriarchs*," 278–81, 297–98. The "daily prayers" quote is in Gordon-Reed and Onuf, page 281.

75. TJ to Gordon, January 1, 1826, Ford, *WTJ* 10:358.

76. TJ to Roger C. Weightman, June 24, 1826, ibid., 10:391–92.

77. On TJ's retirement, see Noble E. Cunningham, *In Pursuit of Reason: The Life of Thomas Jefferson* (Baton Rouge, La., 1987), 322–49, and Andrew Burstein, "Jefferson in Retirement," in Francis D. Cogliano, ed., *A Companion to Thomas Jefferson* (Chichester, England, 2011), 218–33.

78. Malone, *Jefferson and His Time*, 6:498–99; Francis D. Cogliano, *Thomas Jefferson: Reputation and Legacy* (Charlottesville, Va., 2006), 137.

79. JM to Jones, September 4, 1794, *PJM* 3:54; Newspaper Advertisement, Loudoun Land for Sale, October 27, 1809, ibid., 5:750.

80. JM to TJ, February 13, 1826, *WJM* 7:68; JM to Tence Ringgold, May 8, 1826, ibid., 7:83; JM to James McIlhany, January [?], 1827, ibid., 7:91; JM to Hugh L. White, January 26, 1827, ibid., 7:93; JM to Thomas Newton, February 26, 1827, ibid., 7:113; JM to Madison, September 23, 1827, ibid., 7:119.

81. JM to Lafayette, May 2, 1829, ibid., 7:200.

82. Malone, *Jefferson and His Time*, 6:430, 449–51. The "deeply wounded" quotation is on page 451.

83. McLaughlin, *Jefferson and Monticello*, 379–80; Merrill D. Peterson, ed., *Visitors to Monticello* (Charlottesville, Va., 1989), 95, 111, 116, 120.

84. JM to John Quincy Adams, December 17, 1828, *WJM* 7:187; JM to Madison, March 20, 1829, July 2, 1830, April 11, 1831, ibid., 7:192–93, 213, 231–32.

85. The section on JM's years following his presidency draws on Ammon, *James Monroe*, 546–73, and Harlow Giles Unger, *The Last Founding Father: James Monroe and Nation's Call to Greatness* (New York, 2009), 333–47.

86. JM to Madison, April 11, 1831, *WJM* 7:233.

AFTERWORD

1. TP to John Inskeep, February 1806, *CWTP* 2:1480.

2. AH to Sedgwick, July 10, 1804, *PAH* 26:309; JA to John Taylor, Letter 18 (1814), *Works* 6:484; TP, Rights of Man, *CWTP* 1:254.

3. TJ to Samuel Kercheval, July 12, 1816, Ford, *WTJ* 10:37–45.

4. Gordon S. Wood, *Empire of Liberty: A History of the Early American Republic, 1789–1815* (New York, 2009), 702–703; idem., *The Radicalization of the American Revolution* (New York, 1992), 367; Joyce Appleby, *Inheriting the Revolution: The First Generation of Americans* (Cambridge, Mass., 2000), 57–59; Dumas Malone, *Jefferson and His Time* (Boston, 1981), 6:437.

5. TJ to Lafayette, November 4, 1823, ibid., 10:281.

6. TP, *Rights of Man*, *CWTP* 1:343; TP, "To the Citizens of the United States," Letter II, ibid., 2:917. The "art of conquering at home" quotation can be found in Chris Hedges, *Wages of Rebellion* (New York, 2015), 157.

7. TP, *Constitutions, Government, and Charters* (1805), in *CWTP* 2:995; TP, "To the Citizens of the United States," Letter VIII (1805), ibid., 2:956.

8. Pauline Maier, *American Scripture: Making the Declaration of Independence* (New York, 1997).

9. TP, "To the Citizens of the United States," Letter VIII, ibid., 2:949.

INDEX